The American Quest for the
Primitive Church

The American Quest for the Primitive Church

RICHARD T. HUGHES

Editor

UNIVERSITY OF ILLINOIS PRESS
Urbana and Chicago

© 1988 by the Board of Trustees of the University of Illinois
Manufactured in the United States of America
1 2 3 4 5 C P 5 4 3 2 1

This book is printed on acid-free paper

Library of Congress Cataloging-in-Publication Data

The American quest for the primitive church.

Includes index.
1. Restoration movement (Christianity)—Congresses.
2. Protestant churches—United States—Doctrines—
History—Congresses. 3. United States—Church history—
Congresses. I. Hughes, Richard T. (Richard Thomas),
1943-   .
BR517.A54 1988   280′.4′0973   88-5437
ISBN 0-252-01538-X (cloth: alk. paper)
ISBN 0-252-06029-6 (paper: alk. paper)

Contents

Acknowledgments

This volume is the fruit of a conference held at Abilene Christian University (ACU) in July 1985 on the theme "The Restoration Ideal in American History." Gratitude goes first to ACU and to its president, William J. Teague, for support of the conference and for providing facilities and accommodations.

John C. Stevens, chancellor of ACU, spent numerous hours traveling Texas highways, raising the funds that made the conference possible. All who benefit from this volume are both in his debt and in the debt of those who unselfishly responded with generous gifts.

Donors include Mr. and Mrs. Dwain Evans, Mr. and Mrs. Bob Fitts, Mr. and Mrs. Joe Foy, Mr. and Mrs. Bob Gowens, Mr. and Mrs. Harry L. Groves, Mr. and Mrs. David S. Holland, Mr. and Mrs. Jim Hughes, Mr. and Mrs. Rolph Johnson, Dr. and Mrs. Mike McGuire, and Mr. and Mrs. Willis Witt from the Houston area.

Donors from the Dallas-Fort Worth area include Mr. and Mrs. B. Michael Cummings, Mr. and Mrs. Earl Davidson, Mr. and Mrs. Jim Dickson, Mr. and Mrs. George F. Dillman, Mr. and Mrs. R. C. Duncan, Mr. and Mrs. C. E. Groves, Mr. and Mrs. Terry Groves, Dr. and Mrs. John Isbell, Mr. and Mrs. Hulen Jackson, Mr. and Mrs. L. G. Lacy, Mr. Gilbert McCleskey, Mr. and Mrs. Art McNeese, Mr. and Mrs. Brad Mullen, Mr. and Mrs. Ken Nowell, Sr., Mr. and Mrs. Lynn Packer, Mr. and Mrs. Bob Pierce, Mr. and Mrs. Jerry Robbins, Dr. and Mrs. Willis Starnes, Mr. and Mrs. Mack Swindle, Mr. and Mrs. Larry W. Van Steenberg, and Mr. and Mrs. J. McDonald Williams.

From the Austin area donors include Mr. and Mrs. Don L. Baker, Mr. and Mrs. H. R. Davis, Dr. and Mrs. Claude Hocott, Mr. and Mrs. Leslie G. Huff, Mr. and Mrs. John Reynolds, Mr. and Mrs. W. A. Sloan, Jr., Mr. and Mrs. M. I. Summerlin, and Mr. and Mrs. Alvis Vandygriff.

Donors also include Mr. and Mrs. Neil Fry and Mr. James D. Tittle from the Abilene area, and Dr. and Mrs. Terry Koonce of Calgary, Alberta, Canada.

Gratitude also is extended to Mrs. Marisue Meyer, director of the ACU Word Processing Center, who supervised preparation of the manuscript, and to the following people in that office who helped with manuscript preparation: Angie Allen, Carla Claybrook, Lujean Durham, Rhonda Royal, and Connie Spain. Thanks also go to Baker Stephen Covington Taylor and Mark Wentz, graduate students at ACU, who assisted in manuscript preparation in a variety of ways, and to Marcia Geer, who skillfully handled organizational details when the conference was in its early planning stages. I also wish to thank the editorial staff of the University of Illinois Press, and especially Barbara E. Cohen, the manuscript editor for this project, for splendid editorial work. Finally, I am especially grateful to Marlette Estes, who supervised and coordinated all aspects of the conference. Without her cheerful and skillful assistance, the conference and the resulting volume would never have become reality.

The American Quest for the
Primitive Church

Introduction: On Recovering the Theme of Recovery

RICHARD T. HUGHES

RARELY does a theme that is central to the imagination of a culture, or to significant strands of a culture, go almost entirely unexamined by scholars. Such has been the fate of primitivism or restorationism in American life, however. As employed in this book, the notion of "primitivism" suggests that "first times" are in some sense normative or jurisdictional for contemporary belief and behavior. From time to time scholars have pointed to this theme in various contexts, but no one has sought to trace this theme in its various strands through the long and winding course of American religious history. This book is at least a start in that direction.

Recognizing the dearth of literature in restoration studies broadly conceived, in July 1985 Abilene Christian University (ACU) hosted an academic conference on the theme "The Restoration Ideal in American History." The intent was to bring to the university leading scholars who could reflect on the history and meaning of this theme from a variety of perspectives in American religious life. It was natural for ACU to host this conference because ACU is closely related to the Churches of Christ, whose very raison d'être is tied to the restoration sentiment. But beyond the borders of this tradition, where else has the restoration theme flourished? And how has it functioned in American life? These were among the questions we hoped the conference would help answer.

The focus of the conference and of this book is American Protestantism. It is certainly true that there have been strong restoration sentiments in American Judaism, American Catholicism, and in other religious movements in the United States.[1] But it seemed appropriate, if only because of the profound, collective influence that Protestant communities have exerted on the American mind and character, to focus this preliminary inquiry on American Protestantism and related movements. We therefore begin with Puritans and work our way through Baptists, Methodists, and Episcopalians to Pentecostals and Fundamentalists in these latter days, stopping along the way to look at eighteenth-century Enlightenment thinkers, nineteenth-century Bible scholars, Mormons, and the Churches of Christ. As diverse as this beginning may be, it still leaves untouched such obvious Protestant traditions as Mennonites, Plymouth Brethren, and Quakers—all Protestants with a strong restorationist impulse.

As the diversity of traditions the conference explored was impressive, so was the diversity of meanings that, as conferees discovered, these various traditions have given to the theme of restoration. Struck by this dissensus, Henry Bowden finally suggested that "the meaning of the term [*restoration*] is relative to different people who appropriate it, to what they say it means, and to what activities they pursue under its aegis. Based on historical usage of institutional, doctrinal and biblical categories, there is no meaning intrinsic to the title, and we can find no common agreement on any set of organizational forms or ideas." Two conclusions seem implicit in Bowden's remarks. First, restoration is a slippery concept. That much is apparent. But it is also clear from Bowden's remark that if scholars are to use this concept with creative dexterity, they must be less concerned with abstractions and generalizations and more concerned with hearing how insiders—true believers in the restoration ideal—define the concept for themselves.

This is precisely why, in planning the conference, we deliberately left definitional matters relatively open-ended. In the original program agenda, therefore, the terms *primitivism* and *restorationism* were used without distinction. Time and again, conferees wrote seeking definitional guidance particularly with respect to these two terms. I finally responded with two broad guidelines: first, that we allow the terms *primitivism* and *restorationism* to be used more or less interchangeably. Here I cited for conferees a passage from Theodore Dwight Bozeman's recent book, *To Live Ancient Lives,* where Bozeman argues that the various emphases by Puritans upon antiquity "were not stray thoughts, nor evidences of idiosyncrasy. They were characteristic manifestations of a whole facet of Puritan thought that I shall label 'primitivist,' or alternately, 'restorationist' or 'restitutionist.' " Its defining element was a "reversion undercutting both Catholic and Anglican appeals to a continuity of tradition, to the first, or primitive, order of things narrated in the Protestant Scriptures."[2] It seemed to me that Bozeman's defining element, namely, a "reversion" that pointed back "to the first, or primitive, order of things narrated in the Protestant Scriptures" was the heart of what we likely would be about in this conference, and that it would not be productive to quibble over fine distinctions between, for example, primitivism and restorationism.

At the same time, it was apparent to me and to others that there have been forms of the reversional orientation in America that simply have not appealed to the Bible, and that it would be helpful to have some means to distinguish between, say, biblical primitivism and naturalistic primitivism. It seemed to me that the distinction made by Lovejoy and Boas in *Primitivism and Related Ideas in Antiquity* between "chronological primitivism" and "cultural primitivism" might be helpful at this point.[3] "If I were to distinguish between 'restoration' and 'primitivism,' " I wrote to conferees, "I think I would argue that the theme of 'restoration' more closely conforms to 'chronological primitivism' wherein the greatest excellence and happiness existed at the fount of time; and that 'primitivism' perhaps most closely corresponds to 'cultural primitivism' which suggests the yearning of the civilized for a simpler, less complex world." I concluded my missive with the "hope that the use of the two terms in the program will be more suggestive than prescriptive and will add depth and texture to the possible interpretations of this theme in American history." My concern was to provide minimal definitions at the outset and to allow various definitions and distinctions to be drawn by the practitioners within the various groups that we would explore. It would then become the task of scholars, having heard the testimony of the believers, to make sense of the variety of ways in which the reversional orientation has been employed and nuanced in 350 years of American history.

What emerged from this loosely structured format were three days of richly stimulating dialogue concerning this theme. The dialogue took many forms: agreement, mutual exploration, dissent, and even sharp rebuttal. But through it all, it was the dialogue over a theme long neglected by most American historians that provided the depth and texture for which we all had hoped from the project's conception. The quality of the dialogue was doubtless enhanced by what seemed to at least some of the conferees as the simultaneous familiarity and unfamiliarity of the theme at hand. Winton Solberg perhaps put it best: "To recognize familiar ideas under a new label—in this case, primitivism—is like discovering, late in life, that one has always been speaking prose!"

When all was said and done, several key issues had surfaced. Among those issues were (1) the variety of ways in which primitivism can function in a culture or a religion; (2) the relationship of primitivism to history and tradition; (3) the relationship of primitivism to American culture, broadly conceived; (4) the relationship between primitivism and modernity; and (5) the relationship of primitivism to millennial thought. Let me now attempt to sketch the outlines of these issues and to orient the reader to the rich discussion that comprises the rest of this book.

First, it became apparent to the conferees that the restoration or primitivist sentiment has surfaced in unlikely and surprising places. Indeed, I myself had assumed that one base line of the primitivist motif was its aversion to history and tradition. Bozeman made this very point regarding Puritans in the passage previously cited from him. There, Bozeman wrote of the Puritan reversional orientation that it undercut "both Catholic and Anglican appeals to a continuity of tradition." This aversion to history and tradition—this sense of living with one foot in the present age and the other planted squarely in first times—is all too apparent in Bozeman's Puritans, in New England dissenters like Roger Williams, and in Mormons and pentecostals. Indeed, as Leonard Allen and Jan Shipps point out in their chapters, both Williams and the Mormons testified to the complete extinction of the church at an early date because of apostasy from the norms of first times. For them, therefore, Christian history between the times of the original and the restoration was at best the story of progressive corruption and at worst the story of "human invention" proceeding wholly apart from any divine initiative. Similarly, Grant Wacker notes of early pentecostals that their "longing to recover the 'pure fountain' of the New Testament ... fostered the presumption that virtually everything that had happened since the Day of Pentecost was pernicious at worst, irrelevant at best." The same was true of the Churches of Christ and of many of the Baptists studied by Robert Handy.

Given this context, it was striking to learn of Episcopalians, Methodists, and fundamentalists—people who prized the history and traditions of Protestantism—who also appeal to sacred origins to legitimate their existence and identity. Indeed, Bozeman's description of Puritans as essentially primitivist is itself a somewhat shocking claim. After all, Puritans prized history and learning, interacted with the past, and knew well the stories of those epochs that preceded their own.

In this context, Mark Noll was incredulous at Thomas H. Olbricht's contention that biblical scholars like Moses Stuart and Charles Hodge could in any sense be considered primitivists. Indeed, Noll argued, Olbricht's paper was "a puzzle" and fundamentally misleading. Instead of dealing with primitivists, Noll complained, Olbricht "treats us to an extensive discussion of biblical traditionalists who took their bearings from the learning of the church's varied past." If Olbricht's biblical scholars were the only traditionalists made out to be primitivists at this conference, we perhaps would be inclined to accept Noll's complaint at face value. But Bozeman's Puritans, Holmes's Episcopal Evangelicals, Outler's Methodists, and Carpenter's fundamentalists compel us to take another look and to inquire more closely into the possible relation between the primitivist perspective on the one hand and history and tradition on the other.

To begin this inquiry, we perhaps could do better than to cite Fred Somkin, who writes of the American people in the nation's early years, "As record, as deposit, the past undoubtedly existed, but Americans contested the extent of its jurisdiction."[4] Here is the central point: the extent of history's jurisdiction. This way of putting it goes far to explain, for example, how an Episcopal Evangelical, thoroughly conversant with the history and traditions of the Christian faith—and thoroughly committed to some of those historic traditions—could also proclaim that "our movement is 'New Testament Christianity' in its purest essence." Here was a jurisdictional mingling, as it were. The jurisdiction of primitive norms undergirded this seemingly exclusivist claim. At the same time, the partial jurisdiction of history and tradition eroded the exclusivist implications of Evangelical primitivism and led some of those Evangelicals to hold alongside their primitivism a thoroughly ecumenical outlook.

This suggests that primitivism and a commitment to the contents of history are not necessarily mutually exclusive categories. In an earlier essay, I struggled with the possible relation between historical religions and primitivist perspectives, and asked, "How is it possible to apply essentially nonhistorical categories [e.g., the jurisdiction of first times] to a historical religion [i.e., one which takes history and tradition seriously]?" I remain essentially comfortable with the conclusion I drew at that time.

> [A]ny human history, if that history has more than a formal and factual significance, is fraught with mythical and symbolic power. To the degree that the factual history outweighs the power of the myth, and a certain distance is maintained between the particular history that is normative and the believer's own time, then we may speak of a particular religious tradition as being historical. In such a case a certain objectivity remains. But when the normative history is swallowed up in myth to such an extent that the believer loses the clear distinction between his own time and the primal time, then that historic tradition has lost its historicality. At that point, the particular time that was merely normative now has

become the eternally repeatable primordium within which the believer lives and moves and has his being and apart from which life itself has no meaning and significance.[5]

This suggests two very different ways of conceiving the relation between primitivism and historical consciousness. On the one hand, first times can be a normative, jurisdictional guide to proper attitudes, behavior, or doctrine. In this context, further, the jurisdiction of first times can be complete or partial. The Churches of Christ studied by Bill Humble perhaps best reflect an attempt to make first times completely jurisdictional. Among those people, at least in the nineteenth century, nothing specifically religious was undertaken without first asking for an apostolic command, example, or at the very least, a necessary inference. At the same time, the Episcopal Evangelicals are perhaps a classic example of first times exercising partial jurisdiction. For them, the supremacy of the apostolic order was refracted through a secondary "first time," a period that stood squarely within the history and tradition of the Christian faith: the Anglicanism of Edward VI. For the Churches of Christ, no such secondary "first time" existed, at least not at the level of purposeful and conscious deliberation.

First times, therefore, can be normative and jurisdictional, with degrees and levels of jurisdiction. But primitivism can also function so that first times are "swallowed up in myth to such an extent that the believer loses the clear distinction between his own time and the primal time." In this case, believers are not so much following a primal guide as if first times constitute a kind of sacred constitution, as they are actually living through or reenacting the strong events of first times with which they now fully identify. While New England Puritans never lost the clear distinction between their own time and primal time, it is nonetheless clear that they viewed their wilderness enterprise as a dramatic reenactment of the biblical saga. This is precisely the point Bozeman makes when he writes of New England Puritans that "it would be a mistake to designate their [primitivist] procedure simply an act of textual analysis, or to assume that the resulting system was essentially an appeal for rational assent. For in these as in virtually all examples of Puritan utterance holy writ was approached, in the first instance, neither as a technical sourcebook [nor as] . . . a logical structure, but as dramatic event." As if engaged in sacred drama, Bozeman's Puritans did not merely replicate biblical examples; instead they lived in and from the biblical world. This gave to their replication of first-time examples an entirely different texture than would characterize the more legal approach of nineteenth-century Landmark Baptists or Churches of Christ. Grant Wacker makes essentially the same point, though in stronger terms, regarding many early pentecostals: "Indeed, the yearning to re-enter the primitive church—to breathe its air, to feel the exhiliration of its spiritual life—became so intense that believers sometimes found it impossible to distinguish present reality from the imagined reality of the first century." And Joel Carpenter notes, as well, that fundamentalists "infused the here and now with supernatural power and biblical reality of the grandest dimensions."

In the same vein, Jan Shipps correctly argues that the Mormon restoration was no mere replication of first times. It rather was a living reality in which first times mingled with the latter days in ways that defied separation. Indeed, Shipps argues that the ideal of restoration became living, breathing reality precisely when God himself, along with Moses, Elias, and Elijah visited Joseph Smith and Oliver Cowdery in the Kirtland Temple on April 3, 1836. As Shipps notes, "With that the restoration of all things could truly begin." Here, after all, those times that were first and therefore normative for Mormons mingled indiscriminantly with their own.[6]

David Edwin Harrell, then, may well have been correct when he argued that the restoration sentiment, or some form of that sentiment, "may be the most vital single assumption underlying the development of American Protestantism."[7] The temptation, in hearing such a broad and sweeping assertion, is to suggest that if all are primitivists, then none are primitivists, and that finally primitivism is a term with no substantial meaning. To make that sort of judgment, however, is to miss the point entirely. In the first place, not all are primitivists. But in the second place, when studying the vast array of primitivist traditions, what is needed is the recognition by scholars that primitivism may well have various meanings in various circumstances and in various traditions, that it appears with various grades and levels of intensity, that it interacts with history and tradition in a variety of ways, and that the object of the restoration sentiment (i.e., precisely *what* is to be restored) may vary from group to group, movement to movement, and culture to culture. For this reason, typological assessments of the restoration sentiment can be especially valuable.[8] Indeed, to sort out these distinctions and to probe their implications is to take the restoration sentiment in the American context seriously. To fail in this is to neglect a substantive theme in the American experience.

If the restoration ideal is as widely dispersed in American religion as the chapters in this book suggest, then it is certainly worth inquiring concerning the role of primitivism in the larger American culture. One finds here the same diversity of primitivist sentiment as prevails among the various denominational forms of American religion. Indeed, in the larger culture, the first age, when operative, is often merely normative. It sometimes, however, takes on mythical dimensions, eclipsing a sense of history almost altogether.

In the context of the larger culture, none of the following essays is more suggestive than is Winton Solberg's analysis of the role of primitivism in the American Enlightenment. For Solberg, however, the restoration of biblical paradigms is not so much the issue here as is the restoration of the natural order of things, pure and undefiled, fresh from the hands of God. Many Enlightenment primitivists from an early date identified the American landscape as essentially Edenic. Thus Solberg quotes William Bartram, who proclaimed of the American Southeast that it suggested "an idea of the first appearance of the earth to man at the creation"—a statement reminiscent of John Locke's well-known dictum "in the beginning, all the world was America."

According to Solberg, Bartram represents that strand of the American Enlightenment that despaired of civilization and looked instead to primitive, natural models as "the standard of human values." Ironically, however, other Enlightenment thinkers turned the Bartram tradition on its head. Far from juxtaposing civilization and nature, these thinkers argued both implicitly and explicitly that American civilization *was,* in fact, the natural order of things. Thus Thomas Paine could argue that when viewing the new American government, one was "brought at once to the point of seeing government begin, as if we had lived in the beginning of time."[9] And Solberg quotes Governor Morris who, upon attending the Constitutional Convention, regarded himself "in some degree as a Representative of the whole human race." Solberg then concludes: "If paradise had been lost, paradise would be regained. The American mission in history was the restoration of humanity to its primitive glory."

The notion that America was fundamentally natural gained credence in the years that followed because the American system worked, when judged from a purely pragmatic perspective, and paid rich dividends to its most substantial investors. In this, Americans at large were not unlike Albert Outler's Methodists who took their early growth and success "as proof of their recovery of the original power of 'apostolic Christianity.'" Of this persistent tendency of American primitivists to discern the ancient norms by virtue of experience and success, Henry Bowden comments, "This kind of fixation reminds one of George Tyrell's observation about New Testament scholars of the last century who limited their view of Jesus to an incarnation of their own ideals. They could find only a German in the Jew, he said, a professor in the prophet, the nineteenth century in the first. The Christ identified by such a narrow search, looking down through centuries of Catholic darkness, produced only the reflections of a Protestant face at the bottom of a deep well." Similarly, when nineteenth-century Americans peered into the well of nature, what they saw was America.

If primitivism characterized American cultural identity in the nineteenth century, what might be said of America in the modern period? To even raise this question seems, at first glance, to be the very height of presumption, paradox, and irony. Even if one grants that nineteenth-century America had strong primitivist underpinnings, one would guess that the rapid advances of modernity in recent years would have eroded those underpinnings almost altogether. After all, how is it possible for a nation in the vanguard of modernity still to bear the marks of the backward orientation of primitivism?

Nonetheless, hints and suggestions that some sort of connection does prevail between primitivism and modernity abound in popular culture. Roger Rosenblatt, in his recent letter to Americans in the year 2086, perceptively suggested precisely such a connection when he wrote that "we ride on a supersonic vehicle from our century into yours, yet a great many seats are facing backward."[10]

To explore the nature of those connections, it may be worth pondering the theme of seduction. To be sure, several of the papers in this volume comment on the seductive, sometimes illusory nature of the restoration ideal. Henry Bowden, for example, observes the tendency of primitivism to perpetuate "the dream that we can escape historical conditioning" and to encourage "people to believe that they can, by taking thought, add a cubit to their stature." In a similar vein, Mark Noll remarks that the restoration ideal "underestimates the hold of our own times on our vision of the scriptures" and fails to recognize that while "the Bible may be absolute in its wisdom and authority, . . . we [nonetheless] apprehend its treasures as mediated through history."

In this sense, the notion of modernity may be fully as seductive as that of primitivism. Indeed, modernity as an abstraction—as a symbol for jetting into the future—also enhances the assumption that human beings can escape historical conditioning. And like some forms of primitivism, it also "encourages people to believe that they can, by taking thought, add a cubit to their stature." Robert Bellah and his colleagues make this point fully apparent in their *Habits of the Heart.* In this modern world, human beings need not worry over much about the complexities of the human condition—complexities that share deeply interwoven roots in an intricately complicated past. Nor need they tend to that past as a way of unraveling current dilemmas or helping to heal the ills of the present age. Instead, as if they lived in a total vacuum, isolated and insulated from all that has gone before, they need only apply the proper technique or seek the proper therapy, and all will be well.[11] Here the human condition with its ambiguities, its flaws, its inherent contradictions is essentially dismissed. And history, as the vehicle on which those ambiguities have been transported from age to age, and within whose finite bounds members of the human race have addressed those ambiguities, now in this way and now in that, and in which solutions to problems of human finitude have been tried, have succeeded, and have failed—all of this is fundamentally irrelevant to the myth of the modern age. Walt Whitman captured the essential sentiment of modernity in America when he exulted in *Pioneers! O Pioneers!*, "All the past we leave behind, We debouch upon a newer, mightier world, varied world."

But what does all this mean? Even if one grants that both primitivism and modernity may foster the seductive illusions of historylessness, precisely how have these themes interacted in the history of American religion? Answers begin to emerge in the comments by Brooks Holifield on the chapters by Dwight Bozeman on Puritans and by Leonard Allen on Roger Williams. To the contention of Bozeman and Allen that the New England Puritans were not harbingers of modernity as so many scholars have supposed, but rather agents of first times, Holifield suggestively responds that "these papers . . . alert us to the possibility that the whole conception of 'modernization'—like the analogous conception of secularization—might well be far more ambiguous than we have thought. And they alert us to the possibility that an appeal to the primitive might well be a hidden, or barely recognized aspect of the modern."

If primitivism is indeed "a hidden, or barely recognized aspect" of modernity, the point of connection lies precisely in the fact that both can be highly seductive categories which look chiefly to first times (primitivism) and to the present (modernity) for normative jurisdiction, and in that sense frequently refuse to take history seriously. From this angle of vision, Puritans were indeed harbingers of modernity, but not in the sense commonly supposed. For in rejecting history's jurisdiction, Puritans took a step that later Americans would take in a direction altogether unintended by the Puritans themselves. Later Americans not only would reject history's jurisdiction, they also would neglect history as a meaningful shaper and determiner of destiny—a common assumption of the modern temper. Ironically, therefore, Puritans heralded modernity precisely by planting their feet on the path that led to first times. This, I take it, is at least part of what Holifield means when he writes that "the roadway to the modern world is simply not as straight as many historians of Puritanism have supposed."

We should have learned as much from Nathaniel Hawthorne's insightful novel *The Scarlet Letter*. Interestingly, at the heart of a book whose focus rests squarely on Puritan New England, Hawthorne portrays a character that symbolizes Hawthorne's own nineteenth-century America with its characteristic contempt for the past. This character is Pearl, Hester Prynne's illegitimate daughter, who functions in the book as a kind of hinge between the seventeenth and nineteenth centuries. With roots perversely but inescapably enmeshed in Puritan New England, she nonetheless is a harbinger of Hawthorne's own age. In one telling graveyard scene, Hawthorne relates how little Pearl "now skipped irreverently from one grave to another; . . . skipping, dancing, and frisking fantastically among the hillocks of the dead people, like a creature that had nothing in common with a bygone and buried generation, nor owned herself akin to it. It was as if she had been made afresh out of new elements, and must perforce be permitted to live her own life, and be a law unto herself without her eccentricities being reckoned to her for a crime."[12]

Whereas the exhiliration of modernity led some nineteenth-century Americans to dance on the graves of the dead, the continuing spirit of primitivism led other Americans to a similar neglect of the past. Among those nineteenth-century primitivists who essentially scorned the power of history to shape human affairs were the Mormons and the followers of Alexander Campbell—early members of Churches of Christ. And what is more, primitivism led in both cases directly to aspects of modernity. Samuel S. Hill, Jr., commenting on papers by Humble and Shipps, makes this point inescapably clear when he highlights the "if . . . then" theology of both movements. *If* we restore primitive Christianity, Thomas Campbell surmised, *then* we will also restore the unity of Christians. And *if* I ask for the appearance of the true church, reasoned Joseph Smith, *then* I will be shown. What concerns Hill are the peculiarly modern dimensions of this "if . . . then" perspective. "A place in the stream of evolving American values is thus taken by the Mormon and Campbellite movements in the 1810s and 1820s. Jonathan Edwards's 'surprising work of God' had given way to Charles G. Finney's 'new measures.' Thomas Campbell's 'if . . . then . . .' and Joseph Smith's 'if I ask of God . . . it will be given,' were 'modern' or 'liberal' avenues of access to God. . . . Mystery and a trusting providentialism had yielded to common sense, to *quid-pro-quo* reasoning, to certain kinds of rationalistic, mechanical thinking." Here are outstanding examples of the way in which primitivism often, as Bowden notes, "encourages people to believe that they can, by taking thought, add a cubit to their stature." But the fundamental point to be grasped is the essentially modern dimension of this perspective. Indeed, here was a rationalized self-reliance, set free from the constraints of history and born of the search for first times. Clearly, primitivism had encouraged in these instances a profound neglect of history that had become, by the late twentieth century, one of the distinguishing and generalized features of the modern age.

To understand primitivism and modernity as fundamentally connected in this way goes far toward explaining many of the seeming anachronisms of our age that puzzle many observers. It helps explain, for example, how it is that many members of traditions with deeply restorationist roots—fundamentalist, Churches of Christ, Baptist, Mormon, and pentecostal, for example—can embrace the modern world with religious zeal and perceive in that embrace no paradox, no irony, and no contradiction at all. The space-age cathedrals with which fundamentalists and evangelicals of various stripes have dotted the urban landscape across America stand as mute testimony to that embrace, and perhaps symbolize the ironic primitivist/modernist perspective that forms, for many, the substance of their theology. In many of these cathedrals, sophisticated and well-heeled jet-setters and urbanites, thoroughly at home in the world, gather to celebrate the old-time religion that implicitly—and often explicitly—calls for separation from the world. But the ironies regularly go unperceived because a celebration of the modern world, for many in these cathedrals, is at once in perfect harmony with a celebration of the old-time religion. From the perspective of these believers, the world that deserves rejection is a world, and a world view, that takes seriously the complexities, the ambiguities, and the relativities of history. From this world, however, these primitivist/modernist Christians separated themselves long ago. This observation may help, then, to explain "the complex and often internally paradoxical character of the fundamentalist movement and its moderate heirs" of which Joel Carpenter writes so perceptively.

The connection between primitivism and modernity suggests another important relationship that receives attention in this book, namely, the connection between primitivism and millennialism. Rarely have historians of millennialism perceived the relevance of primitivism for their work. If one asks Why not? two possible answers emerge. In the first place, millennialism, like the category *modernity,* suggests a future orientation, not a reversion to the past. And in the second place, historians typically are all too familiar with the complexities, the ambiguities, and the relativities of history and therefore are not well disposed to take seriously utopian notions of recovering first and perfect times. In this, historians commonly share a world view with Thomas Jefferson and other American Enlightenment thinkers who, as Sidney E. Mead reminds us here, harbored deep suspicions of a direct and easy progress to a golden age. Thus Mead cites Jefferson, who was quite convinced that "from the conclusion of this [Revolutionary] war we shall be going downhill." The prevalence of this perspective among the founders, Mead writes, justifies Page Smith's observation that "reading accounts of the debates in the Constitutional Convention is enough to convince one that the founders thought of government as a device for combatting original sin." This suspicion of human abilities, however, rarely has typified the dominant American perspective. Even when it has, it seldom has mustered sufficient strength to counter effectively the American dream that human beings, by taking thought, might well recover a strong and perfect past and launch the millennial age. As Solberg reminds us in his chapter, the founders themselves, in spite of deep convictions regarding human frailties, nonetheless anticipated at certain levels an American *novus ordo seclorum* (new order of the ages).

Puritans likewise nurtured in this regard a profound theological ambiguity. On the one hand, they held tenaciously to the notion of human depravity, but not so tenaciously as to preclude their conviction that they could, through determined and concerted effort, launch a millennial age born ultimately of first times. Thus Dwight Bozeman argues here that in Puritan thought, primitivism and millennialism were of the same cut of cloth. Indeed, Bozeman argues, millennialism was the form of which primitivism was the substance. "We would observe," Bozeman writes, "that Puritan millennialism, while it may in limited ways have pointed towards later doctrines of progress, was in fact the pinnacle of restorationist hope; it projected the finally triumphant reversion to primordial purity and simplicity." Grant Wacker makes precisely the same argument regarding pentecostalism. There is no question, he writes, regarding the fact that "dispensational premillennialism pervaded the movement. Even so, students of pentecostalism have rarely recognized the extent to which historical primitivism undergirded its millenarianism. More precisely, there is substantial evidence that the hope of the Latter Rain came first in pentecostal thinking, which meant that historical primitivism served as the logical and emotional foundation for dispensational premillennialism, not the reverse." What is more, Wacker notes, "the priority of the primitivist vision was plain to many of the first-generation leaders."

Wacker and Bozeman both seem to suggest that the restoration ideal was important to the millennial vision precisely because it supplied its fundamental content. In such cases, the millennium was nothing more and nothing less than the final recovery of the first strong and perfect age. But in the context of this entire sweep of essays, this conclusion presses upon us one final question—a question regarding those contemporary American Christians with a strongly primitivist orientation but who also are thoroughly at home with modernity. In the case of Puritans and early pentecostals, their perception of the primordium provided content and substance for their millennial vision. In the case of those primitivist/modernist Christians of our time, however, one wonders if all of this has not been turned upside down. Perhaps for many of them, modernity constitutes a kind of realized millennium in its own right that in turn works its way backward to provide substance and content for their vision of first times.

The chapters that follow are grouped into four sections: Puritanism and the Enlightenment, Biblical Scholarship and Fundamentalism, European Traditions in America, and Indigenous American Traditions. A response and assessment concludes each section. Some of the responses carry further the line of inquiry found in the chapters. Other responses contain sharp rebuttals and fundamental disagreements.

The disagreements are rooted partially in the fact that the terrain explored here was initially unfamiliar ground to many of the conference participants. It will be unfamiliar ground to many readers as well. One will not find here, therefore, the kind of neat, closely defined history that emerges when a category or theme has been explored and reexplored by scholars over a considerable period of time. One will find instead a volume marked by questions, explorations, suggestions, implications, and by abundant pointers for further research and analysis. Those who have contributed to this volume will be well rewarded if this book becomes a meaningful first step toward understanding the role of the restoration theme in American religious history.

NOTES

1. Good starting points for assessing the restoration theme in New World Catholicism and Judaism are John Leddy Phelan, *The Millennial Kingdom of the Franciscans in the New World,* 2d ed. rev. (Berkeley: University of California Press, 1970); and Jonathan D. Sarna, *Jacksonian Jew: The Two Worlds of Mordecai Noah* (New York: Holmes and Meier, 1981).

2. Theodore Dwight Bozeman, *To Live Ancient Lives: The Primitivist Dimension in New England Puritanism* (Chapel Hill: University of North Carolina Press, 1988), 11.

3. Arthur O. Lovejoy and George Boas, *Primitivism and Related Ideas in Antiquity: Contributions to the History of Primitivism* (Baltimore: The Johns Hopkins Press, 1935; reprinted New York: Octagon Books, 1965), 1–11.

4. Fred Somkin, *Unquiet Eagle: Memory and Desire in the Idea of American Freedom, 1815–1860* (Ithaca: Cornell University Press, 1967), 57.

5. Richard T. Hughes, "From Civil Dissent to Civil Religion—and Beyond," *Religion in Life* 49 (Autumn 1980): 270.

6. See Jan Shipps, *Mormonism: The Story of a New Religious Tradition* (Urbana: University of Illinois Press, 1985), esp. 67–85.

7. Harrell made this judgment in a banquet address that concluded the Restoration Ideal in American History conference. See epilogue.

8. For two typological studies of primitivism in modern and American Christianity, compare Samuel S. Hill, Jr., "A Typology of American Restitutionism: From Frontier Revivalism and Mormonism to the Jesus Movement," *Journal of the American Academy of Religion* 44 (March 1976): 65–76; and Richard T. Hughes, "Christian Primitivism as Perfectionism: From Anabaptists to Pentecostals," in *Reaching Beyond: Chapters in the History of Perfectionism,* ed. Stanley Burgess (Peabody, MA: Hendrickson Publishers, 1986), 213–55.

9. Thomas Paine, *Rights of Man,* pt. 2, in *The Complete Writings of Thomas Paine,* vol. 1, ed. Philip S. Foner (New York: The Citadel Press, 1945), 376.

10. Roger Rosenblatt, "A Letter to the Year 2086," *Time* 129 (Dec. 29, 1986): 24–29.

11. Cf. Robert N. Bellah, et al., *Habits of the Heart: Individualism and Commitment in American Life* (New York: Harper and Row, 1985), esp. chapters 2, 3, and 6.

12. Nathaniel Hawthorne, *The Scarlet Letter* (New York: New American Library, 1959), 132.

PART ONE

Puritanism and the Enlightenment

1

Biblical Primitivism: An Approach to New England Puritanism

THEODORE DWIGHT BOZEMAN

PERRY Miller died in 1963, before the campus revolutions, before the first men stepped upon the moon. Yet with recent social-historical productions as a partial exception, the course of American Puritan studies in the interim has described a continual cycling back to his great synthetic work on the mind of New England. As if reaching testily from the grave, Miller has done much to control the scholarly agenda even of his severe critics. This is certainly true of those who have labored to demonstrate variety and dissensus in Puritan-era New England in contrast to his report of intellectual unity. If no feature of Miller's *New England Mind* has been more influential than its premise that "the first three generations . . . paid almost unbroken allegiance to a unified body of thought,"[1] so an impressively large number of recent students have taken opposition under the banner of pluralism. Everett Emerson sounded the characteristic note, announcing in 1968 that "we now recognize Puritanism as much less unified than Miller made it out to be." And what seemed less unified to Emerson seemed virtual chaos to Kenneth Silverman: in the early settlements he found, perhaps with a touch of hyperbole, "a welter of uncertainty among Puritans themselves regarding practically every religious, political, literary, and social notion entertained."[2]

At no time has the perception of dissensus held the field. Nor would it be wide of the mark to see in the body of scholarship exploring dissensus a welter of uncertainty respecting its sources, configurations, and extent. And yet revision in this vein not only continues unabated, but it has reached something of a climax in Philip Gura's *Glimpse of Sion's Glory*. Bringing to bear the most thorough and integrated knowledge of religious dissent yet attained by any historian, and deploying his data with admirable ingenuity, Gura there devoted some 330 packed pages to illustration of the thesis that "*heterogeneity,* not [Miller's] unanimity" actually characterized the Puritan colonies' religious life and thought.[3]

Gura's monument to the pluralist thesis illustrates anew the problem of definition that ever has impeded understanding of colonial American religion. What distinctively was the "puritanism" that figured so largely, whether as a divisive or unifying force, in early New England? As with the great majority of historians who have turned their attention to the subject, and notwithstanding the many and notorious confusions about the "puritan" differentia which for decades have vexed workers in this area, Gura does not develop and state a working definition. Almost offhandedly, his narrative tends to focus upon the subjective, spiritist, "mystical" strain of piety described by J. Fulton Maclear in an influential essay of 1956 and to assume this as the crucial Puritan axis. Puritanism thus construed was inherently unstable, inevitably generating antinomian and spiritist offshoots. These, in turn, become evidence of "puritan" heterogeneity. Because, in addition Gura sees in the early colonies' official Congregationalism largely an ad hoc, compromising construction designed to co-opt and neutralize radical demands, he reasonably can conclude that the Founders' society was not centered upon a preexisting, positive theological consensus.[4] In so doing, he reinforces the widespread impression that to seek or specify an American Puritan "mind"—a peculiar, coherent, intrinsically powerful, and historically continuous rendering of the Christian redemption—is to traffic in "fallacious concretion." We propose that a more considered attention to definition, to discerning the distinctive Puritan signature within historic English religion, will lead to a different conclusion; and further, that scrupulous attention to definition is a sine qua non of further conceptual advance in any department of American or English Puritan studies.

To elaborate such a definition, drawing upon materials and events through a century and more after the Elizabethan Settlement and locating the Puritan distinctives within the international community of Reformed Protestantism, hardly can be the province of a twelve-page essay. This endeavor will be far more modest. It will be to offer a preliminary sketch of one element in the profile of historic Puritanism that, although arguably the most fundamental, is little observed in existing interpretation: the drive toward origins. Certainly there is no lack of recognition that Puritan voices habitually appealed to the ancient nation of Israel and to the primitive Christian churches. Yet this appeal and its accompanying assumptions, this peculiar reversion back to an "ancient" and "primitive" standard, remains to be pursued at length as a clue both major and structural to the meaning of this most powerful early movement in English-speaking Protestantism.

Keeping the pluralist thesis in mind, I have selected to examine from countless possibilities two points of conflict in the early history of Massachusetts. First, there was the episode of the veils. In 1630 Samuel Skelton, then pastor of the church at Salem, argued that the Apostle Paul's injunction to the Corinthian church that women should worship with their heads covered (I Cor. 11:2–16) should be obeyed by the Massachusetts churches. In this view he seems later to have been joined by Roger Williams, and the practice was begun in the Salem congregation. Contention ensued. In March of 1634, John Cotton, then emerging as the most authoritative clerical voice, decided to address the issue. In a Thursday lecture in Boston he held "that where (by the custom of the place) they [the veils] were not a sign of the women's subjection, they were not commended by the apostle." After the sermon John Endecott, a past and future governor of the Bay Colony, rose to disagree and defend Skelton's position. The argument rose to some heat and after a time Governor John Winthrop intervened to end it. Cotton's view seems to have prevailed. Veils were not introduced in the Boston church and later Cotton journeyed to Salem and preached a sermon that scotched the practice there.[5]

Second, there was the extraordinary circumstance that the first two presidents of Harvard College, entrusted to train in learning and godliness the most aspiring male youths of New England, held and promoted deviant sacramental views. Despite the caustic attitudes of magisterial Protestants—for such were the political and religious leaders of the Congregationalist colonies—towards "anabaptism," both Dunster and Chauncy after their arrival in Massachusetts adopted irregular positions upon baptism. Dunster held that the baptism of infants was unauthorized by Scripture; Chauncy disagreed but maintained that the biblical standard required immersion rather than sprinkling; and to this he added the demand that the Lord's Supper, which in the colony's churches was celebrated on Sabbath morning, be performed in the evening in accord with apostolic archetype. For present purposes it is unnecessary to relate the details, but these variances from established doctrine predictably occasioned much dispute and dissatisfaction during the 1650s and 1660s.[6]

The veiling of women, baptism of adults only, total immersion, and evening communion—these were part of a radical fringe of ideas all

but universally repudiated within the Reformed Protestant interna-
tionale in which New England Congregationalists took their place, and
they were resisted zealously in Massachusetts. And yet their presence
in the Bay Colony is an evidence of dissensus only on one level, for
beneath the surface of dispute there lay a far more extensive area of
agreement. It came to light both in Skelton's appeal to apostolic injunction and in Cotton's reinterpretation of that injunction. It appeared again in Dunster's and Chauncy's assessment of New Testament practice as binding precedent. These and many similar cases
attest that often enough dissenting voices in seventeenth-century New
England shared with the reigning authorities in church and state an
uncontested unanimity of assumptions about the Christian dispensation. Sacred writ of course was the key; the pronounced "biblicism"
of Puritan programs is perhaps their most remarked feature. Yet merely
to note, with so many students of Puritan ideas and deeds, the intense
devotion of precise Protestants to the Bible tells us very little. What
we must perceive is that Puritan perceptions of Scripture emerged from
and were shaped by an underlying sense of reality. Its key assumption—
accepted no less by Skelton, Dunster, or Chauncy than by Cotton,
Thomas Hooker, or John Winthrop—was the supremacy of the first.
The typifying element was a reversion, undercutting both Catholic and
"Anglican" appeals to a continuity of tradition, back to the "first" or
"primitive" order of things narrated in the Protestant Scriptures. Holy
Scripture stood to the fore in Puritan estimation as the great reinvoking
narrative of first, and only thus authoritative, times and ways.

The thesis that the first is supreme was not devised in the American
Colonies. It was a selective continuation of patterns deeply rooted in
historical Western culture. Certainly it was integral to many phases of
medieval thought, especially to ventures in ecclesiastical criticism and
reform and to movements of radical dissent. On English soil from the
fourteenth century it was the structuring ingredient in Lollard devotion
to "the condition of the church when it enjoyed direct conversation
with Christ, the estate of the Primitive Church."[7] In the immediate
background of reformation in early sixteenth-century England stood
Erasmian Christian humanism with its characteristic summons *ad
fontes,* back to the patristic sources and to the pure and simple philosophy of Christ. Pre-Puritan English Reformers, drawing explicitly
upon all of these heritages, developed programmatic appeals to the
"first, original and most perfect state"[8] of things that "in the corruption
of time"[9] had become encrusted and forgotten. It was in the context
of Protestant calls for a "retrograde movement" to biblical originals
that the preparation and gradual popularization of a vernacular English

Bible became the "supreme event" of the English Reformation. Hence orientation to the first and unspoilt was a pervasive part of the intellectual heritage upon which Puritans drew.[10]

Had the circumstances of religious reform in England approximated those of Protestant Switzerland, the Reformed precincts of South Germany, or the Dutch Netherlands, the thrust of the English towards an original purity probably would not have developed with such vigor; indeed, then no pronounced "puritanism" need have arisen. Striving against impossible odds to accomplish structural reform of the church and to move a morally turbid population to repent and amend in accord with terms of the national covenant, and yet sustaining significant access to university, pulpit, and press, such men sifted out their polemical weapons and sharpened them to an unaccustomed degree. Prominent among these were the various components of Christian primitivism. They reflected ideals held by magisterial Protestants everywhere, not excluding Anglican apologists for the churchly arrangements ratified by the Elizabethan Settlement; but Puritan spokesmen took them up with an especial consistency and vigor. From the time of the original vestiarian movement to the 1630s, they could find no more incisive rallying cry than this: "that is true, whatsoever is first."[11] They strove to convince their countrymen that as the stream of history flowed out "distant from the fountain [of biblical times]," the "less pure and clear" it had become; hence a proper reformation must be distinctly a *re*formation, reclaiming ties to the first. Progress in Christian reform was simultaneously a retrogression, for the very means of advance into greater purity and towards the eschatological vindication was retrieval of the ancient and unspoilt. Thus as dissenting voices portrayed the moral and ecclesiastical changes that alone would ensure the national welfare, they called men back to contemplate the moral law, the reforming kings, and the deuteronomic principles of ancient Israel; so too, in their particular fever against the "rags of popery" in the present church, they practically made a career of appealing to "the Apostles' time, when all things were pure," and "before the white came to be speckled and spotted with black errors and stains."[12]

A broad range of theological developments within Puritanism can be traced along a pattern-imitation axis, a product of the assumption that the history of the Old and New Testament peoples was precedential. Certainly this position was held to a greater or lesser degree within the Scottish and continental Reformed churches as well, but under English conditions it came into abnormal prominence. Whereas defenders of the established church busied themselves qualifying and supplementing biblical authority, Puritan thinkers dwelt tirelessly upon the archetypal forms (most notably the Presbyterian and Congregationalist platforms of ecclesiastical polity and "church discipline") of biblical, primitive, and golden days. As John F. Wilson suggests, such preoccupation, although held with varying degrees of programmatic intent, does much to "locate Puritanism within the distinctive tradition of international Calvinism."[13] It does even more to differentiate it as a party of distinct interest within the English church.

Puritanism, to be sure, embodied as well aggressive and high-strung emphases upon *moral* purity; and to that degree its ethical and evangelical dimensions must enter into any definition of the subject. But with an equal degree alike of passion and intellectual coherence, its proponents also wrestled through the decades with problems of loss and restoration, remembrance and imitation. It is an amazing circumstance that these themes stand neglected or unseen in the bulk of scholarly writing in the field. We venture to suggest that they describe a whole and coherent side of the distinctively "Puritan" venture in ideas. Like those of Aristotelian physics or the faculty psychology, the organizing principles of primitivist thinking were assumed so elementally that they rarely appear wholly and connectedly in the written remains of English dissent. Puritans might disagree with Anglican apologists as to the proper identification, scope, and jurisdiction of first-times patterns, but they considered the primacy (and precedential force) of the first to stand beyond debate.

Thus although treatises upon vocational calling, upon preparation for conversion or special providences, were crucial to the movement's propaganda, there probably never appeared a sermon or text devoted per se to the explication of firstness, although a work like William Whately's *Prototypes, or, the Primary Precedent Presidents [i.e., precedents] out of the Book of Genesis* (1627) brought the precedential dimension of Puritan thinking clearly enough to the fore. Hence it might not be evident to the reader of Puritan remains that they presume and rely heavily upon a version of Christian primitivism unless attention were called expressly to the relevant and scattered passages. But once the initial clues are examined and their possible far-reaching implication for Puritan studies is grasped, the inquirer may be lead on from text to text and theme to theme until the profile stands revealed in all its coherence and power. The further analysis of this profile, should it receive its deserved place on the scholarly agenda, will prove a boon to students of early New England. In the largest and most useful sense, it will go far to resolve the definitional unclarity that for so long has impeded interpretation of our early religious history. It will eliminate many misconceptions. And certainly it will bring the issue of unanimity versus dissensus into clearer perspective.

We may consider, first, the terminology through which the aims of the colonial project were expressed. To a far greater extent than usually is realized, participants in the Bay venture spelled out, debated, clarified, and committed to paper their reasons for venturing to a far-flung wilderness. Once their many expressions of purpose are gathered and appraised, a startling result appears: there is no trace of the normally alleged errand into the wilderness on behalf of the world. In the great majority of cases, religiously activated migrants described their departure from England (so far as this was a matter of positive mission rather than of flight) as a search for "liberty of the ordinances"; often this was joined to a venomous critique both of "ceremonies" and of "human invention" in the Church of England.[14] Obviously these are technical terms to be understood within a context of special assumption, and once this is appreciated it is precisely the primitivist configuration that comes into view. In the applicable lingo, "ordinances" were the archetypal forms of evangelism, worship, discipline, and church order given in New Testament days. It was for their recovery and imitation that a "Puritan" interest had labored in vain for nearly three-quarters of a century before the founding of Salem and Boston. Now, in the 1620s, the rise of the Laudian party with its harsher policing of the official liturgy and its gradual introduction of new and semicatholic usages seemed the end of an era. In light of the new zeal for "ceremonies," lingering hopes for a true English *Re*formation no longer could be sustained. Yet more, so grave an error must evoke at last a long-restrained divine punishment upon a convenanted but erring nation.

And what was the crux of the offense that could have such awing result? *Human invention* was the key. This term, a mainstay of Puritan polemic in all periods, identified the fountain of error through which the purity and simplicity of the first Christian churches gradually had been converted into the hideously convoluted affair that was Roman Catholicism; it pointed as well to the misconstruction of Protestant faith that long had blocked and now threatened to destroy the cause of reformation in England. "Invention" in this context meant disruption of biblical-precedential rule over the Christian quest for redemption; more specifically it meant the contrivance of ecclesiastical forms—such as the surplice, that roundly hated post-primordial "novelty" whose retention by the Elizabethan compromise had given rise to the first recognizably Puritan activities in the 1560s—to modify or replace those given and certified primitively in the first, great age.[15] With some bemusement we may remark that *errand,* a term which does not appear in the literature of the Great Migration, has come to be regarded as an essential index of the founders' aims, whereas *invention, ordinance,* and related terms used by the migrants themselves to signal both their deepest "puritan" grievance against the present English church and their fondest hope for the future, almost wholly have been ignored.

If devotion to the first thus looms largest among the conscious and professed purposes of the Great Migration, so we reasonably might expect to find religious ideals and activities in the infant Congregationalist colonies taking on the appearance of a restorationist crusade. Certainly the religious life of the region and period cannot be explained entirely in such terms, but we suggest that a hitherto largely unseen coherence will emerge if the early American Puritan remains be read from the standpoint of the founders' demonstrable zeal for recovery of original ordinances. Here, for example, is the essential clue to comprehending the affair of the veils and the sacramental aberrations of Dunster and Chauncy. In this instance sharp and potentially irreconcilable differences were involved. The wearing of veils was put down, and Dunster was removed from the presidency of Harvard in 1654 by reason of intransigent anabaptism. But as in many similar instances in the early colonies, the issues were fought out upon a common ground of devotion to precedent and imitation. Cotton's rebuttal to Skelton merely revised that zealous Salemite's construction of an apostolic archetype. Chauncy, whose ardor for the first stood high among his qualifications for the college presidency, retained his office in good standing on the condition that it not be made a platform for his views upon immersion and evening communion. Disagreement there was, but it emerged within a larger unanimity of viewpoint as to the exigencies of the Christian movement in a world long fallen from primitive ways.

Once reform-minded immigrants found themselves in a congenial setting far from persecuting bishops, they turned in a hundred ways to recovery of first-times ordinances. Their most visible and sweeping feat was construction of a Congregationalist church order. One of the most firmly established findings of recent research is that the New Englanders did not arrive with a fully worked out ecclesiology. The systematic scheme of the "Cambridge Platform" of 1648 represents a considerable process of exploration, debate, and compromise. The initial unclarity, however, should not be confused with ideological disunity or confusion. Most of the needed concepts were taken over from preexisting Puritan theory, and the remainder were hammered out in the informal consociation of Boston-area clergy. The existence of this group, which began meeting regularly in 1633, was itself a testimony to clerical consensus and cooperation upon most of the important premises.[16]

Of the several early formulations of the Congregationalist way, the fullest and most authoritative were the "Model of Church and Civil Power" (1634 or 1635), John Cotton's *Keys of the Kingdom of Heaven* (1644), John Norton's *Answer* (ca. 1645), Thomas Hooker's *Survey of the Summe of Church Discipline* (1648), and *A Platform of Discipline Gathered out of the Word of God* (i.e., the "Cambridge Platform," 1648). These documents, including the early "Model," reveal an approach to the issues that is determined fundamentally by a primitivist idealism. Negatively expressed, the governing aim in every case was to make the fullest possible withdrawal from the Catholic and Anglican error of "human invention"; in positive terms the authors aspired to the clearest possible display of the "form and pattern of Government" imparted in scriptural narrative of the first Christian churches.[17]

As they pursued this agenda, filling their texts and margins with biblical citations, New England theorists revealed to the full the customary Reformed-Puritan allegiance to the sacred book. And as they brought their material into order, they also displayed a well-known bent for schematic organization. Yet it would be a mistake to designate their procedure simply an act of textual analysis, or to assume that the resulting system was essentially an appeal for rational assent. For in these as in virtually all examples of Puritan utterance holy writ was approached, in the first instance, neither as a technical sourcebook nor—contrary to repeated claims by students of Puritan Ramism—as a logical structure, but as dramatic event. Perception of biblical content as a vividly real world of "primitive times" was essential to the whole enterprise. Only as its panorama of event became alive, familiar and compelling in the believer's imagination, was it able to prescribe "form and pattern" to modern Christian churches. The "parts of church government," as the authors of the "Cambridge Platform" expressed it, "are all ... exactly described in the word of God"; but they were described in the context of sacred event, through enactment, through dramatic exhibition. And so a first task of the expositor was to summon alive the acts of "Paul in matters of Christian liberty," the examples of "Moses, Joshua, David, Solom[on], Asa, Jehoshaphet, Hezekiah, Josiah ... putting forth their authority in matters of religion," the lament of Jeremiah against "false devices [i.e., inventions] of men" in worship, or the authority of "Peter considered not only as an apostle, but an elder also, yea, and a believer too."[18]

Drama, then, the arresting spectacle of first and singular times, was the first postulate. And yet for the case in hand it was but backdrop to the display of precedents. To the intellectual historian, perhaps the most noteworthy feature of the four documents is their underlying assumption that every defining feature of a properly ordered church is delineated in a scripturally given "express example." Everything else, the schematization, the swirls of polemic, the occasionally heavy reliance upon traditional forms of logical dispute, even the obtrusive Ramism of Hooker's *Survey* is secondary to a "right proceeding according to the [biblical] pattern." New England Congregationalism thus took form as imitation of primitive events. As it had been through some eight decades of Presbyterian- and Congregationalist-Puritan dissent, so it was an axiom of the settlers' conscious theory that the defining features of church order had been preenacted in first times. Now at last they were to be reenacted, to be "taken from the pattern set before us" in the covering "case[s]" of first-time drama.[19] Thus the proposition that "the church of brethren has the power . . . to choose their officers" was grounded upon the use of "vote and suffrage" in the selection of Judas's successor in the apostolic band (Acts 1:15); upon the election of elders in the earliest church in Antioch "by lifting up of hands" (Acts 14:23); or upon the Apostles' instructions to the saints gathered in Jerusalem to elect a staff of seven deacons; and similar instances (Acts 6:3, 5, 7). By the same token the "church covenant" by which a Christian congregation was to be formed found its original in "the Covenant . . which made the Family of Abraham and the children of Israel to be a church and people unto God."[20] "Synods" were to echo "the pattern of that precedent of synods, Acts 15:18," in which a dispute concerning the Christian use of Mosaic law was "sent up to the apostles and elders at Jerusalem"; and the like.[21]

If space permitted us to make further inventory of early American Congregationalist theory and practice and to examine the remains from the conceptual angle here suggested, we would find evidence on every hand that the drive toward origins contributed much both to define and cohere an "American Puritanism." Perhaps most important, we better would command an entire complex of the founders' terminology—their constant talk of the "first," "original," "primitive," and "ancient"; of "ordinances" and "ceremonies," of "pattern" and "example," of "purity" and "simplicity" and many cognate expressions. Then we would better comprehend the special ritual and gravity with which the first town settlers organized to enact the "first beginning" of a church. We would discern that the founders' engrained veneration for first times supplies the key to unlock the elusive mystery of the

American Jeremiads, for that key is simply the qualified admission of the founders' time to the realm of the first and great. We would discover that the alleged "enigma of the Bay Psalm Book" dissolves once that landmark of English psalmody is recognized as an effort to repristinate Christian song. We would find John Winthrop and his fellow magistrates engaged in an effort to recover and apply the principles of Mosaic judicial law. We would observe that Puritan millennialism, although it may in limited ways have pointed towards later doctrines of progress, was in fact the pinnacle of restorationist hope; it projected the finally triumphant reversion to primordial purity and simplicity. And noting the orientation of Puritan religious theory to the approved past, its determination to recover and abide in a perfect and therefore changeless pattern, we would much improve our grasp of correlations between the theology and the traditionalist, imitative society revealed in recent social histories of the first New England towns. When viewed as part of a quest towards the first, these and many other issues come at once into clearer focus.

Such findings make it doubtful that the pluralist thesis in any form can stand as a sweeping characterization of Puritan New England in its formative decades. What is at issue is not the presence of dissenting ideas and groups both within and without the Congregationalist orbit, or their probable influence upon the official society, but recognition of an essentially self-sufficient and historically anchored dynamism of ideas at the heart of that society. From Winthrop's "Modell of Christian Charity" to the "Cambridge Platform," the great body of literary evidence remains squarely within the conceptual frame established by the long-lived and certainly coherent tradition of Tudor and Stuart primitivist dissent. Most of the defining features were rooted back in some seven decades (as of 1630) of remarkably cohesive campaigning for *re*formation in the mother country; the essentials were present already in the Presbyterian agitations of the 1570s. Granted that troublesome, even unresolvable conflict at times emerged within the frame—the cases of Skelton, Dunster, and Chauncy again, or the well-known troubles with semi-Presbyterians at Hingham and Newbury, or the rancorous disputes about the Halfway Covenant. But when seen within a larger continuum of intellectual history, these were the arguments of men and women who disagreed upon a single point or two within an encompassing and historic body of concepts they held passionately in common. And at all times, perhaps excepting the brief Massachusetts governorship of Henry Vane (1636–37), the dominant intellectual leaders remained dedicated to an "apostolic" Christianity formed along Congregationalist lines.

We may grant, again, that their demands, made with customary Puritan rigor, for "precise" conformity to objective, disciplinary forms, could provoke rebellion against reformation-by-precedent in the name of freedom and subjective experience—as witness the Antinomian controversy of the first decade or the Quaker challenge of the third. But spiritist radicalism, contrary to a persistent misrepresentation, was not a straight extension of Puritan content. It is therefore dubious evidence of "puritan" heterogeneity. Unquestionably it grew out of Puritanism; however, it may have drawn upon other and shadowy inheritances from medieval and left-wing Reformation sources. If in widely varying degrees, it did carry over familiar Puritan content. But just as clearly it commenced with deliberate and often dramatic repudiation of distinctive Puritan norms. If we measure it alone by the concerns of this essay, we find it thrusting pointedly beyond ordinances, beyond the established Puritan canons of biblical-precedential reform, into the subjectively freer ethos of the spiritist strain of the Radical Reformation. Moreover, excepting partly the Antinomian conflict at its brief peak, spiritist dissensus in earliest Massachusetts, Connecticut, New Haven, and probably New Plymouth bore but dim comparison with the true heterogeneity soon to emerge in revolutionary England.

New England, of course, did not live by restoration alone. A full assessment of pluralist claims must include other dimensions of Puritan thought and practice. Covenantal doctrine, zeal for "effectual calling" (conversion), an elaborately introspective pietism, collective rituals of "humiliation" and repentance, Sabbatarianism, rigorous moral discipline and withal, an extensive sharing of international Reformed divinity—by the time of the Great Migration of the 1630s, such concerns were held in common by a great majority of "precise" dissenters. All became forces for ideological and institutional unity in New England, forces disregarded by those who can see but disarray in the founders' remains. Certainly it is unity that first and most impresses the student of restorationist ideals and practice. If we look alone at that peculiar devotion to firstness that originally constituted and always fundamentally shaped an "English Puritan interest," the established religion of the earliest Congregationalist colonies will be found to embody one of the most positive, entrenched, and coherent theological impulses in all of modern church history. This impulse, as the founders believed and often said, was the largest and most impressive result in either Old or New England of some seven decades of struggle to recapture, to reiterate, and to enjoy golden times and ways.

NOTES

1. Perry Miller, *The New England Mind: The Seventeenth Century* (1939; Boston: Beacon Press, 1961), vii.

2. Michael McGiffert, "American Puritan Studies in the 1960s," *William and Mary Quarterly* 27 (Jan. 1970): 40–41.

3. Phillip F. Gura, *A Glimpse of Sion's Glory: Puritan Radicalism in New England, 1620–1660* (Middletown CT: Wesleyan University Press, 1984), 7.

4. Gura, *Sion's Glory,* viii, 10, 11, 21, 24, 58, 238, 257–58.

5. John Winthrop, *Winthrop's Journal: "History of New England," 1630–1649,* 2 vols., ed. James Kendall Hosmer (New York: Charles Scribner's Sons, 1908), 1: 120–21; for the text of this sermon, see William Hubbard, *A General History of New England from the Discovery to MDCLXXX,* vol. 5 in *Massachusetts Historical Society Collections,* ser. 2, 5: 204–5.

6. Samuel Eliot Morison, *Builders of The Bay Colony,* rev. ed. (Boston: Houghton Mifflin, 1958), 214–16; "Life of the Rev. Pres. Chauncy," vol. 10 in *Massachusetts Historical Society Collections,* ser. 1, 10: 174–75.

7. Howard Kaminsky, "Wyclifism as Ideology of Revolution," *Church History* 32 (March 1963): 68.

8. John Hooper, *The Early Writings of John Hooper,* ed. Samuel Carr (Cambridge, 1843), 83.

9. Thomas Cranmer, *Miscellaneous Writings and Letters of Thomas Cranmer,* ed. John E. Cox (Cambridge, 1846), 528; see also George Joye, *The Unity and Schism of the Old Church* (n.p., 1543), Sig. A5.

10. John N. King, *English Reformation Literature* (Princeton: Princeton University Press, 1982), 151; E. G. Rupp, *Studies in the Making of the English Protestant Tradition* (Cambridge: Cambridge University Press, 1966), 48.

11. Thomas Cartwright, *A Reply to an Answer Made of M. Doctor [John] Whitgift* (n.p., 1573), 104; Thomas Brightman, *A Revelation of the Apocalypse* (Amsterdam: 1611), 113.

12. Brightman, *Apocalypse,* 47; John Cotton, *Singing of Psalms a Gospel Ordinance* (London: 1647), 62; Robert Crowley, *An Answer for the Time, to the Examination* (n.p., n.d.), 21: Thomas Taylor, *Christ's Victory over the Dragon* (London: 1633), 141.

13. John F. Wilson, *Pulpit in Parliament* (Princeton: Princeton University Press, 1969), 144, and see 143.

14. For a sampling of these themes, see "A Model of Church and Civil Power," segmentally reprinted in Roger Williams, *The Bloudy Tenent of Persecution for Cause of Conscience,* in vol. 3 of *The Complete Writings of Roger Williams* (New York: Russell and Russell, 1963), 3: 279; John Allin and Thomas Shepard, *A Defense of the Answer made unto the Nine Questions* (London: 1648), 4; Thomas Shepard, *God's Plot, the Paradoxes of Puritan Piety, Being the Autobiography and Journal of Thomas Shepard,* ed. Michael McGiffert (Boston: University of Massachusetts Press, 1972), 55–56; "John Cotton's Reasons for his Removal," in Alexander Young, *Chronicles of the First Planters of the Colony of Massachusetts Bay* (Boston: 1846), 438–44.

15. For a sampling of Puritan usages, see Thomas Cartwright, *A Commentary Upon the Epistle to the Colossians* (London: 1612), 122; John Udall, *Demonstration of the Truth of that Discipline, which Christ has Prescribed in His Word, for the Government of his Church,* ed. Edward Arber (London: 1890), 6; Richard Greenham, *The Works of the Reverend M. Richard Greenham* (London: 1601), 23; Thomas Hooker, *A Survey of the Summe of Church Discipline* (London: 1648), pt. 4:10; John Davenport, *Another Essay* (Cambridge, MA, 1661), 15.

16. The story is told in full by Robert Francis Scholz, in " 'The Reverend Elders'—Faith, Fellowship and Politics in the Ministerial Community of Massachusetts Bay, 1630–1710" (Ph.D. dissertation, University of Minnesota, 1966).

17. *A Platform of Church Discipline Gathered out of the Word of God,* in *The Creeds and Platforms of Congregationalism,* ed. Williston Walker (Boston: Pilgrim Press, 1960), 203.

18. *Platform of Church Discipline,* 203; "Model of Church and Civil Power," 260; *Platform of Church Discipline,* 236; Hooker, *Survey,* 6; John Cotton, *The Keys of the Kingdom of Heaven* in *John Cotton on the Churches of New England,* ed. Larzer Ziff (Cambridge, MA: Belknap Press of Harvard University Press, 1968), 91.

19. *Platform of Church Discipline,* 198, 233; Cotton, *Keys,* 150.

20. Cotton, *Keys,* 102; John Norton, *The Answer to the Whole Set of Questions of William Apollonius,* trans. Douglas Horton (Cambridge, MA: Harvard University Press, 1958), 115; *Platform of Church Discipline,* 208; Hooker, *Survey,* pt. 1:69.

21. Cotton, *Keys,* 121, 105; *Platform of Church Discipline,* 233; "Model of Church and Civil Power," 390; Norton, *The Answer,* 128, 133; Hooker, *Survey,* pt. 4:1.

2

Roger Williams and
"the Restauration of Zion"

C. LEONARD ALLEN

IN the summer of 1636, six months after Roger Williams had been banished from the Massachusetts Bay Colony, John Winthrop wrote his friend Williams a letter, one of many in the years that followed. He asked simply, "From what spirit, and to what end do you drive?" Williams replied: like you, I "seek Jesus who was nailed to the gallows, I ask the way to lost Zion, I witness what I believe I see patiently . . . in sackcloth."[1] The brief reply sums up remarkably well both the mood and the central themes of Williams's long career as a religious controversialist. It catches up the pervasive restorationist impulse that undergirded his sharp polemics for the next forty years. Without exaggeration we can say that Williams's life was dominated by this search for "lost Zion," that his overriding passion was the quest for God's pure church.

In this central concern, Williams must be placed against the larger backdrop of biblical primitivism as it developed in sixteenth- and seventeenth-century Reformed Protestantism. Roger Williams and the Puritans stood squarely within the Reformed tradition of "reformation by biblical precedent," a tradition that received sharper focus and more vigorous application in Puritan England. Here there developed, as Dwight Bozeman has pointed out, a broad and often taken-for-granted configuration of ideas centered in the primacy of the "first" and the drive toward origins. Scripture was the divine archetype vividly portraying "first" events and directions. The inexorable human proclivity to embellish these first-times directions and to supplement them with "human invention" necessitated an aggressive and continual drive back to the simplicity and undiluted power of the "first." This biblicist primitivism, though largely overlooked as a coherent and pervasive pattern of ideas in Puritan thought, stands near the center of Puritan concern, underlying and shaping most of the typically Puritan issues.[2]

If the primitivist configuration is pervasive in the Puritan tradition as a whole, it is equally or more so in the thought of Roger Williams. Although Williams quickly strikes us as eccentric, even bizarre, in his unceasing and troublesome dissent from orthodox norms, he shared a large common core of primitivist assumptions and terminology with the Bay Colony leaders. His most basic disagreement with the Puritan theologians was not over the primacy of biblical archetypes or the rejection of "human invention," but over the nature and structure of the archetypes themselves. The New Testament alone was the "pattern" for the church, Williams believed, whereas most people since Constantine had set up the "best patternes of the kings of Judah, David, Solomon, Asa, Jehosaphat, Josiah, Hezekiah."[3] The trouble with the Bay Colony ministers, he charged, was a misunderstanding about the Christian archetype, and a lack of courage to live in full conformity to archetypal norms.

Following his banishment, Williams continued even more zealously the debate over archetypes. A central theme of his polemics in the months that followed was the charge that reformation was incomplete in Massachusetts, that Puritans had failed to separate the church from the world and thus restore the purity of the first age. In the years between 1636 and 1644, Williams entered a period of intense theological ferment. In 1639 he was "emboldened" to embrace believers' baptism, but only a few months later left the Baptist congregation at Providence, renounced his baptism, and evidently never associated himself with a church again.[4] His long quest for "the first pattern" of the church, his restless preoccupation with ecclesiastical purity, his efforts to "finish holiness in the fear of God," all now stirred in him a shocking conclusion. Not only had there been a "falling away ... from the first primitive Christian state or worship"—a theme all Puritans accepted in some fashion—but the church in fact had been extinguished, totally desolated by antichristian pollution.[5] The task now, Williams believed, was not to found churches but to denounce religious error and to wait for God's impending restoration of "lost Zion." The Rhode Island wilderness into which he had been banished was now transmuted into a far more desolate spiritual wilderness into which God's people as a whole had been banished.

For the rest of his life, Williams held this primitivist vision with steady resolve. Although he often entered the swirling debates of the time, both in England and New England, and seemed preoccupied with such current issues as liberty of conscience, ministerial authority and regulation, and church/state relations, the primitivist vision always stood behind and controlled his polemics. Near the end of his life, in a striking passage in his printed debate with some Quakers, Williams was more explicit: "There is a Time of purity and Primitive Sincerity, there is a time of Transgression and Apostacy, there is a time of the coming out of the Babilonian Apostasy and Wilderness."[6]

These three phrases, which set out so strikingly the pattern typical of Christian primitivism, provide a convenient framework to build a profile of Williams's restorationist vision.

For Williams, the sacred "time of purity" was the age of the primitive church, and the sacred archetype was the New Testament, which presented dramatically and vividly the first-times events. Because of Christ's incarnation, Williams claimed, the New Testament alone is the "true paterne" for the life of God's people. It contains "the *lights, patternes* and *presidents* to all succeeding ages." Christ and his apostles have given "particular *Rules* or *directions*" for all Christian duties. Every aspect of Christian worship must be authorized "either by way of *command, Promise,* or example" in the New Testament, even down to the smallest detail. Thus baptism should be in rivers "as the first *Christians* and the Lord *Jesus* himself did."[7] Only by imitating this pattern and reenacting these forms could Christians recover the purity of the "first."

Williams's view of the New Testament archetype for the church was dominated, throughout his scattered writings, by several major themes to which he often returned. In one passage he listed four themes that represented four identifying features or "marks" of the primitive church. "Such *persons,* such *Churches*" as bear these marks, he wrote, "are got neerest to *Christ Jesus.*"[8]

1. The first characteristic of those who have "got neerest to *Christ*" was a desire to be cleansed from the "*filthiness* of false *worships.*" God's work of grace in conversion not only should work a personal regeneration and result in a life of moral purity, but it also should sensitize one to God's pattern for church order and worship and thus result in ecclesiastical purity. Authentic conversion, for Williams, was found in "a turning of the whole man from the power of Sathan unto God, act. 26. Such a change, as if an old man became a new Babe ... yea, as amounts to Gods new creation in the soule." To what was essentially the standard Puritan view, he added that this inward spiritual change must be joined with "a true externall conversion" to the New Testament pattern of worship. Before a person is fit material for church membership, therefore, he must not only be regenerate but

must have repented of and turned from all antichristian pollutions which remained in the Church of England or any other church.[9]

In his urgings for full repentance, Williams did not deny the existence of genuine Christians who had not yet recognized the false, polluted ways of their worship and made a full repentance. There had been many thousands of such people in the time following the "captivitie" of the church, people who "in their persons, *Heart-waking,* in the life of *personall grace,* [but who] will yet be found fast asleep in respect of *publicke Christian worship.*" They belong to God and are "most deare and precious" to him, but in matters of worship are still among the "*Babylonians.*" Just as the Jews exiled in Babylon were still God's people, so were those in "mystical Babel" still spiritual, godly people— but they must come out of their exile before they can "build the Temple of his true church."[10]

Most of Christ's holy witnesses throughout history, in fact, had "been ignorant of the *true* Christ, that is, Christ taken for the Church in the true profession of that holy way of Worship, which he himselfe at first appointed." Williams distinguished between Christ known personally through his saving grace and Christ known as head of his church. The godly cannot be separated from Christ in the first sense, but can be in the second sense. Among those thousands of godly people separated in this second sense, Williams asserted, God had revealed various degrees of recognition of antichristian abominations. But they all needed a further experience of God's spirit at work in them, almost a "second kind of Regeneration," to complete their conversions and draw them out of such abominations.[11] To have a church true to the New Testament pattern, all of its members must have their souls plucked out of false worship in full repentance.

2. The second characteristic of those who have "got neerest to *Christ*" is that they attempt to practice, "in their *simplicity & purity,*" all his "ordinances and appointments." They strip away unflinchingly all the "inventions of men" that have clouded the divine pattern. They hold fast, no matter what the price in worldly reputation and position, to every command given by Christ, first and foremost in matters of God's worship, then in all other matters relating to service to God. They reject utterly any practice not commanded in the New Testament, no matter how pleasing and expedient it may seem to human judgment. They cling only to what is "first," and thus to what is unadultered and holy.

The demand for perfect outward conformity in addition to inward regeneration stood near the heart of Williams's ecclesiology. But to some of his opponents, John Cotton foremost among them, such demands appeared to be a return to a covenant of works. The church, Cotton maintained, is built upon the work of Christ, not that of man, and is maintained by the grace of God, not by precise adherence to a rigid pattern of outward forms. Christians can even "break Covenant, yet if they keep close to Christ, they have the Covenant, although they break it."[12] In Cotton's viewpoint, Roger Williams was guilty of preaching a covenant of works in his demand for complete purity in the life of the church. To demand perfection was to nullify the work of Christ and fall into the legalistic heresy of basing justification upon sanctification.

In a letter to John Winthrop several months after fleeing into the wilderness, Williams addressed this issue in defense of his teaching. He made a careful distinction between the personal salvation (regeneration) of a Christian and that person's obligation to seek God's pure worship and obey God's "appointments" (sanctification). He insisted that he was not questioning the sovereignty of God's grace in salvation, nor denying that people still mired in corrupt worship were godly people and thus counted among the elect; but he *was* urging that healthy faith would seek expression in pure forms of worship, that true godliness would yearn after the "purity & simplicity" of God's order.[13] In *Experiments of Spiritual Life and Health,* a devotional guide that Williams wrote for his wife after a serious illness, he stressed that one sign of true godliness was to "mourn and lament" the apostate condition of the church; the healthy soul, he added, was filled with a "holy vehement longing, after the *enjoyment* of *God,* and of *Christ,* in a *visible,* and *open profession* of his own holy *worship* and *Ordinances,* separate from all false *worships,* Gods, and Christs."[14] None of these efforts merited salvation—only Christ did that; but they were all a vital part of the Christian's efforts to "finish holiness in the feare of God."

3. The third characteristic of those who have "got neerest to *Christ*" is that they are "content with a poor and lowly condition in worldly things." In this they were like Christ. He was a glorious king, mighty and full of splendor, but only in his spiritual kingdom; in the world's eyes he had "the esteeme of a Mad man, a Deceiver, a Conjurer, a Traytor against Caesar, and destitute of an house wherein to rest his head."[15] Christ's lowliness and suffering in his worldly estate served as a model for his faithful followers; they should not expect any better treatment at the hands of the world than was given Jesus himself. Thus for Williams one prime mark of the true church was that it was always a suffering church.

In this conviction, he stood within the tradition created by John Foxe and others in the sixteenth century. In Foxe's national myth of the English martyrs, the true church is never the "most multitude" but always the "little flock," marked by affliction, persecution, and suffering. This became a central theme in the apocalyptic tradition of sixteenth-century English Protestantism, although in the later years of the century there arose the tendency to identify the persecuted "little flock," not with the faithful, but with the English nation itself.[16] It also became a prominent theme in the sectarian protests against the established church of England in the seventeenth century. It was not unusual for a sectarian writer to claim that a deep sense of God's approbation had been conferred upon him by an experience of persecution on behalf of cherished beliefs. Williams shared this sectarian experience and outlook. His own banishment from Massachusetts and isolation amid the savagery and hardships of the wilderness served to strengthen his identification with the huddled bands of believers in the early church and throughout history who had faced explusion, hardships, and often death. Furthermore, it bound him to a Christ whom he saw as despised and rejected yet reigning over a spiritual kingdom that could not be shaken.

Williams's deep conviction that the true church was always a suffering and persecuted church pervades his controversial writings and serves to illustrate how his New Testament archetype for the church and for discipleship contrasted with that of Cotton and those of similar views. Cotton, for example, looked to the deuteronomic theology of ancient Israel and saw that earthly peace and prosperity was assured to God's people when they "flourish in *holiness.*" Williams, however, argued to the contrary that those who are most holy and faithful are most persecuted, as "is the most evident in all the new *Testament,* and all mens new and fresh experience."[17] For Cotton, the reforming magistrate was necessary to uphold true religion and thus ensure the peace of the civil state and prosperity in body and goods. Williams retorted that while Scripture does promise that those who seek first the kingdom will prosper in some sense, these promises can by no stretch of the imagination be used to prove that Christ's followers will have outward prosperity in the present evil world. If one makes the proper typological distinction between national and spiritual Israel, thus taking the New Testament along as archetype, it will be evident that God does not promise prosperity for the nation that establishes true religion. He promises instead only persecution for his people, a persecution that seems heaviest for the most zealous and most faithful.

Since the apostasy, Williams believed, the clergy had disdained a humiliated, crucified Christ and had fashioned for themselves "*Pompus* and *Princely, temporall* and *Worldly Christians*" with the goal of attaining authority, wealth, and power. And the nearer they got to worldly wealth and ease through these means, the "further and further have they departed from *God,* from his *Truth,* from the *Simplicitie, Power,* and *Puritie* of *Christ Jesus* and true *Christianitie.*"[18] In contrast, God's faithful disciples must cling unswervingly to the Christ whose lordship is spiritual not temporal and who sets the supreme example of suffering for the truth. Summarizing this spiritual lordship and its implications for discipleship, Williams wrote: "If him thou seekest in these searching times, mak'st him alone thy white and soules beloved, willing to follow and be like him in doing, in suffering: although thou find'st him not in the restauration of his Ordinances, according to his first Patterne. Yet shall thou see him, raigne with him, eternally admire him, and enjoy him, when he shortly comes in flaming fire to burne up millions of ignorant and disobedient."[19]

4. Williams's understanding of Christ's spiritual lordship had far-reaching implications for his view of the relationship between church and state. If for the individual Christian, Christ's spiritual rule meant a lowly worldly estate and a despised minority status, then for the church as a whole it meant that the spiritual and the temporal were two entirely separate realms. From the separation of church and state Williams then drew his fourth characteristic of those persons who have "got neerest to *Christ*": they have a revulsion to persecuting people of different consciences.

In Old Testament Israel, Williams observed, God had used only one government to control both the civil and spiritual realms, but after Christ he had chosen in his wisdom to administer the two realms through two distinct governments, one religious and one civil. Christ's lordship was to be exercised now, not with physical weapons and coercion that were part of the civil realm, but only with the "two-edged sword" of the Spirit. To mingle these two realms, as Williams thought Puritans in both England and New England were doing, was to fall into "*Babylonish* and *confused mixtures*"; it was to ignore the vital typological distinction between the Old and New Testaments, to prefer Moses over Christ.

According to Williams, when one looks at the primitive churches pictured in the New Testament, one does not find the mixing of civil and spiritual as in the Old Testament. Further, one finds no evidence that the early churches had any sort of alliance with the state as had come to be the norm since the time of Constantine. Never, Williams argued, did the Apostle Paul charge civil authorities with spiritual duties. Reduced to its simplest form, his argument against civil interference in spiritual affairs, against religious persecution in matters of conscience, was this: "Christ Jesus never directed his Disciples to the civill Magistrate for help in his cause." Nowhere in the New Testament was there a "*patterne* and *president*" for magistrates as "*Keepers* of both *Tables*."[20] For Williams, one could not justify civil oversight of religion except by mutilating the New Testament pattern, either by going backward to the Old Testament pattern or forward to the Constantinian pattern. To move either direction was to usurp and deny the authority of Christ in his "first" institutions.

Not only did Williams chart the "time of Purity," but he also described the "time of Trangression & Apostasy." Indeed, a central feature of the restorationist outlook is to see in history a constant story of decline, decay of truth and ideals, and illicit "human invention." Protestant exegetes charted this decline in their historicist reading of the Apocalypse and caught up the disastrous results in the pervasive symbol of the Antichrist. Williams intensely held such an outlook, as did most Puritans; he differed from magisterial Puritans however, chiefly in his view of the time and extent of the decline. Because he rejected the common Puritan model of the godly commonwealth as having no basis in the New Testament, he saw in the rise of such a commonwealth under Constantine the beginnings of the fall. Because he felt the New Testament taught that Christ's kingdom was a spiritual kingdom despised in the sight of the world, he saw in its rise to temporal power, approbation, and glory the abandonment of its true nature. Like the Anabaptist dissenters of the sixteenth century, Williams associated all of these changes with the conversion of Constantine and his subsequent efforts to christianize the Roman empire.

Most Puritans, in contrast, worked with Old Testament models of theocratic Israel alongside New Testament models of the primitive church; thus they tended to look with approbation on Constantine as a godly ruler. Magisterial reformers in general followed Augustine in praising Constantine and applauding the progress of the church under the tutelage of godly rulers. They tended to mark the decisive decline of the church at a later point, typically the emergence of papal prerogatives over the temporal realm. The problem was not that godly rulers failed to exist but that they had failed to do their duty in keeping the church pure.

In contrast, Williams saw the decisive fall resulting, not from the failures of godly rulers, but from their very assumption of power over the church. With the rise of the *corpus christianum,* symbolized by Constantine, the pure church of Christ had been opened to the unregenerate and unrepentant and thus her worship polluted, her holy ordinances defiled, and ultimately her very existence threatened. For Williams, the problem was the transposition of pure Christian assemblies into "Christendom" that occurred when Constantine set up a national church. At that point "the Gardens of the Churches of Saints," to use his most famous metaphor, "were turned into the Wilderness of whole Nations."[21] The wall between church and world was breached and the corruption from the world entered, infected, and soon permeated the whole church. The church became filled with hypocrites, began to look more to temporal resources than to spiritual ones for its strength, sought worldly status and splendor, introduced inventions into the worship God had ordained, and began to force people to conform to its teaching and practices.

What set Williams apart from most other Puritan historiographers was his judgment concerning the severity and effect of the church's decline. Puritans who traced the decline of the church differed considerably as to cause and effect, but most agreed that the result had been a serious eclipse, a desolation, a ravaging of the church, and that in its outward manifestation it had fallen largely under control of the antichristian papacy. Some radicalized this perspective and argued that throughout the great period of apostasy a tiny remnant, practically invisible to the world and untraceable in the records of history, had maintained its loyalty to God apart from the visible church. Thus during this time, as Thomas Brightman put it, "the Church abidinge in most secret lurkinge places, was together with Christ."[22] But the validity of the Protestant church, most English reformers believed, did not rest on any such efforts to argue its historical continuity, for even with no enclaves of the faithful to perpetuate it, the true church could be established by preaching the pure gospel and the joining of saints together in a covenant.

For Roger Williams, the corrupting forces unleashed by Constantine had a much more disastrous and permanent effect. They did not just extinguish the gospel, but also the apostolic messengers who alone possessed the authority to preach and to gather churches. When the line of apostolic authority was broken in the fourth century, Christians had been left with no means of forming themselves into legitimate congregations. Any attempt to do so would result simply in "great *mistakes,* and *wandrings* from the first *Patternes* and Institutions of *Christ Jesus.*"[23] It was a position that Williams, it seems, accepted reluctantly, a result in part of his deep sense of the New Testament as pattern and the overwhelming data of history and experience supporting the mutilation of that pattern.

The many theological disputes of his own age confirmed to Williams that the true apostolic church had been lost, for if it were present, it would be clear to all. One would not have to engage in endless and intricate disputes about its form and function, for just as in the first century the church had been established with displays of divine power on every hand, so in the time of the church's restoration the signs of the true church would be clear to all. Once again there would be indisputable displays of divine power, particularly through the ministry of new apostles commissioned to establish churches. In 1650 Williams wrote to John Winthrop that the controversies of the time (particularly those in Connecticut) caused him both "to rejoice and mourn: rejoice that the Lord Jesus his name is more sounded, and mourn that not after the first pattern, in which I find no Churches extant framed, but all (by a dreadful fate) oppressing, disolving &c., [with] breaches and divisions wonderful."[24] The very divisions and debates of the time, he concluded as a close follower and participant, provided eloquent testimony to the fact that God's true church, long since extinguished, was still nowhere to be found. He had desired earnestly to see "any *coal* or *sparks* of true light amongst so many false and pretended candles," but had not been able to see it. Although he had been "a diligent and constant *Observer,*" Williams remarked that he could not "bring in the *Result* of a satisfying discovery, that either the *Begetting Ministry* of *Pastors* and *Teachers,* according to the first *Institution* of the *Lord Jesus,* are yet restored and extant." He concluded that there had been "a total routing of the *Church* and *Ministry* of *Christ Jesus,* put to flight, and retired into the *Wildernesse* of *Desolation,*" and that the hiatus of the church would not come to an end until the "bright appearance" of Christ occurred and new apostles were commissioned.[25]

For the present, God's elect ones were still scattered in the "Wilderness of Desolation." During this time God provided oversight and protection of the elect not through the "ordinary" power dispensed through the ordinances but through his "extra-ordinary" power given directly to individuals. Christian spirituality ordinarily was expressed through the outward, visible ordinances—baptism by immersion, preaching of the word, the Lord's Supper, laying on of hands—but since the fall the spirit and form of Christianity had been split and the forms were now mere husks, impotent as channels of communion with God.

God's direct inspiration, Williams believed, was centered in the figure of the eschatological "witness" (drawn from Rev. 11:3–12). Throughout the centuries since the fall of the church, there had been many thousands of such witnesses who had endured great persecution rather than capitulate to embellished doctrines and invented worships.[26] Throughout the centuries, all the witnesses had "prophecyed and mourned in *Sackcloath* 1260 dayes or yeares (prophetically) I say mourned for the routing, desolating of the Christian Church or Army: and panted and laboured after the most glorious *Rally* thereof, and *Restauration.*"[27] Although many of the witnesses had attempted, mistakenly in Williams's eyes, to gather churches, they still had been God's agents in decrying the pollution of Christendom, in holding up the "first Pattern," and in ministering to his few faithful people.

Such an emphasis on direct inspiration, Williams realized, could be carried easily to dangerous and radical extremes; thus he argued, especially when faced with Quaker claims, that only under the "extraordinary," temporary conditions caused by the fall of the church could the direct and "immediate" call to spiritual vocation be held up as the norm. Furthermore, such a calling paled in comparison to the power of the Spirit when flowing through apostolic ministers and primitive ordinances.[28]

Williams of course numbered himself among this company of witnesses. Keenly aware of his own wilderness existence, Williams was sustained by his unshakable belief that Antichrist soon would be defeated, his "inventions" cast out, and pure worship in a pure church once again offered to God.

All of this would occur when the "time of transgression & apostasy" gave way to the "time of the coming out of the Apostasy & Wilderness," the time when a "restauration of the first pattern" would take place. Williams laid out his view of this process of restoration most clearly in his brief tract *Queries of Highest Consideration* (1644), which he wrote a few months after arriving in England on his first return trip. It was addressed to the five Dissenting Brethren in the Westminster Assembly and the Scottish Commissioners to the Assembly. In January of 1644 both groups had published apologies for their respective reform programs: the Dissenting Brethren had issued *An Apologeticall Narration* defending their Congregationalism, and the Scots had answered with *Reformation of Church-Government in Scotland, Cleered from Some Prejudices* supporting their Presbyterianism. Both groups claimed that their program was founded upon nothing but "the first Apostolique directions, pattern and examples of those Primitive Churches recorded in the New Testament."[29] And while they disagreed on the form of church government, both were agreed in seeking a national reformation conducted by Parliament. In his tract Williams raised twelve queries to these two groups of clergymen designed to test their proposals for reform against the norm of Scripture. By this means, Williams believed, it would be clear to all that neither group had scriptural precedent behind it in proposing a magisterial reformation of the English church.

In his tract, Williams unequivocally rejected such a proposal. Scriptural precedent did not give to magistrates the responsibility of bringing the church into conformity with the primitive church; that was an obligation restricted to the pastors or elders of the individual congregations. Neither was there warrant for reform imposed by Parliament or for an Assembly of Divines appointed to advise Parliament. "What Precept or Pattern," he asked, "hath the Lord Jesus left you in his last Will and Testament for your *Synod* or Assembly of Divines?" The usual prooftext cited for such a practice, he noted, was Acts 15–16 which recorded the proceedings of the Jerusalem Council; but it referred only to the collaboration of individual congregations and was most certainly not "a Pattern for a Nation or Kingdome . . . to reforme or forme a Religion." He further questioned use of the name itself: "in what part of Christes Testament is found that title, *The Assembly of Divines?*" It was a title which, if used at all, should refer to all the children of God as they assembled together in particular congregations.[30]

For Williams the most serious distortion of the scriptural pattern among the Independents and Presbyterians was their conclusion that they were justified in waging a holy war to further reformation. They believed that the welfare of the nation depended upon the establishment of pure religion and that, through such efforts, the "latter-day glory" of the church would dawn. Thus when conflict arose with Charles I, they quickly interpreted the parliamentary cause as a holy crusade against the forces of evil that threatened both church and nation. Williams decried such views as the inevitable result of mixing the temporal and spiritual kingdoms. The fortunes of Christ's kingdom, he believed, were not tied in any way to the fortunes of a nation. Against the advocates of holy war, he wrote: "since the Lamb of God and Prince of Peace hath not in his Testament given us a pattern, Precept or Promise, for the undertaking of a civill War for his sake we Querie how with comfort to your Souls you may incourage the English Treasure to be Exhausted, and the English Blood to be spilt for the Cause of Christ?"[31] Despite "the blood of so many hundreth thousand Protestants, mingled with the blood of so many hundreth thousand Papists, as was spilt some hundreth yeares since in the Waldensian warres," God's people still had not learned that the weapons of their warfare were spiritual.[32]

In most of its major features, Williams strongly opposed the method suggested by the Puritan clergy for restoration of the primitive order of the church. Purification of the church, he believed, was not properly the task of Parliament, the Westminster Assembly, or any other institution outside the particular congregations of saints. Parliament was a secular, representative body charged only with "the Bodies and Goods of the Subject." To allow it to lead reform was to violate the scriptural pattern, underestimate the finitude of human judgment, force consciences, and promote violent holy wars. In contrast, Williams saw the task of restoration as God's alone; only he could repristinate the church according to the original pattern.

Drawing upon the distinction between the "darke" and "light" parts of reformation made by the Dissenting Brethren, Williams restricted all efforts in the present age to the "darke" part. "The Sufferings of Gods Witnesses since the Apostacie," he wrote, "have . . . been only right against the darke part, the Inventions, Abominations and Usurpations of Anti-christ." The "light" part or actual restoration was not a present possibility, for each succeeding reformation was still discovering and decrying more corruption, still attempting to reform the previous reformations, and in this uncertainty and instability all positive efforts at reformation were bound to be incomplete and misguided. The eschatological witnesses could do no more than attack error and denounce corrupt practices. Only after "the finishing of the Testimony, with the slaughter of the Witnesses" would the "light part . . . arise in its brightnesse."[33]

Roger Williams's own experience of suffering and persecution convinced him that he had been chosen as one of God's witnesses. In the opening pages of *Cottons Letter . . . Examined,* which was published as a companion piece to *Queries of Highest Consideration,* he gave an extended account of his banishment from the Bay Colony with all of the hardships it had brought him. The experience stirred in him a deep sense of having been chosen for the honored task of testifying on behalf of the gospel. "It pleased God," he wrote, "to lay a *Command* on my *Conscience* to come in as his poor Witnesse in this great Cause."[34] An essential part of the task Williams understood to be his work as a writer and controversialist. He wrote, it seems, not so much to win people to his viewpoint, for he was not naively optimistic about the chances of that, but to support and strengthen the resolve of fellow witnesses. Williams hoped that his bold controverting of the generally accepted ideas of the godly commonwealth, magisterial reform, religious uniformity, and a millennial rule of the saints would inspire conviction and courage in other witnesses, causing them to be equally bold in their testimony.

Williams's argument for complete liberty of conscience must be understood in this context. In contrast to the Independents, who argued for a limited toleration, Williams argued that only complete toleration would further the cause of reformation. Liberty of conscience would give the witnesses—Christ's true reformers—the freedom to expose all the religious error that was being shielded under the persecuting sword of popes, magistrates, and parliaments. Liberty would speed the task of restoration by giving the witnesses freer course in dividing truth from error, in lifting up the scriptural pattern of the church from amid the jumbled mixtures of church and state. Liberty, in short, would enable the witnesses to complete their testimony in preparation for "the bright appearing of the Lord Jesus" and the restoration of the church.

By separating sharply the "darke part" of the restoration from the "light part," Williams projected the positive work of restoration into an imminent millennial age radically discontinuous with the present. In so doing he departed from the visions of the millennium dominant among the Puritan exegetes and preachers of his day. Although he drew upon the common fund of apocalyptic symbols and used a similiar method of historicist exegesis of the Apocalypse, his periodization of church history and especially his vision of the millennium was given a different shape by his New Testament archetype of the church. By far his most dominant conviction about the millennium was that the pure church of the first century would be restored and that it would duplicate perfectly the "first Patterne." Through his "bright appearing," Christ would commission new apostolic messengers to proclaim the gospel with power and to gather churches. Such churches would be entirely separate from the world, consisting only of the regenerate. Their purity and well-being would be maintained by the elders or pastors as they wielded the sword of the Spirit and not by the civil power wielding the temporal sword. Christ's original ordinances—baptism by immersion in rivers, the Lord's Supper, laying on of hands— would be reinstituted and practiced diligently. Under the Spirit-filled preaching of new apostles, a great influx of converts from the nations of the world would swell the ranks of the church.

In this restored primordial age, the visible signs of God's presence would be evident everywhere just as they had been in the first age. When the apostolic commission and gifts are restored, Williams remarked, "it may please the *Lord* againe to cloath his people with a spirit of *zeale* and *courage* for the name of *Christ,* yea and powre forth those fiery streames againe of *Tongues* and *Prophecie* in the *restauration* of Zion."[35] In the millennium the divine power would be poured out, the primitive pattern of the church repristinated, and God's people again would live fully in the sacred. The inner spirit of Christianity would be joined once again with its external form, and Christians would experience much richer communion with God.

From the late 1630s until his death in 1683, Roger Williams stood virtually alone in maintaining this vision of the Christian primordium. But he firmly believed it to be supported by all "scripture, history, and experience," and so he persisted in his solitary vigil, decrying religious error and awaiting the "restoration of Zion."

Williams's unique and eccentric vision, however, should not blind us to the fact that he shared with the theorists of the New England Way an impressive core of primitivist assumptions. With them, he assumed the primacy of biblical precedent and archetype, the prestige of "firstness," and the illegitimacy of all theological "invention." He shared, in short, the entire fund of primitivist constraints produced by aggressive and prolonged Puritan dissent. Such assumptions led him, as they did John Cotton and his colleagues, ultimately to resist the more radical spiritism that emerged among other dissenters in early New England. Williams, like those who earlier had banished him, maintained a profound passion for the fixed forms and final truths revealed in the biblical primordium and came to share disdain for those who sought the Spirit's guidance into ever new truth. By seeing this profound consensus more clearly, we can also see more clearly the sharp differences that scholars long have attempted to explain.

NOTES

1. *Letters of Roger Williams, 1632–1682,* in vol. 7 of *The Complete Writings of Roger Williams* (New York: Russell and Russell, 1963), 7: 11–12. Between 1866 and 1872 the Narragansett Club (Providence, RI) published a six-volume edition of most of Williams's published works. In 1963 Russell and Russell (New York) reprinted these volumes and added a seventh containing Williams's other known publications. All subsequent citations to his published works are to this edition.

2. George Yule, "Continental Patterns and the Reformation in England and Scotland," *Scottish Journal of Theology* 18 (1969): 305; T. Dwight Bozeman, *To Live Ancient Lives: The Primitivist Dimension in New England Puritanism* (Chapel Hill: University of North Carolina Press, 1988), chap. 1. See also: James C. Spalding, "Restitution as a Normative Factor for Puritan Dissent," *Journal of the American Academy of Religion* 44 (March 1976): 47–63; John

K. Luoma, "Restitution or Reformation? Cartwright and Hooker on the Elizabethan Church," *Historical Magazine of the Protestant Episcopal Church* 46 (March 1977): 85–106.

In my thinking about primitivism, I have been helped by Arthur O. Lovejoy and George Boas, *Primitivism and Related Ideas in Antiquity: Contributions to the History of Primitivism* (Baltimore: Johns Hopkins Press, 1935), and Mircea Eliade, *The Myth of the Eternal Return, or Cosmos and History,* trans. Willard R. Trask (Princeton: Princeton University Press, 1954).

3. *The Bloudy Tenent of Persecution, for Cause of Conscience,* 3: 369.

4. John Winthrop, *Winthrop's Journal: "History of New England," 1630–1649,* 2 vols., ed. James Kendall Hosmer (New York: Charles Scribner's Sons, 1908), 1: 297, 313.

5. *Bloudy Tenent,* 3: 64; *The Hireling Ministry None of Christs,* 7: 158.

6. *George Fox Digg'd out of His Burrowes,* 5: 103.

7. *Bloudy Tenent,* 3: 334, 114, 119–20; *Christenings Make Not Christians,* 7: 36.

8. *Bloody Tenent Yet More Bloody,* 4: 47–48.

9. *Bloody Tenent Yet More Bloody,* 47–48; *Christenings Make Not Christians,* 39, 37.

10. *Mr. Cottons Letter Lately Printed, Examined and Answered,* 1: 82, 348; compare pp. 335, 350.

11. *Cottons Letter . . . Examined,* 68–69, 74, 82, 350.

12. *John Cotton, A Sermon Preached . . . at Salem, 1636* (Boston, 1713), 19.

13. *Winthrop Papers,* ed. Allyn Bailey Forbes and Stewart Mitchell (Boston: Massachusetts Historical Society, 1929–47), 3: 315–16.

14. *Experiments of Spiritual Life and Health,* 7: 82.

15. *Cottons Letter . . . Examined,* 33; also *Bloody Tenent Yet More Bloody,* 468, and *The Examiner Defended,* 7: 224.

16. These generalizations about Foxe are dependent on Richard Bauckham, *Tudor Apocalypse* (London: Sutton Courtenay Press, 1978), 61–64, 132–33.

17. *Bloody Tenent Yet More Bloody,* 79–80.

18. *Bloody Tenent Yet More Bloody,* 381, 404.

19. *Cottons Letter . . . Examined,* 33–34.

20. *Bloudy Tenent,* 3: 119–20, 239–41.

21. *Bloudy Tenent,* 3: 184; also 174–75, 320, 365; and *Christenings Make Not Christians,* 34.

22. Thomas Brightman, *A Revelation of the Revelation* (Amsterdam, 1615), 405.

23. *Christenings Make Not Christians,* 40–41.

24. *Letters of Roger Williams,* 7: 199.

25. *Bloody Tenent Yet More Bloody,* 203; *Hireling Ministry,* 160, 158. Because of his view of the extinction of the church, Williams usually has been grouped with the English Seekers, but he differed from them in such significant ways that the very use of the term may be misleading. Most Seekers were spiritualists who looked for an entirely new order or dispensation for God's people, not for a renewal of the old order; they stood in sharp contrast to

Williams's primitivist vision of a church restored in all of its external forms and fashioned precisely after the "first pattern." Edmund S. Morgan, *Roger Williams: The Church and the State* (New York: Harcourt, Brace, 1967), 53, 152–53, and W. Clark Gilpin, *The Millenarian Piety of Roger Williams* (Chicago: University of Chicago Press, 1979), 62, 184, both point to the tenuous connection between Williams and the Seekers.

26. *Hireling Ministry,* 158, 160–61, 167; *Cottons Letter . . . Examined,* 96–97, 102; *Queries of Highest Consideration,* 2: 262–63; *Bloudy Tenent,* 3: 97–98, 153, 155, 190, 409–10; *Bloody Tenent Yet More Bloody,* 97, 112, 115, 316–17, 327, 330, 353, 380, 383, 386, 464.

27. *Hireling Ministry,* 158. Compare also *Cottons Letters . . . Examined,* 68–69; *Bloody Tenent Yet More Bloody,* 147.

28. *The Hireling Ministry,* 167–68.

29. Thomas Goodwin, Philip Nye, Sidrach Simpson, Jeremiah Burroughes, and William Bridge, *An Apologeticall Narration, Humbly Submitted to the Honourable Houses of Parliament* (London, 1643), 3: compare *Reformation of Church-Government in Scotland, Cleered from Some Prejudices, by the Commissioners of the Generall Assembly of the Church of Scotland* (London, 1644), 5.

30. *Queries of Highest Consideration,* 17–18.

31. *Queries of Highest Consideration,* 26.

32. *Queries of Highest Consideration,* 29; cf. *Bloudy Tenent,* 3: 362–63.

33. *Queries of Highest Consideration,* 29.

34. *Bloody Tenent Yet More Bloody,* 41; compare *Letters of Roger Williams,* 7: 8, 9.

35. *Bloudy Tenent,* 3: 307.

3

Primitivism in the American Enlightenment

WINTON U. SOLBERG

PRIMITIVISM is an attitude of mind that has enduring roots in human nature, and we find examples of it in the American Enlightenment. The leading experts distinguish between two types of primitivism. *Chronological primitivism* generally assumes that the best time in life was the beginning and that the subsequent course of human history has been downward. This theory of decline is often coupled with the belief that there will be a restoration of humanity's primeval condition at some future time. *Cultural primitivism* is the notion that people who live a simple and unsophisticated life have the best conditions of existence. This notion tends to be held by those living in a relatively civilized society who seek their model of human excellence in an existing people far away. Cultural primitivism contains an element of revolt against the familiar and a love of strangeness.[1]

Although this distinction helps in understanding a complex historical phenomenon, life is larger than logic, and in dealing with these issues real people often intermix in their thought elements of both chronological and cultural primitivism. Religious restorationism generally presupposes an earlier golden age and is primarily an exemplification of chronological as opposed to cultural primitivism.

The Enlightenment as an historical movement dates from the late seventeenth to the late eighteenth centuries, and several concepts are central to it. The thought of this phase of Western intellectual history viewed nature as the ultimate source of authority, and it assumed that reason was common to all men. The belief that reason was available to all and that nature could verify everything men needed to know led to other Enlightenment principles such as uniformitarianism, cosmopolitanism, and belief in progress. Another characteristic of eighteenth-century thought was an emphasis on intuition and emotion, a tendency that came to full fruition in the nineteenth century.[2]

Primitivism in the American Enlightenment has received little scholarly attention, and I propose to discuss a wide range of items related to the topic. First I shall examine a variety of views on the physical universe and various forms of life in it. The history of both primitivism and the Enlightenment is closely connected with use of the word *nature* to represent the standard of human values. But the use of nature as a criterion is tricky, for the word has many equivocal and antithetical meanings.[3] Second, I shall discuss government and society as well as religion in the American Enlightenment with a view to identifying their primitivistic dimensions.

"Follow nature" was a slogan of the Enlightenment, and we might well begin by considering how Americans understood nature at the beginning of the eighteenth century. Cotton Mather provided a classic statement on the subject in *The Christian Philosopher*.[4] Scholars agree that this book was the most effective means by which Enlightenment thought was first disseminated in America.[5] Mather's purpose was to show the harmony between religion and the new science associated with Newton. He discussed all of the sciences known at the time. He described the "best discoveries" in nature encountered in his reading and added rhapsodical statements upon the religious significance of the facts and theories presented.

Mather began by recalling the ancient doctrine of the two books of God, "the Book of the *Creatures,* and the Book of the *Scriptures*." God first taught us by his Works, and afterwards by his Words.[6] Mather's treatise on nature was intended to help people understand Revelation. His thesis was the design argument, which held that one may reasonably infer the existence of a purposeful Creator responsible for the universe from evidences of intelligent planning found in physical nature. Plato was the first to give the design argument full expression, and it gained new vitality in England along with the birth of natural science in its distinctively modern form. Mather believed that nature reveals God, but that nature is not a closed system. His belief in the unity of natural and supernatural was deeply rooted in American thought in the early eighteenth century.

William Bartram, the Quaker naturalist, wrote a book near the end of the century that demonstrated how much theories of nature changed during the Enlightenment. His *Travels through North and South Carolina, Georgia, East and West Florida* reveals much in common with Mather's treatise.[7] Both authors stood in the Christian and Neoplatonist tradition, which saw nature as the work of God, as a reflection of divinity. Both shared the widely accepted eighteenth-century belief in the chain of being, the notion of a scale of created forms reaching from the lowest types up a ladder of perfection through man to God. But the Quaker radically departed from the Puritan in many essentials. Mather looked to nature to understand God, exalted man's intellect, and was no cultural primitivist. Bartram substituted nature for God, questioned man's superior place in nature, and was an ardent cultural primitivist. Mather and Bartram provide convenient chronological and intellectual boundaries for our analysis, and by means of Bartram we can understand the direction thought was taking at the time.

Chronological and cultural primitivism were both evident in the simple appreciation of landscape and in the pastoral and agrarian traditions in the American Enlightenment. Mather provided a basis for taking delight in the physical environment. *The Christian Philosopher's* admiration and reverence for the things of the earth made for a relatively new attitude. Mather was indebted to John Ray, the English clergyman and naturalist, whose *The Wisdom of God Manifested in the Works of the Creation* (1691) had rejected the old antithesis between the natural and the supernatural that had led Christians to depreciate nature. Ray's delight in the physical universe was novel, and Mather perpetuated Ray's "insistence upon the essential unity of natural and revealed, as alike proceeding from and integrated by the divine purpose."[8] Mather rhapsodized over minerals, vegetables, and animals, but he did not celebrate sylvan landscapes.

The pastoral is almost any kind of work that idealizes a rural life of innocence and health, and one of its functions has been criticism of the corruption and sterility of city or court life. Pastoralism was a literary and artistic fashion in the eighteenth century, and Americans produced this type of neoclassical literature. Often they followed English models, especially Alexander Pope. William Livingston, for example, a Yale graduate from a prominent New York family, published *Philosophic Solitude: Or, the Choice of a Rural Life,*[9] which revealed the young man's longing for a rural domestic life among friends and books. The author inferred the existence of God from the beauty and harmony of the creation. His book displayed a blend of chronological and cultural primitivism.

The American poet Philip Freneau likewise displayed an indelible strain of both chronological and cultural primitivism.[10] He believed that the natural man was completely happy: "Take all, through all, through nation, tribe, or clan,/ The child of Nature is the *better* man."[11] Man had originally lived in a state of nature in perfect equality. The past was the golden age, and Greece and Rome were Freneau's models. But civilization had moved westward. Freneau had Columbus exclaim on discovering the New World, "here God and nature reign;/ Their works unsullied by the hands of men."[12] America was the favored child of nature. In a series of essays Freneau described the Pilgrim, a philosopher who lived primitively in the forest near Philadelphia, criticizing cities and civilized ways.[13] Freneau's pastoral poems praised the rural contemplative life: "A cottage I could call my own/ . . . A little garden walled with stone,/ . . . Would more substantial joys afford,/ . . . Than all the wealth that misers hoard."[14]

The agrarian tradition in America may be viewed as primarily an expression of cultural primitivism. Freneau believed that nature favored North America in designing it for agriculture rather than mining, and he extolled such agrarian virtues as pruning vines and reaping harvests.[15] Thomas Jefferson's devotion to agrarianism is well known. For Jefferson, the earth was given as a common stock on which man might labor and live, and agriculture was the source of virtue rather than of wealth. In a familiar statement, Jefferson declared, "Those who labour in the earth are the chosen people of God, if ever he had a chosen people, whose breasts he has made his peculiar deposit for substantial and genuine virtue." Dependence begat subservience, and property in land ensured economic security and virtue. Thus agrarianism was essential to democracy.[16]

The most enthusiastic admiration for the beauty of the physical creation came from William Bartram. He spent the years from 1773 to 1777 searching for plants in the Southeast at a time when the region was largely uninhabited wilderness. "The amplitude and magnificence of these scenes are great indeed," he asserted, "and may present to the imagination, an idea of the first appearance of the earth to man at the creation." The whole gorgeous spectacle transported Bartram with delight, and his account is studded with references to the primitive simplicity of the sylvan landscape. Nature seemed to prevail over reason in this "terrestrial paradise," and Bartram was led to exclaim: "O thou Creator supreme, almighty! how infinite and incomprehensible thy works! most perfect, and every way astonishing!"[17]

Cultural primitivism is also found in contemplation of the scale of nature. Mather devoted one essay to vegetables, admiring their utility, medicinal properties, and beauty and seeing in their existence "the Contrivance of our most Glorious Creator."[18] Bartram described the "admirable . . . properties of the extraordinary Dionea muscipula" or Venus's-flytrap, and added that "vegetable beings are endued with some sensible faculties or attributes, similar to those that dignify animal nature; they are organical, living, and self-moving bodies, for we see here, in this plant, motion and volition."[19]

In addition to praising vegetables as sentient forms of life, Bartram believed that the vital principle or efficient cause of motion and action in the animal and vegetable kingdoms may be more similar than we generally apprehend. The most apparent difference between them is that animals have the power of sound and locomotion, whereas vegetables cannot shift themselves from the places where nature has planted them. Yet vegetables move over the whole surface of earth, their seeds being carried by birds or on the wind.[20]

The notion that the life of animals is on the whole superior to the life of humans has been discussed since ancient times. The Latin writers who contributed most to this idea were Pliny and Plutarch. These ancient beliefs were revived during the Renaissance, given currency by Montaigne in the sixteenth century, and elaborated upon by naturalists thereafter. The contrast between animal felicity and human misery was expressed in two antithetical viewpoints by the eighteenth century.

Cultural primitivists used the concept of the "happy beast" in their campaign to lower human self-esteem. These writers, often skeptics, viewed the intrinsic excellence of beasts as arising from their closeness to nature rather than from their reason. They valued instinct over reason. Humans were alienated from nature, their self-consciousness a major cause of their unnaturalness. Antiprimitivists, on the other hand, upheld the Judeo-Christian and Neoplatonic tradition of humanity's cosmic preeminence. They valued reason above instinct and argued that the use of nature as a model for humans was perilous. Human reason was humanity's distinguishing characteristic. To follow nature was to succumb to the animal inclinations in humans.[21]

These ideas found expression in the American Enlightenment. Mather devoted five essays to brute creatures and exhibited familiarity with the issues discussed since antiquity. He admired the images of virtue and duty that animals furnish to minds willing to be instructed by God. Bees in their hives are just to one another, for example, and never lose one day to idleness when the weather permits them to work. In the sea the greater devour the lesser, but fish do not devour their own kind. Similar instances of the kindness of brutes rebuke the rapacity often found in humankind. Most creatures have some quality with which they admonish humans as to what is best. Birds teach neatness; the ant, forecast; the dove, conjugal chastity, and so forth.[22]

According to Mather, animal instinct exhibits an artifice beyond human understanding, and it shows that "*Divine Reason runs like a*

Golden Vein through the whole Leaden Mine of Brutal Nature." Mather described the cleverness of animals and named authors who had given credible relations of reasonable brutes—dogs, foxes, beavers, elephants, and horses. Yet Mather insisted on the distinction between instinct and reason. "There was Humour enough in *Rorarius,*" he wrote, alluding to Jerome Rorario, a late Renaissance Italian author, "who upon hearing a learned Man prefer such a Wretch as *Frederick Barberossa,* before that great Emperor *Charles* V. was thereby so provoked, that he wrote his two Books to prove *that Beasts often have more Use of Reason than Men.*" For Mather, the consequence of such absurd reasoning "carries thousands of *Terrors* with it."[23]

Mather's view probably prevailed during the American Enlightenment. To be sure, Freneau elevated a creature to the status of a man in "On a Honey Bee," but that was poetic fancy.[24] Most Americans distinguished between instinct and reason and reaffirmed the biblical doctrine that man was given dominion over brute creatures. They were, accordingly, not cultural primitivists, however much they might accept pastoralism and agrarianism. William Bartram was an exception. He praised animals and saw in "these finely formed self-moving beings" the hand of God. If the visible, mechanical part of the animal creation is so beautiful and incomprehensible, the intellectual system which secretly operates within must be divine and immortal.[25] Bartram admitted that philosophers had distinguished between brute instinct and human reason, but he blurred the distinction. To him, the parental and filial affections were as ardent in animals as in humans. To illustrate his point he recalled an episode when a cub bear, realizing that its dam had been shot dead, appeared to be "in agony, fell to weeping and looking upwards, then towards us, and cried out like a child. . . . The continual cries of this afflicted child, bereft of its parent, affected me very sensibly," Bartram confessed.[26]

Bartram found "manifest examples of premeditation, perseverance, resolution, and consummate artifice" in the animal creation. Of a spider's efforts to capture a bumblebee, he wrote, "this cunning intrepid hunter conducted his subtil approaches with the circumspection and perseverance of a Siminole [*sic*] when hunting a deer."[27] Bartram endowed Tom, a crow that he reared from the nest, with human attributes. According to Bartram, "It would be endless, to recount instances of this bird's understanding, cunning, and operations, which, certainly, exhibit incontestable demonstrations of a regular combination of ideas, premeditation, reflection, and contrivance."[28]

Bartram tended to see nature as a peaceable kingdom, and he earned a reputation as an advocate of the benevolent disposition of animals.

Once while on a botanical excursion with his father he came upon a rattlesnake coiled and ready to strike. Bartram's fright excited such resentment that he was for the moment "entirely insensible to gratitude or mercy." He dispatched the serpent, but after reflection was sorry for the deed. "He [the rattler] certainly had it in his power to kill me almost instantly, and I make no doubt but that he was conscious of it. I promised myself that I would never again be accessary [*sic*] to the death of a rattlesnake."[29]

He kept his promise when he encountered a formidable rattlesnake once again. As man and beast eyed each other, Bartram's "imagination and spirits were in a tumult, almost equally divided betwixt thanksgiving to the supreme Creator and preserver, and the dignified nature of the generous though terrible creature, who had suffered us all to pass many times by him during the night, without injuring us in the least." Bartram prevailed upon his companions to spare the life of "the generous serpent."[30] As these episodes reveal, Bartram carried primitivism to its outer limit. Surely no American of the Enlightenment surpassed him in looking to animals for models of human behavior.

The Quaker naturalist's emphasis on the dignity of animals led him to question the superior place of humans in the scale of nature. He once wrote, "I cannot believe ... that man who is guilty of more mischief and wickedness than all the other animals together in this world, should be exclusively endued with the knowledge of the Creator, and capable of expressing his love and gratitude and homage to the Great Author of Being who continually feeds and delights us and all his creatures with every good and enjoyment."[31]

Cultural primitivists seek the natural human and, since antiquity, have found him among savages, both real and imagined. Christians were less devoted to pursuit of the noble savage than pagans were, but they perpetuated the search. Discovery and settlement brought Europeans into contact with native Americans, and they devised the image of the noble savage. Sometimes the natives were compared to classical heroes of the mythological golden age or to the ancient Hebrews, and sometimes they were portrayed as children of nature living in an earthly Eden. Writers later devised the image of the rational savage and then drew upon the wisdom of the primitive to criticize convention and artifice in civilized society.

Europeans also developed the image of the ignoble savage. Permanent settlement brought a more realistic assessment of the aborigines, and colonists, judging the red men by the criteria of Christianity and civilization, found them wanting. Negative descriptions of the natives quickly became stereotypes. The Indian was savage and an obstacle to the advance of settlement. The remedy was to civilize and Christianize the savages, or if necessary to destroy them.[32]

The eighteenth century inherited the problem of savagery and civilization, and a number of writers dealt with these matters during the American Enlightenment. Robert Beverley, in his *History and Present State of Virginia,* understood the Indians as natural beings. He drew parallels between savage life and classical precedent in cooking and food, and after describing the custom of offering village virgins to distinguished visitors, he added: "After this manner perhaps many of the Heros were begotten in old time, who boasted themselves to be the Sons of some Way-faring God." As for Indian religion, Beverley termed the natives superstitious and idolatrous. He called their society priest-ridden, implicitly criticizing his own society. Beverley believed that the Indians were "happy . . . in their simple State of Nature, and in their enjoyment of Plenty, without the Curse of Labour." They had good reason therefore "to lament the arrival of the *Europeans,* by whose means they seem to have lost their Felicity, as well as their Innocence. The *English* have taken away great part of their Country. . . . They have introduc'd Drunkenness and Luxury amongst them, which have multiply'd their Wants, and put them upon desiring a thousand things, they never dreamt of before."[33] Beverley proposed to civilize and Christianize the savages, and he favored intermarriage between the races.

John Lawson, writing in *A New Voyage to Carolina,* saw many natural virtues in the Indians. They were "really better to us, than we are to them," although "we look upon them with Scorn and Disdain, and think them little better than Beasts in Humane Shape." Although the tribes were "an odd sort of People under the Circumstances they are at present," Lawson considered them a very happy people and the freest people in the world. But civilization had been detrimental to them. They had learned vices rather than virtues from the English, and were no nearer to Christianity than at the first discovery. Lawson also proposed to convert and civilize them, and he recommended intermarriage.[34]

Cadwallader Colden published *The History of the Five Indian Nations* in 1747. Although he called the Five Nations "a poor and . . . barbarous People, . . . bred under the darkest Ignorance," he likened them to heroes of antiquity. In their courage, patriotism, love of liberty, hospitality, and other noble virtues the Iroquois surpassed the Romans. Colden acknowledged the cruelty of the Indians, but thought the ancients were no better. He exalted the republican government found among the Iroquois and observed that the sachems derived their power from the people. "Here we see the natural origin of all Power and Authority among a free People," he wrote, "and whatever artificial Power or Sovereignty any Man may have acquired, by the Laws and Constitution of a Country, his real Power will be ever much greater or less, in Proportion to the Esteem the People have of him." Primitive society again served as a model for contemporary English society. Colden considered the Indians' propensity for speech-making a natural consequence of republican government, and he reported Indian speeches in tedious detail to illustrate Plutarchian virtue and Ciceronian eloquence.[35]

Civilization, according to Colden, had had a blighting effect upon the nobel savages. Christians had taught the natives vices rather than virtues and had made them worse than they were in the state of nature. Colden's prescription for restoration was in keeping with his Enlightenment ideals. "If Care were taken to plant and cultivate in them that general Benevolence to Mankind, which is the true first Principle of Virtue," he wrote, "it would effectually eradicate those horrid Vices, occasioned by their unbounded Revenge, and then they would no longer deserve the Name of Barbarians, but would become a People, whose Friendship might add Honour to the British Nation."[36]

William Douglass parted company with his friend Colden on the Indians. His book, *A Summary, Historical and Political, of the First Planting, Progressive Improvements, and Present State of the British Settlements in North-America,* published in two volumes between 1747 and 1752, described the Indians as ignorant and lazy. "Like the wild Irish they dread labour more than poverty," he wrote; "like dogs they are always eating or sleeping, excepting in travelling, hunting, and their dances." Unlike the bees and ants who lay up stores, the Indians, Douglass thought, were like rapacious animals who lived from hand to mouth. They were exceedingly barbarous and had neither honesty nor honor, but were "meer brutes in that respect." They seemed to have no government or laws, for they had no compulsive power over one another. Their relations were cemented only by friendship. To Douglass, the Native Americans were "the most barbarous and least polished people upon earth."[37]

Douglass judged the religion of the savages by the only religion he recognized—natural religion. "Our stupid American Indians had no temples, no altars, no idols or images, no set times for worship, if it may be called worship," before the Europeans arrived. English attempts to convert the savages met no success because the colonists zealously pressed Christianity upon aboriginals who were bewildered by the mysteries of the faith. Douglass thought it would have been better to start by instructing the Indians in the principles of natural religion and morality, which were plain and easily comprehended. Historically, religion originated in a few designing men taking advantage of mankind's natural tendency to superstition, Douglass asserted, and he likened Indian powwowers to conjurors rather than to the clergy. Christianity, Douglass concluded, was not likely to find any good footing among the Indians.[38]

These examples demonstrate a close connection between primitivism, both chronological and cultural, and restorationism. If the Indian was a child of nature or a rational creature resembling the heroes of antiquity, he was nevertheless a savage. The solution was to civilize the natives and either to Christianize them or to usher them into the Age of Enlightenment. As for Douglass, his optimism faltered when he considered the future of the Indian in American civilization.

In the late eighteenth century Americans borrowed a new theory to make sense of facts about Indians. Enlightenment thinkers accepted the notion of an orderly universe operating according to regular sequences, and they explained phenomena in naturalistic terms. Humankind was classed as a single fixed species, and human nature was considered as uniform. Environmentalism was introduced to explain the changes in the varieties of human species. Out of these materials Scottish writers postulated that humanity developed in a sequence of stages, and William Robertson applied these ideas to the American Indian in 1777. The Scottish theory taught that the present condition of the Indians resembled that of European society at an earlier age. The Indians were a primitive people; circumstances accounted for their vices and virtues.[39].

This theory conditioned American writing on the natives late in the century. Antiprimitivism remained a preoccupation for many. Joel Barlow, Timothy Dwight, and Francis Hopkinson depicted the bad Indian in their verse,[40] and Dwight restated his view in his *Travels in New England and New York.* Savagery, not innocence, had characterized their condition. Although Dwight thought the Indians better than the Greeks and Romans in some respects, he nonetheless concluded, after observing one tribe on his travels, that "upon the whole, they exhibited the general depravity of human nature under all the disadvantages of profound ignorance."[41]

Primitivism, especially the cultural variety, nevertheless remained fashionable. Hector St. John de Crevecoeur, in his little-known works describing his travels in Pennsylvania and New York, depicted the American Indian as an ignorant barbarian. But in his well-known *Let-*

ters from an American Farmer (1782) he idealized the savage. Crevecoeur, seeking the good agrarian life, realized that under the adversity of the war the American farmer had to revert to a state closer to nature, so he enobled the savage.[42]

Bartram observed the Indians of the Southeast carefully and described those he encountered as physically handsome and possessing exemplary virtues. He believed that a divine light furnished moral guidance to them. Bartram thought that the Indians wanted to become part of white civilization, and in describing Indian institutions and customs, he asserted that "as moral men they certainly stand in no need of European civilization."[43]

Freneau's belief in man's innate goodness was reflected in some of his poems on the Indians as well as in his Tomo-Cheeki essays. But Freneau also realized that the state of nature was often a state of war, and he abandoned his primitivistic, and thus favorable, view of the Indians in his later years.[44] Like many Americans, Freneau was ambivalent on primitivism and on the Indians.

Jefferson emphasized the circumstances that conditioned savage life. One of the main concerns in his *Notes on the State of Virginia* was to refute Buffon, whose theory that nature tended to produce smaller forms of life in America than in Europe led him to charge that the American Indian was feeble, cowardly, lacking in sexual capacity, and deficient in other good traits. Jefferson countered by arguing that the causes of any differences between Indians and whites were in circumstances rather than in nature.[45]

Thus in their attitude toward Indians as well as in their attitude toward other aspects of the physical creation, eighteenth-century Americans exhibited a strain of primitivist thought. The temptation to regard the natives as unspoiled children of nature represented cultural primitivism, but that view was often reinforced by chronological primitivism, a desire to portray the Indians as the counterparts of ancient heroes. Close contact with the natives often gave rise to antiprimitivism, or to the notion that circumstances governed the lives of the savages as well as of the whites.

The question remains as to whether Americans of the Enlightenment demonstrated primitivistic tendencies in thinking about government and religion in the late eighteenth century. "The American revolution grew out of the Enlightenment no less than out of the troubles of its century," Howard Mumford Jones observed, and Enlightenment concepts exerted a major influence in establishing a government for the new nation.[46] The transformation of the colonies into states and the formation of the federal union based on a written constitution were major achievements of the Revolutionary generation, and these two achievements exhibit primitivism in two ways.

One is the appeal to nature as the ultimate source of political authority. In the conflict with Britain from 1763 to 1776, the Americans searched for a line of separation between the powers of Parliament that were valid in America and those powers that were not. This search finally led them to rest their case for independence on the laws of nature. John Locke argued that humans possess rights in a state of nature and that to secure these rights they form government based upon consent. Since the king had violated the social contract, the people were entitled by the laws of nature to establish their own government. This resort to nature as a rationale for civil rights and for the foundation of government may be seen as an expression of primitivism in the American Enlightenment.[47]

The appeal to antiquity in establishing new governments is also testimony to primitivism in the Revolutionary era. The Founding Fathers had read the classics, and they drew inspiration in state-making not from a mythological golden age but from the actual experience of the past. Many principles written into the state and federal constitutions drew upon this legacy. One was the theory of the Roman constitution, which held that the people, not the prince, were the source of political authority. Americans cherished the example of Roman republicanism. Another borrowing from antiquity was the notion of fundamental law, which Cicero was instrumental in transmitting. He grafted the idea of natural law onto the belief that public law is a common engagement of the community, and he taught that nature gives humans reason, which enables them to understand the rules governing the cosmos. This reason was binding on everyone, and therefore no statutory enactment in derogation of the fundamental or "higher" law was binding. James Madison, the most influential of the framers of the American Constitution, had studied the history of ancient confederacies in preparation for the work of the Philadelphia Convention.[48]

The appeal to nature and to the past was closely linked to a vision of the future. Americans wished to establish a government and social order in accordance with the laws of nature and nature's God, and they envisioned their nation as a model for mankind. The birth of the republic gave the people confidence that they were inaugurating a new era in human history, a *Novus Ordo Seclorum* as the motto on the Great Seal expresses it. The Vergilian phrase above both the pyramid and the eternal eye of God on the Seal was *Annuit Coeptis,* a reminder that "He [God] smiles on the undertaking."

Thus, while acknowledging the past, they looked to the promise of the future. As Madison declared, was it not the glory of the American people that while they had paid a "decent respect to the opinions of former times and other nations, they have not suffered a blind veneration for antiquity . . . to overrule . . . their own good sense . . . and the lessons of their own experience?" Posterity would be indebted to America for its innovations. The United States might have perished had its leaders not broken with precedent. "Happily for America, happily, we trust, for the whole human race, they pursued a new and more noble course."[49]

The new republic gave rise to countless expressions of the differences between the corruption of Europe and the bright promise of America. Freneau's "The Rising Glory of America" and Barlow's "The Vision of Columbus" are familiar examples.[50] Gouverneur Morris, one of the Framers of the American Constitution, believed that the republican government established in Philadelphia would serve as a model for mankind. Thus he expressed the conviction that he came to the Constitutional Convention "in some degree as a Representative of the whole human race, for the whole human race will be effected by the proceedings of this Convention." If paradise had been lost, paradise would be regained. The American mission in history was the restoration of humanity to its primitive glory.[51]

As for religion, primitivism and restorationism both had figured prominently in Protestant circles since the Reformation, and the Puritan-Protestants of early America were eager to recover the Word and to erect churches on the biblical pattern. Many Americans continued to express these concerns in the eighteenth century, but the scientific revolution extending from Copernicus to Newton produced a new model for understanding reality, and as a result theology was reoriented. Newtonian science provided a new sanction for natural theology as a respectable body of thought in the eighteenth century.

Natural theology posits the existence of God and an orderly, harmonious universe that reveals the power, wisdom, and benevolence of the Creator. This faith maintains that human reason makes knowledge of the physical universe accessible to all. Natural philosophy or science explains nature, which is considered to operate under Providence but according to regular sequences now called the laws of nature. Newton mathematically demonstrated how these laws work. Revelation was not considered necessary to discern the basic truths of reality.

Natural theology or religion became an essential element of American thought in the eighteenth century. Cotton Mather's *Christian Philosopher* was the earliest physico-theological treatise by an American, and the doctrine it expounded was widely accepted in the eighteenth century. Natural theology together with the design argument provided a large measure of intellectual unity in American culture until the time of Darwin.

While most eighteenth-century Americans accepted natural religion as a way of understanding the physical cosmos, they did not accept natural religion on its own terms. They were not Deists. They believed that nature with its orderly harmony was not self-closed but was part of a larger and higher world of existence from which it could not be separated by any insurmountable barrier. Revelation, they insisted, was necessary to discern the true religion, Christianity. As John Wise declared in 1717, "Revelation is Nature's Law in a fairer and brighter Edition."[52]

Conrad Wright used the term *Supernatural Rationalists* to describe the people who thought in this manner. They erected a superstructure of revealed religion on a foundation of natural religion. Wright maintained that supernatural rationalism was more prevalent than Deism in eighteenth-century America. In any event, if primitivism involves a resort to nature as a standard of human values, then the acceptance of natural religion is a significant manifestation of primitivism in the American Enlightenment.[53]

Deism is natural religion without the superstructure of Revelation, and this system of belief won the allegiance of many leading eighteenth-century Americans—John Adams, Joel Barlow, Benjamin Franklin, Philip Freneau, and Thomas Jefferson to name a few. Deists conceived of the universe as a vast and intricate mechanism that God constantly kept in running order. But they viewed nature as a complete system under divine superintendence and dispensed with Revelation and miracles.

By the 1790s Deists like Thomas Paine and Elihu Palmer became militant apostles of natural religion. They insisted that religious reconstruction must accompany the political reconstruction that had already been effected. Religion as well as government must be placed upon the only true foundation—nature. This radical appeal met little success in a nation so deeply rooted in Christian orthodoxy, but the Deists' program was indicative of a widely shared belief in primitivism and restorationism as the Age of Enlightenment drew to a close.[54]

In summary, a considerable amount of primitivistic thought is evident during the American Enlightenment. With much of it we are already familiar, although usually we know it by other names. (To recognize familiar ideas under a new label—in this case, primitivism—is like discovering, late in life, that one has always been speaking prose!) Fascination with primitivism took many diverse forms in eighteenth-century America. Fascination with nature was of paramount importance, however slippery the meaning of that term. The attempt to understand the various forms of life in the physical creation prompted speculation on the place of plants and animals in the scale of nature, on the relative merits of instinct as opposed to reason in created beings, and on proximity to nature enabling humans to live virtuous lives.[55] Fascination with the Indians gave rise to the myths of the noble savage and the ignoble savage. Fascination with the possibility of creating a "new order of the ages" following the American Revolution prompted the idea of restorationism in religion and in government.

There was much ambivalence with respect to the issues raised by primitivism. Was the best pattern for human life to be found in the ancient past or in remote communities that followed nature's simple plan? The question pulled people in opposite ways. Perhaps some authors were tempted to praise the dignity of animals or the virtues of savages out of dissatisfaction with human nature or conventional society. Those farthest removed from primitive conditions probably found it easiest to sympathize with animals and savages. Many European writers found it fashionable to use primitive peoples as a weapon with which to attack civilized society. Americans usually avoided such literary posturing. Benjamin Franklin and Crevecoeur, writing on the Indians, may have been exceptions.[56]

Primitivism as a mode of thought seems to have increased in America during the eighteenth century. A good reflection of this development is afforded by contrasting Cotton Mather and William Bartram. Mather can fairly be called a cultural antiprimitivist, whereas Bartram can fairly be called a cultural primitivist. A number of forces contributed to the growth of a primitivistic outlook. Classical antiquity was still the standard of thought for educated people in the eighteenth century, and the classics encouraged chronological primitivism by instilling reverence for republicanism in government and for natural theology. In addition, the principles of the Enlightenment contributed to the result. The emphasis on nature as a standard of human values, on reason as the common possession of all, on human nature as uniform, and on the capacity for social progress by the use of reason in reconstructing religion and government in accordance with the norms of nature—all of these beliefs tended to encourage cultural primitivism. And perhaps the qualities of American life—the relative openness of society and of the environment—made it possible for these intellectual influences to find especially favorable conditions for growth in this country.

Primitivism has a close affiliation with restorationism, and the birth of the republic inspired the conviction that the Americans had built their society and institutions on the best models of human excellence afforded by nature and antiquity. Thus the past was prologue, and belief in America's rising glory was widespread at the end of the Enlightenment in America.

NOTES

1. Arthur O. Lovejoy and Georgy Boas, *Primitivism and Related Ideas in Antiquity: Contributions to the History of Primitivism* (Baltimore: The Johns Hopkins Press, 1935; reprinted New York: Octagon Books, 1965), 1–11; George Boas, "Primitivism," in *Dictionary of the History of Ideas,* 5 vols., ed. Philip P. Wiener (New York: Charles Scribner's Sons, 1968–74), 3: 577–98.

2. The literature on the European Enlightenment is enormous, but Arthur O. Lovejoy, "The Parallel of Deism and Classicism," *Modern Philology* 29 (February 1932): 281–99, deserves mention. For America the best account is Henry F. May, *The Enlightenment in America* (New York: Oxford University Press, 1977). Henry Steele Commager, *The Empire of Reason: How Europe Imagined and American Realized the Enlightenment* (Garden City: Anchor/Doubleday, 1977), takes a more limited view of the movement.

3. Lovejoy and Boas, *Primitivism in Antiquity,* 11–16 and appendix.

4. *The Christian Philosopher: A Collection of the Best Discoveries in Nature, with Religious Improvements* (London, 1721). Mather completed the manuscript and sent it to London in 1715; the book appeared in 1720.

5. The best recent studies of Mather are Robert Middlekauff, *The Mathers: Three Generations of Puritan Intellectuals, 1588–1728* (New York: Oxford University Press, 1971); David Levin, *Cotton Mather: The Young Life of the Lord's Remembrancer, 1633–1703* (Cambridge, MA: Harvard University Press, 1978); and Kenneth Silverman, *The Life and Times of Cotton Mather* (New York: Harper and Row, 1984).

6. Mather, *Christian Philosopher,* 8.

7. The first edition was published at Philadelphia in 1791. I have used the London 1792 reprint. *The Travels of William Bartram: Naturalist's Edition,* ed. Francis Harper (New Haven: Yale University Press, 1958), is valuable. On Bartram, see also N. Bryllion Fagin, *William Bartram: Interpreter of the American Landscape* (Baltimore: The Johns Hopkins Press, 1933); Ernest Earnest, *John and William Bartram, Botanists and Explorers* (Philadelphia: University of Pennsylvania Press, 1940); and Edmund Berkeley and Dorothy S. Berkeley, *The Life and Travels of John Bartram: From Lake Ontario to the River St. John* (Tallahassee: University Presses of Florida, 1982).

8. Charles E. Raven, *John Ray, Naturalist: His Life and Works* (Cambridge: Cambridge University Press, 1950), 452–57, 466–67 (quotation at 467). Mather acknowledged his heavy debt to Ray in *The Christian Philosopher,* 3. On "nature reporters" in early America, see David S. Wilson, *In the Presence of Nature* (Amherst: University of Massachusetts Press, 1978).

9. New York, 1747. The work was published anonymously.

10. On Freneau, see Nelson, F. Adkins, *Philip Freneau and the Cosmic Enigma: The Religious and Philosophical Speculations of an American Poet* (New York: New York University Press, 1949); Lewis Leary, *That Rascal Freneau: A Study in Literary Failure* (New Brunswick, NJ: Rutgers University Press, 1941); Philip M. Marsh, *Philip Freneau: Poet and Journalist* (Minneapolis: Dillon Press, 1967); and Mary W. Bowden, *Philip Freneau* (Boston: Twayne Publishers, 1976).

11. "On the Civilization of the Western Aboriginal Country," as quoted in Adkins, *Freneau,* 20.

12. "The Pictures of Columbus," in *The Poems of Philip Freneau,* 3 vols., ed. Fred L. Pattee, (Princeton: The University Library, 1902–7), 1: 117.

13. *The Miscellaneous Works,* in *The Poems (1786) and Miscellaneous Works (1788) of Philip Freneau,* ed. Lewis Leary (Delmar, NY: Scholars Facsimiles, 1975), 281–380 (see the eleven essays treating "The Philosopher of the Forest").

14. "On Retirement," in *Poems of Philip Freneau,* ed. Pattee, 1: 84.

15. "The Rising Glory of America," in *Poems of Philip Freneau,* ed. Pattee, 1: 60, 67, 68–69.

16. Thomas Jefferson, *Notes on the State of Virginia,* ed. William Peden (1787; reprint, Chapel Hill: University of North Carolina Press, 1955), 164–65 (the quotation); A. Whitney Griswold, *Farming and Democracy* (New York: Harcourt, Brace, 1948), 18–46.

17. Bartram, *Travels,* 3, 25, 57 for the quotations. For examples of his ecstatic appreciation of the landscape, see 13, 105, 186, 355, 396.

18. Mather, *Christian Philosopher,* 122.

19. Bartram, *Travels,* xiii–xiv. The Latin name is also spelled *Dionaea muscipula.*

20. Bartram, *Travels,* xiv–xvi.

21. The preceding two paragraphs draw primarily on Lovejoy and Boas, *Primitivism in Antiquity,* 19–22, 389–420; and George Boas, *The Happy Beast in French Thought of the Seventeenth Century* (Baltimore: The Johns Hopkins Press, 1933).

22. Mather, *Christian Philosopher,* 152–55, 179, 218–19.

23. Mather, *Christian Philosopher,* 156–61 (quotation at 161), 213–14. 211.

24. *Poems of Freneau,* ed. Pattee, 3: 284–85.

25. Bartram, *Travels,* xvi–xvii.

26. Bartram, *Travels,* xvii–xviii.

27. Bartram, *Travels,* xviii, xx–xxi.

28. William Bartram, "Anecdotes of an American Crow," *Philadelphia Medical and Physical Journal* 1 (1804): 89–95.

29. Bartram, *Travels* 267–68.

30. Bartram, *Travels,* 264–66.

31. As quoted by Earnest, *John and William Bartram,* 143, from an unpublished manuscript in the Historical Society of Pennsylvania.

32. The preceding two paragraphs draw primarily on Lovejoy and Boas, *Primitivism in Antiquity,* 287–367; Boas, "Primitivism," 3: 591–94; Benjamin Bissell, *The American Indian in English Literature of the Eighteenth Century* (New Haven: Yale University Press, 1925), 1–54; Roy Harvey Pearce, *The Savages of America: A Study of the Indian and the Idea of Civilization,* rev. ed. (Baltimore: The Johns Hopkins Press, 1965), 3–49; and Robert F. Berkhofer, Jr., *The White Man's Indian: Images of the American Indian from Columbus to the Present* (New York: Alfred A. Knopf, 1978), 3–31.

33. Robert Beverley, *The History and Present State of Virginia,* ed. Louis Wright (1705; reprint Chapel Hill: University of North Carolina Press, 1947), 180, 189,195–216, 233.

34. John Lawson, *A New Voyage to Carolina* (London, 1709; reprint, Ann Arbor: University Microfilms 1966), 235, 231, 236, 231–32, 236–37.

35. Cadwallader Colden, *The History of the Five Indian Nations,* 2 vols. (1747; reprint, New York: A. S. Barnes and Co., 1904), 1: x, xi, xxviii–xxxi, xxi–xxii, xvii, xxxiv.

36. Colden, *History,* 1: xi–xii.

37. William Douglass, *A Summary, Historical and Political, of the First Planting, Progressive Improvements, and Present State of the British Settlements in North-America,* (I have used a 1755 edition printed in Boston), 1: 154, 173, 155, 160, 161.

38. Douglass, *Summary,* 1: 168, 166, 162, 165–66, 168, 169. On Colden and Douglass, see also Giorgio Spini, *Autobiografia della Giovane America: La Storiografia Americana dia Padri Pellegrini all' Indipendenza* (Turin: Guilio Einaudi, 1968), 279–96.

39. Pearce, *Savages of America,* 76–104; Berkhofer, *White Man's Indian,* 33–49.

40. Bissell, *American Indian,* 174–77.

41. Timothy Dwight, *Travels in New England and New York,* 4 vols., ed. Barbara Miller Solomon (Reprint, Cambridge, MA: Belknap Press of Harvard University Press, 1969), 1: vii–viii, 86. Dwight began making his annual tours of the region in the 1790s; his four volumes were first published in 1821–22.

42. Pearce, *Savages of America,* 139–42.

43. Bartram, *Travels,* 481–520 and throughout.

44. Adkins, *Freneau,* 25–27; Marsh, *Freneau,* 128–31.

45. Jefferson, *Notes,* 58–63, 64; Pearce, *Savages of America,* 91–96.

46. Howard Mumford Jones, *Revolution and Romanticism* (Cambridge, MA: Belknap Press of Harvard University Press, 1974), 153.

47. Winton U. Solberg, ed., *The Federal Convention and the Formation of the Union of the American States* (New York: Liberal Arts Press, 1958; reprint, Indianapolis: Bobbs-Merrill, n.d.), lix–lxx, lvi–lvii.

48. Solberg, *Federal Convention,* xix–xxii.

49. James Madison, "The Federalist No. 14," as quoted in Solberg, *Federal Convention*, 66.

50. Jones, *Revolution and Romanticism*, 198–203, provides a sample.

51. As quoted in Solberg, *Federal Convention*, 203.

52. As quoted in Conrad Wright, *The Liberal Christians: Essays on American Unitarian History* (Boston: Beacon Press, 1970), 17.

53. Wright, *Liberal Christians*, 6–15.

54. On the developments treated in the two preceding paragraphs see among others May, *Enlightenment in America*, 223–51; Adkins, *Freneau*, 33–57; Harry Hayden Clark, "Toward a Reinterpretation of Thomas Paine," *American Literature* 5 (May 1933): 133–45; and Alfred Owen Aldridge, *Benjamin Franklin and Nature's God* (Durham, NC: Duke University Press, 1967).

55. Students of primitivism in Europe have shown how the premises of cultural primitivism led not only to the cult of the noble savage, but also to the cult of the peasant, the cult of the child, and certain aspects of feminism. See, for example, George Boas, *The Cult of Childhood*, Studies of the Warburg Institute, vol. 29 (London: The Warburg Institute, 1966); and Boas, "Primitivism," in *Dictionary of the History of Ideas*, 3: 594–96. The category of "peasant" is irrelevant to the conditions of American life in the eighteenth century. I have not tried to relate the concept of primitivism to feminism in eighteenth-century America, but I have attempted to ascertain whether a cult of the child emerged during the Enlightenment in America. Although attitudes toward children changed considerably during the eighteenth century, nothing resembling a cult of the child seems to have developed at that time. I draw here on a seminar paper written under my direction at the University of Illinois in the spring of 1985 by James S. Patrick, " 'Innocent Vipers': Children and Youth in Eighteenth-Century New England." In the United States the cult of the child is a twentieth-century phenomenon.

56. Pearce, *Savages of America*, 138–42.

4

Puritan and Enlightenment Primitivism: A Response

E. BROOKS HOLIFIELD
and
SIDNEY E. MEAD

PURITANS: **E. Brooks Holifield** In order fully to appreciate the significance of the two essays by Dwight Bozeman and Leonard Allen, one must set them against a larger background of scholarship about the Puritan past and reflection about its import in American culture. As Bozeman has observed in his larger study of Puritan primitivism, *To Live Ancient Lives,* the interpretations that he and Allen are proposing stand clearly in tension with a popular and time-honored conception of seventeenth-century Puritans as the harbingers of modernity or, in more fashionably current language, as the agents of modernization. Jan Dawson has shown us recently that the quest for a usable past has been one of the primary impulses underlying the conception of Puritanism as a modernizing force.[1] Set in the context of the longer history of interpretation that Dawson has described, the two essays raise anew some old questions. If the Puritans were as preoccupied with the primitivist ideal as Bozeman and Allen suggest, how does that primitivism alter our understanding of their importance within the broader sweep of modern American culture?

In the 1830s, when American scholars first began to muse about their Puritan heritage, both Calvinist evangelicals and Unitarian liberals scrambled to depict their political preferences and ethical predispositions as fruits of the Puritan tradition. They believed that the Puritans were the heralds of modernity because they viewed the Puritan tradition as the source of American civil liberty and public virtue. George Bancroft had no doubt that the Puritan movement was to be viewed chiefly as a source and anticipation of the modern notion of popular sovereignty. Even the midwestern Copperheads and north-eastern Catholics who repudiated Puritanism as the seedbed of civic fanaticism, and the southern conservatives who despised it as the source of fanatic secularity, agreed that the significance of the Puritan past lay in its impulse toward modernity. And after the Civil War, the representatives of the genteel tradition maintained that accent on the modernity of Puritanism by redefining it as a set of universal truths supporting liberty, restraint, and service.

Not until the 1880s did historians first begin to argue that the Puritans embodied not an impulse toward modernity but a regressive enthusiasm for an unsavoury past. Both Brooks Adams, who deplored the "priestly" oppression of New England, and Charles Francis Adams, who conceived of Puritanism as a theological glacier that had to melt before modernity could sail into view, pictured the theologians of Connecticut and Massachusetts as backward-looking reactionaries preoccupied with the ancient and the forgotten. They surely would have welcomed a scholarly demonstration that the Puritans were to be defined by their primitivist inclinations, for they found the Puritans to be very primitive indeed.

By the beginning of the twentieth century, Van Wyck Brooks and George Santayana had resurrected the older view that Puritanism had formed a bridge into the modern world, but unlike the patriarchs of the genteel tradition, they found the bridge to have been excessively narrow and restrictive of modern sensibilities. They thought that the Puritan past had formed the modern literary temper, but with disastrous results.

During the 1920s, Santayana changed his mind. He and Paul Elmer More decided now that the Puritans should be seen as the antagonists of modernity, and they found in that Puritan traditionalism a source of hope that American writers might escape the allure of modernism. It was precisely the antagonism between Puritanism and modernity that made the Puritan past seem appealing. But Santayana, skeptical and somber, could hardly be said to have represented the mood and temper of either Harvard or Main Street in the 1920s. Vernon Parrington was far more representative of the prevailing Progressivism, and his *Main Currents of American Thought* (1927) imprinted in the minds of American students a vivid image of the Puritans as antagonists of the modern temper and of Puritanism as the antithesis of modernity.

Most of us are the heirs of the generation of scholars who read Parrington and found him distressingly bland and disturbingly simplistic. Perry Miller's magisterial synthesis of Puritan thought and culture, *The New England Mind: The Seventeenth Century* (1939), embodied the resurgent conviction that Puritanism represented the grand transition toward modernity. Indeed, a careful rereading of Miller's great volume, in the light of his subsequent scholarship, reveals that the center of his overarching vision was an image of Puritan thought as a subtle and covert movement toward naturalism. In Miller's view, the Puritan covenant theology anticipated modern naturalism through its insight that God would work always through natural means in the natural order. And that protonaturalism reached full coherence when Jonathan Edwards discarded the earlier equivocations and "wove the supernatural into the natural." Edwards made the supernatural "so highly naturalistic that neither new lights nor old lights would have anything of it."[2] Miller's Puritans were modern thinkers, far more modern, in fact, than they themselves could ever have recognized.

Subsequent historians established a profitable cottage industry compiling refutations of Perry Miller, but the conception of Puritanism as a beachhead of modernity has prevailed among the influential interpreters of the Puritan intellect, despite the occasional demurrers of the social historians. Hence we have learned to think of Puritanism as the propaedeutic of modern science, as the breeding ground of modern capitalism, as the nursery of modern political voluntarism, as the forerunner of modern revolutionary political discipline, and even as the engine pulling the whole train of modernization on which we are now perched, for good or for ill.[3]

The history of the interpretation of Roger Williams would correspond closely to the broader patterns. The early Victorian apologists for the Massachusetts Bay Puritans considered Williams to have been somewhat unpleasantly eccentric, but throughout the first half of the twentieth century, at least, everyone who looked at Williams saw a pioneer of liberal democracy, an irrepressible democrat who foreshadowed all the modern political virtues. Only in 1953 did Perry Miller break with that consensus and depict Williams as a pleasantly eccentric interpreter of the types and antitypes of Scripture, a depiction that Edmund Morgan reinforced in 1967 with his lucid account of Williams as a man securely ensconced within the seventeenth century rather than the nineteenth. To some extent, Miller and Morgan prepared the way for us to accept Leonard Allen's further contention that, in some respects, Williams was a man of the first century, not simply of the seventeenth.[4]

It seems clear, at any rate, that Bozeman and Allen present us with an interpretation of Williams and the Puritans that comports uneasily with the popular depiction of Puritanism as a modernizing movement. And yet, unlike their predecessors who accented the discontinuity between the Puritan movement and the modern world, they advance their proposals not to discredit the Puritan past but to appropriate it. Bozeman finds the defining unity of the Puritan tradition in its appeal to a primitive past, and Allen views Williams as an examplar of a restorationism that has deeply influenced American religious history.

In presenting those proposals, Bozeman and Allen raise some of the methodological issues that will recur throughout this volume. They recognize, for instance, that primitivism was only one dimension of the Puritan movement—even if it was centrally important—and that the primitivist impulse distinguished the Puritans only in proportion and degree from their opponents. One is reminded of that voluminous sixteenth-century English squabble between Thomas Cartwright and John Whitgift, in which Cartwright the Puritan argued that since Jesus preached in synagogues, Anglicans must eschew private sacraments and services; and since Paul received Timothy as a minister only after receiving permission from the congregations in Lystra and Iconium, Anglicans must also elect their ministers; and since Matthias was chosen in place of Judas only when there was a shortage in the number of appointed disciples, Anglicans must not "ordain until there be a church void and destitute of a pastor." Whitgift could play the same game. Since Christ wore a seamless robe, he said, Anglican clergy should also wear distinctive copes and surplices.[5]

But in this test case, which exemplifies the common admiration for the primitive among both the Puritans and their antagonists, Bozeman's thesis proves true. Whitgift expressed dismayed surprise that any Christian would condemn any ordinance which "was used and allowed during the time of the primitive church," but he defined the reach of the primitive to include "the next 500 years after Christ," an expansiveness that prompted Cartwright to conclude that "all your proof throughout the whole book is in the authorities of men."[6] Whitgift and Cartwright differed in degree in their adherence to the primitive and in their definition of the primitive, but the difference nevertheless remained crucial.

Both Bozeman and Allen also recognize that the consensus among the Puritans was largely formal: they agreed to appeal to the same primitive source, but they often derived divergent substantive conclusions from that source. In one sense, the two essays restate, with sophistication and detail, the familiar insight that the Puritans were biblicists who sought in the Scriptures clear prescriptions for the ordering of their churches and their piety. And they suggest that the next step in the elaboration of the primitivist thesis might well be to clarify the divergent rules that governed the appeal to a common primitive source.

Allen uncovers one such rule when he observes Williams's preference for the New Testament instead of the Old. I would suspect that a reexamination of Puritan hermeneutics in the light of these two essays would reveal some illuminating interpretive patterns. John Whitgift insisted that Cartwright's prime error was not his appeal to the primitive but rather the rules that governed that appeal. It is never appropriate, he said, "to argue *a facto ad jus* (of a deed or example to make a law)." Christ sat at the last supper, he said: "Doth it therefore follow that of necessity we must needs sit?" Then perhaps the sacrament would be administered "at night, after supper, to twelve, only men and no women, in a parlour, within a private house, the Thursday at night before Easter." Albeit the examples of Christ are to be followed, he continued, interpreters should never "conclude an universal doctrine of one particular and singular example," without the added confirmation of an express commandment.[7] In discerning and analyzing the hermeneutical rules that governed the appeal to the primitive, we might be able usefully to exploit and refine the insights of these essays.

And finally, back to modernity. What do the essays suggest about Puritanism and the emergence of a modern world? Does the recognition of the primitivist impulse entail the conclusion that the Puritan past died in the New England forests without leaving any trace of its imprint on the future? Probably not. The papers do alert us to the possibility that the whole conception of modernization—like the analogous conception of secularization—might well be far more ambiguous than we have thought. And they alert us to the possibility that an appeal to the primitive might well be a hidden, or barely recognized, aspect of the modern. But more clearly they suggest that the roadway to the modern world is simply not as straight as many historians of Puritanism have supposed. Thus they resurrect the familiar idiom of irony, the recognition that the consequences of religious faith have seemed repeatedly to contradict the explicit intentions of the faithful, that a corporate ethos inspired by admiration for the primitive might well have engendered patterns of thought and activity never envisioned by the zealous. And in suggesting that circuitous route from the past to the present, they promise to enrich our understanding of both the present and the past.

ENLIGHTENMENT: **Sidney E. Mead** I begin, first, by noting that comments on a paper usually amount to saying that it is not the paper the commentator would have written on the topic; and, second by confessing that in what follows I do not pretend to rise above the usual.

I have long been intrigued by the way we gather in conferences to discuss something designated by a word or phrase (e.g., "The Restoration Ideal") only to discover that the word or phrase means something different to each person present. Perhaps every conference ought to have an infallible academic pope to tell us what we are to talk about.

In his communication of 5 March 1985, Professor Hughes tried to clarify the topic by noting that in planning the conference he had used the words *restoration* and *primitivism* as "more or less equivalent to one another." He then suggested that Professor Bozeman's definitions set the theme of the conference. Bozeman characterizes "a whole facet of Puritan thought" as " 'primitivist,' or, alternately, 'restorationist' or 'restitutionist' "—words pointing to the ploy of "undercutting both Catholic and 'Anglican' appeals to" the continuity and authority of tradition by arguing that "the 'first' or primitive order of things" depicted in the Bible was normative for all time. Unfortunately, Hughes went on to confuse the definition of "the restorationist ideal" by dragging in Boas and Lovejoy's distinction between chronological and cultural primitivism, thus opening the door to the scores of meanings that primitivism has in different contexts.

Professor Solberg's paper seems to me to be launched on that confusion. He has given us a paper on primitivism defined primarily as the concept of, or feeling for, a supposed agrarian golden age in the past—an image of rustic, bucolic, simple life invoked to contrast with the luxury and titilating sinfulness of the present—or, in brief, "delight in the physical environment" and "the simple appreciation of landscape and agrarian tradition."

In this context the religious primitivism that Hughes and Bozeman were talking about is tangential. Consequently the paper largely ignores the restorationist dimension in the perspective of America's enlightened, deistic gentlemen—e.g., Jefferson's appeal to the pure moral teachings of Jesus to judge his contemporary Christianity; Paine's suggestion that Adam was the first deist and ought to be our example; or Joseph Priestley's two volume *History of the Corruptions of Christianity.*

Solberg defines the Enlightenment as "an historical movement" (as most movements are), primarily bounded by Cotton Mather's *Christian Philosopher* of 1721 and William Bartram's *Travels* of 1791, and asserts that "the thought of this phase of Western intellectual history viewed nature as the ultimate source of authority, and . . . assumed that reason was common to all men." This "belief that reason was available to all and that nature could verify everything men needed to know led to other Enlightenment principles such as uniformitarianism, cosmopolitanism, and belief in progress," while "another characteristic . . . was an emphasis on intuition and emotion."

There is much to question in this neat picture of Enlightenment thought in eighteenth-century America.

For example, I question the claim that nature was viewed "as the ultimate source of authority." As I read some of its outstanding exemplars (e.g., Franklin, Jefferson, Adams, Paine, and Hamilton), not nature but God was the ultimate source of authority, known, to be sure, by study of what Paine called his true book of revelation, the Creation. Confusing the source of the knowledge of God with God's authority, Solberg asserts that the search for justification of separation "finally led" the Americans "to rest their case . . . on the laws of nature" period, overlooking the key phrase in the Declaration of Independence, "the laws of nature and of nature's god." In the Declaration, rights are not rooted simply in nature, but in creation and endowment by the Creator. Jefferson, in pleading for religious freedom, does not appeal to nature as highest authority, but to Almighty God who created the mind free and manifested his will that free it should remain.

In defining *deism* Solberg slips into the common ploy of saying what deists did not believe. Diests, he says, "dispensed with Revelation and miracles" (he should have added the trinitarian formula). This form of defining deism served orthodox Christians to frighten the faithful away from a religious bogey that slighted some of their most precious dogmas, as witness, for example, Timothy Dwight's *Nature and Danger of Infidel Philosophy*. But it tells us nothing about what deists did believe and assert—such as Franklin's list of things he said ˙he never doubted; Paine's elemental creedal belief in one God and no more; Jefferson's elevation of the uniqueness of the pure moral teachings of Jesus as almost to imply divine inspiration. And they did not dispense with revelation; they merely differed from the orthodox respecting its nature. Deists might be known as theistic, radical monotheists, or Unitarian creationists. From the Christian perspective, in the precise terminology current toward the end of the century, they were infidels, not atheists.

Solberg makes one characteristic of Enlightenment thought the "belief in progress." This has to be qualified by noting that the concept of progress in the eighteenth century is often to be seen in the context of a cyclical view of history—the foundation of Volney's much read *The Ruins, or a Survey of Empires* (1791). Jefferson reflects this concept of "progress" in his *Notes on Virginia:*

> From the conclusion of this war we shall be going down hill. It will not then be necessary to resort every moment to the people for support.

They will be forgotten, therefore, and their rights disregarded. They will forget themselves but in the sole faculty of making money, and will never think of uniting to effect a due respect for their rights. The shackles, therefore, which shall not be knocked off at the conclusion of this war, will remain on us long, will be made heavier and heavier, till our rights shall revive or expire in a convulsion.

Our rulers will become corrupt, our people careless. A single zealot may commence persecutor, and better men be his victims.

And this was progress as movement through the persistent cycle of history.

Solberg urges as "testimony to primitivism in the Revolutionary era" (identical with the era of Enlightenment?) the "appeal to antiquity in establishing new governments." But a good case might be made that the founders largely rejected that appeal in setting up their new order of things. Madison's statement, quoted by Solberg, says as much—that while his Americans paid a "decent respect to the opinions of former times and other nations, they have not suffered a blind veneration for antiquity . . . to overrule . . . their own good sense . . . and the lessons of their own experience." Jefferson implied that they studied the ancient forms to find bad examples to avoid and to be convinced that mankind had not found angels to govern them.

Rather they seem to have rooted government in their enlightened view of human nature—in that, Harriet Martineau argued in the 1830s, consisted their genius and originality. Central to that view was what Hamilton spelled out as the "ordinary depravity" of humankind— justifying Page Smith's observation that reading accounts of the debates in the Constitutional Convention is enough to convince one that the founders thought of government as a device for combatting original sin. So when Paine insists that "the only true foundation" of religion and government is nature (as Solberg notes) he most probably had in mind the generally accepted view of *human* nature.

Founding government on this dim view of human nature was at the heart of the Revolution. Augustinian Christians have always argued with their patron saint that Christians alone could support a republic with government by consent, because only they were enabled by grace to overcome their individual pride and selfishness and, in obedience to God, will the common good.[8] This view, spelled out and applied by the founders of Massachusetts Bay, was ploughed into the colonial ethos to become a roadblock in the way toward the new order of things. The founders confronted this Christian tendency to slouch toward theocracy with the scandal of the First Amendment.

In summary, *these* Christians, accepting depravity, argued that democratic-republicanism must be rooted in the altruism enabled by grace.

The founders, generally accepting a similar view of depravity and skeptical of the Christians' altruism after observing their persecutions, concluded that every government must be of sinners, by sinners, and for sinners, that is, erected on the universal selfishness and depravity of humankind. The trick, as Madison saw it, was to contrive government in such a way as to make it the selfish interest of everyone in power jealously to watch the shenanigans of all the others; hence the famous system of checks and balances.

All of this to say that while Solberg has given us a treatise on one slice of the eighteenth century—the reverence of some people of that era for nature and agrarian ideals—we still await an examination of biblical primitivism in the thinking of American Enlightenment figures like Jefferson, Priestley, and Paine.

NOTES

1. Jan Dawson, *The Unusable Past: America's Puritan Tradition, 1830 to 1930* (Macon, GA: Scholars' Press, 1984), 9–144. My description of the movement from Bancroft to Parrington draws on Dawson's useful analysis.

2. Perry Miller, *Jonathan Edwards* (New York: W. Sloan Associates, 1949), 186.

3. Max Weber, *The Protestant Ethic and the Spirit of Capitalism* (New York: Charles Scribner's Sons, 1958); Robert K. Merton, *Social Theory and Social Structure* (New York: Free Press, 1968); Christopher Hill, *Society and Puritanism in Pre-Revolutionary England* (New York: Schocken Books, 1967); David Little, *Religion, Order and Law* (New York: Harper and Row, 1969); Sacvan Bercovitch, *The American Jeremiad* (Madison, WI: University of Wisconsin Press, 1978).

4. Samuel Brockunier, *The Irrepressible Democrat: Roger Williams* (New York: Ronald Press, 1940); Edmund J. Carpenter, *Roger Williams* (New York: Grafton Press, 1909); May E. Hall, *Roger Williams* (Boston: Pilgrim Press, 1917); Emily Easton, *Roger Williams: Prophet and Pioneer* (New York: Houghton Mifflin, 1930); James E. Ernst, *Roger Williams: New England's Firebrand* (New York: Macmillan, 1932); Perry Miller, *Roger Williams* (New York: Atheneum, 1953); Edmund Morgan, *Roger Williams: The Church and the State* (New York: Harcourt, Brace, 1967).

5. John Whitgift, *The Works of John Whitgift*, 3 vols. (Cambridge, 1853), 1:469, 208, 315; 2:14.

6. Whitgift, *Works*, 2:182; 1:427.

7. Whitgift, *Works*, 1:316; 3:94; 2:233.

8. Not long ago one of President Reagan's advisors proclaimed that all non-Christians in the government ought to convert or get out.

PART TWO

Biblical Scholarship and Fundamentalism

5

Biblical Primitivism in American Biblical Scholarship, 1630–1870

THOMAS H. OLBRICHT

I N the first three centuries of American Protestantism, the Bible served as the principal resource for creating and honing the ideal image of the church. In the preacher's repertoire of learning, biblical studies occupied a key position, as is obvious in the requirement that all prospective ministers learn Greek and Hebrew and in the popularity of biblical commentaries. In order to exhibit a church order grounded in the biblical faith it was imperative that the churchman ascertain the true meaning of the biblical text. Not only did the preacher need to work in the original vocabulary and grammar of the Scriptures, he also needed some measure of historical perspective in regard to the settings for biblical materials. These concerns comprised the science of biblical criticism. Although American scholars were not at the forefront of biblical scholarship so as to advance its frontiers, nevertheless in certain critical periods they were abreast of the best biblical criticism available.

I want to focus on the manner in which the construction and defense of theological platforms in the American church fueled the sharpening of skills in biblical criticism. The accelerated interest in biblical criticism is especially obvious in the early American Puritan disputes and in the controversies regarding the trinity in the nineteenth century. In each instance a scholarly exegesis of Scripture was construed as requisite weaponry for carrying the day.

The focus of this book is primitivism. The question must be raised early as to whether an interest in establishing biblical foundations constitutes primitivism. In some measure all the churchmen discussed in this paper were primitivists in that they perceived the final court of appeal for the parameters of life and faith to be ancient documents, that is, the Christian Scriptures. They were all heirs of the Reformation, which placarded the slogan *sola scriptura*. They all had reason for appropriating biblical criticism as contrasted, for example, with twentieth-century Unitarians of humanistic predilections who eschew the normative value of ancient documents. Some were more interested than others in drawing exclusively upon the Scriptures, but even among those who discredited developments past the first century, there were scholars who envisioned cutting-edge biblical criticism as an ally. A case in point was Alexander Campbell who kept up with German, British, and American criticism.[1] Obviously for Campbell, a primitivist vision of faith and life was not inimical to capitalizing upon the grammatico-historical tools of traditional Christianity.

The nature of biblical studies which the Puritans transported to America is critical since these beginnings set the tone for the next two centuries. Then developments in the trinitarian controversies laid the foundations for twentieth-century American criticism. I turn now to characterize biblical studies in these two crucial periods.

Biblical studies came to New England transplanted bodily from England, packed in the soil of centuries of European culture. The plants were not scrubs, the diseased, or castoffs. The people, the tools, and the methods were the best available. Those who did the transplanting had a special interest in biblical studies. It was their aspiration to reform the Church of England along lines which they perceived as replicating the church of the Scriptures.[2] Their home in the New World gave them the opportunity to create a model church which could be copied by the British Parliament. This project demanded an educated ministry, with the result that Harvard College was founded as soon as feasible. The Puritans hoped to train not only the immigrants, but also the sons of those in England who desired a less worldly environment than Oxford and Cambridge.

The model for the church on these shores lay adumbrated in Christian Scriptures. These ancient documents contained the guidelines for personal purity, the congregational blueprint for the church, the foundations for Reformed theology, and the basic data for discerning the signs of the times. The training which ensued focused on the tools for biblical study, especially the original languages of the Scriptures.

The Puritans arrived at the mouth of the Charles River with a culture and church intact. On the ships were educated men, an educated ministry, and the accoutrements of education. In the persons and books of these nonconforming churchmen could be found the front-running tools for biblical studies.

Among the Puritans who migrated to Massachusetts and Connecticut before 1650 were at least 104 who had matriculated at Cambridge and 29 at Oxford.[3] The majority were graduates of Cambridge because the climate there was in some measure favorable to Puritan views. Central to the curricula were the biblical and classical languages and the arts of expression: rhetoric, logic, and dialectic.[4] Instruction in the languages involved lectures in the morning and recitations in the afternoon. Expositions of Scripture occurred early in the mornings and was frequently more devotional than scholarly.

Six of the early ministers who disembarked in Boston Bay received the M.A. from Cambridge.[5] Three of these—Charles Chauncy, John Cotton, and Henry Dunster, along with John Eliot—were singled out for achievement in Hebrew. Chauncy was nominated a lecturer in Hebrew, but served rather in Greek for some years. Cotton won a fellowship at Emmanuel in Hebrew and served as a lecturer for six years.

The training these men received was competent for the times. In the middle of the seventeenth century work in biblical studies in England surpassed that on the continent. As Basil Hall observed, "Almost no grammar, lexicon or commentary by an English scholar won a European reputation before the seventeenth century.... But by the mid-seventeenth century the position had changed."[6]

Several published articles feature the libraries of early New England ministers. In consulting these it is clear that a number of books pertaining to biblical studies appear on most of the lists.[7] John Harvard's library was typical.[8] At least one-half of Harvard's 329 titles were commentaries on the Bible, and several of the remainder were biblical tools such as texts and grammars. Twentieth-century studies have noted the predominance of theological works in the Puritan libraries. Predominant among those works were books on Scripture.

A rigorous study of Hebrew grammar preceded the arrival of the Puritans in America by only about a century.[9] The work of Johannes Buxtorf I (1564–1629) impressed the Puritans and was found in many of their libraries. In addition to grammar, Buxtorf published a lexicon for the Talmud and assisted in bringing rabbinical literature to bear upon Old Testament studies. The Hebrew grammar first used at Harvard, however, was that of Wilhelm Schickard, a professor at the University of Tübingen. His grammar was favored in New England until Judah Monis, a converted Jew, taught at Harvard and published his grammar under the auspices of the Harvard Corporation in 1734.[10]

Hebrew learning in New England employed the same tools as on the continent. Puritans did little to advance these studies, but they were quick to employ them to better understand the Old Testament. Hebraic studies seemed to excite the Puritans more than Greek, but excellent Greek tools were likewise found in the libraries, for example, the grammar of Clenardus, *Graecae Linguae Institutiones*. Other tools for biblical studies found in abundance in Puritan libraries include lexicons and dictionaries in Greek, Hebrew, and English; concordances, critical biblical texts, and various translations.

By far the favorite books transported to these shores were biblical commentaries. Commentaries were various in genre. Several were annotations on the text, some short, some long. The largest number were single volumes on one biblical book. Commentaries were sometimes in a series authored by a single scholar, for example, those by John Calvin. Most were sermonic with a few short introductory remarks. In fact, several were expositions of the text sent to a printer when the sermon series on a specific book was completed. The reason commentaries of this sort were popular was that Puritan ministers were expected to preach a Sunday sermon about two hours in length and lecture for the same amount of time in the middle of the week. They therefore prized commentaries in which another had previously plowed the same territory they must now traverse. So most commentaries were a side-product of sermons written in full and read to a congregation, then handed over to a printer essentially unchanged. Only a few focused on philological and historical observations.

One is surprised over the manner in which the commentaries in the libraries of the Puritans represented the contemporary theological spectrum. Among the books of John Harvard were commentaries by at least forty-five authors, totaling above one hundred volumes. Broughton, Calvin, Lapide, and Piscator were represented by more than one volume. The largest number of authors were Lutheran,[11] although in these years Puritans moved readily back and forth between Lutheran and Reformed. The second largest number were Reformed.[12] At least six of the authors were English Puritans,[13] and Catholic authors made up a surprisingly large collection.[14] Authors represented in Harvard's collection include most of those whose work had considerable circulation. One glaring absence is Erasmus (1466–1536), although his books appeared in other Puritan libraries.[15]

We can get some notion of the commentators read frequently in New England by inventorying the authors cited by John Cotton (1584–1652), probably the most important, if not the most scholarly preacher in New England, who arrived in Boston in 1633. Cotton cited key commentators in his three works on church polity: "A Sermon Delivered at Salem" (1636), "The Keys of the Kingdom of Heaven" (1644), and "The Way of Congregational Churches Cleared" (1648).[16] In these three documents Cotton cited Ainsworth, Ames, Baynes, Bellarmine, Beza, Bullinger, Calvin, Cartwright, Danaeus, Davenant, Luther, Melanchthon, Perkins, Piscator, Rollock, and Zanchi. Of these, those cited the most were Ainsworth, Ames, Bellarmine, Beza, Calvin, Perkins, Piscator, and Rollock.

One is impressed that the Puritans employed the commentaries available from the most scholarly to those chiefly sermonic. Their biblical tools were both international and ecumenical.

Not only did the Puritan fathers transport and import biblical works; they also tried their hand at publishing tools and commentaries. These works were all written in English except John Eliot's translations into the Indian language. For that reason the circulation was largely limited to English-speaking peoples. The international language at this time was Latin. None of the works published exhibited extraordinary scholarship, but none is without merit when compared with similar efforts of the times.

The *Bay Psalm Book* launched New World English publishing efforts in 1640. This famous work is reputedly the first book in English printed in North America. The first edition numbered 1,700. A second printing followed in 1647, with twenty-five additional printings over the succeeding 100 years. The *Bay Psalm Book* was published so the churches could sing the Psalms of David rather than those written by contemporaries. The translation sought to put the Psalms in English meter and rhyme and resulted in certain appealing qualities.[17]

Three of the first-generation preacher-scholars who came to America wrote commentaries, foremost of whom was John Cotton, but also Thomas Parker and Ephraim Huit. Their commentaries were printed in England because of government control on printing, the better presses, and a larger market. It was not until almost a century later that the first commentary was actually printed in America—an honor that likely goes to John Rogers's commentary on Revelation.[18] The earliest commentary published was that of John Cotton on the Canticles (1642), but apparently the first commentary written in America and afterward published, although in England, was that of Thomas Parker on Daniel in 1646.

John Cotton wrote commentaries on the Canticles,[19] Ecclesiastes,[20] I John,[21] and Revelation.[22] These commentaries revealed Cotton more as the preacher than as the scholar. In his commentary on the Canticles, Cotton exhibited an awareness of the original purpose and made certain astute observations on the text that are still viable, but antiquarian observations did not detain him long. The real purpose of these works, in his estimation, lay in a future age, the time of Christ and the church that extended to the present and beyond. It was his task as expositor to lay bare the contemporary threads interwoven into the fabric. There was no hiatus within the document between antiquity and modernity. So Cotton wrote, the "scope is to describe the estate of the church towards Christ, and his respect towards her from his own time to the last judgment."[23] A second edition of the commentary was published in 1648, and a third after Cotton's death in 1655. The commentary on Ecclesiastes, in contrast, commented little on historical and contemporary developments, centering rather on the implications of the text for the development of morals and on God's response to man's corruption. In the commentary on 1 John, Cotton chiefly sought to enhance personal piety. In the commentary on Revelation 13, Cotton, like his Puritan contemporaries, found the history of Christendom adumbrated from the beginning, but especially since the Reformation. He went so far as to assign 1655 as the date of the long awaited day of the Lord, but he was careful about being overly adamant. "I will not be too confident, because I am not a prophet, nor the Son of a Prophet to foretell things to come, but so far as God helps by Scripture light, about the time 1655 there will be then such a blow given to this heart."[24]

Possibly the first commentary written in America and then published was by Thomas Parker on Daniel. Parker wrote other commentaries, but only the one on Daniel reached print. Thomas Parker (1595–1677) was born in Newbury, Berkshire, England. He attended Oxford and Dublin, working at the latter under the famed author of Usher's chronology. He migrated to Holland in 1614 where he studied under William Ames at Leyden, and then went to Franeker where he took the M.A. in philosophy and liberal arts in 1617. He migrated to New England in 1634 and helped found the town of Newbury and served as pastor of the church until his death. He also conducted a school for college prepatory.[25]

Parker only covered the parts of Daniel concerned with the arrival of the kingdom of God. His work indicates considerable erudition. He referred to a number of interpreters including Clement, Origen, Julius Africanus, Tertullian, Pererius, Reinold, Junius, and Broughton.[26] On occasion he quoted Hebrew.[27] He was not sure how to interpret Daniel, but believed that Luther and Wycliff served as points of departure, and that the stone cut out of the mountain was the reformed church which "they began to be cut out, anno 1160, in the Waldenses, and continue so unto this day.""[28] One is amazed by the manner in which Parker construed Daniel. Although an ancient book, it set forth universal history from its own day until the end time. The book thus became a veritable mine of history. If one takes the same path as Parker, history unfolds before one's very eyes.

Little is known about either Ephraim Huit or his commentary, *The Whole Prophecy of Daniel Explained by a Paraphrase.*[29] He matriculated at St. John's College, Cambridge in 1611. He was a curate in Cheshire and Knowle, then settled at Wroxhall, all in Warwickshire. He was silenced by Archbishop Laud for his Puritan views in 1638. He arrived in New England in 1639, was ordained at Windsor, Connecticut, on 10 December 1639, and died at Windsor on 4 September 1644, the same year in which his commentary appeared in London.[30]

Huit's conclusions and methods differed little from those of Parker. He did, however, provide more verse-by-verse comment on the whole of Daniel than Parker. He, like Parker and Cotton, considered circa 1650 pivotal for the in-breaking of Christ's millennial reign.

These commentaries were much like those published in England and on the continent and with much the same purpose. But they were inclined to be more sermonic—more directed to lay interests and problems. For the commentator of the time what counted most was the bearing of the text on his own epoch rather than what it meant in its original setting. These approaches and biblical tools remained much the same in New England and America until about two hundred years later.

We cannot but pause also to mention the unpublished commentary on the whole of the Bible by Cotton Mather, which he titled *Biblia Americana.* The manuscript for *Biblia Americana* has resided at the Massachusetts Historical Society since October 1809. It is in six volumes of about one thousand pages each. In August of 1693 Mather indicated in his diary the intention to commence this monumental work. On 28 May 1706, thirteen years later, he noted that he had "happily finished my great Work." Mather died in 1727, twenty-one years later, without having found a publisher. In the intervening twenty-one years he kept adding materials, desirous for as complete and up-to-date a work as possible. Mather hoped to get the commentary published in England as was typical for works of this size. Furthermore, the prestige of an English publisher increased considerably the prospect of volume sales in Europe. As was the custom, Mather published an announcement enlisting subscriptions.[31] In 1714 he printed *A New Offer, to the Lovers of Religion and Learning.* Cotton's son, Samuel, placed an advertisement in the back of his biography of his father, but his efforts were likewise of no avail.[32]

In his announcements for publication Mather made twelve observations about the contents: (1) the King James translation revised, (2) a rich collection of antiquities, (3) types collated with antitypes, (4) laws and history of Israel, (5) treasures from the Talmud and Jewish writers, (6) natural philosophy called into the service of scriptural religion, (7) a correct chronology, (8) the geography of Palestine and Paradise, (9) a twenty-ninth chapter of Acts, that is, a short church history to the present, (10) the eradication of contradictions, (11) history from all nations showing the fulfillment of prophecy, and (12) "Some essays to illustrate the *Scriptures,* from *experimental piety,* or the observations of *Christian experience.*"

One is impressed with the unlimited surveillance with which Mather searched for materials. His work in the various ancient texts was solid. But because of the future direction of biblical studies his extensive labors only serve antiquarian interests. What he accomplished was essentially an updating of medieval glosses. He utilized the text as the occasion for organizing the spectrum of contemporary knowledge, but manifested little interest in how the text was to be read in light of its own character and milieu. His commentary was not unlike those of the time except that he dwelt more upon curiosities than did Lightfoot, who stressed philological matters, and than did Matthew Henry, who emphasized Christian nurture. Mather was a primitivist in the sense that he believed that an ancient work served as a ready-made file cabinet in which to organize comment upon the contemporary world.

The Puritan search for primitive insight upon the nature of life, faith, and the church set the mold for biblical studies for the next two centuries and beyond. Biblical studies were useful to the church for its piety, its purity, and its prophetic vision. Commentaries and other biblical tools published in America have moved away from a blatant affirming of these ends, but identical goals still underlie many critical efforts.

In a new century—the nineteenth—scholars pursued biblical studies for other reasons, but early predilections persisted. With the rise of Arminianism, Deism, and Unitarianism, other battle clouds darkened the horizon. Early in the nineteenth century the Unitarians perceived that new developments in German biblical criticism portended indispensable weapons for coming skirmishes.[33] These liberals were the first to send their scions to the German citadel to study in depth the new tools and methods. But the traditionalists, that is, the trinitarians, on various fronts soon recognized the battleground and sent their own promising young scholars. The number and significance of the conservative scholars who studied in Germany before the Civil War has not received the attention that Jerry Wayne Brown has given the Unitarians in *The Rise of Biblical Criticism in America, 1800–1870.*

The forces at work in the early part of the nineteenth century laid the foundation for American participation in German biblical criticism which has ruled supreme from that epoch until the present. It is only in the last decade that the vigor of American scholarship may be moving ahead of the German. The nineteenth-century motivation behind the desire to keep abreast of the best in biblical studies reflects the conviction that support from works of antiquity would establish the veracity of any ongoing American confessional group. Not all these confessions were primitivist in the sense of ordering all of life around an ancient vision. But obviously each concluded that the imperative strategy in any theological battle demanded support from cutting-edge biblical criticism. Biblical criticism flourished throughout the nineteenth century in the circles in which this conviction remained intact, and this conviction later served to marshall the scholars who launched the twentieth-century American criticism.

The Unitarians first anticipated victory through the efforts of their promising young men who traveled to Germany to scout out and participate in the rising "scientific" discipline. In his famous address delivered at the ordination of Jared Sparks in Baltimore in 1819, William Ellery Channing set forth his view of the role of Scripture for the Unitarians as they faced the trinitarian polemicists. "We regard the Scriptures as the records of God's successive revelations to mankind, and particularly of the last and most perfect revelation of his will by Jesus Christ. Whatever doctrines seem to us to be clearly taught in the Scriptures, we receive without reserve or exception."[34] While opponents disagreed with their conclusions, the Unitarians rested their case with the primitive Christian documents, and set out to be at the forefront of biblical criticism. In this regard, Conrad Wright, an imminent Unitarian historian, wrote, "Stimulated by a sudden awareness of the riches of German critical scholarship, the liberals were trying to master new principles of biblical study. Their intellectual horizons had suddenly widened, and they were confident that new ways were opening before them for the solution of perennially intractable theological problems. No small part of the enthusiasm with which they attacked orthodoxy stemmed from their confidence that the science of biblical criticism assured the ultimate triumph of liberal Christianity."[35]

The earliest Unitarian encouraged to visit Germany and import the newly developing science to these shores was Joseph S. Buckminster (1784–1812). He made his pilgrimage in 1807 and returned to Boston with 3,000 volumes of European works on the Bible and biblical criticism. In 1818 Buckminster was appointed Dexter Lecturer on Biblical Criticism at Harvard, but died before he could take up the position.[36] Several Unitarians studied in Germany before the Civil War. The first to take a doctorate was Edward Everett, who was given leave to pursue the degree before taking up his teaching post at Harvard. Everett studied at Göttingen under Johann Gottfried Eichhorn (1752–1827), the foremost biblical critic of the day. Upon returning to Massachusetts, he accepted a post teaching Greek and later held political office.[37] George Bancroft followed shortly, receiving the doctorate in 1820. Bancroft taught in prep schools and later became an eminent historian. The common conclusion is that even the Unitarians were not prepared to accept the presuppositions of German criticism and therefore side-railed these able men into other careers.[38]

The hopes of the Unitarians soon reverted to home-trained men such as Andrews Norton, who was named Dexter Lecturer on Biblical Criticism at Harvard in 1813. Despite not having studied in Germany, Norton nevertheless made excellent use of the library acquired by Buckminster. He taught at the Harvard Divinity School upon its founding in 1819 until 1830 and helped shape a program which depended on biblical interpretation rather than dogmatic theology.[39] Before the Civil War the Unitarians produced only a few translations of German critical introductions to the Scriptures, translations of certain books of the Scriptures, and a limited number of exegetical works.[40] They turned out almost nothing which constituted biblical tools or commentaries. The Society of Biblical Literature was founded in America in 1880. Of the thirty-two founding fathers only one—Ezra Abbott—was a Unitarian, and he was educated at Bowdoin and self-trained in biblical criticism.[41] Five of the fathers took degrees from Harvard College, but none from the Divinity School.

The liberals were not only disappointed by the outcome in regard to their young men trained in Germany, but they themselves dropped out of contention for front-running biblical criticism by the time of the Civil War. They soon faced internal battles over transcendentalism and here the battle was not over the Bible, especially from the perspective of the transcendentalists. The result was that after a promising start, the Unitarians were supplanted in biblical criticism by such trinitarians as Moses Stuart, who almost single-handedly shaped the forces leading to post–Civil War criticism.

The trinitarian answer to the Unitarians trained in Germany was Moses Stuart. Stuart received his degree at Yale and for a time trained for a legal career, but coming under the influence of President Timothy Dwight, changed to the ministry.[42] As the result of the direction at Harvard, the conservative (that is, trinitarian) forces in the Puritan church (Congregational) established Andover Theological Seminary in 1809. As the result of the Unitarian charge that Andover would be a purveyor of dogmatic theology—that is, traditional theology apart from a constant look at the Scriptures—a strong effort was put forth to assure a scholarly scrutiny of the ancient biblical documents.

The first holder of the Chair of Sacred Literature at Andover was Eliphalet Pearson, formerly Hancock Professor of Hebrew at Harvard. He resigned after a year and with no heir apparent. Moses Stuart, more because of his abilities than training, was appointed to the post in 1810, which position he held until his death in 1852. As he took up the professorship Stuart had only elementary knowledge of Greek and Hebrew and knew almost nothing about German biblical criticism. But he went to work with great enthusiasm and soon mastered all three. Characteristic of his energy was the publication of a Hebrew grammar for use by his classes three years later in 1813.[43]

Stuart's introduction to German biblical criticism came from books he acquired from the sale of Joseph S. Buckminster's library soon after the latter's death. Among these was Eichhorn's *Einleitung ins Alte Testament*. In order to read this and other works, Stuart taught himself German. According to Brown, "He avidly sought to beg, borrow, or buy any German book dealing with the Bible, and was impatient because he could not read fast enough to avail himself of the material immediately."[44] The result was that Stuart turned out an impressive number of Hebrew and Greek grammars, commentaries, and works on hermeneutics and biblical criticism. He was soon recognized as the most competent philologist, grammarian, and commentator in America.

It was Moses Stuart who trained American churchmen in the ways of German criticism and who in turn whetted the appetites even of lay persons for the latest German developments. The journals of the mainline Protestant denominations report an amazing amount of information in regard to German biblical study. In the *Bibliotheca Sacra,* founded at Andover in 1844, one finds statistics on the theological students studying in European universities, as well as names of the professors.[45] *The Methodist Quarterly Review* listed lectures on biblical criticism in Berlin and supplied information about German books and schools.[46] Regular information in regard to German universities and studies appeared in other journals as well.

One of Stuart's students, Edward Robinson, surpassed Stuart in international acclaim as the result of his topographical studies of Palestine. Born in Connecticut in 1821, Robinson went to Andover to work on an edition of the Greek text of the *Iliad*. From 1823–26 he was instructor in Hebrew at the seminary. He resigned his position, probably at Stuart's encouragement, and left Andover in 1826 to study in Germany. Like Bancroft and Everett, he first made his way to Göttingen, but soon went to Halle where he spent the majority of his time, and from there went to Berlin.[47] He was troubled by what he perceived as the arrogance of the Germans, their critical posture toward Scripture and church, and their nonpuritanical life style. Both Stuart and Robinson held to the principle that "the Bible was *the only and sufficient rule of faith and practice.*"[48] In this manner both men, so influential on American biblical studies, soaked up the technical details of German biblical studies but rejected presuppositions that countered the authority of the Bible in the churches. They were committed to turn aside from presuppositions which placed the primitive Christian documents in a precarious position.

At Halle, Robinson was impressed with the work of the Hebrew grammarian Wilhelm H. F. Gesenius and the theologian Friedrich A. G. Tholuck. The influence of Tholuck on the conservative stream of American biblical studies and theology has not yet been appropriately studied and credited.[49] Robinson returned to Andover, where he remained for three years and worked on a Bible dictionary. Because of failing health he resigned. In 1831 he commenced publishing *The Biblical Repository,* in which he reported the recent developments in American and European biblical studies. After four years Robinson resigned the editorship. Again, in 1843, Robinson worked for and edited the *Bibliotheca Sacra* dedicated to biblical criticism. This connection continued for only a year. In the meantime Robinson worked with American editions of Philip Buttmann's Greek grammar and Gesenius's Hebrew grammar. In 1837 Robinson accepted an appointment to the Union Theological Seminary in New York, recently established under Presbyterian auspices. But before he took up that position he spent four years in Palestine doing pioneering work in topological exploration. For this work, which superseded all prior efforts, Robinson came into the international scholarly limelight, the first American to attain these stellar heights. The legacy of Stuart and Robinson made an indelible impression on training in biblical studies in America.

Before discussing that legacy two other mainline scholars should be mentioned.

Ira Chase of Newton Theological Seminary, a Baptist seminary now Andover-Newton as the result of a merger, traveled to Europe in 1823–24. After study in Germany he introduced German biblical criticism to generations of Baptist seminarians and lay persons. He spent short periods at Halle and Göttingen.[50]

Charles Hodge of Princeton Theological Seminary occupied the same key role among the Presbyterians. Hodge was born in Philadelphia and graduated from the College of New Jersey in 1815 and from Princeton Theological Seminary in 1819. He commenced teaching at Princeton Seminary in 1820 and was appointed Professor of Oriental and Biblical Literature in 1822, which position he held until elected professor of theology in 1840. Hodge was instrumental in founding a "society for improvement in Biblical Literature."[51] In 1825 he founded a journal designated *Biblical Repertory* with the subtitle, "A Collection of Tracts in Biblical Literature." In the *Dissertation* Hodge argued that educators and churchmen should be involved in biblical criticism for two reasons. First, it was necessary in his view for the minister to keep on top of scholarly matters in order to secure and maintain the respect of his parishioners. In that regard Hodge declared that great advancement had been made at Andover by Moses Stuart, and that Princeton must work to catch up.[52] Second, he announced a battle in the making with "a system which we all consider as fatally erroneous." Obviously he had in mind the Unitarians. He was certain that the battle line would be drawn over texts of the Scriptures and argued that insight regarding the integrity of the text would be mandatory.[53] It is clear that Hodge considered biblical criticism prerequisite for tasks confronting the church. Hodge clearly perceived that these primitive documents were the fundamental data out of which the church should construct its theology.

By 1826 Hodge decided that in order to lay the proper foundation for seminary teaching, two years of study in Europe were mandatory. At first he anticipated a year in Paris, then one in Göttingen, but as it turned out, the university at Halle captured a large proportion of his stay. The insistence of Edward Robinson accelerated the arrival of Hodge in Halle. In his letters Robinson impressed upon Hodge the importance of Halle and of Tholuck. In explaining his departure for Halle, Hodge wrote his wife, "There is one very important consideration, that one of its leading theological professors [Tholuck] is a very pious man, the like of which is not to be found elsewhere."[54]

In May 1828, Charles Hodge was back in Princeton ready to take up his life's work. He had become convinced through friendship with Tholuck that a valid, intelligent biblical criticism could proceed which at the same time rejected the presuppositions of the German radicals. Before devoting his life to systematic theology Hodge laid the foundations for biblical studies at Princeton by publishing commentaries on Romans, Ephesians, I Corinthians, and II Corinthians. As an exegete Hodge took pains to keep the larger scene in focus. His philological observations were adequate, although not extensive. He gave attention to the conclusions of others. His purpose was not to exhaust scholarly views, but to circle the passage, noting some of the popular interpretations, then quickly to present what in his view was "the common and only satisfactory interpretation."[55]

It was the conservative, traditional scholars who laid the foundations for American biblical criticism that accelerated in the last quarter of the nineteenth century. Their interest in these primitive documents was premised upon their conviction that the fountain from which the church must drink flowed from ancient days. The key scholar was Moses Stuart. Information was disseminated from the 1830s by the major journals of all the denominations, several of which carried information about developments in Germany in regard to biblical criticism. Chase and Hodge were important for the Baptists and Presbyterians, respectively. The important data establishing the primacy of Moses Stuart is that of the thirty-two founding fathers of the Society of Biblical Literature in 1880; seven were trained at Andover Theological Seminary, many by Stuart himself. Of the rest, four were trained at Union by Robinson who was indebted to Stuart. This means that a third traced their training to Stuart, whose influence loomed larger than any other single person.[56] A further search indicates that at least a half of the remainder were indirectly indebted to Stuart.

My conclusion, I hope, is clear. The authoritative weight of the primitive Christian Scriptures was a major force in shaping the churches of America from the time that the fathers landed at Boston Bay in 1630 until the laying of the foundations for twentieth-century biblical studies in the waning decades of the 1800s. Americans, often polemically inclined, sought to avail themselves of the best in biblical criticism in order to establish their case upon impeccable "scientific" grounds.

NOTES

1. In his works Campbell referred to all the premier biblical scholars of the day. A statement in "Principles of Interpretation" in *Christianity Restored* (1835), 96, cites many of them: "I do not know a single *principle* asserted, that is not already approved by the following: Doctors Campbell, of Aberdeen; Macknight, of Edinburgh; Doddridge of England; Michaelis, of Gottingen; Horne of Cambridge; Stuart of Andover; Ernesti, Lowth, Calmet, Glasius, Harwood, and many other of equal celebrity."

2. See the development of this point in chapter 1: "Biblical Primitivism: An Approach to New England Puritanism" by Theodore Dwight Bozeman.

3. Albert Matthews, "The University Alumni Founders of New England," *Publications of the Colonial Society of Massachusetts* (hereafter *PCSM*) 25 (1922-24):14-23.

4. Mary Latimer Gambhrell, *Ministerial Training in Eighteenth-Century New England* (New York: Columbia University Press, 1937), 9.

5. These six were Peter Bulkeley (1582-1658), Charles Chauncy (1592-1672), John Cotton (1584-1652), Henry Dunster (1609-59), Thomas Hooker (1586-1647), and Thomas Shepard (1605-49).

6. Basil Hall, "Biblical Scholarship: Editions and Commentaries," *The Cambridge History of the Bible* (Cambridge: Cambridge University Press, 1976), 92, 93.

7. See Perry Miller and Thomas H. Johnson, *The Puritans* (New York: American Book Company, 1938), 829-31.

8. Alfred Claghorn Potter, "Catalogue of John Harvard's Library," *PCSM* 21 (1920):190-230. See also the addenda by Henry J. Cadbury, "John Harvard's Library," *PCSM* 34(1933):353-77.

9. Otto Eissfeldt, *The Old Testament: An Introduction,* trans. Peter R. Ackroyd (New York: Harper and Row, 1965), 2.

10. Isidore S. Meyer, "Hebrew at Harvard (1636-1760): A Resume of the Information in Recent Publications," *Publications of the American Jewish Historical Society* 35(1939):145-79.

11. Lutheran commentaries were by Johann Brenz (1499-1570) of Wurttemberg, Joachim Camerarius (1500-1574), Davod Chytraeus (1530-1600) of Wittenberg and Rostock, Conrad Graser (1557-1613), Niels Hemmingsen (1513-1600) of Copenhagen, Aegidius Hunnius (1550-1603) of Wittenberg, Martin Luther (1483-1546), Lucas Lossius (1508-82) of Lunnebourg, Philipp Melanchthon (1497-1560), Heinrich Moller (1530-89), Lucas Osiander the Elder (1534-1604) of Stuttgart, and Abraham Scultetus (1566-89) of Heidelberg.

12. Reformed authors included Theodore Beza (1519-1605) of Geneva, Heinrich Bullinger (1504-75) of Zurich, John Calvin (1509-64), Lambert Daneau (1530-95) of Geneva and Leyden, Antoine de LaFaye (-1615) of Geneva, Johann Jakob Grynaeus (1540-1617) of Basel, Wolfgang Musculus (1497-1563) of Bern, Oswald Myconius (1488-1552) of Basel, Johannes Piscator (1546-1625) of Herbon, and Peter Martyr (1500-1562) of Zurich.

13. English Puritan authors included Henry Ainsworth (1571–1622) of Cambridge and Amsterdam, William Ames (1576–1633) of Cambridge and Franeker, Paul Baynes (　–1617) of St. Andrews Church, Hugh Broughton (1549–1612) of London and Germany, Thomas Cartwright (1535–1603) of Cambridge and Geneva, and John Davenant (1576–1641) of Salisbury. Other Britishers were David Dickson (1583[?]–1622) of Glasgow and Edinburgh, John Dove (1561–1618) of Oxford and London, and Thomas Taylor (1576–1632) of Cambridge and London.

14. Catholic authors included Roberto Bellarmino (1542–1621) of Rome, Corneliusa Lapide (1567–1637) of Louvain and Rome, Francois Feuardent (1539–1610) of northern France, Benedictus Arias (Montanus) (1527–98) of Spain and Rome, Geronimo Osorio (1506–80) of Portugal, Augustin De Quiros (1566–1622) of Spain and Mexico, Joannes (Jean) Royaerds (　–1547) of Belgium, Diego Estella (Stola) (1524–78) of Spain, and Jacques Turin (1580–1636) of Belgium and Holland.

15. Other authors recurring in the lists of other Puritan libraries, although not in John Harvard's library, included Nicholas Byfield (1579–1622) of Chester, John Mayor, John Oecolampadius (1482–1531) of Basel and Bern, David Pareus (1548–1622) of Heidelberg, William Perkins (1558–1602) of Cambridge, Richard Rogers (1550–1618) of Essex, Robert Rollock (1555–99) of Scotland, Thomas Wilcox (1549–1608) of Oxford, Andrew Willet (1562–1621) of Cambridge, and Jerome Zanchi (1516–90) of Strasbourg.

16. These sermons have been brought together and reprinted by Larzer Ziff in *John Cotton on the Churches of New England,* ed. Larzer Ziff (Cambridge, MA: Harvard University Press, 1968).

17. See Zoltan Haraszti, *The Enigma of the Bay Psalm Book* (Chicago: University of Chicago Press, 1956).

18. John Rogers, *The Book of Revelation of Jesus Christ . . .* (Boston, 1720).

19. John Cotton, *A Brief Exposition of the Whole Book of Canticles* (London, 1642).

20. John Cotton, *A Briefe Exposition with Practicall Observations upon the Whole Book of Ecclesiastes* (London, 1654).

21. John Cotton, *A Practical Commentary or An Exposition with Observations, Reasons, and Uses upon the First Epistle Generall of I John* (London, 1656).

22. John Cotton, *An Exposition upon the Thirteenth Chapter of Revelation* (London, 1655).

23. Cotton, *Brief Exposition of Canticles,* 4.

24. Cotton, *Exposition upon Revelation,* 93

25. Cotton Mather, *Magnalia Christi Americana; or the Ecclesiastical History of New-England: 1620–1698* (Hartford, 1855), 482. See also Samuel E. Morison, "The Education of Thomas Parker of Newbury," *PCSM* 28(1927): 261–67.

26. Thomas Parker, *The Visions and Prophecies of Daniel Expounded . . .* (London, 1646), 50, 51.

27. Parker, *Visions,* 30.

28. Parker, *Visions,* 7, 49, 64.

29. (London: Henry Overion, 1644).

30. Frederick Lewis Weiss, *The Colonial Clergy of the Colonial Churches of New England* (Lancaster, MA, 1936), 105.

31. Found in the back of *Bonifacius An Essay Upon the Good as an Advertisement.* The first edition was printed by B. Green (Boston, 1710), 200–206.

32. Samuel Mather, *The Life of Cotton Mather* (Boston, 1729), 183–86.

33. Jerry Wayne Brown, *The Rise of Biblical Criticism in America, 1800–1870* (Middletown, CT: Wesleyan University Press, 1969), 10–26.

34. In *Three Prophets of Religious Liberalism: Channing, Emerson, Parker,* intro. by Conrad Wright (Boston: Beacon Press, 1961), 48.

35. Wright, *Three Prophets,* 14, 15.

36. Brown, *Rise of Biblical Criticism,* 19–26.

37. This is the same man who gave the main address at Gettysburg, long since forgotten, which was upstaged by Lincoln's much shorter Gettysburg Address. See Victor Paul Furnish, "The Historical Criticism of the New Testament: A Survey of Origins," *Bulletin of the John Rylands University Library of Manchester* 56 (1974): 366.

38. For the names of others who studied in Germany between 1815 and 1850, see H. M. Hinsdale, "Notes on the History of Foreign Influences upon Education in the United States," *Report of the Commissioner of Education 1897–98,* 1:591–629.

39. Wright, *Three Prophets,* 17.

40. Brown, *Rise of Biblical Criticism,* 153–79.

41. Thomas H. Olbricht, "The Society of Biblical Literature: The Founding Fathers," unpublished paper read to a session of the society in New Orleans in 1978.

42. John H. Giltner, "Moses Stuart: 1780–1852" (Ph.D. dissertation, Yale University, 1956).

43. *A Hebrew Grammar without the Points; Designed as an Introduction to the Knowledge of the Inflections and Idiom of the Hebrew Tongue* (Andover, 1813).

44. Brown, *Rise of Biblical Criticism,* 49.

45. *Bibliotheca Sacra* 2 (1845):199–200; 4 (1847):209–16.

46. *Methodist Quarterly Review* 32 (1851):178–79; 31 (1849):162–74; 37 (1856):305–9.

47. Brown, *Rise of Biblical Criticism,* 111, 112.

48. Edward Robinson, "Theological Education in Germany," *The Biblical Repository* 1 (1831):1–51.

49. See my article on Charles Hodge in which I affirm the influence of Tholuck: "Charles Hodge as an American New Testament Interpreter," *Journal of Presbyterian History* 57 (1979):117–33.

50. *Dictionary of American Biography,* 4:26.

51. Charles Hodge, *A Dissertation on the Importance of Biblical Literature* (Trenton, 1822), 2.

52. Hodge, *Dissertation,* 41.

53. Hodge, *Dissertation,* 41f.

54. A. A. Hodge, *The Life of Charles Hodge* (New York, 1880), 110.

55. Charles Hodge, *An Exposition of the First Epistle to the Corinthians* (New York, 1857), 211. See my article, "Charles Hodge as an American New Testament Interpreter," (cited in note 49) for additional observations.

56. See my unpublished "The Society of Biblical Literature: The Founding Fathers."

6

Contending for the Faith Once Delivered: Primitivist Impulses in American Fundamentalism

JOEL A. CARPENTER

BACK in the not-so-distant past, when I was about half as old as now, the pastor of my home church began a new series of sermons on the apostle Paul's epistles to the Corinthians by saying something like this: "We at the First Baptist Church of Allegan, Michigan, need to follow Paul's advice to the First Baptist Church of Corinth." The congregation chuckled. Perhaps some of them realized that a comparison of our church to the Corinthian church was no compliment. But most, I suspect, were simply amused to hear the preacher put so literally (although with a twinkle in his eye) what they professed to believe. As Baptists they were a "New Testament church;" and as Bible-believing, fundamental Christians, they were convinced that the apostle's specific counsel was timeless and to be simply transferred to their lives today. Certainly, these commitments display a strong desire to recapture primitive Christianity.

Change the details of this story only slightly, however, and these beliefs could fit most of the groups under study in this volume. Indeed, at first glance, it is hard to identify much that is unique about American fundamentalists' expression of that yearning to restore New Testament faith that has been common to many Christians.[1] Fundamentalism is an eclectic, interdenominational movement that has drawn its constituency from a variety of evangelical traditions, each of which has its own primitivist impulses. In fundamentalist circles, Baptists' claims to have most nearly recovered the earliest Christians' evangelistic fervor, congregational independence, and administration of baptism and the Lord's Supper stood side-by-side with Presbyterians' claims to have restored the apostolic pattern of church government and truly biblical doctrine. In the wake of their controversies with liberals, many fundamentalists appropriated the Plymouth Brethren's preachments against the established churches' apostasy and their attempts to return to the separation and simplicity of the early church. Large numbers of fundamentalists experienced a "Book of Acts" enduement of power through fresh anointings by the Holy Spirit that resembled the Spirit-baptism experiences of their holiness and pentecostal cousins. And like evangelicals of all sorts, fundamentalist congregations sought and enjoyed the "New Testament fellowship" of those whose "like precious faith" resulted from their having been born again.[2]

A closer look at fundamentalism, however, reveals that this movement did put a unique stamp on its attempts to replicate New Testament Christianity, to live out of the Bible. This essay will try to recapture that mood, that set of emphases, which are best stated in a favorite fundamentalist text: "Earnestly contend for the faith which was once delivered unto the saints" (Jude 3). This they took as their task in what they thought were days much like those of the early church and certainly the "last days" of Bible prophecy. If the biblical primitivism of the Mennonites echoed the Gospels, and the pentecostals lived out the Acts of the Apostles, fundamentalists identified with the Epistles. The apostle Paul's admonition to uphold true doctrine and to remain blameless and unspotted "in the midst of a crooked and perverse nation" (Phil. 2:15) resonated powerfully with their experience.

The basis for this biblical primitivism was a principle that was central to fundamentalist thought. As several recent historians of the movement have stressed, fundamentalist intellectual leaders explicitly rejected historicism, a major tenet of modern thought. Historicism, explains Grant Wacker, is "the belief that culture is the product of its own history, that ideas, values, and institutions of every sort are wholly conditioned by the historical setting in which they exist."[3] Whereas this belief became foundational for modern thought, fundamentalists fought tenaciously against it. A few careful scholars, notably J. Gresham Machen of Princeton Seminary, were able to dissect the modernist temper and attack its naturalistic presuppositions, but the average evangelist, pastor, or lay leader knew more intuitively that modern secular life seemed to have no room for God. The most biblically faithful response to historicism, in their minds, was to stress God's ongoing, supernatural presence and activity in and through the Bible, in their Christian experience, and in the prophetic "signs of the times" that they beheld in current events. The result, as we shall see, was a potent popular expression of biblical primitivism and cultural separatism that was uniquely fundamentalist in its nuances of content and expression.

At the same time, however, fundamentalism's primitivist impulse was seriously qualified. Unlike the Mormons, the Churches of Christ, or the pentecostals,[4] fundamentalists valued the Christian past—at least the past since the Protestant Reformation. Fundamentalists assumed that primitive Christianity had already been restored at the Reformation and revived several times since then. Their task, then, was not to recover it, but to defend, cultivate, and promote it—to contend earnestly for it. Some hoped that they, too, would be rewarded for their faithfulness with another great awakening of evangelical Christianity. Primitivist impulses thrived within fundamentalism, but they were tempered and colored by the movement's conservative sense of mission and implicit regard for tradition. Fundamentalists' defense of the "faith once delivered" included both what they considered to be the fundamental, unchanging truths of apostolic Christianity, and more particularly those beliefs as expressed in the evangelical, revivalistic traditions of the modern era.

American fundamentalism is not static, no matter how much some of its leaders insist that it stands unchanged. Thus for the purpose of identifying and examining fundamentalist primitivism, this essay will focus on the movement's career in the 1930s and 1940s. By this time, fundamentalists had clearly established an identity distinct from other closely related evangelical groups such as holiness Wesleyans and pentecostals, and also from the broad federation of conservative cobelligerents in the denominational and antievolution battles of the 1920s, such as the Southern Baptists. Fundamentalism in the 1930s comprised for the most part the smaller, more coherent movement of largely northern Baptist, Presbyterian, and independent millenarians that Ernest Sandeen carefully distinguished from the fundamentalist controversies.[5] Moreover, during this period, fundamentalists were rapidly developing a self-contained network of institutions to sustain their distinctive beliefs and carry forward their agenda.[6] In order to see primitivist impulses at work among fundamentalists, then, we must examine their determined effort to set themselves apart.

Fundamentalists' strategy for living as biblical Christians in a modern setting, for upholding their beliefs in the midst of doubters, was to "come out from among them and be separate" (2 Cor. 6:17). Defeated in ecclesiastical conflict and since the Scopes Trial the laughingstock of secular intellectuals, fundamentalists adopted an alienated stance toward the culture. "These are fighting days for us," proclaimed the venerable president of Moody Bible Institute, James M. Gray, in 1934; fundamentalists would be criticized and ridiculed because "the offense of the Cross has not ceased and never will cease until Satan is chained."[7] The biblical images of God's faithful remnant, as strangers and pilgrims, or as the 7,000 who had not bowed before Baal, held great appeal for them. Baptist militant Oliver W. Van Osdel urged that "in these days of declension and compromise," the movement's program should be to "stand without the camp with the lonely, rejected Son of God, bearing his reproach."[8]

Fundamentalists did not fully agree on what the call to separation demanded, however. To be sure, they expressed it by developing a separate network of Bible institutes, magazines, conferences, and mission boards. Yet for many of them, that was not enough. Rather than remaining in denominations that they perceived as tainted with liberalism and worldliness, they founded new ones or became completely free of affiliation. For these people, the call to ecclesiastical separation seemed so clear and urgent that they doubted the integrity of their comrades who felt compelled to work within the older denominations. Disputes over the implications of separation broke out and caused lingering tensions and resentments in the movement.[9] A study of the fundamentalists' struggle for doctrinal and ecclesiastical purity, based both on bitter experiences and the powerful primitive example set forth in their reading of the Epistles, would be subject enough for this essay.[10] Yet another form of separatism on which all fundamentalists agreed was perhaps more critical to their identity. What they called "the separated life" marked fundamentalists, in their own view, as what the Bible called a peculiar people.

The separated life for fundamentalists meant a variety of things; most visible, of course, was their desire to uphold the behavioral standards of nineteenth-century evangelicals. That was hardly a radical or conspicuously distinct way of life compared to other "peculiar people" in twentieth-century America, notably Hasidic Jews, the Amish, or even some pentecostal groups that forbade jewelry and many rather innocent amusements such as baseball and Coca-Cola. Yet fundamentalists' mores were markedly different from their nonevangelical neighbors. Fundamentalists, wrote Shirley Nelson in her excellent novel about them, "simply spurned the world's frenetic search for empty pleasure. They did not smoke or drink or dance or attend the theater or concern themselves unduly with fashions and fads." The book's major character thought she could always spot a fundamentalist girl on the street, "her face cool and relaxed . . . among the strained and painted, and . . . she could tell the boys too, by a certain clearness in their eyes."[11] Most Protestants probably professed the same ideals, but fundamentalists argued that churches had grown worldly and were allowing more permissive attitudes.[12] In order to uphold these standards, fundamentalists built separate communities where such practices would be enforced. One promoter of Wheaton College assured readers that his school had such standards. He quoted a modernist's nostalgic recollection of a nineteenth-century Protestant college and said proudly that if written in the present tense it would make "an admirable description of Wheaton."[13]

These were but the minimum behavioral constraints for the separated life, however. Along with doctrinal distinctives, they formed the basic boundaries. And in tension with their primitivist yearnings, these practices showed the movement's implicit regard for a particular Christian heritage. But fundamentalists wished to pursue the spirituality that they believed these evangelical standards embodied. A common expression for their ideal was "living with eternity's values in view."[14] Living as New Testament Christians in a modern setting meant counteracting the world's secular consciousness with religious activities and spiritualizing habits of thought.[15]

In order to accomplish this, fundamentalists committed themselves to radically supernatural expressions of Christian doctrine by which they hoped to order their lives. One popular slogan, "the Book, the Blood, and the Blessed Hope," aptly illustrates the movement's separatist and primitivist impulses. By this, fundamentalists meant that they upheld the Bible as the verbally inspired, inerrant word of God; salvation only by the blood shed by Jesus Christ to atone for sinners; and Christ's personal, premillenial, and imminent second coming. These doctrines have been part of other modern evangelicals' belief structures as well; but fundamentalists more than others took their identity and mission from defending and cultivating them. The supernatural character of Christianity was under attack, they believed, so fundamentalists took as their standard these doctrines, which were dramatically opposed to modern historicist assumptions. New Testament Christianity was still available to modern people, fundamentalists insisted, because the Bible spoke timeless truth, because the miraculous new birth still happened through the blood of the Lamb, and because the signs of the times showed that God was fulfilling Bible prophecy in the present age. The foundational ideas behind fundamentalist separatism and primitivism, then, were a radically supernatural understanding of the Bible's original character, blood atonement as the means of miraculous personal redemption, and an ahistorical and maximally literal reading of biblical prophecy.

In the face of modern doubts about God's having spoken any sure and timeless word to humanity, fundamentalists stressed that the Bible, in its original autographs, inerrantly expressed in its very words the mind and will of God and thus should be Christians' final authority. Presbyterian fundamentalist Donald Barnhouse said that the Christian finds in the Bible "God's Word for his daily life and needs. It will ever be, for him, his word, rock, lamp, daily milk and meat, besides the Supreme Court from which there is no appeal."[16] At a time when educated persons widely questioned the inspiration and authority of the Bible, fundamentalists marshalled arguments to defend the Scriptures. Indeed, asserts Timothy Weber, "fundamentalists were self-styled people of the Book who defended against any attempt to undermine its power or prestige."[17]

Historical criticism of the Bible was a major producer of popular doubt, of course. If the Bible was not historically accurate in its accounts and not always written by its purported authors, as Old Testament critics claimed, and if its record of Jesus was colored by the pious elaboration of the early church, as some New Testament critics said, then fundamentalists wondered why anyone should trust the Scriptures to present the sure word of God. Whereas Protestants who accepted the findings of biblical criticism resisted this conclusion and tried to redefine the inspiration and authority of the Bible, fundamentalists and some important secular pundits as well seemed to agree that the new theories had destructive implications.[18]

The way in which fundamentalists defended the Bible's authority is worth pausing to consider. The idea that the Bible was inerrant in its original autographs had been taught by Christian theologians for centuries and had received a new emphasis and clarification over the prior half-century at the hands of the conservative biblical scholars of Princeton Seminary.[19] But among fundamentalist Bible teachers, biblical inerrancy began to take on an altered character. Whereas classical Protestant thought from the days of Luther and Calvin had sought to account for the simultaneous working of natural and supernatural forces in the world,[20] fundamentalists felt so threatened by the naturalistic bent of much current biblical scholarship that they concentrated on the supernatural character of the Bible at the expense of its humanity. Careful attention to matters of culture, history, and philology became rare among fundamentalist students of Scripture.[21]

Two factors contributed to this neglect. First was dispensational premillenialism, the fundamentalists' most common view of God's plan of salvation through the ages. This school of biblical interpretation was by its very nature ahistorical, for it stressed that dramatic changes in history—or new dispensations, as they were called—came not by means of natural forces and human causation, but wholly by supernatural intervention, as God worked out his plan.[22] Dispensationalism's popular attractiveness, however, came less from its view of history than from its interpretations of biblical prophecy. Dispensationalists' predictions of civilization's declension, of "establishment" Christianity's spiritual apostasy, of a global dictator called the Antichrist, and not least, of the Jews' persecution and their restoration of a Jewish state in Palestine—all these have had for many an uncanny resemblance to the history of the twentieth century.[23]

The interpretive assumptions behind this scenario were that the Bible was scientifically accurate in matters of detail and that all of its prophecies would be fulfilled. Dispensationalists believed that they could provide a precise reading of the prophetic clock's advance in history. In so doing, they dispensed with the venerable tradition of figuratively interpreting and historically contextualizing many prophetic texts. Their view of the Bible's verbal inerrancy and supernatural character, then, was considerably more ahistorical and culturally primitivist than that of more traditional Protestant conservatives. As we shall see, fundamentalists' desire to simply live out of the New Testament Epistles was encouraged by a theological system that conflated Bible times and modern times.[24]

The other major force behind fundamentalist biblical primitivism was the movement's popular character. Fundamentalism had its roots much more in weekend Bible and missionary conferences than in theological seminaries. The evangelistic, devotional, and largely dispensational Bible-teaching movement that was transformed into fundamentalism by the 1920s was led in its early stages by a group of eminent pastors, evangelists, and itinerant Bible teachers who were widely respected and, for the most part, well educated, but who cast their visions broadly. They devoted themselves to fostering popular Bible knowledge, lay activism in missions and evangelism, and a widespread personal appropriation of the Holy Spirit's power.[25] As popular promoters, fundamentalists carried forward the nineteenth-century evangelical penchant for simplifying complex issues and playing them out before a popular audience.[26] In their hands, the doctrine of biblical inerrancy lost much of its complexity and especially its carefully nuanced balancing of the Bible's divine and human character. Such nice distinctions would be lost on popular audiences. Either the Bible was God's book or a human creation. People needed to make a choice, fundamentalists insisted, and they were committed to making it appear as simple and as stark as possible. Liberal critics' accusation that fundamentalists taught a "divine dictation" theory of inspiration, then, was often uncomfortably close to the mark.[27]

Thus as historians Mark Noll and George Marsden have shown, popular fundamentalism represented the nadir of a once-respected intellectual tradition. Except perhaps when articulated by its ablest minds, the fundamentalists' religious ideas had become the laughingstock of the American intelligentsia. By the 1930s and early 1940s, a small coterie of younger fundamentalists had begun to work at recovering some credibility in the American academy.[28] But the movement's real focus of attention in these years was popular, and its defense of the Bible's authority turned inward.

Fundamentalists seemed most intent on dispelling doubts about the Bible that had filtered down to the average person. Their favorite apologetic weapons in the 1930s were drawn from archaeology. At that time the field of Near Eastern history and archaeology was blossoming. Archaeologists were verifying biblical place names and story settings once thought legendary and radically revising some of the assumptions of biblical critics.[29] Fundamentalists used many of these examples to confirm their view of the Bible over against "speculative theories."[30] Most fundamentalist laity could not recite the arguments against the higher critics, but fortified with confident rhetoric from the pulpit and in print, they knew that they had some experts who could.[31]

Biblical inerrancy, however, was not an empty shibboleth. It was a defense of a way of life. As people of the Book, fundamentalists made it the central sign and seal of their movement. They labeled themselves "Bible-believing Christians." They prized knowledge of the Bible as the highest learning, so their training schools for Christian workers were "Bible institutes or Bible colleges" where study of the Bible was the major thrust of the curriculum. Bible conferences featuring Bible teachers were popular forms of lay education. "Bible doctrine" was their name for theology, the latter sounding too speculative and human-centered. And hundreds of fundamentalist congregations that had declared their separation from all denominations called themselves "Bible churches."[32]

Fundamentalists believed that the Book had supernatural power. They would resist any claims of magical powers for the Bible, but they insisted that it was God's favored means of salvation. Not only were its words timelessly true and inerrant guides for faith and life, but they would be used by God to change people. When witnessing to others, the sacred words themselves should be preeminent; quoting Scripture was more effective than using one's own phrases.[33] Indeed, in the speech of the more zealous, biblical phrases blended continually into conversation.[34] Fundamentalists took literally, sometimes to vulgar extemes, the biblical promise that "My word shall not return unto me void" (Is. 55:11). They printed Bible verses on billboards, jackknife handles, and automobile spare tire covers; one naturalist wrote them on tags he tied to Canada geese.[35]

The words of Scripture became icons for fundamentalists. They embodied spiritual reality and drew the believer from the mundane world to the sacred.[36] Emblazoned on their church walls or on motto plaques in their homes, biblical phrases were both visual reminders of spiritual truth and badges of separation from a culture whose epigrams were increasingly secular. The mark of being a Bible-believing, fundamental Christian often was carrying at least a New Testament on one's person. It was there not only for convenient reference, but also as the symbol of one's faith, much like a Catholic sister's rosary.[37]

Whereas the Bible was the foundation of fundamentalist communities, the mark of membership was having been "born again." Following the tradition of two centuries of evangelical religion in North America, fundamentalists welcomed to full fellowship only those who testified that they had been washed in the blood of the Lamb. They drew the rebukes of liberal Protestants for their "slaughterhouse religion," their stress on the doctrine of personal salvation through substitutionary blood atonement for one's sins. Modern Christians, liberals thought, should move beyond such crude characterizations and embrace a nobler, more ethically refined understanding of Jesus' redemptive suffering.[38] Blood sacrifice may indeed have seemed primitive and magical to modern minds, but to fundamentalists, insisting on this traditional doctrine was both a matter of faithfulness to the Bible's literal teaching and a way to preserve the miraculous character of redemption. People got saved, fundamentalists argued; they did not merely learn to follow the Master. It was a miracle, a life-transforming experience, an answer to prayer, a supernatural operation of the Holy Spirit made possible by Jesus' sacrificial death.[39]

Certainly fundamentalists produced scores of books and Bible school courses on the methodology of "soul-winning."[40] But even such mechanical and routinized schemes seemed to affect but little the wonder they expressed at the experience of being born again, or seeing another human being come to Christ for salvation. Indeed, the new birth was the most powerful sustainer of fundamentalists' belief that prayers were still answered, that God still intervened in human affairs, or indeed, that the Bible was "sharper than any two-edged sword."[41] Unlike sacramentalists, for whom the most frequent visitation of the holy was the Eucharist, or pentecostals who sought dramatic healings and speaking in tongues, fundamentalists' yearning for miracles was best fulfilled by the new birth. The gospel invitation that pastors gave at the close of evangelistic sermons, calling people to repent and come to Christ, became the high and holy moment of the fundamentalist church service and often took on a quasi-liturgical structure.[42]

In a classically evangelical fashion, the experience of being born again was the matrix of fundamentalist community, its major test of fellowship. The tie that bound congregations together was not simply their kindred minds ideologically, but that common experience of conversion, which initiated them into a new family and transformed their outlook.[43] Fundamentalists' stress on the blood atonement, whatever else it meant, was a theological fencing of their most precious possession in an interpretation that was maximally supernatural, unflinchingly literal, and costly. It was a vivid identification with the biblical company of the blood-redeemed, who would one day gather around the throne and acclaim the Lamb.

In their looking forward to that day when time would be no more, fundamentalists infused the here and now with supernatural power and biblical reality of the grandest dimensions. Fundamentalists believed that at any moment the clouds would part and Christ would appear to take the saints home. He would rescue the faithful, punish the wicked, and establish a reign of perfect peace and righteousness.[44] The grim facts of the 1930s—the Great Depression, the rise of dictators and world conflict, and the persecution of the Jews—confirmed to fundamentalists that the Bible was true and that God was in control.[45] While the press strained to interpret the outbreak of the Second World War in 1939, Donald Barnhouse confided to his readers that "those who know the general lines of Bible prophecy" had an advantage in understanding this event, because "Ezekiel knew more about it than the *Saturday Evening Post*."[46].

At first glance, fundamentalists' close attention to world affairs might seem to argue against the idea that their eschatology was ahistorical and that its effect was to encourage primitivism. Weren't these folk showing a vital interest in the workings of history? Not in any ordinary sense. As mentioned earlier, dispensationalists tended to see human action in various epochs of history as epiphenomenal to the real, spiritual forces at work. The ordinary relationships of contemporary and historical cause and effect paled before the unfolding divine drama.

Armed with prophetic schematizations of the final years before Christ's second coming, fundamentalists read history and current events as if they had been inspired to prophesy in the manner of St. John.

Belief in the imminent, premillennial second coming brought reassurance and hope in troubling times. President James M. Gray of the Moody Bible Institute wrote in his annual report for 1932–33 that although the land was filled with suffering and the institute had its own depression-caused woes, "our times are in His hand. Watch Him draw out our fear!"[47] These were times when people yearned for a way out of their predicament, and fundamentalists believed that they had found it. Said Barnhouse in January of 1932: "The masses can not right things, the leaders can not right things." God's word, he declared, gave the only answer to the world's endless turmoil. Jesus, "God's benevolent despot," must reign. To that end, Barnhouse echoed the Apostle John, " 'Even so, come, Lord Jesus.' "[48]

Fundamentalists' eager correlation of current trends with biblical prophecies went far beyond what they needed to gain a sense of personal deliverance. Constant sifting of world events helped them to put their turbulent and confusing times into a coherent pattern. Chaos became for them cosmic drama. In this respect, the fundamentalist experience closely parallels that of the Marxist Left of the 1930s. In his memoirs of those years, *The Dream of the Golden Mountains,* Malcom Cowley suggests that he and many of his friends converted to Marxism because it made sense of the present mess and gave them a hopeful "long view."[49] They followed events with an eye to how the news portended the coming revolution. Like the Left, the fundamentalists were confident that, as one Bible teacher put it, they could "get the news in advance."[50] Reading current events "in the light of Bible prophecy" thus became a major enterprise for fundamentalists. Not only did this constantly confirm to them the unerring accuracy of their Bibles, but it drew them and their times into the Bible. They were not living merely in modern history, far removed from the biblical world. The pages of Ezekiel, Daniel, I Thessalonians, and the Book of Revelation spoke of their times, of days just around the corner.

With such a powerful trio of mutually supporting foundations for living the separated life, one would expect that the fundamentalist movement would be content to go its own way, to become a self-styled, "faithful remnant" of New Testament Christians in an age of apostasy and decline, with little regard for the fate of society around it. Indeed, that impulse was strong, and one segment of the movement took this stance. But the majority of fundamentalists struggled with competing impulses, which were encoded in their evangelical inheritance. As Samuel S. Hill explains in his seminal essay on restitutionism in American religion, there is a difference between wanting to preserve, defend, and reinvigorate a great tradition, and claiming to be the newly restored, original item.[51] Much as fundamentalists responded to the impulse to leap across history and live out of the Bible, they retained a strong sense of being a people of a place, of a time, with a past. They self-consciously used the term "evangelical Christians" to describe themselves, and although they tended to equate this with "biblical Christianity," they also affirmed Protestant orthodoxy and revivalism, and sought to revive these traditions.[52]

This sense of being champions of the "historic Christian faith" came through most clearly in the fundamentalists' calls for a new spiritual awakening in America. Fundamentalists were heirs to what Grant Wacker calls a "custodial ideal" concerning their role in American culture. They felt compelled to nurture and defend the values that evangelicals had implanted in American life, values which, at least since the 1920s, were rapidly fading.[53] The bitter conflicts of the 1920s had soured fundamentalists on political crusades, and the cataclysmic upheavals of the 1930s, viewed in millenarian perspective, reinforced their pessimism. Yet they tempered the separatist and often primitivist impulse to come out from among their neighbors and their times with calls for revival. Fundamentalists were thus of a divided mind. They looked at the darkness about them and cried, " 'Even so, come, Lord Jesus,' " but they would often insist that time had not yet run out; revival and, indeed, national renewal were still possible.[54] They reached back into their own religious and cultural history for hopeful examples. Hadn't England been saved from revolutionary upheaval by the religious awakening led by Whitefield and the Wesleys? Likewise Finney's and Moody's revivals in nineteenth-century America came to mind; and they cited the more recent religious wildfire in Wales.[55]

Fundamentalists' search for another great revival was of course a manifestation of their desire to confirm divine activity in a secular world. It also marked a yearning to recapture Christian America, that Protestant memory and hope of millennial dimensions that had, by the mid-twentieth century, been seriously punctured by the historical reality of cultural and religious pluralism.[56] Fundamentalists repeatedly invoked 2 Chron. 7:14 ("If my people ... shall humble themselves, and pray, and seek my face, and turn from their wicked ways; then will I ... forgive their sin, and will heal their land"), linking revival with national restoration. Their memory of previous revivals seemed as much mythic as historical in its details and sense of cause and effect. But especially when compared to early pentecostals, who explicitly rejected creeds and traditions and, says Grant Wacker, sought the "wonder-working gospel of the first century" rather than the "old-fashioned gospel of the nineteenth century,"[57] fundamentalists gloried in tradition. Their heritage, they proudly affirmed, was the "old-time religion" of evangelical revivalism. They used its nostalgic appeal repeatedly, as in Charles E. Fuller's immensely popular broadcast "The Old-Fashioned Revival Hour."[58] Their claim that they were the true heirs of the "great tradition" of American Protestantism was an important weapon in their guerrilla war of succession against the liberals.[59] This presumption of standing at the vital center of American Christianity empowered fundamentalist reformers to lead the efforts of evangelicals generally in shaping a "resurgent evangelicalism" since World War II.[60]

A purely primitivist model, then, cannot explain the complex and often internally paradoxical character of the fundamentalist movement and its moderate heirs. George Marsden may have recognized this when he stated that at the core of fundamentalism is a paradoxical tension between "establishment" and "outsider" self-images; and that this conflict made fundamentalists profoundly ambivalent about American Protestant Christianity and, indeed, about American culture.[61] This tension inherent in fundamentalism was, in part, the result of its divided mind regarding the worth of identifying with a particular Christian heritage as opposed to leaping straight to the beginning.

The tension between traditionalism and primitivism helps to make sense of the conflicts among fundamentalism's heirs more recently. Both the more moderate neo-evangelicals, who have formed the strongest party in the postwar evangelical coalition, and their militant separatist opponents, who have claimed exclusive title to the fundamentalist lineage, seem to differ with each other more in regard to these polarities than on basic theology. Neo-evangelical leaders of the 1950s and 1960s such as Carl F. H. Henry, Edward J. Carnell, Harold J. Ockenga, and Harold Lindsell stressed their doctrinal continuity with fundamentalism while criticizing separatists for their hypercritical attitudes, cultural isolation, and anti-intellectualism. These moderate conservatives shunned the fundamentalist label and the movement's prior posture of "separating from apostasy." Instead they eagerly embraced "evangelical" as the name of a noble tradition within Christianity that was rooted in the Reformation and subsequent renewal movements. Their dominant posture became the "revival of evangelical Christianity" that, of course, had been one of fundamentalism's aims.[62] Neo-evangelicals sought a role in their culture and shed some of the anti-worldly alienation that had characterized their fundamentalist parents.

On the other hand, separatist fundamentalists cultivated the culturally pessimistic biblical ethos of the "faithful remnant" that had shaped the movement's outlook in earlier decades. Since World War II, separatists' fears of apostasy and decline have prompted them toward an anti-worldly and conspiratorial stance. The liberal poison, they insisted, had invaded the fundamentalist camp, making neo-evangelicalism, not liberalism, the most dangerous enemy. Separatists sought hard-and-fast doctrinal, ecclesiastical, and behavioral boundaries to stave off such compromise, and thus withdrew further into their own religious communities. They have split into numerous factions, each claiming to have more nearly captured the militant anti-worldliness that they believe the Apostles lived and taught.[63] Witness, for example, the formation of the New Testament Association of Independent Baptist Churches in the early 1960s by dissidents in the Conservative Baptist Association. Led by R. V. Clearwaters of Minneapolis, these extreme separatists charged that the Conservative Baptists, although a fundamentalist breakoff from the Northern Baptist Convention, had compromised their purity by showing sympathy to neo-evangelicalism and supporting Billy Graham's crusades.[64]

Despite these sharp divergences within historic fundamentalism, more recent developments suggest that the internal tension between primitivism and traditionalism has not snapped. The rise of fundamentalist leadership for the religious New Right showed that separatist primitivism had not canceled out the deeply encoded desire for reviving evangelicalism and engaging culture. Jerry Falwell's crusade for a return to the traditional values of a Christian American past may have reflected fundamentalists' acceptance of a particularly potent set of American myths, but it also embraced a tradition and encountered the here and now.[65] The neo-evangelicals, for their part, demonstrated in the recent "Battle for the Bible" (a controversy over biblical inerrancy) that a yearning for divine revelation untouched by ordinary human existence still haunted them.[66] And new primitivist impulses came from those who wished to transcend the legacy of fundamentalism altogether. Certainly primitivism thrived in the Evangelical Orthodox Church (EOC), which arose from house churches established by former staff members of Campus Crusade for Christ. The EOC recently agreed to merge into the venerable Antiochian Orthodox Church. Presiding Bishop Peter Gillquist of the EOC expressed delight that his group would now "be in communion with the faith and practice of the New Testament Church."[67] The stance of the *Sojourners* network of radical Christians bore a certain irony also. They eschewed the evangelical label in favor of "Biblical people," and developed a separatism that, despite its shaping by the New Left and Anabaptism, favored restorationist motifs and strangely resembled the fundamentalism they wished to escape.[68]

Thus the descendants of fundamentalism continued to struggle to understand what it means to earnestly contend for the faith once delivered to the saints. Whether they seek to champion it, to reform it, or to reject it, their fundamentalist legacy haunts them and shapes them. They should grant their fundamentalist forebears credit, though, for instinctively identifying the fundamental problem of being Christian in the timebound twentieth century: how to live in the world and yet not be of it. Fundamentalists failed for the most part to provide an intellectually potent response to the modern historicist temper. Nonetheless their faith in the living Christ granted them, to paraphrase their adversary Harry Emerson Fosdick, the wisdom and courage they needed for the living of their days.

NOTES

1. The citations of those who evaluate the role of primitivism in the Jewish and Christian traditions return eternally to the works of Mircea Eliade, the modern master of the study of the role of archetypes, myths, rituals, and spheres of reality in religions. See his *The Sacred and Profane* (New York: Harcourt, Brace, 1959), 20–113; *The Myth of the Eternal Return* (New York: Pantheon Books, 1954); and *The Quest: History and Meaning in Religion* (Chicago: University of Chicago Press, 1969). Eliade's major point is that primitive religions find only the "sacred time" of myth truly meaningful, and that ordinary time has no real significance unless the sacred is restored periodically through religious ritual. The problem of applying this insight to Jewish and Christian faiths, which are profoundly historical, is discussed in Richard T. Hughes, "From Civil Dissent to Civil Religion—and Beyond," *Religion in Life* 49 (Fall 1980):269–71; and Robert A. Segal, "Eliade's Theory of Millenarianism," *Religious Studies* 14 (June 1978):159–73. Hughes offers a helpful guide: history is more than factual, he says; it has mythical and symbolic power. If "factual history outweighs the power of the myth," and believers maintain a sense of distance between the normative past and their own time, then their faith is historical. But if a believer loses "the clear distinction between his own time and the primal time," then one can conclude that his faith has become ahistorical or primitivist (pp. 270–71). Grant Wacker describes Christian primitivism as a "yearning for pure doctrines, pure beginnings, and pure fulfillments—all untouched by the limitations and corruptions of ordinary existence" ("Primitive Pentecostalism in the Southern Highlands," unpublished paper presented at the annual meeting of the American Historical As-

sociation, December 1983, 8). This essay will rely on Wacker's and Hughes's definitions of Christian primitivism.

2. Two definitive surveys of the types of primitivism exhibited in European and American Christianity are Samuel S. Hill, Jr., "A Typology of American Restitutionism: From Frontier Revivalism and Mormonism to the Jesus Movement," *Journal of the American Academy of Religion* 44 (March 1976):65–76; and Richard T. Hughes, "Christian Primitivism as Perfectionism: From Anabaptists to Pentecostals," in *Reaching Beyond: Chapters in the History of Perfectionism,* ed. Stanley Burgess (Peabody, MA: Hendrickson Publishers, 1986), 213–55.

3. Grant Wacker, "The Demise of Biblical Civilization," in *The Bible in America: Essays in Cultural History,* ed. Nathan O. Hatch and Mark A. Noll (New York: Oxford University Press, 1982), 125. For treatments of fundamentalism and historicism, see ibid., 121–38; Grant Wacker, *Augustus H. Strong and the Dilemma of Historical Consciousness* (Macon, GA: Mercer University Press, 1985); George Marsden, "J. Gresham Machen, History, and Truth," *Westminster Theological Journal* 42 (Fall 1979):157–75; and Paul Carter, "The Fundamentalist Defense of the Faith," in *Change and Continuity in Twentieth Century America: The 1920s,* ed. John Braeman, Robert Bremner, and David Brody (Columbus: Ohio State University Press, 1968), 179–214.

4. Richard L. Bushman, *Joseph Smith and the Beginnings of Mormonism* (Urbana: University of Illinois Press, 1984), 38–39, 53–59, 139–42, 179–88; Jan Shipps, *Mormonism: The Story of a New Religious Tradition* (Urbana: University of Illinois Press, 1985), 1–3, 7–9, 67–85; and Marvin S. Hill, "The Role of Christian Primitivism in the Origin and Development of the Mormon Kingdom, 1830–1844" (Ph.D. dissertation, University of Chicago, 1968), describe Mormonism's disregard for the historic legacy of the church. Grant Wacker, "The Functions of Faith in Primitive Pentecostalism," *Harvard Theological Review* 77, nos. 3–4 (1984):353–75, does the same for the pentecostal movement. Nathan Hatch, "The Christian Movement and the Demand for a Theology of the People," *Journal of American History* 67 (December 1980):545–66; and Richard Hughes, "Primitivism and Culture: New Light Christians in the Upper South," paper presented at the American Historical Association, December 1983, set forth the Christian movement's restorationist position.

5. Ernest R. Sandeen, *The Roots of Fundamentalism: British and American Millenarianism, 1800–1930* (Chicago: University of Chicago Press, 1970), xvii–xviii, 248–69; on fundamentalism's common roots with the holiness and pentecostal movements, see George M. Marsden, *Fundamentalism and American Culture: The Shaping of Twentieth Century Evangelicalism, 1870–1925* (New York: Oxford University Press, 1980), 72–101; and Grant Wacker, "The Holy Spirit and the Spirit of the Age in American Protestantism, 1880–1910," *Journal of American History* 72 (June 1985):45–62. On Southern Baptists' uneasy cobelligerency with northern fundamentalists, see James J. Thompson, Jr., *Tried as by Fire: Southern Baptists and the Religious Controversies of the 1920s* (Macon, GA: Mercer University Press, 1982).

6. Joel Carpenter, "Fundamentalist Institutions and the Rise of Evangelical Protestantism, 1929–1942," *Church History* 49 (March 1980):62–75.

7. James M. Gray, "Fighting Days," *Moody Monthly* (hereinafter cited as *MM*) 34 (February 1934):252.

8. O. W. Van Osdel, "Good Soldiers of Jesus Christ," *Baptist Bulletin* 1 (April 1933):1.

9. For accounts of controversies over ecclesiastical separation, see Bruce L. Shelley, *Conservative Baptists: A Story of Twentieth Century Dissent* (Denver: Conservative Baptist Press, 1960); C. Allyn Russell, *Voices of American Fundamentalism: Seven Biographical Studies* (Philadelphia: Westminster, 1975); George M. Marsden, "Perspectives on the Division of 1937," *Presbyterian Guardian* 29 (January–April 1964):5–8, 21–23, 27–29, 43–46, 54–56; J. Murray Murdoch, *Portrait of Obedience: The Biography of Robert T. Ketcham* (Schaumberg, IL: Regular Baptist Press, 1979); and Edwin H. Rian, *The Presbyterian Conflict* (Grand Rapids, MI: Eerdmans, 1940).

10. For such a study, see Joel Carpenter, "The Renewal of American Fundamentalism, 1930–1945" (Ph.D. dissertation, The Johns Hopkins University, 1984), chap. 2: "The Separatist Impulse," 36–92.

11. Shirley Nelson, *The Last Year of the War* (New York: Harper and Row, 1978), 5.

12. Marsden, *Fundamentalism,* 35–38, 156–59, 162–64.

13. William J. Jones, "A Study in Contrasts," *Bulletin of Wheaton College* 8 (October 1931):7.

14. Jones, "Study in Contrasts," 4.

15. Marsden, *Fundamentalism,* 120, 129, 228; Carpenter, "Renewal," 72–75, 81–83, 249–62.

16. Donald Barnhouse, "The Place of the Bible," *Revelation* 8 (May 1938):195.

17. Timothy P. Weber, "The Two-Edged Sword: The Fundamentalist Use of the Bible," in *The Bible in America,* ed. Hatch and Noll, 102.

18. See, for example, Walter Lippmann's discussion of this issue in *A Preface to Morals* (New York: Macmillan, 1929), 25–35. Typical of fundamentalists' praise for Lippmann's insight are "A New Estimate of Modernism," *Evangelist* 41 (February 19, 1930):4; Donald Grey Barnhouse, "First Century Christianity," *Revelation* 3 (February 1933):44; and Alexander Fraser, "The Indiscipline of the Era," *MM* 40 (September 1939):16. Compare William R. Hutchison, *The Modernist Impulse in American Protestantism* (Cambridge, MA: Harvard University Press, 1976), 257–87.

19. Mark A. Noll, "Introduction," in *The Princeton Defense of Plenary Verbal Inspiration,* ed. Mark A. Noll (New York: Garland Publishing, 1988); and Randall H. Balmer, "The Princetonians and Scripture: A Reconsideration," *Westminster Theological Journal* 44 (Spring 1982):352–65.

20. Lewis Spitz, "History: Sacred and Secular," *Church History* 47 (1978):5–22; B. B. Warfield, "Calvin's Doctrine of Creation," *Princeton Theological Review* 13 (April 1915), reprinted in *The Princeton Theology, 1812–1921,* ed. Mark A. Noll (Grand Rapids, MI: Baker, 1983), 293–98.

21. Marsden, *Fundamentalism*, 122, 224; Mark A. Noll, *Between Faith and Criticism: Evangelicals, Scholarship, and The Bible in America* (San Francisco: Harper and Row, 1986), 32–47, 56–61.

22. Marsden, *Fundamentalism*, 63–65; Timothy P. Weber, *Living in the Shadow of the Second Coming: American Premillennialism, 1875–1925* (New York: Oxford University Press, 1979), deftly outlines dispensational premillennialism (pp. 9–24), which came to dominate fundamentalist eschatology in the 1930s. See also C. Norman Kraus, *Dispensationalism in America: Its Rise and Development* (Richmond, VA: John Knox, 1958); Robert G. Clouse, ed., *The Meaning of the Millennium: Four Views* (Downers Grove, IL: InterVarsity Press, 1977); and Richard Reiter, "A History of the Development of the Rapture Position," in Gleason Archer, Paul Feinberg, Douglas Moo, and Richard Reiter, *The Rapture: Pre, Mid, or Post?* (Grand Rapids, MI: Zondervan Publishing, 1984), 11–44.

23. Sandeen, *Roots of Fundamentalism*, xiii.

24. Ibid., 59–70; Marsden, *Fundamentalism*, 48–66; Weber, *Living in the Shadow*, 9–24, 36–42.

25. Sandeen, *Roots of Fundamentalism*, chap. 7, "The Millenarian Meridian," 162–87, ably surveys the breadth and texture of this popular movement.

26. Nathan O. Hatch, "Evangelicalism as a Democratic Movement," in *Evangelicalism and Modern America*, ed. George M. Marsden (Grand Rapids, MI: Eerdmans, 1984), 71–82.

27. Marsden, *Fundamentalism*, 56, 122.

28. Noll, *Between Faith and Criticism*, nadir: 56–61, early recovery: 91–121; Marsden, *Fundamentalism*, nadir: 4, 7–8, 191, 212–21; and George M. Marsden, *Reforming Fundamentalism: Fuller Seminary and the New Evangelicalism* (Grand Rapids, MI: Eerdmans, 1987), early recovery: 13–82.

29. William F. Albright, the preeminent American scholar of Near Eastern history, summarized the implications of these findings for biblical studies and theology in "Archaeology Confronts Biblical Criticism," *American Scholar* 7 (April 1938):176–88. See also his *From the Stone Age to Christianity: Monotheism and the Historical Process* (Baltimore: The Johns Hopkins University Press, 1940).

30. Fundamentalists used recent archaeological finds to argue for biblical inerrancy in "An Inconsistent Archaeologist," *MM* 31 (May 1931):437–38; "Behind the Times," *Revelation* 1 (September 1931):304; "Archaeology and the Bible Agree Again!" *Sunday School Times* 73 (November 28, 1931):669–70; and "Confirming Moses," *MM* (April 1934):348.

31. Martin Marty, "America's Iconic Book," in *Humanizing America's Iconic Book*, ed. Gene M. Tucker and Douglas A. Knight (Chico, CA: Scholars Press, 1982), 18.

32. This paragraph depends heavily on the observations of Timothy Weber in "The Two-Edged Sword," 102.

33. Phil Saint, "Good for the Soul," *Presbyterian Guardian* 1 (January 22, 1936):150.

34. Nelson, *Last Year of the War*, throughout.

35. Advertisement, *MM* 28 (September 1927): inside cover; John Hay, "A New Society: The S.T.T.L. [Spare Tire Testimony League]," *MM* 37 (June 1937):520; "Gospel Advertising," *Alliance Weekly* 71 (October 10, 1936):646.

36. Marty, "America's Iconic Book," 1–23, helpfully discusses the meaning and function of icons and the role of the Bible for Americans generally.

37. Everett L. Perry, "The Role of Socio-Economic Factors in the Rise and Development of American Fundamentalism" (Ph.D. dissertation, University of Chicago, 1959), 67, 74, 98–99; Thomas Howard, *Christ the Tiger* (Wheaton IL: Harold Shaw, 1967), 75–76.

38. Henry C. Vedder, *The Fundamentals of Christianity: A Study of the Teachings of Jesus and Paul* (New York: Macmillan, 1922), 187–95; Harry Emerson Fosdick, "True Christianity is Progressive," in *Fundamentalism versus Modernism,* ed. Eldred C. Vanderlaan (New York: H. W. Wilson, 1925), 52; Shailer Mathews, *The Faith of Modernism* (New York: Macmillan, 1925), 155–62.

39. Dyson Hague, "At-One-Ment by Propitiation," *The Fundamentals* 11 (Chicago: Testimony Publishing, n.d. [circa 1914]:23–42; J. Gresham Machen, *Christianity and Liberalism* (New York: Macmillan, 1923), 117–56; John Horsch, *Modern Religious Liberalism: The Destructiveness and Irrationality of Modernist Theology,* 3d ed. (Chicago: Bible Institute Colportage Association, 1925), 84–96.

40. Virginia L. Brereton, "The Bible Schools and Conservative Evangelical Higher Education," in *Making Higher Education Christian: The History and Mission of Evangelical Colleges in America,* ed. Joel A. Carpenter and Kenneth W. Shipps (Grand Rapids, MI: Eerdmans, 1987), 118–119.

41. See, for examples, "Tell Me! Oh, Tell Me!" *The Pilot* 10 (May 1930):253; "A Hebrew Christian Testimony," *Moody Church News* 21 (November 1936):7; Will H. Houghton, "Is Life Worth Living?" *MM* 42 (March 1942): 398–99, 429.

42. Daniel P. Stevick, *Beyond Fundamentalism* (Richmond, VA: John Knox, 1964), 57–58.

43. Superb explications of the centrality of the new birth for earlier evangelical communities are Donald G. Mathews, *Religion in the Old South* (Chicago: University of Chicago Press, 1977), 10–38; and George Rawlyk, *Ravished by the Spirit: Religious Revivals, Baptists, and Henry Alline* (Montreal: McGill-Queens University Press, 1984), 109–36. Marsden, *Fundamentalism,* 44–46; and Sandra Sizer, *Gospel Hymns and Social Religion* (Philadelphia: Temple University Press, 1978), 50–82, 112–15, show the continuing importance of a common born-again experience for the evangelical community in Moody's day; while Nelson, *Last Year,* 20–26, portrays a Bible-school setting in the 1940s where young women related their conversion testimonies and experienced a powerful bonding.

44. Cf. Weber, *Living in the Shadow,* 9–24; and other works cited in note 22.

45. Carpenter, "Renewal," chap. 3: "Rapture, Revolution, or Revival: Outlook for a Cataclysmic Age," 93–133.

46. Donald Barnhouse, "Russia Wins The War!" *Revelation* 9 (December 1939):477.

47. James M. Gray, "Drawing Out Our Fear," *Moody Bible Institute Bulletin* 12 (January 1933):3–4.

48. Donald Barnhouse, "Sure Cure for Depression," *Revelation* 2 (January 1932):10.

49. Malcom Cowley, *The Dream of the Golden Mountains: Remembering the 1930s* (New York: Penguin Books, 1981), 31–45, 171–75.

50. Advertisement, quoting Louis Bauman, *MM* 40 (November 1940):135.

51. Hill, "Typology of American Restitutionism," 68.

52. For examples, see James M. Gray, "Scholarship and Evangelical Christianity," *MM* 29 (October 1928):53–55; Editorial, "Are We in a Revival?" *Revelation* 4 (April 1934):135; and Editorial, "Planning the Peace," *Watchman-Examiner* 29 (December 4, 1941):1240–41.

53. Grant Wacker, "Uneasy in Zion: Evangelicals in Postmodern Society," in *Evangelicalism and Modern America,* ed. George M. Marsden (Grand Rapids, MI: Eerdmans, 1984), 17–28.

54. Joel Carpenter, "From Fundamentalism to the New Evangelical Coalition," in *Evangelicalism and Modern America,* ed. Marsden, 3–16.

55. "A Call for Prayer for Revival," *Revelation* 2 (May 1932):205; "Revival Today," *MM* 42 (September 1941):4; "Social Reform and Revival," *MM* 38 (February 1938):296–97; "The Year Closes," *MM* 39 (December 1938):171; S. Paul Weaver, "Pray for Revival," *Sunday School Times* 76 (March 1934):209–10; J. Edwin Orr, *This Is The Victory: Ten Thousand Miles of Miracle* (London: Marshall, Morgan, and Scott, 1936).

56. Robert T. Handy, *A Christian America: Protestant Hopes and Historical Realities* (New York: Oxford University Press, 1971).

57. Wacker, "Primitive Pentecostalism in the Southern Highlands," 8.

58. Daniel P. Fuller, *Give the Winds a Mighty Voice: The Story of Charles E. Fuller* (Waco, TX: Word Books, 1972), is the best account of Charles E. Fuller's career.

59. Robert T. Ketcham, *Facts for Baptists to Face* (Gary, IN: by the author, 1935); John W. Bradbury, "The N.B.C. Fundamentalists," *Watchman-Examiner* 25 (August 12, 1937):916–18; W. B. Riley, "The Denominational Division Among Baptists," *The Pilot* 20 (January 1940):104–5; J. C. Massee, "The Thirty Years War," *Chronicle* 17 (1954):101–10.

60. George M. Marsden, "The Evangelical Denomination," in *Evangelicalism and Modern America,* ed. Marsden, vii–xix; Joel Carpenter, "The Fundamentalist Leaven and the Rise of an Evangelical United Front," in *The Evangelical Tradition in America,* ed. Leonard I. Sweet (Macon, GA: Mercer University Press, 1984), 257–88.

61. Marsden, *Fundamentalism,* 6–7, 11–21, 43–48, 194–95, 204–5, 210–11.

62. Edward John Carnell, *The Case for Orthodox Theology* (Philadelphia: Westminster Press, 1959), 120–212; Edward John Carnell, "Post-Fundamentalist Faith," *Christian Century* 76 (August 26, 1959):971; Carl F. H. Henry, *The Uneasy Conscience of Modern Fundamentalism* (Grand Rapids, MI: Eerd-

mans, 1947); Harold John Ockenga, "Can Fundamentalism Win America?" *Christian Life and Times* 2 (June 1947):13–15; John Ockenga, "Resurgent Evangelical Leadership," *Christianity Today* 4 (October 10, 1960):11–15; Harold Lindsell, "Who Are the Evangelicals?" *Christianity Today* 9 (June 18, 1965):3–6.

63. Robert T. Ketcham, "A New Peril in Our Last Days," *Christian Beacon* 21 (May 17, 1956):2, 6–7; and Charles J. Woodbridge, *The New Evangelicalism* (Greenville, SC: Bob Jones University Press, 1969), expose the neo-evangelical menace; whereas Jerry Falwell, ed., *The Fundamentalist Phenomenon: The Resurgence of Conservative Christianity* (Garden City, NY: Doubleday, 1981), 109–63; and George A. Dollar, *A History of Fundamentalism in America* (Greenville, SC: Bob Jones University Press, 1973), provide helpful maps of the separatist terrain and faithful reflections of the separatist mentality. For a perceptive tour of the separatist subculture by "outsiders," see Frances Fitzgerald, *Cities on a Hill: A Journey Through Contemporary American Culture* (New York: Simon and Schuster, 1986), 121–201, on Jerry Falwell and his Thomas Road Baptist Church; and Alan Peshkin, *God's Choice: The Total World of a Fundamentalist Christian School* (Chicago: University of Chicago Press, 1986).

64. William Vance Trollinger, Jr., "One Response to Modernity: Northwestern Bible School and the Fundamentalist Empire of William Bell Riley" (Ph.D. dissertation, University of Wisconsin-Madison, 1984), 236–40; Dell G. Johnson, "Fundamentalist Responses in Minnesota to the Developing New Evangelicalism," (Ph.D. dissertation, Central Baptist Seminary, Pillsbury, MN, 1982).

65. Richard J. Mouw, "Assessing the Moral Majority," *Reformed Journal* 31 (June 1981):3–4; Richard Lovelace, "Future Shock and Christian Hope," *Christianity Today* 27 (August 5, 1983):16; "An Interview with the Lone Ranger of American Fundamentalism," *Christianity Today* 25 (September 4, 1981):22–23; Falwell, *Fundamentalist Phenomenon,* 179–85, 219–23.

66. Mark A. Noll, "Evangelicals and the Study of the Bible," in *Evangelicalism and Modern America,* ed. Marsden, 103–21; Cf. James Barr, *Beyond Fundamentalism* (Philadelphia: Westminster Press, 1985).

67. Bruce Wollenberg, "The Evangelical Orthodox Church: A Preliminary Appraisal," *Christian Century* 97 (July 2–9, 1980):698–702; David Becker, "A Closer Look at the Evangelical Orthodox Church," *Christian News Encyclopedia,* vol. 2 (Washington, MO: Missourian Publishing, 1983), 875; "Evangelical Orthodox Church to Join Eastern Orthodox Church on Istanbul Trip," *Evangelical Newsletter* 12 (March 15, 1985):1; Bradley Nassif, "Evangelical Denomination Gains Official Acceptance into the Orthodox Church," *Christianity Today* 31 (February 6, 1987):40.

68. Jim Wallis, *Agenda for Biblical People* (New York: Harper and Row, 1976); Jim Wallis, *The Call to Conversion: Recovering the Gospel for These Times* (San Francisco: Harper and Row, 1981); and Jim Wallis, *Revive Us Again: A Sojourner's Story* (Nashville: Abingdon, 1983). These books' titles, no less than their contents, reveal a restorationist agenda.

7

Primitivism in Fundamentalism and American Biblical Scholarship: A Response

MARK NOLL

THE two preceding chapters, despite appearances to the contrary, have much in common. Both are products of mature reflection by historians who have become masters of their subjects. Both also share what is really a common subject. The fundamentalists of Professor Carpenter's chapter defined themselves by contending for the form of biblical religion that is the subject of Professor Olbricht's paper. Almost by definition, fundamentalists were a people who harkened back to American experience of the period 1630 to 1870 as the golden age from which, in the early twentieth century, the nation had now sadly departed. The chapters also share one more feature that provides occasion for the substance of my comment. This is that both chapters finally suggest—Carpenter's explicitly and Olbricht's implicitly—that neither primitivism nor restoration, strictly speaking, played a decisive role in the subjects they examine so well.

Carpenter's chapter is a learned examination of the primitivist influence among American fundamentalists. His conclusion is that while a restorationist element existed among fundamentalists, it was accompanied by other powerful concerns as well. The result was a tradition in which primitivism was always present, but never dominant. At first glance the case that Carpenter makes is a strong one. Along the way he buttresses his argument with a series of penetrating observations, of which three seem to me especially perceptive.

First is his assertion that fundamentalistic primitivism was "tempered and colored by the movement's conservative sense of mission and implicit regard for tradition." Fundamentalists had a definite stake in the peculiar American experience, and so they could not afford the luxury of abandoning all in pursuit of first-century norms. Second, Carpenter wisely describes the sense of proprietorship that fundamentalists felt for American religious life, and indeed American culture more generally. This sense that they were the true heirs of America's finest hours did much to restrain primitivism. Third, I was struck by Carpenter's almost off-hand comment to the effect that when fundamentalists did display a biblical primitivism, they turned to the New Testament Epistles as norms. Other primitivists, Carpenter notes, turned elsewhere, Anabaptists to the Gospels and pentecostals to the Acts of the Apostles. This is a shrewd observation and one that suggests important questions for research. When studying biblical primitivism, it does seem important to ask which part of the Bible functions as the standard, for it is rarely the entire text.

These are only three of the particular virtues of Carpenter's essay that contribute to his general conclusion that fundamentalists experienced chronic tension between primitivism and tradition. At this point, however, I would like to address myself to that conclusion itself, especially to the statement that "it is hard to identify much that is unique about American fundamentalists' expression of that yearning to restore New Testament faith that has been common to many Christians." I wonder if that is so, because it seems to me that fundamentalists did in fact exhibit an intense primitivism in their defense of the Book, of the Blood, and of the Blessed Hope, and in their struggle to recapture a lost Christian America.

In the first instance it is possible to see in fundamentalism what Lovejoy and Boas called "cultural primitivism," a concept that Richard Hughes has summarized as "the yearning of the civilized for a simpler, less complex world." Each of the fundamentalist contentions for the Book, the Blood, and the Blessed Hope took a common form, and each exhibited cultural primitivism. In each case fundamentalists attempted to read experience from a divine angle of vision. In each case they tried to understand the contemporary world as the divinely inspired authors of Scripture had understood their experience. In each case fundamentalists denied that historical process—networks of cause and effect open to public analysis—had anything significant to do with their belief.

Thus when fundamentalists defended the Book, they did so by urging for the inerrancy of the Bible's original autographs, an idea that had been around a long time but which had never assumed such a central role for a Christian group. This belief had the practical effect of rendering the experience of the biblical writers nearly meaningless.

It was the word of God pure and simple, not the word of God through Moses, David, Samuel, Matthew, Mark, Luke, John, or Paul, that was important. Likewise, fundamentalist convictions about the miraculous character of redemption through the blood of Christ reflected age-old Christian beliefs, but expressed them with a heightened concern for nonhistorical elements. When fundamentalists spoke of the new birth, they stressed the unmediated activity of the Holy Spirit. Although in practice they used a wide variety of "means" by which the new birth could be encouraged—cultivation of family worship and nurture, earnestness of preaching, the example of holy living—in theory they continued to stress the immediacy of the Holy Spirit's action. This too reflected a negation of historical process. Finally, the fundamentalist longing for the Blessed Hope treated current global history with a similarly cavalier spirit. If current events were important primarily because they fulfilled biblical prophecy, then the relationships that all could study between contemporary cause and contemporary effect paled into insignificance. Again, fundamentalists were reading history as if they were inspired like the authors of Scripture had been inspired, rather than as believers whom God had commissioned to participate in the ongoing nurture of the church in this time between the times.

The extent of fundamentalist negation of historical process certainly must qualify as a distinct primitivism. Fundamentalist belief in the supernatural, or in the extraordinary action of God in the present, was by no means unique in Christian history. But its way of concentrating upon the numinous at the expense of the natural was distinct. Classical Protestantism, for example, had a number of devices that allowed it to combine supernatural and natural visions of the world. Lewis Spitz has spoken of the *simul* principle originating in Luther by which one could regard events as the simultaneous outworking of both divine and human causation. And Calvin and his heirs used the word *concursus* to denote the same dual approach to explanation.[1] For fundamentalists, however, the natural pole of historical explanation had largely faded from the scene. They were thus exponents of cultural primitivism.

And they were also exponents of "chronological primitivism," which as Richard Hughes suggested, we may define as a belief that "the greatest excellence and happiness existed at the fount of time." They longed to restore an America that—at the "fount of time"—had honored the sabbath, respected godliness, elected saints, and encouraged public righteousness. This does not look at first like a biblical primitivism unless we remember how much framers of America's revival tradition had linked the establishment of the new nation with the recovery of primitive Christianity, a theme amply documented in the essays of Nathan Hatch. When Tom Paine suggested that "we have it in our power to begin the world over again," American Protestants took him at his word and set to work recreating the New Testament church.[2] This was the legacy fundamentalists sought to recapture, and in this they were biblico-nationalist restorationists, chronological primitivists with a vengeance.

Like Carpenter, Olbricht brings to his work a vast familiarity with important sources and a seasoned judgment. In his essay he wants to show that biblical primitivism was a major force in American biblical criticism "from the time that the fathers landed at Boston Bay in 1630 up until the laying of the foundations for twentieth-century biblical studies in the waning decades of the 1800s." And again, like Carpenter's, Olbricht's chapter is studded with gems of insight. As one who has tried to make some sense of academic biblical study by Americans, I am impressed with the breadth of his research. Especially striking to me was the demonstration here of how many Americans, from the very beginning, read the finest results of European biblical study. Wellhausen, Kuenan, and Robertson Smith were far from the first Europeans to dent the consciousness of their country cousins across the Atlantic. In addition, I found most enlightening Olbricht's understanding of how patterns of formal schooling influenced the course of biblical scholarship. For example, it says a great deal for the quality of instruction directed by Moses Stuart that such a high percentage of the founders of the Society of Biblical Literature were his pupils. And I found Olbricht's chapter particularly illuminating in its contention that distinctly conservative leaders laid the foundation for academic biblical scholarship in America, an endeavor that in recent decades the theological heirs of those conservatives have looked upon with considerable suspicion. In this regard, it is worth asking if the process described by Olbricht is not the same sort of process uncovered in earlier monographs by T. D. Bozeman and E. Brooks Holifield, who showed that apologetical procedures developed by conservatives early in the nineteenth century evolved into means to escape orthodoxy at the end of the century.[3]

For all these virtues, however, Olbricht's essay still is something of a puzzle to me. Put most simply, I am at a loss to see how what he describes, and well describes, can be considered biblical primitivism. The efforts to keep abreast of European scholarship, to collect the books of the best critics (as even John Harvard did in his short life), to write 6,000 manuscript pages on the Bible and its milieu as Cotton Mather did, to study German and other exotic tongues with the fervor displayed by Moses Stuart, to undertake the perilous voyage to the Old World in order to sit at the feet of learned Bible scholars—all of these seem like traditionalism instead of primitivism. Although a certain primitivist element was prominent among some of the early Puritans, it was explicitly rejected by the major figures of this essay. Most American Puritans, and certainly the nineteenth-century conservatives like Stuart and Charles Hodge, believed not in "early" or "primitive" or "New Testament" Christianity, but in "historic Christianity." This is the burden of Mather's *Magnalia Christi America,* of Hodge's *Systematic Theology* and most of his polemical essays, and of Stuart's defense against the Unitarians. These conservatives aligned themselves self-consciously with the Christian tradition, often expressed in respected confessions of faith. They did not pine for a lost golden age. They did not want a simpler, less complex world. Especially when it came to studying the Bible, only the best learning would do.

The biblical primitivists of early America, as Olbricht seems to recognize at one point, were in fact the Unitarians who, as he puts it, "rested their case with the primitive Christian documents." Since the early days of the Reformation, Unitarian biblical primitivists had been claiming that if Christians went back to the Scriptures alone, setting aside the husks of tradition, they could rid themselves of irrational notions like the Trinity.[4] To counter this primitivism, conservatives like Cotton, Mather, Stuart, and Hodge drew self-consciously on the historical resources of the church. They defined themselves explicitly in terms that had been developed in the course of that history. Primitivist assaults on that tradition were nothing less than heresy.

Given the title of Olbricht's essay, one would expect fuller treatment of these Unitarian biblical primitivists and also of the restorationists that Nathan Hatch has studied, or of the Mormons, or even of the Methodists who followed John Wesley. For although Wesley was a learned man who encouraged his ministers to study much, he also urged them to seek simplified pristine expressions of faith and life. So he wrote a tract entitled *Primitive Remedies* on health care. And so he embraced the people at large as the object of his sermons. "I now write (as I generally speak) *ad populum*," Wesley wrote in the preface to his *Sermons on Several Occasions,* "to the bulk of mankind—to those who neither relish nor understand the art of speaking, but who notwithstanding are competent judges of those truths which are necessary to present and future happiness. . . . I desire plain truth for plain people."[5] These are the Christian groups who seem best suited to the label of biblical primitivists.

As it is, however, the essay treats us to an extensive discussion of biblical traditionalists who took their bearings from the learning of the church's varied past. No better illustration exists of this kind of traditionalism than Charles Hodge's friend, Joseph Addison Alexander (1809–60) who taught at both Princeton College and Princeton Seminary. Alexander was a linguistic marvel who in the space of a relatively short life learned to speak, read, and write English, Latin, German, French, Italian, Spanish, and probably Portugese, to read and write Arabic, Hebrew, Persian, Greek, Romaic, and Aramaic, to read Ethiopic, Dutch, Sanskrit, Syriac, Coptic, Flemish, and Norwegian, and to make some sense of Polish, Swedish, Malay, and Chinese. Part of his application to language-learning seems to have been a whimsical indulgence of his own genius, but most of it had a definite purpose—to enable Alexander to read more fully what was written about the Scriptures in these other tongues. Here is how his biographer described Alexander during the writing of his great commentary on the Book of Isaiah, which appeared in 1846 and 1847.

> When he was writing his Commentary on Isaiah, he caused to be made two standing desks reaching from one end to the other of his large study. These were two stories high. On the lower story he placed the folios and quartos, and on the upper the octavos. I should estimate that these stands held about fifty volumes, all of them open. He would first pass down the line where the commentaries were, then to the lexicons, then to other books; and when he was through, he would hurry to the table at which he wrote, write rapidly for a few minutes, and then return again to the books: and this he would repeat again and again, for ten or twelve hours together.[6]

Alexander was an unusual case. But he nonetheless embodied the attitude toward Scripture typical of the Puritans and nineteenth-century conservatives whom Olbricht studies. For them, the Bible was a book to be studied *with* the history of the church, not *against* it.

In spite of these strictures, let me hasten to add that there is something to be said in defense of the Puritans and the nineteenth-century conservatives as biblical primitivists. The reason they sought the finest learning about Scripture was because they felt that a better understanding of the ancient biblical world would nurture a better Christianity in the present. In that sense, to be sure, they were primitivists. But in methods for arriving at that biblical understanding, in respect for the centuries that had intervened since the apostles, and in their desire to align themselves with the tradition of orthodoxy as they understood it, they were anything but primitive.

On the fragile bridge constructed by that ambiguity, let me now pass to some general reflections on the subject of biblical primitivism. At this point I am speaking less as a historian and more as a Christian, although one hopes that these categories are not mutually exclusive. And it is only fair to say that as much as I hold the Scriptures to be absolutely authoritative for this as for every age, I am suspicious of primitivist ways of understanding the Bible. This suspicion, which is probably more of a virulent prejudice, arises from personal experience: too many times in recent years I have been shown depths of meaning in Scripture from individuals, living and dead, whose insights had been despised by the community of faith in which I was reared simply because they were part of a supposedly corrupt history. But my prejudice against biblical primitivism also has a theoretical basis. Recent books like Edward Shils's *Tradition* (University of Chicago Press, 1981), Jaroslav Pelikan's *The Vindication of Tradition* (Yale University Press, 1984), and even indirectly Eric Hobsbawm and Terence Ranger's edited collection, *The Invention of Tradition* (Cambridge University Press, 1983) show that the hand of the past can indeed become an incumbrance, a blight rather than a blessing. They show that traditionalism, what Pelikan calls "the dead faith of the living," can strangle vitality and curtail creativity. And they show that cynical leaders are able to manipulate, distort, invent, dismember, or divert traditions for self-serving purposes. But at the same time, such studies also show how essential and inescapable tradition is, especially for those who believe in a religious faith rooted in history. To quote Pelikan once again,

> The dichotomy between tradition (as a bad thing) and insight (as a good thing) breaks down under the weight of history itself. A "leap of progress" is not a standing broad jump, which begins at the line of where we are now; it is a running broad jump through where we have been to where we go next. The growth of insight . . . has not come through progressively sloughing off more and more of tradition, as though insight would be purest and deepest when it has finally freed itself of the dead past. It simply has not worked that way in the history of the tradition, and it does not work that way now. By including the dead in the circle of discourse, we enrich the quality of the conversation.[7]

Nowhere are these principles truer than in the understanding of Scripture.

Primitivism, by contrast, in its search for a pristine fount in biblical time and especially for the simpler, less complicated realities of the New Testament, makes two misjudgments. It underestimates the hold of our own times on our vision of the Scriptures. And it overestimates our ability to get back, to recover that ideal time—the Old Testament for some Puritans, the Gospels for the Anabaptists, the Acts for the pentecostals, or the Epistles for fundamentalists—in its original purity. A comparison of biblical primitivisms shows these things most clearly. In the fifteenth century, followers of John Hus tried to combat the ecclesiastical corruptions of their day by holding up the ideal of what they called "the primitive church." A recent commentator has summarized the content of that primitivist vision:

> The age of the primitive church had been a time when Christians abounded in virtue, when there was a deep devotion to the Eucharist, when the church practiced a community of goods, when the clergy were saintly, when even small children were well versed in the knowledge of Scripture, when the church lived in unity and peace rather than in schism, when doctrine and morals shone with the light of the Holy Spirit, when the fervor of genuine repentance made a resort to indulgences unnecessary, [and] when "imitators of the apostles" avoided the use of philosophy.[8]

Now this Hussite primitivism, to be sure, shares certain features with other biblical primitivisms. But there are also important differences. Few biblical primitivists in the early United States, for instance, would have championed veneration for the Eucharist or assumed the necessity of a distinct clergy. Why was Hussite biblical primitivism different in many particulars? Because the Hussites lived in a different age with different conventions of thought and habits of discourse than biblical primitivists in other ages.

All of this is meant to say that biblical primitivism looks like a slogan whose reach exceeds its grasp. The Bible may be absolute in its wisdom and authority, but we apprehend its treasures as mediated through history. Once that is admitted, the only question is not whether to employ history to understand the Bible, but how much and what kind of historical guidance we will allow, in Pelikan's phrase, to take part in the "conversation."

Yet in conclusion it is impossible—especially in this hospitable place— not to recognize the wonderfully stimulating effect that the primitivist vision has exercised at different times and among different segments of the Christian community. Whether Hussites in the fifteenth century or restorationists in early America, and many more besides, the ideal of recovering a pure and uncorrupted message of Scripture has been a goad to spiritual growth and a stimulus to labor for the Kingdom. Certainly one of the richer, more endearing mysteries in the Christian story is how biblical primitivism itself has become a tradition of great power and lingering effect.

NOTES

1. Lewis Spitz, "History: Sacred and Secular," *Church History* 47 (March 1978):5–22; and B. B. Warfield, "Calvin's Doctrine of Creation," *Princeton Theological Review* 13 (April 1915):190–255.

2. Paine quoted in Henry F. May, *Ideas, Faiths and Feelings* (New York: Oxford University Press, 1983), 194.

3. T. Dwight Bozeman, *Protestants in an Age of Science* (Chapel Hill: University of North Carolina Press, 1977); and E. Brooks Holifield, *The Gentleman Theologians* (Durham, NC: Duke University Press, 1978); this is also the thesis of James Turner's *Without God, Without Creed: The Origins of Unbelief in America* (Baltimore: The Johns Hopkins University Press, 1984).

4. Cf. Jaroslav Pelikan, *Reformation of Church and Dogma (1300–1700),* vol. 4 of *The Christian Tradition* (Chicago: University of Chicago Press, 1984), 326–31.

5. John Wesley, *Sermons I, 1–33,* vol. 1 of *The Works of John Wesley,* ed. Albert C. Outler (Nashville, TN: Abingdon Press, 1984), 103.

6. Cited in E. J. Young, "The Study of Isaiah since Alexander" in his *Studies in Isaiah* (Grand Rapids, MI: Eerdmans, 1954), 10–11.

7. Jaroslav Pelikan, *The Vindication of Tradition* (New Haven: Yale University Press, 1984), 81.

8. Pelikan, *Reformation of Church and Dogma,* 118.

PART THREE

European Traditions in America

8

"Biblical Primitivism" in Early American Methodism

ALBERT C. OUTLER

THERE are several stereotypical ways to misunderstand early Methodism in America that have continued to seem credible to Methodists and non-Methodists alike, even until now. One is to connect its first century in America too closely with its Wesleyan antecedents in eighteenth-century Britain. Despite the Anglican affiliations of John Wesley, Thomas Coke, Joseph Pilmore, and others, Francis Asbury and the bulk of American Methodists in the early decades understood themselves in terms of modified "non-conformity" that set them quite apart from the Episcopalians on the one side and other American Protestants on the other. Their "Arminian" theology set them off from the Reformed traditions generally, and their societal polity (with its "connectionalism," "itinerancy," and monarchical "episcopacy") distinguished them from all the congregationalist and presbyterian traditions. Moreover, they themselves were well content with these "Methodist distinctives," as they called them.

Another misleading stereotype is the supposition that American Methodism in its recent *second* century (1884–1984) amounted to a simple extension of the first. Sweeping social changes and drastic doctrinal reorientations altered the ethos and outlook of mainline Methodism in ways that require a reformulation of almost all generalizations about the early decades, or at least different nuances.[1] Nor will generalizations that are sound enough for "United" Methodism (since 1968) hold without important revision for the other Methodist bodies in America (e.g., the African Methodist Episcopal Church, the African Methodist Episcopal Zion Church, the Christian Methodist Episcopal Church, Wesleyan Methodists, Free Methodists, Nazarenes, and even less for the pentecostalists-in-variety who also acknowledge a "Wesleyan" provenance).

Indeed, the Methodist heritage itself has a more shadowy lineage than one would guess from the myths about John Wesley as its founder, *de nihilo*. It goes back at least to the seventeenth-century negations of High Calvinism (as distilled in the canons of the famous Synod of Dort, 1619), gathered under the misleading umbrella term *Arminian*. Its alternative doctrines stressed grace and free will, along with a variety of notions about "double justification" (as with Martin Bucer and the so-called School of Saumur—e.g., Amyraldus, LeBlanc, Cameron, Peter Baro, et al.). We know about this still obscure tradition largely through its critics—the French Protestant Jean Daillé in his *La foi fondée sur Les Saintes Scriptures, Contre les Nouveau Methodistes* (1634), the English Nonconformist Theophilus Gale in *The Court of the Gentiles* (1672), and the Lutheran Johannes Vlach's *Dissertationes Trias* (1680), one of whose dissertations deplores the doctrines of *nostri novi Methodistae*. An English Puritan critique of this "new *method* in divinity," aimed actually at John Goodwin and Richard Baxter, appeared in an anonymous pamphlet in 1696, *A War Among the Angels of the Churches: Wherein is Showed the Principles of the New Methodists in the Great Point of Justification*. Its author, "A Country Professor of Jesus Christ," was especially incensed by what seemed to him as their "neonomianism," their false doctrines of imparted righteousness in justification and their preference for the doctrine of Christ's atoning death as the "meritorious cause" of salvation, by contrast with the Reformed doctrine of the atonement as justification's "formal cause."

Thus when the brothers Wesley and their friends formed a semimonastic society in Oxford in 1729 and labeled it the Holy Club, this was bound to remind some of their Anglican critics of those old "new Methodists" and this came to be the nickname (appearing first in 1732) that stuck. Nor is it unimportant that Wesley treated the appellation as a nickname (and preferred to speak of his disciples as "the people *called* Methodists").

It was natural enough, therefore, that when the Methodist movement began to spread as a religious society within the Church of England (in 1739 and thereafter), it would appear as an ecclesiastical anomaly, neither Anglican nor Nonconformist. As friendly a critic as Josiah Tucker (afterward dean of Gloucester) could admonish the Methodists against doctrinal confusion and warn them against the dangers of separation and schism.[2]

John Wesley, however, was all the more convinced that the times called for an evangelical alternative to the sacerdotalism of "the Church as *by law* established" and to the Calvinism of Nonconformity. He saw his revival as a providential corrective to the formalism and moralism of the national church; he sincerely believed that the Methodist gospel of grace ("repentance, faith and holiness") was a recovery of apostolic doctrine—still another reform of the Reformation. The Methodists recoiled in horror from the "wars of religion" that had followed the sixteenth-century disruptions. and their memories of religious anarchy in Cromwell's Commonwealth left them suspicious of what they saw as theocratic visions both in Calvinism and in "radical Protestantism."

In America, the Methodists were latecomers (our earliest firm date is 1766), who had blithely lightened their inherited baggage from the Old World. To begin with, many of the first Methodists in the colonies were "Irish" (some of them Palatine Germans who had first migrated to Ireland and become Methodists there before their further transplantation to the New World). Their primitivism consisted largely in their zeal for Scripture as "the *sole* rule of faith and practice" and their sense of "the Apostolic Church" as a perpetual charter rather than as an imitable model.

Once their colonial ties with Britain and the Church of England had been severed, the American Methodists were torn between their tenuous loyalties to John Wesley and their need of a ministry of their own. Inevitably, there were initiatives on behalf of a self-constituted "restoration" (as in the "Fluvanna Schism" of 1782–83). Francis Asbury, the only English Methodist appointed by Wesley who had remained in America throughout the Revolution, held out for some link in legitimation from Wesley and the British Conference. Wesley, in turn, was prepared to reverse his erstwhile negative views of American independence and moved quickly, on several fronts, to provide the Americans with the makings of a church independent, but still linked with its British heritage. It was Wesley the churchman who dared to act as "a Scriptural episkopos" (with what he thought was patristic precedent) and to ordain two elders (Thomas Vasey and Richard Whatcoat), and to ordain his assistant, Dr. Thomas Coke (Ll.D.) as general superintendent for America. This trio was to proceed forthwith to the new country and provide a ministry of "Word, Sacrament and Order" for the Methodist people. With them, he sent along a curious abridgement of the Book of Common Prayer that he had prepared for the new church along with an anti-Calvinist abridgement of the Thirty-Nine Articles; its title was *The Sunday Service of the Methodists in North America* (1784). As a personal blessing and also as an official warrant for all these protocols of continuity, he drafted an open letter "To Our Brethren in America," reflecting his sense of tradition as taprooted in Scripture and developed in his church history: "As our American brethren are now totally disentangled both from the state [the new U.S.A.] and from the English hierarchy, we dare not entangle them again either with the one or the other [note this affirmation of the separation of church and state six years before the First Amendment]. They are now at full liberty simply to follow the Scriptures and the Primitive Church. And we judge it best that they should stand fast in that liberty wherewith God has so strangely made them free."[3] This is the same man who had, a decade earlier, "submitted" his *Collected Works* (1771–74) "to the judgment of Holy Scripture, right reason, and Christian Antiquity."[4]

There can be no doubt that for Wesley, Apostolic Christianity was normative or that its restoration continued as an ideal for him and his people. But he was also immersed in church history; he took some sort of continuity of ministries for granted. Was Wesley, then, a restorationist? The answer here hinges on one's understanding of tradition, continuity, and development in church history since the end of the apostolic age. Even the American Methodists, with a far less vivid or rich sense of tradition, understood themselves as reforming a debilitated church rather than reconstituting one, *de novo*. With remarkable self-reliance, therefore, they constituted themselves into the first independent denomination in the new American nation with a title connoting their polity, The Methodist Episcopal Church (1784). Coke and Asbury were elected as their general superintendents (and promptly took on the title "bishop"). They arranged for an itinerant network, tightly connected, from Maine to Georgia, which then was dominated entirely by Francis Asbury, who reigned without a peer for a full quarter century before his death in 1816.

Wesley had supposed that his brethren in America would wish to continue under *his* spiritual direction and theological tutelage, as British Methodism had done so willingly for the preceding two generations. He also assumed that Dr. Coke, as his delegated *locum tenens,* would be cordially received as the head of the new church, or at the least as Asbury's senior partner. All these assumptions were miscalculations—both of the American temper and of Asbury's temperament.

The Americans were prepared to acknowledge Wesley as their eponymous patriarch, but they were equally resolved upon maintaining their new independence. Asbury assumed the mantle of leadership, quietly eased Coke out of the picture, allowed *The Sunday Service* to fall into disuse—and proceeded to set as distinctive a personal mark on American Methodism as Wesley had done in Britain. His primitivism had no speculative theological basis. He had next to no sense of tradition, but also no strong convictions about a church in apostasy since the end of the apostolic age. It was, rather, that the Bible served him sufficiently in his personal spiritual hungers and in his passion for awakening and converting souls. In typical Methodist fashion, he added the *Book of Discipline* and the *Hymnal* to "the iron ration" of his preachers. What he had learned from John Wesley (from slight acquaintance and only a brief career in the English Conference) was twofold: that the church is best defined by its commitment to mission and that a religious society is best directed by a single head. In America, he came to see how the talents of the preachers could be multiplied by frequent rotation ("itinerancy").

The Methodists were quick to adopt the patterns of revivals and camp meetings and to put them to good use. On their own, they invented the circuit rider—a Christian militiaman, traveling light, meshed into a grid of conferences (from local "charge," to district, annual, and general), subject to appointment and frequent reassignment. Until recent times, Methodist preachers were never "called;" they were sent— never "elected" by a congregation; they were received. It was a strange combination—a focus on Scripture and experience as the fonts of authority, together with a monarchical polity within an egalitarian society. What is more, since this unique polity seemed to work so well— not merely on the frontier but in the towns and cities—the Methodists came readily to believe that they had rediscovered the most adequate contemporary analog to polity in the apostolic church.

The Methodists resisted all ideas of the "invisible church" (this they associated with Reformed notions of *numerus electorum,* "the secret number of the elect"). They did, however, insist on probationary church membership, plus a strict discipline within the church membership. Their "article of religion" (XIII) on the church, adopted from Article XIX of the Thirty-Nine Articles (itself derived from Article VIII of the Augsburg Confession) was suitably ecumenical: "XIII. The visible Church of Christ is a congregation of faithful men in which the pure Word of God is preached, and the Sacraments administered according to Christ's ordinance, in all those things that of necessity are requisite to the same." In his sermon, "Of the Church" (1785), Wesley expanded the same definition.

> The catholic or universal church is all the persons in the universe whom God hath so called out of the world as to entitle them to the character of Christians—as to be one body united by one Spirit, having one faith, one hope, one baptism . . . [then follows a comment on national and local churches]. A particular church may, therefore, consist of any number of

members, whether two or three millions. But still whether it be larger or smaller, the same idea is to be preserved. They are one body and have one Spirit: one Lord, one faith, one baptism, one God and Father of all.[5]

Among American Methodists, this view was focused on "the church of the converted," with constant stress on regeneration and assurance (with frequent allusions to Acts 2:41–47). In Wesley, Scripture and tradition had been integrated, as the mutual interdependence of *revelation* and *interpretation*. No one among the American Methodists, however, knew enough about tradition to appropriate such an integration. Thus Wesley's concept of four-fold authority—of Scripture (as base and font), of tradition and critical reason as hermeneutical pillars, and of experience as confirmation—was drastically altered. Scripture was kept as base and font, but tradition was ignored and reason turned into rationalization (*fides quaerens—argumentum!*). Experience was enlarged beyond its original denotation of "assurance" into emotive concerns of all sorts with an authority of their own (*because* they were emotive). After all, what is there polite to say to a patently sincere assertion: "Deep in my heart, I *know* that . . ."?

Classical restorationism, especially in America, felt bound by "the silences of the New Testament." Methodist primitivism tended to take those silences as concessions to true believers to follow the leadings of their conscience and common sense—within the canons of faith, hope, and love. Methodist ministers were largely self-educated, with biblical perspectives of salvation that discouraged critical study of church history on the one hand and speculative theology on the other. They were bound into a close-knit fellowship in which "membership in full connection" in an Annual Conference was distinguished from ordination—and meant a good deal more, in practical terms. And this distinction persists in the Methodist ethos still.

Besides the Articles of Religion supplied by Wesley, the Americans produced one of their own: XXIII, "Of the Rulers of the United States of America"; they declined to attempt any other statements of official orthodoxy. They stoutly rejected the formalism that they saw among the Episcopalians and Roman Catholics. Their eucharistic theology varied from memorialism to the sort of spiritual realism reflected in Charles Wesley's "Hymns for the Lord's Supper." They retained the Apostles' Creed as an optional usage, but quietly dropped the phrase "descended into hell" from their version of it. Some congregations used "the Creed commonly called Nicene" for Holy Communion.

In 1808 the General Conference adopted a Restrictive Rule that forbade the revocation, alteration, or change in the Articles of Religion as well as the establishment of any "new standards or rules of doctrine contrary to our present and established standards of doctrine"—and then resisted all motions designed to specify what those "present and established standards" were. Indeed this ambiguity still persists. The doctrinal Rule has never been challenged, constitutionally; but this has not prevented Methodist theologians from continuing their theological developments in bewildering variety, with little or no regard to their official Rule. In 1968, when the Evangelical and United Brethren brought their Confession of Faith into the United Methodist Church, it was declared "consonant with the Methodist Articles of Religion" by vote of the General Conference—and a second Restrictive Rule was added that the text of that Confession was unalterable. One might think that this would have made for a stable theological tradition (even a static one!). Everyone knows, of course, that the opposite has actually been the case. In 1972 the United Methodist General Conference approved Wesley's fourfold guidelines as authoritative; in 1984 the conference mandated a "doctrinal commission" to produce "a *new* statement of United Methodist standards of doctrine."

One can, therefore, see in American Methodism a distinctive mingling of primitivism and churchliness. This has generated an ethos all its own: Methodism has been a sect that became a church without ceasing to be a sect, professing a biblical base. Throughout the nineteenth century, Methodists in general accepted Richard Watson's dictum that Holy Scripture is unique "in its power to communicate divine truths on all subjects connected with our moral state."[6] This impulse to improvisation supported the conviction dearest to Methodist hearts: the church defined as mission. Their enthusiasm and zeal for converts attracted enough adherents so that the Methodist growth rate outpaced the population curve for the first half century; thereafter it led the other Protestant denominations, until an unrecorded day in 1924 when the Baptists edged ahead and have continued on the rise ever since. Earlier on Methodists took their cheerful statistics as proof of their recovery of the original power of apostolic Christianity. Since the reversal of these growth curves, they have had to seek other grounds for self-congratulations.

Given their Anglican origins, Methodists have been especially sensitive to the outright rejection of their ministerial orders by the Protestant Episcopalians, their open scorn of the pretensions of a Methodist episcopate and, therefore, of the validity of Methodist sacraments. This generated a large literature, best represented by Nathan Bangs in his major treatise *An Original Church of Christ: Or, a Scriptural Vindication of the Orders and Powers of the Ministry of the Methodist Epis-*

copal Church (1837). It was chiefly an argument with the Episcopalians, but its triumphalism was generalized. Bangs was a primitivist of sorts; his claim was that the Scriptures provide the church more with a charter than with a blueprint: "In the course of this investigation, we hope to derive some assistance from the early history of the church, reminding ourselves, in the meantime, of the fallibility of ecclesiastical writers.... When we take our leave of the inspired writers, we no longer have an infallible guide."[7]

He distinguished between Scripture itself as revelation and "the primitive church as a privileged witness" as chief aid in the business of valid interpretation. Given this distinction he could stake out the Methodist claim to a biblical authority for their doctrine and polity: "Without presuming to condemn others, we [Methodists] think that we have sufficient authority from the *Scriptures* as to the truth of our doctrine—and from the primitive church as to the efficacy of our polity—so as to do what we have done and as we will continue to do."[8]

What was unmistakably clear in the New Testament to Bangs was the Gospel: the revelation of God's grace in Jesus Christ and of the church's mission to provide witnesses to that Gospel in all places and times. "To the Scriptures, therefore, we must make our ultimate appeal.... So far as they lend us their infallible light, and we suffer ourselves to be ordered by it, we shall not be led astray."[9] But note the different nuance here from the similar sentiments of the Puritan Thomas Brooks (1608–80): "I dare not rise above what is written. Where the Scripture is silent, there I love to be silent and where the Scripture hath no tongue, there I desire no ears."[10]

Bangs was, therefore, convinced that Asbury and Coke had been justified "in organizing a church according to the apostolic model." It was a church with a classic trinitarian theology, Christology, soteriology. Yet it was also a church in continuity with the church through the ages. It had itinerant ministers, local elders, and class-meetings led by layfolk. Ministers served under annual appointment without appeal and the bishops shared the same bursary with the other circuit riders. Bangs saw Methodism as a leaven among the denominations, "to revive *pure and primitive Christianity*" (a favorite phrase).

Bangs took pluralism and a sort of "spiritual ecumenism" for granted: "It is possible to cleave to our own institutions and yet exercise a catholic spirit toward all who love our Lord Jesus Christ in sincerity. There are superficial differences between Christian communities, but these cannot be felt at the heights which are above the accidental forms which are created and destroyed, by time."[11]

A generation later, this same tradition was reformulated by a disciple of Bangs, Richard Abbey, in *An Inquiry into the Ecclesiastical Constitution, the Origin, and the Character of the Church of Christ and the Gospel Ministry* (1860):

> The Methodist Church, for instance, is not apostolic because of her confederate character [nor, by implication, would she be if she were congregational in polity]. It is apostolic because, and only because, of her conformity, in faith and practice, to the *religious* doctrines which the Apostles held and taught. This is the test, and the only test, of a *CHURCH OF CHRIST*.

Or again,

> A church is a *society* of Christians, preaching the Gospel, administering the sacraments and otherwise following Christ.

He concluded then,

> that the character of *the primitive church* is to be sought for in the principles of true religion and not in the mode of ecclesiastical association [i.e., polity] into which Christians form themselves.[12]

Both the strengths and weaknesses of American Methodist theology in the nineteenth century may be measured in Richard Watson's *Theological Institutes,* for this single book taught more Methodists what little school-theology they knew than any other (including Wesley's *Sermons* and *Notes*). Its first edition stretched from 1823 to 1829; it then went through five revisions and thirty printings before the century was out. Arminian in substance and Calvinist in form, Watson sought to provide Methodists with what Wesley had chosen not to provide, a systematic theology. His ecclesiology was heavily influenced by William Cave, *Apostolici* (1677)—one of Wesley's favorites. Watson's premise—that "the primitive Christians owed much to what they had learned in the Jewish synagogues"—allowed him to argue that "in all those particulars in which they were left free by the Scriptures, primitive Christians adopted those arrangements for the government which promised to render it most efficient in the maintenance of truth and piety."[13]

These samplings (in the absence of any influential counterstatements) may be taken as representative of American Methodist ecclesiology down through the century—until the "liberal transitions" toward its end. They reflect a special brand of primitivism that was neither magisterial nor restorationist in its typical form. Its distinctive emphasis was on development: the adaptation of "efficient means" to serve the perennial end of the apostolic mission. It served the Methodists in justification of their ministerial order (against the Episco-palians), of their connectional polity (against all congregationalists), and of their "gospel of universal redemption" (against the Calvinists). Not at all incidentally, this sense of a biblical taprootage remained with the Methodists (sometimes in strangely altered forms) throughout the three transmutations that altered mainline Methodism in the twen-tieth century out of all comparison with its origins: (1) its eager, if also belated, embrace of the Enlightenment and its theological spinoffs in Liberal Protestantism; (2) Methodist enthusiasm for the Social Gos-pel—The *Social Creed of the Churches* (adopted by the new Federal Council of Churches in 1908) was an adaptation of a Methodist doc-ument; and (3) the tragic immoderations of the late nineteenth-century controversies between the "liberals" and partisans of "holiness." There is sad irony in the fact that all Methodists in their bitter differences (always to God's greater glory!) have appealed to the same biblical vision of the peaceable Kingdom of God on earth for their authority and vindication, even as they have differed hopelessly in their appeals to the Bible as authority for their rival programs.

After a brief interim of cooperation in the early stages of the Second Great Awakening, the Methodist primitivists and the Reformed res-torationists (both well portrayed in Arthur Piepkorn's *Profiles in Belief,* vol. 2) tended to go their separate ways. Rice Haggard began as a comrade of James O'Kelly (the first American Methodist to rebel openly against Asbury's pious tyrannies) and ended up as a loyal ally of Barton W. Stone. For all their differences, these two quite disparate traditions have shared the conviction that the essence of the true *koinonia tou Christou* is its visible manifestation of faith in Christ and its imperative to be witness to God's self-disclosure in him. This shared tradition is reflected in Thomas Campbell's *Declaration and Address* of 1809— which can have had no direct connection with Wesley's earlier "Ar-ticle." Here is Campbell's definition: "The Church of Christ upon earth is essentially, intentionally and constitutionally one—consisting of all those in every place who profess their faith in Christ and offer their obedience to him in all things, according to the Scriptures, and who manifest the same by their tempers and conduct.[14]

What is to be learned from all this beyond commonplaces about the ironic discrepancies that have always existed between the professions and performances of religious movements? Is it instructive to be re-minded that the restorationists began by eschewing denominational-ism and then fell victim to its virus? What is the moral to the fact that mainline Methodism began by professing as its distinctive aim the "spreading of scriptural holiness over these lands" and then fell into a preoccupation with organization that has put a premium upon maintenance, and then confounded *that* with mission?

This much at least is clear from almost any reading of this history: that both restoration and holiness are ideals so fructifying that even when tarnished by the kinds of entropy with which we are so familiar as church historians, they still retain their regenerative power as ideals—so that, like the Holy Spirit who inspires them, they defy domestication and continue in their power to spark off new insights and new vitalities in later generations. For always there is a remnant who look beyond old formulae to their still living powers of refreshment. It is this vision of apostolic Christianity repristinated in later ages (less by replication than reappropriation) that can always find new relevance in new times and circumstances. And if such an ideal—of a vital community of "new creatures in Christ"—still defines God's will for the unity of Christians in time and space, then it might also continue as an urgent, however baffling, task for his obedient children in whatever history that may still unfold.

NOTES

1. Robert Chiles, *Theological Transition in American Methodism, 1790–1935* (Nashville, TN: Abingdon Press, 1964; Lanham, MD: University Press of America, 1983).

2. Josiah Tucker, *Brief History of the Principles of Methodism: Wherein the Rise and Progress, together with the Causes of the Several Variations, Divisions and Present Inconsistencies of this Sect are attempted to be traced out and accounted for* (Oxford, 1742).

3. John Wesley, "To our Brethren in America," in *The Letters of the Rev. John Wesley,* ed. John Telford (London: Epworth Press, 1931), 7:239.

4. John Wesley, "To the Reader," in *Works of John Wesley* (Bristol: W. Pine, 1771), 1:vii.

5. John Wesley, "Of the Church," in *Sermons,* ed. Albert C. Outler (Nashville, TN: Abingdon Press, 1986), 3: sermon no. 74, par. 14–15.

6. Richard Watson, *Sermons* (New York: Waugh and Mason, 1835), 2:474. Cf. 107, 179, 369.

7. Nathan Bangs, *An Original Church of Christ; or, A Scriptural Vindication of the Orders and Powers of the Ministry of the Methodist Episcopal Church,* 2d ed., rev. (New York: T. Mason and G. Lane, 1837), 10–11.

8. Bangs, *Original Church of Christ,* 9.

9. Ibid., 11.

10. Thomas Brooks, *Works,* 6 vols. (Carlisle, PA: Banner of Truth Trust, 1980), 4:374.

11. Bangs, *Original Church of Christ,* 381–82.

12. Richard Abbey, *An Inquiry into the Ecclesiastical Constitution, the Origin, and the Character of the Church of Christ and the Gospel Ministry* (Nashville, 1860), 33, 80, 112–13.

13. Richard Watson, *Theological Institutes: or, A View of the Evidence, Doctrines, Morals, and Institutions of Christianity* (Nashville, 1860).

14. Thomas Campbell, *Declaration and Address* (Washington, PA, 1809), cited in A. Piepkorn, *Profiles in Belief* (New York: Harper and Row, 1978), 2:629–30.

9

Biblical Primitivism
in the American Baptist
Tradition

ROBERT T. HANDY

THERE is no simple or fully satisfactory way to define or describe the largest denominational family of Protestants in the United States, nor will any one analogy picture the complex situation very clearly. Ralph Barton Perry once observed that "a historical creed is like the sun, appearing as a clear-cut and uniform disk when low on the distant horizon, but revealing itself on closer inspection as a vast caldron of molten matter, emanating gases, and with corona and streamers projecting indefinitely into surrounding space."[1] That imagery does have some uses in depicting the Baptist denominational family in America as it suggests a richly diversified, multilayered tradition that, in its long history, often has been marked by heated controversies. As this congregationally ordered movement expanded through nearly four centuries of history from small, separatist, free-church origins in England through evangelism, migration, and missions to become a major American denominational family, it has projected streamers into most of the nations of earth. Further, with its emphasis on religious freedom and its drift away from its earlier confessions of faith, it has had continually to explain to itself and others what it is that gives this vast movement the identifiability it has.

One familiar way Baptists in the United States have sought to do this is by listing a set of guiding principles; such lists vary in detail, yet overlap at certain points. None of the principles are unique to Baptists; it is in the way that those principles interrelate that the diverse people who call themselves Baptist have certain common characteristics. On most lists of Baptist principles are such matters as the authority of the Bible, the lordship of Christ, the guidance of the Holy

Spirit, the baptism of believers by immersion, the autonomy of the local congregation, associationalism, and religious freedom. Especially important for this discussion of Baptists and biblical primitivism is, of course, the emphasis on the authority of the Bible.

Variously interpreted throughout Baptist history, the authority of the Bible has meant that there has been a certain openness to tendencies toward primitivism or restorationism. Something of the desire to get back to primitive biblical and early church patterns was evident in the first appearance of English Baptists in Holland late in the first decade of the seventeenth century; by 1611 or 1612 a group of them returned to England and presently small congregations of General or Arminian Baptists arose, some forty-seven by 1644. Meanwhile, the Particular or Calvinist Baptists, destined to be much larger and historically (for several centuries) more dominant in both England and America, arose in the late 1630s. By 1677 they adopted as their confession of faith what was basically the Westminster Confession with minor emendations; the position of this Second London Confession was ratified by a General Assembly of Particular Baptists in 1689 in England with 107 churches represented.[2]

In the American colonies, a small General Baptist Association was formed in 1670. Relying heavily on Hebrews 6:1–2, its members called themselves Six Principle Baptists; five of the principles (repentance, faith, baptism, resurrection of the dead, and final judgment) were generally accepted, but the sixth—the laying on of hands after baptism—was distinctive. Of much greater significance for the rise of the denomination was the formation of the Philadelphia Baptist Association in Philadelphia in 1707. For much of the eighteenth century it was the dominant Baptist association, extending northward into New York and Connecticut and southward into Virginia. In 1742 it authorized the publication, with minor changes, of the Second London Confession, which became popularly known as the Philadelphia Confession.

As the Baptist movement grew remarkably in size to become the largest denomination in the United States by 1800, many of the new associations that were formed adopted the Philadelphia principles. The first chapter of the Confession of Faith emphasized that "The Holy Scripture is the only sufficient, certain, and infallible rule of all saving Knowledge, Faith, and Obedience," and found that its authority depended not on the testimony of any man or church, but wholly upon God, "the Author thereof."[3] That strong position, much emphasized in actions of the Philadelphia Association, could and often did serve as an invitation to biblical primitivism by those who were in or attracted to the Baptist movement. Yet the ecclesial context of the Philadelphia Association with its centralizing tendencies as defined in other articles of the long confession tended to limit exclusive or one-sided attention to that first important article. Nonetheless, as the passing decades brought many changes, some groups stressed heavily the authority of Scripture and the desire to restore primitive patterns of church life in accordance with that authority, whereas other aspects of the Philadelphia tradition were minimized.

In the latter half of the eighteenth century the impact of the Great Awakening on the Baptists was strong, and the Calvinist orientation was modified by a shift toward a pietistic and revivalistic evangelicalism, especially among the spate of new associations formed during or soon after that period. All this led to sharp tensions and to divisions between Regular (Calvinistic) and Separatist (revivalistic) churches and associations, the latter insisting on the Bible alone as the platform of their beliefs. As Baptists of various alignments worked together in the struggle for religious freedom and at the tasks of evangelism and mission, however, they were able by 1814 to frame a national organization, The General Missionary Convention of the Baptist Denomination in the United States for Foreign Missions, soon popularly called the Triennial Convention. It represented a fusion of Philadelphia interests with those of the Separates, for many of the local and regional splits had been mended by that period as Calvinistic and revivalistic Baptist evangelicals had found ways of working together.[4] At a time when the religious atmosphere of the country was being much influenced by the Second Great Awakening, many persons questing for a church life based on New Testament and early church patterns were drawn into the Baptist movement as it increasingly found its unity in the emphasis on biblical authority.

Very prominent and controversial among these people was Alexander Campbell. As he sought to find a basis of uniting the various branches of Christendom by the restoration of primitive apostolic patterns, he adopted baptism of believers by immersion, and in 1813 his independent Brush Run Church joined the Redstone Baptist Association of Pennsylvania, an association that had adopted the Philadelphia Confession. Campbell, however, was restive under the Calvinism, confessionalism, and centralizing tendencies of that association, and in 1823 the congregation left the Redstone for the Mahoning Association in Ohio, a much more loosely organized and reforming group. He urged Baptists along with all other Christians to return completely to New Testament patterns of church life with a minimum of organization. His influence spread rapidly as many Baptist congregations joined the ranks of the Reformers, but the two movements were on collision courses, and by 1830 the churches under Campbell influence had largely withdrawn to become a principal element in the indigenous American denomination called the Disciples of Christ. Despite the intense controversies that marked the separation of the two movements, some of the principles and attitudes expressed by the Reformers lingered on among Baptists, particularly the opposition to missionary societies characteristic of the Campbell of the Baptist period—views he later changed as the first president of the Missionary Society of the Disciples. Although the Baptist/Disciples separation was a heated one, there was sufficient continuing similarity between them to lead to at least six periods of conversation on the possibility of union between 1841 and 1952.[5]

What historians record as the antimission movement opposed all missions on hyper-Calvinistic grounds; two of its prominent leaders were long active as Baptist frontier preachers. John Taylor of Kentucky wrote a forceful tract entitled *Thoughts on Missions* in 1819, attacking missionary boards, conventions, societies, and theological schools and their agents who were busy raising money among the churches. Such agents, as Taylor saw them, picking out one as an example, "spoke some handsome things about the kingdom of Christ; but every stroke he gave seemed to mean MONEY."[6] Another antimission Baptist was Daniel Parker of Illinois, a rigorous predestinarian who opposed missionary societies as purely human agencies. Something of the militant and separatist spirit of such hyper-Calvinistic Baptists was typified by the conclusion of one of his pamphlets, "as God never intends to make peace with his enemies, neither does Daniel Parker intend to make peace with his enemies by compromising the truth of God's word."[7]

Intensely Calvinistic, antimissionary, primitivist attitudes swept across the Baptist movement from the middle Atlantic states and across the South to the western frontiers, often dividing or capturing associations and forming new ones. For example, in 1827 the Kehukee Association of North Carolina severed its former ties and became independent, discarding all missionary and Bible societies. The divisive controversy deeply affected congregational and associational life in many parts of the South but not only there; new statements of faith were adopted and new, rather loose ties among the separating bodies were made through letters of correspondence. A significant milestone in primitive Baptist history was a declaration made in 1832 by a group of Particular (Predestinarian) Baptists at the Black Rock Baptist Church of Baltimore, Maryland. The Black Rock Declaration took an emphatic antimissionary stance and objected with great vehemence to tract societies, Sunday schools, and the education of the clergy. The period of intense controversy across the denomination was disruptive of Baptist unity and costly for its missionary efforts. The great bitterness aroused during this period is disclosed in a comment made by a visitor to Tennessee in 1851: "Theological champions meet with burnished swords and cut and hew each other to the wondrous gratification of their respective partisans, who gather in hundreds for successive weeks to these scenes of religious combat."[8] Many of the various Primitive Baptist associations active in the late twentieth century have an honored place in their historical memories for the exciting times of separation and the shaping of this distinctive interpretation of Baptist principles; they often make specific reference to Kehukee and Black Rock.

As we look at Baptist life under our present rubric of biblical primitivism, we see this theme expressed also in movements not usually classed as such. It was, for example, clearly a major ingredient in the Old Landmark movement as it arose in Southern Baptist life in the second half of the nineteenth century. Its central figure, J. R. Graves, prominent Tennessee pastor and editor, forceful writer and eloquent speaker, campaigned tirelessly for the view that only Baptist churches in succession to the original first-century churches were true Christian churches—all others were merely religious societies. Beginning with the Cotton Grove Resolutions of 1851, Graves wrote books and editorials and spoke repeatedly in advocating his controversial views. He stated that the primary purpose of one of his works, *Old Landmarkism: What Is It?* was "to establish the fact in the minds of all, who will give me an impartial hearing, that Baptist churches are the churches of Christ, and that they *alone* hold, and have alone ever held, and preserved the doctrine of the gospel in all ages since the ascension of Christ."[9] But not just any Baptist churches: only "true" ones in succession with the original first-century churches, among which missionary and Freewill Baptists or those who associated with merely human religious societies were not included. True Baptists, he wrote elsewhere, "claim that they are successors to the 'Witnesses of Jesus,' who preserved the faith *once* delivered to the saints, and kept the ordinances as they were originally committed to the primitive Churches. They claim to be the lineal descendants of the martyrs who, for so many ages, sealed their testimony with their blood."[10]

The Landmark position caused great turmoil in the Southern Baptist Convention with its missionary concerns and was finally officially rejected, but not before it made a great impact on that denomination's ecclesiology; as Graves put it in 1880, "I do not believe that there is one association *in the whole South* that would to-day indorse [sic] an alien immersion as scriptural or valid, and it is a rare thing to see a Pedobaptist or Campbellite in our pulpits, and they are no longer invited to seats in our associations and conventions anywhere South."[11] Around the turn of the century schism did occur as separate Landmark associations were formed in Texas and Arkansas; in 1924 they merged as the American Baptist Association, a denomination that claimed over a million members by the 1970s. Its doctrinal statement affirms belief in the infallible verbal inspiration of the Bible. Although opposing missionary societies, the Landmark tradition is not antimissionary, but holds that missionaries should be appointed and supported only by individual congregations. A split-off from the American Baptist Association in 1950 is now known as the Baptist Missionary Association of America and claims over 200,000 members. Hence, although not usually listed among the primitive Baptist bodies, the Landmark denominations do present a distinctive aspect of biblical primitivism among Baptists.[12]

Returning now to Baptist bodies that at present think of themselves as Primitive Baptists or are so regarded by others, we find a very complex situation that presents great difficulties for the historical or sociological interpreter who wants to present a neat classification as to what, where, and how large these groupings are. In volume 2 of *Profiles in Belief,* Arthur Piepkorn included a number of such denominations in his treatment of forty-six Baptist bodies in North America. A serious recent effort at classifying the Primitive Baptists has been undertaken by J. Gordon Melton in volume 1 of the *Encyclopedia of American Religion.* Taking his clues primarily from the history of the nineteenth-century separations, he gathered the materials primarily under the major heading of "Calvinistic Anti-Mission Baptists," but did not hide the difficulties as he pointed to their extreme congregational form of government, reported that for "the overwhelming number of Primitive Baptists, there is no organization above the loose associations which typically cover several counties," and noted that with a few exceptions most such groups have no headquarters, institutions, or official publications, although independent periodicals do provide means of communication among certain doctrinally definable groups in given areas.[13] As there are no official names for like-minded Primitive Baptists above the associational level, Melton chose to run the risk of offense in trying to frame a descriptive label for the larger groupings. Under the subheading of "Primitive Baptists—Regulars" he

gathered some 150 associations of moderate Calvinist Regulars, varying in size from two to more than twenty congregations, along with
almost five hundred independent congregations of similar persuasion.
A second subheading deals with what he styled "Absolute Predestinarians," of which he has located some fifty-one small associations.
The third grouping he called the "Primitive Baptists—Progressive," of
which he has identified some thirteen associations centered strongly
in Georgia that have innovative forms of congregational life.

Melton also listed two main groupings of Black Primitive Baptists.
First under that heading he included some forty-three very small associations, in doctrine and practice very much like the Primitive Baptists—Regulars. The second group, the National Primitive Baptist Convention of the U.S.A., he also found doctrinally like Regulars, but he
also found them to be a much larger group that in 1975 claimed some
six hundred churches with a quarter million members. Efforts to describe that convention illustrate some of the difficulties of the study
of Primitive Baptists. Writing in the early 1960s, Penrose St. Amant
observed that it sponsored missionary societies and Sunday schools
and concluded that it was not Primitive Baptist in the strict sense and
should be separately classified.[14] Piepkorn, however, reported that "the
convention reflects Primitive Baptist positions in its very loose organization," but found that it was somewhat less rigid theologically
than its white counterparts. Although writing in the 1970s, as did
Melton, he reported that it was a much larger body, with nearly 2,200
churches and an inclusive membership of nearly a million and a half,
but characteristically added that "there has been no response to recent
efforts to contact the convention."[15]

After Melton had sought to bring some order into a perplexing area
of study under the main heading of "Calvinistic Anti-Mission Baptists," he found that he had some eleven other groupings that he sub-
sumed under the heading of "Independent Primitive Baptist Associations," many of them very tiny. He included here the Two-Seed-in-
the-Spirit Predestinarian Baptists founded by Daniel Parker, although
I would tend to classify that group, only a remnant of which survives,
with the Absolute Predestinarians.

Wanting to do a little digging in the Primitive Baptist primary sources
for myself, when I learned that a large collection of such materials,
including many association minutes and periodicals, had been gathered
by the Rev. William P. Lewis (1926–84) and recently deposited at the
American Baptist Historical Society in Rochester, New York, I went
there and encountered first hand the difficulties of research in the field.

For I found that some groups not usually included under the category of primitive consider themselves to be such. For example, a periodical entitled *New Testament Christianity,* later renamed *Divine Light and Truth,* shows that the scattered congregations of the General Six Principle Baptists in Rhode Island and Pennsylvania are in the twentieth century members of the London-based Old Baptist Union, which claims that "as a people, we are united internationally, to observe and teach all of the principles of the first Christian church founded by Christ and the Apostles; but for the sake of distinction from other societies we are known as 'The Old Baptists,' for we are indeed true successors of the first Baptists, and hence the oldest Baptists in the world—the church against which 'the gates of hell' have not prevailed."[16] Not a little biblical primitivism persists in another small but complex strand of Baptist life, the Free-Will Baptists, whose very name indicates modification of the Calvinism of so many Primitive Baptists. Although one of the larger of these groups merged in 1911 with what is now the American Baptist Churches, a number of smaller groups that reflect primitivist biblicism, theology, and practice, such as foot-washing, continues.[17]

Even a few hours with the minutes and periodicals of the wide range of Baptist associations and independent congregations that one encounters in researching biblical primitivism among Baptists make it clear that overall generalizations and satisfying classifications are problematic. Most of the congregations are tiny; many meet only once a month. The little periodicals reflect continuing theological debates and controversies, often focused around the issues of predestination. Although the washing of the saints' feet is a practice of many Baptists who may be described as biblical primitivists, some argue against making it a test of fellowship while others do not practice it.

Primitive Baptists, estimated by Loyal Jones to number about half a million in the South,[18] where they are strongest although they are to be found in all sections of the country, are easy to caricature as uneducated, divisive, and backward people, and they have often been treated quite critically if not derisively by modern scholars.[19] But from their associational minutes and publications one sees this much-divided flock as people who care little about the world's judgments: they are in search of the true church on the basis of what they find in the Bible and in the familiar traditions that they believe to be soundly, biblically based. In Jones's words, "in spiritual matters they place trust in no earthly being but in the scriptures and in the Holy Spirit."[20] Knowing that the truly faithful will always be a remnant, they do not worry about small congregations or associations that are ready to divide them further if persuaded that God wills it. Often accused of being otherworldly, they do show a clear sense of the spiritual as opposed to the worldly, and intend to remain faithful to what they are convinced is the biblical and primitive pattern of the church, holding to it against all comers, including those who share their own basic premises but draw different conclusions.

NOTES

1. Ralph Barton Perry, *Puritanism and Democracy* (New York: Vanguard Press, 1944), 65.

2. See, for example, Robert G. Torbet, *A History of the Baptists,* 3d ed. (Valley Forge, PA: Judson Press, 1973), 17–83; William L. Lumpkin, *Baptist Confessions of Faith* (Chicago: Judson Press, 1959), 235–40.

3. Lumpkin, *Baptist Confessions,* 248, 250.

4. Torbet, *History of the Baptists,* 249–51.

5. Franklin E. Rector, "Behind the Breakdown of Baptist-Disciple Conversations on Unity," *Foundations* 4 (1961):120–37.

6. As quoted by Robert A. Baker, ed., *A Baptist Source Book: With Particular Reference to Southern Baptists* (Nashville, TN: n.p., 1966), 80; see also Torbet, *History of the Baptists,* 268–76.

7. As quoted by Arthur Carl Piepkorn, *Profiles in Belief: The Religious Bodies of the United States and Canada,* 4 vols. (San Francisco: Harper and Row, 1978), 2:446.

8. As quoted from *The Biblical Recorder* (August 16, 1851):1, by James E. Tull, "A Study of Southern Baptist Landmarkism in the Light of Historical Baptist Ecclesiology" (Ph.D. dissertation, Columbia University, 1960), 144–45. The Black Rock Declaration is reprinted in part in Baker, *Baptist Source Book,* 82–84.

9. J. R. Graves, *Old Landmarkism: What Is It?* (Memphis, 1880), 25.

10. As quoted by John E. Steely, "The Landmark Movement in the Southern Baptist Convention," in *What Is the Church? A Symposium of Baptist Thought,* ed. Duke K. McCall (Nashville, TN: Broadman Press, 1958), 136.

11. Graves, *Old Landmarkism,* xv.

12. Piepkorn, *Profiles in Belief,* 2:418–21. Fundamentalist Baptist bodies are also not usually listed when primitive groups are being considered, but inasmuch as another paper in this book deals with biblical primitivism in evangelicalism/fundamentalism (Carpenter), I have not discussed it here, although it has been an important part of Baptist life.

13. J. Gordon Melton, *The Encyclopedia of American Religions,* 2 vols. (Wilmington, NC: Gale, 1978), 1:386; cf. 384–91.

14. Penrose St. Amant, "Other Baptist Bodies," in *Baptist Advance,* ed. David C. Woolley (Nashville, TN: Broadman Press, 1964), 378–79.

15. Piepkorn, *Profiles in Belief,* 2:447–48.

16. *New Testament Christianity,* 14 (July 1904): inside back cover.

17. Piepkorn, *Profiles in Belief,* 2:433–37. Although he focuses on Baptists in Appalachia, Loyal Jones, "Old-Time Baptist and Mainline Christianity," in *An Appalachian Symposium,* ed. J. W. Williamson (Boone, NC: Appalachian State University Press, 1977), 120–30, includes Free-Will along with other primitivist Baptist groups.

18. Jones, "Old-Time Baptists," 121.

19. For example, see Jack E. Weller, *Yesterday's People: Life in Contemporary Appalachia* (Lexington: University of Kentucky Press, 1965), esp. 121–33.

20. Jones, "Old-Time Baptists," 129.

10

Restoration Ideology
Among Early Episcopal
Evangelicals

DAVID L. HOLMES

THERE is a story about the first Nestorian missionaries reaching China during the late Middle Ages. Reportedly they told the emperor something like this: "We alone teach—pure and undefiled—the doctrine of the first Christians." Had the emperor known H. L. Mencken, he might have replied with the words that the Baltimore Sage used to send to all of his critics: "You may be right, and you may be wrong."

Since the time of Elizabeth I, the Church of England has been a comprehensive form of Christianity whose broad roof has sheltered various churchmanship parties. Each party has held a different view of what that pure and undefiled doctrine of the first Christians was. This chapter looks at the restorationist ideology of one such group.

Because most restorationists have claimed that the true church must base its teachings preeminently on the New Testament, it is appropriate that this group called themselves Evangelicals. The Anglican or (in America) Episcopal Evangelicals had many shibboleths, and one was that their name should be pronounced with a long *E*. Evangelicals were also very careful to say *A-men* not *Ah-men*. Any Episcopalian who pronounced those words differently was not one of them.[1]

Where the history of Anglican Evangelicalism begins is a question. Some historians start it at Oxford in 1729, when John Wesley took over the leadership of the Holy Club.[2] But as James Spalding has shown, a close tie exists between the Lollards, the Anglican Reformers, the Puritans, and the Anglican Evangelicals, for all had restorationist ideologies.[3]

Whatever its precise origin, Anglican Evangelicalism emerged from the same revival as Methodism, although it remained within the Church of England. John Newton, William Cowper, William Romaine, John W. Fletcher, and Henry Venn were some of its eighteenth-century leaders in England; Charles Simeon, Thomas Scott, the Clapham Sect, and Hannah More carried on the tradition in nineteenth-century England. That it is a different kind of Anglicanism is shown by some of its hymns—"Amazing Grace," "Rock of Ages," and "Just As I Am"— hymns the average layperson today probably thinks of as Southern Baptist.[4]

As for the movement's leaders in eighteenth-century America, if George Whitefield is omitted (in that his relationship to Anglicanism became tenuous in the American Colonies), then Devereux Jarratt and the Methodist preachers such as Joseph Pilmore who stayed within the Episcopal church after 1784 are the major representatives. But the real Evangelical surge in the Episcopal church did not start until the second decade of the nineteenth century. Hence this paper will focus on the program of restoration to the "ancient order of things" that these Episcopal New Lights developed from 1811 until they virtually died out in the later nineteenth century.

The year 1811—the same year in which Thomas and Alexander Campbell formed the Brush Run Church—is the appropriate point to start.[5] In 1811 a Greek-reading farmer named Alexander Griswold (1776–1843) became bishop of the Eastern Diocese (which comprised all of New England except Connecticut). In the same year a patrician named William Meade (1789–1862) entered the ministry of the dying Episcopal Church of Virginia. From that point on, Evangelical Episcopalianism grew in America, until by the mid-1830s the future of the Episcopal church appeared to belong to them.[6] Clergy such as Griswold, Meade, Philander Chase (1775–1852), Richard Channing Moore (1762–1841), James Milnor (1773–1845), Charles McIlvanie (1799–1873), Manton Eastburn (1801–72), Gregory Bedell (1793–1834), and Stephen Tyng (1800–1885), as well as laymen such as Francis Scott Key (1779–1843)—virtually all of whom had undergone a definitive religious experience—were among its leaders. Evangelicals were strong in the older Episcopal dioceses along the eastern seaboard and in the South. They controlled some dioceses in the Middle West, West and Southwest. Virginia Theological Seminary in Alexandria and Bexley Hall at Kenyon College were their leading ministerial training schools. Wherever graduates of those seminaries went in the nineteenth century, they were almost certain to spread the restorationist teachings of Episcopal Evangelicalism.

A restorationist movement not only claims to know what original Christianity is but also tries to reproduce it in the present. What were the restorationist tenets of the early Episcopal Evangelicals? Their program of restoration seems to have embraced at least nine tenets.

First, the Evangelicals firmly took their stand on the New Testament. For them, the New Testament was the norm and standard of Christian faith and practice. "Our movement," an Episcopal Evangelical wrote, "is 'New Testament Christianity' in its purest essence."[7] Thus the overriding point must be that Episcopal Evangelicalism saw itself as thoroughly biblical and sought to mould all aspects of faith and life by the norms of Scripture.

Second, the Evangelicals looked to the New Testament for the characteristics of the true church. And when they did, they found that the Protestant Episcopal church came the closest to approximating its primitive ideals. Insofar as they made few exclusivist claims for Anglicanism, they were "low church." A eulogist wrote of one Evangelical bishop: "He did not approve of some of the ways in which Christ is preached among other denominations. But still it was a pleasant reflection to him that Christ *was* preached."[8] For reasons such as these, the Episcopal Evangelicals cooperated in the United Front.[9]

But if the Evangelicals thought of themselves as Protestants, no one should underestimate their loyalty to the Anglican tradition. They held the restorationist's goal of Christian unity, but they wanted it under Evangelical Episcopal banners. One sees this in Jarratt's disgust and in Pilmore's concern about the departure of the Methodists from Anglicanism;[10] in the tone of the comments many of the Evangelicals made on Wesley, Whitefield, and the Countess of Huntingdon;[11] in the fact that so many of the Evangelicals were converts from other Protestant denominations; and above all in the very small number of Episcopal Evangelicals who followed Assistant Bishop George D. Cummins of Kentucky into evangelical schism in 1873. In the Reformed Episcopal church established by Cummins, the Evangelicals encountered an interpretation of Christianity that truly embodied their beliefs—in nomenclature, in sacramental theology, and in opposition to sacerdotalism. But with relatively few exceptions, the Episcopal Evangelicals simply condemned it.[12]

As for the outward marks of the true church, the Evangelicals adhered to the definition given in Article 19 of the Thirty-Nine Articles: "The visible Church of Christ is a congregation of faithful men, in which the pure Word of God is faithfully preached, and the Sacraments be duly administered according to Christ's ordinance, in all those things that of necessity are requisite to the same."[13]

But the Evangelicals went further; they added discipline as a mark of the true church. Thus unlike the main body of Anglicans from the Puritan Exodus to the Evangelical Revival, they held to a doctrine of the church as virgin. In his study of Puritan restorationism, James Spalding points out that by 1572 the following "three outward marks by which the true church can be known had become commonplace in England": (1) preaching the pure word; (2) ministering the sacraments sincerely; and (3) "ecclesiastical discipline which consisteth in admonition and correction of faults severely."[14]

Spalding's analysis is intriguing because it was precisely their enforcement of severe discipline on clergy and laity alike that caused the Evangelicals initially to be quite out of line with normative Episcopalian practice. And therein lies an interesting story. In the first half of the nineteenth century in America, Episcopal Evangelicals could be admonished, forbidden confirmation, forbidden the Lord's Supper, excommunicated, or deposed (depending on the offense, the frequency, and the diocese or parish) if they did any of the following things: gamble, play cards, duel, swear, drink spirituous liquor, get drunk, frequent taverns, attend a cockfight, attend the theater, attend a ball, race horses, breed horses for racing, deal too much in levity, or observe a continental Sunday.[15]

In other Protestant denominations, of course, such an opposition to worldly amusements was common in nineteenth-century America. But in the twentieth century it is surprising to read of such prohibitions in the worldly Episcopal church. They should be viewed as yet another attempt by the Episcopal Evangelicals at restoration—in this case, of the supposed moral purity of the early church. For their ethical code, the Evangelicals claimed the support of the New Testament and the Anglican Reformation.[16] By enforcing it, they caused the suspension of the bishop of Pennsylvania (for intemperance) and of the bishop of New York (for irregular conduct with women).[17]

Third, the Episcopal Evangelicals believed that they were restoring the faith and practice of the early Christian Fathers. As Samuel S. Hill has written, restorationism "takes the historical character of the Christian religion with the utmost seriousness, in its own specialized way."[18] The problem has always been where to draw the historical line between apostolicity and apostasy, and the Evangelicals were willing to draw that line further into the Patristic period than any other evangelical group.

The Evangelicals claimed that error had infiltrated Christianity very early,[19] and they saw erroneous views—on authority, sacraments, ministry, justification—gain ground in the church as the centuries went on.

But just as Wesley translated the Apostolic Fathers for the use of his preachers, so the Evangelicals took the teachings of the Fathers very seriously, as long as they found that teaching consistent with Scripture.[20] Thus where Alexander Campbell dismissed all creeds as human inventions, the Episcopal Evangelicals insisted that all of their confirmands must believe in the Apostles Creed—not because the Apostles wrote it, but because, as one Evangelical declared, "it contained the sum and substance of what the Apostles believed and taught."[21] Like the continental Reformers, the Evangelicals believed that the Fathers were on their side.[22]

Fourth, as Protestants did in general, the Episcopal Evangelicals thought that the true church had been so added to and so deformed over the centuries that only a great revolution could restore it.[23] They saw one phase of the Reformation—that which occurred in England— as truer to primitive Christian belief and practice than any other. But they also saw one phase of the English Reformation—that which existed under Edward VI—as truer to the original, exact model of Christianity than any of the others. And so in many ways the Evangelicals were Edward VI Episcopalians. G. R. Elton has written that "the Edwardian Reformation went but skindeep."[24] But to that assertion one must add that in Episcopal Evangelicalism two and three centuries later the Edwardian or Cranmerian reformation penetrated to the very soul.

Hence it is not surprising that many of the publications of the Episcopal Evangelicals and of their Evangelical Knowledge Society were reissues of the homilies, the catechisms, and the other writings issued during the reign of the boy king whom they called "the Josiah of the Christian Church."[25] Nor is it surprising that many of the Evangelicals were either professed Calvinists or sympathetic to Calvinism. They found their moderate Calvinism in the Thirty-Nine Articles, which one Evangelical described (in good restorationist fashion) as "a faithful exhibition of Gospel truth."[26] Thus the movement viewed itself not only as a restoration of true Christianity but also as a restoration of the true faith as it had once existed within the Anglican tradition.[27]

Fifth, the Evangelicals believed they had restored the original theology of Christianity. They taught the so-called evangelical summary: "the fall of Adam—[the] consequent impotence of man—[the] sufficiency of the grace of God—bestowed for the sole merit of Christ."[28] Thus they laid great stress on salvation by faith in the atoning death of Christ, and they took original sin very seriously. Shortly before his death, the aged bishop of Virginia could declare that he had "never performed one single act without some sin intermingling with it."[29] For twenty-six years Manton Eastburn addressed the fashionable congregation of Trinity Church, Boston, as "vile earth and miserable sinners, worms and children of wrath."[30] Devereux Jarratt invariably sought refuge in the words, "My grace is sufficient for thee."[31] The bishop of Alabama frequently declared that the lines "in my hand no price I bring/simply to Thy cross I cling" expressed the "sum and substance" of his religion.[32] The bishop of Ohio said that the words of Charlotte Elliott's "Just As I Am" summed up what he had preached throughout his ministry.[33] Thus this was simply a different kind of Episcopalianism than Americans are accustomed to today. It was Protestant Episcopalianism, experiential Anglicanism, primitive Church of England.

Sixth, the Evangelicals restored preaching as the main emphasis of the church. On apostolic grounds, citing St. Paul, they understood the foolishness of preaching to be God's chosen means of spreading the Gospel to sinful humanity.[34] Hence they tried to create a ministry of what the English Puritans would have called "painful preaching pastors."[35] This emphasis on preaching Christ and him crucified and on the power of the pulpit to work conversions was one of the reasons the Evangelicals were so bitter in their opposition to the Oxford movement. On the grounds that such an emphasis falsified biblical religion, they opposed any interpretation of Christianity that emphasized sacramentalism over preaching.

Published sermons give the contents of Episcopal Evangelical preaching. On the whole, their sermons seem to have followed what Jarratt called his preaching "plan": "First, to convince of sin. Second, of inability. Third, to press the convicted to fly to Jesus Christ. . . . Fourth, to exhort those who believe, to be careful to maintain good works."[36]

But historians know less about the style of their delivery, for many of the Evangelicals preached partially or completely extemporaneously and only later wrote down their sermons for publication.[37] In the 1830s a British visitor reported that John A. Clark, rector of St. Andrew's Church, Philadelphia, had a "striking and effective delivery," and that he closed his sermon with "a fervid and high wrought appeal."[38] The sermons of Bishop Moore of Virginia commonly caused congregations to burst into tears, whereas observers described the sermons of Alexander Vinton, rector of St. Paul's Church, Boston, as burning themselves into the memory.[39] "Whenever I heard him preach," a former parishioner at St. Paul's Church Philadelphia, wrote of Pilmore,

> his manuscript was always before him. He began not only by reading, but by reading very deliberately, and with little animation. But he would gradually wax warm, and you would see his eyes begin to kindle, and the

muscles of his face to move and expand, until at length his soul would be all on fire, and he would be rushing onward extemporaneously almost with the fury of a cataract. And the only use he would make of his manuscript in such case would be to roll it up in his hand and literally shake it at his audience.[40]

The description is reminiscent of the advice an old-line Evangelical who was professor of homiletics at Virginia Theological Seminary used to give to his students: "Start low, go slow, rise higher, gain fire, wax warm, *quit strong*."[41]

Also in Philadelphia, one parishioner described the preaching style of Gregory Bedell, first rector of St. Andrew's Church, as a combination of "deep pathos," "sweet yet solemn tones," and "impressive manner."[42] Once, when Bedell preached on the text "This night thy soul shall be required of thee," his message was so effective that a Presbyterian visitor was afraid to stay that night in his room.[43]

The Episcopal Evangelicals stressed sermons as working conversion. Were many converted by their preaching? The answer seems clearly to be yes. So many cadets underwent conversion experiences when McIlvanie was chaplain of West Point that the secretary of war feared that the military academy was going to change into a divinity school.[44] Increased church membership and what by earthly tests would seem to be vital piety accompanied Evangelicalism. Evangelical preachers revived the dying old Established Church of Virginia.[45] To the formal Episcopal church, they restored some of the emotion and excitement of the apostolic period.[46]

Seventh, in the threefold ministry the Evangelicals believed they possessed a New Testament ministry.[47] "I love her," Jarratt wrote of the Episcopal church, "because all her officers and the mode of ordaining them, are, if I mistake not, truly primitive and apostolic. Bishops, priests and deacons were, in my opinion, distinct orders in the church, in her earliest and purest ages."[48]

Unlike High-Church Episcopalians, the Evangelicals refused to disenfranchise nonepiscopal ministries. Some few of them may also have believed that episcopacy was an historical accident. But the earlier view of Bishop William White that the Episcopal churches could temporarily dispense with episcopacy, and the later view of Phillips Brooks and other Broad churchmen that the Christian church had started with the simplest of organizations, were not the views of most of the early Episcopal Evangelicals. [49]

Instead, the Evangelicals believed that they had restored the unsacerdotal, scriptural, Cyprianic episcopate. Their reading of the New Testament indicated that the two duties of a New Testament bishop were *preaching* (which St. Paul always puts first in his directives to Timothy) and *authority*.[50] Thus they held a high view of the historic episcopate, although like other restorationists, they opposed any setting apart of the ministry as a sacred caste. In fact, when Phillips Brooks was elected bishop of Massachusetts in 1891, an elderly bishop of Virginia named Whittle—an old-line Evangelical whose churchmanship was so low that he opposed to the end of his life any use of candlesticks or flowers in Episcopal churches—refused to consent to the consecration on the grounds that Brooks's views of the episcopate were defective.[51]

Sacramental theology was the eighth way in which the Episcopal Evangelicals exhibited restorationist ideology. The Evangelicals were restorationists in the general Protestant sense of returning to the supposed practice of the early church and acknowledging only two sacraments. Other wings of the Episcopal church occasionally waffled on the precise number of dominical sacraments.

In an Anglican context the Evangelicals were sacramental restorationists in removing what they thought were patristic accretions to biblical theology and practice. On scriptural grounds they refused to give any mechanistic or medicinal interpretation to the ordinances (a position they also claimed was identical to that of the Anglican Reformers).[52] Thus they viewed baptism as Christian circumcision, causing no moral change, no new nature, but rather acting as a sign and seal of divine promises; the only "regeneration" they avowed was a conditional title to salvation via engrafting into the church.[53] In the Lord's Supper, the Evangelicals denied any doctrine of eucharistic sacrifice and asserted instead the spiritual presence they claimed to find in the New Testament, in the early Fathers, and in the Book of Common Prayer.[54]

But the last way in which the Evangelicals attempted sacramental restorationism is perhaps the most interesting. What church historians have commonly called the Christian movement divided over how the Scriptures speak on the mode and the purpose of baptism. Most "Christians" ultimately found believers' baptism by immersion to be scriptural.[55] For a virgin church, of course, adult baptism is critical.

The Episcopal Evangelicals, however, lacked a choice between infant and believers' baptism. The Thirty-Nine Articles tied them to infant baptism "as most agreeable with the institution of Christ."[56] Yet at the same time the evangelicals rejected baptismal regeneration on biblical grounds and believed instead that true admission to the church came by personal conversion, by lively faith and repentance, and by a renovation in the heart of the believer. For an infant, godparents could only promise such a future change of heart.

And so the Evangelicals did the best they could. They changed confirmation into the Episcopalian's real renunciation of the world, the flesh, and the devil. Before they would confirm, they usually demanded either personal testimony or signs of conversion. In their parishes the "new birth" became normative.

Inevitably standards varied, but on the whole the ratification of baptismal vows the nineteenth-century Evangelicals demanded of their confirmands was exceptionally strict. Teenage and adult candidates for confirmation would go through a series of scrutinies and long instruction. By the time of the bishop's visit, the classes knew very well the renunciation of the world and its pleasures that confirmation entailed.

That Robert E. Lee was not confirmed until his late thirties has puzzled many biographers. Some have reasoned that Episcopalians in Virginia did not take confirmation seriously, in that they had existed without the rite from 1607 to 1790. Since antebellum Virginia was a bastion of Episcopal Evangelicalism, however, the Episcopal laity of Virginia were taught precisely the opposite view of confirmation. In addition, Lee had been raised under the stern William Meade, who was his wife's cousin and godparent. Thus one might guess that Lee probably knew very well what he was doing when he delayed confirmation.[57]

Hence, in a way that is redolent of the catechumens, the Evangelicals enforced strict rules for membership as a communicant of the Christian church—yet another indication of their restorationist ideology.

A final way in which Evangelicalism displayed restoration ideology involved language and practices. In nomenclature, the Evangelicals consciously tried to use "Bible names for Bible things." They used *table* instead of *altar*; *minister* or *presbyter* instead of *priest*; *ordinances* instead of *sacraments*; and *Lord's Supper* instead of *Eucharist* or *Mass*. They called clergy and laymen *Brother* and often used *Sister* for laywomen.

In addition, the Evangelicals revived early Christian practices. Prayer meetings, extemporaneous prayers, lay prayer leaders, weekday "lectures" (reminiscent of the prophesyings of *The Didache*), foreign missions in keeping with the Great Commission—all came into the Episcopal church from the Evangelical party.

Probably because of their opposition to sacramentalism, the Evangelicals failed to revive weekly Holy Communion, which is biblical. A socioeconomic reason should perhaps be sought for their failure to revive footwashing. A few Evangelicals only seem to have become involved with millennialism.[58]

And even fewer Episcopal Evangelicals seem to have sensed what biblical scholarship has now apparently shown: that the New Testament exhibits a wide diversity of interpretations of Christianity, that even Paul's churches exhibit Catholic as well as Protestant elements, and that if Christians are going to restore the so-called New Testament church, they should consider giving it a very broad roof.[59] Hence the Evangelicals missed a crucial point about the Anglican comprehensiveness that was reemerging in the nineteenth century. A church where Anglo-Catholic, High church, Broad church, and Evangelical interpretations of Christianity coexist might in itself represent a prime example of New Testament restorationism.

"At the time of my entering the ministry," wrote Thomas March Clark of the year 1836, "the growth of the [Episcopal] Church was very much in the Evangelical direction, and it looked as if this party might soon attain a decided ascendancy."[60] But the Evangelicals not only did not win over their church to Edward VI Episcopalianism, they actually died out to the extent that they appeared a surprising curiosity by 1900. Why?

The fading of the vision of the first generations and its crystallization into the opposition Low-church party—"exclusive, intolerant, denunciatory"[61]—had something to do with that failure. So did the departure in 1873 of the Reformed Episcopalians, which placed the Evangelicals very much on the defensive. As the nineteenth century progressed, the bareness of Evangelical worship and architecture also went against the rise of liturgical consciousness among Episcopalians and Protestants in general.[62] Similarly, the teachings of the Evangelicals on worldly amusements appeared increasingly narrow to Episcopalians as the years went on. Even in Evangelical Virginia, much evidence exists that many of the male laity had never supported their clergy on these regulations.[63]

But the principal cause for the decline of the Episcopal Evangelicals seems to be their refusal to come to grips with Darwinism, with the historical-critical method, and with the other new knowledge of their day.[64] Even as criticism undercut their positions, the Evangelicals remained verbal inspirationists, textual infallibilists, wedded to the idea that the Bible not only set forth one consistent theological system, but also that Archbishop Usher had the proper chronology of it. In the words of one of his former students, Joseph Packard (a Hodge-like figure who taught the biblical courses at Virginia Theological Seminary for most of the nineteenth century) "belonged to the pre-Darwinian era, . . . closed his eyes to any indications of . . . composite authorship," and "believed in the historical accuracy of . . . Genesis, . . . Job, and . . . Jonah."[65] Manton Eastburn, who served as bishop of Massachusetts until 1872, boasted that he had not changed his religious views since he was seven years old and refused to read biblical criticism.[66] A Sunday school teacher in an Evangelical parish rejoiced that her students, all under six years of age, "could separately and individually state clearly and explicitly, in theological terms, the entire plan of salvation."[67] The rank and file of the Evangelicals not only did not understand the new knowledge; they were frightened by it. In these matters the future in the Episcopal church belonged to the Broad churchmen and to Anglo-Catholics of the Gore school.[68]

What happened, then, to the Episcopal Evangelicals? By the late nineteenth century, they had divided into three groups: (1) Main-line Liberal Evangelicalism—sometimes called Low churchmen, sometimes called Liberal Evangelicals. These clergy and laity accepted many Broad church positions and carried some of the traditions of the Evangelical movement into the twentieth century;[69] (2) Apocalypticism of the Niagara Conferences type. As recent scholarship has shown, some of the early fundamentalists came from Episcopal Evangelicalism.[70] After the early years of the twentieth century, only isolated Episcopalians of this kind remained; and (3) Reformed Episcopalianism—which steadily declined in the twentieth century and today numbers approximately 5,000 members.[71]

A final reason the Evangelicals declined might be added. Their attempt to evangelicalize the Episcopal church failed, it would appear, because almost from its beginning Anglicanism has been obliged to be a comprehensive church, where the Catholic principle of continuity coexists, often in tension, with the restorationist claims of the Reformation. Thus the Evangelicals represented only one emphasis in the Episcopal church. The year 1811, after all, was also the year of the consecration of John Henry Hobart as bishop of New York. Hobart was also a missionary-minded restorationist, but in his case of High-Church, Patristic-oriented, non–Roman Anglicanism, Hobart thought all Americans would ultimately return to this true church, and he constantly accused the Evangelicals of diluting its exclusive principles.[72]

Moreover, if Hobart was a High churchman who nevertheless shared many Reformation views with the Evangelicals, the Tractarians and Ritualists who began to emerge later in the nineteenth century introduced dress, postures, furnishings, doctrines, and loyalties that were simply antithetic to Evangelicalism. Yet they, too, considered themselves restorationists—in this case, of the medieval Catholic heritage of the Church of England. And in their minds, of course, that heritage was true to the primitive church.[73] Thus the evidence suggests that the Evangelicals ultimately failed to work their will simply because of the nature of Anglicanism.

Episcopal Evangelicalism appears to have been the product of four strands of influence: Anglican Evangelicalism, British Methodism, Puritanism, and the Second Great Awakening. The movement emerged at a time when Episcopalians were a tiny proportion of America's population. The Methodists with their circuit riders and emotional preaching, the Baptists with their democratic polity and critique of infant baptism, and the Christian movement with its sense of restoring the New Testament church were sweeping the nation. Devereux Jarratt was the movement's John the Baptist, but Episcopal Evangelicalism emerged in full force in America only in the second decade of the nineteenth century. In time it won over somewhere between forty and sixty percent of the Episcopal church.

Like other restoration movements, Episcopal Evangelicalism had qualms about ecclesiasticism; but like other schools of Anglicanism, it also stood for historical continuity and liturgical order. It emphasized personal religion over institutionalism and the preached word over the sacraments. As the true entrance to the Christian faith, it favored the heartfelt vows of confirmation over the waters of infant baptism. It tried to make the Episcopal church into the unspotted bride of Christ rather than the forgiving mother of sinners. It had no intention of allowing Anglicanism to be a comprehensive church. Rather, it zealously wished to restore the old paths of what it felt was the true Anglicanism that had existed during the reign of Edward VI. Above all, it must be seen as a return in Anglicanism to the imperishable evangelical strain that, over and over again in Christian history—not simply in the Reformation, but also in the Middle Ages and in the Early Church—has broken out anew.[74]

"I have now, in compliance with the usages of our communion, laid my hands upon you," Bishop Eastburn once declared to a confirmation class at the Church of the Advent in Boston, a parish that had accepted the teachings of the Oxford movement. Eastburn (who thought Rome the Antichrist and who, in the words of an associate, "really believed that the faith which our Lord came to establish upon this earth would die out utterly with the extinction of the Evangelical Party"[75]) had refused in previous years to confirm at the church, for its worship and furnishings included an altar, a cross, golden candlesticks, auricular confession, and genuflection. But a new canon of the Episcopal church had now forced him to confirm, and he spoke to the confirmands with his usual sureness and candor:

> And you have been confirmed. To what extent you comprehend the real nature of the act of dedication, and what instructions you have received respecting it, I do not know. I think it is possible that you have been taught this table is an altar, but it is not so, in as much as no sacrifice has ever been offered here or ever can be. You may have been told by those gentlemen in the rear that they are priests in the Church of God. In any real sense you are as much priests as they are, for we are taught in the New Testament that all the faithful are alike priests in the kingdom of Christ. I made them what they are with a breath, and I can unmake them with a breath. They may have told you that it is your duty to confess your sins to them. You have as much right to insist that they should confess their sins to you. There is but one Being to whom we can go with our transgressions with any hope of being absolved.

And so on and on, and when he had concluded, the Evangelical bishop said, "let us pray," gave the benediction, ended it with "A-men" (not *Ah-men*), and got out of there.[76]

This was the faith the Episcopal Evangelicals thought had once been delivered to the saints.

NOTES

1. William Wilberforce Newton, *Yesterday with the Fathers* (New York: Cochrane Publishing, 1910), 204, 199.

2. G. R. Balleine, *A History of the Evangelical Party in the Church of England* (London: Longmans, Green, 1933), 1.

3. James C. Spalding, "Restitution as a Normative Factor for Puritan Dissent," *Journal of the American Academy of Religion* 44 (March 1976):47ff.

4. John Newton, Augustus Montague Toplady, and Charlotte Elliott, respectively, wrote the hymns. In addition to Balleine, a good study of the Evangelical party is L. E. Elliott-Binns, *The Early Evangelicals* (London: Lutterworth Press, 1953).

5. In his *The Episcopal Church In the United States, 1789–1931* (New York: C. Scribner's Sons, 1951), James T. Addison selects precisely this year as the start of the post-Revolutionary revival of the Protestant Episcopal church.

6. Thomas March Clark, *Reminiscences,* 2d ed. (New York: 1895), 57.

7. *Abiding Values of Evangelicalism* (Philadelphia, 1938), 119–20; cf. 37. For similar assertions, see William Meade, *Reasons for Loving the Episcopal Church* (Philadelphia, 1852), 28. For similar Puritan assertions, see *Abiding Values,* 150.

8. John Johns, *A Memoir of the Life of The Rt. Rev. William Meade, D.D.* (Baltimore, 1867), 527. See also William A. Clebsch, "William Holland Wilmer" (Unpublished S.T.M. thesis, Virginia Theological Seminary, 1951), 59–60.

9. See Charles I. Foster, *An Errand of Mercy* (Chapel Hill: University of North Carolina Press, 1960).

10. See, for example, Devereux Jarratt, *The Life of The Rev. Devereux Jarratt* (New York: Arno Press, 1969), 106, 119; and F. E. Maser and Howard T. Maag, eds., *The Journal of Joseph Pilmore* (Philadelphia: Historical Society of the Philadelphia Annual Conference of the United Methodist Church, 1969), 243–44.

11. See, for example, William Meade, *Old Churches, Ministers and Families of Virginia,* 2 vols. (Baltimore: Genealogical Publishing, 1966), 2:356.

12. See E. Clowes Chorley, *Men and Movements in the American Episcopal Church* (New York: C. Scribner's Sons, 1946), 418–22. Newton, *Yesterday,* 58ff., speaks of the Reformed Episcopalians as the "ultras" and "radicals" of Episcopal Evangelicalism.

13. For an authoritative Evangelical statement on the doctrine of the church, see William H. Wilmer, *The Episcopal Manual,* 3d ed. (Philadelphia, 1841), 39ff.

14. Spalding, "Restitution," 54. John Calvin had the first two marks, and the early English Puritans added the third.

15. For examples of such Evangelical strictness, see Jarratt, *Life,* 7, 23, 30, 42, 54–55, 85, 134; Elizabeth H. Murray, *One Hundred Years Ago* (Philadelphia, 1895), 108ff.; William Meade, *Sermon Delivered at the Consecration of The Right Rev. Stephen Elliott* (Washington, D.C., 1841), 19–20; Johns, *Memoir of Meade,* 278–87; and Clebsch, "William Holland Wilmer," 56ff.

16. Cf. Meade, *Sermon Delivered,* throughout. "No drinking, no gambling, and more of the simple goodness of Jesus," as Francis Scott Key put it; quoted in John Sumner Wood, *The Virginia Bishop* (Richmond: Garrett and Massie, 1961), 143.

17. Both Bishop Henry U. Onderdonk of Pennsylvania and his brother, Bishop Benjamin T. Onderdonk of New York, were High churchmen. The role of party spirit in their suspensions is analyzed in Raymond W. Albright, *A History of the Protestant Episcopal Church* (New York: Macmillan, 1964), 226–42.

18. Samuel S. Hill, Jr., "A Typology of American Restitutionism," *Journal of the American Academy of Religion* 44 (March 1976): 65.

19. See, for example, *Abiding Values,* 145–46. For Meade's views on error, see his *Companion to the Font and the Pulpit* (Washington, D.C., 1846), 54–55.

20. Like Wesley, many of the early Episcopal Evangelicals—especially John Johns—were Patristic scholars. See W. A. R. Goodwin, ed., *History of the Theological Seminary in Virginia and Its Historical Background,* 2 vols. (New York: E. S. Gorham, 1923), 2:3.

21. Typical is Meade's view of creeds in *Reasons for Loving,* 28.

22. Meade, *Reasons for Loving,* 13.

23. *Abiding Values,* 51.

24. G. R. Elton, "The Reformation in England," in *The New Cambridge Modern History: The Reformation,* ed. G. R. Elton (Cambridge: Cambridge University Press, 1965), 2:245.

25. Spalding, "Restitution," 56. See, for example, William Meade, ed., *The Catechisms Usually Styled King Edward's and Dean Nowell's, The Truest Expositions of the Church Catechism and Baptismal Service* . . . (n.p., 1858?), and William Meade, ed., *The Wisdom, Moderation, and Charity of the English Reformers, and of the Fathers of the Protestant Episcopal Church in the United States* (n.p., n.d.).

26. Meade, *Reasons for Loving,* 29–30.

27. A good study is Robert W. Prichard's "Nineteenth Century Episcopal Attitudes on Predestination and Election," *Historical Magazine of the Protestant Episcopal Church* 51 (March 1982): 25–51. A few Evangelicals openly opposed Calvinism, but virtually all allowed a diversity of opinion on four of the Five Points. See Cornelius Walker, *Memoir of Rev. C. W. Andrews, D. D.* (New York, 1877), 196ff.; Goodwin, *History,* 1:163–64, 629–32, 2:3; Chorley, *Men and Movements,* 47; Meade, *Old Churches,* 1:420–21. Moore of Virginia was clearly an Arminian. See J. P. K. Henshaw, *Memoir of the Life of the Rt. Rev. Richard Channing Moore* (Philadelphia, 1843), 207.

28. Greenough White, *A Saint of the Southern Church* (New York, 1897), 122. Cf. Norris S. Barratt, *Outline of the History of Old St. Paul's Church, Philadelphia* (Philadelphia: Colonial Society of Pennsylvania, 1917) 74–75; Goodwin, *History,* 1:351, 2:5.

29. Johns, *Memoir of Meade,* 516–17.

30. Chorley, *Men and Movements,* 48.

31. Jarratt, *Life,* 207; cf. 48–49.

32. White, *Saint,* 159.

33. William Carus, ed., *Memorials of the Right Reverend Charles Pettit McIlvaine,* 2d ed. (London, 1882), 204.

34. George M. Brydon, *Highlights along the Road of the Anglican Church* (Richmond: Virginia Diocesan Library, 1957), 38–39.

35. See, for example, Spalding, "Restitution," 57.

36. Jarratt, *Life,* 89. Cf. Richard Channing Moore's self-description: "My mode of preaching . . . is evangelical; exposing to view the awful degeneracy of man and leading him from every other dependence, to the Lord Jesus Christ for succor and salvation" (see Henshaw, *Memoir of Moore,* 144; cf. 149–50).

37. See, for example, Clark, *Reminiscences,* 102; Jarratt, *Life,* 9; and Heman Dyer, *Records of an Active Life* (New York, 1886), 150.

38. Edward Waylen, *Ecclesiastical Reminiscences of the United States* (London, 1846), 195–96.

39. Henshaw, *Memoir of Moore,* 297, 310–15, 325; Clark, *Reminiscences,* 95.

40. William B. Sprague, *Annals of the American Pulpit,* 9 vols. (New York: Arno Press, 1969), 5:270.

41. Told to the writer by the late George J. Cleaveland, registrar of the Episcopal Diocese of Virginia.

42. Stephen H. Tyng, *Sermons by Rev. Gregory T. Bedell . . . with a Biographical Sketch,* 2 vols. (Philadelphia, 1835) 1:lxxxiii–lxxxiv.

43. Tyng, *Sermons of Bedell,* 1:lxxxv.

44. Newton, *Yesterday,* 32. Cf. Carus, *Memorials of McIlvaine,* 20–30.

45. The story is told in Brewster S. Ford and Harold S. Sniffen, eds., *Up From Independence* (Richmond, VA.: Interdiocesan Bicentennial Committee of the Virginias, 1976).

46. See, for example, Tyng, *Sermons of Bedell,* 1:lxxxi; Jehudi Asmun, *Memoir of the Life and Character of the Rev. Samuel Bacon* (Washington, D.C., 1822), 190; and Carus, *Memorials of McIlvaine,* 93.

47. See Wilmer, *Episcopal Manual,* 3ff; Meade, *Sermon Delivered,* 4ff.; John A. Clark, *A Walk About Zion* (New York, 1849), 78–93; and Joseph Packard, *Recollections of a Long Life* (Washington, D.C.: B. S. Adams, 1902), 177.

48. Jarratt, *Life,* 152; cf. 130.

49. William White, *The Case of the Episcopal Churches in the United States Considered* (Philadelphia, 1783). For the views of Brooks, see Raymond W. Albright, *Focus on Infinity* (New York: Macmillan, 1961), 356ff. Cf. Francis P. Weisenburger, *Ordeal of Faith* (New York: Philosophical Library, 1959), 24, and Newton, *Yesterday,* 194–95.

50. See Meade, *Companion,* 6ff., and Newton, *Yesterday,* 194.

51. Goodwin, *History,* 2:14. For a sketch of Francis M. Whittle, see Goodwin, *History,* 2:9–15.

52. In his *Companion,* Meade declares that the church must go back beyond the views of Cyprian, Ambrose, Tertullian, and other Church Fathers whose views of baptismal regeneration led to such practices as baptizing and giving the Lord's Supper to corpses, as well as to changing baptismal water after each baptism, due to the belief that original sin had defiled it (pp. 54–55).

53. Meade, *Companion,* 8, 11–12, 18–19, 42–43, and elsewhere; Wilmer, *Episcopal Manual,* 124–51. Moore was an exception among the Evangelicals, for he believed in baptismal regeneration; see Henshaw, *Memoir of Moore,* 203ff. Among the "ritualists," William Augustus Muhlenberg did not believe in it; see Anne Ayres, *Live and Work of William Augustus Muhlenberg,* 5th ed. (New York, 1894), 173.

54. Wilmer, *Episcopal Manual,* 161–81; Meade, *Companion,* 14. When Waylen visited St. George's Church in New York on a Communion Sunday in 1838, James Milnor preached against holding "too high or too low" views of the sacrament; see Waylen, *Ecclesiastical Reminiscences,* 183.

55. Winfred E. Garrison, *An American Religious Movement* (St. Louis: Bethany Press, 1966), 57, 74.

56. Article 27. In his *Companion,* Meade sees the failure to present children for baptism as "only the first of a series of harmful neglects which may ultimately lead to a child's ruin" (p. 17).

57. For typical Evangelical discussions of confirmation, see Wilmer, *Episcopal Manual,* 152–60; Carus, *Memorials of McIlvaine,* 144–45, 195; and Meade, *Baptismal Vows and Worldly Amusements* (New York, 1858). For questions about Lee's confirmation, see Margaret Sanborn, *Robert E. Lee: A Portrait* (Philadelphia: Lippincott, 1966), 226; and Marshall W. Fishwick, "Robert E. Lee: Churchman," *Historical Magazine of the Protestant Episcopal Church* 30 (December 1961): 251–65.

58. See Ernest R. Sandeen, *The Roots of Fundamentalism* (Chicago: University of Chicago Press, 1970), 55–56, 147–52 (cf. 8, 25, 146); and George M. Marsden, *Fundamentalism and American Culture* (New York: Oxford University Press, 1980), 61, 82.

59. Typical is Ernst Käsemann, *New Testament Questions of Today* (Philadelphia: Fortress Press, 1969).

60. Clark, *Reminiscences,* 57.

61. White, *Saint,* 73. Cf. Phillips Brooks's description of Eastburn in Alexander V. G. Allen, *Life and Letters of Phillips Brooks,* 3 vols. (New York: E. P. Dutton, 1901), 2:202–3.

62. See, for example, Newton, *Yesterday,* 191–92, 199.

63. A good summary of the conflict between Evangelical clergy and laity on worldly amusements and discipline can be found in Johns, *Memoir of Meade,* 277–88.

64. See, for example, Newton, *Yesterday,* 164, 189–90, and elsewhere.

65. Carl E. Grammer, in Goodwin, *History,* 1:575.

66. Chorley, *Men and Movements,* 48–49; Henry Codman Potter, *Reminiscences of Bishops and Archbishops* (New York: G. P. Putnam's Sons, 1906), 64–65. Cf. Allen, *Life and Letters of Brooks,* 202–3.

67. Newton, *Yesterday,* 191.

68. For an insightful analysis of the reasons for the collapse of the Evangelical party, see Newton, *Yesterday,* 189ff. Newton himself was an Evangelical who became a Broad churchman.

69. See Alexander C. Zabriskie, ed., *Anglican Evangelicalism* (Philadelphia: Church Historical Society, 1943).

70. See Sandeen, *Roots of Fundamentalism,* 55–56, 147–52 (cf. 8, 25, 146); and Marsden, *Fundamentalism,* 61, 82.

71. For a modern study of the Reformed Episcopal schism, see Paul A. Carter, *The Spiritual Crisis of the Gilded Age* (DeKalb, IL: Northern Illinois University Press, 1971), 179ff.

72. See John F. Schroeder, *Memorial of Bishop Hobart* (New York, 1831); and John McVickar, *The Early Life and Professional Years of Bishop Hobart* (Oxford, 1838).

73. Despite its defects, the best single study of Anglo-Catholic history and theology in America is George E. DeMille, *The Catholic Movement in the American Episcopal Church,* 2d ed. (Philadelphia: Church Historical Society, 1950).

74. Powell Mills Dawley, *Chapters in Church History* (New York: National Council, Protestant Episcopal Church, 1950), 129.

75. Newton, *Yesterday,* 150–51.

76. Potter, *Bishops,* 101–2. Harry Croswell, *A Memoir of the Late Rev. William Croswell, D.D.* (New York, 1853), 357 ff., details the conflict between Eastburn and the parish.

11

Perplexity Over
a Protean Principle:
A Response

HENRY WARNER BOWDEN

A NY respondent to such excellent papers as these must consider it
part of his task to draw their separate strengths together. Tackling
the problem of correlation, then, and with due regard for press of time,
let me try to mention a few common points that recur. And let me
sharpen our focus a bit further by saying that I am trying to approach
the topic of restorationism as a student of religious phenomena, not
as a participant in one of its many channels. How can an analyst rather
than an advocate respond in ways that help put this topic in perspective
and give it some definition?

In considering perspectives that might enable historians to come to
grips with "the restoration ideal," we could do worse than to begin
with the old standby questions drilled into newspaper reporters: who,
what, when, where, and why. So perhaps I can best serve you by
pondering aloud some of the perplexities involved in correlating answers to these basic questions. Of the five, I take two as given. The
when and where are largely set by the parameters of the conference at
which these papers were delivered. The when is primarily nineteenth
century, and the where is America—although chronological and geo-
graphical variance make these categories problematic too. For our purposes, however, it is more important to focus on the other three questions, who, what, and why—in that order.

Who. Our authors have approached their separate topics with mutual caution, reminding us that it is difficult to make satisfactory generalizations or accurate classifications among such large groups of people. But at the same time they have also supplied admirable capsule

statements of what these different groups shared. One can catch glimmers of a common identity among them: among those who "are in search of the true church on the basis of what they find in the Bible and in the familiar traditions that they believe to be soundly, biblically based" (Handy); among those dedicated to "ideals[,] . . . even when tarnished by . . . entropy . . . , [that] still retain a regenerative power . . . to spark off new insights and new vitalities . . . [among those] who look beyond old formulae to their still-living powers of refreshment" (Outler); and among those claiming "to know what original Christianity is and [who try] to reproduce it in the present" (Holmes).

As articulations of a general principle, these descriptions help demarcate a basic orientation. More specifically, though, who actually used restorationism as a guideline to the religious work they pursued? Mr. Outler includes Wesley, Asbury, Bangs, Abbey, and Watson in the mainstream of Methodist evangelical primitivists who stressed similarities between their mission and the apostolic church; Mr. Handy starts in the early 1600s and moves through the Philadelphia Baptist Association to a succinct overview of such particulars as Parker and Graves, the Black Rock Church of Baltimore and the Baptist Missionary Association of America; Mr. Holmes locates scores of individuals from clergy like Meade and McIlvaine to laypersons like Key and Elliott who constituted a far-flung party of Episcopal Evangelicals.

So far, so good, but notice too that each author alludes to others—some of them diametrically opposed to those deliberately emphasized—who laid claim to the same general principle embraced by those occupying center stage. Among those in the wings are Methodist cadres who explored the frontiers of liberal theology, who worked to spread the Social Gospel, and who followed the austere allurements of Holiness and pentecostalism. Notice that among Anglicans John Henry Hobart also claimed the role of restorationist while defending High Church standards in sacraments and soteriology, as did Tractarians and Ritualists. When we come to the Baptists, perhaps all we need to do is say that, if veterans like Piepkorn and Melton had trouble identifying restorationists, we less specialized observers need not chafe unduly at the confusion over specifically whom we are talking about.

What do these rich data tell us about who restorationists were? For serious students of religion, setting some limits to this complex subject and its personae is about as hard as nailing jelly to a wall. Judging from the evidence before us, I suggest that almost anyone could claim "the restoration ideal" as their guiding principle. The iceberg's tip scanned herein shows moreover that virtually everyone did claim it, too. There is no way to decide, outside given circles of convictions, which people and programs are legitimate and which spurious. The restorationist-primitivist-evangelical mantle rests on anyone who wants to wear it, and it fits the shoulders of protagonists and antagonists alike with indifferent propriety. So historians have a difficult time identifying restorationists by looking at those who appropriated the term for themselves.

What. Perhaps if we take only those persons highlighted in these essays and confine ourselves to what they said about restorationism, then we might understand it better. Tangible aspects of "the restoration ideal" always have form and content, finding outlet as institutions and ideas. Let us review them briefly in search of at least some common ground, if not unanimity, on questions of faith and order.

Ecclesiastical forms include among many other things an ordained ministry, organized procedures, and programs for outreach. The groups under study agreed that ministers were needed, but they disagreed on origins and legitimacy. Methodists and Episcopalians espoused bishops as a key element in an effective ministry. Primitivism and expediency led Methodists to sanction an *ex nihilo* episcopacy and then to add a flow chart of conferences that knit leaders into a highly structured system. Episcopalians respected the historic episcopate with attendant ordination for subordinate offices. But against these churchmen who felt congruent with apostolic patterns we find Baptists who never acknowledged bishops as mandatory or even legitimate on biblical grounds or based on the wisdom of practical experience. Methodists and Episcopal Evangelicals stressed lay participation, but many Baptists did away with ordained clergy altogether in the name of restoring biblical simplicity. So questions about ministerial status remain unsettled amid these intramural attitudes regarding who embodied the restored ideal of Christian leadership.

Putting aside the issue of clerical preference, Methodists and Episcopalians clearly favored solid organizational structures in their respective spheres. Circuit riders functioned in a network of conferences ranging from local to general; Evangelical priests maintained institutional loyalty within a traditionalism that did not look favorably on Bishop Cummins's schismatic Reformed Episcopalians in 1873. Baptists, on the other hand, were noteworthy for frequent opposition to associational efforts beyond the local congregation. Mr. Handy's paper fairly bulges with examples of those who resisted centralizing tendencies in the name of biblical precepts. Ironically enough, many of those anticonvention factions went on to form their own associations and thereafter gave rise to succeeding generations of reformers who raised again the standard of local autonomy. Whether the question was a central one such as a national coordinating body or incidental ones regarding theological seminaries, tract societies, or Sunday schools, it seems there was considerable disparity over the extent of proper organization.

We are forced to admit that a general principle like scriptural precedent or apostolic example offered no guideline for understanding what kind of ecclesiastical order restorationists wanted to support. Apparently the only way to resolve the matter was for different protagonists to prove the superiority of their view by applying a pragmatic test. Mr. Outler noted that "since it seemed to work so well . . . the Methodists easily persuaded themselves that they had come upon the most adequate contemporary analog to the apostolic church." But pragmatism could be persuasive for Baptist convictions too, and ecclesiastical success endorsed as easily their particular ecclesiological ideas. Episcopal growth must have been large enough to confirm proper polity for them as well and to promise bigger numbers if people worked just a little harder.

All three authors emphasize missions or a strong sense of evangelical outreach as a driving force in primitive Christianity and in latter-day attempts to recapture it. Even here, though, some Baptist primitivists opposed missions on principle; others were antimissionary if associations rather than local churches sustained them. This missionary element is worth remembering, and we will return to it in asking about the content of different gospels being preached. But before we leave the category of institutional arrangement, let us notice that many Methodists and Episcopalians were ecumenically minded. They agreed that the true church is a spiritual one, with no single denomination restricting apostolic sanctity to its particular precinct. As pan-Christian believers envisioning a restored faith in one Lord, they recognized that all those converted to the love of Christ held membership in the City of God. It is worth quoting Bangs again in this regard who said "it is possible to cleave to our own institutions and yet exercise a catholic spirit toward all who love our Lord Jesus Christ in sincerity." Many Baptists were open-minded, too, but some of Mr. Handy's exponents voiced the opinion that theirs were the only churches to reinstate first-century prototypes. So "the restoration ideal" was apparently not enough to dampen parochialism because some advocates set themselves apart, saying "they alone hold, and have alone ever held, and preserved the doctrine of the gospel in all ages since the ascension of Christ."

What was that doctrine, that gospel? In terms of theological systems, deferring the question of whether Americans preserved much capacity for systematic theology in the nineteenth century, restorationist preachers advocated two separate doctrinal emphases. Holmes points to strong Calvinist inclinations among Episcopalians who believed they had restored the original theology of Christianity. Outler alludes to Methodists who supported doctrines usually termed Arminian. Handy rings changes on both, mentioning Particular Baptists who advocated Calvinist principles and General Baptists whose views allowed for freer grace. Some thought the Apostles' Creed sufficed to express content of the faith. Others held out for christocentric trinitarianism. Still more opposed all creeds and confessions, Calvinist or otherwise, because doctrinal formulations that went beyond biblical language seemed pernicious. While some restorationists accepted minimal ideological forms, others resisted them as obstacles to recapturing the sound and simple beliefs of the Fathers.

Many people considered formal expressions of valid faith to be superfluous because the source of proper beliefs was available to everyone. The Bible served as rallying point for all restorationists—no matter what their particular brand of ministry, church organization, attitude about missions, or theological inclination. Biblical precepts were the authoritative standard for everyone. But what did the Bible really say? It is not enough for historians to indicate that restorationists took their stand on the New Testament record as their norm and standard for Christian faith and practice (Holmes); or that the authority of the Bible was especially important for primitivists (Handy). The disconcerting fact is that all these people squabbled between and among themselves over authoritative interpretations of Scripture on its controverted points (Outler). Some decided that biblical silence meant proscription; others thought that lack of canonical directives granted permission to follow common sense and sincere conscience. But approaches to and derivations from a shared Bible never yielded what we might call a unified platform. It seems quite evident that restorationists-primitivists-evangelicals in Europe and the United States did not come close to a common exegesis of holy writ.

The method most people used to derive meaning from the sacred page appears again to have been a pragmatic one. Interpreters usually relied on their own experience or on that of significant voices in their respective communities as litmus paper for textual analysis. Lessons taught by practical testing often turned out to confirm the teaching thought to have been originally recorded in biblical times. This kind of exegesis has certainly been congruent with American emphases on revivalism, pragmatic activism, and personal experience as they have flourished through most of our nation's past. But interpretive permissiveness coupled with numerical success has given priority to both intuition and census figures as guidelines for reading the Bible. This kind of fixation reminds one of George Tyrell's observation about New Testament scholars of last century who limited their view of Jesus to an incarnation of their own ideals. They could find only a German in the Jew, he said, a professor in the prophet, the nineteenth century in the first. The Christ identified by such a narrow search, looking down through centuries of Catholic darkness, produced only the reflection of a Protestant face at the bottom of a deep well. This appears to be the case with restorationists, too. It is a natural and certainly a time-honored phenomenon for people to see their acculturated values confirmed in the Bible. But we despair of finding a correlative basis when so many different people justified their varying principles by appealing to Scripture.

A survey of this evidence forces us to say that "the restoration ideal" is truly a protean concept. The meaning of the term is relative to different people who appropriate it, to what they say it means, and to what activities they pursue under its aegis. Based on historical usage of institutional, doctrinal and biblical categories, there is no meaning intrinsic to the title, and we can find no common agreement on any set of organizational forms or ideas.

So what in the last analysis can we say about this ideal invoked by so many and evocative of such various meanings? It was simply and magnificently that: an idea, prompting old men to dream dreams and young men to see visions. It was an energizing call to further reformation, a hope for return "to that imperishable evangelical strain that over and over again in Christian history . . . has broken out anew" (Holmes). It has appealed to the will and conscience of believers to pursue for themselves "the ideal of apostolic Christianity repristinated in later ages, less by replication than by refreshment" (Outler). Such an ideal was additionally powerful as a symbol that pointed beyond itself to a metaphysical reality, the spiritual gathering into one body of new creatures in Christ. So historians can see that "the restoration ideal" was not just a pious platitude that masked human struggles for power and influence. It was, for all its vagueness and imprecision, a creative conception that pointed to the essence of the true church (variously perceived) "within which all who are named, saved, and sanctified by the grace of our Lord Jesus Christ are one in the Spirit" (Outler).

Why. Let us consider briefly why so many people have employed this conception over such a long period of time. It seems to me that restorationism has been popular among many different groups because it has both positive and negative connotations. We seem to hear this ideal invoked most often on the negative side, and it has proved to be a marvelous weapon indeed for criticism and reform. Superficial observers could easily conclude that primitivist standards are merely a convenient pretext for disgruntled factions to use in opposing whatever they happen to find offensive. But restorationist ideals also serve a positive function by unifying followers once reformed. Reinstated Gospel standards become a platform for cohesion, and while perhaps appearing second in historical sequences, they are by no means secondary in importance. So the positive and negative aspects of restorationism are both important, and the most successful restorationist programs are those able to keep both of these features at work concurrently.

If one were to hazard additional interpretations of why restorationism has exerted such appeal in western history, the following observations might be pertinent. The ideal is a legitimating principle. If one wants to attack something perceived as corruption and purge it from the body of believers, then appeals to earlier rectitude can justify action. If one wants to hold the faithful to efficacious patterns, then an appeal to venerable precedent can enjoin conformity and cooperation. Legitimation accompanies either using a scalpel to lance infection or using sutures to bind up wounds for healing. Whether the outcome of action is rupture or reunion, people carry with them the comforting notion that they are right in acting the way they do. And the satisfaction of *being right* has often been more important in church history than size or recent pedigree.

Restorationism has also appealed to people because it is grand. It allows leaders and followers to settle for impressive-sounding generalities instead of laboring over serious questions of identity and behavior. The ideal offers utopian and possibly even millennial expectations that frequently obscure needs to feed the hungry and visit the sick in God's name. So there is an element of escapism that could explain some types of primitivism where ecclesiastical architects have opted for glittering superficialities instead of the stern task of living the Gospel.

Let me end by touching lightly on one more interpretation, making only a tentative suggestion without intending any well-rounded viewpoint as an alternative: restorationism could appeal to many because it is ahistorical. The ideal of repristinating, refreshing, returning to thoughts and behavior removed from us by two thousand years perpetuates the dream that we can escape historical conditioning. It encourages people to believe that they can, by taking thought, add a cubit to their stature or, by making an effort, determine their nature and destiny. This assumed superiority of will to context preserves an illusion of freedom that has sustained extravagant expectations among people in every epoch. As a critical historian I am more impressed with the limitations that circumstances impose on people—not the least of which are the restricted and biased viewpoints people have in trying to understand the past they wish to emulate. But for all the difficulties involved in this ideal, it is not less effective in stimulating Christian practice despite its unrealistic wish to accomplish the impossible.

PART FOUR

Indigenous American Traditions

12

The Reality of the Restoration
and the Restoration Ideal
in the Mormon Tradition

JAN SHIPPS

THE concept of restoration can be found in the Judeo-Christian scriptural materials from the biblical story's first major turning point, when Eve and Adam were thrust from the garden, to its last, when John the Apostle was banished to the isle of Patmos and there beheld a series of apocalyptic visions. What may properly be described as a restoration motif can be identified in the different parts of the Old Testament, as well as in the New Testament, although its presentation takes different forms. It is especially evident in the Psalms and in the post–exilic materials. Again and again Hebrew psalmists and prophets speak of returning to a paradisiacal situation wherein the earth will be renewed, the blind will see, the lame will leap for joy, hunger will be satisfied, righteousness and truth will prevail, and the covenant between God and his people will be reinvested with meaning. In addition to restoration references of a general character, the Old Testament includes restoration passages that are very specific. Following the division of Israel into northern and southern kingdoms, and after the desolation of Jerusalem, the destruction of the temple, and the Babylonian captivity, Isaiah, Jeremiah, Ezekiel, and other prophetic figures predict the reunion of Jacob's family through an in-gathering of the members of the scattered tribes. With the "whole body of Israel" restored, they look forward to the restoration of the Kingdom of God that would include rebuilding both the city of Jerusalem and the temple, restoring them to the glory they had possessed in King Solomon's day.

In the New Testament, itself the canonized story of a restoration movement, the Old Testament's generalized restoration motif is reflected in the various Gospel accounts that picture Jesus feeding the hungry, healing the sick, making the lame man "take up his bed and walk," and causing the blind to see. Although his followers believed that Jesus was the son of a virgin, that he was Immanuel, whose coming the prophet Isaiah had foretold, the crucifixion frustrated further fulfillment of specific restoration prophecy having to do with the Messiah's bringing about the restoration of a civic Kingdom of God. The cross, signifying the crucifixion, became the symbol of a new covenant that brought Gentiles as well as Jews into a covenantal relationship with the divine. As is detailed in the Acts of the Apostles, the apostolic church became the guardian of the social reality of the new covenant. The concept of the Kingdom of God as a precise place in space and time gave way to the "gospel of the Kingdom of God" and the idea that "the kingdom of God is within you," that is, within the Christian community and by extension within individual Christians. Yet the enormous appeal and continuing power of restoration promises that admit interpretations of great specificity are clearly indicated by the inclusion of the Book of Revelation at the end of the New Testament canon.

Considering the emphasis on restoration found in the Bible—obvious even from the foregoing barebones review—it is not surprising that so many movements within the modern history of the Judeo-Christian tradition have a restorationist base. (In the same vein, in view of its firm rooting in the Judeo-Christian tradition, it is not surprising that the United States has become the primary political agent for the "redemption of Zion" since the close of World War II.)

It is somewhat surprising, however, that so many Christians have understood restoration to be virtually synonymous with New Testament primitivism. Whether it represents little more than a vague longing, a nostalgia for living in Christianity's golden age, or whether it represents a rigorous, full-scale, good-faith effort to restore "the essentials of primitive Christianity" in an institutional context, the search for the restoration *essence* (as it would be stated in Platonic terms) has been concentrated on the apostolic era.

Mormonism is a conspicuous departure from this pattern. Without question the biblical account of the church during the apostolic age was important to seekers who followed the Mormon prophet. But unlike the restorationist understandings of the Campbellite, Seventh-day Baptist, and other American primitivist movements, Mormonism's understanding of itself as a restoration movement began with the belief that the Church of Jesus Christ was removed from the earth when direct communication between divinity and humanity ceased at the end of the apostolic age. Furthermore, Mormonism's understanding of itself as *the* (not "a") restoration proceeded from the assumption that restoration could and would come about when *and only when* direct communication between humanity and divinity was reopened. This is to say that before restoration could occur, one who could speak for God, a prophet, would have to come forth.

The belief that Joseph Smith, Jr., was such a person and that through him restoration was effected arises from an extraordinary set of theological claims that together establish for Mormons *an unbroken line of fulfilled prophecy* from Isaiah, Ezekiel, and Daniel, through Revelation to Joseph Smith and beyond. Whereas from outside the faith these claims may appear as "a silly mess of stuff"—the phrase is from early Mormon leader Parley Pratt—the Mormon conviction that they were directly connected to both Old and New Testament restoration promises, plus the fact that these claims are internally consistent, proved to be a motive force powerful enough to bring a new religious tradition into being.[1]

The main elements of the early Mormon story are very familiar. In addition to the prophet's autobiographical statement, which has been canonized, many historical narratives outline Joseph Smith's career. They describe a First Vision in which the future prophet saw God and Jesus as distinct personages and learned from them that all the churches then existing were false and that he would be the agent of the restoration of the true church. These accounts tell of Smith's finding a set of golden plates on which an ancient record was engraved in "reformed Egyptian;" they tell about his "translating" this record to bring the Book of Mormon forth and describe the establishing of the Church of Jesus Christ. Fundamentally historical rather than theological in nature, these accounts of the beginnings of Mormonism go on to picture Smith leading the Latter-day Saints (LDS) forward into a "new dispensation of the fulness of times."[2] But there is no systematic theological statement on the order of an LDS *Summa Theologica* that organizes and clarifies the theological claims supporting the Mormon restoration.[3]

The Book of Mormon and Smith's early revelations (many of which were published as *A Book of Commandments* in 1835) provided the basis for the Mormon theological system, but Mormon beliefs were elaborated and interpreted in other writings of Joseph Smith, in early Mormon pamphlets, and in LDS sermons and addresses. Of the latter, the most significant were delivered by an important group of LDS leaders between 1847 and 1890. Recorded by scribes, the discourses of Brigham Young, John Taylor, Wilford Woodruff, Lorenzo Snow,

Orson and Parley Pratt, Daniel H. Wells, George Q. Cannon, Joseph F. Smith, and at least a dozen others were published serially in England and distributed in the United States.[4] The members of this group were such influential interpreters of the Mormon belief system that they may well be described as the church fathers of Mormonism.

The intent of this essay is gathering Mormon theological claims from these diverse places, organizing them, relating them to restoration promises found in biblical materials and in the LDS canon of Scripture, and suggesting their impact on Latter-day Saint history.

Before proceeding to that task, however, it is important to take up the matter of the first Mormon prophet's own conception of his role in the Mormon restoration. This is an especially significant issue in view of the results of recent research which is providing direct evidence to establish beyond dispute conclusions that an impressive body of less direct evidence has long suggested.[5] Joseph Smith, his father, and possibly one or two of his brothers were practitioners of folk magic.[6] The future prophet had been actively involved in the practice of using seer stones or "peepstones" as a means of "divining" the location of lost treasures before 1827, when he reported finding a cache of gold plates whose surfaces were covered with engravings and some "ancient seers" known as the "Urim and Thummim." Connecting this report with Smith's earlier divining ventures, many of the inhabitants of the area of western New York where he lived dismissed his prophetic claims and continued to regard him as a folk magician.

The future prophet could very well have been employing the magic arts when he sought treasure in the Hill Cumorah, where he said the plates were found. But since religion and magic were not mutually exclusive in either European or American folk culture,[7] his having been involved in folk magic does not indicate that psychobiographer Fawn M. Brodie was necessarily correct in describing Joseph Smith as a village scryer who engaged in conscious deception.[8] It is entirely possible that rather than being quite aware that he was creating a work of fiction that he afterward came to accept as true, Smith became convinced as the text of the Book of Mormon started to take shape that the words he dictated to his scribe came from the "sealed book" to which Isaiah referred in chapter 29.

Whether this young New York farmer actually found metal plates or whether he worked from plates that he could only see with "spiritual eyes," the future prophet prepared a document containing characters copied off the plates some of which he said he translated "by means of the Urim and Thummim."[9] This he gave to his scribe, Martin

Harris, so that it could be taken to the East for examination by eminent linguists of the day.

In his account of the beginnings of Mormonism written in 1838, Smith reported that Harris returned from visiting Columbia College saying that he had given the paper to a great authority, Professor Charles Anthon, but that Anthon could not read the hieroglyphics on the page. Determining exactly when Smith started to identify himself as the unlearned one to whom a sealed book was delivered is difficult.[10] Yet it stands to reason that Smith recognized the significance of Isaiah 29 when he was dictating the section of the Book of Mormon known as 2 Nephi.

Although the biblical account says only that the unlearned man protested that he was not learned and that the Lord promised to do "a marvelous work and a wonder," a corresponding passage in Smith's "gold bible" is more informative. Chapter 27 of 2 Nephi includes much of the content and even much of the actual wording of Isaiah 29. But it is more explicit about the connection between the unlearned man and the marvelous work, making clear that the unlearned would "read the words which I [the Lord] shall give unto thee."

A 1980 work by Lutheran minister Robert Hullinger, *Mormon Answer to Skepticism: Why Joseph Smith Wrote the Book of Mormon,* made an elaborate and sustained argument that Martin Harris's journey was undertaken by design, that Smith sent him to the East to show the characters presumably copied from the plates to highly respected scholars of the day because their failure to read the document would mean that the Isaiah 29 prophecy was being fulfilled.[11] Hullinger believes, in accordance with Fawn Brodie, that the episode was deliberately set up, as it were, to make Smith's book more appealing by establishing a clear connection between the Book of Mormon and the Bible. Although Hullinger and Brodie differ on the matter of Smith's motive—he believes that the Book of Mormon was written to combat skepticism, whereas she apparently thought that the project was initially a mercenary enterprise—they use similar circumstantial evidence to make their cases. But even if Hullinger and Brodie are right, even if Harris was sent to the East so that Smith could claim that he was the unlearned man who could read what the learned could not, the only available primary source materials—writing in Smith's own hand and the manuscript of a history of these early years written by the prophet's mother—give absolutely no indication that Smith ever doubted that he was the person to whom the ancient prophet made reference. The prophet Joseph believed that this was an incident in which prophecy had been fulfilled and those who followed him concurred.

The first chapter of one of the earliest and most often reprinted LDS proselyting tracts, *A Voice of Warning and Instruction to All People,* is a good example of the significance of this linkage with the Bible. The author, Parley P. Pratt, ranged all across the Old and New Testaments citing example after example of fulfilled prophecy. His intent was to show that "the predictions of the Prophets can be clearly understood, as much so as the almanac when it foretells an eclipse." Moreover, he said, quoting 2 Peter 1:20 as his authority, "no prophecy of the Scripture is of any private interpretation;" prophecies have been and will be *literally* fulfilled. To emphasize the importance of this message, Pratt placed the motto "What is Prophecy but History reversed?" at the head of the *Voice of Warning*'s second chapter, "On the Fulfillment of Prophecy Yet Future." It is a motto that could have stood as well at the head of many of the early accounts that the Latter-day Saints wrote telling their own stories.[12] Such works show that the concept of a literal fulfillment of prophecy was, to borrow a phrase from *A Voice of Warning,* the "definite rule of interpretation" used by the Saints, both in reading Scripture and in trying to comprehend the meaning of their own individual and corporate lives.

A description of the combination of theological elements that serve as a foundation for the Mormon restoration will illustrate the significance to LDS theology of this same "definite rule of interpretation." A caveat is in order, however. In reading this description of the claims supporting the Mormon restoration, one should remember that the various LDS interpretations of events as prophecy fulfilled were not introduced sequentially. Nor were all such interpretations regarded as equally important by the early Saints. Moreover, the elaborate inter-related set of fulfilled prophecy claims are not emphasized in modern Mormonism in the same way they were emphasized in the nineteenth century. The fundamental import of assertions that prophecy had recently been fulfilled and that it continues to be fulfilled was the reassuring message that "the heavens are no longer brass," that direct communication between divinity and humanity had been reopened.

Since the late 1870s and early 1880s, that message has increasingly been communicated to Latter-day Saints through the First Vision story, an account of a theophany in which God and Jesus appeared to fourteen-year-old Joseph Smith in the spring of 1820 in the spot now known as the Sacred Grove.[13] But this episode was apparently not often described during the period of Mormon beginnings; the message that

God was starting to speak again first appeared in Mormonism in very specific claims about fulfilled prophecy.

Identification of Joseph Smith as Isaiah's unlearned man set the stage for the Mormon restoration. The Book of Mormon was identified as the "marvelous work and a wonder" foretold in verse 14 of Isaiah 29. "And in that day," verse 18 of the same chapter reads, the deaf shall "hear the words of the book and the eyes of the blind" shall be opened. "The meek also shall increase their joy in the Lord and the poor among men shall rejoice in the holy one of Israel," verse 19 says, conjuring up one of the many generalized restoration pictures found in the Old Testament materials. But exactly what connection could be established between the coming forth of the book that the learned could not read and the opening of the LDS restoration? The fulfillment of a second prophecy was more specific.

Almost nowhere in the Old Testament is there a more dramatic rendering of the coming restoration of Israel than that found in Ezekiel 37. The hand of the Lord set the prophet down in the valley of dry bones and caused him to prophesy, whereupon the bones were resurrected into the whole house of Israel. Then the word of the Lord came again, instructing the prophet to write [a history] for the "stick of Judah" and another history "for Joseph, the stick of Ephraim." When that was done, the Lord would take the two sticks and "make them one stick" and one nation in his hand. Two passages in the Book of Mormon relate Smith's "gold bible," as his contemporaries called it, to Ezekiel's prophecy. The first, a part of a great vision given to Nephi of the grand sweep of history up to the early nineteenth century, tells of a time when the history of the Hebrew peoples who had come to the New World before the Babylonian captivity would be joined to the "record of the Jews." The other, from 2 Nephi 3:12, says that "the fruit of [the loins of Joseph] shall write"—a clear reference to Joseph Smith—"and the fruit of the loins of Judah shall write" and these writings "shall grow together."

By themselves, these two passages might not have been strong enough to support an interpretation of the Book of Mormon as fulfillment of Ezekiel 37. But other evidence attests to the prominence Mormons gave to this connection during the years when Mormonism was coming into being and when the theological tenets that would undergird the Mormon community were being put in place. In August of 1830, a revelation given through Joseph Smith spoke of Moroni, the angel, as the one "to whom I [the Lord] committed the keys of the record of the stick of Ephraim."[14] In addition, early broadsides advertising the

Book of Mormon described the work as "the stick of Joseph taken from the hand of Ephraim."[15] The message being transmitted ran as follows: because the Book of Mormon was "the stick of Ephraim," its coming forth signaled the beginning of the restoration of Zion.

An examination of references to the new dispensation and the restoration, cited in the index to the sermons delivered by the aforementioned LDS church fathers and published in the *Journal of Discourses,* further indicates how the Book of Mormon was linked to the Bible and how its coming forth was presented as the first step in the restoration. Besides citing Isaiah 29 and Ezekiel 37, these LDS leaders sometimes referred to a third Old Testament passage, "Truth shall spring out of the earth, and righteousness shall look down from heaven," to prove that the Book of Mormon, translated as it was said to have been from gold plates found in the ground, was a fulfillment of prophecy.[16] But of all the biblical passages that they used to make this point, these leaders most often cited a passage from the Revelation of St. John to associate the coming forth of the Book of Mormon and the opening of the final dispensation and the beginning of the restoration. The same August 1830 revelation (*Doctrine and Covenants* 27) that made reference to Moroni's possession of the keys to the record of the stick of Ephraim also indicated that the Book of Mormon contained "the fulness of the everlasting gospel." This phrase directed the attention of early Mormons to Revelation 14:6, and a positive identification was quickly made. The heavenly being that led Smith to the Hill Cumorah was none other, the Mormons came to believe, than the angel that flew "in the midst of heaven having the everlasting gospel to preach unto them that dwell on the earth," and this specific claim was made repeatedly in nineteenth-century LDS sermons and gospel tracts.[17]

The attention that LDS speakers directed to this reference from the Book of Revelation brought the Saints close to the many other American Christians of their day who were mightily concerned about the second coming of Christ and the inauguration of the millennium. Yet it was a proximity more apparent than real. Accepting the Book of Mormon as scriptural fulfillment of Old as well as New Testament prophecy set the Saints on a path that would separate them from other forms of Christianity on the basis of doctrine, as well as from the more obvious perspectives of marriage practice (polygamy), politics, economics, and, in time, geography.

The early Saints also applied literal fulfillment as the definite rule of interpretation to other Mormon Scriptures. Recognizing the Book of Mormon as the "translation" of "an account written by the hand of Mormon upon plates" meant recognizing, in turn, that in the day when the writings of the fruit of the loins of Joseph and Judah "grew together," God would raise up a "choice seer," whose name like that of his father would be Joseph. He would be one who would be mighty among the people, who would "do much good both in word and in deed," who would "work mighty wonders" and bring to pass the restoration of Israel.[18] As a result, his followers not only allowed Joseph Smith, *Junior,* to lead them; they expected him to prophesy, to speak for God. In their eyes this was a sure sign that the Gospel was restored.

Given this Book of Mormon prophecy, the fact that "thus saith the Lord" was the form of address that Smith used in calling his father, his brother Hyrum, Oliver Cowdery, and others into God's service was reassuring.[19] It meant that the heavens were opened, that prophecy was fulfilled then and there, not that it would be fulfilled in some far distant future. The restorations of the ancient priesthoods of Aaron and Melchizedek that Joseph announced were likewise reassuring; they fit clearly into the category of "mighty wonders" that were inaugurating the restoration. Moreover, that this was a restoration of something more than the so-called primitive church was made crystal clear when revelation formally authorized the authority of the Mormon leader. On 6 April 1830, the day when the Church of Jesus Christ was formally reorganized, revelation designated Smith as seer, prophet, and translator, as well as apostle of Jesus Christ and elder of the church.[20] The lack of a carefully drawn distinction between forms of authority drawn from the Old and New Testaments (and from the Book of Mormon) is an early signal that when the Mormon restoration was fully in place, it would be nothing less than the "restoration of all things."[21]

As momentous to Smith's followers as were the restoration of the ancient priesthood and the reorganization of the church, it is likely that the fulfillment of two prophesies uttered by Smith in September 1830 were of greater consequence in turning the Mormon restoration into a literal actual living reality. One of these, now numbered section 27 in the LDS *Book of Doctrine and Covenants,* is a revelation saying that the hour approached when the Lord would come "to drink the fruit of the vine" with his Saints on earth. With him would come Elias and Elijah, and Jacob, Isaac, and Abraham, plus John the Baptist and Peter, James, and John. To Elias, the revelation said, had been committed "the keys of bringing to pass the restoration of all things, spoken by the mouth of all the holy prophets since the world began." To Elijah, continued the revelation, had been committed "the keys of the power of turning the hearts of the fathers to the children and the hearts of the children to the fathers." The second significant prophecy given through Joseph Smith in that same month was a revelation that dealt with the gathering of the Saints and, using the imagery of John's revelation, prophesied the end of time.

Fulfillment of these prophecies came in reverse order. Indeed the gathering of the Latter-day Saints started on the morrow of Smith's announcement of the prophecy, if not before. Prior to the issuing of the revelation about the gathering of the Saints, missionaries had been making preparations to carry the message of the Book of Mormon to the Indians on the Missouri frontier. Smith admonished them to keep their eyes open. Even as they told the Indians how the Book of Mormon revealed that the American natives had a Hebraic heritage, the missionaries should keep watch for a likely place where the Saints could gather. Chapter 29 of 3 Nephi had promised that when the words from the plates should come forth, then would the Saints know "that the covenant which the Father hath made with the children of Israel concerning their restoration to the lands of their inheritance" was beginning to be fulfilled. If a suitable place could be found and set apart, then the Latter-day Saints, God's chosen in the new dispensation, could claim their own inheritances and the building up of God's kingdom in the new world could begin even before the rebuilding of his kingdom in Palestine.[22]

The first gathering place was not to be so far west, however. In early 1831, the prophet and most of his followers left western New York en masse to gather in Kirtland, Ohio, where a Campbellite minister, Sidney Rigdon, had been converted to the "restored gospel" and, in turn, had converted his entire congregation to Mormonism. In the astonishingly short period of two to three years, Smith and his band built up such a thriving settlement that it transformed this tiny hamlet into a good-sized Ohio town. As in ancient days, the Saints constructed a temple to serve as Kirtland's focal point, its center. Thus it was that the early Mormons, believing that the heavens had opened and that prophecy was being fulfilled in their own day, began to bring about the fulfillment of prophecy themselves. As Feramorz Fox, Leonard J. Arrington, and Dean L. May demonstrated in their study of early Mormon communitarianism, *Building the City of God,* this became the LDS pattern.[23] Prophecy was fulfilled: things came to pass because the Saints—believing that the restoration had commenced—made them come to pass.

While this is a process that is certainly related in some manner to the concept popularly known as "self-fulfilling prophecy," it was (and is) by no means an uncomplicated process in which prophecy can be equated simply and directly with stimulus and fulfillment can be equated simply and directly with response. That the issue is far more complex and complicated is indicated by the fact that before this pattern was truly established one more dramatic fulfillment of prophecy occurred to set the LDS restoration firmly on course.

On 3 April 1836, climaxing the week in which the Kirtland Temple was dedicated, Joseph Smith and Oliver Cowdery went behind the temple veil and there, in what can be interpreted as fulfillment of the prophet's September 1830 revelation—although the Saints do not universally interpret it as such—the prophet and the "first elder" of the church were visited, they reported, by the Lord of Hosts. He accepted the temple, said his name should be there, and promised to manifest himself to his people therein. Then, the report continues, Moses, whose coming had not been prophesied, appeared and committed "the keys of the gathering of Israel" to the Mormon leaders. After this, Elias, whose appearance had been foretold, committed to them "the dispensation of the gospel of Abraham," saying to Smith and Cowdery that in them and their seed all future generations would be blessed. Finally, Elijah stood before them, they said, and committed to them the keys of this, the new and last dispensation of the fullness of times. With that the restoration of all things could truly begin.[24]

The outlines of the story of what happened to the Saints as they engaged in the most radical restoration project ever undertaken in the American West are likewise familiar. But only those who find sermons as well as settlement patterns interesting would know that, in spite of the fact that they were driven from the nation, the Saints saw their going out as a literal fulfilling of Revelation 18:4: "Come out of her [the world], my people, that ye be not partakers of her sins and that ye receive not her plagues."

That favorite text from the New Testament, Acts 3:21, was used again and again, most especially by Brigham Young and future church presidents John Taylor and Wilford Woodruff, to describe the character of the Great Basin kingdom. The Saints did not believe that their new dispensation superceded all previous dispensations; it fulfilled them. Flowing into this new dispensation were all that had before been revealed. As is well known, for the nineteenth-century Saints in the West, this dispensation included a political kingdom organized in the manner of the Kingdom of God in Solomon's day, under what they regarded as ancient ordinances administered in temples—most particularly plural marriages and baptisms for the dead—as well as a church organized, they believed, as it had been organized in the days of the Apostles.

It would be saying far too much to say that, as a reality, the radical restoration was an unqualified success. But it was successful enough to lead the Saints to believe that another of Isaiah's prophecies was about to be fulfilled: the kingdom established in the top of the mountains shall "be exalted above the hills and all nations shall flow into it." The Saints had learned, as Woodruff said, "to take God at his word."[25] Moreover, they knew, as Taylor said of the Almighty, that "he does not run on a narrow track as we do," and they depended on the coming reality of Daniel's vision of the stone cut out of the mountain without hands as a means by which the Mormon kingdom would break in pieces and consume all other kingdoms and stand forever.[26]

But history proved that literal fulfillment of this prophecy would not come in North America at the end of the nineteenth century. The Saints' success in building, inside the boundaries of the United States, a Kingdom of God that operated according to ancient principles generated powerful non-Mormon opposition. By the 1890s, this opposition became so intense that, for self-protection, Mormonism had to shift away from its radical restorationist mode to what may best be described as a mode of conservative preservation. Exchanging the political kingdom and the practice of plural marriage for Utah statehood, the Saints preserved the restored Gospel, the restored priesthood, the reorganized church, and the kingdom *idea*. But the LDS civic kingdom was no more.

The fact of the kingdom's demise caused an enormous wrenching within Mormon culture and even within the LDS religious realm. The most visible evidence of the tumult was the bewilderment and chaos infecting Mormon culture after the Saints were directed by the president of the LDS church—their prophet, seer, and revelator—to discontinue their practice of plural marriage. The demise of the Mormon political party and the division of the Saints into the Democratic and Republican parties also generated confusion in the culture. These conspicuous evidences of turmoil in the LDS community were but signals of the critical situation in which Mormonism found itself as it moved away from its period of beginnings, which the Saints had confidently regarded as the "winding-up scene," toward a new world in which the LDS church would be the reality, and the literal restoration as it manifested itself in the Mormon kingdom would be ideal and memory.

In the half-century after 1890 Mormonism changed dramatically. Its ecclesiastical structure was streamlined and its theology systematized, and the everyday experiences of ordinary Saints slowly but very surely started to resemble the everyday experiences of Christians who are Protestants and Roman Catholics.[27] As the LDS church has expanded beyond the confines of the Great Basin, first to California and then to the remainder of the United States and outward to the world, its doctrine has been organized and elaborated in such a way that it can be communicated across linguistic and cultural barriers. As this has happened, the reality of the Mormon restoration seems to have receded in importance, whereas its significance as ideal increases. As that happens the difference in Mormonism and other forms of Christianity become sharper. The apostolic era is an era of great consequence to the Saints, but in most Mormon hearts and minds "restoration" corresponds to an LDS golden age when Zion stood in the tops of the mountains for all to see.

NOTES

1. Parley Pratt's expression is found in *A Voice of Warning and Instruction to All People,* perhaps the greatest of all early Latter-day Saint proselyting tracts. In the 1893 edition, the quotation appears on p. 133. The argument that Mormonism is not a denominational, heretical, or fraudulent form of Christianity but a new religious tradition is made in Jan Shipps, *Mormonism: The Story of a New Religious Tradition* (Urbana: University of Illinois Press, 1985).

2. From the standpoint of the Church of Jesus Christ of Latter-day Saints (LDS), the most authoritative of these quasi-canonized narratives are two composed by General Authorities of the LDS church: B. H. Roberts, *Comprehensive History of the Church of Jesus Christ of Latter-day Saints* and Joseph Fielding Smith, *Essentials of Church History,* both of which were published by presses controlled by the LDS church. The best narrative accounts currently available are James B. Allen and Glen M. Leonard, *The Story of the Latter-day Saints* (Salt Lake City: Deseret Book, 1975), and Leonard J. Arrington and Davis Bitton, *The Mormon Experience: A History of the Latter-day Saints* (New York: Knopf, 1979). However, because these accounts of the LDS past are written from the perspective of a particular form of Mormonism, the fracturing of the Mormon movement after Smith's death is not emphasized. Because quite different understandings of the meaning of the concept of restoration developed between the Saints who followed Brigham Young to the Great Basin and those who stayed in the Midwest and were "reorganized" under Joseph Smith III, the breakup of the movement that occurred between 1844 and 1860 is important here. A new general history of the Reorganized Church of Jesus Christ of Latter Day Saints (RLDS) is being written by RLDS church historian Richard Howard. Until that work becomes available, the best single source for information about the RLDS Church is Inez Smith Davis, *The Story of the Church,* 4th ed. rev. (Independence, MO: Herald Publishing House, 1948).

3. The most important compendia include James E. Talmage, *The Articles of Faith [of the] Church of Jesus Christ of Latter-day Saints* (Salt Lake City:

Deseret New Press, 1901), of which many reprints are available; and Bruce R. McConkie, *Mormon Doctrine* (Salt Lake City: Bookcraft, 1958). A compilation of radio talks presented in 1944 by Joseph Fielding Smith has been brought together in a volume entitled *The Restoration of All Things* (Salt Lake City: Deseret Book, 1973). But while this work enumerates and explains many of the theological points that will be dealt with here, it is in no way a work of systematic theology.

4. These sermons were recorded in shorthand as they were delivered and were published in the twenty-volume *Journal of Discourses* (hereinafter *JD*) published serially in Liverpool and London in the nineteenth century. A photo lithographic reprint of these sermons was published in 1956 (Los Angeles: Gartner Printing and Litho).

5. A summary of the evidence about Joseph Smith's connection with the group sometimes called the "Palmyra magicians" is found in Fawn M. Brodie, *No Man Knows My History: The Life of Joseph Smith: the Mormon Prophet*, 2d ed. (New York: Knopf, 1976), chap. 2 and appendix A; see also Marvin S. Hill, "Brodie Revisited: A Reappraisal," *Dialogue: A Journal of Mormon Thought* 8 (Winter 1972):72–85; Marvin S. Hill, "Joseph Smith and the 1826 Trial: New Evidence and New Difficulties," *BYU Studies* 12 (Winter 1972):223–33; and Jan Shipps, "The Prophet Puzzle: Suggestions Leading Toward a More Comprehensive Interpretation of Joseph Smith," *Journal of Mormon History* 1 (1974):3–20.

6. A narrative description of this connection is found in the early chapters of Richard L. Bushman, *Joseph Smith and the Beginnings of Mormonism* (Urbana: University of Illinois Press, 1984). A more recent publication on this topic is Alan Taylor, "The Early Republic's Supernatural Economy: Treasure Seeking in the American Northeast, 1780–1830," *American Quarterly* 38 (Spring 1986):6–34. In addition, a major book-length study of Mormonism and magic has recently been published: Michael Quinn, *Early Mormonism and the Magic World-View* (Salt Lake City: Signature Press, 1987). Another is underway: John L. Brooke, *Joseph Smith, Early American Occult Traditions and the Origins of Mormonism*, forthcoming from Cambridge University Press. A number of articles about Joseph Smith and folk magic published between 1984 and 1986 are not included here because some of the evidence on which they were based was drawn from documents forged by document dealer Mark Hofmann. It is important to recognize that Michael Quinn's recent book-length work details the Smith family's connection with folk magic without depending on evidence drawn from documents that passed through Hofmann's hands.

7. Hill, "Money-Digging Folklore," 474–75. See also, James Obelkevich, *Religion and Rural Society: South Lindsey, 1825–1875* (Oxford: Clarendon Press, 1976); and Jon Butler, "Magic, Astrology and the Early American Religious Heritage," *American History Review* 84 (April 1979):317–46.

8. Brodie, *No Man Knows*, 49.

9. Joseph Smith, Jr., *History of the Church of Jesus Christ of Latter-day Saints: Period I, History of Joseph Smith, the Prophet*, 6 vols., 2d ed. rev., ed. B. H. Roberts (Salt Lake City: Deseret Book, 1955), 1:19.

10. A clear photostat and a transcription of a note that Smith wrote on the back of a copy of the document Harris is said to have carried to show Professor Anthon is included in Dean C. Jessee, ed., *The Personal Writings of Joseph Smith* (Salt Lake City: Deseret Book, 1984), 284. This document turns out to have been a forgery, however.

11. Robert N. Hullinger, *Mormon Answer to Skepticism: Why Joseph Smith Wrote the Book of Mormon* (St. Louis: Clayton Publishing House, 1980).

12. A particularly important example of such an account is the diary of Wilford Woodruff, one of Smith's first followers who became the fourth president of the LDS church. This diary is being published in typescript by Signature Books, a private press in Salt Lake City. Other examples are found in the writings of Jedidiah Grant published in Gene Sessions, *Mormon Thunder* (Urbana: University of Illinois Press, 1982); and the various writings of LDS women published in *Women's Voices,* ed. Kenneth W. Godfrey et al. (Salt Lake City: Deseret Book, 1983).

13. James B. Allen, "Emergence of a Fundamental: The Expanding Role of Joseph Smith's First Vision in Mormon Religious Thought," *Journal of Mormon History* 7 (1980):43–61.

14. *Book of Doctrine and Covenants, 27:5.*

15. A photograph of one of these broadsides is included in Allen and Leonard, *Story of the Latter-day Saints,* 49.

16. See, for example, *JD* 8:367.

17. References to Revelation 14:6 are found in at least twenty of the talks given between 1855 and 1880 that are printed in the *Journal of Discourses.*

18. *Book of Mormon,* 2 Nephi 3:24.

19. *Doctrine and Covenants,* 2, 3, 6, 8, 10.

20. *Doctrine and Covenants,* 21.

21. This expression, often used to describe the form of Mormonism that included temple ordinances, plural marriage, and a literal kingdom structured on the model of Solomon's kingdom, is adapted from Acts 3:21, which speaks of "the times of restitution of all things which God hath spoken by the mouth of all his holy prophets since the world began."

22. Revelation specifically designated Missouri as the "land of your inheritance" on 7 June 1831; *Doctrine and Covenants* 52:42.

23. Feramorz Fox, Leonard J. Arrington, and Dean L. May, *Building the City of God* (Salt Lake City: Deseret Book, 1976).

24. *Doctrine and Covenants,* 110.

25. *JD* 2:195.

26. *JD* 26:107. The best discussion of the Mormon expectations of their kingdom coming to rule the kingdoms of the world is Klaus J. Hansen, *Quest for Empire: The Political Kingdom of God and the Council of Fifty in Mormon History* (East Lansing: Michigan State University Press, 1967).

27. The most recent and best treatment of this era is Thomas G. Alexander, *Mormonism in Transition: A History of the Latter-day Saints, 1890–1930* (Urbana: University of Illinois Press, 1986).

13

Playing for Keeps: The Primitivist Impulse in Early Pentecostalism

GRANT WACKER

"WHEN I make a word work a lot," Humpty Dumpty once remarked, "I always pay it extra." Because I shall be making two words work a lot in this essay—*primitivism* and *pentecostalism*—it seems only fair to pay them extra at the outset. And because the latter term is somewhat easier to pin down, at least historically, it may be easier to begin there.

Although the origins of the pentecostal movement are still somewhat unclear, historians generally agree that it grew from the merger of four or five distinct theological currents within evangelical Protestantism in the United States and Great Britain in the late nineteenth century. That confluence produced a widespread conviction that the conversion experience was to be followed by another landmark event in the believer's life known as the baptism of the Holy Spirit. The latter was regarded as the foundation for a triumphant Christian witness and the prerequisite for one or more of the nine gifts of the Spirit described in 1 Corinthians 12 and 14. Near the turn of the century, however, a small number of men and women came to a considerably more radical conclusion. They became convinced that the ability to speak in "unknown tongues," as the Apostles had done on the Day of Pentecost, was the one and only incontestable proof that a person had truly received the baptism of the Holy Spirit. Soon known as pentecostals, these ardent believers often called their missions Full Gospel Tabernacles, by which they meant that they (and they alone) preached the "full" gospel of personal salvation, divine healing, the Lord's soon return and, as noted, the necessity of Holy Spirit baptism signified by unknown tongues.

The pentecostal movement grew relatively slowly until World War II, but then expanded extremely rapidly, especially in Third World countries. Today scholars estimate that there are at least 100 million adherents worldwide. More than three hundred pentecostal denominations exist in the United States alone. Most are quite small, yet the two largest, the Assemblies of God and the predominantly black Church of God in Christ, each claim more than two million domestic followers and additional millions in other parts of the world. Since 1900 the pentecostal movement seems to have changed very little in matters of doctrine, but, as we shall see, appearances can be deceiving. Old ideas have acquired new meanings. And important sociological changes have taken place as well. Urban missions and backwoods huts contrast with magnificent suburban churches and a billion-dollar television ministry dominated by pentecostal celebrities. Moreover, since the 1950s divine healing meetings and speaking in tongues have penetrated the Roman Catholic church and many of the historic Protestant denominations, forming a pentecostal subtradition widely known as the charismatic renewal. Even so, despite its sprawling size and bewildering diversity, pentecostalism in all parts of the world is still bonded by a powerful conviction that the miraculous, wonder-working gospel of the New Testament is just as real at the end of the twentieth century as it was in the first.[1]

Before attempting to highlight the patterns of primitivism in early pentecostalism, we need to attend to the other preliminary task: forging a working definition of primitivism. In this essay I shall use that word in a broadly generic manner to refer to any effort to deny history, or to deny the contingencies of historical existence, by returning to the time before time, to the golden age that preceded the corruptions of life in history. Just as primitivism took a variety of forms in American religious history, so too it took a variety of forms in early pentecostalism. I shall isolate three of those patterns and call them philosophical, historical, and ethical. These are, of course, only analytic distinctions. In reality, the three patterns emerged at the same time and functioned as a coherent and mutually reinforcing system. But there was something like a logical progression from philosophical to historical to ethical primitivism, and thus that is the order in which we shall look at them.

Philosophical primitivism might be described as the conviction that believers not only could know but in a very real way possess or lay personal claim to absolute truth. Of course this assumption, or at least something similar to it, was characteristic of all sectarians, but among early pentecostals it flourished in a particularly vigorous and uncompromising way. It fostered the assurance that their ideas and experiences were sanctioned by a tribunal above and beyond all mundane authorities. It prompted them to believe that their ownership of the truth was unencumbered by the limitations of finite existence. By calling this trait philosophical primitivism I do not mean to imply that pentecostals were particularly "philosophical" about the underpinnings of their worldview. Quite the contrary, philosophical primitivism existed mostly at the preconceptual level and, as such, served as the foundation for virtually everything else that they thought about the world and their place in it.

Elsewhere I have tried to assess the role of philosophical primitivism in early pentecostal culture, so here it is necessary only to summarize its principal ramifications. First and foremost, perhaps, philosophical primitivism prompted converts to resist the relativistic assumptions of modern culture in general and of modern biblical scholarship in particular. To pentecostals that meant that the writers of the Bible had not been influenced in any truly significant way by the setting in which they had lived. In the words of one pentecostal biblical scholar, it simply never occurred to him until he entered a secular graduate school in the 1950s that the Bible had not "dropped from heaven as a sacred meteor."[2]

Given the assumption that the Bible originated before or outside of ordinary human history, it was easy for pentecostals to plunge to the conclusion that it was errorless. "I believe in the plenary inspiration of the Scriptures," proclaimed B. H. Irwin, a leading evangelist at the turn of the century. "I detest and despise ... this higher criticism, rationalism, and this seeking on the part of ungodly professors to do away with objectionable parts of the Word of God, and as fire-baptized people we stand on the whole Book, hallelujah!" Older Christian groups knew of course that "standing on the whole Book" was easier said than done, but one mark of the movement's youthfulness was that its leaders seem never to have doubted that their interpretation of the Bible—their theology—was just as inerrant as the Bible itself. "Jesus hates impure doctrine," William J. Seymour, a founder of the famed Azusa Street Mission, trumpeted in the heat of the revival. "There was a time when we were fed upon theological chips, shavings and wind, but now ... we are feeding upon ... the whole Word and nothing but the Word."[3]

Philosophical primitivism encouraged pentecostals to believe, in short, that their own reading of the Bible, no less than the Bible itself, had somehow escaped the vicissitudes of historical construction. It also led them to assume that scriptural interpretation was best when it was as literal—which is to say, as radically present-minded—as credibility could stand. "You absolutely lose your own judgment in regard to the Word of God," Seymour insisted. "You eat it down without trimming or cutting, right from the mouth of God." The practice of handling poisonous snakes, which persisted for many years in and out of the Church of God in the southern Appalachians, was based on an unflinchingly literal reading of Mark 16:17. That and other isolated passages, taken literally, became the basis for drinking lethal doses of poison, handling live coals of fire, and refusing to use prescription medicines even when it meant certain death for oneself or one's children.[4]

The second form of primitivism that structured early pentecostal culture was historical primitivism. Strictly speaking, this phrase is a contradiction of terms, for primitivism is by definition a denial of the relevance of history. Nonetheless I shall use the term—albeit somewhat loosely—to refer to the special way that pentecostals handled church history and their place within it. Briefly stated, they were certain that their movement repristinated apostolic Christianity. At the same time, they were equally certain that it owed nothing to the long history of the Christian church between the second and twentieth centuries. A caveat is needed at this point. Many scholars draw a distinction between the concept of historical primitivism and its kissing cousin, restorationism, but in this essay the difference between these notions is not important, and therefore I shall use the terms interchangeably. Thus for pentecostals the main import of historical primitivism was the conviction that the New Testament provided a workable blueprint for Christianity in the modern world, complete just as it stood, without adaption, interpretation, or translation into the idioms of modern culture. And the reason was simple: the New Testament church *was* the twentieth-century church. The only problem was knowing where to draw the boundaries, knowing who was in and who was out.

In some respects pentecostal historical primitivism was a manifestation of the same restorationist yearning that cropped up among rival groups like the Landmark Baptists and the Churches of Christ. In other respects the pentecostal version represented a highly creative refashioning of familiar ideas. But before we examine the process by which pentecostals used common materials to forge a distinctive theology, we first need to think about the way that unself-conscious attitudes about history made historical primitivism a natural and seemingly logical way to view the world.

To begin with, early pentecostals were uninterested in the academic specialty that is generally known as church history. Contrary to the popular stereotype, they were seriously concerned about theological education, promptly establishing a score of Bible and missionary training institutes in all parts of the country. Yet they paid little attention to church history, and when they did, they did it with virtually no sense of critical method.[5] More significantly, pentecostals remained diffident about their own history. Like most sectarians, they considered their origins miraculous. As William Seymour put it, "the source is from the skies." The *Faithful Standard,* organ of the Tomlinson Church of God, similarly insisted that "THE HOLY GHOST [has been] THE LEADER—not any man." As late as 1949 Donald Gee, arguably the most astute and worldly-wise figure pentecostalism ever produced, wrote that the movement did "not owe its origin to any outstanding personality or religious leader, but was a spontaneous revival appearing almost simultaneously in various parts of the world." If the source was from the skies and if human instruments were irrelevant, there really was not much to write about. Serious historical interests did begin to bloom in the 1950s, but it is significant that even then the first major effort by a pentecostal scholar to reconstruct the history of the Assemblies of God was called *Suddenly . . . from Heaven*—a title that hardly could have been more nonhistorical, if not antihistorical, in intent. With minor exceptions, that attitude did not change until the 1960s when second- and third-generation pentecostals started to enter secular graduate schools and write doctoral dissertations on various aspects of their own tradition. Even so, university-trained pentecostal historians still evinced little desire radically to situate the movement in the social and cultural setting in which it was born. No one traced its continuities with heterodox neighbors such as the Latter-day Saints, or with unwashed cousins such as Frank S. Sandford's Shiloh movement in Maine or Franz Edmund Creffield's Holy Jumpers in Washington state.[6]

Unself-conscious attitudes of this sort were, however, only part of the story of early pentecostals' view of their place in Christian history. Self-conscious, explicit historical primitivism formed the other and undoubtedly larger part. In a word, many pentecostals exhibited a quite deliberate *dis*interest in the subject. The longing to recover the "pure fountain" of the New Testament, as Gee put it, fostered the presumption that virtually everything that had happened since the Day of Pentecost was pernicious at worst, irrelevant at best. The former view—that the history of the church was essentially a tale of sustained apostasy—was particularly strong in the Church of God. For centuries, groused A. J. Tomlinson, the group's founding patriarch, the truth has been "buried beneath the debris of custom, tradition, and unbelief. . . . Creeds, articles of faith, systems, doctrines, false Churches are even now quivering, ready to fall. The True Church of God is going to rise soon above the great host of modern churchianity, and shine out in her glory and beauty with conquering tread."[7]

For most pentecostals, however, the long history of the church was not so much evil as simply irrelevant. By "one great revolutionary wrench," Frank Ewart, a leader of the Los Angeles revival, boasted, "[God] is lifting His church back over the head of every sect, every creed, every organized system of theology, and [putting] it back where it was [on] the Day of Pentecost." The assumptions that nourished this idea were perhaps best summed up by Bennett F. Lawrence in 1916 in a volume significantly titled *The Apostolic Faith Restored*. The older denominations, Lawrence judged, had existed long enough to "establish precedent, create habit, formulate custom."

> In this way they have become possessed of . . . a two-fold criterion of doctrine—the New Testament *and* the church position. [But pentecostals] do not recognize a doctrine or a custom as authoritative unless it can be traced to . . . the Lord and His apostles. This reversion to the New Testament [is] responsible for . . . the absence of any serious effort . . . to trace an historical connection with the primitive church. The Pentecostal Movement has no such history; it leaps the intervening years crying, "BACK TO PENTECOST!"[8]

First-generation pentecostals went to extraordinary lengths to prove that their revival did not merely reproduce, but replicated—albeit on a grander scale—every detail of the Day of Pentecost. For those with sufficient faith, wrote Elizabeth Sisson, a leading evangelist, God promised that he would "repeat . . . the original pattern which He gave in the Upper Room at Jerusalem." Repeating the original pattern therefore became the overarching aim, the pole star by which all beliefs and actions were measured. Indeed, the yearning to reenter the primitive church, to breathe its air, to feel the exhilaration of its spiritual life, became so intense that believers sometimes found it impossible to distinguish present reality from the imagined reality of the first century.[9]

Apostolic imagery framed their world, defined their rhetoric. Converts commonly described their experiences in terms of threes, sevens, twelves, and forties. One of countless examples was Charles Parham's description of the initial falling of the Latter Rain at his Topeka Bible School in the winter of 1901. He wrote that he received the baptism of the Holy Spirit three days after a student named Agnes Ozman first received it, in an upper room of the school, in the midst of twelve ministers also seeking the experience. The school enrolled forty students. Without a trace of self-consciousness—or self-criticism, one might add—pentecostals recurringly identified themselves with Christ and their revival with the Holy Spirit. Parham casually pointed out, for example, that the day he received the baptism he had waited upon the Lord from 9 A.M. until 3 P.M., the very hours that Christ had hung upon the cross. Lillian Thistlewaite, Parham's sister-in-law who was present that night, remembered that some had seen cloven tongues of fire dancing above the heads of those who were speaking in tongues. When A. J. Tomlinson was baptized in water, he heard a voice saying, "This is my son, in whom I am well pleased." Tomlinson never lost that sense of divine identification. After he was made general overseer of the Church of God for life in 1914, he boldly concluded (despite considerable evidence to the contrary) that the assembly's "selection was marked with such demonstrations and manifestations of the Spirit of God that . . . there seems to have been a kind of sacredness thrown around the position." William Seymour liked to point out that the Azusa Mission was located in a run-down part of Los Angeles. "You would hardly expect heavenly visitations there"—we can almost see the grin—"unless you remember the stable at Bethlehem." No believer could have missed Seymour's meaning when he added that the revival was "born in a manger and resurrected in a barn."[10]

The original pattern stood, in short, as the only blueprint for authentic Christianity in the twentieth century or, for that matter, in any century. But pentecostals could not leave it there. Neither lack of interest nor self-conscious disinterest in the long history of the church would have posed a special problem for them if in most other respects their behavior had been continuous with the traditions of evangelical Protestantism. But speaking in unknown tongues, casting out demons, praying for healing, dancing in the Spirit, and occasionally resurrecting the dead were, if not unique, at least so peculiar that pentecostals felt impelled to legitimate themselves in the light of Christian history. Therefore it is not surprising that they sometimes suggested, almost inadvertantly, that their leaders had directly succeeded Martin Luther, George Fox, and John Wesley, or that their revival should be framed in the context of the Wesleyan and Irvingite revivals in England, or that precedents for tongues were sprinkled throughout the history of Christianity. Some writers, such as Bennett Lawrence, shrugged off such attempts to establish continuity with the past by indicating that they were "more for the purpose of providing a ground of expectation that [supernatural power was] permanent in the church . . . than to trace any historical connection with primitive believers." But for most thoughtful believers the problem of legitimacy still nagged.[11]

In order to account for their place in God's "Plan for the Ages," pentecostal leaders therefore forged a complex theory of the effective demise of apostolic Christianity in the second century and its restoration in the early twentieth century. They called it the covenant of the Latter Rain. The Latter Rain theory of history did not, of course, have anything to do with real history, with the publicly accessible data that critical historians seek to organize and interpret. Rather it was a theological rendering of history, based upon Deuteronomy 11:14, Joel 2:23, and James 5:7. In those passages the Lord indicated that he would manifest his power first in an early, preparatory rain, then again in a latter, consummative rain. To pentecostals it was self-evident that those verses referred, respectively, to the charismatic manifestations in the apostolic church and in the current revival.

In the first systematic exposition of pentecostal theology, published in 1907, George Floyd Taylor explained that the land of Palestine received "two special rains each year," one in the early spring, enabling the seeds to sprout, and another just before harvest in the fall, enabling the grain to "mature and mellow." Because God had designed Palestine to be a "miniature world in itself," Taylor argued, it was evident that he intended its meteorological pattern to be spiritually replicated in the "church at large." Thus the early rain, which came at Pentecost, inundated the church with "mighty floods of salvation." But when the church became a "great hierarchy, the long drought began." Taylor allowed that during the Protestant Reformation the "latter rain began to be foreshadowed," and he admitted that the holiness revivals of the 1890s may have been "preliminary showers." "But we know that [those revivals fell] far short of the apostolic revivals—the early rain. . . . So we may expect the latter rain to be much greater and more powerful than the apostolic revivals."[12]

But how did pentecostals know that the current revival was the Latter Rain foretold by the prophets? What made this revival different from countless stirrings in the past? Several answers were common, including the return of the Jews to Palestine, the apostasy of the established denominations, and the increase of natural calamities. The 1906 San Francisco earthquake loomed especially large in their speculations. Elizabeth Baker, a prolific tract writer and apologist for the movement, insisted that the Latter Rain prophecy in Joel could not have been fulfilled on the Day of Pentecost, as Christians usually assumed. According to Acts 2:19–21, she argued, the final fulfillment of Joel's prophecy was to be accompanied by "mighty supernatural signs in nature[,] which did not accompany the early outpouring." Frank Ewart similarly pointed out that just after the Azusa revival began, "an earthquake of frightful dimensions rocked the physical world." In his mind the import was clear: "In all of God's great moves, nature sympathizes." It happened at Sinai, at Calvary, and at Azusa "history again repeated itself." These events were enough to convince Susan A. Duncan, a founder of the Rochester Bible and Missionary Training Institute, that the "dividing line [of history] has been crossed and we are in the time of the latter rain."[13]

Even so, social and natural occurrences of this sort seem to have been afterthoughts, corroborating documentation at best. The hard proof, the evidence that really persuaded pentecostals that the Latter Rain had started to fall, was the fact that the supernatural gifts of the Spirit—the gifts that once had flourished among the Apostles—seemed finally to have reentered the church after centuries of disuse. More precisely, the reappearance of the gifts led pentecostals to believe not only that they were entering the time of the Latter Rain, but also, and more portentously, that they were God's specially chosen agents for bringing it to pass.

In order to understand how this notion arose, we need to remember that pentecostals did not exercise the gifts in an ideational vacuum. Rather they embedded the gifts in an elaborate eschatological scheme called dispensational premillennialism. This meant that powerful religious experiences and the theological interpretation of those experiences became functionally inseparable. This process, this continuous interplay between experience and the interpretation of experience, merits careful examination, for it illustrates how inventive a folk tradition can become when its real life activities smash into an ideological roadblock.

Dispensational premillennialists ordinarily asserted that the gifts of the Spirit, initially given to the Apostles on the Day of Pentecost, were withdrawn when the Apostolic Dispensation came to an end. Since God had abolished the gifts when their purpose had been fulfilled, their reappearance in the twentieth century was a human invention at best and a satanic counterfeit at worst. Pentecostals did not exactly reverse that argument, but they tinkered with it to make it fit their purposes. Briefly stated, they merged the Apostolic Dispensation with the succeeding Church (or Christian) Dispensation. This allowed them to claim that the outpouring of charismatic gifts on the Day of Pentecost was the Early Rain that marked the beginning of the Church Dispensation, whereas the current outpouring of charismatic gifts was the Latter Rain that marked its climax. The general absence of charismatic gifts during the Church Dispensation (except at the beginning and at the end) was not because God had withdrawn them, but because the church's apostasy and disobedience had rendered them inoperative.[14]

The cornerstone of the Latter Rain argument was the assumption that the kind of miracles that appeared at the beginning of a dispensation always reappeared at its end. "On the Day of Pentecost," George Floyd Taylor judged, "the first manifestation was speaking with other tongues . . . and then followed the healing of the sick, casting out of devils, etc. So it would only be natural to expect that in the latter rain, Pentecost should be repeated and followed by the same manifestation." J. W. "Daddy" Welch, an early chairman of the Assemblies of God, similarly concluded that "[today's] glorious manifestations of divine power . . . have proven beyond a doubt that God's time-piece has reached the dispensational hour in which He had promised to pour out His Spirit in *Latter Rain* significance. . . . The last days have come."[15]

But above all it was the restoration of one gift, the gift of speaking in unknown tongues, that proved to first-generation pentecostals that the Church Dispensation was finally drawing to a close. When Susan Duncan asked, "[How] do I know that this is the Latter Rain?" she predictably answered that since tongues was the only sign unique to the Day of Pentecost, its reoccurrence in the twentieth century proved that the end was near. The British Holiness Zionist periodical *Prophetic Age* likewise avowed that the "wonderful sign in 1906 is the restoration of tongues, which must be done before the Gentile Times end." Elizabeth Sisson warned that proper understanding of the dispensational significance of tongues was not a matter of abstract theological interest, but of life or death: "The mightiest of all the signs," she declared, "has been God's beginning sign. . . . As He filled all Jerusalem with the 'sound' of His coming in the former rain, so now He is filling all the earth with the sound of His coming in the latter rain."[16]

Duncan's declaration raises the question of millenarianism. A number of scholars have argued that early pentecostalism is best understood as a millenarian movement. There is considerable merit in that point of view, for it is indisputable that the symbolism of dispensational premillennialism pervaded the movement. Even so, students of pentecostalism have rarely recognized the extent to which historical primitivism undergirded its millenarianism. More precisely, there is substantial evidence that the hope of the Latter Rain came first in pentecostal thinking, which meant that historical primitivism served as the logical and emotional foundation for dispensational premillennialism, rather than the reverse.

The priority of the primitivist vision was plain to many of the first-generation leaders. Charles Parham initially described the new phenomenon as "The Latter Rain: The Story of the Origin of the Original Apostolic or Pentecostal Movements." The first synoptic history of the movement, serialized in the monthly *Faithful Standard* in 1922, carried the title "The Wonderful History of the Latter Rain: Remarkable Repetition of the Acts of the Apostles." The premier tenet of the Azusa Mission's statement of faith declared: "THE APOSTOLIC FAITH MOVEMENT stands for the restoration of the faith once delivered unto the saints." In the second issue of the mission's newspaper William Seymour summed up his view of its place in history in an article revealingly titled "The Pentecostal Baptism Restored: The Promised Latter Rain Now Being Poured Out on God's Humble People." Although some periodicals bore explicitly millenarian titles such as *Bridegroom's Messenger,* and others, such as *Good Tidings,* stressed evangelistic motifs, most underscored the connection, if not the identity, between the Early Rain of the first century and the Latter Rain of the twentieth century: *Apostolic Banner, Apostolic Herald, Apostolic Light, Apostolic Messenger, Apostolic Faith, Apostolic Witness, Latter Rain Evangel, New Acts, Pentecost, Pentecostal Evangel, Pentecostal Power, Pentecostal Testimony, Pentecostal Wonders.* The list could be extended considerably, but this is enough to suggest that terms like apostolic, latter rain, and pentecostal, which had primitivist resonances for their readers, were the ones partisans most frequently used to label their movement. Other periodical titles connoting the idea of the restoration of a primitive place or event, such as *Upper Room,* or the related idea of temporal promise and fulfillment, such as *Meat in Due Season, Christian Harvester,* and *Evening Light,* cropped up from time to time. Aimee Semple McPherson's most popular book bore the explicitly restorationist title, taken from Peter's sermon on the Day of Pentecost, *This Is That.*[17]

The Latter Rain vision gradually dimmed. As the years passed and pentecostals found themselves more and more at home in the evangelical Protestant mainstream, they were increasingly tempted to legitimate themselves by discovering a substantial and continuous tradition of charismatic revivals stretching from the apostolic church to the present. Nonetheless, old ideas died hard. In the 1940s P. C. Nelson, probably the best educated of the second-generation leaders, boldly titled one of his works *The Jerusalem Council: The First General Council of the Assemblies of God.* The first scholarly history of the movement written by a pentecostal, Klaude Kendrick's 1959 University of Texas doctoral dissertation, was called *The Promise Fulfilled*. And in 1984 Vinson Synan, a leading pentecostal scholar with a Ph.D. in history from the University of Georgia, published a survey of the recent world-wide growth of the revival under the title *In the Latter Days*. All this leads to the conclusion that for many years, and to some extent even today, historical primitivism helped pentecostals turn their greatest theological liability—namely their discontinuity with classical Christianity—into an asset. It allowed them the luxury of two histories at once: one pegged outside the corruptions of time, impervious to the scrutiny of critical observers, the other tucked safely within the legitimating canopy of Christian tradition.[18]

This brings us finally to ethical primitivism, the third pattern that informed the culture of early pentecostalism. Of the three, ethical primitivism is the most elusive. For present purposes it is sufficient to say that it was a cluster of antimodern behavior patterns that were related to, if not produced by, the outlook embodied in philosophical and historical primitivism.

To begin with, the cornerstone of ethical primitivism was the assumption that the power of primitive Christianity was inseparable from its form, and the form, of course, corresponded to the guidelines set forth in the New Testament. Therefore, if the modern church was to exercise the power of the apostolic church, it first would have to manifest its form. "There never can be a new church," the healing evangelist John Alexander Dowie insisted, "unless it is a false church. . . . If we are to get back to primitive power . . . we will have to . . . get back to primitive organization, primitive faith, primitive simplicity, primitive purity of life. Primitive power follows all that." The yearning to repossess the wellsprings of apostolic power impelled pentecostals to insist that their movement was not new, but an exact duplication of early Christianity. The movement might be "new to the world in these last days," William Seymour acknowledged, but its "doctrine is old as the New Testament . . . the same old teaching of 1900 years ago."[19]

Replicating the form of the original church meant, first of all, reestablishing the biblical pattern of church government. For many converts, especially in the Church of God tradition, that meant strict episcopal polity. In Tomlinson's words, "Bible Church = absolute government of Jesus." But for many pentecostals, restoring the original pattern of church government meant no government at all. When the Azusa Mission painted its name over the front portal, Frank Bartleman, one of the founders, promptly pulled out, denouncing that act as the first step toward "hierarchism." Yet no one assailed efforts to impose structure upon the movement more vigorously than Parham. "It is a pitiable sight," he growled, "to see a few driveling, spiritual idiots in the shape of would-be Apostolic church organizers drag their slimy, carnal skeletons from mission to mission, trying to rally their followers by vomiting lies and scandal over them.... A demoniacal craving for power and authority has seized certain Apostolic workers, and, drunken with this wine ... they present an array of straw soldiers wandering in the quagmires of creeds, doctrines, fanaticism, wildfire, message giving and false interpretation."[20]

If pentecostals differed about the proper form of church government, they never differed about the proper form of personal conduct: systematic renunciation of the ways of the world. The key to apostolic power was apostolic purity. The first Christians did not have "tobacco, or gum, or coca cola, or picture shows ... to be tempted with," the *Church of God Evangel* allowed, "but if they had, such things would have had no attraction for them, because they were on fire for God." Pentecostals knew that modeling their churches and lives to fit the specifications established by the apostles would not be easy. But the Azusa *Apostolic Faith* assured its readers that Jesus had promised that "He would give us power ... *the same power that he had*." The valences of ethical primitivism were succinctly captured by one L. C. Ebey of Herman, California: "I believe and look for the true restoration of the apostolic faith.... If you keep your hearts pure and open, God will give you the old apostolic power."[21]

Pentecostals quickly discovered, however, that translating apostolic models into the idioms of the modern world was one thing, but living with Christians who did not share those models or who did not share them in the same way was more difficult. If the aim of ethical primitivism was to recapture the power of apostolic Christianity, the effect, as often as not, was invidiousness toward other—and especially toward older, more established—Christian traditions.

Considerable evidence suggests that to outsiders, the movement's most repugnant feature was neither its unconventional theology nor its ecstatic excesses but its elitism, its uncompromising, jut-jawed disdain for customs of denominational Christianity. This trait was most obtrusive in The Church of God, where the definite article in the name was significant. In that tradition the determination to discern and enforce the New Testament blueprint for church government provoked endless polity fights and three major schisms. "We are the only people in the world that are prepared to carry a FULL GOSPEL," A. J. Tomlinson crowed.

> This statement may seem a little egotistical and selfish, but when the matter is simmered down to the cold facts it is too true to be sneered at. . . . We all know [that] the common and popular religion . . . is cold enough to freeze almost any soul. . . . [And] when we consider [other] pentecostal people, only a part of them wash feet. . . . And when we come up to signs and gifts they all stop and shake their heads when the serpents are produced and fire is handled as miracle. And when the powers are demonstrated in a manner that their little minds can't understand, they often cry out "fanaticism."[22]

Until World War II, when the leavening influence of association with men and women of other traditions began to be felt, the various Church of God groups remained militantly exclusivistic. But they were not alone. William Seymour rejoiced that the "real Pentecost that has been hidden for all these centuries the Lord is giving back to earth through some real humble people that have no better sense than to believe God." Given that premise, it was easy to conclude, as one Azusa convert did, that "sanctification makes us holy as Jesus is." Another convert proclaimed that pentecostals were the "elite of the universe." In his monthly magazine Charles Fox Parham routinely misspelled seminaries as cemetaries and mocked professional clergy as "D.D.'s—dumb dogs." Frank Bartleman gave no quarter to his rivals in the nonpentecostal holiness movement. Their problem, he wrote, was that they were "most tenacious of their attainments and position . . . filled with hard-hearted pharisaism . . . with little left but the shell of their profession." Bartleman concluded that "on the whole" the holiness folk had failed God because they had grown "hard, censorious, critical and bigoted." Condescension mixed with overt hostility toward the established denominations and toward other evangelical sects lingered for many years. In 1951 the general superintendent of the Assemblies of God boasted that "God has brought us out of old, dead ecclesiasticism and denominationalism. He has made us free people, and we are not going back into 'Babylon' any more." In the mid 1980s no American pentecostal denomination belonged to the National or World Council of Churches, and individual ministers who displayed conspicuous interest in the ecumenical movement risked rebuke or dismissal.[23]

One effect of religious primitivism was, then, persistent invidiousness toward other traditions. A second, closely related effect is best described as an antistructuralist impulse: a determination to destroy the arbitrary conventions of denominational Christianity in order to replace them with a new order of primal simplicity and purity.

The antistructuralist impact of ethical primitivism was evident first of all, as Roger Robins has argued, in the movement's egalitarian social structure. The acute status consciousness of many modern pentecostal churches makes it easy to forget that in the beginning drifters, day laborers, blacks, and non–English speaking immigrants were welcomed; that women were ordained to preach the Gospel in this country and abroad; that children were accorded a standing probably unparalleled in the history of American Protestantism. "No instrument that God can use is rejected on account of color or dress or lack of education," one pioneer insisted. "That is why God has so built up the work." Another leader proudly pointed out that neither God nor the movement recognized "man-made creeds, doctrines, nor classes of people." It is quite true that the revival soon succumbed to the race and gender prejudices of the environing culture. But that should not obscure the fact that in many churches and in countless ways the old stratifications were razed and a new order erected.[24]

Antistructural influences also were evident in the movement's worship patterns. Believing that the Holy Spirit did not confine himself to established leaders, pentecostals insisted that anyone should feel free to speak, and thus they blurred the distinction between clergy and laity. Believing that the Holy Spirit did not confine himself to the walls of the meeting house, pentecostals insisted that believers must preach the Good News anywhere people might listen, and thus they blurred the distinction between sacred and profane space. Believing that the Holy Spirit did not confine himself to any human instrumentality, pentecostals insisted that singing and praying should be uninhibited responses to the promptings of the Spirit, and thus they blurred the distinction between liturgy and cacophany, between order and anarchy.

The results were predictable. Often, Charles Parham judged, the people "screamed until you could hear them for three miles on a clear night, and until the blood vessels stood out like whip cords." A Pennsylvania evangelist noted that in his meetings the "power was so irresistible that people fell from their seats until the floor was literally covered with prostrate people." Florence Crawford, who founded a splinter group in Portland, Oregon, significantly called the Apostolic Faith, was pleased to say that in her Portland meetings the people "fell screaming to the floor under the power of the preaching." After an Oakland revival Crawford noted with evident satisfaction that the "floor was covered with souls laid out under the power." The report of a missionary pastor in Honolulu was remarkable only because it was so typical: "We had quite a scene at the altar last night," he began. "A demon possessed man who was kneeling at the altar was picked up by demon power, thrown over the altar rail on his head, and when we commanded them to come out of him they barked at us and said that they would not come out of him, but they were cast out in the Name of Jesus and the man was set free." A newspaper reporter who visited Maria Woodworth-Etter's meetings in Muncie, Indiana, recalled that one could not "imagine the . . . confusion." "Dozens lying around pale and unconscious, rigid and lifeless as though in death. Strong men shouting till they were hoarse, then falling down in a swoon. Women falling over benches and trampled under foot. . . . Aged women gesticulating and hysterically sobbing. . . . Men shouting with a devilish, unearthly laugh."[25]

Striking as those descriptions are, the antistructuralist import of ethical primitivism was most compellingly evident in the hallmark of the revival: speaking in tongues, technically known as *glossolalia*. In order to understand this, it may be helpful briefly to consider the import of recent social scientific studies of glossolalic speech. Over the years glossolalia undoubtedly has been the movement's most distinctive—and most misunderstood—feature. Outsiders (especially those who have never heard it) often suppose that it is simply gibberish. Veteran pentecostals and professional linguists both know, however, that the real thing is a baffling and awesome phenomenon precisely because it is not gibberish. Cross-cultural investigations have shown that a glossolalic utterance is drawn from the basic sounds of phonemes of a speaker's native language. Those phonemes erupt, not at random, but in patterns that resemble the phonological patterns of that language. That is why glossolalia is easily mistaken for language: it sounds like it—especially in real-life situations where it competes with other noises and is accompanied by gestures and facial expressions. Linguists insist, however, that glossolalia is not language. Unlike all known languages, living or dead, glossolalia has no grammar. Nor does it have any semantic value, because the "words" are unrelated to the stock of public meanings within the speech community (although they may have a private meaning for the speaker, or a purely connotative meaning for the hearer).[26]

For first-generation pentecostals, glossolalia undoubtedly met a variety of theological and aesthetic needs, but the evidence noted above suggests that glossolalia also functioned as an antistructuralist ritual. It was neither language nor gibberish, but something strangely in-between: a series of utterances poised between patterned communication on one side and unpatterned nonsense on the other. Indeed, if the aim of such rituals was, as some anthropologists have said, to facilitate the transition from one social state to another by drawing attention to the liminal zone between them, it is reasonable to suppose that glossolalia may have been a tangible symbol of the unstructuredness that pentecostals sought in their religious quests or of the marginality they experienced in their social lives.[27]

Other ecstatic rituals common within early pentecostalism also seem to have had an antistructuralist function. A crisscrossing of the line that marked the boundary between ordinary and extraordinary experience was a recurring feature in autobiographical accounts of the baptism event. Repeatedly, the testimonials referred to a rapturous loss of identity or loss of all sense of time and place. Indeed, some converts indicated that they were able to speak only in tongues for days, weeks, or even years afterward. "Biological isomorphism"—the ritual reenactment of death and resurrection through physical prostration—calls to mind another hallmark of early pentecostalism: falling to the floor in a trance or trancelike state known as being "slain in the Spirit." In a typical service, Frank Bartleman recalled, "men would fall all over the [meeting] house, like the slain in battle. . . . The scene often resembled a forest of fallen trees." Indeed, for many years no report of a meeting was complete unless it included a reference to the number of souls who were "saved, baptized, healed, and slain in the Spirit."[28]

Ethical primitivism functioned, in short, as an ambiguous ideal. The desire to recapture the power of New Testament Christianity entailed an emphasis upon personal holiness and an impulsion to share the good news of the Gospel on street corners, in saloons, or anywhere men and women might listen. But ethical primitivism also fostered an attitude toward other Christians (not to mention members of other religions) that was triumphalist at best, morally irresponsible at worst. And it spawned antistructuralist inclinations that were sometimes consistent—and sometimes not so consistent—with pentecostalism's own deepest insights into the meaning of biblical faith.

The last point is particularly important. Early pentecostalism is not adequately understood if we think of it only in sociological terms as an alienated sect inexorably drifting back into the comforts of mainstream Protestantism. There is a measure of truth in that interpretation, but it is equally important to remember that the movement harbored a regressive strain that was, by any reasonable measure of such things, socially disruptive. Its defiance of social conventions, its bellicosity and zealotry, its ecstatic excess and deliberate scrambling of human language, surely reflected a darkly primitivist urge toward disorder. All of this is to say that the impulses that spawned pentecostalism, and to some extent helped to sustain it after the first generation, were both functional and dysfunctional, structural and antistructural, and we have not found the movement, much less deciphered it, until we have come to terms with the simultaneously constructive and destructive forces that energized its religious life.

Nearly a century has elapsed since the first blush of the revival. From the perspective of the 1980s, the movement seems to have changed relatively little. The official doctrinal tenets of the major pentecostal denominations have been amended only in minor ways, and the worldview of the typical believer remains almost as supernaturalistic as it was in 1900. Modern pentecostals generally applaud the spread of the movement into the Roman Catholic church and other Protestant denominations, but they continue to believe that only pentecostals, in whatever fellowship they may be found, have inherited the full teaching of apostolic Christianity. Exorcism, divine healing, and speaking in tongues are more circumspectly practiced, but compared with other evangelical Protestants, pentecostals are still remarkable in the extent to which they cultivate the miracles of the Spirit.

Nonetheless, appearances can be deceiving. The rapid eruption and equally rapid exhaustion of two primitivist, countermodernizing movements shortly after World War II revealed the depth of the changes that had taken place.

The first of those pressures was the New Order of the Latter Rain, a little-known yet influential stirring that started in 1947 in an independent Bible school in North Battleford, Saskatchewan. It quickly spread to the United States and touched pentecostal missions worldwide. Like early pentecostalism, the New Order, as it was commonly called, considered demons the source of most illnesses and therefore equated healing with exorcism. More important in the present context is the fact that adherents construed these and other charismatic gifts as tokens of the restoration of apostolic power that would immediately precede the Lord's return. Unlike early pentecostalism, however, the New Order also emphasized the restoration of the biblical practice of prolonged (preferably forty-day) fasts and the gifts of healing to specially chosen apostles and prophets rather than to the church as a whole. In the mid-1980s, New Order teachers were still playing a conspicuous role in the nondenominational charismatic movement, especially in segments that advocated the restoration of rigidly authoritarian and patriarchal polity structures. For the most part, however, they had been discredited in the more established pentecostal churches as mavericks and extremists.[29]

The second and more important countermodernizing trend was the rise of independent "deliverance" evangelism in the 1950s and 1960s. This was not a wholly new development. Divine healing had always been an important part of pentecostal culture, and although the movement had traditionally insisted that any Spirit-filled Christian could secure healing through his or her own prayers, pentecostals also knew that certain individuals, such as Maria Woodworth-Etter and John Alexander Dowie, possessed special gifts of healing not available to ordinary believers. But shortly after World War II a relatively small group of specially gifted healers skyrocketed into national prominence and acquired a broad following among rank-and-file pentecostals. Most were promptly squeezed out of their denominations by leaders troubled by persistent rumors of financial and sexual irregularity and by the healers' refusal to be held accountable to denominational authorities. But the attempt to ostracize celebrities such as William Branham and Oral Roberts predictably backfired. Unfettered by denominational constraints, many soon established private empires of seemingly boundless power and wealth.[30] The crisis provoked by the independent healers neatly symbolized the fate of primitivism in American pentecostalism at midcentury. It suggested that the movement was torn between ahistorical, countermodernizing forces on one side, and historicizing, modernizing forces on the other. For the former, the conflict proved to be a last gasp, however. By the end of the 1960s the big tents had disappeared and the stars had disappeared or fallen into disgrace. The rise and fall of the independent healers appears to have been a final outburst that marked the exhaustion of the primitivist impulse and the beginning of a new style of life and worship that assuredly was still influenced, but no longer governed, by the original concerns.

Today the major American pentecostal denominations claim millions of upwardly mobile lower- and middle-class members and work with annual budgets that would have staggered the imaginations of their forefathers. More influential—or at least more visible—are the parachurch ministries that increasingly crowd the religious landscape. Pat Robertson's Christian Broadcast Network and University in Norfolk, Virginia; Oral Roberts's University and City of Faith Medical Center in Tulsa; Freda Lindsay's Christian Center and Christ for the Nations Institute in Dallas; and the PTL retirement and vacation complex near Charlotte, North Carolina, are only a few of the independent, pentecostal-sponsored enterprises that, taken together, represent an investment of billions of dollars and the commitment of millions of supporters. But numbers tell only part of the story. The real change is the shift of focus from the "full gospel" of the early days to a preoccupation with conservative political causes and, among a substantial minority, an explicit commitment to the pursuit of health, wealth, and worldly success under the aegis of "prosperity evangelism." Describing the latter aspect of contemporary pentecostalism as a "veritable spiritual Amway movement," historian David Edwin Harrell aptly notes that it offers not healing for the sick but security for the well, not "consolation to the poor but confirmation to the successful."[31]

Scanning the literature of the pentecostal movement from 1900 to the present, one gains the impression that the acculturative process started after World War I, sharply accelerated after World War II, and has continued unabated to the present. But when the revival was young and still vibrant with the hope of the primitivist vision, pentecostals knew that they were legitimated not by human traditions but by apostolic authority and power. They knew, in short, that the movement had been born in the fullness of time to manifest the glory of the Latter Rain.

NOTES

1. The best scholarly study of the origins of pentecostalism in the United States is Robert Mapes Anderson, *Vision of the Disinherited: The Making of American Pentecostalism* (New York: Oxford University Press, 1979). For an overview of the movement worldwide see Walter J. Hollenweger, *The Pentecostals*, trans. R. A. Wilson (German, 1969; Minneapolis: Augsburg Publishing House, 1972). For the numerical magnitude of contemporary pentecostalism, see David B. Barrett, *World Christian Encyclopedia* (New York: Oxford University Press, 1982), 838.

2. "Sacred meteor" is from Russell P. Spittler, "Scripture and the Theological Enterprise," in *The Use of the Bible in Theology: Evangelical Options,* ed. Robert K. Johnston (Atlanta, GA: John Knox Press, 1985), 63. For philosophical primitivism, see Grant Wacker, "The Functions of Faith in Primitive Pentecostalism," *Harvard Theological Review* 77:3–4 (1984):353–75.

3. B. H. Irwin, *Live Coals of Fire,* 13 October 1899, 2, quoted in James R. Goff, Jr., "Pentecostal Millenarianism: The Development of Premillennial Orthodoxy, 1909–1943," *Ozark Historical Review* 12 (1983):19. William J. Seymour, *Apostolic Faith,* October 1907–January 1908:3, and April 1907:3.

4. Seymour, *Apostolic Faith,* January 1907:3.

5. Based upon a curricula survey of pentecostal schools compiled by Ralph M. Riggs, Education Secretary, Assemblies of God, ca. 1950, "History of Education," Assemblies of God Archives, Springfield, MO. To this day, to the

best of my knowledge, no pentecostal scholar has written a synoptic history of either European or American church history.

6. Seymour, *Apostolic Faith,* October 1906:4; *Faithful Standard,* November 1922:8; Donald Gee, *The Pentecostal Movement* (1941; London: Elim Publishing, 1949), 3; Carl Brumback, *Suddenly . . . from Heaven: A History of the Assemblies of God* (Springfield, MO: Gospel Publishing House, 1961).

7. Donald Gee, *The Ministry Gifts of Christ* (Springfield, MO: Gospel Publishing House, 1930), 13; A. J. Tomlinson, *Evening Light and Church of God Evangel* 1 (July 1910):1.

8. Frank Ewart, *The Phenomenon of Pentecost* (Houston: Herald Publishing House, 1947), 87; Bennett F. Lawrence, *The Apostolic Faith Restored* (St. Louis: Gospel Publishing House, 1916), 12. Although Ewart's book was published at mid-century, I would argue that he was a valid first-generation witness given that he moved to Los Angeles in 1907, participated in the initial Azusa Mission revivals, and became pastor of William H. Durham's pentecostal mission in that city in 1912.

9. Elizabeth Sisson, *A Sign People* (Springfield, MO: Gospel Publishing House, ca. 1918), 13.

10. Charles Fox Parham and Lillian Thistlewaite in Sarah E. Parham, comp., *The Life of Charles Fox Parham* (Baxter Springs, KS: Apostolic Faith, 1930), 52–53, 60–61; A. J. Tomlinson in *Diary of A. J. Tomlinson,* ed. Homer A. Tomlinson (Queens Village, NY: The Church of God, World Headquarters, 1955), 3:13; and A. J. Tomlinson, *Answering the Call of God* (Cleveland, TN: White Wing Publishing House [1913]), 21; Seymour, *Apostolic Faith,* November 1906:1, and *Apostolic Faith,* September 1906:3.

11. Lawrence, *Apostolic Faith Restored,* 12. For the point of the last sentence of the paragraph I am indebted to Donald Wilber Dayton, "Theological Roots of Pentecostalism" (Ph.D. dissertation, University of Chicago, 1983), 32.

12. George Floyd Taylor, *The Spirit and the Bride* (Falcon, NC: privately printed, 1907), 21.

13. Elizabeth Baker, *Chronicles of a Faith Life* (New York: Garland Publishing, 1984), 143; Ewart, *Phenomenon of Pentecost,* 18; Miss S. A. Duncan, *The Early and the Latter Rain* (Rochester, NY: Elim Publishing House, ca. 1910), 7–8.

14. See, for example, D. Wesley Myland, *The Latter Rain Pentecost* (1910; Chicago: Evangel Publishing House, 1911), 80–81, 85. The most systematic exposition of the continuities and differences between conventional and pentecostal versions of dispensational premillennialism was Frank M. Boyd, *Ages and Dispensations* (Springfield, MO: Gospel Publishing House [1955]); see esp. p. 46 for a clear affirmation of the continuity of the Apostolic and Church Dispensations. See also Gerald T. Sheppard, "Pentecostals and the Hermeneutics of Dispensationalism: The Anatomy of an Uneasy Relationship," *Pneuma: Journal of the Society for Pentecostal Studies* 6 (1984):5–33, esp. 25. Although Sheppard overstates the difference between the systems, he offers a valuable analysis of the theological implications of those differences. Finally, it should be noted that the prophetic or dispensational significance of the

biblical references to the early and latter rains was only one of three concurrent meanings all such references possessed for early pentecostals. The other two involved (1) literal or historical descriptions of the actual rainfall in the land of Palestine in the first and twentieth centuries, respectively, and (2) spiritual or typical/antitypical descriptions of the promulgation of the Law to Moses on Mount Sinai and the consummation of the Law to the Jews on the Day of Pentecost, respectively (Myland, *Latter Rain,* 6).

15. Taylor, *Spirit,* 91; J. W. Welch, "Introduction" in Lawrence, *Apostolic Faith Restored.*

16. Susan A. Duncan, *Word and Work,* August 1910:239, quoted in D. William Faupel, "The Function of 'Models' in the Interpretation of Pentecostal Thought," *Pneuma: Journal of the Society for Pentecostal Studies* 2 (1980):68; *Prophetic Age* quoted without citation in *Apostolic Faith,* May 1907:1; Sisson, *Sign People,* 9, 12.

17. The quotation from Charles Parham is the title of chapter 7 of *Life of Charles F. Parham;* I owe this reference to Dayton, "Theological Roots," 17. The Azusa Mission creed is printed in *Apostolic Faith,* September 1906:2. The William J. Seymour article is in *Apostolic Faith,* October 1906:1. Bibliographic information on most of the periodicals mentioned, as well as many others, can be found in Charles Edwin Jones, *A Guide to the Study of the Pentecostal Movement,* 2 vols. (Metuchen, NJ: Scarecrow Press, 1983).

18. For the main point of this paragraph, I am indebted to D. William Faupel; P. C. Nelson, *The Jerusalem Council: The First General Council of the Assemblies of God* (Enid, OK: Southwestern Press, ca. 1930); Klaude Kendrick, *The Promise Fulfilled: A History of the Modern Pentecostal Movement* (Springfield, MO: Gospel Publishing House, 1961); Vinson Synan, *In the Latter Days: The Outpouring of the Holy Spirit in the Twentieth Century* (Ann Arbor, MI: Servant Books, 1984).

19. John Alexander Dowie is quoted without citation in Gordon Lindsay, *John Alexander Dowie* (1951; Dallas: Christ for the Nations, 1980), 155, and in *Champion of Faith: The Sermons of John Alexander Dowie,* ed. Gordon Lindsay (Dallas: Christ for the Nations, 1979), 102. Seymour, *Apostolic Faith,* October 1907–January 1908:2. It could be argued that Dowie was not a pentecostal because he did not condone speaking in tongues in his meetings or endorse it as the necessary evidence of the baptism of the Holy Spirit. However, besides the fact that it is somewhat anachronistic to define pentecostalism by those criteria, Dowie qualified as a pentecostal in all other respects. Many of his followers eventually became leaders in the movement.

20. Frank Bartleman, *Azusa Street* (Plainfield, NJ: Logos International, 1980), 68–69, unabridged reprint of *How Pentecost Came to Los Angeles* (1925); Charles Parham, *Apostolic Faith* [KS], October 1912 supplement: 7.

21. *Church of God Evangel,* February 10, 1917:1; *Apostolic Faith,* October 1906:3; L. C. Ebey, *Apostolic Faith,* November 1906:2.

22. A. J. Tomlinson, *Church of God Evangel,* March 10, 1917:1. For a typical account by an outsider in which the elitism of pentecostals was noted—and

scored—see "The 'Tongue Movement,' " *Independent* 66 (1909):1286–89, esp. 1288, col. 2.

23. Seymour, *Apostolic Faith,* February–March 1907:6; "Sanctification makes us . . ." from *Apostolic Faith,* May 1908:2; "Elite . . ." is from *Upper Room,* July 1910:8; for Parham see, for example, "A Critical Analysis of the Tongues Question," *Apostolic Faith* [KS], June 1925:2; Bartleman, *Azusa Street,* 79–80, see also 9, 19, 27; the general superintendent's quotation is from Ernest S. Williams, "Forty-Five Years of Pentecostal Revival," *Pentecostal Evangel* 19 (August 1951):3–4, quoted in Kendrick, *Promise Fulfilled,* 70. I owe the last reference to Roger Robins, "Worship and Structure in Early Pentecostalism," senior seminar paper, Harvard Divinity School, 1984, 24. For a very different interpretation of the history of pentecostal attitudes toward other Christians see Cecil M. Robeck, "Pentecostal Perspectives on the Ecumenical Challenge," paper given to the Society for Pentecostal Studies, Cleveland, TN, 1983.

24. The pioneer was quoted without attribution in Stanley H. Frodsham, *With Signs Following: The Story of the Pentecostal Revival in the Twentieth Century* (1926, Springfield, MO: Gospel Publishing House, 1946), 34; "Manmade creeds . . ." is from Seymour (?) *Apostolic Faith,* September 1906:3. I owe the main point of this and the following paragraph to Roger Robins's exceptionally perceptive study, "Worship and Structure," 23.

25. Parham, "Sermon," *Apostolic Faith* [KS], April 1925:9; "Power . . . irresistible . . ." is from J. E. Sawders, *Apostolic Faith,* February–March 1907:3; the Florence Crawford quotations are from *Apostolic Faith,* February–March 1907:5 and April 1907:4; the Honolulu pastor was H. M. Turney, *Apostolic Faith,* April 1907:1; the reporter's description is from Muncie *Daily News,* 21 September 1885, quoted in Wayne E. Warner, *The Woman Evangelist: The Life and Times of Charismatic Evangelist Maria B. Woodworth-Etter* (Metuchen, NJ: Scarecrow Press, 1986), 55.

26. William J. Samarin, *Tongues of Men and Angels* (New York: Macmillan, 1972), 2, 78–87, 120; H. Newton Maloney and A. Adams Lovekin, *Glossolalia: Behavioral Science Perspectives on Speaking in Tongues* (New York: Oxford University Press, 1985), 26–38. Glossolalia may have been an extension, albeit an extreme one, of the regression from written to oral communication that has been characteristic of many revivalistic and popular religious movements. See the provocative suggestions along this line in Harry S. Stout, "Culture, Structure, and the 'New' History: A Critique and an Agenda," *Computers and the Humanities* 9 (1975):224.

27. See, for example, Victor Turner, "Images of Anti-Temporality: An Essay in the Anthropology of Experience," *Harvard Theological Review* 75 (1982):243–65.

28. Bartleman, *Azusa Street,* 59–60. Additional examples of such phenomena can be found in virtually any issue of the early periodicals. For a handy—albeit somewhat sanitized—collection of autobiographical recollections of traumatic glossolalic speech and other forms of ecstatic experience, see Wayne E. Warner, ed., *Revival* (Tulsa: Harrison House, 1984).

29. Richard Michael Riss, "The Latter Rain Movement of 1948 and the Mid-Twentieth Century Evangelical Awakening" (Master of Christian Studies thesis, Regent College, 1979).

30. The best study of the independent deliverance evangelists is David Edwin Harrell, Jr., *All Things Are Possible: The Healing and Charismatic Revivals in Modern America* (Bloomington: Indiana University Press, 1975).

31. David Edwin Harrell, Jr., "Healing Revivalism Since World War II," paper presented to the American Society of Church History, New York, December 1985. See also David Edwin Harrell, Jr., "Radical Right: Electronic Evangelism," *Occasional Papers* (Collegeville, MN: Institute for Ecumenical and Cultural Research, 1981), 3–7, reprinted in *A Documentary History of Religion in America: Since 1865,* ed. Edwin S. Gaustad (Grand Rapids: Eerdmans Publishing, 1983), 539–44.

14

The Restoration Ideal in the Churches of Christ

BILL J. HUMBLE

THE Churches of Christ in America trace their roots to a restoration movement that began on the American frontier in the first decade of the nineteenth century and whose best-known leaders were Barton W. Stone, Thomas Campbell, his son Alexander Campbell, and Walter Scott. But Churches of Christ are not the only heirs of this heritage. There are now three American churches, whose memberships total nearly three million, with common historical roots in the Stone-Campbell restoration: Disciples of Christ, Churches of Christ, and Independent Christian Churches. The Disciples are now concerned about ecumenical and social issues rather than restoration, but the Churches of Christ and Independent Christian Churches are still strongly committed to the restoration of the primitive church.

The thesis of this paper is that Churches of Christ are most indebted to three leaders for their restoration theology: Thomas and Alexander Campbell in the period between 1800 and 1850, and David Lipscomb during the decades following the Civil War.

Thomas Campbell was a Seceder Presbyterian minister from Rich Hill, northern Ireland, who migrated to America in 1807 (at age 45) and settled in southwest Pennsylvania. Soon after arriving in America, Thomas Campbell was at odds with his church over the authority of Scripture as compared with creeds and the limitations of fellowship at the Lord's table. Campbell left the Presbyterians and in 1809 he wrote a plea for unity and restoration entitled *Declaration and Address*. William Warren Sweet has described the *Declaration and Address* as "a great document; one of the greatest indeed that American Christianity has produced."[1]

There are two themes that recur over and over in the *Declaration and Address,* the unity of all Christians and the restoration of the primitive church. Thomas Campbell was deeply distressed at the tragic divisions within Christendom. In northern Ireland his own church, the Seceder Presbyterians, were divided into Burghers and Anti-Burghers, and he had worked unsuccessfully to heal this division. And in America his passion for unity was one of the causes for his alienation from the Seceders. It is not surprising, then, that the *Declaration and Address* is infused with a passion for Christian unity.

Campbell wrote, "The church of Christ upon earth is essentially, intentionally, and constitutionally one; consisting of all those in every place that profess their faith in Christ and obedience to him in all things according to the Scriptures."[2] Except for the familiar plea "We speak where the Bible speaks and are silent where the Bible is silent," this is probably the best-known sentence that Thomas Campbell ever wrote. Notice the three words Campbell used when he said that the church is "essentially, intentionally, and constitutionally" one. By "essentially" he meant that unity is the essence of the church's being God's people. By "intentionally" he meant that it was the intent or plan of God that his people be one. And by "constitutionally" he meant that unity will come when the church follows the New Testament, the constitution that God has given to govern it.

Campbell believed "that division among the Christians is a horrid evil, fraught with many evils." He called division "antichristian, as it destroys the visible unity of the body of Christ; . . . antiscriptural, as being strictly prohibited by his sovereign authority; . . . antinatural, as it excites Christians to condemn, to hate, and oppose one another."[3]

But how could all Christians ever be united? Campbell's answer was the restoration of the New Testament church. Influenced by John Locke, Campbell believed there were essential truths of Christianity that all Christians could accept, and if the primitive church could be restored on the basis of these truths, denominational divisions would disappear and the church would again be united. The unique significance of the *Declaration and Address* lies in this vision that Christian unity could be achieved through a restoration of the primitive church. As. W. E. Garrison has observed, "The idea of defending or restoring the unity of the church was not new. But the idea of making the first of these the instrument for accomplishing the second was new."[4]

If Christians were ever to be united, according to Campbell, nothing could be bound as an article of faith or test of fellowship unless it was "expressly enjoined" by the authority of Christ or his apostles "either in express terms or by approved precedent." He concluded, "Nothing ought to be received into the faith or worship of the Church, or be made a term of communion among Christians, that is not as old as the New Testament."[5] Campbell often called the New Testament a perfect pattern or constitution for the church. He viewed the Old and New Testaments as the perfect revelation of God, but he saw the New Testament as a perfect "constitution for the worship, discipline, and government of the New Testament church" just as the Old Testament had been for the Old Testament church.

Campbell recalled that the first Christians walked "in the fear of the Lord in holy unity and unanimity," and he said that if we would erect churches "in an exact conformity to their recorded and approved example," we would enjoy the same unity they had. The only way to overcome religious division was by "simply returning to the original standard of Christianity, the profession and practice of the primitive Church, as expressly exhibited upon the sacred page of New Testament scripture." He urged, "Let us do as we are there expressly told they did, say as they said; that is, profess and practice . . . in every possible instance, after their approved example, and in so doing we shall realize and exhibit all that unity and uniformity that the primitive Church possessed."[6]

Thomas Campbell was a man with a vision: the unity of God's people would be realized by restoring the primitive church. The *Declaration and Address,* with this vision, has probably had a greater influence on Churches of Christ than any other single document in American history.

If the Churches of Christ are indebted to Campbell for their vision of restoration, they are indebted to Barton W. Stone, far more than to Campbell, for their numerical strength across the South. After the historic revival at Cane Ridge in 1801, Stone left the Presbyterians and began establishing independent churches. By 1811 the Stone movement had churches in twelve states stretching from Arkansas to New York, whereas Thomas Campbell had established only the small Brush Run Church by 1811. Stone's passion for Christian unity is well known, but he also saw a return to biblical authority as the road to unity. Stone wrote, "The Bible alone in heart believed, and in the spirit obeyed, is doubtless the means of Christian union."[7] Those words might have come from Thomas Campbell.

When Thomas Campbell's family joined him in 1809 in Washington, Pennsylvania, his eldest son Alexander was already wrestling with doubts about his Presbyterian heritage. The younger Campbell had been a student at the University of Glasgow, and there he had met

James and Robert Haldane and Greville Ewing who had left the state church of Scotland and were establishing independent congregations in Scotland and England. The younger Campbell was challenged by their views on biblical authority, congregationalism, and weekly communion. He raised questions about this spiritual heritage, groped for answers, and refrained from communing with the Seceders. Just before the Campbell family arrived in America, the *Declaration and Address* had come from the press. When Alexander studied it, he found his answers and his mission. He embraced his father's vision, and soon the mantle of leadership shifted from father to son.

The task of applying the restoration concept to the everyday questions of church life became the major work of Alexander Campbell's life. What did it mean to restore the primitive church? What would be practiced, and what abandoned, in a restored church? What about baptism, church polity, or worship? These questions, and countless others, were neither raised nor answered in the *Declaration and Address*. Thomas Campbell had written a bold visionary statement of principle, a program for the future, a call for unity through restoration. His son was a man of different temperament, an iconoclastic, pragmatic restorer whose task was to apply the restoration principle to the practical questions of faith and life.

One of the first questions to arise concerned baptism. According to an autobiographical article by Alexander Campbell, he was talking with a Presbyterian minister about restoring the primitive church and, specifically, about the idea that nothing could be accepted in the church unless it was "expressly enjoined" in the New Testament either in "express terms" or "approved precedent" (command or example). The Presbyterian responded that on this basis Campbell would become a Baptist. Campbell reported that he was mortified that he could not produce a New Testament passage authorizing infant baptism.[8]

The result was an intensive year-long study of baptism. When the younger Campbell was convinced that the primitive church practiced immersion, Thomas Campbell agreed. But he saw no need for them to "unchurch and paganize" themselves and make a new profession of immersion. For some months Alexander yielded to his father's views. Soon, however, his convictions demanded action, and on 12 June 1812, he was immersed by Matthias Luse, a Baptist minister. And he was not alone. Seven others, including his father, joined him in Buffalo Creek, and within a few weeks the Brush Run Church, the Campbells' first congregation, was a church of immersed believers.

Fifteen years later, Walter Scott was serving as evangelist for the Mahoning Baptist Association in Ohio and began preaching a new insight into the purpose of baptism. According to Scott, baptism was "for the remission of sins," and the immersed believer then received "the gift of the Holy Spirit" (Acts 2:38). Scott's new evangelism was a sharp break with the prevailing Calvinistic view of conversion. According to Scott, Calvinism stated the Gospel "wrong end foremost." Faith was not the mystical fruit of the spirit in the heart of one depraved and incapable of believing of one's own volition, as Calvinists taught. Rather, faith was the heart's response to the proclamation of the Gospel, and baptism was the act that completed one's obedience to Christ. Scott argued that the gift of God's spirit came after baptism, not before faith as Calvinism taught.[9]

What appealed to the people of the frontier about Scott's evangelism was the positive assurance of salvation. Whereas Calvinism often left them with interminable uncertainty about the state of the soul, Scott's message gave positive assurance that the immersed believer was numbered among God's elect. Many other preachers of the Campbell and Stone movements embraced Scott's new evangelism. Thousands were baptized, and the Campbells' restoration knew rapid growth for the first time. It should be noted that baptism by immersion for the remission of sins has continued to be emphasized among Churches of Christ.

Thomas Campbell had assumed in the *Declaration and Address* that the restoration of the primitive church would bring unity. However, the acceptance of immersion revealed a possible tension between unity and restoration. Earlier Thomas Campbell, like John Locke, had assumed that most Christians believed the essential truths of the Christian faith. But now, there was one doctrine, baptism by immersion, that the Campbells saw as important in restoring the primitive church, but which most Christians did not accept. The Campbells' immersion did open Baptist doors, and for the next fifteen years (1815–30) the Campbells worked as reformers within the Baptist church.

Alexander Campbell's first periodical, the *Christian Baptist,* was published during these years (1823–30). The goals of unity and restoration are both found in the *Christian Baptist,* but the priority is on restoring the primitive church, whereas the goal of Christian unity recedes into the distance. This is seen in a series of thirty articles entitled "A Restoration of the Ancient Order of Things," which Campbell began in 1825 and continued through 1829.

In the first article in this series, Campbell tried to distinguish between restoration and reformation. Many reformations had been attempted since the Middle Ages, and although Campbell often paid tribute to the Reformers, he believed their attempts had fallen short. In Campbell's view, human systems of religion, creeds, and clergy were subjects of reformation, but not the Christian religion: "Every attempt to reform Christianity is like an attempt to create a new sun." Campbell envisioned his goal in these words:

> A RESTORATION of the ancient order of things is all that is necessary to the happiness and usefulness of christians. . . . To bring the societies of christians *up* to the New Testament is just to bring the disciples, individually and collectively, to walk in the faith, and in the commandments of the Lord and Savior, as presented in that blessed volume; and this is to restore the ancient order of things. Celebrated as the era of Reformation is, we doubt not but that the era of Restoration will . . . transcend it. . . . Just in so far as the ancient order of things, or the religion of the New Testament, is restored, just so far has the Millennium commenced.[10]

Campbell believed that a new day was dawning. The restoration of the primitive church would reunite Christians and usher in the millennium. Campbell was so optimistic that he named his new journal, begun in 1830, the *Millennial Harbinger.*

Walter Scott made the same distinction between restoration and reformation that Campbell did. He began a new paper, *The Evangelist,* in 1832; and he wrote in the first issue that there was a rapidly growing party that was pleading "not for a *reformation* only, but an entire and unqualified *restoration* of every thing warranted in the holy scriptures, comprehended under the two titles of *ancient gospel* and *ancient order.*"[11] Scott defined the "ancient gospel" as including everything necessary to win disciples and add them to the church, and the "ancient order" as the doctrines relating to the life of the church. Churches of Christ today do not use the vocabulary of "ancient gospel and ancient order," but they still do emphasize soteriology and ecclesiology in their attempts to restore the primitive church.

It should be noted, however, that by the 1830s Campbell and the other leaders began to use the terms *reformation* and *restoration* interchangeably and often referred to their work as "the current reformation."

Campbell was concerned about how people became citizens of Christ's kingdom, and he discussed this in another article in the series, "A Restoration of the Ancient Order of Things." This article, like others in the series, was strongly anticreedal, and Campbell insisted that if we are to restore the primitive church, we must accept the New Testament as "the constitution of the kingdom." Citizens must be received into the kingdom today "just as they were received by the apostles into it." To illustrate how this was done, Campbell used the analogy of naturalization, a result, perhaps, of his being a naturalized citizen of the United States. How did the Apostles receive people into Christ's kingdom? According to Campbell, they demanded that human beings acknowledge the King's supremacy by confessing him as the Son of God and expressing their allegiance in an act of naturalization—baptism.[12] And Campbell concluded that men and women become citizens of Christ's kingdom in this same way wherever the primitive church is restored.

Campbell explored a wide variety of subjects in his thirty articles on "A Restoration of the Ancient Order of Things." Three articles were devoted to the authority of Scripture and to criticizing Protestant creeds. Three articles discussed church organization; six, the worship of the church; and seven, church discipline. Others dealt with hymnody, the spirit of the early Christians, New Testament requirements for church membership, love feasts, and official names and titles.

In another article in the series Campbell acknowledged a hermeneutic problem that every restorationist must face, and this is the question of determining which practices of the primitive church are important for today. What does the New Testament bind on all ages? And what may be dismissed as the culture of an ancient world? In March of 1826, Campbell printed a letter he had received from an Indiana reader, Joseph Hostetler, who identified himself as a German Baptist or Dunkard. Hostetler commended Campbell for being "so great an advocate for primitive christianity," but he wondered how Campbell could disregard the commands for foot-washing, the kiss of charity, and trine immersion.[13] In his response to Hostetler and other critics, Campbell tried to study each New Testament passage in its context to determine what was "essential" (a common practice that seemed to be required of all the churches) and what was "circumstantial."[14] Campbell's treatment of the subject must have satisfied Hostetler, for in the early 1830s Hostetler and fifteen German Baptist churches in southern Indiana and Kentucky became a part of Campbell's restoration movement.[15]

Others were not satisfied. Sidney Rigdon believed that the community of goods of the Jerusalem church was binding on later ages, and he tried to practice it at Kirtland, Ohio. After Campbell opposed him, Rigdon left the Campbell restoration and became a very influential Mormon.

In summary, Thomas and Alexander Campbell envisioned the restoration of the primitive church as a means to achieve the ultimate goal of Christian unity. They believed that they stood on catholic ground where all Christians could unite. The younger Campbell wrote, "While endeavoring to abolish the old sects, let us be cautious that we form not a new one. This may be done by either adding to, or subtracting from, the apostolic constitution a single item. Our platform must be as long and as broad as the New Testament."[16] The Churches of Christ, however, have not followed the Campbells' teaching on every point, and they would resent being called "Campbellites." Still, the Campbells' commitment to biblical authority, their dream of restoring the primitive church, and their agenda for "restoring the ancient order of things" have had a great influence on Churches of Christ. Alexander Campbell gave this simple definition of restoration: "The thing proposed, is to bring the christianity and the church of the present day up to the standard of the New Testament."[17] It would be difficult to find a better statement of the continuing commitment of Churches of Christ than in those words of Campbell.

The four decades following the Civil War were a time of travail for this restoration movement. The period stretches from 1866, when Alexander Campbell died, until 1906, when the United States Census listed the Churches of Christ and Disciples of Christ separately. The dream of Thomas Campbell and Barton W. Stone had been the unity of all believers. Ironically, the "unity through restoration" movement they began suffered division, and after the schism there were two churches. The Disciples of Christ or Christian Churches were larger and stronger, especially in the North. The Churches of Christ were located mainly in the South and often distinguished themselves from their northern brethren by their refusal to use instrumental music in worship. The division had many causes: the tension between unity and restoration, doctrinal disputes about church organization and worship, socioeconomic differences, Civil War alienation, and the challenges of liberal theology.

The most important leader among the southern Churches of Christ during these decades of division was David Lipscomb, a Nashville, Tennessee, preacher-editor. Lipscomb was editor of the *Gospel Advocate* for the forty years from 1866 until 1906, and his paper had a greater influence than any other journal among the southern churches.[18].

There are two facets of Lipscomb's thought that are important for this study. The first is his deep, almost childlike faith in the authority of Scripture. Lipscomb's life was driven by an unwavering conviction that the Scripture was God's word and must be followed.

For example, in 1867 Lipscomb and Thomas Munnell, an influential Kentucky preacher, carried on a written debate in the *Gospel Advocate* about missionary organizations. According to Lipscomb, the New Testament taught that mission work should be done by the local churches.

The churches might cooperate, but this would not require missionary societies. Munnell responded by challenging Lipscomb to tell how churches could cooperate in a "business-like way" without some kind of organization. Lipscomb's answer is typical of his effort to rely on Scripture:

> We do not know that God proposed to convert the world in a business-like way. Wise men, intent on the accomplishment of a great object, would scarcely choose a babe, born out of wedlock, cradled in a manger, as the efficient superintendent in the accomplishment of that work. Business men . . . would have hardly sought out unlearned, simple hearted fishermen as their agents . . . would not have chosen the infamy of the Cross, and the degradation of the grave. . . . This is so unbusiness-like that, business men, entering in strive to change it to a more business-like manner. . . . God's ways are not man's ways . . . and the foolishness of God is wiser than man.[19]

Nearly thirty years later, on the thirtieth anniversary of his becoming editor of the *Gospel Advocate,* Lipscomb reflected, "The cardinal thought in my religion has ever been to follow the will of God, as expressed in precept or by approved example; to stand on safe ground; to be sure of the approval and blessing of God." And "guided by this principle," Lipscomb opposed practices that he saw as inconsistent with the restoration of the primitive church.[20]

The second aspect of Lipscomb's thought was his continuing commitment to the restoration of the primitive church and his sense of continuity with the work of the Campbells. This is illustrated in an exchange of letters between Lipscomb and S. N. D. North in 1907 that led to the separate listing for Churches of Christ in the religious census. North was director of the U. S. Census Bureau, and as he prepared for the 1906 religious census, he wrote to Lipscomb and asked whether there was "a religious body called 'church of Christ,' not identified with the Disciples of Christ." And if there was, North wanted to know how it originated and what its distinctive principles were.

Lipscomb's lengthy reply recounted the work of Thomas Campbell and quoted extensively from the *Declaration and Address.* This shows that Lipscomb viewed himself and Churches of Christ as standing in continuity with Thomas Campbell's commitment to restoring the primitive church. Having made this clear, Lipscomb answered North's question: yes, the Churches of Christ were a separate church from the Disciples.

Why had the separation come? According to Lipscomb, it had come because some of the churches had abandoned the principle of restoring the primitive church. He told North that as the movement had grown in numbers and wealth, some of the churches adopted practices that had been opposed earlier: "a general organization of the churches under a missionary society with a moneyed membership, and the adoption of instrumental music in worship." Lipscomb called these "a subversion of the fundamental principles on which the churches were based." And Lipscomb told the director of the Census that it was controversy over these issues and "the principle of fidelity to the Scriptures" that had divided the churches.[21] Lipscomb was concerned about the impact of theological liberalism on the restoration movement in the North, and his reference to "fidelity to the Scriptures" probably reflects this concern.

Lipscomb wrote hundreds of editorials and articles for the *Gospel Advocate,* but he did not often write specifically about restoration. There is nothing in Lipscomb comparable to Alexander Campbell's thirty articles on "A Restoration of the Ancient Order of Things." Lipscomb's voluminous writings focused on the study of Scripture and practical issues of Christian conduct. He wrote commentaries and answered countless questions from readers of the *Gospel Advocate.* But underlying every article that he wrote, there was a commitment to the authority of Scripture and to the dream of restoring the primitive church. What Thomas and Alexander Campbell had begun, he was resolved to continue. And when others introduced practices that he saw as subversive of the restoration dream, he opposed such "innovations" with long suffering forbearance, but he did not waver.

The dream of restoring the primitive church has appeared many times in Christian history. The dream has taken many forms in our own country's religious heritage, as illustrated in this book. The Churches of Christ share this dream. For their restoration commitment and agenda, the Churches of Christ are indebted to Thomas Campbell for the goal of unity through restoration, to Alexander Campbell for a restoration agenda that grew out of decades of study and controversy, and to David Lipscomb for an unwavering determination to remain true to Scripture and the restoration dream when others, in his judgment at least, were forsaking this heritage. There are debts to many others, of course, but to none more than to these three.

NOTES

1. William Warren Sweet, "Campbell's Position in Church History," *The Christian Evangelist* 76 (8 September 1938):969. This was a special issue of

The Christian Evangelist commemorating the one hundred and fiftieth anniversary of Alexander Campbell's birth.

2. Thomas Campbell, *Declaration and Address* (St. Louis: Bethany Press, 1960), 44.

3. T. Campbell, *Declaration and Address,* 46–47.

4. Winfred E. Garrison, *Heritage and Destiny: An American Religious Movement Looks Ahead* (St. Louis: Bethany Press, 1961), 80. Other historians have noted Thomas Campbell's unique treatment of unity and restoration as complementary; cf. William E. Tucker and Lester G. McAllister, *Journey in Faith* (St. Louis: Bethany Press, 1975), 111–14; David Edwin Harrell, Jr., *Quest For A Christian America* (Nashville, TN: Disciples of Christ Historical Society, 1966), 10; and Thomas J. Liggett, "Why the Disciples Chose Unity," *Lexington Theological Quarterly* 15 (January 1980):24. For a recent dissenting opinion, see Leroy Garrett, *The Stone-Campbell Movement* (Joplin, MO: College Press, 1981), 6–11, 146–59; Garrett argues that Barton Stone and Thomas Campbell gave such priority to unity that restoration is an aberration whenever it appears in the history of the movement. The data on the Campbells' view of restoration included in this chapter shows that Garrett is mistaken in giving such priority to unity.

5. T. Campbell, *Declaration and Address,* 46.

6. T. Campbell, *Declaration and Address,* 45, 62, 77.

7. James Mathes, ed., *Works of Elder B. W. Stone* (Rosemead, CA: Old Paths Book Club, 1953), 262.

8. Alexander Campbell, "Anecdotes, Incidents and Facts," *Millennial Harbinger,* ser. 3, 5 (May 1848):280–83.

9. Dwight E. Stevenson, *Walter Scott: Voice of the Golden Oracle* (St. Louis: Christian Board of Publication, 1946), 59.

10. Alexander Campbell, "A Restoration of the Ancient Order of Things, No. I," *Christian Baptist* 2 (7 February 1825):136.

11. Walter Scott, "The Reformation," *The Evangelist* 1 (2 January 1832):20.

12. Alexander Campbell, "A Restoration of the Ancient Order of Things, No. III," *Christian Baptist* 2 (4 April 1825):174.

13. Alexander Campbell, "A Restoration of the Ancient Order of Things, No. XI," *Christian Baptist* 3 (8 March 1826):162–63.

14. Alexander Campbell, "A Restoration of the Ancient Order of Things, No. VII," *Christian Baptist* 3 (5 September 1825):29–33.

15. David Barry Eller, "The Brethren in the Western Ohio Valley, 1790–1850: German Baptist Settlement and Frontier Accommodation" (Ph.D. dissertation, Miami [Ohio] University, 1976), 199–201.

16. Alexander Campbell, *The Christian System* (Nashville, TN: Gospel Advocate Company, 1979), 84.

17. A. Campbell, "Restoration, No. I," 136.

18. Two good biographies of Lipscomb are available: Earl Irvin West, *The Life and Times of David Lipscomb* (Henderson, TN: Religious Book Service, 1954); and Robert E. Hooper, *Crying in the Wilderness: A Biography of David Lipscomb* (Nashville, TN: David Lipscomb College Press, 1979).

19. David Lipscomb, "Discussion—Missionary Societies," *Gospel Advocate* 9 (14 March 1867):208.

20. David Lipscomb, "Thirty Years Work," *Gospel Advocate* 38 (9 January 1896):4.

21. The correspondence between North and Lipscomb is reprinted in full in "The 'Church of Christ' and the 'Disciples of Christ,' " *Gospel Advocate* 49 (18 July 1907), 457. Publication of this religious census did not appear until 1910.

15

Comparing Three Approaches to Restorationism: A Response

SAMUEL S. HILL, JR.

T WO aspects of this comparison of the three approaches to restorationism in the preceding chapters bulk largest. First, it is necessary to assess the depth of the commitment to the restoration ideal or impulse in the pentecostal movement, the Churches of Christ, and the Latter-day Saints church—an ideal to which all three papers call attention. This commitment is given expression in belief, conviction, normative teaching, incentive for mission, and ideological distinctiveness. Second, it is necessary to recognize the variety of particular traditions that honor this commitment. There is not only a diversity, mind you, but a variety—Mormonism, the pentecostal movement, and the Churches of Christ are about as various as one could ask for. The design of this section, with an essay on each of the three, requires that I deal with all and seems to imply that this response should move in compare/contrast categories, at least to a degree. This response seeks to address that need. Here, however, the promise of fruitfulness easily shades into contrivance. Let us all beware.

Jan Shipps's analysis of Mormonism emphasizes its uniqueness. Mormonism is not in essence a derivation or a deviation or a reactionary response. In fact, it is even more than a configuration of components found elsewhere. It is a *sui generis* religious tradition (with parallels of course). Shipps tells us what we teachers have learned through practice, sometimes the hard way, that classification schemes widely applicable and genuinely illuminating do not work well for Mormonism.

All the criteria that Shipps uses for that particular religious movement, in the "history of religions" mode, should apply to pentecostalism and the Churches of Christ brotherhood as well. Well, they do and they do not, since those two groups are denominations of Christianity. In her terms, they and their kind are distinguished from Mormonism along the qualitative lines that separate "radical restoration movements" from "restoration movements." New beginnings characterize the former; reformation and revitalization the latter. By intention, the pentecostal movement and the Churches of Christ are unique, radical, and in a sense *sui generis*. Yet they really do not so qualify. They may be no closer than distant cousins to each other and to other Protestant bodies, but the bloodline is manifestly the same. Common classifications do work for illuminating these two denominations. Their respective orientations to organization, society, doctrine, and the like admit of comparative analysis. As intimated, even Mormonism is subject to some comparative treatment; all religious movements are.

In attempting to compare these three religious groups, one construct that may yield insight is the compression theme, impulse, or factor. Compression—drawn together, the reopening of the heavens—is a very different motif from "collapsed" as in the sense of collapsed into each other. By this coinage I refer to an attitude toward the relationship between the primary phenomenal norm and the practice of the people who accord honor to the norm. In one set of cases, a horizontal compression occurs, in the other a vertical compression is characteristic. This way of formulating attitudes is meant to sharpen perspectives on the role of history and to reveal similarities between variant forms of restorationism. As such, it has a chance of refining the category of "ahistorical" on which Mircea Eliade, Sidney Mead, and Richard Hughes have relied. What I am casting about for is a description that is an alternative to ahistoricality through being more inclusive than a merely historical frame of reference. To anticipate my argument: although these three share much, they build their cases on different forms of affinity between the norm and the practice, the pentecostal movement being less directly concerned with the issue of history than the other two. They all "compress," draw heaven and earth close together, but in different ways.

Restorationism in all its forms has something important to do with views of history. Pointedly, how do we get from the normative primitive Christian period to a believing tradition's present time? The horizontal kind of compression is preoccupied with the ancient and the current. It repudiates all intervening history, rarely as fact, but as holding any theological significance. Its goal instead is more the exaltation of the original than the demeaning of the subsequent. Still, the net effect is the repudiation of a section of God's providential guidance of the affairs of humankind. Moreover, it implies a vigorous confidence in one or another "modern" special act of Providence; that is, either radical restoration or restoration. The status of history is what is at issue for the horizontalists. The historical process is seen as subordinated to the will and work of God, as being eminently susceptible to his intentional presence or his not-so-tolerant judgment; it enjoys little independence from his direction; not so much life of its own. Furthermore, sacred and secular are clearly distinguished. So much greater weight is given to the normative, in its original manifestations and the restoration of the original, that all other history is largely stripped of divine significance. Most notably, such-Christianity-as-there-was is ignored (at best) in the practice of authentic church life and sometimes branded as a centuries-long aberration.

Compression for horizontalists means then that roots and conformity to roots, in practice and in institutional life, are magnified. Propriety prevails over power. Definition supersedes mystery. Fastidiousness is commended. Adaptation and improvisation are condemned. The drawing together of two periods of history gives character to each and to the remainder of the historical process. This kind of compression carries with it its own index terms, its values, its categories for perception and responsibility.

Compression can occur on another plane as well, the vertical. Pentecostals share the compression factor with other restorationists, but in their hands, its expression takes a quite divergent shape. (It is worth remarking, parenthetically, that Christian Science is a third cousin to the pentecostal movement, morphologically.) What are drawn close together in this model are heaven and earth, God and people in the world. There is some looking back to the original historical period in the interest of duplication or restoration, as Grant Wacker's paper informs us. Restorationism has not always been acknowledged as the lifeblood or watchword of pentecostal people, however, as with our other two movements. But in the early days that theme was a frame of reference often and in explicit fashion, and more recently it stands as an animation for realizing the power of miracles that characterized the church in the days of Christ and the Apostles.

Pentecostalism departs from the organization-authority-practice nexus of the Churches of Christ and Mormonism. Far less institution-minded than they, it has little incentive to assess the church of the era between primitive and twentieth-century Christianity. It did the next best thing, of course, in its determination to repudiate the tepid and lifeless, overorganized, and elitist features of late nineteenth-century Evangelical churches—features they felt had smothered the Evangelical fire. But the vision of a new dispensation focused on power, zeal, and the free flow of the Spirit. The principal manifestation of this release of the supernatural into the natural realm was speaking in tongues along with other gifts of the Spirit. This kind of penetration of the eternal into the temporal simply outflanks the issue of history. Theophanies occur to individuals, not to and for institutions—although we must take care to note that pentecostal experience takes place in a group of persons who have gathered with fellow worshippers. It has to do with dynamic personal experience, not with observance of specific constitutional directives. In a certain sense, pentecostalism has far more in common with Mormonism in this regard than with the Churches of Christ. The last is grounded in constitution and principles and in responsibility to conform to a strict construction. Mormonism's essence is contained in narrative but those are congealed into a primary proposition, true authority, with numerous subpropositions of gospel and law.

Pentecostalism's genius is better represented as an explosion than as a grounding. Reference to the history of primitive Christianity here has the effect of modeling, of exemplifying, and of generating.

The use of theory on comparative schemes is regularly illuminating in the study of religious movements. Very often, it also discloses something about a particular movement that is different from its self-conception and even apparently inimical to its intentions. The analysis of our three movements just presented shows a side of each of which each may be unaware. We may call it the "if . . . then . . ." approach. In less pleasing terms, it may be described as mechanical. Bill Humble's paper perceptively points up Thomas Campbell's claim that: *if* we restore the features of primitive Christianity, *then* we will restore the unity of all Christians. Comparably in the Mormon tradition: *if* Joseph Smith, Jr., asks for the appearance of the true church, *then* he is (in time) shown the one (indeed is himself the instrument of its founding). Pentecostalism is somewhat more committed to mystery, to the "surprising work of God," there being less reliance on a formula for bringing about fruition. Yet conduciveness, preparation, and expectation are attitudes characteristic of pentecostal services also. All three movements demonstrate a vigorous conviction about free will, about the participation of the human agent in the work of God.

A place in the stream of evolving American values was thus taken by the Mormon and Campbellite movements in the 1810s and 1820s. Jonathan Edwards's "surprising work of God" had given way to Charles

G. Finney's "new measures." Thomas Campbell's "if . . . then . . ." and Joseph Smith's "if I ask of God . . . it will be given," were "modern" or "liberal" avenues of access to God. The compression factor was at work making spiritual achievements regular, predictable, and logical. In the new dispensation, God was working in less strange ways, epistemologically at least. Mystery and a trusting providentialism had yielded to common sense, to *quid-pro-quo* reasoning, to certain kinds of rationalistic, mechanical thinking. Recent scholarship on Mormonism especially has established the discontinuities between these "old new religions" and their surrounding culture, but it remains unassailably true that they are profoundly American and modern.

Where limited vision shows up most commonly is in the eyes of scholars of Christianity who insist on interpreting these nineteenth-century American developments by reference to the standard canons of church history study and without reference to the movements' own views. In a variety of ways they are all dispensationalist. A new dispensation has begun, a new order in the ages; time has reached its fullness. A dispensationalist outlook rather naturally employs many new features, teachings, practices, and means. In the area of doctrine, it pleased God to replace the Augustinian-Thomist-Reformation stress on divine freedom and divine sovereignty with convictions about human freedom and agency. With respect to means, restoration ideology often makes joyful use of "mechanical," "rational," "logical" strategies of the "if . . . then . . ." sorts to which we have referred. Thus the attributes of "American" and "modern" establish no fault, no violations or compromise. Instead the nouns they modify, being designs of God, simply incorporate those adjectives. The spirit of this reconstruction is: in these last days, in this new time, God has replaced old wineskins with new, the timeless truth having been placed in new earthen vessels.

This line of analysis ushers us directly back to the issue of history. What distinguishes a restoration movement is, of course, the understanding of and attitudes toward the historical process. And this very hallmark item throws up barriers in the path of others' comprehension. Yes, these movements are culture-shaped, if one looks at them from such perspectives as classical Christian history or the standard study of history or social science. One has noted something important in pointing that out, when viewing these movements from any such conventional perspective. But viewed from the inside, these movements only suggest that the God of the ancient order continues to confound the wise through revealing teachings, practices, and means that, by being his own, upset human expectations—and discredit "man-made" traditions, "human inventions."

In rereading Jan Shipps's studies of Mormonism, I find that my analysis here is an elaboration of her depictions of that movement as radically restorationist. Naturally I hope that something significant has been added to our understanding, but much about this serves to confirm her treatment.

By indirection, attention to papers on these three quite different movements guides us to see the pentecostal phenomenon in a somewhat fresh light. In a nutshell, I judge it the least radical of the three. Mormonism is radically restorationist and a "new religious tradition." The Churches of Christ are restorationist and a new departure within the range of historic orthodoxy centering everything in a single hermeneutic principle. Pentecostalism stands closer to the classical tradition, more revitalizationist than restorationist, and a variation on Protestant orthodoxy. Its special concern and unique thrust is to associate full Christian discipleship with the gift of speaking in tongues.

Nevertheless, all three cases compress by bringing into the closest correlation the That and the This. While retaining a serious dualism, they embrace an uncritical notion of revelation. Heaven and earth do indeed draw very close together.

Let me, as a means of summarization, suggest a practical test for this formulation, a test focusing on the conservation or ecology concern or cause to which Americans have lately begun to pay much attention. The issue is: how does the natural order fare in a complex of the natural and the supernatural where the two are compressed into dynamic proximity? Lack of familiarity with the range and depth of these three movements restrains me from carrying out the test. But champions of all these might do well to reflect on how physical nature fares where confidence about the knowledge of the supernatural abounds and in a setting in which redemption outranks creation. At any rate, I would like to know about the positions held by the Churches of Christ, Mormons, and pentecostals on how close heaven and the physical environment are drawn and whether a sense of stewardship directs concern to the physical environment. This matter is an important ethical item in its own right, but it may also serve as a template for discerning the character of the three movements.

Epilogue

DAVID EDWIN HARRELL, JR.

*E*DITOR'S NOTE: David Edwin Harrell, Jr., noted student both of American evangelicalism and of religion in the American South, graciously accepted the difficult assignment of delivering an extemporaneous address at the conclusion of the conference, in which he responded to some of the major themes the conference had raised. His address, however, was far more than a response to the conference presentations. It also was a primary document in its own right. Clearly confessional, this document testifies to the continuing power of the restoration ideal in American life.

I have reflected some in the past few months about my selection to deliver this address. It is clear to me that there are two explanations for my having been assigned this task. First, I have written two books and several scholarly articles about the history of the Disciples of Christ and Churches of Christ. Perhaps more important for this occasion, however, is the fact that since age twelve I have been a member of the Church of Christ. In fact, my convictions are those of the strictest and most conservative members of this tradition—inorganic, anti-premillennial, anti-institutional. I come, therefore, to give you the musings of an insider on the occasion of three days of brooding about the central commitment of my life.

One indelible impression I take from this conference is that the restoration ideal has been a powerful motif. In fact, it may be the most vital single assumption underlying the development of American Protestantism. Equally important, the restoration ideal continues as one of the most compelling ideas in modern Christianity. The spread of pentecostalism around the world is striking testimony to the continued appeal of restoration thinking. All over the world millions of Christians still seek a restoration of the church's lost purity.

The presentations at this conference have laid bare the problems in such thinking as well as highlighting the power of the idea. These are problems which every honest restorer has engaged in personal combat. It is clear that the idea is still marketable in the twentieth-century world, but is it defensible? The questions asked of us here stretch on and on: Is the first-century purity we seek an illusion rather than a restorable reality? Was the early church intended as a model? Is the New Testament a blueprint or is it a divine drama? Can we escape our own culture in pursuit of a pristine past? Should we try? It is well that we have come to the point at which such questions can be asked at a place like this; I can tell you that I have long felt compelled to answer them in the quiet of my own conscience. I shall understand, in the end, if my personal confessional does not satisfy all doubters. I suspect that all those who through the centuries have embarked on a journey toward a more holy past have done so as an act of faith rather than because of an empirical imperative. But, a bit later, without retreating into total obscurantism, I shall give you my testimony.

To speak of restoration is to speak of movements, not of one movement. The methods of all restorers have not been the same; the variations from Puritans to pentecostals to Mormons have been vast. But they all have been united by the primitivist notion that one must reach back to the beginning to find the truth. That idea has carried with it consequences for both good and bad. Every restorer has both gained comfort and solace and paid an intellectual and psychological price.

Restorers, we repeatedly have been told, live in an ahistorical world, a world with sharp disjunctions and dark ages. The past, save for that divine moment at the conception of Christianity, is corrupt. Such a view of the past has consequences; it runs easily to anti-intellectualism and the deprecation of the arts and esthetic beauty. Restoration is a serious business, little given to levity or humor.

I confess that I recognize such a religious canvas. Liturgy and elegance might inspire those from other traditions, but they seem inherently decadent to me. I stand in awe, but ill-at-ease, in the nave of Notre Dame of Paris. One of my graudate students recently taped an interview with me which I fear may sooner or later appear in the outrageous publication *Wittenburg Door*. I rattled off a sequence of practiced punch lines about the lighter side of American religion before being asked at the end of the interview, "How about saying something funny about the Church of Christ?" I asked my interrogator to turn off his recorder while I thought. After several minutes I finally admitted that I did not know anything funny about the Church of Christ. We take ourselves with deadly seriousness. It is the nature of our business.

It is intriguing to speculate on the practical and psychological consequences of a restoration childhood. Those intent on restoration eschew many of the myriad of intellectual paths offered in the modern world—theology, biblical criticism, speculative science. Places such as Abilene Christian University, where there is an honest effort to encounter both past and present, find themselves living in delicate tension. Although some individuals thrive in that tension, for the most part such institutions form bridges that transport people back and forth from one cosmos to another.

If one confesses that some of life's alternatives are closed to restorers, it is well to assert that others are enriched by the heritage. I certainly cannot name all of the strengths of restoration thinking, and they are probably different for each restoration stream, but I can offer some guesses based on a lifetime of observing the maturing of a generation reared in Churches of Christ. Ours is an intensely rational movement, hewn out in debate, logical argument, preaching, and proof-texting. If disinterest in theology and speculative thought is anti-intellectualism, then the label fits. But I would guess that the Churches of Christ in the twentieth century—filled with upwardly mobile lower-middle class people—have produced more than their share of scholars. The movement reaches to the first century for models, and it has been preoccupied with understanding its own history. Though out of step with modern thought, it has encouraged diligent and regimented study. The restoration ideal has determined the direction in which these energies are expended. The Churches of Christ have produced Bible commentators, translators, linguists, historians, debaters, polemicists, and Bible students of no mean ability. Look in the universities of this nation and you will find them there. But do not look for theologians and theoretical scientists.

Further, restoration fosters surety. It is no mean blessing to be able to lay hold on those first sure truths that form the basis for Christianity. It makes you part of a divine drama in the midst of the most irrelevant life. In the rural churches of the South, in neatly kept little weatherboarded Churches of Christ, I have seen the faces of those entrusted with cosmic missions in the midst of the grapes of wrath. And I have seen the same sense of destiny etched on the weathered faces of the partners of Oral Roberts. I have beheld them standing, gazing at Tulsa's space-age buildings that were the products of Oral's vision and their money. They were little people who had thought big thoughts because of their faith.

And surety has served equally well many of us who have left the farms. We have wandered into the world; we have seen it; and we have found ourselves ill-at-ease in it. It is not easy to sleep soundly in the lodge at Pebble Beach when your boyhood was spent on a sultry farm in South Georgia. But such journeys seem less hazardous if one's traveling case is filled with memories of staunch and sturdy Christians who in a leaner childhood withstood the fierce buffeting of an unfriendly world. The personal shock of our encounter with modernity cannot dislodge memories of family and friends and of sure truths that are full of comfort.

But I must now turn to the most serious flaw we have discovered in restoration thinking: its tendency to self-righteous and opinionated divisiveness. This conference has been about restoration movements, a pluralistic statement that unsettles those of us reared in *the* restoration movement. Clearly the idea of restoration raises as many issues as it resolves. What is it that is to be restored? Are you an Old Testament or a New Testament restorer? Are you restoring the life, the piety, the miracle-working power, the ordinances, or the church order? Serious restorers have divided about countless, seemingly trivial things. Years ago I made a speech on pentecostalism at a Mennonite school, Goshen College. Illustrating the divisiveness of early pentecostalism, I told them of the fire-baptized schism over the "neck tie issue." After the lecture, one of the young Amish students informed me: "We divided over the neck tie issue, too. But we also divided over the one-suspender and two-suspender issue." That's creative. But it hardly outstrips the countless issues that have divided members of Churches of Christ. There are about half a dozen major streams coming out of the Campbell-Stone restoration movement, and there are scores of minor variations. One could pardon an outsider for suggesting that there must be a fatal flaw in the restoration principle.

One of the perverse assumptions of my life, however, has been that every man's belief, however curious, deserves consideration. In a speech I made nearly twenty years ago at the Disciples of Christ Historical Society, I began by noting Elmer T. Clark's comment in his book *The Small Sects in America* that it is "a peculiar type of mind which is convinced that God is interested in whether worshipers sing with or without instrumental accompaniment." I thought, I retorted, that it was "a peculiar type of mind" which thinks it is "a peculiar type of mind" which believes that God cares whether people sing with or without instrumental music. Curiosity is in the mind of the beholder. Historians surely must shoulder some responsibility in helping us understand one another's eccentricities.

Everybody's restoration is the product of a labored tradition. That does not make it true; it does not make all restoration movements equal; but it does say that every "peculiar type of mind" has its own integrity and logic and deserves a respectful hearing. Grant any zealot five assumptions and his or her eccentricities become a consistent, logical, and thoughtful platform upon which to build a holistic and sometimes heroic life.

Restoration is in many ways the ultimate modern expression of intellectual individualism. A historian could hardly visit these stern and rugged plains of west Texas without thinking back to historians Frederick Jackson Turner and Walter Prescott Webb who theorized that the American frontier brought humankind to history's culmination of individualism, optimism, and freedom. It seems eminently sane that on these plains should have flourished a religion that claimed the individual ability, right, and obligation to seize one's destiny with a Wild-West will to be just a Christian.

Candor demands that I confess that such an individualistic Christianity has had a less heroic side. One preoccupied with little questions may refuse consideration of important ones; restoration fervor has often been substituted for preciseness in exegesis. And restoration movements sometimes have been plagued by a gunfighter mentality. The search for truth has often been combined with unfortunate doses of intolerance, irascibility, and provincialism. Restoration demands individual judgment. It is time to confess, I believe, that the idea generates religious division. But I am not willing to concede that it necessarily breeds rancor and the abandonment of civility.

While decrying bigoted intolerance, it should be acknowledged that narrow-mindedness is not the peculiar property of biblical primitivists and restorers. Intolerance oozes rather evenly across the religious and political landscape; it knows few doctrinal barriers; religious liberals are no more immune to it than conservatives. And while many biblical primitivists have been myopic, most have embraced the concept of a universal church defined only in the mind of God. But such intuitions in no way changed their responsibilities to truth and its restoration.

What often has struck outsiders as intolerance may be better understood as conviction. My heritage has given me convictions; truly held and seriously followed, they have life-molding powers. They have been my gyroscope through the years. It is the role of conviction in my own life, I believe, that explains the paradox of my becoming the biographer of Oral Roberts. Pentecostals were the arch enemy of the Churches of Christ when I was a youngster. I remember well when a Roberts tent meeting invariably would invoke an advertisement from a local Church of Christ offering $1,000 reward to anyone who could prove that a miracle had taken place. And yet, I was fascinated by Roberts. I think

I know why. It is because I feel comfortable in the presence of conviction, right or wrong. I understand it; and I like it.

In conclusion, I agree with Professor Bowden and others who have reminded us forcefully that restoration was an ideal, nothing more. It still is. It is an ideal that pervades modern Protestantism. It is fitting that this conference acknowledge the frustration about the failures and anomalies of the past felt by thoughtful heirs of restoration slogans. But it is also fitting for us to acknowledge that the recurrent search for New Testament purity calls to account institutional churches grown rich and flabby, spokespersons for God who have grown ambivalent and messageless, and Christians so thoroughly captured by the world that they have neither the desire nor the ability to judge it. The quest for purity can only exist alongside a perception of unfaithfulness. The people who make such judgments of their times surely act partly in self-defense, asserting their own individuality in the face of the perceived arrogance and patronizing of their betters. In so doing, they sometimes speak foolishly and fall victim to charlatans. They may become captives of their own cultural prejudices. But the presence of such protest may be the closest this besieged nation shall come to hearing a prophetic witness. I have long been convinced that ideas are not the primary movers of history, but that history reaches out for the ideas needed at the time. Our times continue to breed a hunger for a Christian message that stands in judgment on humanity's imperfections, as we imagine the Gospel did in the first century.

I am a restorer—unbowed, undaunted, extremist, and eccentric—a period piece in a Disciples of Christ movement grown increasingly uncomfortable with the intellectual, social, and psychological pitfalls of restoring New Testament Christianity. The centerpiece of my intellectual universe is biblical primitivism, a search for the first pure truths and ordinances. I am seeking that illusive, pristine image of Christianity as it came from the mind of God. You say it is not there; it is an illusion. I have decided to seek it anyway. We live in a world of illusions. You say I will not find it because I carry on my back the baggage of my own past, of the culture in which I live, of the language with which I think. Self-consciously and with as much self-awareness as possible, I have decided to try. You say I shall fail and be disillusioned. So far, I have not.

In a sense all restorers are seekers, though sometimes we may think otherwise. Yet I shall not become cynical and despairing because all truths are not readily apparent, but rather I am joyous and thankful that we have come this far by faith. To be a restorer has always meant to be an explorer in search of Zion, bound to grope in our own human and cultural maze, never finishing our task, but ever learning through struggle and commitment to the truth. But I have never been alone; God has provided others of like mind to be my fellow travelers. It has been a rigorous journey, but I know existentially no other way. The search has served me well, and should you come to look for me, you will find me a bit further down the same road.

Notes on Contributors

C. LEONARD ALLEN is an associate professor in the College of Biblical Studies, Abilene Christian University. He is co-author with Richard Hughes of *Illusions of Innocence: Protestant Primitivism in America, 1630–1875* (1988) and has published several articles dealing with aspects of American religion.

HENRY WARNER BOWDEN is a professor of religion, Rutgers University. A past president of the American Society of Church History, he has authored *Church History in the Age of Science* (1971), *American Indians and Christian Missions* (1981), and the *Dictionary of American Religious Biography* (1977).

THEODORE DWIGHT BOZEMAN is a professor in the School of Religion and the Department of History at the University of Iowa. He is author of *Protestants in an Age of Science: The Baconian Ideal in Antebellum America* (1977), *To Live Ancient Lives: The Primitivist Dimension in Puritanism* (1988), and various articles on aspects of religion in American history.

JOEL A. CARPENTER is an associate professor of history and administrator of the Institute for the Study of American Evangelicals at Wheaton College. He previously served the history department at Trinity College, Deerfield, Illinois. He is co-editor with Kenneth Shipps of *Making Higher Education Christian: The History and Mission of Evangelical Colleges in America* (1987) and has written numerous articles dealing with fundamentalism and evangelicalism in American life.

ROBERT T. HANDY is Henry Sloane Coffin Professor Emeritus of Church History, Union Theological Seminary in New York City. He is a past president both of the American Baptist Historical Society and of the American Society of Church History and has authored, among other volumes, *American Christianity* (2 volumes with H. Shelton Smith and Lefferts A. Loetscher, 1960–63), *A Christian America: Protestant Hopes and Historical Realities* (1971, rev. 1984), and *A History of the Churches in the United States and Canada* (1977).

DAVID EDWIN HARRELL, JR., is University Scholar in History at the University of Alabama at Birmingham and has taught previously at the University of Arkansas, the University of Oklahoma, the University of Georgia, and East

Tennessee State University. Among the books he has authored are *Quest for a Christian America* (1966), *White Sects and Black Men in the Recent South* (1971), *The Social Sources of Division in the Disciples of Christ, 1865–1900* (1973), *All Things Are Possible: The Healing and Charismatic Revivals in Modern America* (1975), *Oral Roberts: An American Life* (1985), and *Pat Robertson: A Personal, Religious, and Political Portrait* (1987).

SAMUEL S. HILL, JR., has taught at Stetson University and the University of North Carolina, Chapel Hill, and is currently a professor of religion, the University of Florida. Among his books are *Southern Churches in Crisis* (1967) and *The South and the North in American Religion* (1980). He is the editor of and a major contributor to *Religion and the Solid South* (1972) and *Varieties of Southern Religious Experience* (1987), among others, and editor of the *Encyclopedia of Religion in the South* (1984).

E. BROOKS HOLIFIELD is the Charles Howard Candler Professor of American Church History at Emory University. His books include *The Covenant Sealed: The Development of Puritan Sacramental Theology in Old and New England, 1570–1720* (1974), *The Gentlemen Theologians: American Theology in Southern Culture, 1795–1860* (1978), *A History of Pastoral Care in America: From Salvation to Self-Realization* (1983), and *Health and Medicine in the Methodist Tradition* (1986).

DAVID L. HOLMES is a professor of Religion and a member of the American Studies faculty at the College of William and Mary. He has taught at Carnegie-Mellon University and the University of Virginia. He is church reviews editor of *Anglican and Episcopal History* and is completing a history of the Episcopal church for the Denominations in America series of the Greenwood Press.

RICHARD T. HUGHES is a professor in the Religion Division at Pepperdine University and previously taught at Abilene Christian University and Southwest Missouri State University. He is co-author, with Leonard Allen, of *Illusions of Innocence: Protestant Primitivism in America, 1630–1875* (1988).

BILL J. HUMBLE is chairman of graduate studies in the College of Biblical Studies and director of the Center for Restoration Studies at Abilene Christian University, where he also has served as vice president for academic affairs. He earlier taught at Florida Christian College. His works include *Campbell and Controversy* (1954, 1987), *The Story of the Restoration* (1969), *Addresses of R. S. Bell* (editor, 1987), and a documentary film, *Light from Above: The Life of Alexander Campbell* (1988).

SIDNEY E. MEAD has taught at the University of Chicago; Meadville Theological School; Southern California School of Theology, the Claremont Colleges; and the University of Iowa. He served as president of Meadville Theological School and of the American Society of Church History, and is currently retired from full-time teaching in Silver City, New Mexico. Among his publications are *The Lively Experiment: The Shaping of Christianity in America* (1963), *The Nation With the Soul of a Church* (1975), and *The Old Religion in the Brave New World: Reflections on the Relation Between Christendom and the Republic* (1977).

MARK A. NOLL is a professor of history at Wheaton College and previously taught history at Trinity College, Deerfield, Illinois. He is the author of several volumes, including *Between Faith and Criticism: Evangelicals, Scholarship and the Bible in America* (1986), editor of *The Princeton Theology* (1983), and editor with Nathan Hatch of *The Bible in America: Essays in Cultural History* (1982).

THOMAS H. OLBRICHT chairs the Division of Religion at Pepperdine University and previously taught at Harding University, The University of Dubuque, the Pennsylvania State University, and Abilene Christian University. He has served as president both of the Southwest region of the American Academy of Religion and of the Southwest Commission on Religious Studies. Among his books are *The Power to Be* (1979), *He Loves Forever* (1980), and *The Message of Colossians and Ephesians* (1983).

ALBERT C. OUTLER is a professor emeritus, Perkins School of Theology, Southern Methodist University. He has taught at Duke University, Yale University, and Union Theological Seminary in New York City, and is a past president of the American Theological Society, the American Society of Church History, and the American Catholic Historical Association. He has authored *Psychotherapy and the Christian Message* (1954), and *The Christian Tradition and the Unity We Seek* (1957), among others, and has edited *St. Augustine: Confessions and Enchiridion* (Library of Christian Classics, 1955), *John Wesley* (Library of Protestant Thought, 1964), and *The Works of John Wesley*, vols. 1–4 (1984–87).

JAN SHIPPS is a professor of history and religious studies and the director of the Center for American Studies at Indiana University/Purdue University at Indianapolis. She is a past president of the Mormon History Association and the Indiana Academy of Religion. She has published extensively on Mormon history and is author of *Mormonism: The Story of a New Religious Tradition* (1985).

WINTON U. SOLBERG has taught at the U.S. Military Academy, Yale University, and Macalester College, and is currently professor of history at the University of Illinois. He has been vice-president of the American Association of University Professors and president of both the Mid-America American Studies Association and the American Society of Church History. His publications include *The Federal Convention and the Formation of the Union of the American States* (1958), *The University of Illinois, 1867–1984: An Intellectual and Cultural History* (1968), *Redeem the Time: The Puritan Sabbath in Early America* (1978), and *A History of American Thought and Culture* (1983).

GRANT WACKER is associate professor and director of undergraduate studies in the Department of Religious Studies, University of North Carolina, Chapel Hill. He has written *Augustus H. Strong and the Dilemma of Historical Consciousness* (1985) and numerous articles dealing with nineteenth- and twentieth-century American religion with particular focus on the history of American evangelicalism and pentecostalism.

Index

Economic democracy and financial participation

The ideas behind economic democracy and financial participation are not new; the International Congress on Profit sharing first met in Paris in 1889. The practical objective of many profit sharing schemes was increased labour management co-operation. Some also had an ideological objective – the resolution of a perceived contradiction between concentrated wealth and power and the democratic ideal.

In *Economic Democracy and Financial Participation*, Daryl D'Art has two objectives. First, to examine if, and under what conditions, profit sharing schemes and employee shareholding can motivate workers and generate cooperative striving. Second, he identifies the schemes of financial participation which have the potential to realise economic democracy within the individual firm and wider society. To fulful these objectives the author draws on the results of research carried out in the USA, Sweden, Denmark and Ireland. By making a comparative international study he contrasts an individualist approach to economic democracy with a collectivist approach. He also offers an analysis of recent Irish employee shareholding legislation and concludes with an overall examination of the effectiveness of these various schemes. The final result offers an international, in-depth analysis of financial participation at both a theoretical and practical level.

Daryl D'Art is currently Associate Lecturer in Industrial Relations at The National College of Industrial Relations, Dublin. He has extensive lecturing and research experience in industrial relations, labour history, management and organizational behaviour.

Economic democracy and financial participation

A comparative study

Daryl D'Art

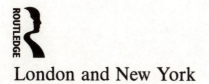

London and New York

First published in 1992
by Routledge
11 New Fetter Lane, London EC4P 4EE

Simultaneously published in the USA and Canada
by Routledge
a division of Routledge, Chapman and Hall, Inc.
29 West 35th Street, New York, NY 10001

Typeset in Times Roman by
Falcon Typographic Art Ltd, Edinburgh & London
Printed and bound in Great Britain by
Mackays of Chatham PLC, Chatham, Kent

British Library Cataloguing in Publication Data
D'Art, Daryl
  Economic Democracy and Financial Participation
  I Title
  331.2164
  ISBN 0–415–06215–2

Library of Congress Cataloging in Publication Data
D'Art, Daryl., 1943–
  Economic Democracy and Financial Participation: A Comparative
  Study/Daryl J. D'Art
  p. cm.
  Includes bibliographical references and index
  ISBN 0–415–06215–2
  1. Profit-sharing – Case studies   I. Title
  HD2971.D37   1992
  331.2'164 – dc20

to Anne and Daryl
and in memory of my father

Contents

Figures

Tables

Foreword

THE IDEA

The basic idea of providing employees in organisations with a share in the surpluses generated by work activities sounds seductive in its simplicity and apparent common sense. Not surprisingly, it has been argued that this will act as a work incentive and will promote co-operation. The assumption of such reasoning is rooted in judgements about the unfairness and conflictual nature of *laissez-faire* capitalism, based on capital provided by those with surplus wealth and wage labour provided by those with appropriate skills and knowledge. As the author of this new comparative analysis of 'financial participation' makes abundantly clear, the debate on the utility of such an approach has existed right from the beginnings of the joint stock corporation system in the nineteenth century; yet protagonists of financial participation have continually produced new schemes and methods of employee shares in such surpluses. The technical basis for financial participation schemes in different societies has varied considerably and has also clearly reflected very different ideologies and perspectives. One consequence of this, is that debate on the issues of financial participation has become confused and ambiguous. It is argued that financial participation is essential for economic democracy, but equally that it is a way of preventing democratic control. It is seen as a basis for employee motivation, but also as a way of reducing managerial power and shareholder influence. It is seen as a way of reshaping capitalism, but also of preserving and defending it. What was simplistic logic has turned into conceptual confusion and a discussion of tax law and pension practice. Why did this happen? The answer to this question must lie with the way that financial participation conflates a number of major issues of political and social philosophy.

THE LEGITMACY OF ECONOMIC POWER

The first major issue underlying decisions over the necessity for financial participation is the question of how far economic power, exercised through free labour, product and capital markets, is legitimate, *sui generis*. Markets depend on the social acceptability of contractual economic relationships, freely negotiated by the parties to the contract. Such contractual relationships, both between producers and sub-contracted suppliers and between producers of goods and services and customers, depend on the development of contract law and market institutional arrangements. Wherever 'capitalism' has emerged in its mature forms, in different parts of the world economy, there has always been an agreed political context which protects property rights and the rights of contract partners. The regulation of employer–employee relations, especially in large enterprises, has frequently been the weakest part of this political consensus. This is not surprising as labour contracts imply dependence and the acceptability of managerial hierarchies and control mechanisms. Such dependence could easily be seen as 'exploitation' in the Marxist paradigm, or even for non-Marxists it can mean a need for mechanisms, such as collective bargaining, to restore a degree of power balance to employer–employee relationships. The invention of the joint stock corporation and of limited liability for shareholders clearly did nothing to solve this question of employee dependence.

The three main answers to this issue have all proved to be inadequate as solutions. The socialist emphasis on the need for public ownership can now be seen as broadly irrelevant to the creation of greater managerial legitimacy, even if it is seen as necessary for macro-economic planning. The creation of institutional forms of representative democracy within the enterprise – co-determination and co-operation councils – also does not necessarily develop greater managerial legitimacy. Market adjustments mean a need for managerial action, which is frequently against the short-term interest of particular employee groups. In times of recession and rationalisation it is difficult to maintain the acceptability of managerial actions, especially from those who may be about to lose their jobs, even if works councils discuss the broad lines of redundancy programmes.

The third answer of relying on union power and collective bargaining has two major defects; unions do not represent all levels of employees equally and also themselves suffer from problems of inadequate democratic representation. The problem of managerial legitimacy is therefore compounded by problems of the legitimacy of union representation.

Behind these issues is the fact that enterprises themselves, created to exploit economic opportunities, are not unitary institutions but could be depicted as a set of Chinese boxes, all of which have different identities and conflicting economic objectives and interests. Legitimacy must be related to the actual roles and behaviour of managers and management systems, and this is frequently beyond the influence of policies of public ownership, co-determination and collective bargaining.

THE LEGITIMACY OF REWARD SYSTEMS

Financial participation is proposed frequently as a means of improving the legitimacy of remuneration packages or systems, rather than that of the managerial system. It is argued that wage and salary systems are too closely related to individual job or task levels, and do not recognise the claim of employees to benefit from the overall success of the enterprise. The problem here, of course, is again twofold. First, what exactly is the nature and size of the surplus created – the accounting issue. Second, how can the competing claims of stakeholders be reconsidered – how much should be paid to those loaning their capital to the enterprise, how much should go back to customers in terms of lower prices, how much should flow to suppliers in terms of increased prices and how much to employees themselves? It is also clear that employees are not a homogeneous group and that managers and core employees may demand a greater slice of surpluses than temporary or peripheral employees.

The legitimacy of reward systems is therefore inevitably related to the acceptability of enterprise business strategy and the acceptability of those taking such decisions. Paradoxically, financial participation for employers may be acceptable only when employees are 'detached' from the enterprise and accept their rewards simply as extra rewards for their work. We have seen from our earlier analysis that this is unlikely for key employees in large organisations.

THE LEGITIMACY OF CAPITAL ACCUMULATION PROCESSES

The third issue underlying the debate on financial participation is that of the legitimacy of the arrangements in society for savings and capital accumulation. Three distinct problems for policy makers need to be distinguished here. In the first case, how should society organise its arrangements for supporting dependents and those who are not working in economic organisations? Savings are necessary for family expenditure on education, housing, holidays, sickness and retirement. Even if the state takes responsibility for all these objectives, it is clear that in advanced societies personal savings are still going to be crucial to set beside public provision out of taxation. The opportunities for savings are defined by financial and capital market opportunities, and enterprises could provide special opportunities for stimulating, supporting and protecting employee savings.

Second, there is the issue addressed by wage earner funds, namely providing a balance of economic power between capital which is controlled by private institutions, banks and security houses and capital raised by employees and citizens. The growing power of pension fund trusts is a critical issue here.

Third, there is the broader issue of how far employees need to have special opportunities for investing their capital in their own enterprises – in order to promote commitment – and how far the capital investment process should be a totally distinct universal system separated from employee-relationships. The financial scandals of the last decade has illustrated the problems arising from deregulation by the state and the issue of conflict between short-term profitability objectives of financial institutions and the need for long-term invest-ment strategies for world competitiveness are both consequences of promoting completely free capital markets.

THE UTILITY OF THE COMPARATIVE APPROACH

The usefulness of this fresh analysis of financial participation by Dr D'Art lies primarily in his comparative approach. Most discussions of financial participation to date have been carried out by protagonists who have argued for the need for a particular institutional approach of employee shareholding or cash bonuses. This study demonstrates the limitations of such an approach. The author shows clearly that the historical and political context of financial participation schemes in each society shapes the actual objectives of the parties pursuing such an approach. The reality is that when financial participation schemes are introduced into organisational systems there is no valid a priori reasoning which will allow conclusions on the effects of these schemes to be drawn – unless there has been a previous analysis of the nature of the micro-political system which actually exists within the organisation and unless the analysis can be set in its macro-economic, political and social context. The general debate on the schemes is therefore of little value, unless it is set in a proper perspective.

It is important to see that this conclusion also applies to the author's search for testing how far financial participation can be linked to actual employee participation in managerial decision making. He is able to show that in the evidence surveyed, for example in the USA there is little or no connection between these two phenomenon. This does not mean, however, that financial participation could not be linked to employee participation *under certain conditions*. It is fairly clear that prior commitment by management to employee participation is one of these conditions. This is, in itself, unlikely in many Western societies as presently constituted, but again is not impossible.

The achievement of the author is therefore that he provides a basis for a new debate on financial participation through his national case studies and his comparisons. The reader is bound to ask how far actual employee participation is bound to include an element of financial participation and to enquire about the conditions which would allow both forms of participation to co-exist. It is clear that these conditions include both macro- and organisational policies. We are certainly going to be able to use this analysis as the debate on 'European' forms of participation is brought to a climax in discussions on the Social Charter and the new Directives planned by the European Commission.

Keith Thurley
Professor of Industrial Relations
London School of Economics
October 1991

Abbreviations

AFL-CIO	American Federation of Labor and Congress of Industrial Organizations
AIF	Annual Improvement Factor
CII	Confederation of Irish Industry
COLA	Cost of Living Allowance
CONRAIL	Consolidated Rail Corporation
CPSI	Council of Profit Sharing Industries (USA)
DA	Dansk Arbejdsgiverforening (Confederation of Danish Empoloyers)
DLR	Daily Labor Report (issued by AFL-CIO Washington)
EEC	European Economic Community
ERISA	Employee Retirement Income Security Act 1974 (USA)
ESAP	Employee Stock Appreciation Plans
ESOP	Employee Stock Ownership Plans
ESOT	Employee Stock Ownership Trust
FUE	Federated Union of Employers
GAO	General Accounting Office (USA)
GM	General Motors (USA)
HUD	Department of Housing and Urban Development (USA)
I	Industriradet (Federation of Danish Industries)
ICTU	Irish Congress of Trade Unions
IDE	Industrial Democracy Europe
IMS	Irish Marketing Surveys
IPC	Irish Productivity Centre

IRC	Internal Revenue Code (USA)
IRS	Internal Revenue Service (USA)
LO	Landsorganisationen i Danmark (Federation of Danish Trade Unions)
LO	Landsorganisationen i Sverige (Swedish Confederation of Trade Unions)
NCEO	National Center for Employee Ownership
PAYSOP	Payroll-Based Stock Ownership Plan
PS	Profit Sharing
PSCA	Profit Sharing Council of America
PSRA	Profit Sharing Research Association (Ireland)
PSRF	Profit Sharing Research Foundation (USA)
SAF	Svenska Arbetsgivareforeningen (Swedish Employers' Confederation)
SAMAK	Arbetarrorelsens Nordska Samarbetskommitte (Joint Committee of the Nordic Labour Movement)
SAP	Socialdemokratiska Arbetarepartiet (Social Democratic Party) Sweden
SBL	South Bend Lathe
SD	Socialdemokratiet (Social Democratic Party) Denmark
SI	Sveriges Industriforbund (Federation of Swedish Industries)
SPP	Socialist Peoples' Party, Denmark
TCO	Tjanstenannens Centralorganisation (Swedish Central Association of Salaried Employees)
TRASOP	Tax Reduction Act Stock Ownership Plan
UAW	United Auto Workers (USA)
UFCW	United Food and Commerical Workers' Union (USA)
USWA	United Steel Workers of America
WEF	Wage Earner Funds

Acknowledgements

Much of the research for this book was carried out during my term as research fellow in financial democracy at the School of Business and Administrative Studies, Trinity College, Dublin from 1983 to 1985. The fellowship was funded by the Planned Sharing Research Association. I am very grateful to Dr Jack Fitzpatrick, president of the PSRA, and to John Brady, SJ of the College of Industrial Relations, Donal McCullogh and other members of the Association for their patience and encouragement.

Work was still in progress at the end of my tenure in TCD and its completion owes much to the facilities and financial assistance provided by Aer Lingus and the Irish Productivity Centre. Aer Lingus funded my field trips and in the persons of Dominic Coleman and John O'Neill responded favourably to requests for study leave and other special arrangements. Also, I am grateful to my comrades of the Instrument Section, Maintenance and Engineering, Dublin Airport, whose banter frequently revived my flagging spirit. Gratitude is equally due to The Irish Productivity Centre which provided me with a temporary home, Arthur Coldrick for his interest and encouragement, and Tom Lyons who kindly allowed me to share his office. Ms Breda Finnerty was also helpful in a variety of ways.

The research undertaken in North America was greatly facilitated by the unstinting assistance and hospitality of Bert L. Metzger, President of the Profit Sharing Research Foundation. Bert allowed me unrestricted access to the files of the PSRF at Evanston and arranged some of my interviews and very pleasant accommodation with Mr and Mrs Marum. Gratitude is also due to David Ellerman of the Industrial Cooperative Association, Sommerville, Mass.; Luis Granados, ESOP Association of America; Corey Rosen, National

Center for Employee Ownership; John Zalusky, American Federation of Labor and Congress of Industrial Organizations; T.E. Parfitt and J.W. Cooper, Harris Trust Bank; Dean Boyle, Warner Gear; R.L. Wilson, Chicago and Northwestern; and other individuals and companies who gave time to this research but wished to remain anonymous.

The willingness of trade union officials, business spokespersons and politicians to supply material and answer innumerable questions made the Scandinavian chapters of this book possible. In particular, I am grateful to Svend Auken, leader of the Danish Social Democrats; Bo E. Carlsson, SAF; Jorgen F. Hansen, Danish LO; Kenneth Kvist, Left Party Communists, Sweden; Clas Nykvist, TCO; Lars-Olof Petterson, Swedish LO; Torben A. Sorensen and Ole Olsen, DA; Bjorn Pedersen, Left Socialists, Denmark; Peter Vognbjerg, Wage Earners Cost of Living Fund, Denmark; Mrs Anne Wibble, Liberal Party Sweden.

Initially this study was supervised by the late Professor Charles McCarthy until his sudden and untimely death, and then by Dr Ferdinand Von Prondzynski. I am deeply grateful to both for their patient assistance and encouragement. Other colleagues in the School of Business and Administrative Studies, Dr Geoffrey MacKechnie and Mr P.J. McCabe, made helpful comments. The Secretary of the School of Business, Ms Susanna Cunningham, was always extremely helpful, far beyond the call of duty. Alan Matthews, Department of Economics TCD, despite a crowded schedule, kindly translated the 1986 Wage Earner's Fund proposal of the Danish labour movement. Alan also read large sections of the work. Finally the staff of both the Lecky and Berkeley libraries were always most helpful and obliging.

It is a truth universally acknowledged that Ph.D. students make tiresome companions. Conversation on any topic with such individuals seems to terminate inevitably in their particular area of study. In my own case all conversational roads led to economic democracy. Despite being sorely tried, many of my friends remained loyal, for which I am grateful. My friend and colleague Brendan McPartlin, SJ, College of Industrial Relations, made useful observations and gave excellent advice. Dr Bill Toner, SJ, rendered invaluable assistance at a crucial juncture. The College librarians, Fiona Murray and Mary Buckley, were always most obliging. Other friends and comrades were helpful and supportive in various ways, in particular, my friends of long standing Maura and John O'Riordan, Ms Eileen Colgan who typed the final draft, Paddy Gillan, Leslie McKay, Des Geraghty,

Kevin Quinn, Herdis Skov, Mae and Mike Sullivan, John Barret and Brid and Jack Hanna.

Finally my deepest gratitude is due to the ultra loyalists, my wife Anne and son Daryl. Daryl's humorous and quizzical scepticism regarding the whole endeavour was refreshing. Any credit for the eventual completion of this study is largely due to Anne. It was Anne who typed and retyped earlier drafts, who translated some of my more convoluted sentences into readable English, who cured my incipient Luddism regarding the word processor and who was always supportive. A mere typed acknowledgement of these labours is a poor recompense.

The zeal of this witness for Profit Sharing had stood the test of personal maltreatment. He attended a meeting of miners at which a Union lecturer denounced Messrs Briggs' system as a device for 'cheating the men'. 'When he had finished', Mr Toft (a working miner) told the Commissioners, 'I got up to defend the principle because it is dear to my life. I believe it is a good thing and is calculated to do good and I have taken it up not for any amount of interest or flattery or benefit I might get from the Masters by advocating it, but because I believe it is destined to do a great amount of good. They would not let me continue to speak and overpowered my voice, and I had a clod come at my head.'

(Mr Roebuck – 'I hope it did not strike you')

'it did not hurt me, only my feelings were hurt.'

Statement on Messrs H. C. and A. Briggs
profit sharing scheme before the Royal
Commission on Trade Unions 1868[1]

'What do you think of profit sharing?' Carol ventured.

Mr Elder thundered his answer . . .

'All this profit sharing and welfare work and insurance and old age pension is simply poppycock. Enfeebles a workman's independence – and wastes a lot of honest profit. The half baked thinker that isn't dry behind the ears yet, and these suffragettes and God knows what all buttinskis there are that are trying to tell a business man how to run his business, and some of these college professors are just about as bad, the whole kit and bilin' of 'em are nothin in God's world but socialism in disguise. And it's my bounden duty as a producer to resist every attack on the integrity of American industry to the last ditch. Yes – SIR.'

Sinclair Lewis, (1921)[2]

Introduction

Schemes of financial participation such as profit sharing or employee shareholding within individual enterprises generally have two principal objectives – to stimulate worker effort and labour–management co-operation. Often, schemes of employee shareholding have an additional macro objective – the resolution of a perceived contradiction between wealth and power concentrated in the hands of a minority and the democratic ideal. This contradiction, it is asserted, can be resolved by the diffusion of individual share ownership among the maximum number of employees and citizens. Broader ownership of productive assets, in establishing a type of financial or economic democracy, will create conditions in contemporary capitalist economies that will tend to complement rather than contradict political democracy. Can profit sharing motivate workers and can the individualist and voluntarist approach of employee shareholding become a vehicle for the realisation of economic democracy, or could one argue for a compulsory collectivist approach? These are the questions addressed and hopefully answered by this book. However, before outlining the approach and methodology, setting the development of financial participation in historical perspective will give concrete form to the issues addressed.

EMPLOYER/EMPLOYEE RELATIONS AND THE INDUSTRIAL REVOLUTION

An endemic problem for employers, particularly since the Industrial Revolution, is the control and efficient direction of labour.[3] The factory system was at once a response both to the new technology and to the problem of control.[4] However, gathering formerly scattered groups of workers within single enterprises under a harsher work discipline threw into sharp relief the widening social gulf and the changed relations between masters and men.[5] Furthermore, pressure from an increasingly competitive market, structural change and vulgarised versions of the new political economy prompted many employers to purge the employment relationship of all personal and particularistic bonds, considerations and sentiments.[6] There began to emerge in mine, mill and factory a pattern of employer/employee relations which has become characteristic of western industrial society. According to Fox, it was a pattern marked by increasingly impersonal and narrowly contractual attitudes and behaviour, by mutual distrust and grudging calculation, and by the decay of whatever diffuse bonds of obligation that might have mitigated the harshness of employer/employee power relations in earlier times.[7] Relations between the parties had been reduced to the cash nexus.

Some employers were critical of these developments from paternalist, humanitarian or Christian standpoints. Yet for many of their colleagues only the advantages of the simplified employment relationship were apparent. Freedom from traditional encumbrances allowed a rapid and more effective response to signals from the market. Initially, any negative aspects of the arrangements were obscured by the power of employers and the weakness of workers.

From the 1880s onwards, the drawbacks were more evident in the industrialised countries. Combination was increasingly resorted to by employees. The trade unions were both an expression of divergent interests aggravated by the employment relationship of the cash nexus, and an attempt to modify market forces and the absolutism of employers. Beyond the enterprise in the wider society, gradual extensions of the suffrage and the rise of socialism presented employers with a potentially more fundamental challenge. These developments raised the spectre of political power captured by a socialist labour movement threatening the operation of the free market and the expropriation of capitalists. There began a search for a philosopher's stone to cure these social and industrial ills. Profit sharing and its variants has since that time figured intermittently as one possible solution.

PROFIT SHARING AS A STIMULANT TO CO-OPERATIVE STRIVING

The classic definition of profit sharing was formulated and adopted by an International Congress on Profit Sharing in Paris in 1889.

Profit sharing, Congress declared, is 'an agreement freely entered into, whereby employees receive shares, fixed in advance, of the profits'.[8] Subsequent definitions of the concept have mostly been commentaries or expansions on the original.[9] Similarly, the objectives of profit sharing have tended to multiply. At the outset, the aims of the measure were in the main comparatively modest, being confined to the individual enterprise. According to one Victorian proponent, profit sharing was 'a singularly efficacious means of obtaining enhanced industrial results, and of stilling the disastrous antagonism between employers and employed.'[10] The assumption was that workers receiving a share of company profits in addition to wages would be encouraged to work harder, more diligently and in co-operation with their employers. Increased effort, increasing profit and returns to workers, would unite employers and employees in harmonious pursuit of a common objective.

PROFIT SHARING/EMPLOYEE SHAREHOLDING SCHEMES – A SOCIAL CEMENT

With many of these early schemes the individual employee profit share took the form of a cash bonus. A more sophisticated version distributed the employees' profit share not in cash, but in an equivalent number of their own company shares. Like their cash counterpart, share-based or co-partnership schemes, as they were called in Britain, sought to create harmony and efficiency within the enterprise. There was also the hope expressed by one pioneering practitioner that 'trade unions would wither away as anachronisms'.[11] Yet share-based schemes had an additional objective which was altogether more ambitious. The experience of ownership or co-partnership through shareholding would inspire worker loyalty not just to the firm but to the prevailing economic arrangements. With the diffusion of share ownership, the formerly propertyless labourer would now have a tangible stake in the system. The attraction of unionism and the siren calls of socialists for the expropriation of the propertied classes might lose much of their appeal. Thus the potentially explosive combination of unionism, socialism and democracy would be defused. Employee shareholding – the industrial version of peasant proprietorship – would, some expected, have the same stabilising and socially conservative effect.[12]

Given the above objectives, the popularity of profit sharing with employers was likely to be at its highest during periods of industrial and social unrest. A historian of nineteenth- and early twentieth-century

British profit sharing has shown how the number of schemes adopted varied in phase with the cycle of labour militancy. Only 40 schemes were adopted between 1865 and 1888. Yet in the three years from 1889 to 1892 which witnessed the rise of new unionism and the revival of socialism, 88 schemes were established.[13] A second peak in the number of profit sharing schemes (1911–14) coincided with the flourishing of syndicalism and the triple alliance of miners, railwaymen and dockers.[14] Another historian of the period has concluded that profit sharing was merely an extension of anti-union paternalism, a method of combatting labour unrest and had little to do with philanthrophy.[15]

In America, during the last two decades of the century, profit sharing impressed some employers as a possible cure for the ills of industrial government, and in 1892 an association to promote the measure was established.[16] Profit sharing was to figure as a weapon in the arsenal of American employers during their open shop campaigns from the turn of the century to the 1920s.[17] With the Wall Street crash and the temporary fall from grace of capitalism and businessmen generally, the salvationist aspect of profit sharing was to the fore. A 1939 Senate committee on the topic saw profit sharing as saving the free enterprise system. Making every worker a capitalist through profit sharing, the investigating committee believed, would ensure employee support for American capitalism and opposition to state socialism.[18]

PROFIT SHARING, EQUITY AND DEMOCRACY

The objectives of profit sharing are not solely instrumental, manipulative and ideologically conservative. Even an implacable foe of profit sharing has acknowledged the sincerity of its proponents and allowed that its business and philanthropic aspects are confused and difficult to disentangle.[19] The philosophy of profit sharing, one American authority claimed, is a combination of ethical idealism and hard practicality.[20] A nineteenth-century advocate seemed to suggest that the schemes would enlighten economic science with the spirit of the gospel.[21] Possibly one of the earliest examples of profit sharing was introduced not with any conservative intention but to give a fuller and deeper expression to the democratic ideal. Albert Gallatin, secretary of the Treasury under Jefferson and Madison, established profit sharing in his Pennsylvania glassworks in the belief that 'the democratic principle upon which this nation was founded should not be restricted to the political processes, but should be applied to the industrial operation.'[22] The primary motivation for profit sharing at the Rowntree works was the conviction that it constituted justice for employees. Furthermore, the company was at pains to stress that the scheme would not alter the position of trade unions, which it announced were desirable both for the firm and its employees.[23] Another example of profit sharing inspired by considerations of equity is the scheme operated by the John Lewis Partnership. Here also the attitude towards unions is positive.[24]

PROPONENTS AND PRACTITIONERS OF FINANCIAL PARTICIPATION

In these examples the proponents or advocates of profit sharing are also its practitioners. This is not always the case. More often profit sharing or its variants are advocated by individuals or groups whose connection with industry and commerce may be less than direct. Their advocacy may be primarily motivated by considerations of equity or what one historian called a 'hunger for harmony'.[25] On the other hand, the aims and concerns of the actual practitioners of profit sharing, namely employers, may not always accord with those of its proponents. For instance, the advocacy of profit sharing is sometimes justified by the assertion that workers have a right to share in the profits. As will be seen, many American employers would emphatically reject such a contention.[26] Nevertheless, such disagreement has not apparently hindered the prolific growth of profit sharing and employee shareholding schemes there. The gap between theory and practice, proponents and practitioners, has given rise to the contradictions, distortions, confusion and abuses that have dogged these schemes since their inception.

Yet this dichotomy between proponents and practitioners of financial participation requires some refinement. Proponents of profit sharing or employee shareholding can be roughly subdivided into idealists and pragmatists. Idealist or altruistic proponents of these schemes tend to insist that they be implemented according to the letter and spirit of orthodox prescriptions. A primary objective of pragmatic proponents is the widespread adoption of these schemes. Consequently, they tend to the latitudinarian, possibly fearing a strict interpretation will alienate potential practitioners among employers. This book will suggest that the many failures of profit sharing or employee shareholding to motivate workers and engender co-operative striving can be ascribed to shortfalls between prescriptions and practice. An example would be the recommendation that schemes be established as additions to prevailing wage rates and fringe benefits. This is most commonly flouted in American schemes of financial participation, where a majority, it will be shown, function as pension substitutes with a consequent loss of motivational potential.[27] Yet this is mainly a characteristic specific to American schemes, and is partly explained by the weakness there of organised labour.

As will be seen, there are other equally important recommendations or prescriptions for successful financial participation. Nevertheless, many employer practitioners of financial participation in America, Scandinavia and Ireland either oppose or consider unnecessary the implementation of these prescriptions.

THE PARADOX OF MANAGERIAL SCHEMES OF FINANCIAL PARTICIPATION

There is general consensus, it will be established, among proponents and researchers of financial participation on the crucial importance of employee involvement in the implementation and operation of these schemes. According to one expert, the heart of profit sharing will be found in consultative procedures, co-operative formulation, free discussion of ideas and joint consideration of company financial and production problems.[28] He admits that these participative requirements, essential for a scheme's success, are a high price to pay for those managers or employers who prize traditional prerogatives.[29] The American, Scandinavian and Irish chapters of this book will show that few employers or managers are prepared to pay anything like such a price. This reluctance will be manifest even in those schemes that require a very modest dilution of managerial prerogative and an extremely limited sharing of control. Stripping these schemes of their participative elements will emasculate any potential they might have to stimulate worker motivation and co-operation.

There are wider ramifications of employer unwillingness to share information and control, particularly with regard to employee share holding. Such schemes are often expected to perform a dual function: first, to stimulate employee effort and co-operation within the enterprise; second, through broadening share ownership, to resolve a perceived contradiction between concentrated wealth and power, and the democratic ideal. A rough approximation to this ideal would involve rule by the majority, accountability of the rulers to the ruled, and a fair measure of equality – or at least the absence of gross inequality. Though largely realised in the political sphere, oligarchic control characterises most western economies. Diffusion of share ownership, it is sometimes suggested, would mitigate this imbalance.

FINANCIAL PARTICIPATION, DEMOCRACY AND CONTROL

It seems paradoxical that employers opposed to sharing control and information within the enterprise can adopt schemes that will ostensibly democratise capitalism. The contradiction, however, is more apparent than real. Some employers, while adopting these schemes to avail themselves of tax concessions, attempt to restrict the franchise of worker shareholders. In those cases where employee shareholders exercise all the rights and privileges of conventional shareholders, their combined shareholding is usually insufficient to influence economic decision making to any significant extent. One British advocate of employee shareholding could assure employers contemplating its introduction that, to date, there was no evidence of its likely interference with the entrepreneurial control of a business.[30] Just as in the majority of cases there is no real democratisation of control within the enterprise, this is also the case in the wider society. There is evidence to suggest that the diffusion of share ownership, far from dispersing control, consolidates its exercise in the hands of a few large capital owners.[31] Generally, schemes of individual employee or citizen shareholding effectively divorce ownership from control. Their intention, it seems, is more to legitimise the existing exercise of oligarchic control than to extend democratic decision making to economic activity.[32]

COLLECTIVE PROFIT SHARING – A TRADE UNION VERSION OF FINANCIAL PARTICIPATION

The Scandinavian chapters of this book will provide some support for the above contention – that the diffusion of individual share ownership tends to consolidate rather than challenge the existing exercise of economic control. One objective of the Swedish and Danish labour movements' collective profit sharing or worker fund proposals was greater accountability in economic decision making both within the enterprise and in wider society. It was an attempt to extend the democratic process beyond its political straitjacket. According to Macpherson, a fully democratic society requires democratic political control over the uses to which the amassed capital and the remaining natural resources of the society are put.[33] This attempted extension of democracy met with fierce opposition from employers, capital owners and their spokesmen in both countries.

Their counter-proposal, which, it will be shown, would have left their oligarchic control intact, was the diffusion of individual shareholding among citizens and employees.

The Webbs dismissed profit sharing, peasant proprietorship and similar initiatives as types of individualist radicalism which are passing away.[34] The persistent vigour of profit sharing/employee shareholding schemes in America and their possible resurrection in these islands apparently confounds prophets of their demise. Yet the Scandinavian examples will suggest that these schemes, confined to some individual firms, offer no solution to the problems and contradictions of capitalist economies operating within a democratic framework. Of course, these contradictions only become acute when a strong, unified, and socialist labour movement captures political power. In such circumstances the Webbs might yet be vindicated.

Aim and approach of the book

The central question of this study is under what circumstances profit sharing and employee shareholding can motivate workers and what scheme of financial participation has the potential to realise economic democracy within the individual firm and wider society.

At the outset, some justification must be offered for the comparative approach adopted by this study. This is particularly necessary given that some commentators have questioned the value and indeed the enlightenment to be gained from comparative studies of industrial relations. The reader, it is claimed, is taken on a grand tour and presented with a diverse selection of systems in various countries but left to draw his own conclusions. This practice has been likened to a tour of an industrial relations zoo. Another critic identifies comparative industrial relations as an area abounding with pretension and superficial generalisations.[1]

The choice of two apparently polar opposites – America and Scandinavia – might seem to leave the approach adopted by this study vulnerable to the above charges. Yet from the viewpoint of the study, both share an important characteristic and problem. As capitalist democracies, both exhibit a considerably uneven distribution of wealth. Some individuals or groups in both countries regarded this concentration of wealth and power in few hands as contradicting if not undermining political democracy, and they were sufficiently disturbed by this phenomenon to initiate remedial action. This action can be viewed as an attempt to establish a form of economic democracy, complementing or supporting its political counterpart.

A central concern of this book is to identify a form of financial participation possessing the potential to realise economic democracy within the individual firm and the wider society. American and Scandinavian approaches represent respectively the individualist and collectivist answers to the question. A comparison and contrast of both approaches seem more likely to produce a balanced consideration than an exclusive and lopsided focus on one or the other. Indeed, a comparative examination of the strengths and weaknesses of individualist and collectivist approaches to economic democracy could assist in evaluating their ultimate effectiveness. Furthermore, it raises the question as to why the individualist approach should flourish in America, while there is a pronounced preference for the collectivist approach in Scandinavia. Explaining these preferences in terms of the balance of social forces or the hegemony of a particular economic ideology, focuses attention on the outcomes desired by proponents of alternative approaches to reform. To establish whether a chosen method of reform is designed to perform an integrative or transformative function, may illuminate its effectiveness as a vehicle for economic democracy.

None the less, the comparative approach remains open to criticism. For instance, it could be argued that the points of comparison between America and Scandinavia are narrowly based and the similarities superficial. In America, apart from a handful of enthusiasts, there is no popular movement or demand to establish economic democracy. Among American employers who took up employee stock ownership, a concern with economic democracy in the workplace or wider society hardly figures on their list of priorities. In Denmark and Sweden, on the other hand, economic democracy is an integral part of labour movement policy, and its implementation is sought with some vigour.

Nevertheless, despite these differences, the American experience with employee stock ownership has a relevance and can contribute to an understanding of the Scandinavian debate on economic democracy. When debating economic democracy, Scandinavian labour movement spokesmen frequently cite American schemes of financial participation as examples of how not to democratise production ownership. Again, a Swedish union spokesman dismisses attempts to broaden individual share ownership as a sham solution to the problem of concentrated wealth and power. Yet the alternatives to collective profit sharing put forward by Scandinavian employers are similar in many respects to American schemes of financial participation. Consequently, a familiarity with the practice and results of American schemes of financial participation can assist in evaluating the effectiveness of alternative approaches to economic democracy in Scandinavia.

PLAN OF THE STUDY

A prerequisite for any coherent discussion or examination of economic democracy is some definition of democracy itself. Thus, the conception of democracy adopted by this book is developed in the opening sections of Chapter 1. From this it follows that any genuine scheme of economic democracy must allow for the exercise of employee influence and control on economic decision making. Various schemes of financial participation are then examined against this criterion. Employee shareholding, apparently offering the greatest potential scope for the exercise of employee influence and control on economic decision making, is identified as a likely vehicle for the realisation of economic democracy within the individual firm, or at a micro level.

Chapter 1 also reviews the motivational assumptions underlying financial participation. Among proponents and commentators on profit sharing there is a large measure of agreement on the necessity to establish certain preconditions if the motivational potential of a scheme is to have any hope of realisation. These five requirements or preconditions were gleaned from a review of the profit sharing literature and are listed in detail in Chapters 2 and 6, and sources cited. They can be summarised as employee involvement in the initiation, implementation and administration of a scheme. Furthermore, a scheme should function as an addition to wages and fringe benefits rather than as a substitute. The presence of these requirements and preconditions, the profit sharing literature suggests, is essential if the motivational potential of a scheme is to be realised. In the light of modern developments in motivation theory and the erosion of certainty that there is 'one best way', these assumptions may appear extremely problematic. Yet a recent British investigation of incentive payment systems, which adopted a contingency approach to motivation, surprisingly confirmed that consultation and employee involvement in their implementation is of central importance to the success of these schemes. These findings are considered in detail in Chapter 1.

Once a claim has been established for the importance and continuing relevance of traditional prescriptions, the latter can serve as a useful tool or template in assessing existing profit sharing schemes. The presence or absence of these prescriptions in a particular scheme can give an initial indication at least of their probable motivational effectiveness.

Chapter 2 discusses the claim that profit sharing can motivate or positively alter employee behaviour. North American profit sharing is chosen as the testing ground for this claim because of its world leadership regarding the number of existing schemes and their continuing growth. A 1973 survey of 702 profit sharing plans, a 1981 survey of 521 plans plus a survey of 13 companies conducted for this study, and interviews with business people, trade unionists and profit sharing experts are used to construct a detailed picture of the operation of these schemes. The schemes are then examined to see if they meet certain requirements and establish certain preconditions. Their absence, it was assumed, would augur ill for the motivational potential of American profit sharing.

In the majority of American schemes surveyed, one or more of the traditional preconditions or requirements was absent, pointing to the likely failure of American profit sharing to motivate workers. Examination of evidence to the contrary did little to challenge this initial prognosis. Three studies were reviewed in which favourable comparisons on a number of indices (index of earnings per common share, index of dividends per share, etc.) were made between profit sharing and non-profit sharing companies. On some of these indices the performance of profit sharing companies was superior. Yet the evidence that profit sharing had made the significant contribution to superior financial performance was at best ambiguous. One of the studies, which attempted to assess the effect of the company's profit sharing schemes on employee performance, found them to be negligible. This is hardly surprising, given the absence of many traditional preconditions in the majority of American profit sharing schemes. Indeed, this may explain their motivational failure. One example is the frequent use of profit sharing as a pension substitute. This was the practice in 70 per cent of the schemes surveyed. Nevertheless, a case study of the Warner Gear Company demonstrates that profit sharing can motivate workers. It also confirms the importance of implementing traditional prescriptions.

While a majority of American deferred profit sharing schemes function as pension substitutes, in an even greater number of cases there appeared to be an almost total absence of employee involvement in their initiation, implementation and administration. If a reluctance to implement these participative requirements, or to share information and control, is generally characteristic of managerial schemes of financial participation, then it is unlikely that employee shareholding will motivate workers or realise economic democracy within the individual firm.

Chapter 3 assesses the potential of employee shareholding to motivate workers and realise economic democracy within the individual firm. The methodological approach is similar to that adopted in Chapter 2. Again, American employee stock ownership plans, or employee shareholding schemes, are the chosen example because of their comparatively large and growing number. Surveys and interviews are used to profile these schemes. They are then examined to ascertain the extent to which they implement traditional prescriptions. These requirements or prescriptions are the same as those applied in the profit sharing chapter, along with two additions specific to employee shareholding. The additional requirements are that employee shareholders have the right to vote shares allocated to their accounts, and that their combined shareholding represents a significant percentage of company equity. Unfortunately, there is no agreement among experts as to what constitutes a significant percentage, it being variously estimated at 10 per cent, 14 per cent, or possibly a minimum of 50 per cent. None the less, a number of traditional prescriptions proved to be absent in the majority of schemes.

Consequent scepticism as to the motivational potential of American employee stock ownership plans was paradoxically confirmed by surveys which attempted to prove otherwise. Yet a case study of the Rath Packing Company employee shareholding scheme, which implemented traditional prescriptions, demonstrates the potential of employee shareholding to motivate workers and realise economic democracy within the individual firm. The explanations for the failure of the generality of American employee stock ownership plans to realise their motivational potential are the familiar ones – their use as substitute benefits and the reluctance of employers or managers to share information and control. Indeed, in many instances, managers retained voting rights on shares distributed to employees. A second case study of the South Bend Lathe Company suggests that the above strategy will not only neutralise the potential of these schemes to motivate workers or realise economic democracy, but could sour labour–management relations.

Chapter 3 also considers the macro aspect of employee shareholding. Some American proponents of these schemes see the diffusion of individual share ownership as resolving a perceived contradiction between wealth concentrated in few hands, and the democratic ideal. The Rath Packing Company case study illustrates a weakness in this approach. Despite achieving a substantial degree of internal democratisation through individual share ownership, both the firm and its employees remained creatures of external economic forces.

The subjects of Chapters 4 and 5 are the Swedish and Danish labour movements' proposals for collective profit sharing or economic democracy. A study of these proposals is useful for the following reasons. First, they represent an alternative labour movement approach to financial participation, at both a macro and micro level. Second, comparison and contrast of union and management proposals will deepen understanding of both. Finally, an examination of collective profit sharing brings into sharper focus questions concerning the exercise of influence and control within the workplace and wider society. Can the implementation of collective profit sharing in one or more of its forms realise economic democracy at a macro and micro level? How well founded are the Swedish and Danish employers' criticisms of these proposals, and could their counter-proposal – the diffusion of individual share ownership – be equally effective in establishing economic democracy? These are the questions addressed by Chapters 4 and 5.

The methodological approach adopted in both chapters is conditioned by the novelty and unfinished form of the labour movement's proposals and a consequent dearth of empirical data. For instance, since 1973, Danish wage earner funds, or collective profit sharing, have undergone a number of modifications, yet they remain mere proposals. Though a Swedish version of collective profit sharing was eventually implemented in 1984, it is a shadowy manifestation of the 1975 original. Consequently, the approach adopted was largely historical and descriptive. First, the particular historical, social and economic developments which gave rise to the Danish and Swedish labour movements' demands for collective profit sharing are outlined. Second, the proposals are examined and trade union spokesmen and politicians interviewed in an attempt to gauge the adequacy of collective profit sharing, as both a response to specific problems and as a vehicle for the realisation of economic democracy. However, before reaching any conclusion, employer criticism of collective profit sharing and their counter-proposals are examined. This examination is based on a number of interviews with employers and a review of their publications on collective profit sharing. From these conflicting perspectives, tentative conclusions are drawn regarding the likely effect and effectiveness of collective profit sharing, while the Danish and Swedish employers' approach to financial participation is shown to be remarkably similar to that of their American counterparts.

A final chapter reviews profit sharing/employee shareholding in Ireland where legislation to encourage the general adoption of these schemes is of very recent origin. Indeed, the virtual absence of a tradition of employee financial participation is an important factor in choosing the Irish example. In such conditions, the employer response to profit sharing/employee shareholding can be seen developing, rather than already formed by custom and practice. Consequently, an examination of Irish employers' responses to these schemes tests a claim of this book that the majority of employers are reluctant to implement the participative requirements of these schemes or to share information and control.

The approach adopted in the Irish chapter is as follows. First, the legislation to encourage growth in the number of profit sharing/employee shareholding schemes is examined. It was found to impose no obligations on employers, regarding employee involvement in the administration of the schemes. Second, three attitude surveys designed to elicit employer responses to various aspects of profit sharing/employee shareholding are reviewed. The review establishes that Irish employers, like their American and Scandinavian counterparts, fear these schemes may involve disclosure of information and loss of control to employees. Thus, as vehicles for the realisation of economic democracy, managerial schemes of financial participation are, in general, unlikely to prove effective.

Finally, throughout this book, various legislative enactments on profit sharing or employee shareholding are considered. Much of this technical detail is at best peripheral to the main argument. Nevertheless, its exclusion would have made examination and discussion of these schemes less than comprehensible.

1 Financial democracy and financial participation

Industrial or Economic Democracy is a phrase that figures in so many quasi utopias that it has retained very little precise meaning. Mainly, I think, it means two things: first, the trade union rule over industrial relations; second, democratization of the monarchic factory by workmens' representation on boards or other devices calculated to secure them influence on the introduction of technological improvements, business policy in general and, of course, discipline in the plant in particular, including methods of 'hiring and firing'. Profit sharing is a nostrum of a subgroup of schemes.

J.A. Schumpeter (1943)[1]

Profit sharing is a method invented by the middle-class mind in conformity with the ideas of the middle classes . . . it [PS] proposes to leave the control of the business in the hands of the employer and to give to the operatives a part only of the profits of the business.

D.F. Schloss (1898)[2]

One object of this chapter is to identify among the various schemes of financial participation the one with the greatest potential for the realisation of financial or economic democracy. In pursuit of that object the chapter will be structured as follows. First, the conception of democracy adopted by this study will be outlined. (Some conception of democracy would seem a necessary prerequisite to any consideration of financial or economic democracy.) Second, financial participation and some of its variants will be examined with a view to selecting a likely vehicle for economic democracy. The principal criterion used in this process of elimination or rejection of unsuitable schemes will be the conception of democracy already adopted. Finally, the macro and micro approaches to financial democracy will be introduced and the focus of subsequent chapters outlined.

DEMOCRACY

Democracy is a word with a long history and its meanings have been varied and complex. The literal meaning of democracy is simply the rule of the people.[3] According to Williams, up to the end of the seventeenth century several uses of the term indicate a form of popular class rule, or democracy as a state in which all had the right to rule and did actually rule.[4] Similarly, for Rousseau democracy apparently involved all citizens actively participating in framing laws for their own governance within a context of approximate social and economic equality.[5]

Today, the above conception of democracy implying popular and direct participation in political and economic decision making would probably be regarded by many as an unrealisable ideal. Direct democracy has been superseded by representative democracy – that is the opportunity for all citizens periodically to elect representatives to Parliament. Undoubtedly, the size and complexity of the modern state make the practical arguments for representative democracy extremely persuasive.[6] Yet a cost of this procedural efficiency is the extent to which it diminishes the political power of individual citizens in comparison with their power in a direct democracy. To describe the periodic participation of citizens in elections as instances of ruling, does seem, Dunn remarks, a little strained.[7] Some might view this dilution of popular rule or control as a serious defect of contemporary capitalist democracies. Yet the adoption of remedial measures, designed to increase popular participation, influence and control in political and economic decision making at all levels, would likely be opposed by proponents of democratic elitism as impractical and potentially destructive of democracy.

The theory of a political elite was developed in Europe towards the close of the nineteenth century and formed part of a doctrine opposed to the spread of socialism and democratic notions.[8] Elite theorists argued that the people or the governed never in any real sense participate in government but merely submit.[9] The possibility of government by the people was denied.

In the twentieth century the most influential exponent of this view has been Joseph Schumpeter. Most recent work on democratic theory, it has been claimed, is elaborated within his framework and based on his definition of democracy.[10] Schumpeter began his examination by discarding the traditional democratic doctrine of equality as factually unsound.[11] Dispensing with its ideological or normative content, he redefined democracy as 'a political method or arrangement for arriving at legislative or administrative decisions'.[12] Owing to the complexity and size of modern societies, these decisions are taken by elected representatives. Therefore the will of the people is the product, not the motive power, of the political process.[13] The sole function of the electorate is to choose between elite groups competing for political power.[14] Action, Schumpeter insists, is the prerogative of the politician. Consequently, electors must refrain from lobbying or attempting to instruct their representatives.[15] Schumpeter would strictly confine the operation of this method to the electoral process. No responsible person, he insists, can view with equanimity the consequences of extending the democratic method, that is to say the sphere of politics, to all economic affairs.[16]

At least two objections might be advanced against Schumpeter's analysis. First, in modern western democracies it is no longer possible, if such was ever the case, totally to isolate economic and political decision making. Indeed, the ills of capitalist economies in the US and Europe alike are increasingly ascribed to what has been called 'the excess of democracy'.[17] It would be mistaken to interpret this complaint as simply a reaction from devotees of *laissez-faire* to state intervention. In many western democracies, business is partially dependent on a range of government subsidies, incentives and concessions.[18] Britain and Ireland are cases in point.[19] The apparent paradox has been explained by Crouch. A continuing problem for *laissez-faire*, he claims, is that it has to try and put economic decisions beyond the reach of democratic politics – not beyond all politics, because it will be important that government takes political measures necessary to sustain the *laissez-faire* system, but beyond democratic pressures for full employment and social services.[20] So, despite Schumpeter's injunction, economics and politics in many western countries are closely intertwined; thus limiting democratic decision making and participation to the exclusively political process of voting in local and general elections may create a lacuna in the modern democratic polity. As will be seen, wealth and consequently power are concentrated in a few hands in some contemporary capitalist democracies.[21] These powerful economic oligarchies and monopolies, while capable of influencing governments and markets, are themselves virtually free of popular accountability and control. Public policy, it has been claimed, necessarily tends to be oriented, especially over the long run, in a direction which is fundamentally in line with the interests of giant corporate enterprises.[22] A truly democratic society would seem to require the extension of democratic procedures, processes and control to the economic arena.[23]

Second, in rejecting the ideal of equality and insisting that there should be only a minimum of popular participation, is not Schumpeter draining democracy of its essence, a form without content? According to Bachrach, the emphasis in classical democratic theory upon citizen participation in all public affairs was based on the premise that such involvement is essential to the full development of individual capacities.[24] It is reasonable to assume, he continues, that the full development of adult men and women requires the opportunity and challenge to participate in public life beyond the ballot box and dues collection.[25] This developmental conception of democracy which demands the maximum possible participation of citizens in political and economic decision making is the one adopted by this study. Consequently, schemes of industrial and economic democracy which increase the accountability of managerial or economic elites through greater worker/citizen participation and control are viewed as devices making for the realisation of the democratic ideal.

From Schumpeter's perspective, schemes to maximise popular participation would probably appear as irresponsible folly. As soon as the typical citizen enters the political field, Schumpeter asserts, his mental performance drops to a lower level, his arguments are infantile, his behaviour primitive, and he tends to yield to prejudice and impulse.[26] During the 1970s, proposals of the Bullock Committee for worker representation on company boards prompted a similar response from the director general of the British Institute of Directors. He condemned the proposals as irrelevant, dangerous and having as much justification as the Emperor Caligula's idea of making his horse a consul.[27] Findings of some postwar political sociologists might appear to confirm the wisdom of Schumpeter's preference for minimum popular participation.

Data from large-scale empirical investigations in many western countries revealed that the outstanding characteristic of most citizens, especially those of low socio-economic status, was a general lack of interest in political activity. Furthermore, the existence of non-democratic or authoritarian attitudes was found to be wide-spread, again particularly among the lower socio-economic groups. One conclusion drawn was that an increase in political participation of these normally apathetic groups would endanger the stability of the democratic system.[28] Apathy then seemed to be a political good.[29] It was not the people but the privileged elites, one political scientist concluded, who were the bastions of democratic defence.[30]

The above view has been described as a static conception of democracy.[31] Nevertheless, its proponents might argue that it provides some stability and the maintenance at least of democratic forms. Liberal or capitalist democratic theory, Dunn claims, accepts capitalist democracies as imperfect devices for fending off worse fates.[32] The alternative dynamic or developmental concept of democracy, stressing maximum popular participation in political and economic decision making, is rendered unworkable by characteristics apparently common to the working class – apathy and authoritarianism. Increased participation by an authoritarian working class might in the long run prove inimical to the survival of liberal democracy. However, if these supposedly proletarian characteristics are to a large extent structurally determined rather than innate, then there may be a way out of the developmental democrat's dilemma.

PARTICIPATION – AUTHORITARIANISM AND DEMOCRACY

It is a fundamental idea of sociology that the institutions that exist in the different spheres of society are not merely co-existent, but are connected with each other by relations of concordance or contradiction, and mutually affect each other.[33] This would suggest that a person's experience within the family, the education system or the workplace can influence his or her attitude and behaviour regarding the wider society. Dahrendorf claims that apart from the state, no other imperatively co-ordinated organisation can compare with the industrial enterprise in the number of persons affected by its structure and the intensity of its influence.[34] The particular significance of large-scale industry is further emphasised by the fact that those who earn their living in industrial enterprises spend a large part of their lives there and are under the influence of the social relations characteristic of industry.[35] These relations could be described as autocratic, hierarchical and exhibiting gross inequalities in the distribution of power.[36] The workplace, it has been asserted, is the most authoritarian milieu in democratic societies.[37] Such an environment is likely to be productive of alienation, feelings of powerlessness and insignificance among shopfloor workers. Furthermore, the contradiction between the autocratic workplace and the apparently democratic egalitarian nature of the wider society may serve to deepen apathy and cynicism. Workers' attitudes and behaviour in the wider society are likely to be significantly influenced by such experience. There is some evidence to support this contention.

Lipset ascribes the authoritarian disposition of the working class to poor education and insufficient experience of participation in political or voluntary organisations.[38] A study of 400 autoworkers found that those with low job satisfaction were generally passive and did not vote or participate in community organisations.[39] Generally, jobs of such workers are highly prescribed, machine paced and routinised, leaving little scope for the exercise of initiative or control. There is ample evidence to show that as a result of these conditions, individual workers lose interest in themselves and the collectivity.[40] Conversely, a Norwegian study consistenly found that democratised authority in industry resulted in more workers attempting to control the circumstances of their own lives both in the plant and the wider society.[41] This could be described as the development of a sense of political efficacy – i.e., a belief among individuals or groups that it is possible to exercise some control over their circumstances through involvement and participation in the political process. A study of five countries – Britain, W. Germany, Italy, Mexico and the US – concluded that opportunities to participate in decisions at one's place of work were crucial to the development of political efficacy.[42] There is little novelty in such a conclusion. Confronted with the inevitability of universal suffrage, John Stuart Mill was concerned as to how the newly enfranchised working classes might participate in the state. He suggested that the educative effect of participation at local level and in the workplace would prepare workers for involvement in the wider political arena.[43]

One writer appears to suggest that authoritarian decision making and hierarchical power structures, common features of most workplaces, could be the principal explanation for the supposedly authoritarian nature of the working class.[44] In that case, a move towards more democratic structures and decision making within the workplace might check any tendency among working people towards authoritarianism. This would appear to set democracy on a firmer foundation than basing its survival on the continued apathy and non-participation of the working class. Thus it could be argued that the developmental democrats' insistence on maximum popular participation in political and economic decision making at local and national levels might, in the long run, tend to conserve and strengthen democracy rather than encompass its destruction. Yet the fears of democratic elitists for the survival of liberal democracy in such circumstances are not entirely without foundation. Liberal democracy, as Macpherson points out, has at least two meanings: '"liberal" can mean freedom of the stronger to do down the weaker by following market rules; or it can mean equal effective freedom of all to use and develop their capacities. The latter freedom is inconsistent with the former.'[45]

For instance, a substantially uneven distribution of wealth and power (a characteristic of modern capitalist democracies) may allow few citizens to experience equal and effective freedom to use and develop their capacities. Espousal of a developmental conception of democracy would seem to involve the downgrading – if not demise – of the market capitalist version of liberal democracy. Participatory democracy, Heilbroner suggests, may be uncongenial or destructive of the attitudes and behaviour patterns on which the business system has traditionally rested.[46] An examination of democracy and self-determination by one political scientist prompted him to question the compatibility of private ownership in the means of production with any significant approximation to equal self-determination.[47] As will be seen when the Swedish and Danish labour movements' proposals for economic democracy are considered, the above remarks become more than purely speculative.

PARTICIPATIVE DEMOCRACY

The conception of democracy adopted in this book can now be briefly outlined: it is that all citizens should have an equal and effective right to participate actively, either directly or through elected representatives, in political and economic decision making in the workplace and wider society or at micro and macro levels. Yet equal and effective participation is only likely to be realised within a context of social and economic equality. What is posited here is approximate rather than absolute equality. By approximate equality is meant that any difference in wealth, education or access to knowledge should not be so considerable as to result in the permanent subordination of some groups of citizens to others, or to create great inequality in the exercise of decision making rights.

The object in formulating a conception of democracy is to use it as an aid or benchmark in distinguishing among the various schemes of financial participation the one with the greatest potential for the realisation of economic democracy. At the outset, the above formulation can be used to establish some essential requirements. Obviously, the operation of any suitable scheme must promote a more equitable distribution of wealth or ownership of productive assets. However, this alone would be insufficient; power, the concomitant of wealth, must also be correspondingly dispersed. Thus, a more equitable distribution of wealth and power will enable employees and citizens to participate in, influence and, to some extent, control economic and associated decision making at the level of the individual firm or in the wider society. The most developed form of economic democracy will enable subordinate participants to deploy an upward exertion of control on decisions at both levels. Various schemes of financial participation can now be set against these criteria to discover a likely vehicle for the potential realisation of financial democracy. The word potential is used advisedly. It is not intended to apply the above criteria with excessive rigidity and automatically exclude from consideration all schemes that do not immediately realise full-blown economic democracy.

A secondary purpose of this and following chapters will be to identify those schemes most likely to fulfil the practical expectations of financial participation. These are: more harmonious industrial relations and a highly motivated workforce who identify, and are involved with, the fortunes of the firm. Yet it would be wrong to assume that the practical and ideological objectives of financial participation are independent or mutually exclusive. Indeed, this book will suggest they are complementary and interdependent. Schemes of financial participation devoid of a genuinely participative element, it will be shown, are unlikely to stimulate worker motivation and labour–management co-operation.[48] Employee participation in decision making, a key variable of financial democracy, is equally important if the motivational potential of financial participation is to be realised.

FINANCIAL PARTICIPATION

Financial participation is an imprecise term. For instance, it could be argued that employees in receipt of wages already experience financial participation. In this book only those schemes whose payments to employees, either in cash or shares, are additions to standard wage rates and fringe benefits, will be considered as falling within the category of financial participation. Yet within that category the schemes are many and varied. However, the primary purpose of this section – to identify a scheme potentially able to realise financial or economic democracy – will serve to restrict the area of investigation. Such a scheme, to conform with the conception of democracy already adopted, must have the potential at any rate to share not only wealth but power. In other words, any scheme of economic democracy while benefiting employees financially, must simultaneously increase their influence and control over a wide range of decision making.

The search for a scheme of financial participation that could serve as a vehicle for economic democracy will be conducted as follows. Schemes will be graded in an ascending order according to the scope they allow for the exercise of employee participation, influence and control. The one with the potential to maximise employee participation, influence and control over a wide range of economic decision making through financial participation will be the most likely vehicle for economic democracy.

In all, four schemes of financial participation will be examined. These are – the Rucker Plan, cash-based profit sharing, the Scanlon Plan and employee shareholding. This examination has a twofold purpose. First, it will give some concrete form to the concept of economic democracy adopted by this study. Second, it will show that any scheme of economic democracy must have at least the potential to redistribute wealth and power simultaneously.

The above procedure will also facilitate some examination of the motivational potential of financial participation. Indeed, many managers would probably regard the expected stimulus to employee effort and productivity as the principal object of these schemes. Finally, possible trade union responses to these schemes will also be considered.

THE RUCKER PLAN AND VALUE ADDED

One comparatively simple form of financial participation is the Rucker Plan for productivity based on added value. First, it is necessary to distinguish between value added and profit. Essentially, the difference lies in the method of calculation. Profit is the sum remaining after the total costs of goods, services, wages and salaries have been subtracted from the total sales revenue. Value added is the sum remaining after the price of bought-in goods and services – excluding wages – has been subtracted from the total sales. This remainder is the wealth created by the use of company plant and machines by the workforce and management. A historically constant ratio between this production or added value and total wage costs was discovered in the 1930s by Allen W. Rucker, an American management consultant. Rucker proposed to simply maintain the historical ratio of payroll to value added by increasing the total payroll fund exactly in proportion to every increase in value added. This, he believed, would stimulate the workforce to greater productivity as measured by added value, because remuneration would automatically increase in proportion. A more direct link between worker effort and reward, proponents of the plan would suggest, give it an advantage over some schemes of financial participation. Yet the participative element for employees in the Rucker Plan is negligible.[49]

CASH-BASED PS

Under the cash-based system of profit sharing, a bonus is paid to employees, usually calculated on a fixed predetermined percentage of pre-tax profits. With an increase in profit there is a corresponding increase in the worker's bonus. It is assumed that such incentive will spur the employees to greater efforts, thus increasing the profitability of the enterprise.

Though providing more scope for employee participation than the Rucker Plan, two objections would make difficult the inclusion of cash-based PS under the heading of financial democracy. First, even under the best possible circumstances of full employee participation in the organisation and administration of the scheme, their role would be strictly limited. No potential would exist for employee input into the wider financial affairs of the company. Apparently, the majority of cash-based schemes make little claim to be participative. In Britain less than half the companies with cash-based schemes claim to have consulted employees on its introduction, while in Ireland, in nearly all cases it was found that there was no employee participation in the management of PS in the initiation of the scheme or any form of consultation.[50]

A second objection to such schemes would be purely practical. An expert maintains that PS can be included in any comprehensive classification of incentive payment systems.[51] If this is so, it may be one of the less effective of such systems. The connection between the effort or efficiency of workers and the profit earned by an organisation is not direct. Assuming maximum employee efficiency, profit can still fluctuate from year to year. A fall in the price of raw materials or a general trade recession can increase or reduce profit margins independent of employee effort.[52] Possible results could range between greater employee understanding of market forces or apathy and even resentment. According to Latta, such criticisms are irrelevant, for he points out that promoters of PS do not regard the schemes as a direct incentive to greater employee effort. Rather, they see PS as motivating the employee as a member of a team, creating a more positive working environment and improving labour relations.[53] Nevertheless, these expectations appear to be grounded in a belief in the power of financial incentives, even though they may be indirect or remote.

Sociologists generally remain sceptical of claims made by managers and economists for the efficacy of monetary incentives. In their view, the failure to appreciate the complexity of human motivation would be the outstanding weakness of every system of financial incentives so far practised or proposed.[54] Marriott claims that employee responses to financial measures represent complex reactions to the total situation, both past and present, and the wider environment in which incentive schemes are applied.[55] Another expert dismisses traditional incentive wages and profit sharing as quite inadequate in terms of modern psychological theory.[56] Possibly mindful of these caveats, all contemporary promoters of PS are agreed that the schemes cannot succeed as substitutes for good industrial relations, adequate pension schemes, sick benefits, good working conditions, and wages at union rates. There is unanimity on the necessity for these basic requirements if PS is to succeed. Yet, even the fulfilment of these essential preconditions, with the addition of PS, may be insufficient to trigger a spontaneously co-operative spirit among employees towards the enterprise or stimulate effort above minimum acceptable levels. For instance, Whyte suggests that the success of plant-wide incentives depends upon the institution of human relations changes and he proposes a formula: no change in human relations, no worker response to plant-wide incentives.[57] The central thesis of his work is that responses to incentives depend in large measure on the organisational context in which they take place.[58] This is a contention with particular relevance for Ireland. Whelan found that Irish trade unionists display extremely high levels of distrust towards management, with over 70 per cent of manual workers believing that management would 'put one over' on workers if they got the chance.[59] Under such conditions, the results of a cash-based PS scheme introduced without consultation and requiring minimal participation, would likely disappoint even modest managerial expectations.

Alan Fox would argue that PS will not make any significant difference in employee behaviour, even with the implementation of changes suggested by writers of the human relations school. Despite the persistent belief that a share in profits will arouse the desired spirit of involvement, identification and commitment, Fox contends there is no evidence of any lasting effect upon employees whose jobs remain fragmented, highly prescribed and subject to hierarchical inspection and control.[60] There are grounds for believing, he continues, that in western society the individual's degree of moral commitment, identification and involvement is associated with the degree of discretion his job affords him.[61] From this radical perspective, PS can achieve little without fundamental change in the power and trust relations in the workplace.

Despite the above objections, cash-based PS schemes continue to be used by management. In Britain, a survey of 246 companies operating some form of employee financial participation found 70 per cent of the schemes were cash based. Almost all the respondents that operated cash based PS considered them to be fairly or very successful. Of the wide variety of reasons given for the success of the schemes, the two most prominent were (i) they encouraged employees to identify with the company and (ii) they provided an incentive for greater effort.[62] On the face of it, this would appear to be impressive evidence for the success of cash-based PS. However, Reilly, who conducted the survey, acknowledged the difficulty of creating objective tests to determine the success of the schemes. Consequently he was forced to rely upon the subjective judgement of the companies concerned to indicate whether the schemes proved helpful.[63] It is most likely that the questionnaire would have been completed by the personnel manager or some other member of the managerial strata. In that case the evidence may be flawed by ideological bias. The use of incentive schemes in many firms, Behrend found, rests on faith in, rather than proof of, the effectiveness of financial incentives.[64] Apparently, most managers rely on impressions and beliefs when making judgements about the effectiveness of financial incentives.[65]

The work of two organisational theorists would suggest a more limited usefulness for the cash-based scheme. Katz examines the assumption that the liking for an organisation created by system rewards (bonuses, cash-based PS, etc.) will generalise to greater productive effort within the enterprise. Such a generalisation of motivation may occur, he allows, but to a very limited extent. It would not be a reliable basis for the expectation of higher productivity. System rewards, Katz maintains, are more effective for holding members within the organisation than for maximising other organisational behaviour.[66] Echoing Katz, Galbraith concludes that system rewards have their largest effect on encouraging people to join and remain in an organisation.[67]

Evidence from research on the John Lewis Partnership which surveyed rank-and-file as well as managerial attitudes would support the above conclusions. Top management in the partnership is ideologically committed to the sharing of wealth, power and knowledge with all employees, subject to the commercial success of the business.[68] The mechanism through which it is intended to realise these aims are a somewhat limited representative system, a profit sharing scheme that is in reality cash based and a partnership Gazette and Chronicle.[69] Working conditions and pensions are good: the rate of pay is above average and management attitude to unions is one of friendly neutrality.[70] Not surprisingly, employees regard the partnership as a good employer.[71]

These are favourable conditions under which to test the assumption that a sharing of profit will encourage employee identification with the company, which in turn will translate into greater effort and higher productivity. The findings of research on the John Lewis Partnership would confound both assumptions. An attitude survey of rank-and-file partners suggests that the general ethos of employment relations within the partnership is not essentially different from that which prevails in employing organisations of a more usual kind.[72] Nor, apparently, was there an increase in employee productivity above normally acceptable levels. Management still felt some form of individual employee incentive was necessary.[73] The partnership's achievement in combining commercial success with satisfactory employment should not be underrated. However, in producing a fundamental alteration in employee attitudes or effort, its effects appear to be insignificant. Overall, the partnership's concrete result may be limited to enticing employees to join and remain in the organisation. In purely instrumental terms, this would further limit the usefulness of cash based PS to situations of full employment where labour is at a premium.

Yet the lacklustre performance of PS may be due more to defective practice than to theory. Proponents of profit sharing would probably ascribe its failures to improve worker productivity or engender labour–management co-operation as being primarily due to inept application. Certainly, a review of the profit sharing literature shows general agreement among proponents and commentators on the necessity to establish certain preconditions if the motivational potential of a scheme is to have any prospect of realisation. These are:

1 *Broad coverage* A PS or share scheme must embrace the maximum number of employees.
2 *Consultation* Employees must be consulted by management in formulating the plan and involved in its administration.
3 *Predetermined formula* The cash bonus or share allocation must be distributed to employees according to a predetermined formula worked out between management and workers.
4 *Additional benefit* The profit share or share allocation must be an addition to standard wage rates and fringe benefits and not a substitute for either.
5 *Communication* Continuing emphasis on the merits and details of the plan and a willingness on the company's part to disclose financial information.

These requirements or preconditions are discussed in detail in Chapter 2 but can be conveniently summarised as employee involvement in the initiation, implementation and administration of a scheme.[74] The absence of one or more of these requirements, proponents would argue, explains the motivational failure of many PS schemes. In the light of modern developments in motivation theory and the erosion of certainty that there is 'one best way', these assumptions appear extremely problematic. Yet a recent British study of incentive payment systems, though it adopted a contingency approach to motivation, could be interpreted as confirming a continuing importance for traditional prescriptions for successful PS.[75]

This Department of Employment research paper set out to answer a number of questions regarding the effectiveness of incentive payment systems. It attempted to discover the percentage of cases where the introduction of a new incentive scheme led to an improvement in employee performance and how this performance could be quantified, measured and monitored. Also, it investigated the extent to which variations in improved performance are affected by different situations and whether there is a significant relationship between altered performance and factors in the scheme's method of implementation. Other influences which might have a bearing on the effectiveness of a payment system were also considered, i.e., behavioural factors, technology and the external economic environment in which the firm was trading.[76]

In all, 63 firms in the manufacturing and service sectors which had introduced incentive payment schemes during the period 1977–80 were surveyed. They ranged in size from organisations employing less than 35 blue collar workers to those employing over 3,000 workers. A wide variety of schemes were in operation. While some linked the bonus to individual performance, the majority awarded the bonus on a group or company-wide basis. There were some cash based PS schemes in this latter category.[77]

Beginning with a review of classical and human relations motivation theory, the researchers rejected as fundamentally flawed the advocacy of panaceas for all management situations. Research evidence demonstrated, they pointed out, that improvements in productivity could be obtained with one technique in one situation, and different techniques in another situation where the first technique did not work.[78] For instance, the Wage Payment Systems Research Team, led by Tom Lupton at Manchester, conducted a series of studies of payment systems in operation, to learn about the factors which could influence the way a pay system worked. This work led to guidelines being proposed for the design of wage systems which took account of some 29 factors in the organisation and its environment, known to have an influence on wage system effectiveness.[79] Therefore, there could be no single technique or panacea for motivating employees. Instead, they adopted a contingency approach to the assessment of incentive payment systems. At the heart of contingency theory is the simple idea that there is no single best way of organising and no single ideal management system.[80] Consequently, the researchers assumed that the effectiveness of a payment system will be influenced by the behavioural, structural and environmental factors within which it operates.[81]

First, the research confirmed previous findings that some employees will respond better to certain types of reward systems than others. There were major differences in the extent to which blue collar, white collar and supervisory staff valued a range of possible rewards. Blue collar employees were found to have a more or less instrumental attitude to work, while there was some doubt about the appeal of direct financial incentives to white collar and supervisory groups. Second, the type of incentive payment scheme and the size of the organisation within which it was introduced also influenced blue collar employee productivity and output. A negative association was found to exist between short-term variable bonuses based on individual performance and employee output. The strength of this negative association increased with organisation size. Conversely, short-term variable bonuses awarded on a group basis were positively associated with improved work attitudes and output. Yet, this association seemed likely to weaken with an increase in the size of the enterprise.[82]

Some tentative inferences can be drawn from the above findings. Collective bonus schemes such as cash-based PS seem more likely to positively affect employee performance than bonuses awarded on an individual basis, i.e. piece-rates. Yet a significantly positive outcome from the application of cash-based PS can apparently only be expected under certain conditions. These would be small firms with a predominantly blue collar workforce in which there was a frequent distribution of the profit sharing bonus. With regard to white collar and supervisory staff, a profit sharing scheme in which the bonus is distributed in the form of shares rather than cash might have greater appeal.

Overall, there was considerable variation between the performance of organisations in the researchers' sample.[83] They attempted to identify a key variable or variables explaining these differences. There was no advantage, they found, in selecting one type of payment scheme over others with regard to variations in the rate of technological change in particular firms.[84] Furthermore, the amount of performance variation between firms explained by the type of incentive scheme installed was not great.[85] The researchers were not perturbed by these findings, because they were consistent with a contingency approach to organisation theory which suggested that the characteristics of the environment and organisational situation would have a major impact on the degree of incentive scheme success.[86] Indeed, a significant amount of the relevant success of the schemes resulted from the buoyancy of the market and various other organisation and environmental characteristics operating at the time. The particular type of incentive payment scheme introduced added to these factors.[87]

Finally, the researchers re-examined their data to see whether any other factor explained performance variations more effectively than those already considered. They adopted a different approach on this occasion. Instead of applying a hypothesis based on previous theory, a hypothesis was developed from the data collected. This approach identified 'time spent in consultation about the incentive payment system' as the variable explaining different results better than any other factor.[88] As the researchers remarked, 'this most striking finding' did not relate easily to the technological/structural approach to contingency theory.[89] Nevertheless, of all the variables tested in the study for an association with beneficial results for the organisation deriving from their new payment system, the degree and extent of consultation during the process of design and implementation of the scheme was the one most closely associated with benefits to the organisation.[90] The kind of consultation that showed itself to be worthwhile was not simply a management style or an exercise in democratic procedures. It was rather the expenditure of management effort in detailed discussions about a specific change that was planned, which was modified as a result of these discussions and was eventually implemented with the understanding of those to whom it was to be applied.[91] The relation between the extent of consultation and the effectiveness of an incentive payment system, the researchers admitted, was not something they had set out to test, but it was such an important factor that it virtually pushed its way out of their data.[92]

The above findings suggest that the traditional prescriptions for successful PS, emphasising employee involvement in the initiation, implementation and administration of a scheme, remain both relevant and significant. Of course, this is not to deny that behavioural, structural and environmental factors can also influence the outcome of such schemes or even render their application inappropriate. Earlier, it was noted how improved employee performance, resulting from schemes such as cash-based PS, can be enhanced in certain circumstances, i.e., small firms with a predominantly blue collar workforce. Yet the extent of consultation with employees was found to be the most important factor explaining the success of an incentive payment scheme.

This is a weighty finding with regard to incentive schemes generally and profit sharing in particular. First, it tends to confirm the validity of traditional prescriptions for successful PS. Second, it underscores the necessity to implement these prescriptions if the scheme is to have any prospect of securing a positive alteration in employee behaviour. Lastly, given the importance of these prescriptions, they can serve as a useful tool in assessing existing PS schemes. The presence or absence of these prescriptions in a particular scheme can give an initial indication at least of their probable motivational effectiveness.

Yet, even assuming the wholehearted implementation of traditional prescriptions, it might be questioned whether cash-based PS can be considered as a form of financial democracy. Doubts on this matter principally arise because the participative element in cash-based PS is so severely restricted. There is little scope to extend employee influence and control beyond the confines of the scheme to the wider financial affairs of the company. Even simply as a financial incentive to greater productivity, cash-based PS (because of the remoteness and ambiguity of the relationship between employee effort and profit) may be less effective than the Rucker Plan. There are schemes, however, which, in meeting some of the above objections, might qualify for inclusion under the heading of financial democracy.

THE SCANLON PLAN

A crisis in the American steel industry of the late 1930s brought many companies close to bankruptcy. The president of the local Steelworkers' Union, Joseph Scanlon, took action to save his members' jobs.[93] This resulted in a formula for labour–management co-operation in which both parties would share in future increases in productivity. Appropriately, the formula was dubbed the Scanlon Plan.

In the method of calculating the bonus, there is some similarity between the Rucker and Scanlon Plans. The unique feature of the Scanlon Plan is its emphasis on participation. Nothing is as important, Lesieur insists, as the participative aspect of the plan.[94] The first step in its application is to find the normal labour cost for the plant over a period of time (usually a year). When payroll is compared with the sales value of goods produced, a norm can then be set. An increase in production and sales would alter the relationship between payroll and sales. The difference between norm payroll and actual payroll would constitute the bonus pool. In the two earliest versions of the plan, all of the bonus was paid to labour, but in later plans 25 per cent accrued to the company.[95]

The advantage claimed for the Rucker Plan over PS has already been noted. Similar claims have been made for the Scanlon Plan in that employees can easily discern the relationship between payroll and sales, and therefore between effort and reward. The economic rewards of the plan are related to factors in the work situation which are controllable by employees. Elimination of waste or employee attempts to streamline work practices will maximise production and potential sales, thus increasing the bonus pool.

Two aspects of the plan enhance its acceptability to the workforce and possibly its efficiency. As with PS and the Rucker Plan, the bonus is awarded on a group rather than an individual basis. Such an arrangement avoids the drawbacks associated with individualistic and competitive incentives, such as piece-rates.[96] More importantly, under the Scanlon Plan this putative co-operation is realised by formally establishing an area of collaboration and machinery to give it expression. Through a combination of production committees and a screening committee, management and workers co-operate to increase productive efficiency and thus the amount of the bonus.

Each major department has a production committee on which management and workers are represented. The function of the production committee is twofold: first, to discuss ways and means of eliminating waste, or better ways of doing a job; second, to process suggestions from employees or unions on more effective work practices. The screening committee is composed of top management and worker representatives drawn from the production committees. Its primary purpose is to examine the figures from the previous month's sales and payroll, and to announce the bonus amount to be shared among the employees. The screening committee also ratifies suggestions adopted by the production committees or reassesses those that have been rejected, or whose usefulness has been disputed. In keeping with the co-operative ethos, no individual reward is made for any suggestion, but is regarded as a contribution to group welfare. Individuals whose suggestions have been rejected are personally contacted and the decision explained. Lastly, the screening committee keeps employees informed of any developments that may affect the bonus, for example the sales success of a new product. On both committees there is no voting on suggestions or decisions, for management has the right to veto.[97]

With its involvement of the workforce through a participative approach and the establishment of a more direct link between effort and reward, the Scanlon Plan might appear to meet the principal practical and ideological objections levelled against cash-based PS and the Rucker Plan. Scanlon enthusiasts vouch for the effectiveness of the plan. A survey of ten companies that operated the plan over a two-year period found an average increase in productivity of 23 per cent.[98] A vital factor in the rapid attainment of better performance, Puckett suggested, may have been the change in attitude and a *new esprit de corps* among the workforce.[99] By 1958 the scheme was installed in over 50 companies and its success, Turner claims, was unaffected by plant size, technology, or by the presence or absence of a union.[100]

There is a dearth of research on the use or experience of the Scanlon Plan beyond that published by the enthusiasts for the scheme. Evidence from more neutral sources question, if not contradict, the above findings. A 1962 report by the Industrial Relations Counsellors Incorporated on six firms operating the plan concludes that it is of very limited application in American industry, but this fact has been obscured by its success in a few highly publicised cases.[101] In Britain, variants of the Scanlon Plan applied in the motor industry have not been notably successful.[102] A drop in body sales, which adversely affected the bonus of the Scottish plants, was later held partly responsible for a round of industrial disputes.[103] An information note issued by the British Institute of Management (1964) suggests a similar mediocre performance for Scanlon in other industries.[104] However, one contemporary researcher has taken a more positive view of the plan. Reviewing forty years of mostly American research on the Scanlon Plan, Schuster is in agreement with its proponents that the Scanlon concept is 'important', 'significant', 'bold' and 'spectacular'. Yet empirical evidence to support these claims is, he admits, not yet available. Nevertheless, he cites some studies which suggest the plan may increase productivity and organisational effectiveness, and encourage people to work harder. Additional research is required, Schuster concludes, to give greater support and credibility to existing findings.[105]

Given the above contradictory, though scanty evidence, it is reasonable to conclude that the Scanlon Plan cannot claim any spectacular advantages over other group incentive schemes. Yet, could it not be argued that the comparatively elaborate participative arrangements, combined with the wealth-sharing elements of the plan, would qualify it for inclusion under the heading of financial or economic democracy? Indeed, the Scanlon Plan has been described as 'existentialism for workers'.[106] Apparently, this suggests the plan would allow workers to take decisions that would shape their destiny. Furthermore, it is claimed 'the plan is a revolution in the sense that initiative can now come from the lowest levels of the organisation.'[107]

In fact, both the participative and wealth-sharing aspects of the plan are extremely limited. The initiatives Turner sees coming from the lowest levels of the organisation are confined to suggestions on increasing efficiency, and even these are subject to managerial veto. A redistribution of wealth and power within the organisation is neither the intention nor could it be the result of the Scanlon Plan. Rather, its implicit assumption is that the traditional portions of the wealth generated within the enterprise that accrue to capital and labour is equitable or at least acceptable. Starting from this baseline or the status quo, Scanlon proposed that a substantial portion of any further wealth generated by labour's effort would automatically accrue to labour. Viewed from a radical perspective, the plan could be seen as a device to secure labour's co-operation in its own exploitation. Whyte takes a more moderate, though not essentially different, view of the plan. Its implementation, he believes, would leave managerial prerogative untouched and it could reduce or eliminate resistance to change.[108] Under the co-operative relationship established by the plan, workers and foremen would no longer need to protect themselves from higher management. Thus, Whyte concludes, it would become possible to achieve a degree of management control of the production process that has not hitherto existed.[109] Labour's participation in the Scanlon Plan is restricted to suggestions for increasing its own productivity or checking on the calculation of its bonus. A genuinely democratic element can be said to be non-existent.

VALUE ADDED, SCANLON, RUCKER AND THE TRADE UNIONS

Today, claims made for the participative or wealth-sharing aspects of the above schemes would be subject to more critical scrutiny. This is due to a variety of factors. Both the Rucker and Scanlon Plans originated in the America of the 1930s and may now be anachronisms. Scanlon himself was very much the business unionist.[110] American business unionists unquestioningly accept the capitalist system and the right of management to manage. They see the primary function of trade unionism as increasing workers' share of the wealth produced, which a scheme like the Scanlon Plan might go some way to satisfy. On the other hand, some European trade unions, cast in a socialistic mould, seek to advance the interests of the entire working class through social and economic transformation.[111] Consequently, the Scanlon Plan might not flourish in a European context. Again, changes in managerial thinking have rendered obsolescent aspects of the plan. Its participative aspects, for instance, are very much of the human relations tradition, and its techniques are no longer highly regarded as effective managerial tools. In a comparatively recent publication which considers employee financial participation, a section devoted to the Scanlon Plan makes no reference to its participative paraphernalia.[112] Rather, it is simply regarded as a company-wide incentive scheme or productivity plan. The original enthusiasts of the plan were at pains to stress the centrality of its participative aspects. Among managerialists, the reduction in status of the Scanlon Plan to a group incentive scheme may be in part a response to higher expectations and aspirations among European trade unionists.

Like Scanlon, the value added concept and the Rucker Plan all appear to share a common implicit assumption and common starting-point. They assume that of the wealth generated within the enterprise, the traditional portions that accrue to capital and labour are either equitable or the result of immutable economic necessity. Thus, it is believed that an automatic sharing of any increase in wealth, on the traditional ratio between capital and labour, will promote higher productivity and industrial peace. Redistribution is not envisaged or contemplated. Furthermore, the absence of any element of control or influence for workers, beyond greater productive effort, would render invalid any description of these schemes as democratic.

FINANCIAL PARTICIPATION AND CONTROL

Schemes like the Scanlon or Rucker Plans and value added, when operating within the enterprise or wider society, may increase the amount of labour's share, but leave the relative shares of labour and capital intact. The increase in the amount of labour's share is expected to secure its acquiescence in the existing exercise and distribution of power and wealth. This may explain the attractiveness of such approaches for technocrats and managerialists. However, where unions or workers aspire to exercise some control over economic decision making within the firm or wider society, the inadequacy of these versions of financial participation becomes immediately apparent. A brief review of an article by two Irish managerialists, Mulcahy and McConnell, and the Congress response, will go some way to substantiate this claim.

An urgent priority for the Irish economy identified by Mulcahy and McConnell was an increased rate of growth. Increased growth, they argued, would mean increased value added from which all would benefit. One factor retarding growth was conflict among the stakeholders in an organisation attempting to maximise their share of added value. Notwithstanding these efforts, the authors demonstrated that over a decade the relative shares of management, workers and shareholders had remained substantially the same. Once labour accepted this fact, not only might it lessen industrial conflict, but it could serve as a basis for company-wide incentive schemes. Workers could be guaranteed their traditional share of any increase in value added. Mulcahy and McConnell went on to suggest that the concept could be extended to provide a measuring procedure in the creation of democratic industrial structures.[113] The whole scheme bears a remarkable resemblance to the Scanlon Plan.

In reply, O'Riordain, an official of the Irish Congress of Trade Unions, welcomed the Mulcahy–McConnell article as a contribution to an overdue debate on income distribution and the democratisation of decision making in the economy. On the necessity for higher growth rates and the contention that labour's share of value added had remained relatively static, O'Riordain was in agreement. In fact, he expanded the Mulcahy–McConnell period by citing figures from 1951–70 to show there had been no redistribution of income from capital to labour. However, he did not regard increasing labour's share of value added as an adequate remedy. Extrapolating from a Congress resolution of 1973, he concluded 'the issue can no longer be that of workers sharing the cake, they must now become increasingly involved in democratically controlling the shape and size of the cake as well.'[114]

Some tentative conclusions can be drawn from the above exchange. Scanlon, Rucker or value added schemes of financial participation are unlikely to satisfy a labour movement seeking the democratisation of economic decision making. Indeed, the Swedish example will demonstrate the limitations of these approaches. In that country from the mid-1930s to the early 1970s the national representatives of capital and labour evolved a *modus vivendi* which in essence operated as a macro Scanlon Plan. An important factor precipitating its eventual breakdown was a labour movement demand for greater influence on economic decision making within and beyond the enterprise.[115] In such circumstances the usefulness of Rucker, Scanlon and value added will be confined to the category of group financial incentives. In that role, because of a more direct link between effort and reward, they appear to have the advantage over cash-based profit sharing. As a stimulus to greater productivity, their ultimate success will depend on a variety of factors not only within but external to the individual firm.

EMPLOYEE SHAREHOLDING OR EMPLOYEE STOCK OWNERSHIP

Cash-based PS, because it allows no scope for employee input into the firm's economic decision making, has already been excluded from the category of financial democracy. There is, however, another method of sharing profit. Rather than a cash award, individuals could be granted the equivalent value in company shares or equity. Alternatively, employees could purchase their own company shares. One version of this approach is the executive share option or incentive scheme. As the title suggests, the allocation of the option to purchase shares is restricted to senior management. Such an arrangement is likely to exacerbate the already uneven distribution of wealth and power within the enterprise. Consequently, its effect would be to retard, rather than promote, economic democracy. More appropriate would be a share-based profit sharing scheme in which all staff could participate. The possession of company shares could secure for workers the right to vote at shareholders' meetings, and thus exercise some influence on financial policy. This combines the elements of both ownership and control. Thus worker shareholding can create the conditions, within the individual firm at any rate, for the potential realisation of economic democracy.

FINANCIAL DEMOCRACY: MICRO AND MACRO OR INDIVIDUALIST AND COLLECTIVIST APPROACHES

There are two possible approaches to financial democracy. One approach is to distribute shares to individual workers within single firms. Admittedly, the object of many such schemes is not to alter fundamentally the exercise of control but to give workers a financial stake in their enterprise. None the less, employee shareholding has the potential to redistribute wealth and power. Consequently, it could become a vehicle for the realisation of economic democracy, at least within individual firms. One drawback of this approach to economic democracy is that it could create new inequities and anomalies between groups of workers in the wider society. For instance, those employed in the public sector would be excluded from participation in these schemes, while the benefits for workers in more profitable firms would be greater than that of their counterparts employed in the less successful firm.

A second approach to financial democracy through collective profit sharing would aim to remedy these defects. Under this scheme, various company shares are distributed to workers not as individuals but as a group or collective. Shareholder franchise is exercised by worker representatives at local and national level. The object is to democratise decision making not only in the enterprise but in the economy as a whole. These approaches can be conveniently described as the micro and macro or the individualist and collectivist.

In the next two chapters, practical examples of deferred profit sharing and employee stock ownership or employee shareholding in North America will be examined. The investigation will have a twofold purpose. First, to discover if under the operation of these schemes financial democracy at a micro level is, or can be partially or fully, realised. A second line of enquiry will attempt to gauge the practical usefulness of these schemes. Do they, for instance, alter employee attitudes, facilitate greater co-operation between labour and management, and so lead to increased productivity and profitability? Collective profit sharing, or the macro approach to economic democracy, will be the subject of the Scandinavian chapters.

2 The practice, function and results of North American profit sharing

Management selection of a profit sharing trust as an expedient alternative to determinate pension benefits for employees is not likely to arouse worker enthusiasm for profit sharing. Certainly in the past the use of 'profit sharing' schemes as a seeming alternative to paying prevailing wage scales proved both a fallacious and damaging practice . . . It is to be hoped that yesteryear's misuse of profit sharing will not be paralleled by myopic applications of profit sharing to today's retirement problem. Although 'profit sharing' has a generous sound, labour is at present too cognizant to be misled as to its true content and purpose.

K.M. Thompson (1949)[1]

As noted in the introduction, commentators generally agree that profit sharing is an amalgam of practical business sense and altruism. Indeed, in the British examples of profit sharing at the Rowntree Works, or the John Lewis Partnership, altruism or philanthropy, tinged with paternalism, appeared as the dominant elements. In the contemporary western context of political democracy and strong union movements attached to egalitarian notions, profit sharing schemes, redolent of paternalism, may encounter a cool reception. Many American practitioners of profit sharing have purged their schemes of altruistic, philanthropic or paternalist elements. However, as will be seen, pragmatic or good business sense versions of profit sharing may prove even less acceptable to organised labour.

This chapter will be divided into three sections. The first section will deal mainly with the nature and function of American profit sharing (PS), and legislation affecting its development. A second section will consider its success as a stimulant to greater employee effort, and its effect on labour–management relations within an enterprise. American profit sharing practice will be examined to ascertain the extent to which it conforms with or departs from traditional prescriptions. The implementation of these prescriptions (which will be detailed later) have long been deemed essential prerequisites if a scheme is to motivate workers and stimulate labour–management co-operation. A comparison between prescriptions and practice will allow tentative conclusions to be drawn regarding the motivational potential of American PS. Furthermore, setting these conclusions against the available empirical evidence may serve to confirm or deny the importance of traditional prescriptions. A third section will deal with the American labour movement, its attitude to PS, and recent developments in the area. Finally, deferred profit sharing as a vehicle for the realisation of financial democracy will be considered.

THE PHILOSOPHY OF AMERICAN PROFIT SHARING

It has been suggested that the aims and philosophy of profit sharing are generally the same in Europe and the US.[2] In fact, the American and European approach both in theory and practice are fundamentally different.

Reviewing the arguments for PS, two Irish writers concluded that in their view equity was by far the most important element.[3] Wallace Bell, director of the Industrial Participation Association in Britain maintains that the real argument for employee PS is based not on its supposed incentive effect but on equity.[4] A memorandum adopted by the European Commission identifies the overall aim of employee participation in company profits as sharing out the fruits of productive activity more equitably.[5] There is evidence to suggest that some PS schemes have been initiated to give these sentiments practical effect. A British survey of 90 cash-based schemes embracing all employees found that in 27 firms the primary reason for its introduction was the belief that employees have the right to share in the wealth of the company.[6]

In sharp contrast, an altruistic element is virtually absent from American PS schemes. Sharing for the sake of sharing, one PS consultant has warned, may be the antithesis of capitalism.[7] Apparently this is a view shared by many American PS companies. A study of 38 large companies by B.L. Metzger lists the principal reasons why these concerns have established PS plans. The 123 responses were grouped under 13 headings. To provide long-term security and retirement income was the most frequently mentioned reason. Equity as a reason for establishing a PS scheme was mentioned only once.[8]

TRUE PROFIT SHARING

A plan in which all employees are eligible to share and which would be an addition rather than a substitute for adequate employee benefits has been defined by one American consultant as 'true profit sharing'.[9] Automatically excluded from this category would be PS plans that were used as a major vehicle to protect workers against the economic hazards of death, disability, illness and old age. Reviewing American PS practice of the early 1970s, Wood noted that many employers used their plans as a replacement for other benefits. Few PS plans, he concluded, are true plans by any stretch of the imagination.[10]

In a majority of cases, it seems, the primary function of American PS plans is to provide a pension or retirement income for employees. Again the contrast with European practice is striking. The aim of relating retirement income to profit, Latta remarks, is entirely unknown in Europe.[11] A survey by the Profit Sharing Council of America in the early 1970s of 702 plans found that in 446 companies there was no pension plan in effect. In other words, 63.5 per cent of companies surveyed were using PS as a substitute for a pension plan.[12] Apparently the use of PS in lieu of pensions is a continuing trend. A 1981 survey by independent consultants of 521 firms operating PS found just over 70 per cent offered no pension plan.[13]

Table 2.1 Profit sharing and pension plans in 521 companies

No. of employees	1–99	100–499	500–999	1,000–4,999	5,000+	Totals
Companies with PS only	194	106	33	22	10	365
Companies with PS+ pension	46	50	12	26	22	156
No. of companies	240	156	45	48	32	521
% of companies without pension	80.8	67.7	73.3	45.8	31.2	70

Source: Based on figures from *1982 PS Survey*, Hewitt Associates, 1982.

INCIDENCE AND TYPES OF PROFIT SHARING PLANS

It has already been suggested that the primary function of many American profit sharing schemes is to provide a pension for employees. Some indication of the incidence and types of profit sharing plans in operation will add weight to this contention. It will show that the type of scheme most suitable for use as a pension benefit tends to predominate.

Cash-based profit sharing

Where the main function of PS is to provide a pension, the annual, semi-annual or quarterly bonus typical of the cash-based scheme would hardly be appropriate. It could only succeed if there was a regular and substantial bonus which workers would carefully dissociate from weekly pay and set aside for retirement. In many western countries the pressure of advertising urging immediate consumption would likely frustrate such an outcome. Not surprisingly, cash-based schemes account for a small and declining percentage of American PS schemes. In 1973 cash plans represented only 4.7 per cent of plan types.[14] By 1981 this figure had fallen to 2.4 per cent.[15]

Combination plans

Combination plans represent 16 per cent of plan types. As their title suggests, these plans combine both the elements of cash-based and deferred PS. Usually a portion of the profit sharing bonus is paid in cash to the employee and the remainder is deposited in a trust. In 7 per cent of combination plans, division of the shared profit between cash payout and deferred payment is predetermined. Of the remaining 9 per cent the portion of shared profits to be paid in cash can, within limits, be determined by the employee.[16]

Deferred profit sharing

Representing 82 per cent of plans, deferred profit sharing is the dominant form of American PS.[17] Under a deferred PS plan the employer's contribution or the amount of profit to be shared is credited to employees' accounts with no optional cash payout. In the majority of plan types (94 per cent), the company contribution is credited to employee participants according to their wages or a combination of wages and length of service.[18]

In many cases, employees can also make a voluntary contribution, and the percentage of deferred and combination plans with this facility has shown a long-run tendency to increase. From 4 per cent in the early 1950s, plans with employee voluntary contributions had risen to approximately 60 per cent by 1981.[19] These contributions can vary from 1–10 per cent of employees' pay.[20] In a tiny and decreasing minority of plans, employees' contributions are mandatory.[21]

Contributions of the employer and, when present, of the employee, are invested in securities by a trustee and the participants are credited with the earnings on the investment. While there is a variety of funds in which PS assets can be invested, the most commonly used is the balanced fund. This consists of various common stocks, bonds or preferred issues. Plans with over 1,000 participants usually have more than one investment fund. This can be of advantage to participants near retirement who wish to switch their account to a more conservative investment. Finally, in some plans (20 per cent) up to 50 per cent of total assets are invested in employer stock.[22]

DEFERRED PROFIT SHARING – WHO BENEFITS?

Profit sharing, if devoid of an altruistic element, must appear at least to benefit both employer and employees in roughly equal measure. If the benefits of a scheme are evident for the employer but ambiguous for employees, this may adversely affect its motivational potential. This may be the case with deferred profit sharing.

As already noted, under deferred PS the employer's profit sharing contribution, instead of being paid directly to employee participants, is invested on their behalf. Provided these various investments turn out well, the participant will benefit. If, on the other hand, the investments depreciate in value, then the participant loses. Many surveys over the years by the Profit Sharing Council of America of small, medium and large PS companies demonstrate that the majority of deferred plans have retirement benefit as a primary aim.[23] Thus, participants in deferred PS plans cannot be assured of definite benefits upon retirement. Such an arrangement runs directly counter to European PS prescription and practice. A good pension scheme, Wallace Bell asserts, ranks only second to a good salary structure. Pensions, he insists, should come before profit sharing.[24] Nevertheless, many American employers prefer to provide a retirement income from PS because it avoids the financial commitment and actuarial complexities of a defined benefit pension plan.[25] Furthermore, employers believe an additional advantage of this approach is that it provides encouragement to employee performance, an incentive absent in conventional pension plans which guarantee a specific retirement income.[26] A pension, one executive has claimed, 'destroys incentive' and he advises employers to 'go the PS route'.[27]

OBJECTIONS TO DEFERRED PROFIT SHARING

Criticism of, or objections to, deferred PS as practised in the US would probably come from two quarters. First, proponents of orthodox or 'true' PS would be sceptical of the motivational power of deferred PS, partly because it operates as a substitute rather than as an additional benefit. Though the linking of pensions to profit may be economically convenient to employers, it might appear to employees as a negative incentive, placing greater emphasis on the stick rather than the carrot. Promoters of PS have generally stressed its value as a positive incentive. Second, deferred PS as a pension is likely to conflict with a major trade union goal: the promotion of employee security. In this pursuit a guaranteed pension annuity has been an important objective. Since the 1950s the announced policy of American labour unions has been to seek management provision for employee security assessed on the income of the business as a cost of operation.[28] However, once it could be convincingly demonstrated that deferred PS can both stimulate superior employee performance and provide adequate retirement benefits, the force of the above objections would be weakened.

DEFERRED PS – AN ADEQUATE PENSION?

Since the early 1970s there has been some debate on the adequacy of PS as a retirement income. Writing to B.L. Metzger, president of the Profit Sharing Research Foundation, T.H. Paine of Hewitt Associates, a firm of consultants in employee benefits, expressed the need for basic pension benefits which would guarantee workers a certain needed level of retirement income. A pension, he argued, can be geared to adjust benefits, to changes in compensation, to update past credits, and to provide income for the retiree that he knows will continue for the rest of his life. It was his experience that PS plans had difficulty in fulfilling the objectives of basic retirement income. He admitted many features could be added to PS to offset some of its weaknesses in this respect. Nevertheless, it was the opinion of Hewitt Associates that PS did not comprise a good form of basic retirement income.[29]

In reply, Metzger explained that many managers believe that the best and only sound basis for 'guaranteeing' any retirement benefit is through a partnership incentive programme directly linked to the profitability of the firm. Companies also felt they were able to undertake a more generous programme where contributions are directly related to profit or the ability to pay. Furthermore, many companies, Metzger argued, have been successful in providing very substantial benefits under the aegis of PS far in excess of those normally guaranteed under a fixed benefit pension plan. Finally, he implied, the passage of time would render the objections of Hewitt Associates groundless. There was a growing trend, Metzger asserted, for companies to use PS and pension plans in combination.[30] In fact, between 1973 and 1981 the trend apparently has been in the opposite direction. By 1981 the number of companies with PS but no pension plan had increased by almost 7 per cent.[31] The provisions of the Employee Retirement Income Security Act of 1974 may have significantly influenced this development.

EMPLOYEE RETIREMENT INCOME SECURITY ACT 1974 (ERISA)

Any examination of pensions, profit sharing or employee stock ownership plans in the US would be incomplete without some review of ERISA. Indeed it can be seen as a watershed. Also, consideration of employer responses to the act illuminate the nature of American PS. It will confirm that many schemes function as cheap pension substitutes in which the principal beneficiary may be the firm rather than its employees.

The origin of the legislation can be found in a continuous flow of complaints from participants regarding specific private pension plans. Dissatisfaction mainly centred on the following: severe age and service requirements before eligibility for a pension; inadequate funding by employers; termination of plans without funds to assure pensions to qualified employees; and the diversion of pension funds for private purposes by employer or union involved.[32] Almost all business leaders and many union officials were actively hostile to the proposed reform.[33] Union leaders feared new standards would make pension plans prohibitively expensive. This attitude was to change, possibly as a result of rank-and-file pressure, and gradually the number of unions interested in pushing the legislation increased. After more than ten years of lobbying for pension reform the Employee Retirement Income Security Act became law on 2 September 1974.[34]

The basic thrust of the legislation is to ensure that employees of companies with pensions get something out of these plans.[35] A fundamental of the law is that pension fund investments must be for the sole benefit of the participants and their beneficiaries. While pensions comprise the primary focus of the legislation, PS, stock bonus, saving and employee welfare plans are also subject to some of its requirements. The legislation, it has been claimed, put into effect the most sweeping overhaul of pensions and PS plans in history.[36]

ERISA – A SUMMARY OF ITS MAJOR PROVISIONS AFFECTING PS

The act expects that PS plans will not be unduly exclusive and will seek to include as many employees as possible. The maximum waiting period for participation in a pension or PS scheme is one year of service. Plans are prohibited from establishing eligibility requirements based on age where an employee is 25 years or over. A part-time employee who has worked more than 1,000 hours during the year must be treated as though he had worked the entire year.

Vesting

The law establishes new minimum standards for vesting of employees. Vesting, or a vesting standard, sets the maximum length of time an employee must work before a non-forfeitable right to the accrued benefit in his PS, stock ownership or pension plan account is established. The employer must choose from three vesting schedules. Employees must be 100 per cent vested after 10 years service. Alternatively, a graduated schedule can be used which would demand 25 per cent vesting after five years of service and reaching 100 per cent in the following 15 years. Lastly, there is the rule of '45' not generally used by PS plans. Under this schedule the accrued benefit of a participant with five or more years' service will be 50 per cent vested when his age and years of service equal 45. By the end of the following five years the participant must be 100 per cent vested.

Forfeitures

Forfeitures are linked to breaks in service. An employee who works for less than 500 hours in one year will be considered to have broken service. The employee then forfeits the non-vested portion of his account. Provided the former employee is not rehired within a year of his termination date, the forfeitures are either credited to the remaining participers or used to reduce subsequent company contributions to the plan.

Investment and fiduciary responsibility

Under ERISA, a person who manages a pension or PS plan, who renders advice for a fee, or who has any authority or responsibility in the plan administration, is defined as a fiduciary. Fiduciaries are obliged to act responsibly and in the interests of the plan participants and beneficiaries. The 'prudent man' standard requires fiduciaries to diversify plan assets to minimise the risk of losses unless it is obviously unwise to do so. Not more than 10 per cent of pension plan assets may be held in employer securities. Stock bonus and PS plans are exempt from this limitation. Under the act, plan participants can initiate civil actions for breach of fiduciary responsibility.

Reporting and disclosure

A plan administrator is required to publish a summary plan description, written so that it will be understood by the average plan participant. Each participant must be provided with a copy. Also the plan administrator must file an annual report with the Internal Revenue Service.

Tax Concessions

The employer's contribution to pension or PS plans is tax deductible. Where employee contributions are made, these are tax free. Employee earnings in a deferred PS account are not taxed until the money is disbursed. Lump sum contributions can receive capital gains treatment on amounts attributable to participants' pre-1974 participation. Amounts attributed to post-1973 participation are taxed at the ordinary rate. Only those plans submitted to and approved by the Internal Revenue Service (IRS) as complying with ERISA regulations can qualify for this favourable tax treatment.[37]

ERISA: THE EMPLOYERS' RESPONSE AND ITS EFFECT ON PS

Initially, the passage of ERISA into law was regarded by some among the PS community as a setback. The years between 1974 and 1977 have been described as the terrible three.[38] Terminations for PS plans in

1975 were 75 per cent above the rate for the previous year. For pension plans, the termination rate was even higher. In the following year, 1976, the failure rates of both pensions and PS plans accelerated. Most of these failures were concentrated in smaller companies.[39]

With PS, the requirements of ERISA were only partly responsible for the spate of liquidations. Two years of bear markets on Wall Street had exacerbated the crisis. The rate of return on investment of the major PS funds dropped to minus 15 per cent in 1973 and to minus 22 per cent a year later.[40]

Balances in the PS accounts of many participants were drastically reduced. Disgruntled beneficiaries in the Marriott Corporation and Tappan and Co. took legal action under ERISA against their employers.[41] Some companies reacted by replacing PS with a pension plan. Large concerns like Sears Roebuck and Co. and Burlington Industries supplemented their existing PS schemes with pension plans. Signode did not introduce a pension plan but guaranteed a minimum investment return on PS accounts. Similarly, the Xerox Corporation guaranteed its employees that their PS funds would be large enough on retirement to meet a basic pension standard.[42] Though praiseworthy, such guarantees highlight the contradictions involved in using contingent contributions to fund a retirement benefit. Yet by 1980 the Profit Sharing Council of America was sanguine concerning ERISA. Overall, it claimed ERISA had a relatively minor effect on the vital provisions of PS (eligibility and vesting) but a much greater and more costly effect on pension plans.[43]

While ERISA stopped short of making pensions mandatory, it did impose exacting standards on existing or future pension plans. Fiduciary responsibility, diversification of assets, and in many cases accelerated funding to cover past and future liabilities, became necessary requirements. The law also established a government pension insurance fund to which employers were obliged to contribute an annual premium of $1 per participant. In the event of plan failure, the fund would honour financial commitments made to employees. Defaulting companies were liable to reimburse the fund for monies paid out up to a maximum of 30 per cent of their gross worth.[44] For pension plans, these were burdensome administrative and financial provisions. In contrast, all PS plans were exempt from funding, diversification and insurance requirements.

The advantage to employers of PS as a flexible and economic method of funding a retirement income in which any possible losses are borne by employees has already been noted. Pension plans, however, guarantee employees a definite retirement income based

Figure 2.1 Percentage of new approvals for pensions and PS pre- and post-ERISA

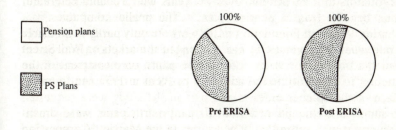

Source: Participative Developments in the US, Metzger, 1978

Figure 2.1 represents the PS/pension universe before and after the passage of ERISA. Of the annual number of newly approved employee benefit plans, PS and stock bonus plans usually accounted for 44 per cent. Pensions accounted for 56 per cent of newly approved plans. Within four years of the legislation's enactment there had been a shift of 8 percentage points in favour of PS. Pension's share of new approvals had shrunk to 48 per cent while PS had grown to represent 52 per cent.[45]

on their earnings and years of service. Thus, any loss due to poor performance of pension fund investment must be borne by employers. In its stricter regulation of pension plans, ERISA was to emphasise sharply this difference between PS and pensions. For employers, the attractiveness of PS as a pension substitute because of its controllable costs and comparative freedom from government regulation may have become more pronounced.

Speculating on the likely effect of the new law, two observers believed it would encourage a trend away from defined benefit pensions towards plans where the employees equity was limited to funds set aside by the employer. Because they avoided the costs or provisions of the legislation, they believed PS plans would become more prevalent.[46] Again, a writer in the *Harvard Business Review* considered the alternatives open to employers in the wake of ERISA. Because current costs are controllable, and future options open, he concluded that those companies with PS plans may be in the best position of all.[47] Many employers, it seems, acted on this advice.

DEFERRED PS AS A PENSION BENEFIT DEFENDED

Doubts expressed by consultants in employee benefits as to the adequacy of deferred PS as a retirement income have been noted.

Such scepticism has not been confined to the experts. Executives have been hard-pressed to convince their own employees and union negotiators that PS benefits over the years will probably be greater than benefits from a pension plan.[48] The president of the Profit Sharing Research Foundation in his work *Profit Sharing in 38 Large Companies* (Metzger 1975) has challenged the sceptics. Retirement benefits from deferred PS and pension plans were compared in an attempt to demonstrate the adequacy of PS as a retirement income. Each of the 38 companies taking part in the study were requested to supply one example of PS dollars paid out to a non-management participant who retired in 1976. Of the 38 companies, 33 responded with the necessary information. The next step was to set a hypothetical pension standard. Only after a review of the relevant literature and the actual benefits being provided by pension plans in 1976 was the standard set. This accomplished two objectives. First, it ensured the pension standard set was reasonable. Second, it anticipated criticism of the standard as either too niggardly or too generous.

Once the pension standard had been set, this was then compared with PS benefits on a percentage basis. The percentage was calculated by dividing the annual PS income by the annual pension standard. Out of the 33 companies in which comparisons were made, 19 provided both a PS and pension plan. In the remaining 14 companies, PS was the sole retirement vehicle. Six of the companies with both PS and pension plans fell below the pension standard by a maximum of 41 per cent and a minimum of 2 per cent. Of the remaining 13 companies in this group, PS benefits exceeded the pension standard by between a minimum of 12 per cent up to a maximum of 498 per cent. In the 14 companies without pensions, PS benefits exceeded the pension standard by a maximum of 911 per cent and a minimum of 2 per cent.[49]

This is apparently impressive evidence of the superior performance of PS compared with a standard pension. Yet it is questionable if these findings are applicable to PS plans generally. Metzger himself disclaims any intention to assert that all PS participants end up as well as in the examples quoted.[50] In fact, the unrepresentative nature of the companies chosen severely limits the usefulness of the PS pension comparisons. Of the 38 companies surveyed, 34 were among *Fortune* magazine's listing of the 500 largest industrials, retailing companies and banks.[51] The numbers participating in each company's PS plans roughly averaged 25,000.[52] A study of 702 PS companies in 1973 found those with 1,000 or more plan participants represented 13.2 per cent of companies surveyed.[53] Again, a 1981 study of 521 companies found that those with 5,000 or more plan participants represented 6 per cent of the sample.[54]

It was firms with 500 or less participants that accounted for 75 per cent of companies surveyed. Though this is a statistic of the 1981 study, it is consistent with previous surveys.[55] Finally, only 25 per cent of these small companies offer a pension and PS plan, while 57.9 per cent of the companies surveyed by Metzger offered this combination.[56]

The examples chosen by Metzger are not typical of the average PS company in the US. Therefore it is reasonable to conclude that the case for PS as a superior or even adequate retirement income has not been proven. All that can be said with certainty is that the benefits of PS are uncertain. Inadvertently, maybe, Metzger has underlined this fact. If, he argues, a company consistently contributes around the median input of 8–10 per cent of pay into a PS trust and the investment returns over the years fall at least in the 6–10 per cent range, employees should receive enough in PS to fund their retirement programme adequately.[57] In the face of these equivocations, employees who are free to choose are likely to opt for the guaranteed security of a pension. This may be particularly the case in America, where in many instances employers' PS contributions are discretionary and not calculated according to a predetermined formula.[58]

THE MOTIVATIONAL EFFECTIVENESS OF AMERICAN PS

Reviewing the PS pension landscape in the aftermath of ERISA, the president of the PSRF detected some merit in the use of PS and pension plans in tandem.[59] It was a combination that he expected to become more common.[60] Now is the time, he urged, to stop thinking of PS solely as a retirement income; rather the focus should be on the essence of PS, its motivational dynamics.[61] From the evidence presented earlier, it is apparent that these expectations have not been realised nor these exhortations heeded. In a substantial and increasing number of cases, PS continues to be used primarily as a pension substitute.[62] This and other characteristics of American PS may significantly reduce its possible effectiveness as a spur to increased worker effort or efficiency.

There is general consensus, it will be shown, among researchers and proponents of PS that its potential success as a motivator or stimulant to improved industrial relations depends on adherence to certain principles. These can be summarised under five headings:

1 Broad coverage
2 Consultation
3 The use of a predetermined formula to calculate the PS bonus
4 PS should be an addition rather than a substitute for prevailing
   wage rates and fringe benefits
5 Communication

1 Broad coverage

This means that a PS plan should embrace the maximum number of employees. Apart from reasonable exceptions, rules governing eligibility for participation should be generous. Few should be excluded on the grounds of rank, seniority or income, and no individual or group should be excluded because of trade union membership. In short, the overwhelming majority of employees should be eligible to participate. Exclusion of particular groups is likely to breed resentment – a sentiment inimical to co-operative striving which PS aims to promote.[63]

Unfortunately, it is difficult to establish clearly whether coverage in American PS is generally broad or restricted. A 1973 survey of 702 plans found the majority (80 per cent) included all employees.[64] However, the same study noted that most new PS plans limited coverage to salaried or clerical employees and excluded unionised workers.[65] In Metzger's *Profit Sharing in 38 Large Companies*, 24 of these had varying levels of unionisation. In 19 of these companies, union members were allowed to participate in the PS plan while in the remaining five they were excluded. Apparently, eligibility of union members to participate in these companies' PS plans depended on union strength among employees. Metzger found that when 11 per cent or more of the workforce was unionised, then union members were included in the companies' PS plans.[66] The 1973 survey, which implied that broad coverage was common in most PS schemes, has not been supported by more recent findings. In a 1981 survey of 521 companies operating PS plans, the total employee population numbered just over 1.5 million. Yet only 49 per cent of these employees participated in a PS plan.[67]

The survey conducted for this study examined 13 companies with PS, employee stock ownership plans or a combination of both. In the seven non-union companies, all employees were eligible to participate in the PS or stock ownership plan. The remaining six companies were subdivided into three groups reflecting their degree of unionisation.

In the first group, unionised workers represented 70–90 per cent of the workforce and all employees participated in the company PS or stock ownership plan.

Unionised workers in the next two companies represented 90 per cent and 15 per cent of the workforce respectively. In both companies, union members were excluded from the PS plan. This was not simply a case of anti-union bias: as the primary function of both PS plans was to provide a retirement income, it was reasonable to exclude union members who were already covered by their own pension plan. One of the companies also offered a stock purchase plan, and this was open to all employees.

In the last group, each company had over 30,000 employees and unionised workers accounted for only 1–2 per cent of the workforce. Both companies excluded union members from their PS plans. One company offered employees PS, stock ownership and a savings plan, but union members were excluded from all three.

Taken together, the above evidence would suggest that coverage in American PS schemes may be less than generous. There is apparently a tendency to discriminate against union members when they represent a minority of the workforce.

2 Consultation

Broadly this is taken to mean that employees would be consulted in the formulation and involved in the administration of a PS plan. It is generally agreed that the absence of employee involvement in a PS plan will reduce its effectiveness.[68] Employee sharing in the installation and administration of a scheme is expected to have several beneficial effects. First, such involvement will minimise any sense of paternalism or arbitrary philanthropy. Second, the sharing of administration between employers and employees will, it is hoped, foster a co-operative spirit.[69] Even this amount of employee involvement may be inadequate. One researcher has suggested that successful PS with organised labour may necessarily involve some co-operation between employer and employees in determining what constitutes profit. The nature of profit, he points out, is vague and within business circles its definition is disputed. Consequently, labour–management conflict on what constitutes profit could be more frequent and intense. This could be avoided, he suggests, by some labour influence in the determination of profit or alternatively a degree of independent supervision of accounting practice.[70] More modestly, findings of American consultants show that group meetings or personal contact are the best methods of selling a PS scheme to employees.

That American PS practice fails to satisfy these requirements is not surprising. Generally, American management is jealous of its prerogative, or right to manage, and there is little obvious enthusiasm in the labour movement for representation on boards of management. Compared with Europe, industrial democracy in the US has made little or no headway. The evidence available on the installation and administration of American PS reflects this climate.

The thirteen companies surveyed for this dissertation were questioned on the extent of consultation with employees before the introduction of their PS or stock ownership plans. Three companies where unionised workers accounted for 80–90 per cent of the workforce were discounted. This was done because, under US labour law, if more than 30 per cent of employees are represented by a union they must be included in the PS plan and the company is obliged to bargain with the union on its provisions.[71] In two of the remaining ten companies, 1–15 per cent of employees were unionised, while the other eight were non-union. Management response in these companies, it was felt, would give a truer indication of the prevalence of consultation.

Of the ten companies surveyed, only one held a general meeting with employees before the introduction of its PS plan. In the remaining nine the introduction of PS or stock ownership plans was by management fiat. There was no consultation with employees, who were informed of the *fait accompli* by company notice board. Only in one case – at a routine quarterly meeting – were employees verbally informed of management's decision. Of course, the evidence from such a numerically small sample can make no claim to be definitive. Nevertheless, its suggestion of little employee involvement in the mechanics of PS schemes is borne out by more comprehensive surveys.

A 1973 survey which examined the administrative provisions of 702 PS plans found 95 per cent were operated by either an administrative committee (51.5 per cent) or fund trustees (43.9 per cent). Plans in which an employee advisory committee was fully responsible for their operation accounted for 3.4 per cent of the sample. In another 1.2 per cent of plans, responsibility was shared between employees and an administrative committee or fund trustees. Overall, plans which involved employees in their administration represented only 4.6 per cent of the sample or approximately 32 plans out of the 702 surveyed.[72]

Though these are statistics of a decade ago, it is unlikely there has been any significant change in the interim. Changes that have taken place point in the direction of less rather than more employee involvement. Of plans in the 1973 survey which had operated for 25 years or more, 7.6 per cent had an employee advisory committee. This percentage decreased to 5.1 per cent of plans whose ages ranged between 10 and 25 years, and to 4.1 per cent of plans which had been installed in the previous 5–10 year period. Not one of the plans installed after 1968 made any provision for an employee advisory committee.[73] Employee involvement in either the installation or operation of American PS schemes appears to be negligible.

This conclusion could be faulted for its failure to acknowledge that employees in some plans can choose a particular investment fund for their PS credits. In 42.8 per cent of the plans surveyed by Hewitt Associates, there was only one investment fund for employer and, if present, employee contributions.[74] Obviously, in these cases there was no possibility of employee choice. However, in 57 per cent of plans, the number of investment funds available for the company PS contribution, and if present, the employees, ranges between two and four funds.[75] Employees can choose between funds invested in high-risk, high-return securities, own company stock, government bonds, or a combination of these. In 66 per cent and 41 per cent respectively of these multi-fund plans, participants can determine how their own contribution and those of the employer should be invested.[76]

Commenting on the choice available in some multi-fund plans, one PS executive has claimed it enables employees to control their own destinies.[77] This is hardly accurate. It has already been noted that in the vast majority of plans, participants have no say in their administration, and the choice involved in fund election may be more akin to a lottery than an exercise of influence and control. In schemes (20 per cent) where employers' and/or participants' contributions are invested in own company stock, the potential does exist for the exercise of employee influence. In practice, however, it is likely to be minimal. First, this is because not all participants in PS plans that hold company stock are automatically granted voting rights. Whether employees can vote company stock credited to their PS accounts appears to be a function of management discretion. In Metzger's study of 38 large companies, 36 of these invested an average of 45 per cent of plan assets in their own company stock.[78] Participants in 19 firms had voting rights on the shares in their accounts. In the remainder, shares were either voted by the trustees or administrative committee. Participants' shares in one company in this group had no voting rights.[79]

Second, even given participants' voting rights, their block of shares is not likely to represent a significant portion of company equity. Of 104 companies with part of their PS fund in employer securities, only 18 invested over 50 per cent of plan assets. Another 52 invested 10–50 per cent, while in the remaining 32, less than 10 per cent of plan assets were so invested.[80] Finally it must be remembered that investment of PS funds in employer securities is mainly confined to large companies and consequently is not a major feature of American schemes. Undoubtedly there may be individual schemes which combine employee voting rights, fund election and involvement in the administration, but they will be isolated exceptions. Their incidence will not be sufficient to modify to any great extent the original conclusion that employee involvement or control in American PS is negligible.

3 The PS bonus and the predetermined formula

It is generally agreed that the PS bonus, or the amount of the company contribution to be shared among employees, must be calculated according to a predetermined formula. There are many variations, e.g. a percentage of pre-tax profit; a percentage of profit shared after prior capital reservations; or a sliding scale in which the amount of profit shared can increase with an increase in profit beyond certain set figures. Ideally, there should be consultation between management and workers on the particular formula to be used before the installation of the scheme. Yet the essential factor crucial to the success of the plan is how the company contribution is determined. Schemes without a formula, where the frequency or amount of company contributions is arbitrary, or at management's discretion, have little chance, it is believed, of motivating workers.

A formal agreement on the amount of profit to be allocated, an Australian Department of Labour report maintains, is essential if a PS plan is to have any incentive value and avoid misunderstanding.[81] A more recent report to the Canadian Department of Labour makes a similar recommendation. Employees, it warns, must not feel the company contribution is subject to the whim of management. The profit sharing formula of a successful plan, it concludes, is fixed in advance.[82] Employees, the president of the PSRF notes, do not favour discretionary bonus plans that depend upon management decisions to which they are not privy and over which they have no control. The formula approach, he contends, is superior.[83] This advice has been ignored by many practitioners of American PS.

Figure 2.2 Percentage of PS plans in which employer's contribution is discretionary

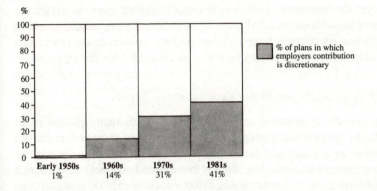

Sources: Guide to Modern Profit Sharing, Curtis, 1973, p. 225; *1982 PS Survey,* Hewit Associates

Figure 2.2 illustrates the percentage of plans surveyed over a 30-year period in which the employer's contribution is discretionary. Not shown is how company size appears to determine the method of PS contribution. Only 13 per cent of plans with 1,000–5,000 participants use discretionary contributions, whereas 5.3 per cent of plans with less than 100 participants use this method.[84] In 47 per cent of plans with 500 or less participants, the company contribution is discretionary. This group accounted for 76 per cent of plans surveyed by the Hewitt Associates' study.[85]

An early 1950s study of American PS schemes examined plan changes and attempted to identify emerging trends. Some companies surveyed had changed over from arbitrary contributions to a fixed formula. The study detected an unmistakable trend in the direction of a formula.[86] Since that time the movement has been in the opposite direction. The percentage of American PS schemes in which the employer's contribution is discretionary has shown a long-run tendency to increase.

Many American companies, it appears, determine their PS contributions on a discretionary basis. Such a practice, it is generally agreed, will seriously impair the motivational effectiveness of PS. A monograph written in the early 1950s expressed a different view. It maintained there was no appreciable difference in the lifespan of plans with a predetermined formula and of those that provided for arbitrary allocations.[87] This can be discounted for two reasons: first, because it runs directly counter to the majority of research findings; second, only 1 per cent of PS schemes in the early 1950s determined company contributions arbitrarily. Therefore, the appearance (even in small numbers) of PS schemes using discretionary contributions among discontinued plans would support rather than challenge the conventional wisdom on this matter. Finally, the prejudicial effect of discretionary contributions on employee motivation can only be exacerbated where the primary function of PS is to provide a pension.

4 PS as an additional rather than substitute benefit

This fourth requirement would demand that PS must function as an addition to prevailing wage rates and standard benefits: it cannot succeed as a substitute for either.[88] Extensive American use of PS as a pension substitute has already been noted. Inevitable European scepticism as to its motivational effectiveness would be justified only if the majority of American workers regard a pension as a standard benefit. In the two decades since 1945 the provision of pensions for employees has been converted from a progressive practice into a standard practice.[89] Consequently, a pension, though funded through PS, will be received by many employees as nothing more than their due. Few are likely to regard this version of PS as an example of company generosity. Even as early as 1949, Thompson noted that management's selection of a PS trust as an expedient alternative to pension benefits for employees is not likely to arouse worker enthusiasm for PS.[90] Therefore, as a pension substitute, the motivational potential of PS is likely to be considerably reduced, and because of its uncertain benefits could even become a source of employee resentment.

There is another characteristic of American PS that would militate against its success as a motivator. Critics have identified the distribution of profit at fairly lengthy intervals as a weakness common to most PS schemes. According to an Australian Department of Labour report, it is well established that a distant reward is not an effective incentive to increased day-by-day effort.[91] If this is accepted, it would be difficult to entertain rational expectations that American PS would significantly influence employee motivation, because the majority of schemes (82 per cent) are of the deferred variety in which the reward is postponed until retirement. Noting its frequent use as a pension substitute, one PS consultant has concluded that its utility as a tool for improving productivity may be diminished.[92]

There appears to be a general awareness of this inherent defect in deferred PS plans. Because they do not provide immediate reward and feedback, the incentive value of deferred payout plans, a Canadian report suggests, may be considerably reduced.[93] This difficulty, it is believed, can be overcome by an effective and regular communication programme with employees.[94]

5 Communication

Among American proponents of PS, confidence in the power of communication is unbounded. The amount of profit shared, Metzger claims, ranks second in importance to the manner in which PS is communicated. You can sell an inferior plan with communication, he asserts, better than a marvellous plan with no communication.[95] B.A. Diekman, president of the Canadian Institute of PS, identifies communication as a key ingredient in its success.[96] A PS plan without communication, he warns, will simply create an expense from which the company will get no return.[97] That communication is an integral part of PS, Diekman illustrates in the anecdotal, homiletic style favoured by many of his colleagues.

A company owner, he relates, telephoned to apply for membership of the Institute as he was about to install a PS scheme. It was to be a cash plan with no predetermined formula, and no regular period of cash payout. Both, the caller decided, would be at his discretion and depend on company profitability. With such a high discretionary content, Diekman pointed out, it would be difficult to set targets for employee effort, and how, he queried, was the plan to be communicated? It was a Gordian knot the caller did not intend to untie, for he replied, 'I'm not going to tell the bastards anything.' This, Diekman comments, is the antithesis of PS and he advised management that the best way to communicate with their employees is to be completely open and frank.[98] Such a radical pronouncement may have shocked his audience, for it was immediately qualified. Employers who are reluctant to disclose sales, costs and profit figures, he suggests, can still communicate with their employees by using percentages.[99] With some exceptions, it is generally acknowledged that communication with employees is an essential element in the possible success of PS – or indeed in the maintenance of stable industrial relations.[100] However, the expectations of human relations theorists that effective communication would prove a panacea for industrial conflict have not been realised. The degree of success of managerial communication with employees as a stimulus to greater effort or in fostering company loyalty and solidarity will be determined by a variety of factors within and external to the enterprise. Consequently, even the most energetic response to Metzger's injunction 'communicate the hell out of it' may inadequately compensate for the inherent weaknesses of deferred PS.[101]

Its first weakness is its use as a pension substitute. Apart from the drawback of an excessive deferral of gratification, it would be difficult, short of outright bamboozlement, to arouse employee enthusiasm for what has come to be regarded as a standard benefit. A second weakness would be the use of discretionary contributions in a substantial minority of schemes. Diekman's anecdote illustrates the difficulty this provision creates for effective communication. In the absence of a defined commitment, Metzger comments, companies will have a difficult hurdle to leap: namely, to convince employees they will share equitably in ongoing company success.[102] Finally, a third weakness would be the nature of the communication process itself. According to the Bullock Report, purely advisory arrangements where workers are given information, and can express opinions but exercise no influence, are not likely to create much enthusiasm or interest.[103] Though these findings refer to the experience with works councils, nevertheless the one-way communication process described is reproduced exactly in American PS schemes. It has already been noted that consultation with workers is at best perfunctory and their influence either in the installation or operation of the vast majority of schemes is negligible. In the final analysis, it may be this absence of employee influence rather than poor communication or the deferred element in American PS that will militate most against its success as a motivator. The amount of deferred gratification, even sacrifice, involved in workers' co-operatives, does not figure high on the list of reasons for their failure.

Expert opinion would maintain that the five principles or requirements outlined above are basic preconditions for the potential success of any PS scheme. In practice, a large majority of American PS schemes fall below these requirements. Coverage, it appears, is less than generous, and consultation or involvement of employees is negligible. In respect of consultation, the failings of American PS practitioners may be no worse than that of their European counterparts.[104] However, the trend towards discretionary contributions and the use of PS as a pension substitute in compounding these deficiencies must severely circumscribe the effectiveness of many American PS schemes. Even the best of communication programmes may be insufficient compensation for these defects. In many cases, managerial communication with employees may be less than frank. Economic convenience can only partly explain the increasing popularity with employers of discretionary contributions. Another advantage of this method would be circumvention of the necessity to disclose company financial information. The above factors combined augur ill for the motivational effectiveness of American PS. Yet there is some evidence to the contrary.

PROFIT SHARING – SOME EVIDENCE FOR ITS SUCCESS

A study by Metzger and Colletti compared the financial performance of PS and non-PS companies between 1952 and 1969.[105] It was an expansion on two earlier studies which had considered the question, 'Are PS programmes detrimental to stockholders' interests?'. From *Fortune* magazine's listing of the 50 largest merchandising companies in the US, 14 were selected. Of these, eight operated a PS scheme while the remaining six did not share profits. Over a 17-year period, the performance of the companies in the PS and non-PS groups were compared against nine measures, e.g. index of dividends per common share, companies earnings per employee, etc.[106] The researchers found that on all measures the PS group outperformed the non-PS group by substantial percentages. Within the PS group of companies, those with broad coverage outperformed those with coverage limited to certain categories of employees.[107] In all eight companies, the PS scheme had been installed as a retirement or retirement partnership incentive programme.[108] Managers were asked to rate the effectiveness of their PS plans in relation to specific benefits. Only four replied. As a pension benefit, three companies rated their schemes as very effective and one as moderately effective. In creating a feeling of partnership between employees and management, one company rated its scheme as very effective while the remaining three categorised theirs as moderately effective. As an aid to improving morale, teamwork and co-operation between employees, one company rated its PS plan as very effective, another as moderately effective, and the remaining two characterised its effect as doubtful.[109]

Earlier it was noted that increased worker effort is only one of many factors favourably influencing company profitability. Admittedly, Metzger and Colletti make no extravagant claims and they warn it would be wrong to accept PS as the cause of superior performance in the companies surveyed.[110] They allow that more competent management may be the major factor, but suggest PS is an important contributor to the exceptional profitability and growth of these companies.[111] Yet from their own findings it would appear that the real success of PS was in providing a pension. Factors most likely to boost productivity, improved management–worker relations, morale and co-operation, were generally mediocre to poor. This consideration might tend to devalue the contribution of PS to these companies' success. Yet when management was asked whether they felt their PS schemes had contributed in an important way to their company's financial success, five answered in the affirmative.[112] The most appropriate conclusion encompassing this paradox might be that PS may have favourably influenced company performance, but not as an incentive to greater employee effort or cooperation.

In *Profit Sharing in 38 Large Companies*, Metzger again compared the performance of PS and non-PS companies. There were only two points of comparison in this study: return on sales and return on equity. While a larger number of companies were sampled, their performance was measured over a shorter period, 1973–6. From *Fortune*'s listing of the largest industrials and 50 largest retailers, 23 and 9 PS companies were chosen respectively.[113] When the medians of returns on sales and equity were compared, the PS group achieved higher percentage returns on both than did comparable non-PS companies. For Metzger, this finding combined with that of the earlier study, would indicate a positive though not perfect correlation between PS and superior corporate performance. It was PS, he concluded, that contributed to these better results.[114]

Criticism of these claims would be similar to those made already. Though PS was the sole retirement vehicle in less than half of these companies, management rated their schemes as very effective in providing economic security for employees.[115] As an aid to cutting costs or increasing efficiency their effect was considered moderate to doubtful.[116] Metzger sees no contradiction here, rather he regards these responses as reaffirming PS more as a participation incentive than a stimulation incentive.[117] The validity of this distinction is questionable.[118]

The economic evidence for the superior performance of PS companies over their non-PS counterparts is not altogether clear-cut and unambiguous. Undoubtedly the PS group of companies show a consistently higher percentage return on both equity and sales in the years 1973–6.[119] Yet over that three-year period, even allowing for fluctuations, these percentages declined to below their original starting figures. This trend was reversed in the non-PS group of companies. Over the same period the percentage return on equity and sales in these companies rose above the original figure. The exception was the return on sales in the retailing companies which began and ended with the same percentage.[120] To view the relative decline in returns on equity and sales in the PS group of companies as a reversal of Metzger's claims would be unwarranted. Nevertheless, the evident ambiguity does imply that the influence of PS on these variables may be slight.

Another more comprehensive survey than either of the two outlined above again examined the financial significance of PS.[121] Over a 19-year period, ten measures of performance were used to compare PS and non-PS companies in six industries.[122] Of a total of 202 companies, 75 shared profits and 127 did not. No attempt was made to evaluate personnel factors such as labour turnover, days lost because of work stoppage, or morale and employee attitudes.[123]

Of all ten measures, six were used to compare the trend and level of performance in the PS and non-PS companies. The remaining four measured only the trend in performance between the two groups.[124] The PS group was superior to the non-profit sharers on two-thirds of the measures used to evaluate company performance. However, the superior performance of the PS companies remained relatively static. When trends of relative improvement or decline in each group were compared, they were found to be the same. Also, the superior performance of PS over non-PS companies was not consistent in all six industries. In department stores, food stores and chemicals, PS companies were superior. In drugs and publishing, however, PS companies were neutral, while in the domestic oil industry they were inferior.[125]

Virtually every activity of a firm's employees, Howard maintains, affects its financial results and ultimately its profit. The extent to which PS affects these activities, he admits, is not directly measurable. Nevertheless, he claims the strong showing by PS companies in the above study would indicate that PS plans have an important bearing on the final result.[126] Yet the poor showing of PS companies in one industry, and their neutral performance in two others, makes such a conclusion questionable. Greater consistency in the performance of PS companies across all six industries would be expected if PS is to be upheld as a significant element in company success. Howard's concluding remarks may tend to overstate the beneficial effects of PS in the companies surveyed.

The weakness of the above studies is they do not definitively establish, but merely suggest, that PS is a significant factor in company profitability. As measures of the success of PS, they may be rather crude. Furthermore, the applicability of the evidence to the generality of American PS is questionable.

In the two studies by Metzger and Colletti, not one of the companies surveyed employed less than 2,000. The numbers employed in each company from both studies roughly averaged 22,000.[127] Unfortunately, Howard does not give the numbers employed in the companies he surveyed but it is likely they had similar employment levels. As such, companies in the three surveys are typical of only a minority of American PS schemes.[128] Apart from numbers employed, there are other important differences between small and large PS companies.

In 69 per cent of companies with 5,000 or more employees, the PS plan is an additional benefit. This is the case in only 24 per cent of small companies employing 500 or less. Over three-quarters of these smaller companies use PS as a pension substitute. Again, the use of discretionary contributions is more prevalent in smaller companies.[129] If these differences between the larger and smaller companies and the prescriptions for successful PS are considered, then the larger companies would, apparently, be better circumstanced to use PS as an employee incentive. Therefore, evidence for the success of PS in the larger companies is hardly applicable in the case of smaller companies. Yet despite these criticisms, evidence for the financial significance of PS in larger companies cannot be dismissed.

PS AND COMPANY PROFITABILITY – A DIFFERENT APPROACH

To the question of PS as a factor in improving company profitability, the survey conducted for this study took a different approach. It attempted to discover what effect PS had on various aspects of employee behaviour, e.g. absenteeism, timekeeping, staff turnover, individual or group output, etc. A significantly favourable effect, it was assumed, would likely contribute to improved company financial performance.

As the focus in this section is on PS, those companies using only employee stock ownership plans were discounted. Only eight PS companies remained. Within this group a distinction was made between the practitioners of 'true PS', and those that used their PS schemes as a substitute benefit. The belief that the motivational effectiveness of PS is likely to be improved when used as an additional rather than a substitute benefit, was the basis for this categorisation.

Companies (three) using PS as a substitute benefit

While one company in this survey (Northwestern Railroad Chicago) did operate a PS scheme, it was not intended, nor did it function, as an incentive. Non-unionised employees had expressed a wish for a pension, and a PS scheme was introduced as the least costly way of funding such a benefit. In the opinion of the vice president, the scheme had worked well, but there was no expectation it would stimulate employee effort.[130] Another of the companies operated a cash-based scheme as its only employee benefit. Though it claimed the scheme had successfully motivated employees, it could produce no statistical data in support. Finally, Braun and Co. used their PS scheme primarily as a pension benefit, but also expected it would stimulate employee effort. Evaluating the scheme, the company stressed its success as a pension and as an aid to the retention and recruitment of staff. The vice president was also of the opinion that employees had a feeling of involvement and were interested in company profits.[131] Again, there was no statistical data on any relevant aspects of employee behaviour.

True PS Companies (five)

Companies were included in this group because their PS plans were additional rather than substitute benefits, e.g. a pension. Such companies it is believed would be better circumstanced to use PS as an incentive to greater employee effort. As can be seen from Table 2.2, this was a motive frequently mentioned by companies when accounting for the introduction of their PS schemes. However, equally important emphasis was placed on PS as an aid in the attraction and retention of staff.

Table 2.2 Frequency of reasons mentioned for introducing a PS scheme in five companies

Reason for PS introduction	No.
Incentives to employees to work harder.	4
To attract and retain staff.	4
To improve industrial relations.	2
To reward those who contribute to company profits.	2
To identify employees with business.	1
To educate employees as to how company performs.	1

Source: Survey conducted for this book.

One exception in this group was the Harris Trust and Savings Bank of Chicago. Though its pension scheme was separate and independent of an ESOP and PS plan, there was no attempt to use either of these additional benefits as incentives. According to the vice president, the primary purpose of the PS scheme was the attraction and retention of employees. In his opinion, the individual effort of an employee could not affect bank profit. Employing over 3,000 people, the bank was too large, he believed, for PS to function as a motivator.[132] These sentiments were not reflected in the bank's annual PS report to employees: 'As large and varied as the Harris is', employees were told, 'each of us can do something about profits'.[133]

Of the four remaining companies, three expected a dual benefit from their PS plans, namely the attraction and retention of staff, and an incentive to greater employee effort. All three companies claimed their schemes had achieved the objectives originally set for them. Yet when asked to elaborate, the incentive effect of PS did not figure prominently in their replies. For one company, PS had reduced the rate of staff turnover, which it believed would probably have been greater without the scheme. A second company claimed their employees were happy with the PS plan. This company ascribed the continuing high turnover of employees to its policy of hiring employees with high expectations who eventually moved on. A third firm believed its PS scheme had made it competitive with other employers in attracting and retaining staff. The problem of employee motivation, this company explained, was still being worked on. None of the three companies could provide any statistical data on employee absenteeism, sickness, productivity, etc.

The fifth and last company among the practitioners of 'true PS' is unique not only to this group but to all eight companies surveyed in that it could produce some statistical evidence for the incentive effect of PS. Though only one example, it does suggest that the request for statistical data was reasonable, provided the main intention of a PS scheme was to stimulate employee effort and co-operation. Secondly, the comparative success of this particular scheme would underscore the relevance of traditional prescriptions for successful PS outlined earlier. A brief examination of the scheme will highlight these points.

WARNER GEAR – A CASE STUDY IN SUCCESSFUL PS

The Warner Gear factory located in Muncie, Indiana, is a subsidiary of the Borg Warner Corporation. It manufactures automobile gearboxes, industrial and marine transmissions. The total workforce numbers 2,306 which is comprised of 1,800 manual workers, 500 clerical workers and six executives. Since 1937, the manual workers have been organised in the United Auto Workers' Union. Wages are at union rates with an additional annual improvement factor paid every year. The AIF usually involves a 3 per cent increase in basic wages. All employees are covered by a pension scheme, the benefits of which are calculated on length of service and salary in the last five years prior to retirement.

During the 1970s, relations between management and union were 'typically adversarial'. There was a strike in 1979 and another three-week stoppage in 1980. Management responded by initiating changes in industrial relations policy. First, an attempt was made to overcome the mutual hostility between clerical and manual workers. Despite opposition, both groups were brought together on a company picnic which, management claims, undermined traditional antagonisms. This was followed up by employee involvement and 'quality of work-life' programmes established in 1981. Management also co-operated in an employee welfare programme which dealt with alcoholism and drug abuse.[134]

Though industrial relations improved, management was unhappy with the level of plant productivity. When management emphasised the necessity for increased productivity, the union responded by suggesting a PS scheme. Management was agreeable, and the scheme was installed in January 1983. Simultaneously, a joint panel on productivity and quality was set up, on which management and union were equally represented. Its function was to monitor the operation of the scheme and improve its efficiency.

The PS plan was cash-based with a monthly payout. Coverage was generous: with the exception of six executives, all workers were eligible to participate. The PS bonus was calculated according to a predetermined formula. Usually the PS bonus is distributed among workers according to their salary; at Warner Gear the allocation was on the basis of the individual number of hours worked. It was a strategically adroit provision, and probably prevented a resurgence of antagonism between clerical and manual workers. Furthermore, it may have helped to create a feeling of equality which fostered a spirit of co-operation. Interviewed by the press, the president of the UAW local said of the scheme: 'I think it is very good for all employees. It is the only way all of us can get the same amount of money whether you sweep the floor or manage the plant.[135] Finally, communication of the plan was excellent. Along with the worker–management panel, a monthly newsletter was distributed which gave details of achievements or failures to reach particular targets and generally exhorted all to greater efforts.

Figure 2.3 Improvement in productivity in Warner Gear, January–December 1983

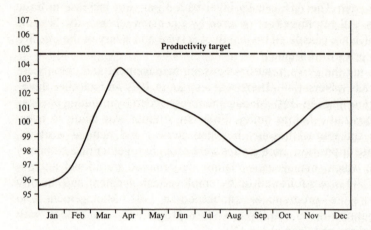

Source: Warner Gear monthly staff newsletter from files at the PSRF, Evanston, Illinois

According to the firm's vice president of human relations, the scheme had achieved many of its objectives. Management relations with the UAW, whom he characterised as 'good business people', were now he claimed 'super'.[136] During the 1970s, union grievances had averaged 207 per year, but they were now reduced to 30. Union–management co-operation had eliminated many unnecessary procedures and identified the need for machine changes which had resulted in cost savings of $250,000 a year. Timekeeping improved and the rate of staff turnover declined.

In some respects the PS scheme fell short of expectations. The incidence of absenteeism and sickness among staff remained static. Though a vigorous campaign of communication was carried on against losses through waste and scrap, there was no improvement. Rates of productivity did improve, but failed to reach the desired target.

Allowing for other developments within the firm, this improvement in productivity was quite substantial. During 1983 Warner Gear hired 800 new employees. Because of an initial learning period, productivity usually declined. Formerly, management claimed, this drop had been in the order of 15 per cent. Yet during 1983, despite the influx of new employees, there was a consistent overall improvement in productivity.[137]

Admittedly, the PS scheme at Warner Gear has only been in operation for a short duration. Yet given that it favourably influenced productivity and changed some aspects of employee behaviour, it can be reasonably described as a success. However, improvements in industrial relations and co-operation among various groups in the plant cannot be claimed exclusively for PS. Management efforts to reach an understanding with the workforce and establish a relationship of trust were probably crucial preconditions for its success. Another important factor was a favourable disposition among union members towards the PS concept. That the scheme itself, both in its installation and operation, followed closely the prescriptions for successful PS can only have enhanced its potential viability.

The Warner Gear scheme cannot be regarded as even remotely representative of American PS. That cash-based plans account for only 2 per cent of schemes in operation would be its most obvious disqualification. Yet aspects of its comparative uniqueness may provide some insight into American PS.

At Warner Gear the primary purpose of the PS scheme was to increase employee productivity. That productivity levels were recorded, and traditional prescriptions for successful PS followed, would imply that management was sufficiently serious in this endeavour. A substantial majority of American PS schemes either neglect these prescriptions or, indeed, even flatly contradict them. Cases in point are the frequent use of PS as a pension substitute and discretionary employer contributions. Again, of the PS companies interviewed for this study, six expected PS would, among other things, act as an incentive to employee effort. Yet only one could produce any statistical evidence to that effect. Such a casual and unorthodox approach by many managers calls into question the seriousness of their endeavours or intention to use PS as a motivator. This is hardly surprising, for it was demonstrated earlier that the majority of American PS schemes fail to establish the basic preconditions required if the motivational effectiveness of PS is to be realised.

AMERICAN PS AND EMPLOYEE MOTIVATION – A CONCLUSION

What then is the purpose of American PS if it does not significantly change employee behaviour or stimulate increased productive effort? In 70 per cent of cases the primary function of American PS is to provide the least costly method of funding a pension. Among smaller companies, an even higher percentage uses PS as a pension substitute.

For those companies that already provide a pension, the function of PS is to encourage employees to join and remain in the organisation. This is evident from the replies of companies surveyed for this study. The above functions are not mutually exclusive. A potential employee is more likely to join an organisation with some type of pension than one without this benefit. Also, a deferred PS scheme can serve to complement or top up a pension on retirement.

Yet does not such a conclusion fail to account for the three studies examined earlier which suggested a link between superior company financial performance and PS? Could it not be argued that this superiority is due to the incentive effect of PS on employee effort? This might be plausible using the Howard study but only because of its exclusive focus on financial data. However, the remaining two studies also considered the effect of PS on employee behaviour and the results provide little support for this argument. The majority of companies in both studies rated the effect of PS in improving morale, team-work, co-operation, or as an aid to cutting costs and increasing efficiency as mediocre to doubtful. Therefore, though these studies apparently establish the superior performance of PS companies over their non-PS counterparts, this superiority cannot have been due to PS significantly changing employee behaviour or stimulating greater effort. It was as a pension benefit, or for providing economic security for employees, that managers of companies surveyed rated their PS schemes as very effective or successful. Consequently, their strongest effect would be in encouraging employees to join and remain in the organisation.

Such a conclusion is easily reconcilable with the apparent superior financial performance of PS companies. First, a PS benefit, in increasing the attractiveness of a company for potential employees, creates a wider constituency from which they can be selected. Thus management is freer to use various criteria in selecting what it considers the most suitable candidates for the available work. Second, PS, in encouraging employees to remain in the organisation, can help reduce the disruptive effect of high turnover on productivity and morale. Despite its propagandists, the real purpose and function of American PS is either to provide a pension, or to encourage employees to join and remain in the organisation. There may indeed be a third aspect.

PROFIT SHARING AND THE AMERICAN UNION MOVEMENT

Unlike some of their European counterparts, American unions generally neither espouse nor are influenced by a socialistic ideology.

The only operative ideology of the American labour movement, it has been claimed, is its commitment to the business enterprise system.[138] If, as Metzger suggests, PS offers 'a piece of the action for participants', a favourable reception to these schemes might be expected from American unionists.[139] Latta remarks that there is no reason to believe that unions in the US could not find PS consistent with their general social and economic views.[140] The reality, however, is altogether more ambiguous.

The American Federation of Labor and Congress of Industrial Organizations (an equivalent of the British TUC or the Irish Congress of Trade Unions) does not have an official policy on PS.[141] Unions affiliated to the AFL-CIO are free to determine their individual responses to the concept. Yet traditional union attitudes to PS have been either hostile or indifferent. Proponents of PS argue that organised labour has gradually modified this position, and continually cite in support the example of Walter Reuther and successive presidents of the United Auto Workers' Union.[142] In its enthusiasm for PS, the UAW remains an exception.[143] Most unions have avoided the PS concept.[144] Union leaders in general are not strong advocates of PS plans.[145] This coolness stems not from any ideological objections to the precepts of PS but rather from how it functions in the American context.

For unions, probably one of the more unattractive aspects of PS is its frequent use as a pension substitute. Its inevitable uncertainty as a retirement benefit runs counter to a standard union concern with security. According to J.W. Cooper, vice president of the Harris Trust Bank, and treasurer of the PSRF, unions have consistently pushed for defined benefit pension plans rather than PS.[146] A very large international union gave its opinion on PS as a pension benefit. Employees have no guarantee that a company will earn sufficient profit during any year to add credit to a retirement fund, and because many factors affect company profitability over which employees have no control, they consider it unfair they should be asked to operate such a plan.[147] It may be significant that of the companies interviewed for this study, those with the largest percentage of unionised workers provided a pension separate and independent of ESOP or PS plans. In one of these companies, the pension of non-unionised managerial staff was funded through PS, while unionised employees were separately covered by a defined benefit pension plan.[148]

Another union objection to PS, especially when used as a pension substitute or flexible wage, would be the union's lack of any substantial voice in the forces that shape profits.[149] Decisions affecting profits are the exclusive prerogative of management, over which workers have little control. Even at a lower level, employee involvement in the installation or administration of PS plans is rare. That more recent PS plans make no provision for employee involvement would confirm rather than counter union objections.

Many unions also appear to be suspicious of PS as being inimical to their efforts to organise workers. In an attempt to determine union opinion of the effect of PS on organising drives, a researcher wrote to 19 of the largest international unions in the US. Only ten replied. With one exception all felt the existence of PS plans was restrictive of organising efforts.[150] However, these were intuitive feelings or based on personal experience, and were not supported by any statistical evidence. To remedy this defect, the researcher concerned examined the success of union organising drives in 759 PS companies. Under US labour law, workers in non-union plants can be represented by a union only if a majority elect to do so. All such elections are monitored by the National Labour Relations Board. In the PS companies, unions won 44.3 per cent of union elections. This was below a five-year average of all other union victories in NLRB elections of 59.8 per cent.[151] Even allowing for other factors beside PS that could materially influence the outcome of such elections, Czarnecki concluded that the union's percentage of organising victories is significantly less in plants with PS than those without.[152] The study, he claims, reinforces the notion held by many industrial-relations managers and union officials that it is harder to organise a plant that has a PS plan in operation.[153]

The above finding would receive some support from interviews of personnel managers of non-union PS companies carried out for this study. One company bluntly stated it would oppose any attempt by its staff to join a union. Another two believed unions to be anachronisms, particularly in their own companies where wages were above union rates and management was socially responsible. While Mr T.E. Parfitt of the Harris Trust Bank was not opposed to the union concept, he believed unions were unnecessary at the bank and any attempt by staff to organise would be opposed. Only one or two banks in the US, he pointed out, were unionised. Benefits at the Harris Trust Bank (ESOP-PS-Pension) were typical of banking generally; employees were well treated and these factors combined, Mr Parfitt believed, had kept the unions out.[154]

It would be wrong to assume all PS schemes either operate as pension substitutes or union deterrents. Obviously this would not be the case in companies that already provide a pension and in which a high percentage of the workforce is unionised. The introduction of PS in such companies is unlikely to provoke a hostile union response. Proponents of PS often point to the variety of unions involved in company PS schemes as indicative of a developing favourable labour attitude to the concept. What is more likely is the existence of two distinct union attitudes. Where PS is used as a deterrent to organising drives or as a pension substitute, union attitudes are likely to be hostile or suspicious. On the other hand, PS offered as an additional benefit is likely to receive a favourable union response. One union has explained that its resistance to the concept is because instances where PS is sincerely used by employers to benefit employees are the exception rather than the rule.[155] However, another union is unequivocal in its support for PS, and confidently believes its introduction will benefit its members.

PROFIT SHARING AND THE UNITED AUTO WORKERS – A NEW DEPARTURE?

Recent developments in industrial relations in the US would appear to offer a new role for PS beyond a pension substitute, or as a benefit to encourage employees to join and remain in the organisation. Whether PS in its new guise will become a permanent feature of collective bargaining contracts it is too early to say. Yet some indication of its long-term prospects may be gained from a review of the UAW experience between 1980 and 1984.

The UAW ranks among the larger international unions in the US. Most of its members are employed in the four corporations that constitute the American automobile industry. Over the past 25 years the usual procedure has been for the union to negotiate a three-year, no-strike contract. Though negotiated separately with each corporation, all agreements contain the same basic terms.[156] The union has secured a pension as a standard provision for its members. Common to all contracts is an annual improvement factor (AIF), and a cost of living allowance (COLA). The AIF traditionally involves a 3 per cent wage increase each year, while COLA keeps wages abreast of rises in the consumer price index. As an enthusiastic proponent of PS, the union leadership since 1955 has continually attempted to negotiate a PS plan on contract renewal, but this was resisted by the auto companies.[157] Yet by June 1982, Ford and General Motors had installed PS schemes, while another was already in operation at Chrysler. However, these schemes may not have been exactly what the union originally intended.

From the late 1970s, the American auto industry was being ground between the millstones of recession and foreign competition. By 1981 sales had fallen to the lowest level for 20 years, while in the same period the number of licensed drivers had increased by 75 per cent. Foreign imports accounted for more than 26 per cent of the US auto market. Losses in the industry, it was estimated, would exceed $5 billion in 1981.[158]

The first corporation hit by recession was Chrysler. In 1980 threatened bankruptcy was averted by union wage concessions in return for PS.[159] As the crisis deepened, General Motors, and in particular Ford, experienced increasing difficulty. Wage reductions were a solution favoured by both corporations, but this was rejected by the unions as simplistic. Nevertheless, the union agreed to consider renegotiation of existing contracts with the corporations, though they were not due to expire until September 1982.[160]

Representatives of UAW members at Ford and GM met separately in January 1982. By this time nearly 300,000 workers had been laid off in the industry, and union leaders were willing to begin negotiations.[161] Though authorised to proceed by both groups, a minority of GM delegates were unhappy with the decision. They claimed the union leadership had lost touch with the rank-and-file and promised to oppose any concessions to the corporation.[162] Negotiations at Ford were speedily completed, and when the new agreement was submitted to the membership it was ratified by a three-to-one majority.[163] At GM negotiations were protracted, breaking down once.[164] Finally, after the closure of more of the corporation's plants, agreement was reached between the parties. Despite endorsement by the union leadership, the new contract was ratified by a narrow margin; 52 per cent for, 48 per cent against.[165] The contracts at Ford and GM were to remain in force until September 1984.

The UAW agreements with Ford and GM were essentially similar. In both corporations, wages were in effect frozen. For the duration of the contracts AIF increases were relinquished. While COLA was maintained, quarterly payments were deferred for 18 months. The nine days' extra holidays which the UAW had secured in previous contracts to increase employment were given up. In return, both corporations guaranteed a two-year moratorium on plant closedowns, and promised every effort to maintain employment and find work for those laid off through subcontracting. The principle of equality of sacrifice was accepted, which meant any reductions in compensation or benefits would apply to all, irrespective of rank. Quality of work-life programmes were to be extended, and labour–management forums established.[166] A comparatively novel feature in both contracts was the introduction of PS.

In both corporations the schemes were cash-based, and rules governing eligibility were generous. All hourly workers and non-bonus salaried employees were covered by the plans. While the formulas used to calculate the PS bonus were different, both were predetermined. At Ford a sliding scale was used. When pre-tax profits exceeded 2.3 per cent of sales, then 10 per cent of that sum would be shared among participants; above 4.6 per cent and 6.9 per cent of sales, then 12.5 per cent and 15 per cent would be distributed respectively. At GM profits were to be shared after a specific minimum annual return. This would be realised when company profits exceeded 10 per cent of net worth plus 5 per cent of other assets. Beyond this threshold, 10 per cent of pre-tax profits were to be distributed among participants. In both corporations, allocation to individual employees was on the basis of hours worked. Both plans were scheduled to come into effect on 1 January 1983 with the first payout a year later.[167] When the president of the UAW was interviewed about PS at GM and Ford, he conceded that the corporations had agreed to introduce the plans when there was no profit to share.[168] Yet he remained committed to PS.

Undoubtedly, the depressed state of the industry and the probability of more layoffs significantly influenced the course of negotiations and their conclusion. Yet the agreement at Ford was hailed by the union leadership as 'a historic breakthrough'.[169] Union response at GM was muted. The main virtue of the contract, union leaders stressed, was its protection of members' jobs, a claim substantiated by GM's chairman.[170] It was a move in a new direction, he believed, 'away from confrontation towards co-operation . . . away from our adversarial past towards a new alliance for the future'.[171]

In June 1982 the above developments were the subject of a labour–management conference.[172] Many participants argued that the concessions made by the UAW at Ford had put the labour movement on the defensive and would lead to a deterioration in labour–management relations. Many firms outside the auto industry, they claimed, were now insisting on similar concessions. The Ford agreement was defended by Donald Ephlin, vice president of the UAW, as improving labour–management relations and providing job security for his members. A labour lawyer asserted the concessions had been inspired by necessity rather than co-operation. He was supported by the president of the United Food Workers local, who expressed scorn for companies who preach co-operation but support union-busting organisations. However, a Harvard professor of industrial relations believed that the more mature bargaining relationship established at Ford might help shift American management emphasis from short-term gains to long-term solutions.[173] Events of the autumn were to challenge the more optimistic interpretations of developments in the auto industry.

Two years earlier, the UAW at Chrysler had accepted a wage freeze in return for PS. In September 1982 the contract came up for renewal, and the corporation offered the restoration of COLA and the continuation of the quarterly PS bonus. The union sought an increase in basic wages to restore parity with workers at GM and Ford. Other union objectives were the restoration of COLA and the continuation of PS. Negotiations broke down, and the general membership voted overwhelmingly for strike action. Eventually the company agreed to increase the basic wage rate and restore COLA, but the PS plan was terminated. Forced to choose, the rank-and-file at Chrysler had sacrificed PS for an immediate wage increase.[174]

Though the new contract at Chrysler was a setback for PS as a flexible wage, the concept continued to have powerful advocates. Writing in the *Wall Street Journal*, Peter Drucker considered the options open to smokestack unions (autos and steel) when existing contracts came up for renewal. Because of economic recovery, he thought it likely unions would seek restoration of concessions granted during the recession, plus an increase in basic wages. Such a course, he believed, would result in wholesale job losses, primarily because the poor competitive position of autos *vis-à-vis* their European and Japanese rivals was due to a labour cost disadvantage. Smokestack corporations, he warned, had the alternatives of increased automation or relocation to Mexico or Third World countries where labour was cheaper. If the unions were to avoid a rapid decline in jobs and members, they must adopt a more pragmatic approach to wages and benefits. One solution, Drucker suggested, was that one-third of the present basic wage should be flexible. In times of high corporate profits, workers would receive the flexible portion of the wage and possibly much more. During a recession, wages could fall to the basic two-thirds, thus the corporations would remain competitive and layoffs could be avoided.[175] An ideal vehicle for this contingency income would be PS.

Drucker's article evoked a favourable response in government circles. The chairman of the Federal Reserve Board, Paul Volker, urged management and unions to overcome their resistance to PS.[176] Another member of the Board suggested that the installation of

PS plans could moderate wage increases and curb inflation.[177] The recently retired president of the UAW added his voice to the chorus. In the future, he predicted, PS could replace the AIF if the formula was improved.[178] The PS concept received another boost with the widely publicised first cash payout at GM.

Early in February 1984, both Ford and GM announced their returns for the previous year. Ford's profits for 1983 of $1.87 billion, the chief executive claimed, represented the greatest turnround from a loss position in US corporate history. His speech contained no reference to the company's PS plan with its employees.[179] Roger B. Smith, chairman of GM, was much more expansive. Addressing the National Press Club in Washington, Smith announced an all-time record profit of $3.7 billion for the corporation in 1983.[180] This remarkable recovery, he admitted, was due to many factors, but the most important, he claimed, was the new spirit of co-operation and dedication among employees. Nearly a third of a billion dollars, he promised, would be shared among all salaried and hourly workers.[181] No other company anywhere in the world at any time in history, he claimed, had ever distributed such a large amount of profit.[182] Many unionised companies, he granted, shared profits but the entry of GM into the field was significant. First, because of the unprecedented size of the payout. Second, because GM was among the largest of unionised companies.[183] The PS plan at GM, he asserted, marked a new milestone in employee relations.[184] Not only would it make every employee an entrepreneur, but it represented a true sharing of ownership and a further democratisation of industry.[185] Smith emphasised the importance of successful PS at GM: it would stand as an example of what a group of citizens engaged in private enterprise can accomplish when they know their combined efforts to increase productivity will be rewarded with a just and equitable share of profits.[186] Finally, he hoped that by other companies adopting PS and introducing a flexible component into employee total compensation, American industry would become increasingly competitive.[187]

The chairman's euphoria was not matched by the union response. At Ford, the UAW vice president was pleased his members would receive a share of the profits. However, he expressed concern at the disparity between amounts earned by workers and those paid to company executives in bonuses, salary, stock options and other forms of compensation.[188] Though closely identified with the promotion of PS and co-operation, these sentiments were echoed by Donald Ephlin, vice president of the UAW at GM.[189] Anticipating the summer round of negotiations for a new contract, the union announced it would seek improved PS formulas as well as wage increases and the continuation of COLA.[190] It was a repetition of demands made in earlier negotiations with Chrysler. Apparently the crisis was now past the union at Ford, and GM intended to revert to its original position on PS as an addition to COLA and AIF rather than as a substitute for either. On this point union resolve may have been stiffened by rank-and-file unrest.

Over the life of the contract, pay concessions by the average UAW member at Ford and GM promised to be substantial. By forgoing the traditional 3 per cent, AIF employees would sacrifice about $2,200 over term. In addition, each member deferred nearly $1,300 in COLA over an 18-month period. The first PS payouts due in March 1984 would only represent a small fraction of these concessions. Each eligible worker, it was reckoned, would receive $440 at Ford and $640 at GM.[191] From the beginning there had been little enthusiasm for the contract at GM, and in the interim a rank-and-file movement had arisen whose object was 'to restore more in 84'.[192]

If developments at Chrysler and union demands at Ford and GM constituted a check to PS as a flexible wage, then management action at GM may have delivered the *coup de grâce*. A fortnight after the chairman held up industrial relations at GM as an example to American industry and hailed the rise of the entrepreneurial employee, a confidential company document was leaked to the union and press. The paper was written by Alfred J. Warren Jr, GM's vice president of labour relations, and it outlined corporate bargaining strategy and targets for 1984. Top of the list was the elimination of annual raises AIF and COLA; these were to be replaced by PS. This was directly contrary to union strategy. Suspension of AIF and the deferral of COLA were originally granted by the union and very reluctantly at GM as temporary expedients during the recession. Already there was pressure for their restoration along with the retention and improvement of PS. Another of the corporation's objectives may have provoked even deeper resentment among union members. The corporation was now preparing to revoke the guarantee of job security, which from the union viewpoint was one of the positive features of the contract. Apparently, GM intended to lay off 80,000–100,000 workers by 1986.[193]

The document also considered how GM could sidestep 'the restore more in 84' movement, rapidly gaining ground among the rank-and-file. It would be difficult, Warren admitted, because of record profits in 1983, the $2.80 billion paid out in shareholders' dividends, plus the fact that executives' bonuses would be at an all-time high.

To stop the restoration movement, the corporation would have to convince workers that the real issue was not how much GM made, but how much it needed for business. It would also be necessary to explain that executives' bonuses are earned and are not some special privilege. Warren's suggestion for circumventing these difficulties when published struck a fatal blow at union–management co-operation. The corporation was 'to influence the UAW leadership' to bring the general membership round to its point of view. Whatever the truth of the matter, the document conveyed the impression that Ephlin, vice president of the UAW, was in the corporation's hip-pocket. Ephlin had already been accused by some of his members of being too close to the company.[194]

Not surprisingly, labour–management relations at GM deteriorated. One commentator described them as presaging a new Ice Age. Some union locals threatened to withdraw from the quality of work-life programmes, and strike action was contemplated. The corporation's public relations people attempted to dispel the gathering anger and resentment by suggesting the leaked document did not necessarily reflect the views of the executive committee. It did, however, accurately reflect those of chairman Smith, who had made no secret of his conviction that all workers at GM should become entrepreneurs through PS.[195] However, despite their apparent commitment to the business system, the union members at GM had shown a marked reluctance to don the entrepreneurial mantle if the result was a reduction in wages or benefits.

Those of a left-wing political persuasion may be content to point to the débâcle at GM as another example of capitalist devilry. Some unionists may recall the remark of J.L. Lewis, one-time president of the CIO, that PS is a delusionary snare.[196] According to B.L. Metzger, the development at GM was 'dreadful and a setback for PS'.[197] Such conclusions, appearing to suggest a dramatic change in industrial relations within the corporation, exaggerate the effect of the leaked document. Initially a substantial minority of union members at GM had opposed any concessions, and even before the contract's expiration, union leaders were demanding their restoration.

Subsequent revelations can have only hardened the union line. Certainly the developments at GM were a setback for PS as a flexible wage. Yet in all three corporations the UAW retained its enthusiasm for 'true PS' or PS as an additional benefit. It must be remembered the union desired not only the restoration of COLA and AIF but the retention and improvement of PS. While union and management were favourably inclined towards the PS concept, there was a fundamental disagreement on its interpretation and application.

American management tends to view PS as a substitute for pensions or, latterly, for wage increases. Unions traditionally seek security through fixed standard benefits to which PS, because of its contingent nature, can only be an addition. This dichotomy explains the unenterprising attitude of many American labour unions towards PS. Given the UAW experience of 1980–4, a similarly cautious attitude is likely to develop among the union leadership.

PROFIT SHARING AND THE FLEXIBLE WAGE

The above review prompts the conclusion that PS as a flexible wage will suffer the same fate as PS as a pension substitute, i.e., union rejection. Union members or their representatives would not be alone in looking askance at such versions of PS. According to one nineteenth-century British expert, employers who adopt PS on condition that employees consent to receive lower wages cannot be considered to practise what is properly known as PS. He characterises flexible-wage PS as minus or negative participation.[198] Reviewing previous American management attempts to use PS as an alternative to paying prevailing wages, Thompson concluded that it proved to be both a fallacious and a damaging practice.[199] None the less, despite past failures and contemporary difficulties at GM, a new champion of profit sharing as a flexible component in wages has arisen. In his book *The Share Economy*, Professor Martin Weitzman argues that if roughly 20 per cent of basic wages were contingent on company profitability, this would allow firms to hire more workers, thus reducing unemployment.[200] Professor Weitzman's proposal has attracted a lot of attention. Many commentators regard it as a novelty, apparently unaware of its former less-than-happy history.[201]

Yet the assumption that this dubious version of PS will be inevitably rejected by unions may be too absolutist. Under certain conditions, the introduction of PS as a flexible component in wages might prove acceptable. As a first condition, there should be full and frank disclosure of company financial information and rigorous implementation of the equality of sacrifice principle. Second, employees' representatives should be able to exercise some control over employment policy and the distribution of the surplus. The establishment of such conditions would, of course, involve a radical restructuring of traditional relations within industry. Any prospect of success for 'true PS' would require both capital and labour to vacate the comfort and security of their entrenched positions.

OBSTACLES TO SUCCESSFUL PS

The most common obstacles to the potential success of PS can be summarised under three headings. These are: employer reluctance to implement the participative requirements of these schemes; employer reluctance to disclose company financial information; and union distrust of PS. Regarding employers, the validity of these generalisations would be confirmed by the fate of the Vredeling proposal in Europe.[202] From the viewpoint of American unions, few PS schemes have worked to their advantage. Even as early as 1939, a US Senate committee, though favourable to the PS concept, admitted that it had been 'misused and abused in design, motive and administration'.[203] Apparently, there has been little change since. In the US, the main function of PS is to provide a pension. Only by the establishment of 'true PS' can union distrust be assuaged. Finally, the paradox at the heart of PS must be recognised: though long regarded as a management tool, the establishment of 'true PS' would inevitably involve some dilution of managerial prerogative.

AMERICAN PS AND FINANCIAL DEMOCRACY

Because of the absence of employee influence and control, an earlier chapter concluded that PS cannot be considered as a form of financial democracy.[204] The negligible involvement of employees in either the installation or operation of American PS schemes would substantiate this conclusion. Even if Metzger's recommendation to integrate employee participation and PS were followed, it would do little to promote genuine democracy – financial or industrial – simply because the participation envisaged involves no employee control over management decision making. Management must set goals and use employees' unique human resources to help them manage the business better, but Metzger warns they should not cease to manage and never lose control of the business. This is not, he admits, parity or even non-parity co-determination, but participative management.[205] Metzger's participation amounts to no more than that involved in the Scanlon Plan. As a vehicle for the realisation of financial democracy, the inadequacy of that plan has already been explored in an earlier chapter.[206]

CONCLUSION

Overall, this chapter may have conveyed the impression that PS in the US is a failure. Certainly, the evidence for its success as a stimulant to greater employee effort, productivity, or co-operation is not only scant but ambiguous. However, behind the rhetoric it is doubtful if this is, or ever has been, the primary purpose of the majority of plans. Again, unions appear to have rejected PS both as a pension substitute and as a flexible component in wages. In the long run, because of declining membership, union hostility to these versions of PS may be of no great significance. Statistics show a steady increase in the number of new PS plans.[207] Obviously, many employers have confidence in PS, and not without reason. In fostering a degree of organisational loyalty among employees, as an economical pension benefit, and as a union deterrent, PS has been successful. Many non-unionised employees also benefit, for undoubtedly a pension funded through PS is preferable to no pension at all. It may be one of those ironies of history that the prevalence of PS-funded pensions can largely be ascribed to successful union pressure for defined-benefit pension plans.[208] Nevertheless, taken on its own terms and from the viewpoint of employers and non-unionised employees, American PS can be regarded as a success.

Finally, few American schemes can be regarded as 'true PS' plans or fulfil the basic preconditions for their success. Therefore any general conclusion based on American experience as to the success or failure of PS would be unwarranted.

3 Employee stock ownership plans (ESOPs) in the United States – worker capitalism?

Over 100 years ago Abraham Lincoln signed the Homestead Act. There was a wide distribution of land and they didn't confiscate anyone's already privately owned land. They did not take from those who owned to give to others who did not own. It set the pattern for the American capitalistic system. We need an industrial Homestead Act . . . It is time to formulate a plan to accelerate economic growth and production and at the same time broaden the ownership of productive capital. The American dream has always been to have a piece of the action.

President Ronald Reagan (1979)[1]

Being labelled owners drew out the cynicism in many workers. 'To me its just a glorified name for a tax write-off.' – 'We're not partners, we're not owners' – 'It's not ownership – we have no say in it, we can't do what we please with it, like a house you own.' 'We are not owners at all – that's just a pretty name. We're owners in name only – on paper.'

Workers' attitudes in a company they own through an employee stock ownership plan[2]

Earlier it was suggested that employee shareholding had the potential to redistribute wealth and power, thus realising economic or financial democracy within the individual enterprise.[3] This chapter, in examining the operation and results of American employee stock ownership, will test the validity of the above hypothesis, and the effectiveness of the micro approach to economic democracy.

Its structure will be as follows: an introductory section briefly reviewing the history of American employee shareholding or stock ownership; the ideas of Louis Kelso; and recent legislative enactments designed to revive and promote the widespread adoption of these schemes. The following section will detail the actual operation of employee stock ownership plans and assess their motivational potential. Beneficial ownership, that is ownership without control, it will be suggested, can do little to encourage employee co-operative striving. Yet the attachment of many employers, managers and their spokesmen to beneficial ownership, whatever its motivational deficiencies, will be evident. A reluctance to share information and control is the most likely explanation for this attachment. Indeed, this unwillingness to share information and control, the paradox at the heart of many managerial initiatives in employee financial participation, underscores a recurrent theme of this study.[4] Finally, the two remaining sections of the chapter will consider the American union movement's response to employee stock ownership, and the proposition that these plans can realise economic democracy.

EMPLOYEE STOCK OWNERSHIP – A HISTORICAL REVIEW

Since 1974, there has been a comparatively rapid growth in the number of employee stock ownership plans in the United States. These contemporary plans, sophisticated and flexible, can serve a variety of functions. Nevertheless, their central concept – that of workers owning shares in the company which employs them – is hardly a novel one. Furthermore, neither have the arguments for, or the expectations from, these plans changed greatly in the interim.

Employee stock ownership was practised in the New England factories of the 1840s and these plans were promoted by William Merideth, the then secretary of the US treasury.[5] However, these early attempts to interest employees in the purchase of their own company stock were largely unsuccessful. It was not until 1893 that a plan proposed by the Illinois Central Railroad found favour with its minor executives and employees which resulted in substantial purchases of company stock.[6] Other companies followed this example, and employee share ownership became less unusual in the years preceding the First World War. During that conflict, government issues of liberty bonds, the purchase of which was facilitated by instalment payments deducted at source, familiarised many workers with stock ownership and helped to popularise the idea. In 1915 about 60 concerns operated employee stock purchase plans. By 1929 nearly 1,000 firms had installed such plans, covering approximately

1 million waged and salaried workers.[7] Many factors contributed to the proliferation of these plans.

During the war years and into the post-war period, a rapid rise in real wages made possible employee purchase of company stock, and rising stock prices made such purchases attractive.[8] It was a desire some employers were anxious not only to satisfy but to encourage. The American labour movement had emerged from the war confident and aggressive. Membership of the American Federation of Labor had more than doubled since 1914. By 1920 the AFL had over 4 million members – a figure never surpassed in the 57 years between 1881 and 1938.[9] Another manifestation of labour's strength was the emergence of a broad-based movement for industrial democracy. The recent revolution in Russia increased employer unease. A response by some companies was to initiate employee stock ownership plans.[10]

In the absence of federal regulation, these plans differed widely in the kind of stock offered, eligibility and purchase limits, and in the availability of employee voting rights. Yet common to all broadly based plans were certain managerial expectations. Within the individual enterprise, employee stock ownership was expected to increase productivity, worker commitment to the firm, and improve labour–management relations, leading possibly to the irrelevance of union representation. Some industrialists viewed stock ownership as a non-revolutionary means of providing industrial democracy. Employees, they suggested, could come to own the means of production, not through immediate expropriation, but by gradually becoming owners and employers.[11] Concerned with the wider society, politicians of both parties advanced employee stock ownership as the salvation of America from communism and socialism through the transformation of workers into capitalists.

Despite the growing popularity of these plans, they were denounced by socialists as capitalist snares, while labour leaders characterised them as anti-union. Critics also contended that owning stock gave workers little control over corporate decision making, and was a very risky investment. The collapse of the market in 1929, and the sharp decline in stock values exceeded the most pessimistic predictions. Between 1929 and 1932 the index of common stock prices fell by 75 per cent. A sample portfolio of stock sold to employees through corporate plans had by 1932 fallen to 15 per cent of its 1926 value.[12] Confronted with unemployment or wage cuts, employees sold their shares into the weakest market of the century and realised enormous losses. Not only had the risk element in worker shareholding proved substantial, but the amount of ownership or control achieved was apparently negligible. Even when these plans were at their peak, employees owned about 1 per cent of the outstanding stock of all concerns and about 4.5 per cent of stock in companies operating such plans. In not one of these cases did employees own more than 18 per cent of the company's outstanding stock.[13]

By the mid-1930s, 90 per cent of employee stock ownership plans had been discontinued. Those that survived restricted eligibility to upper-income employees or executives. Managers issued apologetic recantations, former enthusiasts for the plans fell silent, and publications on the subject ceased to appear. Broad-based employee stock ownership, Patard claims, was not just destroyed but discredited for a generation.[14] In recent times the revival and rehabilitation of the concept can largely be ascribed to the work and writings of one man, Louis O. Kelso.

LOUIS O. KELSO –
TWO-FACTOR ECONOMICS AND WORKER CAPITALISM

The thinking behind the present employee stock ownership plans (ESOPs) was developed in a number of publications by Louis Kelso, a one-time San Francisco lawyer and now investment banker. Central to Kelso's theory is a rejection of Marxian or socialist claims that labour is the sole generator of wealth or value. According to Kelso, Marx erred in his failure to acknowledge the productive power of capital. Kelso regards as a mystification the Marxian contention that the apparent productive power of capital is in reality the productivity of congealed labour.[15] Not only are there two factors of production, but because of modern technological developments, the productive power of capital is steadily rising compared with that of labour.[16] Today, Kelso asserts that physical labour accounts for 10 per cent and capital instruments for 90 per cent of wealth production.[17]

If capital produces most of the economy's wealth and if income were distributed on the basis of input, then those solely dependent on the wages of labour would hardly reach subsistence level. Full employment policies, government welfare programmes, corporate taxation, and labour unions keep wages artificially high.[18] Yet such mechanisms have not altered the maldistribution of income. A congressional committee of 1976 found 6 per cent of the American people owned over 70 per cent of privately held corporate wealth.[19] Such concentration Kelso ascribes to the corporate practice of internal financing. Between 1955 and 1965, he points out, less than 5 per cent of new capital was financed by the issue of securities to the general public. The remaining 95 per cent was internally generated from withheld earnings.[20] This concentration of economic power, Kelso believes, is perilous to freedom and democracy.[21]

Kelso rejects socialist solutions of expropriation or redistribution. It is not private property in itself that is harmful, he explains, but the fact that so few own any significant amount of it.[22] Furthermore, the principle of private property must be upheld, he maintains, for private property in the means of production is the bulwark of free societies and free lives.[23] Neither is redistribution an option, for it is incapable of bringing into existence any significant amounts of new capital.[24] For Kelso, capital produces most of the goods and services in the modern industrial economy.[25] Therefore his solution is to broaden the ownership of future capital wealth. This can be done through a variety of credit mechanisms which would foster broad ownership of newly created wealth by the average citizen. The most well-known of the Kelsonian mechanisms is the employee stock ownership plan (ESOP). This technique facilitates the acquisition of equity capital by the corporate employee, while simultaneously providing a greatly improved source of finance for the corporation.

With the establishment of broadened share ownership, every worker will become a capitalist, increasing his productivity and his attachment to both the firm and the prevailing economic system. As owners, workers will receive dividends as well as wages. A greater return to capital will be reflected in improved dividend payments. Thus, it is hoped, capital ownership will come to dominate workers' economic attitudes and lessen the upward pressure on wages.[26] In the long run it is expected ESOPs will be anti-inflationary. Finally, widened share ownership would likely create pressure for a reduction in corporate taxation, and the 'natural order' of returns to investment will be restored.

THE FIRST KELSO ESOP

In 1954 a US Internal Revenue Service ruling allowed a qualified employee trust (e.g. a profit sharing or stock bonus plan) to borrow money for investment in employer securities. Two years later the founders and owners of Peninsula Newspapers Inc. of California decided to retire, and the concern looked certain to be absorbed by a large newspaper chain. Using the 1954 IRS ruling, Kelso organised an employee purchase of the retiring shareholders' equity and blocked the impending takeover. The employees had become owners of their employer's stock without having to put up their own money. This idea of using debt or financial leverage for such a purpose is the hallmark of what has been termed the ESOP philosophy.[27] Other practical demonstrations were to follow. However, as there was no legal definition or regulations dealing specifically with ESOPs, companies introducing such plans had to negotiate the details with the local IRS office.[28] There appeared to be little prospect of changing this situation, and Kelso's theory and practice were either dismissed or ignored. It was not until the early 1970s when Kelso secured a powerful ally in Congress that ESOPs became a subject of national attention and some controversy.

SENATOR RUSSELL B. LONG AND THE LEGISLATIVE DEVELOPMENT OF ESOPs

Kelso's release from the obscurity in which he had languished during the 1950s and 1960s came through a meeting with Senator Russell Long, a Louisiana Democrat. Converted by Kelso's arguments, Long as chairman of the Senate Finance Committee was powerfully placed to push for a legal definition of ESOP. This was partly achieved in the Rail Reorganisation Act of 1973 which amalgamated seven insolvent railroads into the Consolidated Rail Corporation (CONRAIL). Senator Long included in the bill a provision requiring the organisers of CONRAIL to consider the ESOP as a method of funding some of the corporation's capital requirements. Though ultimately rejected as impractical, nevertheless Congress had recognised the existence of ESOP.[29]

From this salient, Long launched an amibitious and ultimately successful legislative programme designed to promote the general adoption of these plans. An examination of the legislative enactments listed below will firmly place Long and Kelso among the pragmatic proponents of employee share ownership. Pragmatists, it was suggested in the introduction, are chiefly interested in encouraging the maximum number of employers to introduce such schemes. Consequently, the emphasis of legislation sponsored by pragmatic proponents of employee shareholding is usually on tax advantages for companies, while requirements regarding employee voting rights, participation in administration, or that schemes function as additional benefits, are either minimised or ignored. While such a minimalist approach may increase the attractiveness of schemes for employers, it is a strategy fraught with serious shortcomings. Absence of employee involvement in the administration of these schemes, or their use as substitute benefits, will very likely vitiate their motivational potential. The resultant mediocre effect of the schemes as stimulants to employee effort or co-operative striving confirms critics of worker shareholdings in their scepticism. Similarly, their use as pension or other substitute benefits, allowed by loopholes in the legislation, will reinforce traditional union suspicion of such schemes. As will be seen, the Long/Kelso legislation tends to sacrifice quality for quantity – a failing the Irish chapter will show as not exclusive to America.

Employment Retirement Income Security Act 1974 (ERISA)

The background and provisions of this act have already been dealt with in some detail.[30] Essentially, it sought to regularise the operation of pension plans to ensure they would exclusively benefit participants. Under the act, 'a party in interest' (e.g. an employer or major shareholder) extending credit to an employee benefit plan, enabling it to obtain a loan for the purchase of employer securities, was deemed to be a prohibited transaction. This provision, superseding the original IRS ruling under which the first leveraged ESOP had been created, rendered any such future schemes illegal. Senator Long succeeded, however, in amending this section of ERISA to provide an exception for ESOPs.[31]

The act defined ESOP as a technique of corporate finance that utilised a stock bonus plan designed to invest primarily in employer securities. To this end the ESOP trust was allowed to borrow money, repayment of which was guaranteed by the employing company. This ability to use company credit is central to the ESOP concept.

Though a technique of corporate finance, ESOPs are simultaneously an employee benefit plan. A plan with such dual functions could give rise to conflicts of interest. In recognition of these potential problems, the act recommended that all ESOP transactions be subject to special scrutiny by the Department of Labour and the Internal Revenue Service to ensure they were primarily beneficial to participants.[32]

To a great extent, ERISA merely codified and clarified the way existing ESOPs had been operating.[33] Yet it represented an achievement for the Long/Kelso partnership and laid the foundation for further legislative measures favourable to the growth of these plans.

A brief review of the measures listed below will confirm observations already made regarding the Long/Kelso approach. The main thrust of the legislation is to provide tax advantages as an inducement to companies to install employee stock ownership plans. Indeed, as will be seen, anything considered an obstacle to the widespread adoption of these schemes, i.e. attempts to ensure that the primary beneficiaries are employees, received short shrift.

Trade Act 1974

The purpose of this act was to provide federal government guarantees for loans made to companies damaged by foreign competition. Senator Long amended the act to give preferential consideration to companies agreeing to channel 25 per cent of their loan through a qualified leveraged ESOP,[34] a qualified plan being one that complied with the rules of ERISA.

Tax Reduction Act 1975 (TRASOP)

Under this act the normal investment tax credit available to corporations was increased from 7 to 10 per cent. Again the influence of the ubiquitous senator is evident. A section of the act allowed companies to claim an additional tax credit of an amount equal to 1 per cent of the corporation's investment, provided such an amount was transferred in employer stock to an ESOP. Thus an 11 per cent tax credit became available to companies that installed these plans. The act in effect had created a new type of ESOP – a Tax Reduction Act stock ownership plan (or TRASOP).

An additional tax credit of 1 per cent may appear insufficient to foster the growth of these plans. For a large, capital intensive corporation this could amount to a significant concession. The Tax Reduction Act of 1975 has been identified as the main stimulus for employer interest in ESOPs.[35]

Tax Reform Act 1976

This act increased the 1 per cent investment tax credit granted in the 1975 legislation by 0.5 per cent. Corporations with TRASOPs could qualify for this additional credit if they increased their stock contributions to the plan by an equivalent amount, and if this increase was matched by cash contributions from employee participants. In meeting these requirements, a company could claim a total investment tax credit of 11.5 per cent.

The act also contained an unusual Congressional directive. Apparently the IRS had taken to heart ERISA's instruction that it endeavour to ensure participants were the primary beneficiaries from the operation of these plans. In pursuit of this object the IRS issued various regulations. These, the Congress declared, were burdensome and contrary to Congressional intent: the IRS was directed to rewrite them. For many companies these revised regulations greatly increased the appeal of ESOPs.[36]

Revenue Act 1978

This was mainly concerned with participants' voting rights, 'put options', and 'the right of first refusal'. These will be discussed presently.

Economic Recovery Tax Act 1981 (PAYSOP)

Essentially this altered the basis of the TRASOP, originally created by the Tax Reduction Act of 1975. Under that act, the value of the extra 1 per cent or 1 per cent tax credit granted to the firm that installed a TRASOP depended on the extent of its capital investment. The Economic Recovery Tax Act of 1981 ruled that future tax credits would be calculated on a payroll basis. Beginning in 1983, companies contributing stock to a tax credit ESOP would receive a tax credit amounting to 0.5 per cent of plan participants' payroll. In 1985 the tax credit would increase to 0.75 per cent of participants' payroll. Appropriately, this modified tax credit ESOP was termed a payroll-based stock ownership plan (PAYSOP).

This switch from a capital investment to a payroll basis was designed to achieve two objects. First, to make tax credit ESOPs equally attractive to all companies, not just capital intensive ones. Second, a tax credit based on payroll would encourage employers to maximise the number of plan participants.

THE GROWTH OF ESOPs

The United States Congress views ESOPs as 'a bold innovative method of strengthening the free enterprise system and to solve the problem of securing funds for necessary capital growth while bringing about stock ownership by all corporate employees'.[37] Listed above is some of the legislation enacted by Congress to promote their growth. Regarding the proliferation of these plans, this strategy has been successful. As one commentator remarked, 'ten years ago employee ownership was a utopian theory spouted mainly by academics and

Figure 3.1 Growth in number of ESOPs 1975–84

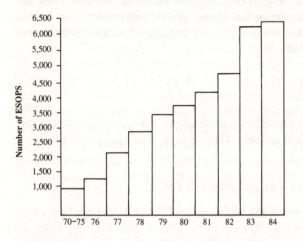

Source: National Center for Employee Ownership (NCEO)

political fringe groups. Today it is a fast spreading gospel of pragmatic capitalism.'[38]

What factors can account for the rapid growth of ESOPs? Undoubtedly Senator Long's exertions resulting in favourable tax treatment for these schemes were of crucial importance. Yet the senator's policy was not without its critics, for Kelso's ideas had failed to win universal acceptance. In some quarters they were bitterly opposed.

ECONOMISTS, BUSINESSMEN, POLITICIANS AND KELSOISM

Early in 1975, New York's famous fringe newspaper, *The Village Voice*, published an article entitled 'Crazy Louis and his creeping two-factorism'. Noting Kelso and Long's appearance on television, the newspaper commented 'When Russell Long put his arm around Louis Kelso on television a few weeks ago the academic economists reacted with predictable distress. Crazy Louis was back. For 20 years reputable economists have been telling America that Kelso was a self deceiving charlatan, a utopian fool and a registered crank.'[39] Despite the humour, the article accurately described some economist's reactions to Kelsoism.

Milton Friedman has described Kelso's two-factor economics as a crackpot theory. Instead of claiming labour is exploited as Marx did, Kelso says capital is exploited. According to Friedman, this is worse than Marx, it is Marx stood on his head.[40] Paul Samuelson, Nobel Laureate in economics, has subjected Kelsoism to more rigorous scrutiny. Testifying before a Congressional committee, Samuelson maintained that Kelsoism is not accepted by modern scientific economics but regarded as an amateurish and cranky fad. In support, he cited many prestigious economic journals which have withheld recognition or approval from the doctrines of Kelso. Its central tenet is contradicted by the findings of economic empirical science, which estimates the contribution of labour to the totality of GNP is in the region of 75 per cent with only 25 per cent attributable to land, machinery and capital. Furthermore, Samuelson continued, in modern economics an increasing proportion of labour productivity is attributable to the investment of human capital in the form of education and skill enrichment. Finally, he concludes, this 75/25 per cent breakdown is diametrically opposed to Kelso's presuppositions which are purely speculative and not based upon econometric analysis.[41]

Another economist has examined Kelso's suggestion that ESOPs would reduce unit labour costs and therefore be anti-inflationary. Roth demonstrates that the expected dampening effect on wages is at best problematic. Broad a priori assumptions about ESOP's probable effects are, he warns, ill advised, and suggests analysis should proceed on the basis of individual firms. Thus, he concludes, the case for a systematic policy designed to encourage widespread ESOP adoption is somewhat weakened.[42]

The scepticism of economists was shared by Peter Drucker, though for different reasons. Kelso's proposal to convert American workers into capitalists by making them employee owners, was dismissed by Drucker as the old industrial democracy plan all over again. History had demonstrated that such schemes almost guaranteed industrial bitterness rather than concord. Tying employees' retirement benefits to the fortunes of employer stock was a hazardous practice. Even the most prosperous concerns, he pointed out, can experience years when stock prices are down. Employees retiring in these periods are likely to be discontented and hostile critics. Recent ESOP legislation he characterised as an incentive to expropriate workers' pension funds to finance companies unable to raise capital from conventional sources. Lastly, Drucker regarded Kelso's project of turning workers into capitalists as superfluous. Through their pension funds, workers already owned over 30 per cent of American business, and this had been achieved without the cost or risk inherent in Kelso's scheme.[43]

Within business circles, those of Drucker's opinion were in a minority. *Fortune* magazine believed national policy should encourage the growth of ESOPs. Broadened capital ownership had many advantages. With the benefits of corporate wealth more widely distributed, a reduction in corporate taxation could become politically palatable. One of the biggest problems of business, Burck asserted, was the extent to which it was misunderstood by society. Receiving the financial information that comes with ownership would likely increase employee understanding of how business operates. This general increase in awareness would improve the prospects for the long-run survival of capitalism.[44] Similar points were made by *Forbes* magazine, which hailed Kelso's scheme as a solution to the democratic dilemma. Incentives (tax concessions, cheap loans, etc.), while stimulating wealth creation and building a healthy economy, have the side-effect of making the rich richer. This situation makes life easy for left-wing demagogues. Consequently, those of a left-wing political persuasion are opposed to the use of incentives, while those on the right demand more. With widened share ownership, incentives would be used to make everybody richer.[45]

Despite the tone of these reviews, it may be doubted that the popularity of ESOP's with spokesmen of business interests sprang primarily from a concern with the reformation of free enterprise capitalism. As one pension consultant wryly remarked 'No one is putting in an ESOP just to be a nice guy.'[46]

Kelsoism struck a responsive chord with politicians of both parties. This is hardly surprising, for a recurring theme of American political ideology is the support of the small man in his struggle with the concentrated power of big business or government.[47] The concept of broad ownership of productive capital, it has been remarked, runs through the writings of the leading thinkers of the American revolution and is embodied in the land policies of the first hundred years of the nation's existence.[48] A great advantage of ESOPs, one commentator observed, is they are such a natural from a political viewpoint. Who, in populist Washington, he asked, whether liberal or conservative, would knock the idea of spreading corporate ownership? Prophetically, another observed that Kelsoism is the only economic doctrine introduced in a generation that could become a plank in either the Democratic or Republican platforms.[49]

Nevertheless, the early 1970s were a propitious time for the rebirth of worker ownership. Economic *malaise* appeared unresponsive to Keynesian prescriptions. A reduction in the role of government in economy and society was one solution that increasingly gained credence. It was a climate in which worker ownership, with its associations of decentralisation and local control, could flourish.[50]

Since 1974, despite changes in administration, ESOPs have consistently received bipartisan support. President Reagan was a particularly enthusiastic advocate of the concept.[51] Worker ownership has won approval across the political spectrum because, it has been suggested, it dovetails neatly with American cultural values.[52] Yet this broad consensus on ownership may eventually fracture on the question of control.

If ideology, the economic climate and the influential Senator Long all combined to promote the legislative development of ESOPS, generous tax concessions have fostered their growth. Indeed, this success has prompted some economists to regret their opposition, and argue for a more pragmatic approach to Kelsoism. Broad capital ownership, they contend, could have many beneficial effects. Such schemes might eventually eliminate income maintenance and transfer programmes, while providing an alternative to redistribution or some form of socialism. A broader distribution of future wealth has enormous potential for strengthening capitalism by making it a moral and equitable system consistent with political democracy. Finally, they note, expanded capital ownership is now part of national policy. Therefore they recommend their colleagues to ignore the errors of Kelso's theory, and instead concentrate their analyses on ways to improve this policy. Will economists, they ask, continue to stand idly by and allow lawyers and politicians to restructure the economy, or will they enter creatively into shaping policy for the expansion of capital ownership?[53]

ESOP ORGANISATIONS

Along with creating a lively debate, ESOPs have also brought into being new organisations. The ESOP Association of America is a national association of ESOP companies and specialist practitioners. Describing itself as the national voice of these companies, the association is based in Washington and maintains close links with Louis Kelso and Senator Long. Keeping a watchful eye on Congress and lobbying congressmen to smooth the passage of favourable legislation is an important part of its function.[54] Through publications and surveys, it keeps its membership abreast of developments in the field.

The National Center for Employee Ownership, which is also located in the Washington area, eschews all political lobbying. The centre is dedicated to increasing the awareness and understanding of employee ownership. Its main activity is concentrated on researching the theory and practice of employee ownership.[55] The centre has links with academics in various universities.

Within these institutions, ESOPs have captured the attention of many and promoted investigation of worker ownership and industrial democracy similar to studies undertaken in Europe during the late 1960s. Harvard University has set up a study group on worker ownership and participation in business. Finally, the Industrial Cooperative Association of Somerville, Mass., while not directly concerned with ESOPs, has produced many incisive papers dealing with the question of ownership and control.

TYPES OF ESOPs AND THEIR OPERATION

The leveraged ESOP or Kelso Plan

The characteristic which makes the leveraged ESOP unique is its ability to establish an employee stock ownership trust (ESOT) which can borrow money for the purchase of employer securities. It is from the trust's capability to float a loan that the term 'leveraged' derives. The debt incurred by the ESOP trust is repaid with annual contributions from the employer. These transactions are illustrated in Figure 3.2

Figure 3.2 The financing technique of the leveraged ESOP

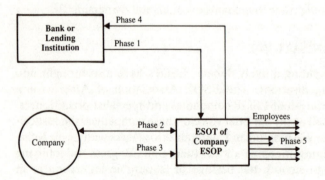

Phase 1
The company sets up an ESOP, and the plan trust ESOT raises a loan from the bank which is guaranteed by the company.

Phase 2

The ESOT passes the money it has borrowed to the company directly. In return, the company issues an equivalent amount of new shares or stock to the ESOT. To comply with the rules of ERISA, the stock sold to the trust must be at current market value. The trust now holds these shares in a 'suspense account'. Allocation to the accounts of individual employees cannot begin until the first instalment of the loan is repaid.

Phase 3

In setting up a leveraged ESOP, the employer has agreed to make annual contributions sufficient to repay the loan, usually within a five-year period or less. The employer begins his annual cash contributions to the trust.

Phase 4

On receipt of the company's annual contribution, the ESOT transfers this amount to the lender, and over a period repays the loan.

Phase 5

With the repayment of each instalment, a block of shares of equivalent value is released by the ESOT and allocated to employees' individual accounts. By the time the loan is repaid, all the shares originally purchased by the trust will have been allocated to participants. The company, if it wishes to raise new capital, can begin the cycle again.

The advantage of this method over conventional techniques of finance (i.e. borrowing directly from the bank) is the tax saving. While interest payments on a loan raised in orthodox fashion are tax-deductible, the principal is repaid out of after-tax revenue. The leveraged ESOP, though a financing technique, is also an employee benefit plan. Employer contributions to all qualified employee benefit plans are tax-deductible up to 15 per cent of participants' payroll.

A unique concession granted only to the leveraged ESOP has raised this ceiling to 25 per cent.[56] Therefore, provided company contributions remain within this limit and are sufficient to repay the loan within the agreed period, then both principal and interest payments are tax-deductible. Compared with orthodox methods, the leveraged ESOP can apparently provide a company with cheaper capital.

The non-leveraged ESOP

As its title suggests, this type of ESOP does not utilise its debt financing capability, i.e. it does not borrow money to purchase employer stock. Nevertheless, the non-leveraged ESOP can become leveraged if the trustees so desire. Because of this facility, employer contributions are not based on profit, though they are tax-deductible at the standard rate common to most employee benefit plans. Employer contributions to the plan can be either in shares or cash. If paid in shares they must be employer securities, if in cash it must be used to purchase employer securities.

When employer contributions to the non-leveraged ESOP are in the form of newly issued shares, this can amount to a considerable tax saving and increased liquidity for the company. Contributions in this form do not require any cash outlay, yet the firm can deduct from its tax bill an amount equivalent to their market value. With the non-leveraged ESOP there is no 'suspense account' holding unallocated shares obtained through debt financing. Therefore allocations to the accounts of individual participants begin immediately.

Tax credit ESOPs, PAYSOPS and TRASOPS

The working of these plans has already been outlined in the section dealing with ESOP legislation. Like the leveraged and non-leveraged ESOPS, tax credit ESOPs are designed to invest primarily in employer securities. Simply, the employer establishes a plan and contributes an amount of shares based on the available tax credit. However, tax credit ESOPs cannot use the leveraging facility common to other ESOPs.

Specific requirements for ESOPs as qualified plans

A qualified or approved ESOP is one which implements the requirements listed below. Subsequent approval from the Internal Revenue Service allows a company to deduct part of its ESOP contribution from its taxable income.

Participation and eligibility

While companies operating ESOPs are not obliged to include all employees, the plan must not discriminate in favour of officers, shareholders, or highly compensated personnel. This requirement is satisfied if at least 70 per cent of employees are covered by the plan. Before applying this percentage test, two groups may be excluded from consideration. These are union members already covered by a pension plan, and employees who have not met the plan's minimum age and service requirements.[57]

Allocation of shares to participants' accounts

All ESOPs must provide a definite formula for the allocation of employer contributions to participants' accounts. Companies operating leveraged or non-leveraged ESOPs may adopt any formula, provided it does not discriminate in favour of highly compensated personnel.[58] Within these terms, a simple formula would be to credit an equal amount of shares to each participant. However, tax credit ESOPs (PAYSOPs/TRASOPs) must allocate employer contributions in proportion to participants' total pay up to a ceiling of $100,000. Pay in excess of this limit may not be counted for allocation purposes. Though this formula results in greater stock allocations to more highly paid employees, it has been deemed to be non-discriminatory.[59] Among all ESOPs the tax credit allocation formula is the one most widely used.

Vesting

As qualified plans, leveraged and non-leveraged ESOPS must use one of the three minimum vesting standards established by ERISA. These schedules have already been detailed in a previous chapter.[60] Tax credit ESOPS are exceptions in that all shares allocated to participants' accounts must be immediately 100 per cent vested.[61]

Voting rights

Prior to the Revenue Act of 1978, only TRASOPs were required to provide voting rights for participants. Since its enactment, participants in nearly all types of ESOPs must be allowed to direct the voting of employer stock allocated to their accounts. In other words, voting rights can no longer be retained by trustees but must be 'passed through' to participants. When applying this rule, a distinction is made between publicly traded and closely held companies.

A publicly traded company is one whose shares are traded on the stock exchange, the prices of which are determined by willing buyers and sellers. Participants in an ESOP established by this class of company must be allowed to vote shares allocated to their accounts on all corporate issues. A single exception is the non-leveraged ESOP, in which voting rights may be retained by the trustees. In all other ESOPs the vote is 'passed through' to participants who direct trustees how to vote their stock. Trustees or fiduciaries may not vote stock already allocated to a participant who fails to exercise his right.

A closely held company is one whose shares are not traded or quoted on the stock exchange. Voting rights of ESOP participants in these companies are restricted. Participants are entitled to direct trustee voting only on corporate issues which by law or company charter require more than a majority vote of all shareholders. Mergers, acquisition or dissolution would be examples of such issues.[62] Consequently, opportunities for ESOP participants in closely held companies to exercise their franchise would be rare.

Dividends

A company paying dividends on its shares that subsequently installs an ESOP must also pay dividends on shares allocated to participants' accounts. These payments can be made in several ways. They can be 'passed through' the trust and paid directly to participants. In that case they will be taxed at ordinary rates. Alternatively, they may be used by a leveraged ESOP to supplement repayments of the debt incurred by the trust. Finally, they can be retained by the trust for the purchase of employer securities which would be then allocated to participants' accounts.[63]

Distribution

As qualified plans, all ESOPs must provide a formula for the distribution of vested benefits in the accounts of individual participants. Normally, vested benefits are distributed on death, disability or termination of employment. Benefits on distribution may be in stock or cash or a combination of both. Participants, however, must be informed in writing of their right to demand distribution in stock.

Shares of closely held companies may not be saleable outside the firm. Consequently, participants of a leveraged or tax credit ESOP in this class of company are entitled to require the employer to repurchase distributed shares at a fair market value. This is termed a 'put option'. In turn, to maintain the private nature of the company, a plan can grant a closely held employer the 'right of first refusal'. This would oblige participants to offer their distributed stock for sale to the ESOP trust first. Because of a readily available market for their distributed stock, publicly traded companies are not subject to 'put options', nor can they require a 'right of first refusal'.[64] Finally, lump sum distributions may receive favourable tax treatment such as ten-year averaging and capital gains rates for appreciated stock.

THE USES OF ESOPs

Usually companies establish employee benefit plans for one or two purposes. These may be to provide a pension plan, or to stimulate greater employee effort and improve labour–management relations. The company that adopts an ESOP can transcend these limitations. Because of its unique features, the ESOP can be utilised to serve a variety of other purposes, as illustrated below. However, with some uses of these plans, for instance as pension substitutes or providing a market for closed company shares, their benefit to employees is questionable. In such circumstances, the motivational potential of a scheme will be weakened. Additional safeguards, or a stricter interpretation of existing legislation to ensure that ESOPs primarily benefit employees, could avoid this outcome. Yet, as will be seen, corrective action suggested by one government department was trenchantly opposed, while a bill to prevent the use of these plans as pension substitutes failed to win support. It is very likely that opposition by proponents of employee shareholding was fuelled by fears that implementation of these modifications would render the installation of ESOPs less attractive to many employers. Thus the schemes remain open to abuse, and in some cases are ambiguous benefits for employees. The list below, which details the various possible uses of an ESOP, testifies to the versatility and complexity of the scheme.

1 A technique of corporate finance

The working of the leveraged ESOP has already been examined. For companies its main benefit is the provision of a loan, the principal and interest of which is repayable with pre-tax earnings. While this can involve substantial savings, there are some drawbacks, principally the dilution of shareholders' equity resulting from the issue of new stock to employees. This can be particularly severe if the issue occurs when market prices are temporarily below the book value of the stock. Furthermore, contributions to an ESOP will be listed as an expense on the company's profit and loss account. The combination of additional expense and dilution will reduce reported earnings per share. Consequently, potential investors may place a lower value on such stock, a result detrimental to the company and its shareholders. Simply using the ESOP as a financing tool, it has been claimed, is likely to prove dearer than almost any of the available alternatives.[65] This caveat, however, is mainly applicable to the publicly traded company.

2 The creation of an in-house market for shares

A difficulty confronting major shareholders who wish to liquidate their holding in a closely held or private company is the absence of an established market for their stock. Remaining shareholders may be unable to raise the capital required, or an outside purchaser may be unavailable. Given the possibility of takeover, such a purchaser may not even be sought. Thus, the shareholder can only look to the company to redeem his stock. For neither party is this an attractive alternative. First, as the company repurchase or redemption will be made with after-tax revenue, liquid assets will be correspondingly reduced. Second, monies accruing to the selling shareholder from the redemption are treated as dividends and taxed accordingly.

If, however, the company establishes an ESOP, the trust can purchase the shares with tax-deductible employer contributions. The shareholder also benefits in that cash realised from the sale of stock to an ESOP will be treated as capital gains, which is taxed at a lower rate than dividends. In effect, the ESOP has created a private market for the stock of the employer or major shareholders. However, the rate of stock redemption will depend on the type of ESOP. Using a non-leveraged ESOP, redemption will be by instalment. With a leveraged ESOP, the purchase can be completed in one transaction with a loan raised from an outside lender.

The use of an ESOP as an in-house market for closed company shares can create for the employer problems of compliance with the Internal Revenue Code, Treasury regulations and ERISA. For instance, regulations require that all qualified employee benefit plans be established for the exclusive benefit of employees or their beneficiaries.[66] Yet the major beneficiary of an ESOP used in the above fashion appears to be the selling shareholder, who is assured of liquidity for his stock. Again a requirement of ERISA is that employer stock sold to an ESOT must be at fair market value.[67] The shares of a public company traded in an established market are easily valued. For the closely held company with no market or price for its shares, valuation becomes problematic. Therefore these firms must consider all relevant factors when determining a fair market value for its stock. Incorrectly valued employer stock sold to an ESOT will be deemed a prohibited transaction.[68] In that event, the employer will be subject to special excise taxes, the plan will lose its qualified status, and contributions will no longer be tax-deductible. Lastly, the closed company sponsoring a leveraged or tax credit ESOP must grant participants a 'put option' on distributed shares.[69] The employer must ensure sufficient cash is held in reserve to meet this contingency.

3 Estate planning

For the sole owner or major shareholder in a closed company, the problem of stock marketability outlined above can be critical on retirement. In anticipation of this event, the ESOP can be used to provide liquidity for the holding. Again, the ESOP is being used to create an in-house market for closed company shares. Though the retiring owner is gradually liquidating his holding, he can still maintain control through the establishment of stringent vesting and participation requirements.

4 Alternative to going public

For the company wishing to remain closely held but short of capital, the ESOP offers an alternative to listing its shares on the public exchange. Instead, some or all of the capital required can be raised through a leveraged ESOP.

5 Neutralising takeover bids

Shares can be contributed to an ESOP to block unfriendly tenders or takeover bids. This defence can be augmented by a leveraged ESOP purchasing outstanding shares. The crucial requirement for the success of this strategy is that incumbent management retain voting rights on the stock.[70]

6 Corporate divestiture

In recent years, observers of American corporate behaviour claim to have detected a change in management criteria for evaluating corporate performance. Evidence is available to show that divisions or subsidiaries of large corporations are now required to meet annual profit targets or hurdle rates. While this practice may be unobjectionable, criticism has focused on what is considered unreasonable rates. Frequently these targets, or hurdle rates, may be over 20 per cent. Failure to achieve these rates of return will result in the subsidiary being divested, i.e. sold or shut down.[71] Closure will mar the corporate image, involving a loss of face with its workforce and the community. Furthermore, such occurrences encourage critics who argue that the corporation has some obligation to the community which has provided the infrastructure and tax concessions for its operation.[72] The corporation can avoid these mildly unpleasant consequences by arranging an employee purchase of its subsidiary through a leveraged ESOP. The method used is simply a variation on the ESOP financing technique.

Figure 3.3 Corporate divestiture using a leveraged ESOP

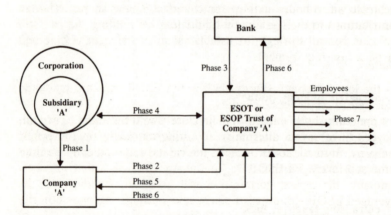

Phase 1

The corporation hives off its subsidiary A to create a new shell company – company A.

Phase 2

Company A now creates its own ESOP trust (ESOT).

Phase 3

The ESOP trust now raises a loan from a bank or lending institution guaranteed by the parent corporation.

Phase 4

Using the proceeds of the loan, the ESOP purchases from the parent corporation all the assets of shell company A.

Phase 5

Having purchased the assets, the trust then exchanges them with company A for an equivalent amount of shares.

Phase 6

No longer a legal fiction, company A can now begin to repay the trust with tax-deductible contributions. The trust passes these contributions to the bank to repay the loan.

Phase 7

As the loan is repaid, shares held by the ESOP trust are gradually allocated to employees' accounts.

Apparently both parties benefit from this transaction. The employees have saved their jobs and will eventually own the new company. In turn, the corporation has rid itself of a possibly troublesome subsidiary. Furthermore, as the stock issued is that of a new company, the parent corporation will avoid the handicap of the leveraged ESOP – dilution of equity and earnings. As one authority noted, corporations will find ESOP financing an attractive method of divestiture, especially for subsidiaries with limited profitability and marketability.[73]

7 Transfer of company ownership to employees

The use of the ESOP to create an in-house market for closed company shares has already been reviewed. In that instance, the trust bought out a major shareholder and the employees became part owners of the company. For a complete transfer of ownership the same method is used, the only difference being that the trust will probably have to raise a larger loan. As a vehicle to liquidate the interest of a sole owner or major shareholders, the leveraged ESOP is ideal. Especially when it is only the superior smaller companies who find they can go public or be acquired at attractive prices. Among many smaller companies, it has been suggested, the transfer of ownership to employees through a leveraged ESOP is likely to increase.[74] Such transfers, whether the result of corporate divestitures or the retirement of a sole owner, can create the conditions within the individual firm for the realisation of financial or economic democracy. Later, a consideration of some practical examples will indicate the likelihood of this promise being fulfilled.

8 In lieu of a pension

Employer cash contributions to a pension or profit sharing (PS) plan are tax-deductible. Nevertheless both plans, but particularly a pension, involve a continuing drain on company revenue. Indeed, one reason for the popularity of PS plans as pension substitutes is that they allow employers to base the frequency and amount of their contributions on company profitability. The ESOP possesses an even greater advantage in that no cash outlay is required. Employer contributions in the form of newly issued shares will receive the same favourable tax treatment, thus effecting an increase in company cash flow. For smaller companies short of revenue, the ESOP is an attractive pension surrogate. For employees the benefits are dubious.

The uncertain nature of pension benefits funded through a PS plan have already been considered.[75] Even with diversified investment of PS plan assets, the eventual pension benefit is still subject to the vagaries of the stockmarket. Using an ESOP in lieu of a pension magnifies this risk element. Given ESOP assets are invested mainly in employer securities, the employee's pension is entirely dependent on the fortunes of his individual firm. In the event of company failure, the employee will lose both his job and pension.

Apparently, Congress intended that the ESOP should primarily function as a method of providing stock ownership for employees. It was not designed or expected to serve as a pension plan.[76] Taking his stand on a Revenue ruling of 1979, one benefit consultant insisted that the objective of ESOP is shared ownership not retirement benefits.[77] According to a Department of Labour pension specialist, one intention of ERISA was to protect the employee by splitting his financial fortunes from those of his employer. An ESOP used as a pension benefit, he maintains, suspends this protection.[78] Though an ESOP used in this fashion may be in breach of the spirit, it is still within the letter of the law. As will be seen, many employers have exploited this lacuna. Yet as early as April 1976, Senators Humphrey and Javitts tabled a bill that would have effectively closed this loophole. Under their proposed act, companies intending to introduce an ESOP would first be required to have a pension plan in operation. The measure failed to win the necessary support and was withdrawn.[79] Thus the intentions of Congress regarding ESOPs and pensions became another paving stone on the road to perdition.

9 Compensation for wage reductions

Since deregulation in the American airline industry, many companies have experienced economic difficulty. For some, survival has depended on the willingness of employees to accept wage reductions. In some instances, employees have been compensated with a share in the airline through an ESOP. Pan American workers agreed in 1981 to a wage freeze and reduction in return for a 13 per cent share in the company. The amount of stock allocated to the individuals is equivalent in value to the wage cut. Workers were also granted one representative on the board of directors, and the five members of the ESOP administrative committee are drawn from the five unions in the airline.[80]

10 Motivation and Productivity

Common to all ESOPs of whatever type, whether operating in a closely held or publicly traded company, is the traditional assumption that a share in ownership will stimulate employee motivation and productivity. Employees who have a stake in the company, it is reasoned, will work harder to ensure its success. Furthermore, it is hoped that sharing ownership will alter employee perceptions of their role within the enterprise. This changed perception is expected to undermine employee loyalty to antagonistic unionism, and to improve labour–management relations.

Though these venerable expectations have rarely been realised, it might be precipitate to dismiss them as unreasonable or the theory behind them as unsound. The many failures of such schemes can be ascribed more to poor practice than to defective theory. With American PS, for instance, the prescriptions necessary for its potential success have rarely been followed.[81] Yet the fulfilment of these, plus additional requirements, are equally essential if there is to be any prospect for the success of worker shareholding. Whether the prescriptions for successful worker shareholding have suffered the same fate as those of PS can be gauged from a review of these plans' actual operation.

THE REAL WORLD OF ESOPs

The theory of ESOPs, how they should operate, and the variety of their uses have now been explored. In contrast, the purpose of this section will be to provide a description based on a number of surveys of their actual operation and use in many firms. From this broadly representative picture, conclusions can be drawn as to the likelihood of their success as stimulants to productivity, improved industrial relations and the possible realisation of financial democracy. Where relevant, criteria used to evaluate American PS practice will be applied.

Company classification and size

Kelso originally intended the ESOP to act as a mechanism for the dispersion of concentrated capital ownership. To that end he envisaged the installation of these plans in large successful corporations.[82] In reality, the ESOP is much more common in the small, closely held company.

A survey of 229 ESOP companies conducted by Marsh and McAllister for the *Journal of Corporation Law* found 81 per cent, or 186, were closely held.[83] Students of the University of California who surveyed 180 companies operating these plans found 88 per cent, or 158, were privately owned.[84] The ESOP Association of America, surveying 229 of its member companies, listed 84 per cent, or 192, of them as private.[85] Not only were the majority of companies closely held, they were also small. In the Marsh and McAllister study, 75 per cent of companies had less than 500 employees.[86] Of the companies surveyed by the Californians, 82 per cent employed less than 200 workers.[87] Contrary to Kelso's design, the typical ESOP company is likely to be a small, closely traded concern with less than 500 employees. This is a profile remarkably similar to that of the typical PS company.[88]

Employee Coverage

All benefit plans designed to stimulate productivity and labour–management co-operation must of necessity include the maximum possible number of employees without discrimination against particular groups. We have seen that employee coverage in American PS practice is less than generous.[89] With ESOPs this pattern has been repeated. The Corporation Law survey found only 45 per cent of plans included more than 75 per cent of the workforce.[90] For all 219 plans the median employee coverage was 68 per cent.[91] This tendency to exclude a group of employees is pronounced in the case of union members. Admittedly the majority of ESOP companies are non-union. Of the companies that comprised the three above surveys, 31 per cent, 27.3 per cent and 34 per cent respectively were unionised.[92] However, within this minority of unionised companies, at least half would appear to exclude all organised workers from their ESOP.[93] Generalising from their study, Marsh and McAllister conclude that the mean employee coverage among companies decreases as the percentage of employees represented by a union increases.[94]

Consultation

The importance of consultation and employee involvement in the genesis, implementation and administration of PS has already been considered.[95] Given the element of ownership, this would be an equally if not a more important requirement with ESOPs. Nevertheless, the scant amount of employee involvement characteristic of American PS appears to have been reproduced among the generality of these plans. In 90 per cent of the companies surveyed by Marsh and McAllister, the ESOP trustees are appointed by the board of directors. Plans in which trustee appointment was solely the prerogative of participants (3 per cent) or a decision of participants and directors (3 per cent) accounted for only 6 per cent of the sample.[96] Predictably, this restriction on employee involvement extended to voting rights. Of the closely traded companies surveyed by the Corporation Law and the ESOP Association studies, 77 per cent and 90 per cent respectively did not allow participants to vote shares allocated to their accounts.[97] Instead, shares were voted by the trustees. Publicly traded companies appear more willing to enfranchise participants. Both surveys alternately found 63 per cent and 80 per cent of public companies allowed participants to vote their stock on all corporate issues.[98] Yet it is not the publicly traded, but the closely held concern that is the representative ESOP company. Therefore employee involvement, influence, or control in the majority of these plans is not likely to be significant.

A substitute benefit

The bleak prospects for employee benefit plans that are expected to function simultaneously as a substitute benefit and a stimulant to productivity and co-operation has been noted.[99] They are more likely to fall between two stools. A classic example is the PS plan used as a pension substitute. Used for the same purpose, the ESOP possesses even greater advantage for employers. Indeed, one survey found 33 per cent of ESOPs were conversions from PS plans.[100] In many cases, it has been claimed, ESOPs have come to replace other forms of employee benefits linked to retirement.[101] Unfortunately, the extent to which these plans are used as pension substitutes can only be established indirectly. None of the companies surveyed was bluntly asked whether their ESOP doubled as a pension, possibly because such a practice is officially disapproved of. Rather, companies were required to list their various benefit plans. Of the companies surveyed by the ESOP Association, only 31 per cent maintained a pension plan in addition to an ESOP.[102] For many smaller companies, the study noted that in the absence of an ESOP employees would receive nothing other than a wage.[103] Again, for 73 per cent of respondents in the Californian study, the ESOP was the only benefit.[104] Taken together, these surveys suggest that perhaps over 70 per cent of companies use their ESOP partly as a pension surrogate. For the small, closely traded firm this may be a conservative estimate.

Communication

Managerial communications with employees as an essential element in the possible success of employee benefit plans has already been acknowledged.[105] Given the complexity and sophistication of ESOPs, a clear explanation of the concept is absolutely crucial to trigger any of its possible motivational effects. Companies that fail on employee communication claim much less impact on worker motivation and productivity. Annual reports, employee meetings, ESOP handbooks, and personalised letters are the most frequently used methods of conveying ESOP information.[106] As a general rule, the larger the company, the greater the variety of methods used. However, only a minority of employers (44 per cent) professed themselves satisfied with their employee communications programme. The majority (56 per cent) were either dissatisfied with or uncertain of its effectiveness.[107] In the Californian study, 71 per cent of companies rated employee understanding of their ESOP as poor to fair.[108] Another aspect of effective employee communications is employer readiness to disclose company financial information, particularly so with ESOPs, where employees as shareholders are entitled to such information. Nevertheless, a substantial minority of employers (44 per cent) refuse to disclose any information beyond what employees would normally receive in a conventional firm. In small, closely traded companies this percentage was even higher at 48 per cent. Probably the most remarkable statistic of all is that in 43 per cent of companies in which the ESOP owns over 50 per cent of the equity, management continues to withhold financial data from employee owners.[109] Such secrecy has bedevilled many schemes of labour–management co-operation, not just in America but throughout Europe.

THE GENERAL ACCOUNTING OFFICE REPORT ON ESOPs

At the request of the US Senate Finance Committee, the General Accounting Office (GAO) conducted a study on the operation of ESOPs.[110] Published in June 1980, the report was highly critical of these plans, and in turn itself became the object of criticism. A prominent member of the ESOP Association questioned both the methodology and objectivity of the report.[111] Admittedly, only 16 companies were examined, yet the report's findings are not contradicted by surveys with larger samples. Though also sceptical of the GAO study, the managing director of the ESOP Association did concede that some of its criticisms deserved discussion.[112]

The GAO report reviewed the operation of ESOPs in three publicly traded and 13 closely held companies. Generally, it found companies did not operate these plans in the best interests of participants.[113] The report focused on the closely traded concern where this failure was evident. Problems identified in companies of this type were stock valuation, its marketability and voting rights.

Stock valuation

The difficulties involved in valuing closely held company stock have already been alluded to. Yet ERISA requires that such stock, sold or contributed to an ESOP, must be at a fair market value which has been determined in good faith. Good faith determination, the regulations define, are at least an annual appraisal independently arrived at by a qualified person.[114] A valuation agent must not be connected in any way with the company or parties to the ESOP. The GAO found the appraisal arrangements in many companies lacked such independence. In four of the 13 firms, the board of directors or company officials valued the stock sold to the ESOP.[115] This was also the practice in about 18 per cent of closely held companies surveyed by the Californians.[116] Even when appraisals were undertaken by independent experts, the GAO argued that good faith determination was more apparent than real, mainly because appraisers failed to take account of the limited marketability of such stock, or did not consider it relevant.[117] A recognition of this factor would reduce the value of closely held company stock. All 13 firms, the report claimed, sold or contributed stock to their ESOPs at questionable prices.[118]

The sale or contribution of overvalued stock to an ESOP can adversely effect the interests of participants. First, they will be misled as to the ultimate value of their benefits. Second, it will increase the amount on which participants will be taxed when stock is distributed. Finally, ESOP assets can be drained off if stock is acquired at more than fair market value.[119]

Marketability

On distribution, if closely held company stock is to be of any value, a 'put option' must be available for participants. Private companies operating a leveraged or tax credit ESOP are legally obliged to provide this facility. Of the 13 companies in the GAO report, two were subject to such an obligation.[120] In the remainder, repurchase was at the employer's discretion. Nevertheless, GAO investigators were assured by respondents of their intention to repurchase. When examined, such assurances lacked credibility for there was little evidence that employers had made provision to carry out their intent. Only three companies had prepared a forecast of future cash needs for the redemption of stock distributed by the ESOP. Generally, the remaining companies had neither identified nor provided financial resources to meet such a contingency. Trust holdings in these companies consisted mainly of employer securities with little or no liquid assets available for repurchase.[121]

Despite the small sample, the GAO findings have some validity. Of the private companies surveyed by Marsh and McAllister, 41 per cent did not grant participants a 'put option'.[122] This was also the case in 57 per cent of the companies surveyed by the Californians.[123] Exceptions were the closely held companies surveyed by the ESOP

Association, in that a minority (12 per cent) did not provide a 'put option'.[124] However, within the group who provided this facility, only 38 per cent had commissioned an actuarial study to establish future cash needs for the redemption of distributed stock.[125]

The GAO investigators found no instance where ESOP participants were deprived of pension benefits due to an employer's inability, or refusal, to repurchase stock. This was not, they suggested, the result of obligations honoured but of time. None of these plans, they claimed, had been in operation long enough to require companies to meet the substantial financial commitments to participants.[126]

Voting rights

Of the 13 private company ESOPs examined by the GAO, 12 held voting stock. Within this group only one company 'passed through' voting rights to participants. In the remainder, a committee or trustees appointed by the employer voted shares in participants' accounts.[127] Generalising from these examples, the report concluded that the majority of companies provide no mechanism through which employee shareholders can influence the decisions of ESOP trustees.[128] The accuracy of this observation is confirmed by other studies.[129]

The above situation, the GAO believed, was totally at variance with Congressional intent. Congress, it pointed out, created ESOPs partly as a way of transferring capital ownership to employees. Full capital ownership, the report argued, is withheld from employees if shares sold or contributed to an ESOP are non-voting or if voting rights are retained by trustees. Thus employees are forced to rely on a trust appointed by management to vote the stock in their best interest.[130]

GAO CONCLUSION AND RECOMMENDATIONS

Overall, the GAO report concluded, ESOPs have been used for their tax concessions and to provide a market for closed company stock.[131] Companies have used these plans not primarily to benefit participants but for their own advantage.[132] Three recommendations were made to minimise the latitude for possible abuses. The report had demonstrated that the primary guidance available for the valuation of closely held company stock was inadequate.[133] Consequently it called on the secretaries of Labour and Treasury to issue specific guidelines designed to correct this deficiency.[134] Second, it recommended that Congress enact legislation requiring all private company ESOPs of whatever type to grant participants a 'put option'.[135] Finally, it advised that closely traded companies be legally bound to 'pass through' full and unrestricted voting rights to participants in all ESOPs on employer stock allocated to their accounts.[136]

ESOPS: THEIR MOTIVATIONAL POTENTIAL CONSIDERED

Coverage, consultation, communication, etc. would be basic pre-conditions necessary for the success not just of ESOPs, but of any benefit plan designed to stimulate employee motivation and productivity. These preconditions are absent among the majority of ESOPs. Furthermore, for the generality of participants, the benefits of these plans are ambiguous. Combined, these factors augur ill for the ESOP's potential positively to influence employee behaviour. However, this would be an initial prognosis, for there are possibly two additional preconditions specific to these plans which must be considered.

Michael Conte and Arnold Tannenbaum of the University of Michigan conducted a study of 98 companies which had some component of worker ownership. The researchers tentatively concluded that employee ownership could favourably influence worker attitudes, productivity, and company profitability.[137] They identified at least one condition apparently crucial to this outcome. A significant amount of company equity should be owned by workers. This was the variable they found most closely associated with above average levels of profitability.[138] In other words, the more stock owned by workers, the greater the motivational effect. The presence of a second condition – the right of workers to vote their shares – might be expected to be equally beneficial. However, evidence for a significant connection between direct ownership or voting rights for workers and company profitability was ambiguous in that it did not confirm or deny the importance of this condition. The amount of equity owned by employees seemed to be the key variable. Yet companies in which workers held a high proportion of equity also tended to provide voting rights for worker owners and representation at board level.[139]

The absence of these two additional preconditions (worker voting rights and their ownership of a sizable portion of company equity) in the real world of ESOPS would, it might be assumed, tend to confirm the pessimism expressed earlier as to their motivational dynamic. Unfortunately such a straightforward conclusion is not possible because the motivational significance of these provisos have either been challenged or are uncertain. An example is the question of voting rights. Despite the ambiguity of Conte and Tannenbaum's findings, common sense would suggest that withholding voting rights from employee shareholders will diminish worker involvement and therefore motivation. Given these rights are retained by trustees in the majority of private company ESOPs, their motivational effectiveness might be expected to be be negligible. However, as will be seen, the relationship between worker productivity and voting rights has been disputed.

A more important proviso identified by Conte and Tannenbaum was that employee shareholders should own a significant amount of company stock. This of course begs the question as to what constitutes a significant amount. Among ESOP consultants there is general agreement that the amount of stock owned by employees must be above a certain minimum to trigger the motivational potential of these plans. This threshold has been variously estimated at between 10 and 15 per cent.[140] Some companies would be unable to satisfy this criterion. In the public companies surveyed by Marsh and MacAllister, the median percentage of employer stock held by their ESOPs was 9 per cent.[141] The ESOPs of closely traded companies which own on average 32 per cent of equity would appear better circumstanced to realise the motivational effectiveness of these plans.[142] Apparently this could be the case if the critical threshold estimated by ESOP consultants is correct. Yet their percentages may be altogether too low.

The evidence for a positive correlation between the amount of company equity owned by the ESOP and its motivational effectiveness was originally produced by Conte and Tannenbaum. Their finding is based on a study of 87 companies in which relevant data were available. In 67 (78 per cent) of them, employees owned between 50 and 100 per cent of the firms' equity. Within this group, 34 companies (40 per cent of the whole sample) were 100 per cent owned by employees.[143] Obviously, the link established by these researchers between motivation and equity ownership was based on companies in a substantial majority of which employees held 50–100 per cent of their equity. Therefore, if it is possible to propose a necessary minimum, it may be more in the region of 50 per cent than the 10–15 per cent figure advanced by ESOP consultants. In that event there would be few ESOP companies that could meet this requirement.

Combined, the number of companies in the Marsh and McAllister and the ESOP Association surveys total 431. In 235 (54 per cent) of these companies, ESOP equity ownership varies up to a maximum of approximately 24 per cent. Companies in which the ESOP owns 50 per cent or more of employer's equity accounted for 67 (15.5 per cent) of the combined sample.[144] It may be that the ESOPs of most companies hold an insufficient amount of equity to arouse a positive employee response.

CONCEPTS OF OWNERSHIP – MOTIVATION, VOTING RIGHTS, AND THE QUESTION OF CONTROL

Two British ESOP enthusiasts have defined employee ownership as follows: a form of industrial organisation where generally at least part of the equity is owned by the workforce, who also assume a considerable degree of responsibility for the survival of the firm, although they may have little formal control.[145] Holding an individual or group responsible for a situation over which they have little or no control would appear contrary to the principles of natural justice. As both writers later admit, responsibility usually goes hand in hand with some ownership of equity and a degree of control over the enterprise.[146] There would, in any case, probably be few organised workers who would accept the burden of responsibility without being simultaneously able to exercise control. These considerations apart, Bradley and Gelb's definition, though possibly an accurate description of the majority of ESOPs, is nevertheless inadequate. Employee ownership can take at least two forms – beneficial or direct.

With beneficial ownership, employees own shares in their company but these are voted by a group of trustees appointed by management. Under direct ownership, employees retain and exercise voting rights as do ordinary shareholders. Trustees voting shares on the instructions of employees would still come within the definition of direct ownership.

Both types of ownership have their champions and critics. Louis Kelso, prophet of worker capitalism, favours beneficial ownership. Manager employees, he asserts, should manage, and non-manager employees should be beneficial owners. European co-determination plans, he maintains, by foisting amateur management on the corporations have added enormous confusion to the business scene.[147] Amateur management is defined by Kelso as the making of management decisions by people lacking qualifications. Generally, he claims, amateur management benefits no one, but this is particularly the case in a concern where employees are also shareholders.[148] Norman Kurland, a former associate of Kelso and persistent ESOP advocate, holds similar opinions. He recommends employee-owned companies to pay regular dividends, but not to involve employees in management. He believes union representation on the board of directors involves a conflict of interest.[149]

Much of the criticism of beneficial ownership has come from academics, or groups outside the ESOP fraternity. The ESOP promoted by Kelso and his colleagues has been alternatively characterised as a spurious form of worker ownership, or a cynical twist of the concept.[150] Conceived in the world of anti-union politicians, investment bankers, corporate lawyers and top management, the ESOP, David Ellerman claims, bears the indelible marks of its origin. Intrinsic to the concept, he maintains, is a subordinate role for labour. The trust mechanism is cited in support of this contention. Trusts, Ellerman argues, are used where beneficial owners are children or legally incompetent. In all cases, ownership is placed in trust because the ultimate owners are not trusted. Within these broadened ownership schemes, there are he claims, two classes of ownership – a first-class ownership for the elite, and a second-class beneficial ownership for the workers. While control is a concomitant of the first, it is absent in the second class of ownership. The insulation of control from workers, Ellerman claims, underlies the ESOP vision.[151] Yet despite this critique, some ESOPs, albeit a minority, do confer direct ownership on employees.

Preference for either version of ownership or arguments for the superior merit of the preferred type appear to be largely a function of the proponent's political persuasion. The intention here is to avoid entanglement in this morass. Rather, the merits of the alternative types of ownership will be assessed according to their motivational effectiveness.

Kelso and his colleagues implicitly assume that 'a piece of the action' or ownership will be sufficient to motivate employees. For them, employee ownership is the acme of financial incentives for worker productivity. Against this, it is argued, the word ownership has many connotations, the most common being control. Consequently, a company that installs an ESOP and tells workers they are now owners may raise expectations which, if unfulfilled, could be counter-productive. If, for instance, employees cannot vote their stock, it has been suggested that they may become resentful towards management, especially in difficult periods when their co-operation is most needed.[152] Indeed, there is some evidence to suggest that this is a realistic possibility. A majority employee-owned firm investigated by Kruse, in which voting rights were retained by trustees, was threatened by a strike. Management warned such action would reduce profits distributed to employee owners. Workers responded: 'We don't vote, we don't control the money, we don't care.' The strike went ahead.[153] To avoid disappointing employees' expectations, Norman Kurland has come forward with a novel proposal. Plans without participation rights, he proposes, should not be described as ESOPs but ESAPs – employee stock appreciation plans.[154] Though many ESOPs are in reality ESAPs, is it inevitable that their motivational effectiveness will therefore be correspondingly reduced?

In an overall review of their study of 229 companies, Marsh and McAllister concluded that their results did not reveal a relation between voting rights and improved productivity.[155] The ESOP Association survey, also of 229 companies, came to the opposite conclusion. Voluntarily providing employees with 'pass through' voting rights, it believed, may have favourably influenced productivity.[156] Findings of studies that focus on a single or small number of firms in which employee attitudes are surveyed are more consistent. Long examined three firms recently converted to employee ownership. The beneficial consequences of the conversion varied across the three. Their maximisation, he found, depended on the degree of ownership, and the extent to which traditional patterns of employee influence and participation in decision making changed subsequent to the conversion.[157] Again, in one firm Long attempted to assess the relative importance of share ownership versus control on employee attitudes. Share ownership in itself, he concluded, does appear favourably to affect employees' attitudes to their job. However, participation in decision making, he found, had a generally stronger effect.[158] Based on a detailed study of two employee-owned firms, Kruse outlined the conditions necessary to maximise an ESOP's organisational effectiveness. Employees must be involved in the initial installation of the plan, and there must be an intensive educational programme. Furthermore, employees should participate in decision making, and the financial rewards of ownership should be substantial.[159] These most recent findings would confirm many of the prescriptions traditionally deemed essential for the success of ESOPs and similar plans.

Participation, or the exercise of some control by employees, the weight of evidence would suggest, is an important element in the motivational success of worker ownership. If the intention in installing an ESOP is to improve productivity and foster labour–management co-operation, the one that confers direct ownership is more likely to succeed.

Having reviewed the record of employee ownership, O'Toole concluded that the effect of an ESOP on employee morale, motivation and productivity appears most positive with the establishment of three conditions:

1 Ownership is direct (that is, not through a typically designed ESOP trust).
2 Ownership is widespread (that is, almost all workers are shareholders, not just managers or those workers sophisticated enough to take the initiative to invest).
3 Ownership is broadly held (that is, when all workers have significant not just nominal equity).[160]

He advises managers who are uncomfortable with wide-scale authentic employee participation in ownership and management to avoid these plans. Worker capitalism, he claims, can only succeed with a full and unstinting managerial commitment to all its ramifications.[161] A minimal expectation would be that employee shareholders could vote stock allocated to their accounts.

There are three arguments for the extension of voting rights to employee shareholders. First, granting such rights is very likely to improve the motivational effectiveness of employee ownership. Second, the GAO recommendation that voting rights for employee shareholders, particularly in private companies, are necessary to protect their interests. Finally, the withholding of voting rights from a group of shareholders may be in breach of an unwritten rule of the stockmarket. Stock exchanges around the world apparently generally disapprove of unequal classes of stock as an infringement of shareholder democracy. However, in the face of employer reluctance to pass through voting rights, such reasoning counts for nothing.

According to Granados, the leading argument against pass-through voting rights is the dampening effect such a requirement would have on the growth of ESOPs.[162] One company president told the GAO investigators he would terminate his ESOP if obliged to grant participants voting rights.[163] The extent of employer resistance on this issue can be gauged from their reaction to the Finance Act of 1978. This enactment extended restricted voting rights to participants in private company ESOPs. Its provisions fell far short of later GAO recommendations on shareholder franchise in these companies. Nevertheless, the act roused employer resistance and the ESOP Association lobbied extensively for its repeal. In 1981, a majority in the Senate voted for repeal but this was blocked in the House of Representatives.[164] Despite this defeat, the campaign continued with undiminished vigour, strongly supported by employers. Of the 225 companies surveyed by the ESOP Association in 1983, only 8 per cent were opposed, while 68 per cent favoured repeal. The remainder were uncertain. Within the group of closely traded companies, an even higher percentage (75 per cent) favoured repeal of the 1978 act.[165] Three-quarters of repealers, when asked to indicate the strength of their feelings on this matter, rated them as 'very strong'.[166]

Owners of small, closely traded companies have usually spent a lifetime building up the concern. Of course, this could equally apply to many of the firm's employees. However, employers who install an ESOP in this class of company obviously find it difficult to transfer control as well as ownership to employees. While major shareholders may be willing to sell to an ESOP, they are reluctant to relinquish control. A resolution to this dilemma, it has been suggested, is to appoint trustees who will then vote the wishes of management or former shareholders.[167] Hence the popularity of beneficial ownership, and the opposition of employers to pass through voting rights which would effectively abolish this facility. Yet beneficial ownership, the evidence suggests, is much less likely to alter employee attitudes or behaviour. Given that ESOPs can serve a variety of functions, this defect may not be of crucial concern.

The result of the above review, and discussion of the actual operation of the typical ESOP can be briefly summarised as follows. In a majority of plans, traditional preconditions (communication, consultation, etc.) essential for their motivational success are absent. These weaknesses are exacerbated by insufficient equity ownership and the retention of voting rights by management appointed trustees. Furthermore, in a number of schemes the employer appears to be the principal beneficiary. For many employees, beneficial ownership may be a misnomer. Consequently, in bringing about a significantly positive alteration in employee behaviour, the effect of ESOPs as currently operated is likely to be negligible. Nevertheless, some evidence has been advanced to the contrary.

ESOPs – THE EVIDENCE FOR THEIR SUCCESS

The study most often cited in support of ESOPs' motivational effectiveness is that by Conte and Tannenbaum. They found employee-owned companies were 1.7 times more profitable than their conventional counterparts.[168] This tentative conclusion was based on 30 companies in which profit data were available. Yet it was doubtful if the companies that compose this study can be considered as a representative sample. In a substantial majority, the ESOP held 50 per cent or more of employers' equity, while about a quarter of these companies were directly owned by employees.[169] A profile of the typical ESOP company based on numerically larger samples would be altogether different. Only one-tenth would be directly owned, and the percentage of employer stock held by the trust would be much smaller.[170] The findings of the Conte and Tannenbaum study may not be readily applicable to the generality of ESOPs.

Of the 180 companies surveyed by the Californian students, many believed their ESOP made no difference to the level of employee motivation.[171] Some employers qualified this opinion by claiming their plans had not operated long enough to make a final judgement.[172] The average age of the plans surveyed was three years.[173] Only 20 per cent of respondents claimed their plans had reduced employee turnover, the remainder registered no effect.[174] Unless the work atmosphere and employer/employee communications were already good, the ESOP by itself, the researchers concluded, did not seem measurably to improve employee morale or motivation.[175] Despite this lacklustre performance, the majority of respondents expressed a high degree of satisfaction with their ESOP, believing it was important to the company and had come up to expectations.[176] This is a paradox that will be examined at a later stage.

The ESOP Association survey also attempted to assess the influence of these plans on employee motivation and productivity. Findings were based on the opinion of managerial respondents in 229 companies. The results, the association concluded, supported the idea that ownership brings out the best in people.[177] This may be an overly optimistic interpretation. Companies who claimed their ESOPs had 'strongly improved' employee motivation and productivity accounted for 16 per cent of the sample. A little over half (56 per cent) of the companies rated these aspects of employee behaviour as 'somewhat improved'. More than a quarter (28 per cent) were either uncertain (15 per cent) of these plans' effects, or reported them as having 'no impact' (13 per cent).[178] Only in a small minority of companies was the ESOP an unqualified success. In the majority, its effect on employee behaviour was mediocre to insubstantial.

The *Journal of Corporation Law* survey made a more thoroughgoing attempt to test the theory that ESOPs can improve employee motivation and output. Three indicators of performance were used. First, the annual average productivity of ESOP companies was compared with the national average in ten major industries between 1975 and 1979. Overall, the productivity of ESOP companies was 1.5 per cent above the national average.[179] Yet in the mining, construction, and service industries ESOP companies were below the national norm.[180] That no explanation is advanced for this discrepancy calls into question the usefulness of such comparisons. Indeed, given the method used to calculate ESOP companies' productivity as an indication of employee effort, it is far from exact. Productivity figures were obtained by calculating the annual percentage change in the ratio of total compensation to total sales. The volume of sales can be influenced by many factors beyond the control, and independent, of employee effort.

A second approach based on the opinion of personnel managers attempted to evaluate the effect of ESOPs on workplace atmosphere. A majority of managers (59 per cent and 79 per cent respectively) believed that its effect on employee morale and their interest in company progress, was good. A minority of managers (37 per cent and 34 per cent respectively) believed the ESOP had a positive effect in increasing co-operation among employees, and also increased the volume of their suggestions.[181] There is an inconsistency here. It might be expected that increased employee interest in the company would be reflected to some extent by an increased volume of suggestions. While 79 per cent of companies claimed increased employee interest, only 34 per cent reported an increase in employee suggestions. This may be a carping criticism and it may be unreasonable to expect a greater correlation between these percentages, which after all are based on the subjective opinion of managerial respondents.[182]

It was the survey's third approach to evaluation which promised greater exactitude and more concrete evidence. Personnel managers were asked to compare, on the basis of company records, employee performance before and after the introduction of the ESOP. In those companies that maintained records, the plan's effect on five measures of employee performance were rated (see Table 3.1).

Marsh and McAllister interpret Table 3.1, and their survey generally, as support for the theory that ESOPs can improve employee motivation and output.[183] A large number of companies, they state, have experienced improvements in employee turnover, quality of work, grievances, etc., since their adoption of an ESOP. The number of companies reporting improvements is, they note, far greater than those reporting a decline in employee performance.[184] While this is undoubtedly true, it is not quite to the point. The important point, they eventually concede, is that the majority of companies registered no improvements on any of the above measures.[185] In other words, in the majority of companies, the ESOP had no effect on employee behaviour – a finding broadly consistent with other studies already reviewed. Yet in many industries, Marsh and McAllister found, ESOP

Table 3.1 Measurement of employee performance since the adoption of an ESOP

	No. of companies	Percentage better	Percentage same	Percentage worse
Employee turnover	165	36	59	5
Quality of work	166	32	67	1
Employee grievances	144	18	81	1
Employee absenteeism	153	10	89	1
Employee tardiness	151	8	91	1

Source: Marsh and McAllister, 1981, p. 612, Table 34

companies had above average levels of productivity. Obviously, this was not the result of altered employee behaviour or increased effort. The link between productivity as defined by these researchers and the motivational effectiveness of an ESOP must be an extremely tenuous one. A more accurate criterion of an ESOP's effectiveness is the extent to which it positively alters employee behaviour. Profitability or productivity figures, as they can be influenced by many factors beyond the control of employees, may be at best the crudest of indicators. This may explain how another study could conclude ESOP firms were less profitable than their non-ESOP counterparts.

Livingstone and Henry examined the economic performance of 102 companies over a ten-year period. The total sample was equally divided between ESOP and non-ESOP firms. Comparing both types, they found non-ESOP companies were more profitable than their ESOP counterparts.[186] The introduction of an ESOP, the researchers concluded, does not encourage better employee performance as defined by higher profits. Their data, they claim, clearly demonstrate that the opposite occurs. They suggest that differences in profitability can be ascribed to less profitable firms introducing an ESOP in the hope it will improve their competitive position through increased employee motivation. Either this has not occurred, they speculate, or the cost of the plan has outweighed the net financial benefit to the company.[187]

It would appear from the evidence reviewed above that the motivational effect of the majority of ESOPs is negligible or at least doubtful. Nevertheless, the continued growth of ESOPs would indicate that they must provide some useful benefits. Employers in a survey already considered, expressed satisfaction with these plans despite their failure as motivators.[188] This is a paradox familiar to those acquainted with employers' evaluation of PS plans. In many cases,

PS was simultaneously expected to provide a pension and act as a stimulus to employee effort. Failure to achieve this latter objective with many employers did not disqualify these plans from being considered successful. The ESOP provides even greater versatility, and a wider variety of applications. Consequently, for employers a plan's motivational failure may be more than compensated for by other benefits. This is evident from Table 3.2.

Table 3.2 Relative importance of different reasons among employers for adoption of an ESOP in 229 companies.

Reason	Per cent very important	Per cent somewhat important	Per cent not important
To provide a benefit for employees	84	16	0
To improve employee productivity	51	43	6
To take advantage of tax incentives	51	34	15
To finance company growth	35	26	39
To provide a private market for shareholders	31	31	38
To provide an estate planning tool	24	38	38
To finance employee purchase of company	19	22	59
To avoid unionisation or strikes	8	23	69
To avoid merger or shutdown	4	5	91

Source: Marsh and McAllister, 1981, p. 602, Table 23

All employers installed an ESOP to provide a benefit for employees. Unfortunately, it is impossible to ascertain whether these plans were substitutes or additional benefits. On evidence examined earlier, it would be reasonable to assume a substantial number were pension substitutes. If so, then their motivational potential would be much reduced. None the less, they would be useful to the employer as a less financially burdensome pension plan.

Among a majority of employers, an important reason for the establishment of an ESOP was to stimulate employee effort or motivation. Almost equally important was a desire to benefit from the available tax concessions. These goals are not necessarily mutually exclusive or contradictory. Given managerial commitment to the concept of employee ownership, and a willingness to establish the basic preconditions essential for its success, these objectives can easily be harmonised. From surveys already reviewed, however, many would seem to lack this commitment, and few have troubled to create conditions necessary for the ESOP's motivational success. A small survey conducted by the National Center for Employee Ownership provides further support for this contention.

The centre questioned 49 ESOP consultants as to how they perceived their clients' attitudes to these plans. In their view, altruistic employers were in a minority. About 7 per cent of their clients, the consultants believed, would have introduced employee ownership even without the available tax concessions. They divided the remaining 93 per cent into two categories. First, those who approved of employee ownership, but without the tax break would not have introduced a plan (50 per cent). Second, those who would prefer to receive the tax and financial benefits of employee ownership without making employees owners (43 per cent). Many companies, the survey concluded, lacked a commitment to employee ownership.[189]

For a majority of employers, looking to an ESOP to influence employee behaviour positively, may be more a pious hope than a rational expectation. Indeed, whether the ESOP is used as a pension substitute, a financing technique, a tax break, etc., motivation is apparently merely a hoped-for incidental benefit. Consequently, the ESOP motivational stimulus may not figure as a crucial consideration when evaluating the success or failure of these plans.

ESOPs AND MOTIVATION – A CONCLUSION

The above review might prompt the conclusion that ESOPs are a motivational failure. For a variety of reasons such a verdict would not only be mistaken but unfair. First, in a majority of plans the basic preconditions necessary for their potential success were absent. The implementation and operation of many schemes precluded in effect any motivational potential. Second, it is doubtful if many employers were primarily concerned with ESOP as a tool for improving employee morale or increasing productivity. A case in point is their refusal to pass through voting rights, despite the evidence that such a facility enhances motivation. Finally, a tiny minority of companies in all surveys reported a significantly favourable alteration in employee behaviour. This would suggest that with the establishment of the preconditions outlined above, the motivational potential of an ESOP can be realised.

The employee-owned company – two case studies

Some concrete form can be given to the above discussion by examining conversions of two companies to majority employee ownership.

Admittedly, these examples are not representative of the typical ESOP. Nevertheless, the course and consequences of these conversions will highlight the possibilities and limitations of worker capitalism. Furthermore, these case studies will demonstrate the continuing relevance and validity of traditional prescriptions for the motivational success of these and similar plans.

South Bend Lathe

In the last decade the most widely publicised example of employee ownership was a small company located at South Bend, Indiana. Founded in 1906, South Bend Lathe (SBL) manufactures metal cutting lathes and other machine tools. Since 1945, the company's 300 blue collar workers, representing 60 per cent of the workforce, have been organised by the United Steelworkers of America (USWA). In 1959, SBL was acquired by a Chicago based conglomerate, Amsted Industries Inc. By the early 1970s, Amsted had become dissatisfied with the deteriorating performance of its subsidiary, and advertised its sale. It was evident that prospective purchasers intended to liquidate the company. The threat of immediate unemployment confronted the entire workforce.

Mr J.R. Boulis, the chief executive originally appointed by Amsted, sought a way to buy the doomed company. It was a colleague who suggested an ESOP. Within three months – on 3 July 1975 – the employees became the 100 per cent beneficial owners of SBL through a stock ownership plan.

Finance for the purchase of Amsted's subsidiary came from two sources. A US government agency, the Economic Development Administration, gave a $5 million grant to the City of South Bend. This grant was then passed on to the ESOP trust of the company (SBL). It was to be repayable at 3 per cent interest over 25 years. These favourable terms were offset to some extent in that another $4.5 million had to be raised from conventional sources. According to Boulis, interest payments on a major portion of that loan were seven points above prime lending rates.[190] The total capital raised was then passed to Amsted in return for its subsidiary.

In the initial stages of the purchase negotiations, Boulis informed local union officials of his intentions. They were asked to treat this information as confidential, since disclosure, he warned, might endanger the buyout. Not until the purchase was well advanced did the international union officials become aware of the transaction.[191] Meanwhile the ESOP was fashioned by Boulis and his attorneys without negotiation or any union input. It was eventually presented to the workers as a *fait accompli* which they could either accept or reject.

From a union viewpoint the plan had many unsatisfactory features. First, the ESOP was to double as a pension benefit. Employees were confronted with the stark choice of their pension benefits or their jobs.[192] It was impossible, they were told, to have both. Second, the amount of stock annually allocated to a participant's account was to depend on remuneration. Finally the ESOP trust, the members of which were to be appointed by the board of directors, would hold all company stock. Only vested stock would carry voting rights. Vesting, however, did not begin until a plan participant completed three years of company service. At that point he would be 30 per cent vested and could vote an equivalent percentage of the stock already allocated to his account. If, for instance, 100 shares had been allocated to an employee's account, then he could vote 30 of these. On completion of ten years, service, a participant would be 100 per cent vested and entitled to vote all shares allocated to his account. In the meantime, voting rights on all non-vested shares would be retained and exercised by the trustees. By 1980, after five years of operation, only 22 per cent of the shares held by the ESOP were vested and eligible for participant voting.[193] As Boulis himself explained, 'We tell our people they have all the advantages of ownership without any of the headaches of management.'[194]

The international officials of the steelworkers' union were unhappy with the loss of pension benefits. However, workers at the plant, though ignorant of the ESOP and its minutiae, then a comparatively novel concept, had little time for reflection. Furthermore, many remembered the shutdown of the Studebaker plant ten years earlier, and its devastating effect on the local community.[195] Acceptance of the ESOP as given by local union officials and the rank-and-file was the inevitable outcome.

For a time, South Bend Lathe became the bright star in the employee ownership movement. A little more than a year after the buyout, the plant was visited by *Time* magazine's business correspondent. In its first year of employee ownership, he reported, pre-tax profits had risen by 10 per cent, and there had been a 20 per cent increase in productivity. Company president Boulis was described as 'exultant' and his conviction was quoted that 'worker owned companies are the way to go.' Union members at the plant displayed none of the ambivalence of labour leaders, but were enthusiastic about the ESOP. Restriction of output was apparently no longer approved of. Slacking was not tolerated, for, as one union steward explained, 'It's, hey, you've got your hand in my pocket if you don't do your job',[196] a quote that was to be taken up and faithfully reproduced in many articles by ESOP enthusiasts.

Testifying before the Senate Finance Committee in 1978, Boulis provided a potted economic history of SBL since its conversion to employee ownership. Profits had improved each year and were now approximately 10 per cent. In three years, sales had increased by 34 per cent. Within 22 months the $4.5 million borrowed from the banks had been paid off. These financial accomplishments, Boulis pointed out, were not achieved at the expense of employee shareholders. Earnings per share had more then trebled from $20 in 1975 to $69 in 1978. Average employee earnings,including bonuses, had increased by 43 per cent since the conversion. Employee productivity, he believed, had very substantially increased and there was definitely better rapport and better morale. The only blemish in this otherwise perfect picture, Boulis conceded, was the unavoidable loss of pension benefits and the resultant wrangle with USWA.[197]

Ostensibly, the union local and its members at SBL had agreed to relinquish pension benefits in exchange for an ESOP. Nevertheless, some were disappointed when no pension money was forthcoming. An explanation for this irrational behaviour may lie in the complexity of the ESOP, the absence of any union influence on its eventual form, and the secrecy surrounding its negotiation. According to one observer, the ESOP document at SBL is drafted in incomprehensible language, and reads like the most baffling of insurance policies.[198] The international of the steelworkers raised the pension issue with the company chairman and president, Boulis, who refused to negotiate with the union, however, or to take the case to mandatory arbitration. The union instituted legal proceedings to name SBL as the successor to Amsted and oblige the company to reinstate the pension plan. While Boulis ignored the international, he continued to negotiate with its local at the plant. This strategy, it has been claimed, was designed to drive a wedge between the international and its local union. Apparently, Boulis tried to convince employees that an ESOP rendered a union superfluous. Responding to the challenge, the international sought and won a National Labour Relations Board election. Workers at the plant voted overwhelmingly that their representation by the USWA should continue.[199] In the opinion of one local steward, workers voted the union back in because they felt they needed its protection.[200] From late 1977 Boulis was legally obliged to negotiate with the international whatever his personal preference might be. In June 1980, SBL was again the subject of a magazine article by Irwin Ross of *Fortune*. By comparison with the earlier write-up in *Time*, it is possible to detect a deterioration in labour–management relations. While Boulis still maintained that employee ownership boosted morale, its permanent effect, he now believed, was confined to managerial and clerical workers. Among blue collar workers considerable disillusion had developed. Despite a slight fall on the previous year, productivity as measured by sales was still high. Though now Boulis admitted he was unable to decide whether this was due to new capital equipment or employee *élan*. Employee ownership, Ross noted, left the traditional hierarchy of decision making at the plant virtually unchanged. A year earlier Boulis had instituted monthly meetings with a 35-member rank-and-file committee to report on various aspects of the business. According to Ross, only information that Boulis did not classify as strictly confidential was disseminated.[201] Among items so classified was Boulis's own salary, the amount of which he refused to disclose to fellow shareholders.[202]

At the end of July 1980, SBL's collective bargaining agreement with the USWA was due for renewal. In negotiating a new contract, the company offered a 10 per cent wage increase and a Christmas bonus, but refused to alter the current cost-of-living allowance (COLA). The resultant strike by union members against the company they owned was a source of amusement to many. More perceptive observers argued that COLA or wage rates were not the real issues. Rather, the conflict sprang from rank-and-file animosity in the make-up of the company ESOP.[203] As the president of the local steelworkers bitterly complained, 'We were promised a piece of the action and we got a misunderstanding.'[204]

Along with COLA, the major issues of the strike were the right of workers to have more than one representative on the board of directors and greater stock voting rights. Three years earlier, workers had unsuccessfully demanded co-determination. A particular focus of resentment was the stock allocation formula through which higher paid personnel received a greater portion of stock. The inequity of this arrangement was highlighted by one striker who pointed out that executives did not pay one more penny for the company than the workers. A revision of this formula was demanded.[205] President and company chairman Boulis ascribed the strike to the malevolence of USWA and the unwillingness of the workers to think and act like owners.[206] A machinist at the plant who had played a prominent part in persuading his colleagues to accept the ESOP countered with the claim that the workers were not real but merely nominal owners.

> What we had there [SBL] for the last five years is ownership without control . . . We've bent over backwards since 1975 to make a good product and keep it selling . . . We've kept our mouths shut, covered up our differences with management to avoid publicity . . . But all we got was the same treatment we had before the ESOP, maybe even worse. We made no decisions. We have no voice. We're owners in name only.
>
> Whyte and Blasi[207]

Boulis was adamant that employee ownership did not mean employee management. Somebody, he believed, had to give the orders to make things happen. You can't run a business, he was convinced, by committee.[208]

Yet did the dispute centre on a struggle of managerial versus worker control? None of the workers interviewed by the *Washington Post* expressed a desire to manage the plant *per se*. But they did expect ownership to confer on them a collegial equality with management, where their opinions would be listened to and their views sought.[209]

The debacle at SBL is the perfect paradigm confirming the observations of W.F. Whyte on the course of many buyouts. Whyte leads the programme at Cornell University on 'New Systems of Work and Participation'. Buyouts or conversions to worker ownership, he found, pass through two stages of development. The first stage – the honeymoon period – is marked by fraternal affection between workers and management. Euphoria is probably heightened by the realisation of jobs saved. In the second stage, a mood of disenchantment spreads among the workers. This is not, Whyte suggests, because they had any concrete ideas of how they should be involved in control or decision making; rather they had vague expectations they would be treated with more dignity and their input into decisions would be respected and requested. As workers see management decision making continue in the style of the old regime without any reference to them, they gradually recognise the inherent contradiction in sharing ownership without sharing control.[210] Over time such a version of worker ownership may be more conducive to bitter resentment than a stimulus to motivation and co-operation. Apparently, to succeed, worker ownership must involve some organisational change and a dilution of managerial prerogative. Yet most managers, it seems, have proved unwilling to change the power relationships in their organisations in response to altered patterns of ownership.[211]

During the strike, Norman Kurland – the consultant who designed the ESOP at SBL – admitted the folly of not consulting the USWA. Local workers, he explained, were just happy to be saving their jobs but had the company involved the international union, an ESOP could have been designed to gain lasting acceptance from all parties.[212] Of course, Kurland's realisation of the importance of consultation and participation have long formed part of the traditional lore of all schemes of labour–management co-operation. Nevertheless, Kurland's position is somewhat paradoxical. His opposition to employee shareholders' involvement in management has already been noted. Yet had the ESOP at SBL been structured in a more democratic fashion, a likely outcome of union input, then some employee involvement in management would have been inevitable.

Finally, an anecdote from the strike that throws into sharp relief the doubtful status of employee ownership at SBL. Management went to court during the stoppage in order to restrain employee owners from trespassing on company property. An injunction was granted against the employees on the grounds that it was the ESOP trust and not the employees that owned the shares of the company.[213]

The Rath Packing Company

Rath is a meat packing company specialising in pork products and located in Waterloo, Iowa. With a workforce of over 2,000, it is the second largest employer in the town and surrounding countryside. During the 1970s the company lost over $20 million. To avoid closure, a capital investment of $4.5 million was required for plant modernisation. Owing to previously dismal economic performance, the cost of raising such a sum in conventional capital markets was prohibitive. Local community officials proposed that the US Department of Housing and Urban Development (HUD) grant the city money, which in turn could be passed to Rath. The department agreed to advance a loan on condition it was complemented by new equity investment.[214]

One entrepreneur who was prepared to invest money put forward a plan for restoring the company to profitability. The collective agreement negotiated for the industry by the United Food and Commercial Workers' Union should be suspended. Workers at Rath represented by local 46 of the international could then agree to substantial cuts in wages and benefits. Union members were being asked to relinquish important and hard-won gains.

That further concessions might be required in the future remained a possibility. The union was in a dilemma. An insistence that present wage levels and benefits were sacrosanct would involve inevitable closure and unemployment. Community leaders and the employer exerted considerable pressure on the union to grant the required concessions and save the plant.[215]

In March 1979 the union came forward with its own rescue proposal incorporating a way to provide the needed equity. Local union leaders were aware that for the past ten years, nearly 2 million shares of common stock, equalling approximately a 60 per cent interest in the company, were available in authorised but unissued treasury stock. They suggested workers should purchase this equity by taking temporary pay and benefit cuts. Each employee would be credited with ten shares in lieu of a $20 pay deduction until all outstanding shares were purchased. Within two to three years, it was estimated, employees would own a 60 per cent stake in the company. Until agreement on this proposal could be finalised, deferred vacation, sick pay and pension increases would be kept in a company account and used for plant modernisation. The union was to retain a veto to ensure expenditure was solely for that purpose. Ultimately these deferrals were to be returned to employees through a profit sharing plan.[216] Finally, the union proposed an enlargement of the company board from 6 to 16 members, the majority of whom would represent the workers.[217] In June 1981 the union plan won official approval from the stockholders and the employees at Rath.[218]

The union proposal sought to encompass a variety of objectives. First, through new investment it would secure the HUD loan and thus save its members' jobs. Second, it desired to limit concessions, protect the pension plan, and gain some control of the company and management decision making. Lastly, it wanted to counter the proposed buyout that would have included drastic wage and benefit cuts without giving the union or employees any control over the company.[219] Some academics assisted the union in drawing up its proposals. According to one of these, 'the lack of any bottom-up power', or its continuing concentration at the upper level of the managerial hierarchy in firms such as South Bend Lathe, were important anti-models.[220]

Initially the local union officials intended to establish a workers' co-operative, but this would have required their 100 per cent ownership of company equity. A second alternative was a democratic ESOP in which individual participants irrespective of the amount of stock held would have only one vote. Legal difficulties forced the abandonment of this scheme. The eventual compromise was an ESOP that fulfilled the various legal requirements while maintaining some element of democratic control. All Rath employees participating in the plan elect the ESOP board of trustees on the basis of one man one vote. The trustees have two functions. First, to elect or appoint ten members of the company board of directors. Second, to vote participants' shares in a block. Trustees vote these shares on instructions emanating from a meeting of employee shareholders.[221]

Workers had now gained majority ownership in a firm that was in effect bankrupt. Labour–management co-operation would be an important element in any attempted return to profitability. Consequently, practical and ideological consideration combined to promote a joint union–management problem-solving programme. A steering committee of top union and management personnel was established, and its first act was to negotiate and draw up a charter.

Its purpose was to delineate clearly the scope and limits of the co-operative programme and agree upon procedures for its extension to various departments. While the collective bargaining contract continued to regulate wage negotiations, the charter governed relations between the parties in the mutually agreed areas of co-operation. Also established was a long-range planning committee on which the company and local union president work out future company strategy.[222]

At departmental level, action research teams were set up. The usual format of labour–management co-operative committee – where workers make suggestions and criticisms to which management is expected to respond – was avoided. Instead, each team goes through a series of stages. A first meeting confronts and lists the problems of workers and management, e.g. productivity, or quality of working life. Subsequent meetings establish an order of priority in which these problems will be tackled and responsibility is assigned to small groups for the development of information and ideas. Finally, the proposed solution of the problems studied is presented to management for implementation.[223]

This co-operation between middle management and shopfloor workers has met with some success. In one department the work of an action research team reduced the down time on machinery by two-thirds. Nevertheless, the major shift of power at the top of the organisation has caused some problems of adjustment. There have been occasions when workers have flatly refused to follow the orders of middle management or foremen. Some in this group, unable to tolerate changed circumstances where their authority appears to be insecurely based, have resigned. Management and union have combined to find a solution. Union leaders have instructed their members to obey supervisory directives. Managers and supervisors on the other hand are attempting to develop a more participative style.[224]

From losing $1.5 million in 1979, company net earnings a year later stood at $3.3 million. Improved profitability was a direct result of reductions in wages and benefits. Sales, however, were at a record high and output per worker was up. The value of Rath stock had also risen. By the end of 1980 there had been a 10 per cent increase in the numbers employed.[225] Yet these improvements were only temporary. An unfavourable pig market and excess capacity in the industry created grave financial difficulties for the company.[226] In December 1981 an article in the *Wall Street Journal* queried worker morale and commitment at the plant. Over 75 per cent of Rath workers signed a spontaneous protest and sent it to the *Journal*.[227] Economic difficulties persisted, however, and in September 1982 60 per cent of the union membership voted for the termination of their pension plan to save the company and their jobs.[228]

The Rath case illustrates not the failure of worker ownership but its limitations. Majority ownership and the democratisation of the power structure within the company seemed to exercise a benign influence on workers' motivation, co-operation, and commitment to the firm. This is evident from their willingness to make initial and subsequently significant economic sacrifices. Undoubtedly these concessions helped to postpone the imminent collapse of the company. Yet, in the long run, its fate may be decided by forces beyond the control of either workers or management. If a glutted market forces its closure, this cannot be seen as a failure of worker ownership.

Throughout the conversion to employee ownership and beyond, the international union (UFCW), while supportive, was an uneasy and unhappy collaborator. The UFCW does not encourage employee ownership because, as an official explained, 'we find it hard to be bosses and workers at the same time.'[229] Furthermore, the concessions granted by the local union at Rath were a derogation from the industry-wide agreement negotiated by the international. Workers agreed to halve their holiday pay, to accept wage cuts, to temporarily suspend and ultimately relinquish altogether their pension benefits. The union feared similar concessions would be sought by other employers in the industry. A moment's reflection on the amount of control extracted by the local in return for these concessions and deferrals would have shown such apprehension to be groundless. As one international official was later to admit, no other company has used Rath Packing as an example when seeking concessions.[230] Rath, it has been claimed, is one of the few examples in the US of worker ownership and worker control in the same company.[231] It is an example few ESOP advocates and even fewer employers have been anxious to follow.

ESOPs AND THE AMERICAN LABOUR MOVEMENT

The American Federation of Labor and Congress of Industrial Organizations (AFL-CIO) has no official position either for, or against, ESOPs. In 1976 the AFL-CIO did circulate a memorandum on the topic to all its affiliates. These plans, it warned, contain many pitfalls for workers and should only be considered within the context of a collective bargaining agreement. Unions should ensure ESOPs are not used to divert attention from improvements in wages and other benefits, particularly pensions. Many small, closely traded companies, the memo notes, use these plans to raise capital. This can amount to workers being asked to accept risks that private investors or financial institutions are unwilling to bear. Nevertheless, the memo concedes, an ESOP used in this way is not necessarily contrary to workers' interests. Rather it indicates the necessity for unions confronted by these plans to be cautious, sceptical and to evaluate critically each individual proposal.[232]

Not all union affiliates shared the temperate attitudes of the AFL-CIO. The president of the International Association of Machinists characterised Kelsoism as a fraud and a hoax, merely a formula for ripping off working people. Large successful corporations, he claimed, don't need ESOPs because it is a method of shifting the burden of loss-making concerns from the financial community to the workers. Any attempt to substitute ESOPs for broadly based pension plans, he warned, would be opposed. All union members were advised to be extremely sceptical of these plans, and local representatives were to resist employer attempts to foist them on the membership.[233] Yet was this just union rhetoric or does it have any basis in reality? Recently the ESOP Association admitted that in some cases these plans are used less to give workers a productive asset, but more to abuse them of their right to benefits.[234]

Generally, remaining unions have been thrown on the defensive by ESOPs, reacting on an *ad hoc* basis when these plans are presented to their members. Few have evolved a policy or strategy to deal with the challenge of worker capitalism. A notable exception is the United Auto Workers' Union. Its position on these plans is evidently based on a detailed study. Provided they are subject to the collective bargaining process, the union has no policy of opposition to ESOPs. Indeed, in some circumstances, and if the terms of these plans are carefully bargained, the ESOP, it is believed, can be a valuable benefit to union members.[235] However, in recognition of the looseness of government regulations and the potential for abuse, the union has issued a number of guidelines for its locals negotiating ESOPs. Some of these are reproduced below.

1 Locals should prefer pensions or other concrete benefits to an ESOP substitute.
2 Union representation on the ESOP trust or administrative committee is a must. At the very least, union representation must equal that of management appointees.
3 The method of allocating stock to employees' accounts on the basis of compensation only should be replaced by a more equitable formula.
4 On stock already allocated to accounts, the local must demand that full and unrestricted voting rights be 'passed through' to individual participants.
5 For the union to make an informed decision on the ESOP proposal, it must have access to all relevant company financial data.
6 Before reaching a final agreement, all locals are advised to submit detailed plan provisions to the UAW Social Security Department for analysis and evaluation.[236]

Given the GAO report and its detection of various ESOP abuses, the UAW position is a reasonable one. Apparently, the union seeks to protect its members by ensuring they can exercise some control or influence on the form and operation of these plans. Incidentally, the union's implicit espousal of direct over beneficial ownership owes little to a left-wing ideological perspective. As the chairman of the UAW Employee Shareholder Committee at Chrysler explained, 'I'm no socialist, but if a guy works for a company he just works for it. If he owns it, he has a right to call the shots.'[237]

No matter how reasonable the UAW position may be, it would be anathema to a majority of ESOP employers who evidently favour beneficial ownership. Yet one ESOP expert has claimed that without significant union support, the widespread adoption of these plans is unlikely.[238] This exaggerates the importance of American unionism, for the percentage of the workforce it represents continues to decline annually. Nevertheless, Marsh and McAllister are of a similar opinion, believing marginal union involvement in ESOPs may be a factor inhibiting their growth. This obstacle can be overcome, they suggest, by finding a way to encourage unions to request or accept ESOPs in contract negotiations.[239] The UAW has evolved such a method, though it is unlikely to please many employers. In that case, it may be the employer rather than than the union that stifles ESOP growth.

As union enthusiasm for their version of the concept waxes, so employer's enthusiasm will wane. The reverse of course is equally true. However, as the examples of the Rath Packing Company and Pan American Airways demonstrate, compromise is possible.

Even under the best possible circumstances, where a union can shape an ESOP to its satisfaction, there remains a latent uneasiness in dealing with employee ownership. Most American unions have eschewed involvement in corporate decision making, and there is little rank-and-file demand for worker directors. Union members on the board, it is feared, will be co-opted by management. An even greater source of anxiety is the perception that union members in an employee owned firm would undergo an identity crisis with detrimental effects on collective bargaining. Workers might become more interested in the long-term maximisation of profit and less in immediate wage increases. As workers identified more with the fortunes of the company and management's viewpoint, a union would be rendered superfluous. Such anxieties, according to Stern and O'Brien, who investigated union attitudes to employee ownership, were mainly expressed by officials without pay bargaining experience in this class of company.[240] Yet for Kelso, the eventual irrelevance of unionism was an expected by-product of worker capitalism. Some employers have installed ESOP as a union antidote.

Most unions with members in an ESOP or employee-owned firm have found changes in the collective bargaining process to be negligible. However, there are some exceptions where the union experience has been an uncomfortable one.[241] Kruse, in his study of two employee-owned firms, tested the hypothesis that under such an arrangement the importance of the union is likely to decline. He found no evidence to support this contention.[242] The evidence from one firm appeared to suggest the opposite effect was more likely, namely that the importance of the union under employee ownership would increase.[243] South Bend Lathe, a 100 per cent employee-owned firm, is another example of such an occurrence. Drawing on his own and a variety of other studies, Kruse argues that the continuing survival of unions in employee-owned firms can be considered a strong and safe conclusion.[244]

Further support for the utility of a union for employee share-holders has come from an unlikely quarter. The ESOP Association survey notes that full 'pass through' voting rights for participants is more common where union members participate in these plans.[245]

While ESOPs may pose no threat to established unionism, does their existence in a non-union firm present an obstacle to unionisation? Unfortunately, there is apparently no empirical data available comparing the success of organising drives in non-union firms with and without ESOPs. However, the higher failure rate of union organising drives in non-union plants with profit sharing plans may be similar in non-union ESOP companies. Kruse has speculated that it may be more difficult to convince unorganised employee owners of their need for union representation. On the other hand, he suggests, unionisation might be easier where employee owners have no voting rights and are excluded from decision making. The fact that four firms have been organised after conversion to employee ownership, he concludes, indicates that it is at least feasible.[246]

Finally, a union lawyer has suggested that the labour movement evaluate ESOPs on an individual basis. In some cases they can be used to save jobs and keep a viable if not sufficiently profitable plant going. Even where the ESOP proposal undercuts industry-wide agreements, this can be offset by more worker or union control over management and investment decisions. Indeed, as the Rath ESOP demonstrates, a trade-off that involves substantial worker control may be sufficient to deter managements elsewhere from seeking similar concessions. The ESOP, Olson concludes, is not a panacea or the primary answer to plant closure, but is a flexible mechanism which unions and workers should understand and be able to use or fight with sophistication.[247]

Since the mid-1970s a less negative attitude towards ESOPs has developed among many union leaders. Essentially, their position on these plans would now be closer to that espoused by the UAW. Unfavourable economic circumstances rather than an insight into the merit of these plans, would be the main agent of change. It would be wrong to assume unions will now look more kindly on the representative or typical ESOP. They are very likely to remain implacably opposed to plans with the configuration of those already outlined in the real world of ESOPs. Yet, even an ESOP shaped to the union's desire may require some modification in a traditional adversarial stance.

FINANCIAL DEMOCRACY

The intention of ESOP legislation, it has been claimed, was to broaden ownership by making workers stock owners and not to extend notions of political democracy to the economy.[248] Recalling the profile of the typical ESOP would be sufficient to confirm the accuracy of this observation. One writer has dismissed management fears that an ESOP might diminish its control. He points out that through the trust mechanism, and even with majority worker ownership, the firm can be controlled exactly as it was before the implementation of the plan. Furthermore, as shares are allocated in proportion to relative compensation, this will favour highly compensated key employees. He insists the ESOP can add to, rather than dilute, managerial control.[249] Yet as the Rath Packing Company shows, a democratic ESOP is a practical possibility.

For the realisation of financial democracy within the individual firm through an ESOP, there would appear to be at least three requirements. First, the plan should embrace all employees. Second, the trustees should be democratically elected and vote shares on the instructions of all participants, not just the management group. Finally, allocation of shares to participants' accounts should be on an equitable basis. A simple solution would be to credit an equal amount of shares to each participant. According to a US Senate Finance Committee booklet, such a formula is flawed because it fails to recognise that employee benefit programmes, like salaries, are intended to reward the more productive employees.[250] Differing rewards to various categories of employees may owe more to the concentration of power at the top of the managerial hierarchy than to objective evaluation.[251] It is usually the most highly paid employees who evaluate the productivity and consequently the remuneration of other employees.[252] Given that the rationality or rightness of salary structures may be questionable, the best course would be to avoid its reproduction in the allocation of shares.

There is a more practical argument for equal distribution. Through the salary structure or other benefits, employees have already been compensated for their more or less productive or responsible jobs. The ESOP is supposedly an additional plan, which by conferring ownership is expected to stimulate a co-operative team spirit. A formula that allocates shares on the principle of 'to him who hath more shall be given' will, for many rank-and-file workers, signal the continuance of the old regime and not a new departure. Thus the egalitarian team spirit which the plan strives to promote will be undermined. Such a formula was a source of deep resentment at South Bend Lathe. Of course, this is not to insist that an equal amount of stock credited to all employees is the only method of distribution. Differing amounts of stock allocated on lengths of service would probably be equally acceptable.

Equal distribution of stock to all employees and their democratic control of the trust would, it is suggested above, be sufficient for the realisation of financial democracy. David Ellerman and his colleagues would be sceptical of such an outcome. Attempts to democratise the economy through wider share ownership, they argue, must fail because capital always tends to reconcentrate. A preventive measure suggested by democratic ESOP advocates – that departing or retiring workers should be obliged to sell shares back to the firm rather than on the open market – Ellerman points out, infringes the right of capital ownership. The ESOP democrats have also attempted to separate the amount of share capital owned from voting power. They have put forward a two-tier scheme where each employee would receive only one vote irrespective of the amount of shares owned. This scheme, Ellerman suggests, is potentially in conflict with ESOP legislation and again constitutes an infringement of capital ownership rights. The solution, he suggests, is to divorce voting rights altogether from capital ownership. Just as a citizen's right to vote is now independent of his ownership of property, so an employee's right to vote should be a personal right, independent of capital ownership.[253]

While the logic of this argument may be impeccable, it ignores existing political and economic realities and the absence of any significant pressure for fundamental change. Despite Ellerman's criticism and the intention of its originator, the ESOP concept has proved to be sufficiently flexible to potentially realise financial democracy within the individual firm.

Even on the assumption that employee shareholding remains substantial and continues to be widely dispersed among the entire workforce, there is nevertheless a deficiency in this micro approach to financial or economic democracy. Such an approach might tend to reinforce rather than alter the existing uneven distribution of wealth and power in the wider society. As the value of employees' dividends depends on company profitability, those employed in enterprises with a low or falling rate of profit would be at a disadvantage, possibly through no fault of their own. New groups of financially privileged and underprivileged workers might be created. Yet even firms under democratic control, unless monopolist, will remain creatures of unregulated market forces, as was the case with the Rath

Packing company. Furthermore, sources of investment or finance for such firms may be controlled by an unaccountable economic elite. The macro approach to financial democracy attempts to solve these problems by focusing on the distribution of wealth and power not only within the individual enterprise but throughout the whole of industry and society. An examination of this approach will be undertaken in the following chapters.

SUMMARY AND CONCLUSION

Kelso's theories or a desire to reform capitalism are of very minor importance in fostering the growth of ESOPs. These plans are less concerned with reformation than encouraging an acceptance of the free enterprise system. In America at any rate, the redundancy of such an endeavour is immediately apparent. Among the broad mass of the people, and within the labour movement, there seems to be a general acceptance of the business system. According to Okun, the bourgeois aspirations of the poor reveal the deeply ingrained market ethic of American society.[254] A hallmark of the American labour movement, despite occasional criticism of sharp business practice or monopoly, has been a willingness to accept capitalist premises and work within the system to maximise their members' interests.[255] The increase in the number of ESOPs can owe little to their supposed merit as a restorative or preservative of free enterprise.

Undoubtedly, generous tax concessions are the primary stimulus to the growth of ESOPs. For the closely traded employer these plans can provide cheaper capital, an in-house market for shares, an inexpensive pension benefit, or all three simultaneously. Who benefits is a question frequently asked concerning ESOPs. Where the plan is an additional rather than a substitute benefit, both employers and employees can be beneficiaries. Employers receive a tax concession and enhance their ability to attract and retain staff, while employees receive an additional and possibly in the long term valuable benefit. Usually only the large publicly traded corporation can afford this munificence. Yet the typical ESOP company is a small, closely traded concern with less than 500 employees. Consequently, the ESOP as an additional benefit over and above standard wage rates and pensions, is likely to be a rarity.

Even where these plans serve in lieu of a pension or compensate for wage cuts, union involvement in their negotiation can ensure a balanced trade-off. Employers benefit from installing a cheaper pension or paying reduced wages, while union members may have saved their jobs and gained substantial control over management decision making. However, not only are the majority of ESOP companies closely traded, they are also non-union. Unchecked by a union, the employer in this class of company becomes the main beneficiary of an ESOP, as the GAO report demonstrates. In these circumstances, the ESOP confers on employees beneficial ownership devoid of control and a high-risk pension benefit. For the employers, the ESOP provides an even cheaper and more flexible pension plan than one funded through profit sharing, greater liquidity and other potential benefits. The marked reluctance of organised workers to adopt an entrepreneurial role was noted in a previous chapter.[256] This was because it involved the introduction of uncertainty and flexibility into formerly fixed wages and benefits. Where employees are represented by a union, worker capitalism in the guise of the typical ESOP is likely to meet a similar reception.

The ESOP is an ambiguous benefit for the majority of employees. This ambiguity is very likely to affect its motivational potential adversely. Moreover, few employers have made a serious effort to establish the basic preconditions necessary for its success. Insufficient equity ownership and the general absence of employee voting rights further militates against the ESOP's motivational potential. After a review of the available literature and discussions with employees and company officials, the GAO investigators confessed they were unable to determine whether ESOPs improved employee motivation and productivity.[257] Apparently, the only tangible benefit of these plans may be to the employer struggling to hold down the cost of employee benefits. Ultimately the cost of ESOPs, an AFL-CIO economist argues, is borne by the taxpayer.[258] During 1979 the revenue forgone by the Exchequer due to ESOP tax concessions has been conservatively estimated at between 1.5 and 2.3 billion dollars.[259]

Further tax concessions granted in 1984, while generating another surge in the growth of these plans, represents a further reduction in revenue from taxation and thus increased their expense to the taxpayer. Earlier this year (1985), the treasury department proposed to eliminate the 1984 provisions along with other cuts in ESOP tax incentives. Senator Long and other members of the Senate Finance Committee have successfully blocked this proposal.[260] Yet the future of ESOPs and worker capitalism may be uncertain.

4 Economic democracy and the Swedish labour movement

Overweening economic power in the hands of one limits freedom for the other. A more egalitarian distribution of power and influence within the economic realm increases freedom there, in the same way that universal and equal suffrage did in the political realm.

Ernst Wigforss (1881–1977)
The foremost ideologist of Swedish social democracy[1]

No Swedish businessman can deny the socialists have made good tax laws for companies . . . . The Swedish tax system is one of the best in the world for companies . . . . Sweden's socialist governments have preserved a system of corporate taxation that might have been drafted by a company treasurer . . . . The socialist party is the party of business.

Opinions of Swedish businessmen in 1976[2]

Two previous chapters examined American profit sharing and employee shareholding as epitomising an individualist approach to economic democracy. The two chapters that follow will deal with the collective approach. In particular, the subject of this chapter is the controversial proposal of Rudolph Meidner, a Swedish trade union economist, for employee wage earner funds or collective profit sharing.

On the face of it there would appear to be little in common between the countries of Sweden and America. While America can be regarded as the archetypal capitalist country, Sweden for 44 years (1932–76) was governed by a socialist party. One observer of a monetarist persuasion has characterised Sweden as a socialist country.[3] Swedish Marxists, on the other hand, have claimed that social democratic policy has not only conserved but reinforced capitalism.[4] According to Lindbeck, it is anachronistic to characterise modern economic policy of the Swedish type as either capitalist or socialist.[5] Up to the mid-1970s, at any rate, there seemed to be few Swedish businessmen who believed they operated in a socialist economy. As a board member of the Swedish Employers Federation and chairman of two major companies remarked:

> Sweden is a funny country to call socialist. In France or Austria the government owns a much larger share of industry and I would expect that in a socialist country personal income taxes would be low and company taxes high, whereas in Sweden it is the opposite. It has the world's highest personal income taxes and it's a tax haven for companies.[6]

Until recently, there has probably been less publicly owned or nationalised industry in Sweden than any other west European country. In fact, 90 per cent of firms are privately owned.[7] It has been estimated that the concentration of share ownership among a comparatively tiny minority is greater in Sweden than in either Britain or the United States.[8]

Like America, Sweden can, with some qualification, be fairly described as a capitalist country. Admittedly, the prolonged dominance of the Social Democrats has created in Sweden the most highly developed example of welfare capitalism. Nevertheless, both countries, as capitalist democracies, despite varying degrees of welfare policy, union and reformist political action, exhibit a common contradiction. Alongside formal political equality, there persists inequality of wealth, and consequently power, concentrated in the hands of a few.

Some individuals or groups have been sufficiently disturbed by this imbalance to initiate corrective action. Yet the solutions adopted for a problem common to Sweden and America are fundamentally different. The American remedy epitomised by the Long/Kelso partnership is to broaden share ownership among citizens and employees. This is expected to mitigate the contradiction between political democracy and economic oligarchy: an expectation, some would argue, that will inevitably be disappointed. The dispersion of shares, it has been claimed, far from favouring a democratic development, strengthens the dictatorship of large capital owners.[9] American readiness to accept a possibly ineffective remedy for concentration can partly be ascribed to a strong tradition of individualism, a weak union movement with an almost exclusive focus on wages and conditions within the individual enterprise, and the absence of a socialist party. Additional factors of equal importance are the vastness of the continent and a large heterogeneous population. On all these points, exactly the opposite conditions prevail in Sweden. Not surprisingly, the Swedish remedy for concentration is based on the collective rather than the individual.

Yet these divergent approaches can probably be best explained by reference to the originating party. Employers or their managerial representatives in America (or, as will be seen, in Sweden, Denmark and Ireland) favour voluntarist schemes of employee shareholding confined to individual firms. European unions who take up the question of economic democracy generally favour collective profit sharing schemes, where a firm's contribution goes direct to a central fund largely controlled and administered by the labour movement.

One object of this and the following chapter will be to point out again the inadequacy of individualist schemes of employee shareholding as vehicles for the realisation of economic democracy. In debate, it will be seen, Swedish and Danish employers conceded as much. However, this admission did not deter employers advancing various schemes of individual employee shareholding as antidotes or system-maintaining alternatives to apparently revolutionary wage earner funds.

SCANDINAVIA AND COLLECTIVE PROFIT SHARING

Why should collective profit sharing, or wage earner funds, originate within the Scandinavian labour movement while development of a similar idea by its American counterpart is virtually inconceivable? The feebleness and continuing decline of American unionism, along with its acceptance of the dominant business ideology, are the obvious explanations. Evidence for this latter claim is provided by the unions' response to managerial schemes of employee shareholding. While technical details of the schemes were critically scrutinised, their underlying philosophy of economic individualism was not questioned.[10] The apparent success of American capitalism and its capacity for seemingly continuous expansion may have helped to stifle the development of an indigenous and popular socialist critique. Certainly, the developments in Europe after 1945 that challenged free market assumptions were much less pronounced in America. One commentator has seen these postwar developments as politicising areas of activity earlier regarded as the exclusive concern of the market.[11] Intervention through political and union channels in the process of income determination, he claims, has grown in importance.[12] A notable movement in this period, according to Goldthorpe, has been for citizenship rights to be further developed in the industrial sphere, e.g. rules governing redundancy, unfair dismissal, worker participation, etc. This extension of citizenship rights into the actual organisation of production, he suggests, raises new and very divisive issues concerning managerial prerogative and the basis of authority and responsibility within the enterprise.[13]

Any manifestation of these developments in America took on an innocuous and very attenuated form. Consequently, nineteenth-century schemes of individualist employee shareholding, at the peak of their popularity in the 1920s, could without incongruity be revived as practical policy. In Sweden, and somewhat less so in Denmark, the above developments had reached their furthest extent. It was in that context that wage earner funds, or economic democracy, became a feasible proposition with good prospects for its legislative enactment. Yet it was a committee appointed by Sweden's first social democratic government that initially formulated the demand for economic democracy.[14] A brief historical review of the Swedish labour movement will explain the proposal's prolonged gestation before its partial embodiment in contemporary legislation. Such a review will also show how schemes of employee shareholding scattered among groups of workers and firms – the epitome of economic individualism – clash on a theoretical and practical level with the collectivist orientation of the Swedish labour movement.

SWEDISH CAPITALISM, LABOUR AND THE HISTORIC COMPROMISE

Compared with other European countries, industrialisation came late to Sweden, though once take-off was achieved – in the early 1870s – economic growth was rapid and sustained.[15] This process stimulated the growth of organisations characteristic of many industrial societies. In 1889 the various socialist clubs coalesced to form the Social Democratic Party (Socialdemokratiska Arbetarepartiet – SAP). Initially, the party saw its main task as fostering the growth of a socialist trade union movement, and for a while these organisations were indistinguishable. However, the necessity of broadening the appeal of unionism to non-socialist workers led to a separation of the industrial and political wings of the labour movement with the establishment of the Swedish Trade Union Confederation (Landsorganisationen i

Sverige – LO), in 1898. Nevertheless, socialist ideology remained very influential and was instrumental in encouraging the LO Congress of 1912 to adopt industrial unionism. Furthermore, LO and SAP remained organisationally linked at local level. Indeed, the idea of a united movement whose political and industrial struggles were completely interdependent, was to remain deeply embedded in the ideology of the party and the LO at all levels. Writing in 1974, Elvander noted that at regional and local level, co-operation is so intimate and the amount of overlapping membership so great that it is sometimes impossible to distinguish trade union and political elements.[16]

Confrontation with a burgeoning union movement and the threat of a socialist party seeking greater economic and political equality through public ownership of the means of production, galvanised employers into action. In 1902 the Swedish Employers Confederation (Svenska Arbetsgivareforeningen – SAF) was established, and launched a counter-union offensive. Though there were some attempts to find a formula for mutual co-existence, they were less than successful. Up to the early 1930s Sweden had the highest levels of strikes and lockouts among European nations.[17] Yet from the mid-1930s there began a sharp decline in industrial strife that was to make Sweden, up to the late 1960s at any rate, a paragon of co-operative relations between capital and labour. This transformation Korpi ascribes to the political success of the Social Democrats and a corresponding decrease in the power resource difference between the two antagonists, forcing a reassessment of earlier strategies of conflict.[18]

In 1938 conciliatory speeches by the SAP minister of finance to stockbrokers and industrialists signalled a new departure in socialist strategy. It must be recognised, the minister argued, that neither the labour movement nor private capitalists could hope to suppress the other altogether. Consequently, both should co-operate to promote their common interest – greater efficiency in production.[19] Conciliation and compromise in the political sphere was paralleled in that of the industrial. In the same year, the LO and SAF hammered out a basic agreement at Saltsjobaden. This established a mutually agreed framework for the regulation of industrial conflict. Only wages and conditions, it was agreed, would be subject to negotiation. In essence, the LO had accepted paragraph 32 of SAF's constitution, which claimed that decisions concerning the organisation of work, or the hiring or firing of labour, were entirely a function of managerial discretion. According to one commentator, Saltsjobaden was to leave

Swedish workers with considerably less control in the workplace than their counterparts in other countries.[20]

Apparently, both wings of the labour movement were now agreed on the maintenance of the free enterprise system. Business was to be encouraged to invest and expand. Labour and capital were to co-operate in promoting economic growth, thus making the pie larger so there would be more to share. There had been a shift from a zero sum conflict to a positive sum or win-win strategy. The seed of the historic compromise had been sown which would mature and blossom in the postwar period.

THE HISTORIC COMPROMISE MATURES

With the return of peace, a move by SAP to revive traditional labour movement policy of nationalisation and economic planning roused a storm of opposition from the bourgeois parties.[21] The result was a reaffirmation of the prewar compromise which secured the dominance of market capitalism and free trade. Decision making in the sphere of production and the initiative to increase economic growth was left almost wholly to the representatives of capital. Distribution of the increasing product, according to the criteria of social justice, welfare policy and the maintenance of full employment, became the responsibility of the socialist government.

Committed to full employment, SAP was confronted by a classic dilemma. Labour scarcity would strengthen workers' bargaining power, pushing up wages in the more successful firms, resulting in inflation and increased inequality among wage earners. The LO devised a strategy to assist its ally in government.

There were three elements to the plan, or Rehn Model as it came to be called, adopted by the LO Congress of 1951.[22] First, the LO promised to consider the macro-economic effects of movements in wages and co-ordinate pay bargaining in accordance with a policy of wage solidarity. Essentially this sought equal pay for equal work, regardless of an employer's ability to pay, and a reduction in differentials between different types of work.[23] Solidarity wage policy was simultaneously expected to promote labour movement cohesion and standard wages by squeezing profits hardest in the least efficient firms, driving them from the market.[24] Second, a labour market policy was devised to rehabilitate casualties of wage solidarity. Displaced workers would be indemnified, retrained, and relocated to the most productive enterprises. Finally, there was a requirement to increase public sector saving. This was to offset an expected decline in business saving due to the profit squeeze. The combination of solidarity wage policy, a profits squeeze, and the growth in government share of saving was expected to reduce economic inequality and contibute to the labour movement's long-run egalitarian goals.

THE REHN MODEL – ITS IMPLEMENTATION

The success of any immediate implementation of the Rehn Model would have been extremely problematic. To govern, the Social Democrats were dependent on the Agrarians who were likely to oppose interventionism outside a recession. Also it was questionable if the LO could co-ordinate pay bargaining. However, at the request of SAF, the LO agreed to participate in centralised wage negotiations. Beginning in 1952, centralised wage agreements were continually renegotiated up to the 1980s.[25] According to one authority, these agreements amounted to a privately operated incomes policy.[26]

Without a high degree of centralisation within union and employer federations, effective national wage agreements would hardly have been possible. Indeed, the degree of autonomy surrendered by unions or employers to their executives, is greater, some observers have claimed, than would be acceptable in other countries.[27] Yet while the union movement participated in shaping national policy, its influence at plant level was very limited.

The establishment of centralised bargaining represented a partial implementation of the Rehn Model. Further advance was blocked by SAP's dependence on the Agrarians. When SAP, in response to LO pressure, attempted pension reform, the measure roused intense political controversy. In the subsequent election, the Social Democrats and Communists were returned with a tiny majority.[28] It was sufficient to legislate for pension reform.

A National Pension Fund, while primarily an employee benefit, also fulfilled another requirement of the Rehn Model, i.e. increased public sector saving. Furthermore, electoral success freed SAP from its dependence on the Agrarians, allowing the establishment of a Labour Market Board and the introduction of a sales tax. By the mid-1960s, the implementation of the LO strategy, or Rehn Model, was complete.

At this point, the achievements of the historic compromise were undoubtedly impressive. There had been a measurable improvement in the standard of living since the war. Social welfare provisions were unmatched by any other country in Europe. Though a high wage economy had developed, and unemployment remained low, the incidence of official strikes were the lowest among western nations. Working hours had been reduced from 48 to 40 and vacations had doubled in length to four weeks.[29] There were, however, some imperfections.

Admittedly, the solidarity wage policy was slowly eroding differentials.[30] The policy probably squeezed profits hardest in the least efficient firms, though it is difficult to discover if it forced the closure of any plant.[31] Yet, at the opposite end of the scale, highly profitable companies escaped with lower pay bills and higher profits than would have been the case if wage policy had operated on the principle of ability to pay. The existence of an untapped potential for wage increases tended to contradict the distributional policy of the labour movement – a tendency inadvertently exacerbated by SAP's pro-investment bias.

This arose from the government's attempt to control or dampen fluctuations in the business cycle and so maintain a consistently high level of employment. Corporations were allowed to deposit 40 per cent of their annual profits tax free in a blocked account at the national bank. These non-interest-bearing deposits could be reinvested only with the government's permission, otherwise the tax exemption was forfeit. Permission was usually forthcoming during an economic downturn.[32] A liberal tax regime for retained corporate earnings may have enhanced economic stability, but an unwanted side-effect was a stimulus to the concentration of wealth. The defects of wage and corporate taxation policy did not become generally apparent until the end of the 1960s.

THE WITHERING OF THE HISTORIC COMPROMISE

Beginning in the early 1960s the Swedish economy experienced intensified international competition. For Swedish industrial capital to maintain its market share, concentration in larger, more efficient firms was essential. The decade witnessed a fourfold increase in the number of mergers.[33] Greater capital intensity, competition and high wages combined to bring about a fall in the rate of profit and a corresponding decline in industrial investment. A 1970 long-term survey identified the provision of risk-bearing capital and measures to stimulate investment in private business as priorities of government economic policy.[34]

Nevertheless, concentration, rationalisation and more efficient work practices steadily increased industrial productivity.[35] Yet there was no corresponding increase in employment.[36] Initially, the LO gave complete support for rationalisation, though the extent, rate and intensity of subsequent change may have far exceeded its calculations. Within industry, increasing levels of absenteeism and labour turnover may have indicated discontent with deteriorating working conditions.[37] A government commission of 1968 found employees generally considered their work physically heavy, dirty, psychologically demanding, and the workplace atmosphere very bad. Greater dissatisfaction was expressed by LO members than the working class as a whole.[38] Blue collar workers, it seemed, were bearing the brunt of structural change, and given the weakness of union influence at plant level, there was little they could do to modify or control its course.

The emergence of the New Left in Sweden during this period of transformation and its criticisms of the labour movement may have partially articulated rank-and-file discontent. An increasingly bureaucratised labour movement, it claimed, no longer represented workers' interests.[39] Union observance of 'no strike' clauses in wage agreements and its acceptance of paragraph 32 of SAF's constitution was questioned. Whatever its original merits, leftists claimed the Saltsjobaden agreement now called for worker submission rather than mature co-operation, and the chief beneficiaries from its operation were employers.[40] Solidarity wage policy was disparaged as 'socialism in one class'.[41] Some radicals attacked the Social Democrats and the LO for not being true socialists but collaborators with capitalists and employers.[42] The finding of a 1968 government commission on industrial and economic concentration gave an edge to some of these criticisms.

THE COMMISSION ON INDUSTRIAL AND ECONOMIC CONCENTRATION 1968

The rapid increase in the number of mergers during the 1960s has already been noted. Not surprisingly, the commission found concentration in industry and commerce to be considerable, exceeding the levels attained in the US or West Germany. The proportion of the workforce employed by the 200 largest private companies had risen from 29 per cent in 1960 to 32 per cent by 1964.[43] Yet the two peaks of merger activity in the decade (1965 and 1969) had still to be reached.[44]

The commission estimated that 5–9 per cent of taxpayers, owned stocks or shares.[45] To illustrate the pattern of shareholding, 15 publicly quoted companies were selected. Within these companies, 0.1 per cent of shareholders held one-quarter, and 1 per cent held one-half of the share capital. Approximately 10–11 per cent of shareholders held three-quarters of the equity capital in these companies.[46] In a larger sample of 282 companies a single family, the Wallenbergs, had majority dominating or strong minority interests in companies with a total of 150,000 employees, accounting for 15 per cent of the total manufacturing value of industry. Seventeen groups of owners had majority dominating or strong minority interests in companies employing 400,000 and accounting for 36 per cent of total manufacturing value.[47] Comparisons with similar investigations in the US and Britain showed a greater concentration of share ownership in Swedish industry.[48] A more recent study would suggest such concentration has become more pronounced.[49]

At shareholders' meetings of about three-quarters of the companies quoted on the stock exchange, between one and three people held a majority of votes. In no quoted company were more than ten shareholders required to obtain a majority of votes.[50] If shareholders' meetings exercise any influence, then, the commissioners concluded: 'it is with only few exceptions exercised by a very small number of people, usually representing the interests of the largest shareholders who are often members of the board of directors.'[51]

Finally, the commission examined the distribution of income and wealth in society. Some extremely modest equalisation of income seemed to have occurred in the years preceding the early 1950s. Since then the distribution of income has remained more or less static.[52] Tax assessment statistics showed the distribution of wealth between 1945 and 1965 remained fairly stable and unequal.[53] The distributional policy pursued by the labour movement in its long tenure of office now appeared to have been largely ineffective. From a left-wing perspective, the findings of the 1968 commission could be construed as an indictment of social democratic postwar policy. Indeed, any Swede who shared Kelso's conviction that concentrated economic power threatened freedom and democracy would have been disturbed by the commission's disclosures.

RANK-AND-FILE REVOLT AND RE-ORIENTATION WITHIN THE LABOUR MOVEMENT

The adverse consequences of structural change were felt not only in the workplace but in the wider society.[54] Criticism from the radical left, the Liberal and Centre Parties (formerly the Agrarians) focused discontent on the Social Democrats. In the local elections of 1966, SAP received its sharpest electoral setback since the advent of universal suffrage.[55] Both SAP and the LO were quick to respond.

At the party Congress of 1967 the future prime minister, Olaf Palme, and the LO chairman, Arne Gieger, made notable speeches on the topic of social and economic inequality. Dynamic development, Gieger maintained, was a prerequisite for economic and social progress, but he continued:

> We must demand that the additional product created by us all is not used to widen the income gap . . . Inequality is documented not only in income statistics but also in social conditions in the labour market. Those with the lowest wage have also as a rule the longest hours, the worst environment, the dirtiest and heaviest jobs and also the highest age of retirement.[56]

In the general election of the following year, SAP was returned to power on a platform of 'greater equality'.[57] For the LO, its radicalisation or rediscovery of socialism proved to be altogether more traumatic and, therefore, probably more durable.

In December 1969, 40 workers at the nationalised iron ore mining works in northern Sweden took unofficial strike action. The strike rapidly spread throughout the ore field to become the biggest strike in Swedish postwar history. Initially the strikers sought improved wages and working conditions, the abolition of piece-rates and an end to an authoritarian style of management. As the strike progressed, a further demand was made for an open, directly democratic system of industrial relations, to prevent decisions being taken over the heads of workers.[58] Prolongation of the conflict, it has been suggested, was due more to differences between the unofficial strike committee and the union hierarchy than between strikers and the company.[59] For the LO, the strike was a direct challenge to its authority and the policy of centralisation pursued since the 1950s.

Rather than an isolated act of defiance, the miners' strike triggered a burst of wildcat or unofficial actions shattering the fabled calm of Sweden's labour market. Of the 216 strikes in 1970, all were unofficial. In the following year, 93 per cent of strikes were illegal.[60] The LO appeared to have lost control over its affiliates and general membership.

The most plausible explanations for the wave of unofficial strikes between 1969 and 1971 have been advanced by Korpi: first, the erosion of wage increases by inflation; second, the deterioration in working conditions; finally, as protests against an increasingly authoritarian exercise of managerial prerogative.[61] In any event, it was essential for the LO to re-establish its authority if the cohesion of the labour movement was to be maintained. To this end, and as a solution to members' discontent, the LO espoused a revitalised solidarity wage policy – economic and industrial democracy.

These were hardly novel proposals. Industrial democracy had been part of the labour movement's programme since the 1920s. The LO Congress of 1966 had appointed a committee to report to the future 1971 Congress on industrial democracy. Proposals for collective profit sharing, or a wage earners' fund, had been heard at LO Congresses in the 1950s and 1960s.[62] Now, however, various factors such as rank-and-file unrest, leftist criticism, and the disclosures of the Committee on Industrial and Economic Concentration combined to suggest the appropriate moment had arrived for the implementation of such measures. At about this time too, a new generation more receptive to these ideas came to power within the LO.[63]

THE LO CONGRESS 1971 – INDUSTRIAL AND ECONOMIC DEMOCRACY

The programme of industrial democracy adopted by Congress in 1971 aimed to bring the whole range of managerial decisions at all levels of the enterprise within the scope of collective bargaining. However, paragraph 32 of SAF's constitution barred the way to greater local union power. Managers were prepared to go some way to allay shopfloor discontent as the famed work reorganisation projects at Saab and Volvo testify. Yet they wished to retain the initiative and ultimate power to decide what could, and what could not, be done.[64] Consequently, employers were unwilling to relinquish paragraph 32 voluntarily. The LO had no option but to call on its ally in government to legislate for the abolition of managerial prerogative.

Once SAP accepted the LO programme of industrial democracy, its embodiment in labour legislation was remarkably rapid. The laws laid down in the previous 60 years governing relations in the labour market were almost entirely replaced between 1972 and 1978.

Board representation for employees 1973

This act gave employees of companies with more than 50 workers the right to elect two representatives to the board of directors. Amending legislation of 1976 extended the application of the earlier act to companies with 25 or more employees.[65]

Act on shop stewards 1974

This gave union stewards better employment security and strengthened their position in the workplace. They were also allowed time off in pursuit of union business.[66]

Work safety law 1974

This granted the elected safety steward the right to halt any process he or she regarded as dangerous, pending judgement from a state safety inspector. The law introduced the principle that the union view of a disputed matter should prevail. Thus the prerogative of interpretation was transferred from the employer to the union, totally reversing traditional practice. Employers were obliged to give advance warning of contemplated changes in plant layout, equipment or employment conditions. Their implementation could be forestalled by the safety steward.[67]

Security of Employment Act 1974

This act obliged employers to justify objectively the dismissal of any employee. In cases of disputed dismissal, the employee in question retains his or her job with unchanged benefits until adjudication by the labour court. Also, employees were entitled to receive from one- to six-months' notice of termination of employment. The necessary minimum period of notice varied with the age of employee. Finally, the act contained a set of rules governing the order of layoffs in the event of insufficient work.[68]

Act on employee participation in decision making 1977

It was this piece of legislation affecting the formal abolition of managerial prerogative regarding hiring, firing and direction of work that laid the axe to the root of the historic compromise. All matters, the act ruled, affecting relations between employer and employee, including the process and results of production, became subject to collective bargaining. On request, a union must be given access to books, accounts and all relevant documents bearing on the company's operations. Management was obliged to initiate negotiations pending any change in operation such as reorganisation, expansion or contraction of the business. Only in disputed wage issues was the prerogative of interpretation to be retained by employers, but then only for a limited period. If the parties could not reach agreement, the matter was to be referred to the labour court.[69]

Opinions differ as to the significance of the above legislation, but particularly with regard to the 1977 act. Social Democratic Prime Minister Palme has described this act as 'the most important piece of Swedish legislation since the enactment of universal suffrage'.[70] Others maintain changes have been few and small. The ordinary employee, it is claimed, cannot see any changes in his work situation connected with the act.[71] Overall, the legislation was welcomed by unions, though these measures alone, some believed, were insufficient for increased wage earner influence.[72] While it would be premature to draw any definitive conclusion, taken together the enactments between 1972 and 1978 appear to open up the possibility for a significant redistribution of workplace power.[73] In that event, the LO will have strengthened local union power without weakening its authority at the national level.

ECONOMIC DEMOCRACY

While industrial democracy reforms may have been a partial solution for problems encountered at enterprise level, other difficulties confronted the labour movement on a macro level. A report on wage policy to the 1971 Congress identified some of these problems. Wage drift in highly profitable firms, it warned, undermined the policy of wage solidarity and labour movement unity. A way had to be found, it urged, to skim off surplus or excess profits in these firms and so reduce their margin for paying more than the agreed rate.[74] The union movement was also conscious of the wide measure of inequality existing throughout society. The LO, the report announced, had become increasingly concerned with the problem of redistribution, not only of income but over the entire social field.[75] Finally, as already noted, there was the continuing decline in investment which had to be reversed if Swedish industry was to remain internationally competitive.

The necessity for increased investment was largely accepted by Congress delegates, but with important qualifications. A motion from the Metal Workers' Union rejected conventional financing of investment because it increased the concentration of wealth and power in the hands of a few. Only investment that did not exacerbate the maldistribution of wealth would be acceptable.[76] Other resolutions demanded that the LO act to bring excess profits in the most expansive sectors of industry under the control of wage earners.[77] The huge National Pension Funds – already a source of loan capital – would, it was now decided, also provide some equity capital to industry. A fourth pension fund was established expressly for that purpose.[78] However, this left the problems of wage policy and inequality unsolved. Congress authorised a group headed by Rudolph Meidner to work out a proposal that would simultaneously solve these problems.

The Meidner Plan

The task of Meidner and his associates was to work out a plan of redistribution that would accomplish three objectives:

1 To complement or reinforce the wage policy based on the principle of solidarity.
2 To counteract the concentration of wealth stemming from self-financing.
3 To increase the influence that employees have over the economic process.[79]

Yet the eventual shape and operation of the plan was subject to certain restrictions. First, it must not conflict with the central trade union demand for full employment. A high level of capital formation is an important prerequisite for the realisation of this aim. Therefore, the proposal could not aggravate the problem of providing investment. Second, it had to be neutral with respect to costs, wages and prices, all potential sources of inflation.[80] Combined, these preconditions and objectives ruled out as solutions a higher rate of corporation tax or profit sharing schemes confined to individual companies.

Higher corporation tax rejected

Increased wealth among the owners of capital was, Meidner admitted, an unwanted result of fiscal measures to stimulate private investment. Likewise, direct government assistance to firms as part of industrial and employment policy accentuated maldistribution. Yet, he pointed out, investment decisions in Swedish industry, overwhelmingly privately owned, are made by private individuals chiefly interested in profitability.[81] Consequently, it is illusory to imagine that a higher rate of corporation tax can achieve major redistributive gains without hindering government promotion of growth and full employment. While some increase in the rate of corporation tax is always possible, it can never be increased to the extent that self-financing and the accompanying growth of wealth in the hands of asset owners, becomes impossible. The labour movement must accept, he urges, that profit and self-financing are necessary features of a growth economy.[82]

Instead of stiffer corporation tax, Meidner proposed that employees share in increasing wealth through the gradual allocation of profit to a central fund owned and administered by themselves. This would avoid the damaging effect of progressive taxation on profits and the adverse distributive consequences of government investment incentives. In addition, a fund system would enable employees to achieve greater influence within industry.[83]

Company profit sharing plans rejected

As a method of achieving the above objectives, profit sharing schemes confined to individual firms were rejected on economic and ideological grounds. Given differing levels of profitability, company PS schemes would likely create new disparities in income, undermining wage solidarity.[84] Furthermore, Meidner argued, such schemes – encouraging enterprise consciousness or cohesion among small groups – would be at variance with the broad socio-economic perspective of the labour movement.[85]

Meidner also faulted company PS schemes on economic criteria. Every PS system, he claimed, involved funds being removed from the enterprise and transferred with or without an interval to employees. This represented a cost to the firm equivalent to a wage increase and could be used to justify higher prices.[86] Furthermore, granting an employee the right to dispose of his profit share was a doubtful benefit, Meidner insisted, not only to the individual but to the whole community, because it represented a drain on resources. It cannot be overemphasised, he remarks, that the portion of growing assets which accrue to employees must remain as working capital within the enterprise. This would avoid a drain on company revenue and ensure continuing influence for employees on economic decision making. Therefore, individual or group withdrawals from the capital of the proposed employee investment fund would only frustrate its object and must be prohibited. In making this a fundamental requirement, Meidner disclaimed any authoritarian intention to limit the individual's free right of disposal in favour of a bureaucratically governed group. It was a choice, he insisted, not between the individual's right to dispose of his profit share and collective power, but between illusory and real profit sharing.[87]

This conviction of Meidner has received support from an unlikely quarter. An employers' group investigating the question concluded:

> If capital or profit sharing systems are to be an effective instrument for creating a broader distribution of wealth and increasing employee influence in companies, some sort of fund must be built up and limits must be placed on the rights of individuals to cash in their shares.[88]

Share ownership and its distribution, Meidner insisted, was more than a question of social justice. It was also a matter of ensuring employees have a greater say in shaping economic and industrial policy. He referred those who advocated broadening individual share ownership as a way of increasing the influence of the small shareholder to the Committee on Industrial and Economic Concentration.

That report demonstrated that despite the presence of thousands of small shareholders, most Swedish companies are dominated by one to three major shareholders.[89] A more recent example would suggest little has changed in the interim. Of the 52,300 shareholders in Electrolux, 92 per cent own fewer than 500 shares.[90] As an antidote for economic oligarchy, or as a way of making industry truly democratic, spreading share ownership, Meidner concludes, scarcely merits even being termed a sham solution.[91]

A wage earner's investment fund – its operation

Meidner proposed that 20 per cent of pre-tax profits in certain firms be annually transferred to a central employee wage earner fund.[92] Publicly owned enterprises and consumer co-operatives were exempt from this requirement because neither facilitate the concentration of wealth among a few shareholders. Furthermore, Meidner believed, transferring a public company to employee ownership, from the citizens as a whole to a particular group, would be a retrograde step. Likewise, he was opposed to any alteration of ownership structure in consumer co-operatives which were already expressions of economic democracy.[93] Of the remaining companies, only those with 50 or more employees would be obliged to allocate 20 per cent of their profit to the fund.[94] Out of a total number of 250,000 companies, Meidner estimated that about 4,000, or 1.7 per cent, would be affected by his proposal.[95]

The central fund

Though less than 33 per cent of the workforce would be employed by eligible profit sharing firms, the operation of the fund was to benefit all workers collectively.[96] Consequently, the various profit sharing contributions were to pass initially to a central equalisation or clearing fund. These contributions were to be in the form of particular company shares, their number being equivalent to the cash value of the profit sharing levy.[97] Thus, the issue of wage earner shares would allow capital to remain within the production circuit, having no adverse consequences for company liquidity.

Directors of this central or clearing fund were to be appointed by the national unions. Smaller unions and those with many small firms in their jurisdiction, Meidner recommended, should be over-represented.[98] Essentially, the fund was to function as an administrative centre, allocating dividend income derived from its shareholdings. The money was to be spent in two ways. Half was to be used for the purchase of shares from companies already participating in the scheme. Purchases would only take place in the event of such companies issuing new shares. Participation in rights issues was crucial if the wage earner fund was to maintain its existing proportion of equity capital in the company.[99]

The remainder of dividend income was to be used for the provision of research and educational services to all local unions and the boards of sector funds. Success of employee funds, according to Meidner, depended on raising the educational level among those who would eventually assume part of the functions of ownership. Education, he believed, was also the most effective counter to bureaucratic unionism and could close the gap between full-time officials and the rank-and-file.[100] Finally, improved educational services could assist workers in maximising the benefits of recent labour law reforms.

Sector funds and local employee influence

While the central fund administered dividend income, it could not vote shares. Yet an important object of the fund proposal was to increase employee influence over the economic process. This could be achieved, it was decided, through representation on the company board of directors. The proportion of labour representatives on the board would depend on the extent of central fund shareholding in the individual company. However, in electing directors, shareholder

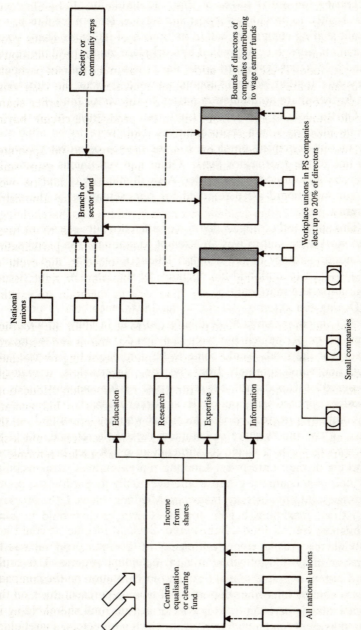

Figure 4.1 LO proposal for wage earner investment fund

Source: R. Meidner, *Employee Investment Funds. An Approach to Collective Capital Formation*, p. 104

franchise was to be shared between an industry or sector fund and local unions in profit sharing companies.

During the initial stages of share accumulation, the sector fund was limited to providing support and services for worker directors in profit sharing companies within its branch of industry. These board members were to be appointed by workplace unions until the central fund held 20 per cent of the particular company's total equity capital. Beyond this point, power to appoint additional worker directors based on further share accumulation passed to the sector fund.[101]

On the board of the sector fund itself, a majority of seats were to be filled by union representatives. Half were to be appointed by unions organising employees in the branch of industry covered by one of the four sector funds. Other national unions outside the industry appointed the remainder. A small minority of seats on each sector fund board were reserved for representatives of the public interest.[102]

This apparently complex division of influence between sector funds and workplace unions was an attempt to maintain the broad socio-economic strategy of the Swedish labour movement, and simultaneously satisfy rank-and-file demands of the late 1960s for decentralisation and more control.

During the autumn of 1975, some 18,000 members (1 per cent) of LO unions examined Meidner's proposal in study groups, and their views of the scheme were canvassed. Only a few expressed fears that the funds would come to be dominated by full-time officials and ruled remotely from the top. Nevertheless, a majority favoured local appointment of representatives for company boards.[103] Meidner opposed a pronounced local worker emphasis in the selection of company directors. Board members who are appointed on the basis of the fund's share of company capital, he argued, ought to be responsible to a wider constituency of employees beyond those working in their enterprise. Limiting representatives' responsibility to their own company group would eventually jeopardise the policy of wage solidarity. In many instances, Meidner believed, the pressure to extract maximum benefit for one's own group would become irresistible.[104]

While eschewing the development of a self-centred enterprise consciousness, it was essential that individual employees feel the fund system operated to make their workplace more democratic. Yet it was equally important that all employees experience the funds as democratising decision making concerning macro-economic change. The sharing of fund influence on company boards between workplace unions and sector funds was the resultant compromise. Possibly, to reassure sceptics, it was decided that appointment to company boards by workplace unions or sector funds could be vetoed by either party.[105]

Wage earner funds, Meidner claimed, were only one of the instruments deployed by democratic socialism to create a better society for the majority of people.[106] They would provide an opportunity to democratise those decisions which are taken within enterprises, but affect a firm's relationship with consumers, local authorities, the environment and the whole community. Meidner envisaged the funds as a new stratum of democracy lying somewhere between government industrial policy on one hand, and labour law providing for co-determination within companies on the other.[107]

Other advantages of the fund system were more pragmatic. Solidarity wage policy could now be pursued free of its hitherto maldistributive aspect. The greater a firm's profit, the faster would wage earner shares accumulate in the fund. Thus wage restraint by workers in the most profitable companies would not benefit private owners.[108] Similarly, industrial self-financing and government incentives for capital formation would become more acceptable, as part of growing assets would accrue to employees collectively.

In conclusion, Meidner reflected on previous receptions accorded to proposals for reform. It is a familiar pattern, he remarked, that a reformist proposal such as that for employee investment funds is distrusted by social revolutionaries as a defence of the old class order, and by conservatives as a social revolution.[109] Events were to prove it a prescient observation.

The reception of the Meidner Plan

Meidner and his colleagues published a first draft of their proposal in 1975. As a result of the study campaign and consultation with a sample of LO union's rank-and-file, some alterations were made. A majority of members sampled (91.6 per cent) were opposed to company-based profit sharing schemes – instead many (94.6 per cent) favoured a collective use for such funds.[110] There was less unanimity on other aspects of the proposal. As has been seen, a compromise was worked out on the extent of local employee influence. However, the minimum size of firms to be included in the scheme now became an open question. Fund policy and procedure regarding foreign multinationals operating in Sweden remained vague. Nevertheless, the modified report was accepted in principle by the LO Congress of

1976.[111] Congress left development of the technical details necessary for the practical implementation of the plan to a government commission on wage earner funds appointed in the previous year.

THE SOCIAL DEMOCRATS (SAP)

The existence of a commission was no happy accident. Indeed, it had been established by the Social Democrats to postpone temporarily a definitive party decision on the funds.[112] Various circumstances combined to promote a policy of equivocation. First, the proposal had been exclusively developed within the LO. There had been unusually little contact or consultation with SAP.[113] On publication, its apparent novelty evoked a divided party response. Many of its aspects were unclear, its long-term economic effects uncertain, and the reconciliation of union power in firms with national economic policy decided at the political level was, for some party members, problematic.[114] Second, the LO proposal seemed critical of traditional labour movement strategy. It was no longer sufficient, it implied, simply to manage capitalism humanely. Rather, it placed the issues of power and ownership of the means of production on the political agenda, and produced a plan to change gradually the uneven relationship between capital and labour. The party had striven to avoid confrontation on these issues since the 1930s.[115] Now SAP was caught in a cleft stick.

Repudiation of the LO proposal would involve for SAP the loss of an invaluable electoral ally. Furthermore, such unprecedented action would arouse intense opposition within the party itself as a retreat from its recent radicalisation. Though it contained no specific proposal for its attainment, economic democracy was an important goal of the new party programme adopted in 1975.[116] Yet open support for the Meidner Plan seemed likely to cost the party dearly in the forthcoming general election. Already, publication of the draft proposal had triggered tumultuous reactions. It had been characterised by Hans Werthen, chairman of Electrolux, as the biggest confiscation ever seen in the western world.[117] The Communist Party dismissed the plan because it was based on the old capitalist relations of production and did not change the class hierarchy in society.[118] In short, the LO proposal had sparked off an intense debate on socialism and socialisation, similar to the planned economy controversy of the late 1940s or the pension dispute of a decade later. As a device to remove wage earner funds from the arena of electoral politics and quell the uproar, the government commission was not a success.

Opposition to the fund proposal from the business community and the Conservative Party continued up to the eve of the 1976 autumn general election. The result ended a 44-year tenure of office for the Social Democrats. According to one observer, the fund proposal and the ensuing debate were the main reasons for the socialist defeat.[119] A contention rejected by the LO Congress of the following year, which reaffirmed the union's goal of 'employee participation in the profits they create'.[120] Data examined by Korpi from pre- and post-1976 election surveys tend to favour the LO view. The Social Democrats' commitment to the use of nuclear energy and some well-publicised scandals within the party were the crucial factors influencing voter choice.[121] Apparently, wage earner funds were of minor importance in the defeat of SAP.

The fund debate conducted during the election campaign probably generated more heat than light. Yet it would be unfair to assume that opponents of the measure were simply content with strident condemnation. Various individuals and groups considered the Meidner Plan in detail and some advanced counter-proposals.

THE RESPONSE OF THE TCO (TJANSTEMANNENS CENTRALORGANISATION)

Influenced by the debate in Denmark, the TCO or Congress of white collar trade unions took up the question of wage earner funds three years before the publication of Meidner's draft proposal. Since 1972 Congress has published five discussion documents on the topic but up to the present time has refrained from making any official announcement of its position. Yet the TCO shares many of the LO concerns. It would be equally anxious to mitigate the maldistributive aspect of solidarity wage policy, increase employee influence within firms and check the concentration of wealth. Like the LO, the white collar Congress has rejected individual company PS schemes as an ineffective method for achieving these objectives. Instead, the TCO would appear to favour some form of collective PS – any difference with the LO being one of emphasis. A primary objective for wage earner funds in the earlier TCO report was to increase investment and capital formation. In later discussion documents this objective has been combined with those of the LO.

Given there is broad agreement between both Congresses on a fund system, how can the subsequent vacillation of the TCO be explained? Unlike the LO, membership of the white collar unions is not politically homogeneous. Approximately 48 per cent of TCO members support SAP, while the remainder divide their loyalties between the three bourgeois parties. As the fund debate continued, positions on the measure became more polarised. Eventually, all three bourgeois parties, Conservative, Liberal and Centre, united in opposition to any proposal for collective funds. In these circumstances, a decision on the funds might have seriously strained TCO unity. Congress postponed taking any decision on the issue until after the general election of 1985.[122]

SOME ECONOMISTS AND THE MEIDNER PLAN

Ingemar Stahl, Professor of Economics at Lund University, was critical of the Meidner Plan because of its potentially damaging effect on the shareholders' function and private investment. Stahl views shareholders as risk takers and allocators of capital, whose remuneration is totally dependent on profit. While the returns to employees and creditors are regulated by contract, shareholders accept a high degree of uncertainty and fluctuation in income. The risk borne by employees or creditors is limited to the collapse of the enterprise. Shareholders, on the other hand, experience every vicissitude in the fortunes of the firm. Yet their willingness to accept the residue after all other contracts within, and external to, the firm have been satisfied, is the guarantee of security for these contracts.[123] However, Stahl warns, the shareholder's role is only sustainable under certain conditions. First, that no other party within the enterprise can acquire sufficient power to affect the allocation of dividends. Second, there must be no obligation to share systematically the residue or profit with other groups while the risk of loss is exclusively confined to shareholders. A gradual takeover of equity capital by wage earner funds would negate both conditions.[124]

Another shareholder function is the allocation of resources between different companies, industries and regions. This allocation, or investment, is decided on the criterion of profitability. As shareholders' income is determined by profit, it is only natural, Stahl asserts, that the assessment of profitability is closely linked to capital ownership.[125] For other parties 'i.e., employees', such conditions of remuneration would normally be unacceptable. Furthermore, he maintains, they lack the capacity to initiate the type of resource reallocation required for a co-ordinated profitability prospective.[126] Yet the effective performance of this shareholder function is again conditional. The owners of equity capital must exercise a unified influence within the company so they can forcefully impress upon all groups the importance of profitability in any investment decision. Also, shareholders must be reasonably independent of political pressure from above and from that of local interests from below. Profit sharing systems, whether collective schemes of the Meidner type or ones that issue shares to individual employees, violate these conditions and so are damaging to the shareholder's functions outlined above. Therefore, it is suggested, both should be avoided.[127]

Professor Stahl's picture of the shareholder as heroic risk taker may be overdrawn and more applicable to early nineteenth-century capitalism. Today it is common practice for shareholders to minimise their risk through a portfolio of diversified holdings. A poor return on investment in one enterprise may be more than compensated by high profits in another. In these circumstances, a company collapse might involve a greater loss for its employees than its individual shareholders. Again Stahl's fear that employee shareholders will conflict with, or distort the function of, conventional company shareholders may be exaggerated. In the US for instance, one motive for the introduction of PS and employee stock ownership plans is the belief they will improve company profitability. Admittedly, many American schemes neutralise any potential conflict between employee shareholders and other equity owners through management retention and exercise of employee voting rights. Yet even where employee shareholders are enfranchised, their combined shareholding is usually insignificant and on any disputed investment decision, their influence would be negligible.

Regarding the operation and consequences of a collective PS fund, Professor Stahl's apprehension is more solidly grounded. Undoubtedly, were the Meidner Plan introduced, it would come in time to limit traditional shareholders' discretion. Indeed, others along with Stahl have warned of its negative effect on the private individual's propensity to invest.[128] While these warnings have been characterised by Meidner as painful reactions to the prospect of power and ownership changes in industry, he does allow the possibility of an investment strike.[129] Meidner was confident such a development could be countered, but many participants in the LO study campaign were less sanguine.[130] The government commission on wage earner funds has examined the likely effect of their introduction on the stock market. Its investigation was inconclusive. Share values, it found, would decline in certain companies, while in others they were likely to remain stable or increase.[131]

PROFESSOR ASSAR LINDBECK – HEAD OF THE INSTITUTE FOR INTERNATIONAL ECONOMIC STUDIES, UNIVERSITY OF STOCKHOLM

Professor Lindbeck was critical of the Meidner Plan on three counts. First, he believed its implementation would undermine Sweden as a pluralist society. The LO plan is designed to counteract the concentration of ownership and power. Yet its long-term operation, Lindbeck claimed, would result in a more extreme form of power concentration. A number of company owners would be replaced by one owner – the trade union. How decentralised decision making might be within the union was, he claimed, irrelevant – the important point being that power and ownership would pass to a single organisation. This would violate Lindbeck's cardinal principle of pluralism – that no single organisation should dominate society.[132]

The spectre raised by Lindbeck of a trade union state has been dismissed by Meidner. He claims that not only is such a development improbable, but unions have given assurances that this is neither intended nor desired. Even when employee funds take indirect responsibility for running a considerable part of the economy, they would, like other economic decision makers, be subject to the primacy of political control and the will of the people embodied in Parliament. The interests of employees, Meidner was convinced, would prove easier to reconcile with socio-political aims than those of large capital owners.[133] Other considerations might weaken the force of Lindbeck's objection. Many small, privately owned firms, co-operatives and state companies would not be touched by the LO's proposal. Also, the funds provide substantial decentralisation of decision making, aiming to balance employee influence and interest at enterprise level with those of other unions and community representatives at industry level.

Another of Lindbeck's contentions which has figured prominently in the fund debate is that the implementation of the LO proposal would destroy the trade unions and their traditional role in collective bargaining. The principal function of unionism, he argues, is to protect wage earners' interests against companies, employer organisations and the state. Under the Meidner Plan, unions would become the dominant owners of equity capital and, in effect, the new employer's federation. Unions would now negotiate wage agreements for their members in companies which they owned and controlled.[134]

The suggestion that the fund would impose an insupportable dual role on unionism evoked an irritated response from its spokesmen.

Many of those, it was pointed out, who now worried about the debilitating effect of the fund on unionism were normally opposed to a strong union movement.[135] Indeed it was Lindbeck's conviction that unions in many European countries were now so strong that they threatened to dominate these societies.[136] None the less, the introduction of a fund system appeared to involve some change or enlargement in the union's traditional role. As Gunnar Nillsson, chairman of the LO remarked, 'Obviously, we can't maintain private capitalism just in order to preserve the present relationships between capital and labour.'[137]

Meidner, however, believed the fund would not demand a radical reorientation for unions, but merely an extension or development of existing practice. There was no feeling within the unions, he claimed, of being threatened by a conflict of loyalty or of serving a dual role if a fund system were introduced. This was because the Swedish trade union movement had long since transcended the narrow limits of an interest organisation and already played a dual role. With a large membership and decades of co-operation with the ruling political party, the union movement was simultaneously representative of the general interest and the group interest. Union wage policy was pursued at the national level, taking the whole economy for its orientation. The economic and socio-political aims of the movement were determined not by the egotistical wishes of a group, but by policies relating to the whole society. It would be a denigration of the tasks and significance of the Swedish union movement, Meidner asserted, if its existence were to be regarded as dependent on the continuance of capitalist employers.[138]

Despite these indignant protests, Meidner did allow that tensions would arise if employees and their organisations took on new functions and responsibilities through co-ownership of the means of production. Yet he was confident a strong and ideologically consolidated union movement could cope. Though performing a dual role, the union would continue to protect employee interests against employers – irrespective of who exercised this function. This would be achieved by the existence of two separate bodies – one dealing with fund administration, the other representing employee interests in the workplace.[139] An additional assurance that employee interests would continue to be effectively represented might be the industrial democracy reforms designed to strengthen shopfloor power introduced during the 1970s.

Yet the fears for unionism expressed by Lindbeck and others, though possibly disingenuous, are not entirely without foundation.

Similar apprehensions have been entertained by American labour unions confronted by schemes promoting employee ownership. Though American unions were necessarily required to go beyond their normal adversarial role, employee ownership did not apparently condemn them to irrelevance or encompass their destruction. In some instances, new employee owners felt a greater need for a union presence within their firms. There is, of course, a big difference between ownership by individual employees and collective ownership by the unions. Though weak and in decline, with a perspective focused on the workplace, American unions appear to have contained the challenge of employee ownership. Meidner's confidence then – that a much stronger Swedish union movement with a broad social economic and political perspective can successfully meet the greater challenge of collective ownership – may not be displaced.

Finally, Lindbeck was critical of the fund system for its likely stultifying effect on a free enterprise economy. Economic growth in developed western countries, he argues, has mainly arisen through the efforts of entrepreneurial individuals and not by government order or central planning. Innovative economic developments have been possible only because private individuals have been relatively free to embody their ideas in a profit making concern.[140] One basic precondition for the success of such initiatives, Lindbeck claims, is a pluralistic administration of capital, or the existence of a decentralised capital market. A variety of independent owners and administrators of capital will facilitate entrepreneurial acquisition of finance for new projects. However, a centralised administration of capital dominated by the state or, in the case of the fund proposal, the trade unions – would tend to impede or stifle such initiatives, mainly because new enterprises, products and production methods often disturb the system, i.e., they threaten established producer interests. Economies without a decentralised capital market, Lindbeck warns, risk reaching a stage where energetic and creative individuals can no longer take the initiative.[141]

Another drawback of union control of equity capital, Lindbeck implied, was the limited nature of unionism's perspective. This was apparently the result of labour being remunerated through the wage contract.[142] It was essential, therefore, that some body existed with the responsibility for maintaining a satisfactory return on capital invested. As has been seen, a similar point was made by Professor Stahl, and he was convinced private shareholders were best fitted to perform this function. In the absence of some such group, Lindbeck feared, there would be little to prevent the allocation of capital to prestige projects, to companies run by personal friends, colleagues and political associates, or companies kept in business without justifiable reason.[143]

The weakness of the above arguments against employee investment funds is their reliance on some questionable assumptions. For instance, the assumption that private initiative provided the main impetus for western industrialisation and economic growth may only hold good for Britain and America. From the beginning, industrialisation in Continental Europe, it has been claimed, was a political imperative.[144] Whatever may be argued about nineteenth-century industrialisation, it is undeniable that postwar European economic growth has largely resulted from an alliance between government and industry. Again, Lindbeck assumes a decentralised capital market is a prerequisite for the realisation of innovative entrepreneurial initiative which state or union control of the capital market would tend to smother. Yet innovation and economic growth has continued in Sweden despite a very high concentration of capital among a small minority of private owners. As will be seen, Lindbeck's proposal for citizen funds was designed to counter not only the Meidner Plan but also the excessive concentration of capital in the Swedish economy. Thus, in the obvious absence of a decentralised capital market, implementation of the LO proposal would involve little change beyond the transfer of ownership and control from a small group of private owners to the trade union movement. Furthermore, is it always the case that state control, or at least involvement, in the supply of risk capital will stifle private initiative? Indeed, it could be argued that such involvement has now become a necessity.

In many western countries there has been a long-run tendency for the supply of capital from individual private investors to decline. Admittedly, this has been offset to some extent by the growth of institutional investment. These institutions, however, generally pursue a conservative investment policy and avoid untried projects. The onerous requirements associated with many bank loans may place them beyond the reach of the aspiring entrepreneur. In these circumstances the state may be the only available source of risk capital. The Irish government, through the agency of the Industrial Development Authority, has financed the initiatives of many entrepreneurs unable to raise capital from conventional sources. Again, the establishment of the fourth National Pension Fund was an attempt by the Swedish trade union movement to compensate for declining investment.

Both Professors Stahl and Lindbeck believe the limited perspective of labour necessitates the existence of a separate independent group primarily interested in return on investment and profit. Union control of investment, they suggest, might result in nepotism or a misallocation of resources. Yet the Swedish union movement at any rate has long since moved beyond an exclusive concern with wages and conditions at the individual workplace. This is evident from the postwar history of the movement. Even so, Meidner recognised that employee investment funds would impose additional responsibilities on unions, hence his emphasis on education.[145] Any tendency to nepotism was likely to be checked by the division of influence between unions in particular firms and those on industry fund boards.

Nevertheless, given Stahl and Lindbeck's investment criteria, union control of capital could very well result in its misallocation. This is not to deny the evidently responsible nature of Swedish unionism. Indeed, it is very likely that profit and return on capital would figure as important considerations in any of its investment decisions. However, other considerations, such as the maintenance or creation of employment, might also influence such decisions. Therefore, as strict union adherence to orthodox investment criteria cannot be guaranteed, capital misallocation could result.

From a purely economic viewpoint, the Stahl/Lindbeck investment criteria are unquestionably sound. Yet the feasibility of their consistent and rigorous application in economies operating within a democratic political framework is doubtful. During Sweden's economic crisis (1976–80) the governing bourgeois parties, despite their evident commitment to free enterprise, brought more failing industries under state control than had been achieved in the preceding 44 years of Social Democrat rule.[146] Difficulties in reconciling the operation of a free market with political democracy are not exclusive to Sweden. A recent British attempt to solve the problem by removing political constraints on market forces seems likely to founder. Thus, in modern western economies, the putative investment criteria of the unions may be the more pragmatic or realistic.

In one respect, the Stahl/Lindbeck concern with a union investment policy is something of a red herring. Under the original Meidner Plan, the funds were simply to hold shares in participating enterprises. Any future investment or share purchase by the fund would be confined to these companies. Consequently the importance or necessity for a union investment policy is not apparent. It was only when capital formation became an additional objective of later fund proposals, that the issue of investment policy arose. Finally, the central weakness of the Stahl/Lindbeck critique is its ideological bias. Their criticism of the Meidner Plan is often based on an idealised or mythical version of the economy which bears little relationship to reality. A preference for the status quo may lie at the heart of their quarrel with the fund proposal.

CITIZEN FUNDS – PROFESSOR LINDBECK'S COUNTER-PROPOSAL

As has been seen, the intense concentration of ownership and control in the Swedish economy was documented by the government commission of the late 1960s. It was imperative, Lindbeck believed, to create a more decentralised capital market and a much broader distribution of individual ownership. He rejected the LO fund proposal in the belief it would exacerbate concentration. Personally, Lindbeck favoured schemes to increase the number of small shareholders. However, he agreed with Meidner that such a policy could not effectively disseminate economic power.[147] Instead, he proposed that the state create a number of independent funds.

Taxation revenue and contributions from the state pension fund would be the sources of finance for these 'citizen funds', and not levies on company profits. As citizen funds, their boards, Lindbeck suggested, should be representative of a broad spectrum of society. Members could be appointed by trade unions, by associations of small enterprises, by agricultural organisations, pensioners' associations, institutions of higher learning, cultural associations and popular movements of various kinds. The aim of these boards would be similar to that of private investment funds, namely to achieve a satisfactory return on capital invested. Simultaneously they would facilitate the transfer of capital, Lindbeck insists, to companies with the most worthwhile projects from a socio-economic viewpoint.

Citizen funds were expected to accomplish three objects. First, they would establish a decentralised capital market. Second, individual citizen involvement would safeguard the capital allocation system from distortion which union dominance would likely introduce. Finally, they would provide all citizens with a share in economic growth.[148]

Citizen funds did not address the problems of solidarity wage policy or enhance employee economic power in the workplace. Nor did they dilute or make accountable concentrated private capital ownership. Furthermore, the individualisation of economic power envisaged by the proposal was foreign to the collective ideals of the labour movement. Anyway, some of its spokesmen were sceptical of any attempt to decentralise the economy into small independent capital markets. Modern industrial production, they pointed out, is carried on in large factory units, which as capital intensive projects require massive investment.[149]

Within the labour movement there appeared to be little obvious enthusiasm for Lindbeck's proposal. Yet for a minority of Social Democrats, citizen funds seemed to be more in keeping with the party aim of placing the determination and distribution of production in the hands of the entire nation.[150] Some supporters of wage earner funds defended the dominance of employee influence by reference to the Marxian labour theory of value, while others simply pointed to the fact that most people spend most of their waking time at work.[151] This debate, in which citizens' rights have been juxtaposed in opposition to workers' rights, has been characterised as unreal. Implementation of the Meidner Plan, it is claimed, would place in the hands of the nation the determination and distribution of production through a combination of decentralised worker control and state control of significant parameters of economic activity.[152]

LEGAL OPINION ON THE MEIDNER PLAN

Stig Stronholm, a legal theorist and jurist, has examined the wage earner proposal. In terms of relevant legal perspectives and existing law, he claims that the Meidner Plan is entirely new and alien to the Swedish legal system. The proposal entails 'a compulsorily regulated transfer of property from one legal subject to another', or in other words, an intervention into the ownership rights of shareholders. In its present framework, the legal system does not allow for such a transfer, nor can it be accommodated within the existing complex of rules. Possibly, he allows, there are certain principles which justify co-determination for workers over their own labour contribution, but there is no support in law for their appropriation of the results of labour. If the holders of political power wish to realise the fund proposal and make compulsory transfer compatible with positive law, then Stronholm was convinced a constitutional amendment would be necessary. This would amount, he concluded, to an extremely far-reaching intervention.[153]

Eventually, when a fund system was implemented, it was by act of Parliament and not through a constitutional amendment. However, the Employers' Confederation SAF have asked the European Court to judge if 'wage earner funds are compatible with the provisions for the protection of property in the European Convention on Human Rights'.[154] Judgement from the court is awaited.

EMPLOYERS, THE WALDENSTROM REPORT AND ECONOMIC CRISIS

In 1974, a year before the completion of Meidner's first draft proposal, the Swedish Federation of Industries (SI) and the Swedish Employers' Confederation (SAF) jointly established a working party to consider the implications of profit sharing and wage earner funds for the economy and the business community. The group was composed of four managing directors of major Swedish companies, two professors of economics, and was chaired by Erland Waldenstrom, board chairman of Grnages, another large company.[155] When the group's deliberations were published in 1976, though entitled *Company Profits, Sources of Investment Capital and Wage Earner Funds*, it became generally known as the Waldenstrom Report. By that time, however, the organisations jointly sponsoring the report appeared to differ as to its original objectives.

According to SAF, the report was to analyse the motives commonly cited for the introduction of profit and capital sharing systems, to discuss the advantages and drawbacks of certain models, and to assess their impact on the economy and business community. It was not, the employers insisted, expected to produce detailed proposals.[156] In contrast, the Federation of Swedish Industries appeared to expect concrete proposals from the Waldenstrom group. This organisation saw the group task as developing solutions to questions of how ownership in companies can be constructed, and how power and production can be redistributed to win majority acceptance. Any practical proposal, the federation assumed, would retain the advantages of the present economic system.[157]

The report began with an international review of proposed and existing systems of profit sharing. In Sweden, it pointed out, equity capital ownership represented a very small proportion of total economic wealth. Consequently, its redistribution would have a negligible effect on the distribution of wealth as a whole. Not only would profit sharing be ineffective in a distributional sense, but it could have negative consequences for the supply of risk capital. Yet it must be remembered, the Meidner Plan was not intended by its proponents as a substitute for general policies of redistribution, but aimed at the democratisation of economic power. Nevertheless, mandatory profit sharing envisaged by the LO proposal was sharply criticised and its introduction, the report claimed, would fundamentally alter the entire economic system.[158]

Despite these reservations, the report acknowledged the exceptionally unequal distribution of equity ownership. Both from a general political viewpoint and in terms of business and industry's own perspective, this imbalance constituted a serious problem. Wealth, resulting from improved company profitability, accruing to a minority of shareholders, was unacceptable in the wider society. A more balanced distribution would generate an increased tolerance for profits. This was the most weighty argument, the report believed, for profit or capital sharing[159] (an argument, it may be noted, remarkably similar to that made by some American business spokesmen in favour of employee stock ownership plans).

The report outlined the essential requirements for an appropriate system of profit or capital sharing.

1 It should be compatible with an efficient and decentralised decision making process in industry which would continue to be based on the individual ownership of equity capital.
2 It should facilitate the supply of risk capital within the economy, ensure the maintenance of a capital market based on voluntary saving and deem maximum economic benefit to be the criterion for the allocation of investment capital.
3 It should entail neither the taxation nor the confiscation of current owners' equity capital.
4 Finally, while an appropriate system would promote a broader, more evenly distributed ownership structure within companies, its introduction would be entirely voluntary.[160]

Obviously, the Meidner Plan would fail to satisfy many of these requirements. One approach considered by the report was the profit sharing scheme confined to the individual firm, and it made certain recommendations as to its operation. Formulas which simply allot a fixed percentage of profit to employees, it advised, should be avoided. Instead, only profit above a certain threshold (e.g. a rate of return on capital equal to inflation, plus an annual 2 per cent) should be shared. Of this amount, one-third should be shared among employees, one-third to regular shareholders and the remainder should be held for taxation. Calculation of this three-way division should be based not on the annual, but on the average profit over the preceding five years. This additional refinement was designed to account for annual fluctuations in many companies' profits. Any profit shared with employees, the report assumed, would be tax-deductible for the company.[161]

Though suggesting a profit sharing formula for company-based schemes, the report remained sceptical of the concept. All profit sharing systems, it claimed, unless accompanied by compensatory measures, lower the original shareholders' dividend and decrease their willingness to invest new capital.[162] The system outlined above would only be suitable in companies with a high level of earnings, or where profit sharing can positively affect worker motivation and productivity. Such an effect would compensate for the lower yield to shareholders.[163] The great disadvantage of these schemes, the report believed, was their limited application. In the private sector, only those employed in companies with high profit levels could expect to benefit. Employees in the public sector would be excluded altogether. It would be better therefore, the report concluded, to introduce a nationwide capital sharing system based not on profits, but wages.[164]

The key recommendation of the report bore no relation at all to profit sharing. Rather than employer contributions based on profit, it was proposed that employees should save a portion, possibly 1 per cent of their salaries or wages. These savings would be placed in a number of funds owned and administered by employees, who would also elect fund board directors.[165] Once in operation, the funds would provide venture capital or investment for business and industry. Wage-based funds were expected to achieve two objectives. First, they would broaden share ownership and disseminate economic power.[166] Shares owned by employees, the report recommended, should be concentrated in sufficiently large funds to give them genuine influence.[167] Second, wage-based funds would free the state from using taxation revenue to make up for the shortfall of savings in the Swedish economy.[168] Unlike individual company profit sharing schemes, all employees, irrespective of the company size, profitability or its location in public or private sector, would be eligible to participate in a wage-based fund system. Fund participants, the report urged, should be obliged to hold savings for at least five years. Beyond that period, taxation on encashed savings or shares should be progressively reduced to encourage an even longer retention.[169]

While the report favoured the general introduction of wage-based fund systems, this preference did not exclude the operation of profit sharing schemes in suitable companies. However, were either system to flourish, state subsidies, it claimed, were an essential prerequisite. Company or employee contributions, it suggested, should be tax-deductible. In conclusion, the report eschewed any element of compulsion in the adoption of these schemes, which it stressed should be wholly a function of managerial or employee discretion.[170]

THE FATE OF THE WALDENSTROM REPORT

As Waldenstrom's principal proposal was similar to Lindbeck's citizen funds, there appeared to be little prospect of agreement between capital and labour. Yet an unequivocal endorsement of wage-based funds by industry and employer organisations might have forced a union rethink. A possible result in that event may have been a negotiated compromise. Apart altogether from tradition, other factors favoured such an outcome. Within SAP at any rate, opinion was divided as to the merits and feasibility of the Meidner Plan. Furthermore, some common ground existed on which negotiations could begin. Both parties agreed that the concentration of equity ownership was excessive and needed correction.

Neither the Federation of Swedish Industries nor the Employers' Association officially endorsed the Waldenstrom report.[171] In September 1977, almost 16 months after its publication, the Employers' Congress considered the question of wage earner participation in industrial capital formation. The idea won unanimous approval. Even its realisation would be welcomed, provided its implementation and operation were in conformity with the requirements already outlined by the Waldenstrom group. As the Meidner Plan contravened many of these principles (e.g. voluntarism) it was flatly rejected, and Congress declared it could not be regarded as a basis for discussion between the labour market parties.[172]

Though apparently enthusiastic for employee participation in capital formation, Congress neither adopted the Waldenstrom recommendations nor produced a specific proposal of its own. Instead it urged the Executive to initiate a campaign of information and education among the membership on this complex matter. At a later date, suitable proposals could be worked out in co-operation with other business organisations.[173]

ECONOMIC CRISIS

Changed circumstances may explain the leisurely approach now adopted by employers to questions of profit or capital sharing. Since the publication of the Waldenstrom Report, a government commission had been established to examine wage earners' funds, and the Social Democrats had been replaced by a bourgeois coalition government more sympathetic to business. These developments may have diminished the urgency for a decision on employee financial participation. More importantly, the effects of international recession were now manifest. Swedish industry experienced a fall in exports, production and profit. In 1977 industrial investment fell by 17 per cent, registering the biggest drop in the postwar period. Yet in the following year there was an even greater decline of 22 per cent:[174] a climate in which any proposal for profit sharing seemed particularly inopportune.

New investment, it was generally agreed, was the solution for Sweden's economic problems. Capital was necessary to expand existing industry, to finance new products, or to replace those sectors and products unable to compete with new producers in the world market. Not surprisingly, the business community looked to private savings to finance this expansion. However, this would require a dramatic recovery in investment, which was unlikely unless companies became sufficiently profitable. Profitability levels in companies could be raised either through increasing demand or controlling, if not reducing, costs. As demand in the world market accounted for nearly 50 per cent of Sweden's industrial output, the scope for manipulation of this variable was severely restricted.[175] The alternative of reducing labour costs was made difficult by the existing system of centralised bargaining and solidarity wage policy. Nevertheless, electoral defeat of the union's political ally and the installation of a government sympathetic to business improved the prospect for the success of this strategy.[176] Apparently, disenchantment with the historic compromise was pervasive.

Many in the business community expected the new government to 'restore the effectiveness of markets' which had been impaired, they believed, by the interventionist policies of the Social Democrats.[177] Already, President Reagan and Prime Minister Thatcher were showing the way. These expectations were largely disappointed. Various constraints prevented the coalition government embarking on any drastic reversal of past economic policy. As the first bourgeois government in almost half a century, it could not afford to appear less concerned than Social Democrats about full employment, or about the economic security of pensioners and other dependent groups. Anyway, among the electorate at large there was some appreciation of, and attachment to, the achievements of socialist economic and welfare policy.[178] Within the coalition, only the Conservatives, the party closest to business, may have had the stomach for disciplining labour by allowing unemployment to rise.

The crisis management strategy adopted by the government was a 15 per cent devaluation to increase the competitiveness of exports, the abolition of some payroll taxes on employers to reduce labour costs, and an increased VAT rate to dampen domestic demand. Any restrictive elements in this strategy were not allowed to affect employment adversely. The labour market policy of its predecessors – retraining and the provision of temporary employment for displaced workers – was not only continued but expanded. Labour hoarding was encouraged by wage subsidies to firms keeping on workers who would otherwise have been laid off. Government expenditure on loans and grants designed to keep ailing companies afloat vastly increased. Finally, the government purchased a number of companies, especially in steel and shipbuilding, introducing an unprecedented degree of what one commentator has described as 'ashcan' or 'lemon' socialism.[179] In assisting the recapture of Swedish exporters' market share, keeping unemployment low, and stimulating some recovery in investment, government policy was a success. Though there was a 4 per cent increase in industrial investment during 1979, this was almost entirely due to public sector firms.[180]

For the rigidly orthodox free marketeers among employers, some of the above developments can only have been distressing. Yet given the balance of social forces and the strength and coherence of the opposition, an open and partisan government espousal of capital's interests was hardly possible. None the less, government by a bourgeois coalition was preferable to one run by Social Democrats. At the very least, it could be expected to remain benevolently neutral. This likelihood and the severity of the economic crisis stiffened employer resistance to the claims of labour.

By the end of 1979, with a bourgeois coalition again in office, SAF refused to negotiate a new agreement with the LO on the grounds that there was no room at all for pay rises and therefore talks would be meaningless.[181] The resultant strike and lockout of May 1980 was Sweden's largest labour dispute to date. It is estimated to have cost unions SKr. 350 million in strike pay and employers SKr. 2.5 billion in lost production.[182] To reduce labour's squeeze on profits, employers were attempting to dismantle or decentralise a wage determination system that had existed for over two decades. Additional demands from labour not only for a share in profits, but for the exercise of some economic influence, had to be firmly resisted. The somewhat conciliatory stance of the early 1970s had gradually given way to outright opposition.

A MODIFIED MEIDNER PLAN – THE LO/SAP PROPOSAL, 1978

As has been seen, the Meidner Plan was not a significant factor in the 1976 electoral defeat of the Social Democrats. Nevertheless, during the election post-mortem, the failure of party and unions to co-ordinate their ideological positions on the issue of economic democracy was deplored. Indeed, on this matter, LO President Nillsson admitted the unions were far ahead of the party. In future, he promised, they would be more circumspect, taking greater heed of electoral politics. After all, he concluded, it is the party which will win back governmental power.[183]

This appraisal resulted in the establishment of a joint union/party working group charged with the preparation of a new proposal on wage earner funds. Of the six group members, two were drawn from SAP while the remainder, which included Rudolph Meidner, were from the LO. The completed report, 'Wage Earner Funds and Capital Formation', was presented at the Social Democrats' 1978 party Congress.

This new proposal simultaneously attempted to disarm criticism of the original plan and provide a solution for declining investment. The collective profit sharing scheme underwent some modifications. While the formula for contributions remained unchanged, the limit above which companies were obliged to participate was raised from 50 to 500 employees. Companies under the limit could, after negotiations with the unions, voluntarily affiliate to the fund system and, to this end, were to be offered a variety of inducements such as tax concessions. Those choosing to remain outside would pay a co-determination levy amounting to 1 per cent of payroll, which would be used to finance union activity within these firms. The original shareholder, it was now suggested, should be compensated, to counter possible cries of confiscation.[184] Though claims that his plan would lead to a centralised trade union state were dismissed by Meidner, the 1978 proposal sought to dispel such fears. Industry or sector funds were to be replaced by 24 regional councils – one for each Swedish county. Each council would be composed of at least 300 members appointed by direct union election. Power to elect directors in profit sharing companies would be shared in the same proportion as before between local employees and the new regional councils. The LO was to assist in co-ordinating the activities of councils through the provision of advice and expertise. At the top of the pyramid, an employee Congress would exercise a general supervisory role over the entire system. Members of this Congress were to be appointed by the regional councils.

The 1978 proposal went beyond a mere modification of collective profit sharing. To the three objectives of the original plan, a fourth was added, namely 'to contribute to collective saving for productive investment'.[185] The concern of the LO with declining investment has already been noted. Indeed, the institution of the fourth national pension fund as an additional source of risk capital attempted to reverse the decline. That initiative, and record company profits returned in 1973 and 1974, may explain the exclusive focus of the 1976 fund proposal on strengthening employee economic influence, the problems of wage policy, and concentrated equity ownership. By that time, however, capital shortage was about to recur with a vengeance. Consequently, capital formation became an important supplementary objective of the 1978 LO/SAP wage earners fund.

The proposed system of capital formation was to be financed by a 3 per cent annual payroll contribution from employers. Accumulated monies would be channelled to two national development funds and 24 regional funds. Again, the proposal sought to placate those who complained that a fund system would result in excessive union power. On one national development fund board, union representatives were in a majority, while on the other, citizen or community interests were dominant. Unions were to have minority representation on regional fund boards – the majority being appointed by the governing political party.[186]

While the employee Congress appointed union representatives on the various boards, it also served to link the autonomous systems of collective profit sharing and capital formation. Revenue accumulated by the funds from the payroll levy was to be used as a source of investment capital for industry. It has been estimated that the amount would be equivalent to almost half the gross annual investment spending of all Swedish industry. Fund investment criteria were only partially orthodox. While any proposed capital spending project would have to satisfy 'certain overall yield requirements', consideration of the 'economic interests of the community and industrial policy' would also influence such decisions.[187]

The 1978 LO/SAP proposal was unique in its failure to please either labour or capital. Labour movement response to the modified plan was not enthusiastic. The plan has been characterised as complicated and unwieldy.[188] Furthermore, the levy financing the capital formation system was to be deducted from the resources available for pay. Therefore it could be regarded, Meidner argued, as a contribution from the wage earners themselves.[189] While the Party Congress endorsed capital formation as an additional goal for wage earner funds, it took no position on the concrete proposals of the modified plan. Wage earner funds, it decided, required further investigation and deferred consideration of the question to the 1981 Congress. The effect of this postponement was to leave the decision to the National Commission on Wage Earner Funds, which had been deliberating on the topic since 1975.[190]

Despite the provision of an additional source of investment capital, and the dilution – if not downgrading – of collective profit sharing, employer distaste for such schemes was undiminished. According to one spokesman for SAF, the same consequences would result no matter what version of the Meidner Plan was introduced. The 1978 proposal, he claimed, would give rise to the same concentration of power and the same risks for political democracy.[191]

THE 1979 ELECTION AND THE NATIONAL COMMISSION ON WAGE EARNER FUNDS

The fund question as an election issue was almost entirely neutralised during the 1979 campaign. In surveys conducted prior to polling, the greatest proportion of citizens (24 per cent) rated the use of nuclear power as the most important issue, 17 per cent chose unemployment, and only 4 per cent gave priority to wage earner funds.[192] Different explanations have been advanced to account for the fund's low public profile. The relegation of the question to the National Commission, one commentator has claimed, largely blunted it as an electoral issue.[193] It was the efforts of the Social Democrats and the LO, another insisted, which shifted the focus of debate from technical details such as fund structure to one of principle, i.e. should a more even distribution of wealth and greater economic influence for employees be pursued?[194]

Even if it had been deprived of the fund bogey, the bourgeois coalition could still face the electorate with some confidence. It had succeeded in maintaining a low level of unemployment, and the continuing use of nuclear power was to be decided by referendum. A second electoral victory over the socialists demonstrated that coalition confidence was not altogether misplaced. Yet there was little room for triumphalism. The 4-percentage-point lead and an 11-seat parliamentary majority won by the bourgeois coalition in 1976 was now reduced to one-fifth of a percentage point and a single-seat majority.[195] Such a result augured ill for future coalition successes.

The National Commission on Wage Earner Funds was expected to produce a proposal towards the end of 1980. To facilitate that outcome, the various interest groups were invited to outline clearly their respective positions. The final submission of the labour movement closely resembled the 1978 LO/SAP scheme. A voluntary tax-subsidised saving plan was suggested by the Conservative Party and employers. Both Liberal and Centre Parties favoured a compulsory saving scheme where the proportion of salary to be saved would be decided annually by Parliament.[196] Unfortunately, commission personnel were unable to reach agreement or even a majority decision regarding the design of the report. In February 1981 the chairman resigned. Exhorted to continue, the commission produced its final document in September of that year. It contained extensive background material on individual and collective profit sharing schemes, but made no proposal.[197]

Despite the interim publication of several expert reports on many aspects of the fund question, the commission in the final analysis was unable to produce any proposals or recommendations. In retrospect, its emasculation is hardly surprising. Divided counsel within the labour movement, together with political and economic developments, all combined to stiffen employer resistance to collective profit sharing. Early in 1980 the employers replaced their representative on the commission. The new appointee was unencumbered by even a remote involvement with any fund proposal. Now SAF announced that the only satisfactory alternative to a fund system was none at all.[198] These moves have been interpreted by some observers as indicating a hardening of employer attitudes.[199] Employers, on the other hand, deny alteration and point to their consistent opposition to the funds since their inception.[200] In the Waldenstrom Report, however, the business community had seemed willing to countenance remedial action for concentrated equity ownership.

A shift in the stance of commission members representing some bourgeois political interests is more apparent. Admittedly the Conservative Party steadfastly opposed the fund system from the early 1970s. Yet within the Liberal Party, a substantial number responded positively to the Meidner Plan. The Centre Party was initially neutral. After 1976, the fashionable dominance in some quarters of a resurrected nineteenth-century political economy and conservative gains at the expense of its coalition partners, may have influenced change. In 1979 the Liberal Party's representative on the commission, who was favourably disposed to some form of collective profit sharing, was replaced.[201] By 1980, employers, Conservative, Liberal and Centre Parties were very near to sharing a common platform of outright opposition to wage earner funds.

WAGE EARNER FUNDS – A TURNING POINT
IN THE CONFLICT

While the commission on wage earner funds continued in existence, the Social Democrats could always avoid a definite commitment to any concrete proposal. Indeed, the Party leadership may have fondly hoped the commission would eventually produce a proposal winning broad acceptance. By the summer of 1981 any such hopes had been dashed. Imminent failure of the commission was evident, and the Party would be obliged to grasp firmly the nettle of wage earner funds at its forthcoming conference. Further equivocation would be likely to alienate large numbers of the rank-and-file. In the meantime, the LO/SAP committee had produced another proposal for presentation at the 1981 Congresses of Party and unions.

There was little novelty in the 1981 proposal. In essence, it was simply a variation on the 1978 plan. The scope of the collective profit sharing scheme was widened to embrace all limited companies. However, a firm's 20 per cent profit sharing contribution was now to be calculated not on the basis of its normal, but of its excess, profits. Depending on company preference, this contribution could be in the form of either cash or shares – though cash would be used by the wage earners fund to purchase shares.

The capital formation system was to be financed by a special additional contribution to the National Pension Fund. This amounted to a 1 per cent levy on payroll, payable by all employers. Accumulated monies when transferred to the wage earner funds would be used for capital investment. The establishment of a link between pension and wage earner funds was a new departure.

Finally, the administrative structure of the funds remained largely unchanged. There was, however, some uncertainty whether union representatives on regional fund boards should be appointed or directly elected.[202]

When the LO/SAP committee's latest proposal was presented at the 1981 Congresses, it was accepted by Party and unions. The four goals for wage earner funds were also endorsed. As to the detailed technical construction of the funds, both Congresses declined to make a decision. Indeed, one prominent member of the Parliamentary Party urged that questions concerning some form of individual connection to the funds and their democratic basis should be left open.[203] Nevertheless, SAP was clearly committed to the introduction of some form of collective profit sharing if returned to power. Yet the obvious willingness of the party to compromise counted little with opponents of the measure.

There now began a debate on wage earner funds rivalling in intensity that of 1976. It was to continue beyond the September election of 1982. At best the bourgeois coalition had been an uneasy alliance. Differences between the three non-socialist parties were now submerged by their unanimous and absolute rejection of any type of collective funds. Wage earner funds, they insisted, would fundamentally alter Sweden's economic system and concentrate excessive power in the hands of unions.[204] One commentator had described their criticism of the LO/SAP proposal as violent.[205] Yet the politicians' anti-fund campaign may have been outclassed by that of industrialists. According to one Social Democrat, the stridency of the business community warnings to voters of the dangers of 'fund socialism' reduced the bourgeois parties 'to a chorus of humming birds'.[206]

Apart from their well-publicised fear that wage earner funds would transform Sweden into an East European dictatorship, employers were critical of other aspects of the proposal. SAF characterised one of its objectives – the counteraction of declining investment – as superfluous. Capital, the confederation maintained, was not in short supply. The success of tax-linked share investment schemes, launched by the government in 1980 was cited in support of this contention. Thousands of people had been encouraged by the scheme to purchase shares amounting to SKr. 1 billion. The Confederation estimated annual investment requirements during periods of industrial expansion at about SKr. 2 billion. Provided share purchase was made sufficiently attractive, voluntary saving could produce just as much risk capital as compulsory collective saving. Therefore, the Confederation argued, wage earner funds were unnecessary for the generation of risk capital.[207]

The employee share ownership scheme referred to by employers had already been condemned as a political ploy. Many in the labour movement believed that the scheme's real purpose was to undermine support for wage earner funds – a conviction that may not have been altogether paranoiac. When the measure was first introduced by the Conservative minister of finance, it was generally recognised as an alternative to the LO proposal. Indeed, the eventual legislation was described by one newspaper as a bourgeois Meidner Plan.[208] While such tactical aims were disavowed publicly by the scheme's sponsors, it has been claimed that they were acknowledged privately. It was obvious, one commentator has asserted, that companies involved in promoting share ownership had joined with the government in an effort to erode support for wage earner funds.[209]

Despite these charges, employers continued to argue with apparent justification that declining investment was not due to a lack of capital. The real reason for the decline, SAF explained, was a lack of profit. If capital investment in productive assets were to increase, then profitability levels would have to be raised. Wage earner funds profit sharing and payroll levies were regressive because they would impose higher costs on business and thus lower profits.[210] To achieve any further expansion of industry and commerce, creative innovative companies must be permitted to retain their profits.[211] Strengthening the free market economy and broadening voluntary private ownership, the Confederation concluded, was the way out of economic crises.[212]

When the occasion demands, the above venerable formula for recovery is commonly offered by employers or their spokesmen in many western countries. Its credibility will usually vary inversely in a given country with the strength of the indigenous union movement and socialist Party. The formula had operated successfully in Sweden for a number of years, but by the early 1970s it had become increasingly threadbare. Its distributional deficiencies and the relegation of labour to a passive co-operator in managerial strategies had eventually given rise to demands for economic and industrial democracy. Within that context, the expressed wish of SAF for the continued and future operation of its formula appeared unrealistic. Similarly circumstanced was the concession of broadening individual share ownership. Not only had this approach been flatly rejected by the LO, but the efficacy of such schemes in redistributing either wealth or power had been questioned in the employers' report of 1976. Yet SAF's complaint that the levies of the latest fund proposal would reduce company liquidity might have been made by Meidner. The original proposal, it will be recalled, attempted to avoid such an outcome by insisting that all PS contributions to the fund be in the form of share certificates. It was ironic that fierce employer resistance to the 1975–6 proposal partially influenced the adoption of modifications they now complained of.

However, an emphasis on the inconsistencies or even impracticality of the employers' argument may obscure its *raison d'être*. The declared aim of SAF was to remove once and for all the question of wage earner funds from the political agenda.[213] Effective campaign slogans for the forthcoming general election would assist in the attainment of that object. The great virtue of the employers' polemic was the ease with which it could be distilled into powerful rallying cries. Few in the business community and many in the wider society would remain unmoved by appeals to defend private ownership and initiative or the free market economy.

THE 1982 ELECTION

Employers spared no effort or expense in attempting to make wage earner funds a pivotal issue in the 1982 general election. The amount of money poured into the campaign was without precedent in Swedish electoral history.[214] Expenditure by industrialists has been variously estimated at £8–10 million.[215] It was an investment which yielded some, though ultimately not a dramatic, return. In August 1981, a poll carried out by the Swedish Institute for Opinion Research found 26 per cent of the public supported wage earner funds, 37 per cent were opposed, while 36 per cent were uncertain. Exactly a year later, on the eve of the election, public support for the funds had dropped to 15 per cent while those opposed to the measure had grown to 57 per cent. Over a quarter of those surveyed (27 per cent) remained uncertain.[216]

Many Social Democrats wilting under the ferocity of the employers' offensive took refuge in evasion. Increasingly, Party spokesmen stressed the openness of the proposal and their willingness to discuss the fund question with the non-socialist parties and industry after the election. The Party appeared to have forgotten its commitment to the 1981 LO/SAP proposal.[217]

Though employers won the propaganda battle, they lost the war. Despite their concerted efforts, unemployment and not wage earner funds became the important issue of the election.[218] An extensive interventionist policy by the coalition government had kept the rate of unemployment at 3 per cent – among the lowest in Europe.[219] Nevertheless, a majority of the Swedish electorate must have regarded it as unacceptably high. The Social Democrats were returned to office with a three-seat parliamentary majority over the bourgeois parties. If the usual Communist support was forthcoming, the socialist bloc would have a 23-seat majority.[220] After a six-year impasse, the way was now clear for a legislative enactment on wage earner funds.

THE ROAD TO LEGISLATIVE ENACTMENT

During the winter of 1982–3, the government appointed three groups of experts. The task of the first group was to draft proposals for collective profit sharing. A second group, the Investment Commission, was to sketch out an investment policy for the funds. Finally, a third group at the Ministry of Finance was to draw up proposals for the organisation and administration of employee funds. By the summer of 1983 the work of these groups was complete. The government then issued invitations to the representatives of the three non-socialist parties and representatives of industry and commerce to take part in discussions on employee investment funds.[221]

Employers were undismayed by the socialist victory. The elections, they pointed out, had turned on the issue of unemployment, not wage earner funds. Therefore the result could not be interpreted as popular approval for the fund proposal. It was quite the opposite, they insisted, and cited in support the last public opinion poll.[222] Only by ignoring that opinion poll could government proceed with the measure. Anyway, the Federation reiterated its categoric rejection of any attempt to introduce wage earner funds in Sweden. Consequently, it declined the government's invitation to discuss the matter.[223] The bourgeois parties had already turned down the government's overtures.[224]

Despite these rebuffs, the government appeared determined to introduce legislation in the autumn. The business community reacted by setting up a committee of 24 businessmen drawn from large and small enterprises throughout the country. This so-called 'October 4 Committee' was to organise broad resistance to the proposal, culminating in an anti-fund demonstration on the day Parliament convened.[225] It was remarkably successful. On the appointed day, 75,000 businessmen and their supporters assembled in protest. Employers claimed it was the largest manifestation of public opinion in Sweden during modern times.[226] Undeterred, the government pressed ahead with its bill in the teeth of bitter and sustained criticism from the opposition benches.

A collective profit sharing and employee investment fund, the government argued, was now more essential than ever. Since its return to office, the Party had embarked on a programme of economic reconstruction in which production, investment and employment had priority over consumption.

High profitability and a reduction in costs and inflation were identified as necessary preconditions for industrial growth. Government action in the winter of 1982–3 in devaluing the krona and encouraging a relatively slight increase in wage costs had led to high company profits. Yet the government warned that the negative effect of devaluation on real earnings and the highly positive effect on company profits and share prices were already imposing strains on distribution policy.[227] Rapidly rising profits not only exacerbated distributional problems between capital and labour, but could undermine the stability of wage determination and disrupt solidarity between different groups of workers. Such potential conflict and instability threatened economic recovery. However, measures giving workers a share in company profits could play an important part in reconciling conflicting interests and improve prospects from restraining rising costs. Employee investment funds would assist in creating a distributively acceptable policy of growth and stabilisation. Thus the vicious cycle of high profits leading to substantial wage drift, accompanied by inflation with a consequent deterioration in growth potential, could be broken.[228]

Apart from equitable distribution, employee investment funds would also foster sustained economic growth. The appearance of these funds on the stock market would increase the supply of capital. Normally in an expanding economy a rising demand for risk capital tends to elevate yield requirements on investments. This tendency can inhibit the expansive capacity of an enterprise. Employee investment funds would counteract this development by providing an additional source of risk capital. These funds, the government claimed, by tackling distribution problems, providing investment and increased economic influence for employees, would help resolve the powerful contemporary conflict between capital and labour.[229]

Finally the government turned on its opponents. Those who portrayed employee investment funds as a threat to the market economy were sharply criticised. The real threat to such an economy, SAP claimed, stemmed from its inability to accommodate human and social considerations. This was evident not only in Sweden but elsewhere during the 1970s. Applying a policy of *laissez-faire* at that time would have eliminated all the big Swedish shipyards, practically the whole steel and mining industry, along with a great deal of pulp and paper manufacturing. Mass unemployment and social and regional disasters would have resulted. The then bourgeois coalition government, the socialists pointed out, contrary to its frequently professed confidence in the infallibility of market forces, intervened to counter their catastrophic effects. Interference was so extensive that many leading economists believed the coalition parties were bent on dismantling the economic system. Yet it was not *laissez-faire*, the socialists insisted, but active reforming efforts checking the destructive elements of the market economy that were prerequisites for its continuance. This was particularly the case, they believed, in societies characterised by political democracy. Employee investment funds were simply an extension of traditional social democratic reformism which had always sought to safeguard human and social values along with the basic function of a market economy. Indeed the funds, it was claimed, could not operate without an open and vigorous risk capital market. Employee investment funds, the government concluded, presupposed a market system.[230]

While spokesmen from both wings of the labour movement publicly defended the fund proposal, there were some within the Party who may have remained privately sceptical. An anecdote from the televised parliamentary debate on the funds illustrates the persistent distaste or unease of some elements in the Party regarding the measure. While opposition speakers enlarged on the evils of the proposal, a cameraman noticed the Social Democrats' minister for finance busily engaged writing. Zooming in for a closer look, the minister's production was displayed for the nation. It was a vulgar piece of verse which roughly translated read 'wage earner funds are a lot of bullshit and now we are stuck with them.'[231]

Eventually, on 21 December 1983, the government bill on employee investment funds became law. All 164 members of the Social Democrats' Parliamentary Party voted for the measure, which was opposed by the combined vote (158) of Centre Liberal and Conservative opposition parties.[232] The Communists abstained. They were unable to support the fund proposal because, they explained, 'it encouraged false reformist illusions.'[233]

THE ACT ON EMPLOYEE INVESTMENT FUNDS

The act ruled that a system of five independent employee investment or wage earner funds be established within the framework of the national supplementary pension system during 1984. Company profit sharing contributions and a payroll levy were to be the two sources of fund finance. Annually accumulated monies would be used for share purchase. The system was to be built up over a period up to and including the year 1990. While the funds would remain in existence beyond that time and continue to administer their shareholdings, capital contributions would cease. An overview and evaluation of the reform would then be undertaken on which unions, firms and the general public could plan future strategy.[234] In the meantime, the LO expected employee investment funds to accomplish five objectives:

1 To facilitate the wage policy of solidarity by allowing employees to share in profits which this policy creates in parts of the economy.

2 To counteract the concentration of wealth and power.
3 To strengthen employees' influence.
4 To contribute to capital formation.
5 To strengthen the pension system by financing a portion of future pensions.[235]

Fund Structure

Finance

The profit sharing tax was set at 20 per cent of a company's profit above a certain minimum level. However, the anxiety of legislators to tax the real rather than the nominal profit of an individual enterprise, made for some initially complicated calculations. First, a firm's nominal profit was defined. To the firm's taxable income for national tax purposes was added its various tax allowances plus its transfers to reserves. The company's national and municipal tax for the year was subtracted from this total to give its nominal profit.

A second stage was to restate this nominal profit in terms of real profit. To this end, adjustments for the annual inflation number are made to the firm's stocks, fixed tangible assets, monetary assets and liabilities. When appropriate additions or subtractions are applied to the nominal profit, the result is a statement of real profit. Though the company's real profit may have been established, there is a final calculation before the profit sharing tax is applied.

Every enterprise participating in the profit sharing scheme is granted a basic allowance of SKr. 500,000, or 6 per cent of wages and salaries paid. As the form of this exemption is optional, it ensures that labour-intensive companies with small profits are treated equitably. The exempt amount is then deducted from a company's real profit before the profit sharing tax is computed. Thus the profit sharing tax base equals real profit minus the exemption.

All limited companies, including foreign multinationals operating in Sweden, incorporated societies, savings banks and mutual property insurance companies, are liable for the profit sharing contribution. In practice, almost all small companies would be exempt because of the basic allowance. Co-operatives or municipal housing companies, life insurance companies, people carrying on business as sole traders or in the form of a partnership or family foundation are not affected by the profit sharing provision.[236]

A second source of revenue for employee investment funds are employer contributions to the pension system. All employers will now pay an additional 0.2 per cent of the total wage bill. Provision is made for possible subsequent increases up to 0.5 per cent. Money thus collected will be passed through the pension system to the employee investment funds. The combined amounts from the profit sharing and pension contributions will be divided equally among the five funds.[237]

Organisation and administration

Five independent employee investment funds, each with its own central office, are to be located in five broadly defined regions of northern, central, eastern, western and southern Sweden. This arrangement is designed to ensure a decentralised fund administration. A funds investment, however, is not restricted to industries within its particular region. The management board of each fund is to be composed of nine members and four deputy members, but all must be either resident or at least connected in some way with the region concerned. At a minimum, five board members and two deputy members are to represent the employee interest. All members will be appointed by the government.[238]

Investment policy

The combined amount from the profit sharing tax and payroll levy that will accrue to employee investment funds had been estimated at approximately SKr. 2,000 million annually up to 1990. Nevertheless, a ceiling of 400 million had been set at the maximum allocation to any one fund in a particular year. Each fund is required to make investments in the risk capital market by buying shares. They can also supply some risk capital for co-operatives. The funds are expected to diversify their holding in different companies and industries. Indeed, the holding of any one fund in a listed or publicly quoted company cannot exceed 8 per cent of that company's voting rights. This limitation is designed to prevent a fund acquiring such extensive ownership that it could become responsible for a company's daily operation.[239] It was a far cry from Meidner's original proposal.

One fundamental aim of the legislation was to improve the supply of risk capital for the benefit of Swedish production and employment. Therefore, fund purchase of shares in foreign companies is prohibited. Finally, while it is intended that share acquisitions should primarily

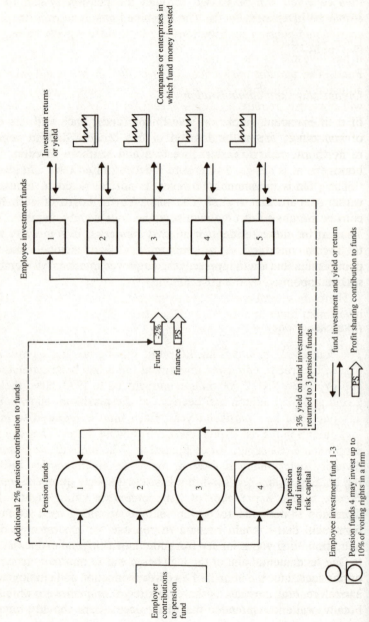

Figure 4.2 **Employee investment funds and the national pension system**

be long term, funds are not prevented from buying and selling in the short term if considered necessary.[240]

Investment yield and the National Pension Fund

Every year, each fund will be obliged to transfer a return on the capital it has invested to the management boards of the National Pension Fund. The amount must equal 3 per cent of fund capital invested, adjusted for inflation. Given this yield requirement, employee funds will obviously require a minimum real return of 3 per cent on any of their investments. Surplus fund capital resulting from a dearth of investment opportunities meeting this criterion can be temporarily transferred to the first three pension funds for investment in bonds.[241]

The yield requirement for employee investment funds seemed to cause some uneasiness within the LO. Congress worried that it might convey the impression that the funds intended to act as capitalists. The aim of these funds, it reminded members, was to contribute to Swedish production and employment. Furthermore, Congress pointed out that their investments would be long-term rather than speculative.[242]

There are several reasons for the interconnection between employee investment funds and the national pension system. First, the pension funds were expected to experience a shortfall in collective savings during the 1980s which capital transfers from employee investment funds could offset. Underfunding of the pension system was partly a result of coalition neglect.[243] A second reason for the link with the pension system was to ensure that all employees would receive a direct return on money invested by the funds. Finally, the location of employee investment funds within the pension system gave them a legal and constitutional status which had been tried and tested.[244]

Local employee influence

Company shares purchased and held by the employee investment funds will carry voting rights. On request, a fund must transfer half the voting rights of its shareholding in a particular company to the local union organisation. These shares can then be voted by the local union and employee investment fund at the company's annual general meeting. Thus, it is expected, employees will gain both a local and regional influence.[245] Given the 8 per cent limit on a fund's shareholding in an individual enterprise, employee influence is likely to be negligible, or as the LO admitted, limited in scope.[246]

UNION AND EMPLOYER RESPONSE TO FUND LEGISLATION

To veteran campaigners for economic democracy, the 1983 enactment on employee investment funds probably seemed but a ghostly manifestation of the original Meidner plan. The LO was obviously disappointed. These funds, Congress stated, did not fulfil all the union movement's ambition for economic democracy, but it conceded that they were a step on the way.[247] One aspect of the legislation of which Congress sought an early revision was government appointment of investment fund board members. These, the LO urged, should be directly elected. Furthermore, Congress argued that as they were employee funds, their board members should only be elected by employees. The Parliamentary Party, on the other hand, wished all citizens to be enfranchised.[248]

Early in 1984 the government appointed a committee to construct a system of direct elections to employee investment fund management boards, and to investigate the feasibility of a similar arrangement for the four pension funds. In both cases, the possible composition of the electorate also became a subject for investigation.[249]

The substantial dilution of the LO's initial fund proposal could be largely attributed to strong and sustained resistance from employers. Yet they were unmoved by this achievement. Despite the comparative mildness and provisional nature of the legislation, the business community and its political allies remained actively and implacably hostile. The leaders of the three non-socialist parties announced their intention of abolishing wage earner funds if they won the 1985 election. In anticipation of that event, they established a joint working group whose task was to draw up a procedure for dismantling the funds.[250] Caution was necessary to minimise any disruptive effect of fund abolition on the stock market. Meanwhile, employers vowed to continue their campaign of influencing public opinion in favour of fund abolition. Success, they believed, was assured because

> Both the extensive criticism, founded on facts, which the 'wage earner funds' have met in the debate during many years, and the strong public opinion against the funds speak for a final outcome where the 'wage earner funds' will only be an unfortunate parenthesis in Sweden's history.[251]

Continued resistance and protests by the business community and the bourgeois parties to the relatively innocuous fund legislation may appear disproportionate. Yet employers were not convinced the funds would terminate in 1990. They feared the legislation was merely the thin end of a permanent wedge which would be driven in over time by extending the scope of the measure – fears that were not totally insubstantial. Sections of the labour movement were critical of the limited nature of fund legislation, and tended to regard it as merely an initial step on the road to economic democracy.[252]

Government response to the renewed anti-fund offensive by employers and opposition was ambiguous. The Social Democrats announced that they would permanently abandon wage earner funds if the Party was defeated in the forthcoming general election (September 1985). Some have interpreted this announcement as indicative of Party distaste for the measure, and its desire to be rid of it.[253] Others have suggested it was a device to rally the faithful.[254] If so, it was successful. The Social Democrats were returned to office, though with a slightly reduced majority.

It is estimated that by 1990 SKr. 14,000 million will have been paid into the five wage earner funds. This will be approximately equivalent to 5–6 per cent of the total value of all listed shares.[255] Apart from union attachment to the funds, this large shareholding makes any future attempt at abolition problematic. Selling off fund shareholdings could adversely affect all share prices in the market. It would appear, therefore, that wage earner funds may become a permanent feature of the Swedish scene.

SUMMARY AND CONCLUSION

Swedish economic and industrial policy between the late 1930s and the early 1970s may represent the most sustained and relatively successful attempt to implement a favourite managerialist prescription for prosperity. The formula can be briefly summarised as labour–management co-operation (with the former as junior partner) to increase productivity and generate additional wealth, thus making the economic pie (and the partners' relative shares) larger. Its extended hegemony and acceptance by the Swedish labour movement can largely be ascribed to the welfare and distributional policies pursued by the socialist government. Eventually, the limitations of this managerialist strategy became apparent. Its tendency to concentrate wealth and power among a minority of capital owners, combined with growing rank-and-file aspirations to exercise greater influence in the workplace and economy, brought about its demise. The resultant legislation for industrial and economic democracy posited a new and more equitable relationship between capital and labour.

Unfortunately, any conclusion as to the effectiveness or concrete achievements of the above legislative programme must, of necessity, be purely speculative. This is particularly so with regard to employee investment funds, not simply because of their very recent establishment but because their present form and shape is, it seems, far from final. Yet, given the restricted nature of the funds as presently constituted, they fall far short of realising financial or economic democracy. Nevertheless, in legitimising an employee's right to share in profits and to exercise some influence on economic decision making within the enterprise and wider society, the funds are an important and practical step in that direction.

One noteworthy aspect of the Swedish debate was the generally sceptical view of employee share ownership schemes in single companies as vehicles for economic democracy. Rather, there was broad agreement that some type of collective fund was an essential requirement. A disadvantage of this arrangement may be its remoteness for individual employees, especially those working in firms in which the funds have no investment. Possible feelings of alienation, or non-involvement for employees so situated, may be offset in two ways. First, all employees will ultimately benefit from the funds through their connection with the pension system. Second, the industrial democracy reforms, by facilitating greater employee influence on enterprise decision making, may increase involvement and participation. The Swedish labour movement views industrial and economic democracy not as separate but interdependent and complementary reforms for the democratisation of the economy.

While wage earner funds are to secure for workers a share in both economic decision making and profit, they also provide capital investment. In their criticism of the funds, industrialists and employers have tended to focus on this latter function as epitomising the revolutionary nature of the proposal which, they believe, will ultimately lead to the socialisation of economic activity. Fund legislation, socialist spokesmen insist, is not a system transforming but a system maintaining reform.[256] Socialist assurances on this point would appear to be supported by the prestigious authority (until recently at any rate) of J.M. Keynes. Eventually, he predicted, the only means of securing an approximation to full employment will prove to be a somewhat comprehensive socialisation of investment. However, the necessary measure of socialisation, he confidently expected, could be introduced gradually without a break in the general traditions of society.[257]

Other commentators have been less sanguine. Attempts to dampen the characteristic oscillations of capitalist development and maintain employment through government or popular control of investment alters the basic motivation of production. Such intervention, Strachey argued, introduces a new overall social purpose for economic activity.[258] Indeed, Martin predicts that the long-term consequences of Swedish partial collectivisation of investment will be far-reaching. It will mean the gradual but inexorable erosion of private property institutions as the basis for organising economic activity. He concludes that private property will be displaced throughout the industrial core of Sweden's economy by a form of social, not state, ownership.[259] Admittedly, the presently restricted nature of the funds hardly warrants such an extrapolation. Yet, it must be remembered, the Swedish union movement looks to the future to extend and widen their scope. In the final analysis, Swedish capital may justly fear the proposal.

The lurking nemesis for capitalism in Sweden was avoided in other western countries during the 1970s, mainly because the Keynesian pursuit of full employment was jettisoned in favour of monetarism. Many of the classic remedies for recession – wage cuts and the removal of rigidities in the labour market – which had been discredited after 1929, were rehabilitated. The ease or completion of the transition depended on a variety of factors. Generally, where union movements were weak, with a narrow socio-economic perspective and with poor or no political representation, the triumph of the new orthodoxy was virtually complete. Within Sweden, even some Social Democrats may have been influenced by these trends. However, popular attachment to full employment and welfare policies and a strong union movement with a powerful political wing, barred the advance of monetarism there. That no attempt was made to implement its policies by the non-socialist parties (its most likely converts) is a case in point. The bourgeois coalition governments surpassed the socialists in applying Keynesian-type remedial measures for recession and unemployment. Yet the same political factors that checked monetarism in Sweden also made collective profit sharing and a wage earner investment fund a politically feasible proposition. Given the absence of these conditions in many European countries, a workers' fund system of the Swedish type will have a very limited application. As the following chapter demonstrates, without a political ally as the governing party, even a strong unified union movement will fail to secure the implementation of such a proposal.

5 Economic democracy in Denmark – postponement or cancellation?

Nor would an incomes policy which would likely leave the distribution of income unchanged ensure union acceptance. If the unions happen to be actively dissatisfied with that distribution their offensive behaviour could be reflected in inflation. . . . Conversely . . . an attempt to obtain [wage] restraint through concertation can be counted on to provoke disagreement over the distribution of income. It can awaken sleeping dogs.

Ullman and Flanagan (1971)[1]

Congress declares that the time has come for the democratisation of ownership. Greater equality must be achieved in income capital and control. The trade unions cannot accept that the capital that we acknowledge is required for the growth of investment and production should be procured in a manner that results in a continued and considerable inequality in the distribution of assets and capital. Employees must claim a share of the growth in capital that by their efforts they help to create.

Resolution adopted by the 1971 Congress of Danish LO[2]

Commentators have generally focused on Sweden as the representative example of Scandinavian schemes for economic democracy. This exclusive approach can be defended by reference to the historic association and links between the Nordic countries and their similar, if differently paced, socio-economic developments. For a variety of reasons, but primarily because of its seminal nature, the Danish labour movement's proposal for economic democracy merits separate consideration. The British Labour Party's document of 1973, *Capital and Equality*, put forward a version of the Danish fund idea as a solution for the maldistribution of wealth. Furthermore, the Danish example, it has been suggested, encouraged the Swedish LO to take up economic democracy again.[3] Second, though the collective profit sharing concept may have been revived by the Danish labour movement, it has so far been unsuccessful in securing its practical implementation, despite possessing an important advantage over its Swedish counterpart. The Danish fund proposal was a joint production of the unions and Social Democratic Party, and the division that may have slowed progress of a similar measure in Sweden was avoided.[4] Nevertheless, economic democracy, albeit in attenuated form, has been realised in Sweden while in Denmark it remains in limbo. Consequently, a review of the Danish experience will illustrate the crucial necessity for labour's parliamentary dominance if the formidable and apparently universal resistance of employers to collective PS is to be circumvented. Third, there are some differences between the Swedish and Danish proposals regarding the extent of worker influence at enterprise level. Finally, it will be shown how extensive economic intervention by the state, and co-operation with unions in shaping national wage policy, can render questionable the existing distribution of wealth and power.

THE BACKGROUND

There are many similarities between the Danish and Swedish labour movements. Like its Swedish counterpart, the Danish Trade Union Confederation, LO (Landsorganisationen i Danmark), maintains close links with the Social Democratic Party, SD (Socialdemokratiet). Though Danish social democracy falls short of the dominance achieved by its Swedish exemplar, nevertheless after 1945 there opened a long period in which it became the 'natural party of government'. From 1947 to 1973 Danish socialists were almost continuously in power, spending a total of less than six years in opposition.[5] Yet there are some differences in detail between the two labour movements. For instance, craft rather than the industrial unionism of Sweden, predominates in the Danish LO. Danish Social Democrats are more dependent in Parliament on the support of small farming interests represented by the Radical Liberals. Many of these differences can be ascribed to the particular development of the Danish economy. Indeed it has been suggested that the industrial revolution of the nineteenth century may have bypassed Denmark.[6]

Up to the 1950s a dynamic agricultural sector producing for an international market was the engine of growth in the Danish economy. Danish industry, on the other hand, characterised by a multiplicity of small firms catering for a domestic market, was virtually stagnant. Sluggishness was compounded by declining industrial investment.[7] During the 1950s these conditions were drastically altered. Other countries, in order to assist their own agriculture, imposed various restrictions on agricultural imports, adversely affecting demand and prices for Danish produce. The crisis proved to be a continuing one, for by the mid-1960s, state support for agriculture had grown to represent 34 per cent of agricultural income.[8] It was these difficulties that influenced the new direction taken by government economic policy.

Essentially, this strategy aimed to lessen the country's dependence on agricultural exports. A conscious national policy of fostering manufacturing industry in larger units was adopted by the government.[9] Owing to the prevailing shortage of capital and the low level of saving by private enterprise, the expansionary programme required substantial state investment.[10] The achievements of the policy were impressive. After 1958 and into the early 1970s, growth in national income averaged 5 per cent annually – a 3 per cent increase. Industry overtook agriculture as the most important source of foreign earnings. Near full employment was achieved and labour shortages became the norm. Rapid economic growth and increased government expenditure on social welfare and education raised the standard of living in Denmark to rank among the highest in the world.[11] Yet these achievements were attended by recurring difficulties.

UNIONS AS THE KEYSTONE OF NATIONAL ECONOMIC POLICY

The tendency to crisis in the Danish economy again became acute in 1962. Rapidly rising wages and prices were its main components. Government responded by establishing an Economic Council which recommended a freeze on all money incomes. When unions and employers failed to agree on a method of implementation, the government resorted to legislation.[12] This so-called 'totality solution' envisaged a virtual two-year freeze of the whole economy, encompassing wages, prices, profits, dividends and directors' fees.[13] In Parliament, the measure was opposed at every stage but eventually passed by a narrow margin. Once implemented, the policy succeeded in stabilising the economy in 1963 and 1964. A crucial factor in its effectiveness was the support of the LO.[14]

The Danish union movement's willing acquiescence in government imposition of an incomes policy is not surprising. Since the war, once Social Democrats were in office, the LO had encouraged wage restraint and sought to prevent strikes.[15] The object was to forward government economic strategy. Now that the party had embarked on an expansionary programme to promote economic growth and full employment, there was greater need for wage moderation to check inflation and promote price stability. Deflation and unemployment were the unpalatable alternatives. Given that the labour movement had never seriously considered expropriation, an improvement in material standards for the working class could only come from increased economic growth.[16] Indeed, many unionists believed that maldistribution was largely due to high unemployment and economic stagnation.[17] Yet there was no question of unions being presented with a *fait accompli*. The very initiative to establish the economic council had been previously proposed in secret talks between the Social Democrats and the LO.[18] Admittedly, the incomes policy was a decree of a coalition government, but one in which the socialists were the dominant partner. Finally, controls on prices, profits and dividends gave unions some assurance that employers would not unfairly benefit from their restraint.

Once statutory restraints were lifted, movements in wages and prices tended to resume their old course.[19] However, the Economic Council remained in being and prior to negotiation of central wages agreements, published a series of pay norms. Voluntary wage restraint now became the key element in stabilisation policy. For reasons already outlined, the LO was willing to continue co-operation, but the drawback of this stance soon became apparent. First, adherence to pay norms, in the absence of statutory controls, could inadvertently boost the employer's surplus. As the chairman of the Economic Council ruefully admitted, 'The trouble with an incomes policy operated by persuasion is you can't really promise anything as to profit.'[20] Second, the publication of pay norms seemed to relegate unions to a purely passive role, straining relations between the union leadership and rank-and-file. The number of working days lost through wildcat strikes, mainly in pursuit of higher wages and improved working conditions, trebled.[21] Under the terms of the September agreement, union leaders were bound to oppose unofficial action; this placed them in the embarrassing position of policing their members.[22] Some shopfloor workers reacted by accusing union leaders of being co-opted. Wage restraint, previously practised by unions in an informal and discreet way, now became more problematic. Repeated recommendations from the Economic Council limiting wage increases to 3 per cent had no effect.[23] The incomes policy was in disarray.

The response of union leaders to these difficulties was to oppose further publication of pay norms, and press for statistics on the personal distribution of income and assets in ever-increasing detail.[24] The data were destructive of the belief that economic growth and full employment would facilitate a more equitable distribution of wealth. While wages had risen with the growth in national income, the shares going to capital and labour remained proportionately the same. Some capital owners appeared to have made windfall gains.[25] This was all the more disquieting in the context of a strong union movement with its political ally in government. State redistribution policy, despite public expenditure accounting for over 30 per cent of GNP, seemed to have comparatively little effect.[26]

In 1950, 70 per cent of all householders owned 6 per cent of the declared wealth in Denmark. By 1970, the share of this group had increased to 11 per cent. Within the same period, the share of the top 5 per cent of householders had declined from 55.5 per cent of declared wealth to 47.5 per cent.[27] These revelations instigated a debate within the labour movement on maldistribution, the outcome of which was a proposal for collective profit sharing or economic democracy.

INCOMES POLICY AND ECONOMIC DEMOCRACY

LO spokesmen today emphasise that economic democracy originated in demands for a more equitable distribution of wealth and increased influence for workers. The suggestion that the union's difficulties with incomes policy contributed to the proposal's evolution would be regarded as erroneous.[28] Nevertheless, it is tempting to argue for at least a tenuous link. An essential ingredient of a successful incomes policy, commentators claim, is consensus on the existing distribution of income within and beyond the bargaining sector. Its absence in Denmark, they contend, partly explains the failure of the policy there during the latter half of the 1960s.[29] Yet the LO remained committed to supporting socialist government economic strategy which, notwithstanding its distributional deficiencies, had raised living standards and reduced unemployment. Wage restraint was, and is, an important element in that strategy. Apparently, once socialists governed, union leaders were willing to persist despite growing difficulties in encouraging wage moderation.[30] Writing in 1971 and reviewing the less than successful attempts of the previous decade, two observers could conclude that 'the Danes were not yet ready to give up on income policies.'[31]

However, given the dissatisfaction with the existing distribution of wealth that had become evident during the 1960s, further attempts at wage restraint could generate fissiparous tendencies within the union movement and growth retarding industrial unrest. Furthermore, a new party (the Socialist Peoples' Party) had arisen on the left of the Social Democrats, and was critical of incomes policies and prepared to articulate rank-and-file discontent.[32] Economic democracy, in tackling maldistribution, could lay a basis for consensus while reassuring workers that wage moderation would not exclusively benefit capital. Thus the promotion of incomes policies in the future would become a less hazardous activity for the party and union leadership.

INDUSTRIAL AND ECONOMIC DEMOCRACY

Maldistribution was not the only concern of the labour movement towards the end of the 1960s. As in other European countries at that time, Danish workers aspired to exercise greater influence on decision making within their enterprises. A proposal for worker representatives on company boards of directors was well received within the labour movement, though some regarded it as inadequate. Without a simultaneous democratisation of ownership, they argued, there would be no significant power shift in favour of workers. It was felt that co-ownership through collective profit sharing would achieve both genuine influence for workers and a more equitable distribution of wealth.[33] In 1969, an LO working party was given the task of reporting on the problem of influence and rights for workers in relation to capital.[34]

The report of the working group was presented at the 1971 LO Congress. It contained the broad outlines of a proposal for economic democracy. However, the conventional idea of profit sharing through share allocations was dismissed as 'nothing but an evasive measure intended to support the existing system'. Economic democracy, it claimed, was more than a question of profit sharing and the accumulation of capital. Instead it was concerned with the 'democratic influence of the entire society on economic development'. The proposal's objective was, in short, 'the democratisation of the economy'.[35] After some discussion, the report was approved and adopted by an almost unanimous vote of the delegates.[36] According to employers, the debate was relatively brief and there was no absolute agreement as to how the unions' demand for economic democracy should be formulated.[37] Nevertheless, a joint LO/SD committee proceeded to draft a legislative proposal for co-ownership or economic democracy based on the 1971 report. Congress also decided to press for worker directors. Such experience was necessary, it was reasoned, as workers would eventually take power under the operation of economic democracy.[38] For the Danish labour movement, at any rate, industrial and economic democracy are inextricably linked.[39]

CO-OPERATION COMMITTEES – THE EMPLOYERS' RESPONSE

Though employers baulked at worker directors, they were prepared to countenance greater employee participation in decision making. Arrangements for joint consultation had existed in many firms since 1947. An agreement in 1970 between the LO and DA, for the establishment of co-operation committees, substantially extended the scope of the earlier arrangement.

Committees were to be set up in enterprises employing 50 or more workers on request from management or a majority on the shopfloor.[40] Both parties would be equally represented on this body. However, the committee chairperson would be a management appointee, while workers representatives elected the vice chairperson.[41] The committees were expected to improve competitiveness and increase job satisfaction and labour–management co-operation. Management and worker representatives would exercise co-determination on the organisation of local work, safety and welfare. Co-determination would also be exercised in formulating company personnel policy regarding unionised workers. General production policy, work planning or the implementation of major change, would be subject to 'co-influence'. Committee members would also receive financial information on the present position and future prospects of the enterprise.[42] To maximise employee involvement, each co-operation committee would encourage the establishment of departmental sub-committees to deal with specific issues, e.g., training.[43]

Danish co-operation committees apparently provide a wide range of decisions in which employees can participate. Yet it is difficult to gauge exactly the extent of worker influence. One commentator was unable to decide if the committees were consultative or participative bodies, and so classified them as lying somewhere in between.[44] This equivocation is understandable. Co-determination, for instance, is defined as 'an obligation on both parties to strive for agreement', while co-influence is described as 'timely consultation'.[45] Any matter on which the co-operation committee cannot agree is referred to the National Co-operation Board on which the central organisations of employers and employees are equally represented. Continuing deadlock at this level will be resolved by an umpire appointed by the labour court.[46]

Researchers have found that management expressed greater satisfaction with the operation of co-operation committees than workers. Some union stewards have complained they received information concerning proposed management action too late to exercise real influence. Yet overall, stewards seem to place a higher value on the function of these committees than do workers. Worker representatives sitting on these committees over time, observers suggest, tend to be co-opted. Rank and file workers, on the other hand, feel their interests are ignored.[47] Nevertheless, they appear to have proved popular. By 1979, co-operation committees had been established in 1,100 firms out of a potential maximum of about 1,400.[48]

The establishment of co-operation committees left the LO's enthusiasm for worker directors undiminished. Continued opposition from employers was swamped by consensus among the parliamentary parties on the virtue of such a measure.[49] A 1974 enactment required that all private and public companies with 50 or more employees must include two worker representatives on its board of directors. In effect, this was minority representation for employee interests, as shareholders in Danish companies elect at least three board members. The right of workers to elect directors was contingent, the law declared, on at least 50 per cent of the workforce wishing to exercise that right.[50] In consequent referenda in almost 2,000 firms, employees in about four companies waived their right to elect directors.[51] These results, suggesting widespread support among the rank-and-file for worker representation at board level, are reinforced by a survey in the metal trades. Turnout of workers in that industry eligible to vote in worker director elections, ran at 80 per cent.[52] Worker directors themselves were equally positive. They found board meetings interesting and instructive, though none reported increased influence.[53]

Employee board members seem to have played a rather passive role to date. Some worker directors believe this is owing to inexperience and their minority position, but are optimistic for the future.[54] Researchers generally agree that the Danish worker director scheme has made no significant contribution to a redistribution of power in favour of employees.[55] This would bear out the contention of some in the Danish labour movement that only a combination of industrial and economic democracy will be sufficient to alter workplace power relations. Yet, if the voyage of industrial democracy from proposal to legislative enactment was short, uneventful and successful, that of economic democracy was in the tradition of the Flying Dutchman.

THE 1973 BILL TO ESTABLISH ECONOMIC DEMOCRACY

The proposal on economic democracy jointly produced by the political and industrial wings of the Danish labour movement was tabled as a bill in Parliament by the governing Social Democrats on 31 January 1973. It had three principal aims:

1 To secure for employees a reasonable share of future capital growth.
2 To strengthen the right of co-determination and increase employee influence on managerial decision making in their particular enterprise.
3 To promote increased capital formation and investment in the economy.[56]

The first two of these objectives were responses to demands made at the end of the 1960s for a more equitable distribution of wealth and greater influence for employees in enterprise decision making. Regarding this latter demand, the bill on economic democracy was not to be viewed in isolation but as complementary to, or interconnected with, the legislation on worker directors which was simultaneously introduced in Parliament. The third objective was an attempt to compensate for the continuing low level of private investment in the economy.

As has been seen, state expenditure stimulated the economic expansion of the 1960s. The resultant boom did not substantially increase private capital investment, and the low level of saving that characterised many private sector Danish firms persisted. In fact, both private saving and private investment declined between 1970 and 1977. A considerable part of the private capital available was invested in property and government bonds.[57] Returns from industrial investment were apparently much lower than the effective interest on bonds. During this expansionary period, the share market accounted for only 3–4 per cent of the capital supplied.[58] Yet higher levels of manufacturing investment were essential if economic stagnation and unemployment were to be avoided. Thus, economic democracy was to secure a more equitable distribution of wealth and power while providing an additional source of risk capital.

Economic democracy – its operation

Fund finance

All employers in the public and private sector would be obliged to make an annual contribution based on a percentage of their total wage and salary bill to the employees' investment and dividend fund. Initially, the contribution was to be fixed at 0.5 per cent in 1974, but would then increase yearly by a half percentage point until 1983. Beyond that date, employer fund contributions would be fixed at 5 per cent of their annual labour costs. Contributions would be deductible from the taxable income of the enterprise.[59]

Fund government and administration

The fund was to be controlled and administered by a board of governors, an executive committee and a management committee. Supreme authority over the fund would be exercised by the board of governors who would lay down guidelines for its activities in accordance with the provisions of the act. Of the 60 members on the board, 24 will be government appointees, while the remaining 36 will be employee representatives. The LO will nominate 18 of these employee representatives, the Organisation of Public and Private Salaried Employees will nominate six, while the Organisation of University Graduates, the Association of Supervisors and Technical Employees, the Society of Engineers and the Organisation of Civil Servants will nominate the remainder. Employee and government representatives on the board of governors will elect six and four of their members respectively to the executive committee. The ten-member executive committee will be responsible for fund administration on lines laid down by the governing body. In turn, the executive committee will appoint management and other supervisory personnel charged with the daily direction of the fund.

Members of the governing body and executive committee will be elected for a three-year term. The accounts of the fund shall be audited by at least two chartered accountants and published. Finally

Figure 5.1 Fund government and administration

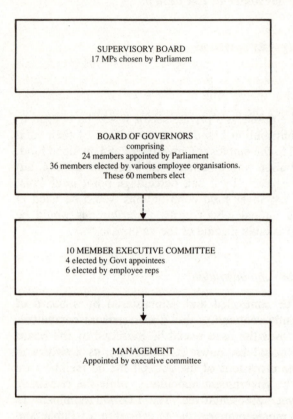

SUPERVISORY BOARD
17 MPs chosen by Parliament

BOARD OF GOVERNORS
comprising
24 members appointed by Parliament
36 members elected by various employee organisations.
These 60 members elect

10 MEMBER EXECUTIVE COMMITTEE
4 elected by Govt appointees
6 elected by employee reps

MANAGEMENT
Appointed by executive committee

a supervisory board, comprising 17 members of Parliament elected by their peers, will oversee the management and activities of the fund. This board can demand any information from the fund it deems necessary for effective supervision, and will report and comment regularly on its operation to Parliament.[60]

Swedish critics of the Meidner plan, it will be remembered, focused on union dominance in the control and administration of the fund. Even some Swedish Social Democrats feared contradictions might arise between union fund policy and national economic policy. This criticism was anticipated and avoided by the Danish fund proposal in its provision for substantial representation of political or community interests on the board of governors. It did little, however, to placate Danish opponents of wage earners funds.

Fund investment policy

The principal use envisaged for employer fund contributions was investment as responsible employee capital in business concerns.[61] According to the legislators, this implied compulsory investment of fund resources in all contributing enterprises.[62] Yet equity investment in public sector companies was precluded, possibly on ideological grounds. Furthermore, the division of private sector companies into three categories opened the way for additional exemptions. Compulsory investment, it was decided, would be confined to major joint stock companies, i.e. those employing 50 or more persons. In all, about 2,800 companies, accounting for about 43 per cent of the sum of earnings in the private sector, would be covered by the compulsory investment provision.[63]

The proposal was that two-thirds of the annual employer fund contribution from major joint stock companies would be automatically invested in these concerns, while the remaining third would pass directly to the fund. Each year the invested sums would be converted into ordinary share capital or in proportion to the existing classes of shares. As registered owner, the fund would receive any dividends from these shares. Fund contributions from major joint stock companies would continue in the above form until employee or fund capital accounted for 50 per cent of total share capital in the company. Thereafter the total annual company contribution would go directly to the fund as a cash payment.[64]

A second category of enterprise, the minor joint stock company, i.e. those employing less than 50 but more than 20 persons, was exempt from the compulsory investment provision.[65] Numbering approximately 2,600, these companies accounted for roughly 6 per cent of the wage and salary sum in the private sector.[66] Such concerns could choose to retain two-thirds of their annual contribution for investment as share capital, or pass the entire amount in cash to the fund. Retaining the portion of fund contribution was conditional on approval from a company general meeting and agreement to employee representation on a board of directors.[67] The choice allowed to minor joint stock companies regarding their fund contribution was likely seen by many Danish employers as being of the Hobson variety.

A third category of company was also exempt from compulsory investment. These were private business concerns, including joint stock companies employing at least 10 but less than 20 persons. About 20,000 undertakings fell within this classification and accounted for about 24 per cent of the total sum of earnings. Such companies could pass their entire annual contribution to the fund in cash, or retain two-thirds for investment as loan capital.[68]

Finally, the cash contribution from the above companies, plus dividends and interest which passed directly to the fund, became its so-called 'free resources'. Where possible, these 'free resources' were to be invested in industry as shares or some form of responsible capital. The remaining monies would be loaned to private and public sector companies and used to acquire real property.[69] A small portion of free resources would be used for the purchase of government bonds to maintain fund liquidity. Fund investments were expected to yield an average dividend of 4.5 per cent per annum on the purchase price of shares and a return of 9 per cent interest on loans.[70]

Employee influence

The rights and privileges attached to any class of share was equally to accompany those owned by the employee investment fund. Yet fund ownership was to remain largely beneficial or confined to the receipt of dividends. Actual voting rights on shares acquired by the fund through compulsory or voluntary conversion of employer contributions, or purchased from 'free resources', would be exercised by employees in the particular company. Thus fund share capital, the legislators maintained, would have a directly democratic effect. However, in exceptional circumstances, the fund board of governors was empowered to exercise this franchise.[71]

Within appropriate firms, employees will influence decision making in two ways. First, employees will elect representatives to attend the general shareholders' meeting. Proposals before the meeting will be supported or opposed by these representatives block-voting the relevant portion of fund equity. To ensure optimum use of this franchise, the fund will institute an educational programme and provide expert assistance in managerial economics and accountancy. Board representation will be a second avenue of employee influence. As has been seen, the 1973 legislative proposal on economic democracy was simultaneously accompanied by a bill proposing to grant workers in public and private companies employing more than 50 persons the right to elect board representatives. The bill on economic democracy intended to extend this provision to those minor joint stock companies voluntarily retaining two-thirds of its fund contribution. Election of additional, or more than two, employee representatives to the boards of minor or major stock companies would depend on the

Figure 5.2 Flow of money in wage earner funds (WEFs)

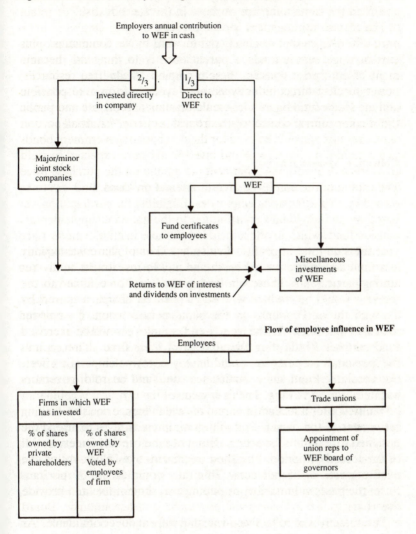

extent of fund shareholding in the individual firm. For very small private companies outside the above categories and in receipt of fund loans, other arrangements would be made for worker participation in decision making.[72] Regarding increased employee influence in public sector enterprises, the bill on economic democracy was vague.

Public sector employees, it simply stated, would, where possible, be accorded the same influence as those in private industry.[73]

The Danish arrangement for the exercise of local employee influence differs from that originally put forward by the Swedish proponents of wage earner funds. Apprehension concerning the development of enterprise consciousness prompted Meidner to divide the power to elect directors between employees in individual concerns and the sector fund boards. These contrasting approaches may reflect the weaker central control of the Danish LO over its affiliates.

Collective co-ownership

The capital of the employee investment and dividend fund was to be owned by all participating employees. Eligibility for participation was based on an individual's contribution to the national supplementary pension fund, which in effect included all those in employment. Each year the sum total of profits, dividends and employer contributions, less fund administrative expenses and any losses, would be divided among participants. Those who had worked for 32 weeks or more in the year would be credited with equal portions. Employees working a minimum of 16 weeks in the same period would be credited with half portions. At the year's end, employees would receive a fund certificate indicating the amount of their share. Though now the personal property of each employee, ownership rights were not absolute. Fund share certificates could not be sold or used as collateral for borrowing. The cash value of the certificates could only be realised after a locked-in period of seven years, or on the death or retirement of the owner. Prohibition on immediate encashment was designed to promote the accumulation of fund capital. On expiration of the locked-in period, encashed certificates would be subject to a fixed tax rate of 35 per cent. This rate would fall to 25 per cent for participants voluntarily postponing encashment for an additional five years.

The objectives of collective ownership were at once both ideological and practical. As employees did not own shares in a particular enterprise, the collapse of any concern and the subsequent loss of fund investment would, to some extent, be borne by all participants. Also the free resources of the fund could be invested for the general benefit of participants and the wider society. Equal shares for all, irrespective of the individual's wage or place of employment, would facilitate labour mobility and reinforce the principle of solidarity.[74] Obviously, schemes promoting worker shareholding in individual firms would find little favour with the Scandinavian labour movement. Indeed, one Danish Social Democrat claims that the profit sharing schemes of the United States are frequently cited in the Scandinavian debate on worker influence as an example of how *not* to democratise production ownership.[75]

Assuming a successful passage through all stages of the parliamentary process, the bill on economic democracy would become law on 1 July 1973. The first fund contribution from all firms would fall due in January of the following year.[76] Fund shareholding in 1981 would account for approximately 10 per cent of the total share capital of joint stock companies. This would have increased to 35 per cent by 1986.[77] These were merely tentative projections. The government was at pains to emphasise that the legislation now before the house did not constitute the final development of economic democracy. Rather, the novelty of the proposal required a gradual implementation, so that employees, companies and society could experience, and become familiar with, its operation.

Furthermore, the government promised to consider a suggestion from the Metal Workers' Union that future fund contributions be no longer solely based on a company's payroll but partly on its profits.[78] Yet the apparent willingness to modify aspects of the proposal was constrained by a commitment to its essentials. This was evident in the government's declared intention eventually to extend the compulsory investment provision to all private companies.[79] It was also evident in its declaration that the legislation was only a first step in the introduction of a system providing for interrelated co-ownership, participation in decision making, and increased capital formation on a large scale.[80]

RESPONSE OF DANISH BUSINESS TO THE LO/SD PROPOSAL FOR ECONOMIC DEMOCRACY

Even before the drafting of the bill on economic democracy and its introduction in Parliament, the Federation of Danish Industries and the Employers' Confederation had subjected the labour movement's initial proposals on the topic to careful scrutiny. Two booklets were the results of this examination. The first, *Co-worker – Co-owner*, a discussion paper on economic democracy, was published jointly by the Employers' Confederation and the Industry Federation in March 1972. A second publication, *The Consequences of Economic Democracy*, was issued by the Employers' Confederation alone in January 1973, the month in which the measure was tabled in Parliament.

Co-worker – Co-owner

The discussion document opened on an optimistic note citing the 1970 agreement on co-operation committees as an example of labour–management compromise on worker participation. Might not the parties, it reasoned, arrive at a similar accommodation regarding economic democracy.[81] Of course, with hindsight, one can see this optimism was misplaced. The establishment of co-operation committees did not diminish union pressure for worker representation at board level. Nevertheless, the document identified features in the idea of economic democracy appealing to private industry. First, the goal of increased savings to relieve the prevailing shortage of capital. Second, increased employee interest and involvement through their investments in industry. These objectives, readers were reminded, had long been sought by the business community.[82] Furthermore, traditional methods to achieve a more equitable distribution of wealth had not only ceased to be appropriate, but were now counter-productive. If pursuit of this goal were to continue, then, the document claimed, economic democracy was probably the least harmful approach – mainly because it avoided the inflationary and stultifying effect on initiative associated with wage and taxation strategies for altering income distribution.[83]

The surprisingly broad agreement between capital and labour on the aims of economic democracy was more apparent than real. This was evident in the business community's interpretation of the concept that workers would increase their savings and invest them in industry.[84] As has been seen, the labour movement rejected individual employee shareholding as destructive of solidarity and ineffective in strengthening workers' economic influence. Anyway, the redistributive element in such a scheme was negligible. However, when the discussion document turned to examine the actual proposals on economic democracy, the differences between the parties was thrown into sharp relief.

Compulsion and tutelage if not confiscation, the document claimed, characterised the union fund proposal. Under its dictat, wage earners would be forced into the system, and, rather than encouraging co-operation, it would weaken the natural community of interest between the establishment and employees. Likewise, the initial proposal to finance the fund through profit sharing would have many adverse consequences. It would constitute a body blow to a company's will and ability to invest, possibly leading to a flight of capital. Levying a firm's profits would deprive employees of the rewards of increased effort, thus dampening motivation and undermining their identification with the firm. While the document conceded that the fund system would promote a more equitable distribution of means, it was nevertheless unacceptable. Not only was it at variance with industry's objectives for economic democracy, but it could not be regarded as a practical proposal to achieve that end.[85]

Before outlining the business community's alternative proposal, the above objections require examination. It was somewhat disingenuous to envisage the fund scheme as being imposed on employees. The proposal, after all, was a joint production of the unions' representative organisations of employees and the Social Democratic Party, which had consistently received a substantial portion of the working-class vote. Only the business community could reasonably view the scheme as an imposition. Again the document's confident assumption of a natural community of interest between employees and management is questionable, or at least requires qualification. The common interest that does exist is likely narrowly based on the survival of the enterprise. In attempting to even the distribution of the surplus and increase employee influence on decision making within the firm, it could be argued that the fund system might tend to broaden rather than narrow the area of common interest between the parties. Finally, there was the claim that wage earner funds would curb the propensity to invest.

The weight of this objection largely depends on the extent and volume of private investment in industry. As already noted, an enduring weakness of Danish industry is its low level of private saving and investment. The fund system, in accumulating capital for productive investment and inducing companies to reinvest, would seem more likely to repair rather than exacerbate this defect. Though industrialists stigmatised the union proposal as impractical, the traditional prescriptions for raising the level of private investment in the economy had not proved notably successful. Indeed, the business community's own proposal for economic democracy (essentially a refurbishment of failed remedies) may be equally suspect as a practical policy.

A counter-proposal

Employers and industrialists favoured the adoption of a multi-stranded solution to the problem of economic democracy. This would combine profit sharing, employee shareholding and investment associations or unit trusts. They believed a solution confined to any one of these schemes would prove ineffective.[86] This scepticism was based on reviews of the operation and results of these plans at home and abroad.

A Norwegian government committee of 1964, investigating the international experience of profit sharing, concluded that it had not been a significant incentive to increased production, the creation of greater prosperity, or to the improvement of labour relations within establishments. Another government report of 1971 discussed the question of investment and influence by employees. Despite a provision in Norwegian company law of 40 years' standing, designed to encourage employee shareholding, the report found that few wage earners had availed themselves of the opportunity.[87] In France, though certain companies were legally obliged to share profits, a survey showed there was little inclination among employees to use their profit share to purchase equity in their employer's concern.[88] Finally, the business community's discussion document turned to consider similar experiments in their own country. A Danish law of 1957 established a tribunal representative of capital and labour whose function was to promote the idea of profit sharing. The tribunal acted as a source of guidance and advice to those wishing to establish schemes; it issued a number of publications and made recommendations of various kinds, including legislative amendments. There were, however, few practical results from these activities.[89] Summarising the Danish and international performance of these schemes, the industrialists' document recognised that they had not appreciably broadened share ownership nor altered the pattern of wage earners' savings or their attitude to industry.[90]

Danish industrialists did not attribute the lacklustre performance of profit sharing or employee shareholding schemes to any intrinsic defect, but to poor returns from investment in industry. Returns from such investment, they claimed, compared unfavourably with the interest on savings or on the yield from insurance policies or government bonds. This largely resulted from negative governmental attitudes towards business which had found expression in discriminatory taxation of shareholding, company legislation, and taxes on prices, profits and active industrial investment. Furthermore, government welfare legislation had deprived wage earners of sufficiently concrete incentives to save. Therefore, if the multi-stranded solution set out below were to succeed, then industrialists argued that radical change in a climate that apparently stifled initiative was essential.[91]

Profit sharing

Mindful of past failures, the discussion document laid down three essential conditions for effective profit sharing. First, that the amount of profit to be shared among employees should be calculated only after an acceptable definition has been produced and a budget has been drawn up for a reasonable return on capital invested. Second, distributing profit in the form of a cash payment should be avoided. Instead, it must be an absolute condition that the wage earners' profit share be invested in the firm either as share capital or outside capital. This was necessary as the profit sharing scheme was part of an overall strategy for the realisation of economic democracy which, whatever its form, assumes that wage earners acquire co-ownership in the means of production. Cash payments from surplus profits inviting immediate consumption would not promote that objective. Another advantage of share-based profit sharing over its cash variant was the avoidance of employee discontent generated by a fluctuating surplus. Finally, the third requirement for the success of these schemes was greater disclosure of company financial information and improved employee understanding of accountancy.[92]

Employee shareholding

This approach was especially directed at all employees of joint stock companies. Like profit sharing, it had the dual aim of securing co-ownership for employees and strengthening their identification with the firm. Employers would invite employees to invest a portion of their wage in their particular company. The fixed annual amount invested, between a minimum of DKr. 300 and a maximum of DKr. 1,200, would be identical for all employees and tax-deductible provided it was not withdrawn within five years. After the first two years, wage earners would be offered the choice of converting future deposits into employer stock, or allowing them to continue as outside share capital. Irrespective of the alternative chosen, employees were guaranteed the official market rate on their investment plus 2 per cent. Furthermore, a savings premium would partly compensate employees purchasing their own company equity for any negative difference in yields between those shares and government bonds.[93]

These incentives for wage earners were designed to offset the modest returns from equity investment and stimulate a general interest in shareholding. Nevertheless, the attainment of widespread employee shareholding, the document warned, would require energetic efforts to overcome existing obstacles.[94]

Investment associations or trusts

A weakness of the above schemes was their limited application. They could not, for instance, be operated in the public sector. Yet if economic democracy were to be realised through broadening share ownership, then it must involve the maximum number of participants. Consequently, a third element in the industrialists' strategy was to encourage the establishment of investment clubs or trusts. Groups of public sector employees, or those working in unquoted private companies, could pool their savings for investment with limited risk in a diversified portfolio of shares. Indirect possession of shares in many establishments would increase understanding of industry while contributing to a diffusion of production ownership. These trusts, the document admitted, might do little to stimulate employee interest in their own companies. Also, few Danish savers had made use of existing investment trusts.[95] Tax concessions, the industrialists believed, could overcome this reluctance.[96]

Industrialists claimed that implementation of their tripartite proposal for economic democracy would have many beneficial effects. The net increase in employee savings would ease pressure on the capital market and the financing difficulties experienced by companies. Furthermore, an increased volume of private saving might reduce claims on public expenditure and slow the growth of public saving. Admittedly, the impossibility of predicting net savings' increase and the loss of revenue to the exchequer through tax concessions were drawbacks. Yet industrialists were confident that the overall economic effect would be favourable.[97]

If wage earners' invested savings were to establish future capital ownership on a broader foundation, would this secure for employees greater influence and control over the economic process? This would be one expectation of any genuine form of economic democracy. Their proposal, industrialists claimed, allowed employees some influence on managerial decision making, though they conceded it would be limited in extent. This was not regarded as a serious shortcoming. First, under modern conditions, the document suggested, share ownership and influence are no longer closely connected. Contemporary shareholders – passive, anonymous and primarily concerned with returns on their investments – are content that management assumes total responsibility for the daily conduct of the enterprise. Second, the 1970 LO/DA agreement on co-operation committees already provided a channel through which wage earners could participate in management. In short, democratic management and consultation would compensate for restricted employee influence in the industrialists' version of economic democracy. Given an altered approach by the legislature to earnings from industrial investment, then, the document argued, owner democracy and democratic management could develop in tandem. Thus, imposition of a single panacea for the manifold problems of ownership and management would be unnecessary. Instead, many different voluntary forms of owner-democracy could evolve, gradually winning acceptance of employees, owners and managers in particular companies.[98]

THE EMPLOYERS' PROPOSAL – A CRITICAL REVIEW

The different methods advanced by the business community and the labour movement for the achievement of economic democracy epitomise the individualist and collectivist orientations of these groups. Exactly similar disagreement on the methodology of economic democracy would emerge between capital and labour in Sweden. Yet division between parties went beyond a mere dispute over means – there were fundamental differences regarding the ends of the measure and the future course of social political and economic development. For instance, the Danish labour movement's proposal for economic democracy aimed to provide additional investment capital while simultaneously securing a more equitable distribution of wealth and power. Control of industrial capital would pass from the hands of private individuals to unions and government, leading gradually to a partial socialisation of investment. The proposal could be viewed as a logical development of existing state investment and redistribution policy, rather than as a revolutionary new departure. The Danish industrialists' proposal for economic democracy, on the other hand, sought a radical reversal of these trends.

First, the redistributive element in the industrialists' proposal was negligible. Broadened share ownership was to come about not through a sharing of excess profits, but from increased employee savings. Admittedly, the proposal did contain a provision for profit sharing. However, its introduction in particular firms would be a function of managerial discretion, and its likely piecemeal application could create new income disparities between similar groups of employees in different companies. Second, industrialists themselves conceded that the diffusion of production ownership might do little to augment employee control over the productive process. Evidence from the US would suggest that not only is this a likely outcome, but even the modest expectation of greater employee interest and understanding of industry would be disappointed. According to management consultant Peter Drucker, American workers through their pension funds are the true owners of the means of production. Workers' pension funds in 1976 owned 25 per cent of American business equity. Drucker estimated that by 1985, pension fund shareholding would have more than doubled.[99] American employees, he notes, may own American business, but they do not know, perceive or experience that fact.[100] Drucker concluded that the impact of this form of worker ownership on industrial relations or American power structures and institutions can only be described as trivial.[101] Obviously, without machinery through which worker owners can co-ordinate and exercise their potential influence, then even the maximum diffusion of share ownership will not realise the substance of economic democracy.

Such a deficiency was evident in the Danish industrialists' proposal for economic democracy. They argued that the contemporary division between ownership and control, along with the establishment of co-operation committees, minimised the significance of restricted employee influence. Yet has the separation of ownership from control wrought any change in the conduct of business? Despite this development, management apparently continues to pursue traditional goals, among which shareholders' interests figure prominently. Thus, for conventional shareholders, the separation that has arisen between ownership and the exercise of control may be of little consequence.[102] This cannot be the case, however, for employee shareholders, simply because their interests and those of conventional shareholders and management may on occasion sharply diverge. Forced to choose, employee shareholders might, for instance, prefer to maintain stable employment at the expense of profits and dividends. Therefore, for employee shareholders, the right conferred by ownership to exercise control, particularly if they possess more than a token shareholding, remains important. Co-operation committees or democratic management would inadequately compensate employees for the loss of this franchise.

Apparently, the establishment of co-operation committees has not significantly increased worker influence. A similar result can be expected from democratic management. Unfortunately, the industrialists' discussion document offered no explanation or definition of this concept. Extrapolating from the opposition of many in the business community to worker representation on company boards, it seemed unlikely to involve a fundamental power shift in favour of employees. The practice of democratic or participative management in the US usually emanates as an alteration in managerial style. Privileges (such as special parking or canteen facilities, different starting times, or other trappings of managerial status that emphasise distance from employees) are abolished. Management becomes less formal, more approachable, and is familiar with shopfloor workers, actively seeking their opinion on a wide range of enterprise issues. An open-door policy is introduced, allowing direct access for all workers to the chief executive.[103] Undoubtedly, in removing some of the more grotesque manifestations of hierarchical power and privilege, democratic management is laudable. Nevertheless, it leaves untouched the existing power imbalance between workers and management, creating a democratic ambience devoid of content.

In many respects, democratic management parallels a common managerialist approach to economic democracy. The schemes advanced by Danish and Swedish employers and the worker capitalism promoted by their American counterparts are essentially similar. All seek to broaden individual share ownership. Danish employers believed that ensuring a connection between this ownership and the exercise of control was unimportant, while Americans expressed forthright opposition. Control is apparently to remain with the large capital owners or their agents. While the financial benefits of share ownership may become more widespread, the existing skewed power distribution is retained intact. The object of this strategy for economic democracy is neither change nor an extension of democratic control, but securing popular commitment to the prevailing economic arrangements.

Earlier it was claimed that Danish industrialists sought to reverse state socio-economic policy radically. The radicalism of the industrialists' approach lies, not in their multi-stranded proposal for economic democracy, but in the preconditions for its success. These demanded reduced taxes on profits and dividends coupled with a relaxation or less stringent application of company law. A further requirement – the removal of disincentives to employee saving – seemed to imply the abolition or severe curtailment of state welfare provision for unemployment and old age. Establishment of these conditions posited a return to a *laissez-faire*, nineteenth-century capitalism. Ironically, it was the social, economic and distributional deficiencies of such a system that spawned the political restrictions and supports industrialists complained of. Nevertheless, like their American colleagues, Danish industrialists were sanguine that broadened share ownership would neutralise the deficiencies of a revivified free market.[104] This was doubtful, given that the extension of share ownership was to proceed in a voluntarist piecemeal fashion while the exercise of employee control would be restricted in scope. Finally, the success of the Danish industrialists' proposal for economic democracy appeared to hinge on dismantling much of the labour movement's legislative achievements. Such a move, likely to arouse implacable resistance, called into question the practicality of the industrialists' proposal.

The Consequences of Economic Democracy

As already noted, publication of this employers' pamphlet coincided with the parliamentary launch of the labour movement's proposal for economic democracy. The pamphlet's primary function was to warn of the consequences that would follow on enactment. Not all union members, employers believed, were enthusiastic adherents of the measure, and some of their predictions may have been directed at this group.[105]

Uncharacteristically, employers expressed the fear that fund operation would effectively limit the room for wage increases. Firms attempting to offset exactions of the payroll levy would be obliged either to raise prices or limit employees' earnings. Eventually, employees would pay for the fund system through reduced earnings or higher prices and taxes.[106] Furthermore, employers pointed out that the payroll levy was discriminatory, imposing a heavier financial burden on labour-intensive as against capital-intensive industry.[107] However, they believed the alternative of partly raising fund finance through profit sharing would create new anomalies and administrative difficulties.[108]

Regarding the redistributional goals of economic democracy, employers adopted a Janus-like stance. They appeared both to accept the necessity for the measure and suggest it was superfluous. They agreed that capital distribution was 'undoubtedly uneven', but they claimed government exaggerated its extent. If, they argued, wage earners' capital in pension funds and insurance was taken into account, this would demonstrate that 'considerable equalisation had already taken place'.[109] Even if this were the case, which is doubtful, there is unlikely to have been a corresponding equalisation of power. Generally, employee control over these assets is non-existent.[110]

Inconsistency in the employers' position was not limited to matters of redistribution. While one part of their pamphlet foretold the depressing effect of fund operation on wage levels, another appeared to predict the opposite. Standard payouts from the fund, employers asserted, would promote income equalisation among wage earners. Employees formerly in receipt of above-average earnings would demand compensation for eroded differentials. Inflationary wage drift, they concluded, would ensue.[111] Such an outcome in the Danish context may be less than certain. The union movement's policy of wage solidarity was, after all, designed to narrow wage differentials. Just as all workers, irrespective of income, received the same cash compensation for rises in the cost of living, so a universally standard fund benefit was consciously chosen to complement wage solidarity. Indeed, there was even some willingness among rank-and-file unionists to support wage moderation. Admittedly, the weight of stabilisation policy borne largely by the unions during the 1960s made continuance of wage restraint and solidarity increasingly problematic. The fund system, in shifting some of the burden to employers, might assist union pursuit of these policies, thereby serving to check inflation.

Turning to another objective of fund operation, employers were sceptical that it would lead to a general increase of employee influence on decision making. Co-determination in business management, they pointed out, would mainly be exercised by employees of major joint stock companies. In certain circumstances, it might be extended to workers in minor joint stock companies. Yet at best, employers estimated, it would enable approximately 25 per cent of the workforce to participate in decision making in their particular firms.[112] The narrow scope for employee influence contained in the employers' own proposals gives this criticism a hollow ring. Nevertheless it cannot be entirely dismissed. Within the labour movement, there seemed to be an awareness of this defect and an intention to correct it. Any subsequent modifications might be constrained by attempts to balance the interests of employees in individual firms and the collective interest of society and the labour movement.

It was this wider aspect of the fund proposal that inspired the employers' most ominous forecasts. Power over investments in trade and industry, they warned, would be concentrated in the hands of a fund management appointed by trade unions and government. Individual influence would be negligible.[113] The possible intrusion of political considerations into economic decision making would interfere with the natural development of the economy.[114] Within such a system there would be no place for private enterprise, independent establishments, or the dynamic development of economic life.[115] Such claims ignored the already valuable contribution of the state to industrial progress.[116] Very similar arguments and predictions would be deployed by Swedish business spokesmen when confronted by wage earner funds in their country. These have already received detailed examination. Danish employers were to anticipate the findings of their Swedish colleagues in declaring the implications of the fund proposal to be revolutionary. They were incredulous that responsible politicians could contemplate legislative enactment of such an untried novelty. They recommended that before any decisive political action be taken, the entire issue of economic democracy should be subjected to careful scrutiny and analysis.[117] Dramatic and unforeseen developments combined to enforce the employers' recommendation.

DANISH SOCIAL DEMOCRACY IN THE EARLY 1970s

Though the bill on economic democracy was introduced in Parliament at the beginning of 1973, by the year's end there had been no debate on the measure. The difficulties that beset the governing Social Democrats within the party, Parliament and outside, may explain their cautious approach.

On the left, the party's hegemony was no longer absolute. Undoubtedly, there was the consistent challenge posed by the Danish Communist Party, but excepting the 1945 election, this had never proved serious. Its loyalty and rigid adherence to the Moscow line ensured its electoral sterility. However, in 1959 Aksel Larsen, general secretary of the party, urged on his comrades the adoption of a middle course lying somewhere between social democracy and Kremlinism. Expelled for his pains, Larsen founded the Socialist Peoples' Party. On its first electoral outing, the party garnered 6.1 per cent of the poll made up mainly, it has been claimed, by disaffected Social Democrats. In the general election of 1966, the SPP more than doubled this percentage, winning 20 seats. Receiving 1 per cent of the vote, the Communist Party failed to win any seats.[118] Ominously for the Social Democrats, a decline in party membership coincided with the advance of the SPP.[119] Co-operation between the SD and SPP in the so-called Red Cabinet of 1966–8 precipitated a split in the latter party and the formation of the Left Socialists.[120] Despite this setback, the SPP won 17 seats in the election of 1971, demonstrating that the menace on the left flank of social democracy had become permanent if not formidable.[121]

The Social Democrats responded to the SPP challenge with a shift to the left. Organisational changes in 1969 devolved greater decision making power to rank-and-file members at branch level.[122] A new party leader, Anker Jorgensen, was elected in 1972. Jorgensen, formerly head of a large general workers' union, was to the left of his predecessor.[123] In 1973 the party Congress called for the preparation of a new programme.

Adopted in 1977, the programme condemned private and state capitalism alike, committing the party to the pursuit of further equality, freedom and solidarity. While acclaiming the improvement in working-class living standards, the document declared it was imperative to counteract the continuing concentration of power in few hands. Major emphasis was placed on the achievement of economic democracy as a solution to this problem.[124] The programme was revolutionary compared with its antecedent of 1961.[125]

While these developments may have stemmed encroachment from the left, they were productive of unease among the right wing of the party. One prominent Social Democrat, Erhard Jacobsen, had already opposed the party's parliamentary collaboration with the SPP. The choice of a new leader gave substance to his complaints of undue union influence on the party's deliberations.[126] Economic democracy and the calls for a new radical programme may have fuelled the fears of Jacobsen and like-minded members that the party had swung too far left.

Division within social democracy was not confined to a right/left dimension. The debate, referendum, and Denmark's subsequent entry to the EEC (in January 1973) sowed dissension at all levels of the party and within the unions.[127] Parties of the right and centre were also ruffled by the controversy. In fact, the early 1970s witnessed growing popular discontent with the established parties of right, left and centre. High levels of personal taxation were an important source of dissatisfaction.[128] Public expenditure in 1965 accounted for 29.9 per cent of GNP. By 1970 this had risen to 40.2 per cent and five years later had climbed to 48.2 per cent.[129] Though this upward spiral had continued unchecked under the bourgeois coalition government of 1968–71, Social Democrats as architects of the welfare state received much of the blame.[130] Predictably, they were attacked from the right but the smaller socialist parties were also critical of welfarism for its failure to eliminate poverty and maldistribution.[131]

Obviously, a party or group that harnessed popular unrest with high taxation could expect, initially at any rate, to prosper electorally. Indeed, employers attempted to direct this discontent against economic democracy by suggesting it was another tax.[132] However, it was most effectively exploited by Mogens Glistrup, tax lawyer and accomplished evader, with the foundation of his Progress Party in 1972.[133] The initial assault of the party was quickly broadened beyond taxation to include bureaucracy and the established parties. By the summer of 1973, opinion polls gave the Progress Party 25 per cent of the vote.[134]

Within the parliamentary arena the Social Democrats were ill fitted to take arms against this sea of troubles. The 1971 election result had been inconclusive. Returned with 70 seats, the Social Democrats were the largest party, and with SPP support the combined parliamentary strength of the left could total 87. On the right, Conservatives and Agrarian Liberals held 61 seats, while Radical Liberals with 27 uneasily occupied the centre.[135] There was little unusual in this configuration. Since the advent of universal suffrage, no single party had won sufficient seats for an overall majority.[136] Consequently, inter-party negotiation and compromise became the essence of Danish parliamentary government. Yet, from the late 1960s, this *modus vivendi* had come under increasing strain. Social democracy's leftward shift and collaboration with the SPP soured relations with its old parliamentary ally the Radical Liberals, edging that party closer to the bourgeois block.[137] So, on taking office as a minority government in 1971, the Social Democrats' room for manoeuvre was further restricted by sharpened ideological division.[138] In these circumstances, pressing ahead with a controversial issue such as economic democracy could unite the bourgeois parties and Radical Liberals in opposition. Even so, defeat was not inevitable. On this particular issue, support from the SPP was a possibility, giving the socialists 87 votes against the non-socialists' 88. Occupants of the four remaining seats representing Greenland and the Faroe Islands had since 1971 usually voted with the government. Ultimately, it may have been the enemy within the socialist camp that prevented economic democracy being put to the test.

If the Social Democrats' less than vigorous parliamentary pursuit of economic democracy was meant as a conciliatory gesture to its right wing, it proved futile. The party's leftward shift probably appeared irreversible to these malcontents. The last straw was a government proposal to increase taxes on house owners. Erhard Jacobsen resigned in protest, but promised to support his former party in Parliament. However, he was absent during a crucial division and the government fell.[139] In the run-up to the December general election of 1973, Jacobsen formed his own party, the Centre Democrats.[140] The years between 1971 and 1973 had witnessed the arrival of three new

Table 5.1 Election returns for established parties in 1971 and 1973

Party	1971		1973		Losses	
	Seats	% votes	Seats	% votes	Seats	% votes
Agrarian Liberals	30	15.6	22	12.3	−8	−3.3
Con. Peoples' Party	31	16.7	16	9.2	−15	−7.5
Radical Liberals	27	14.4	20	11.2	−7	−3.2
Social Democrats	70	37.3	46	25.7	−24	−11.3
Soc. Peoples' Party	17	9.1	11	6.0	−6	−3.1
Total	175	92.1	115	64.4	−60	4

Note: Beneficiaries of these electoral reverses were the new parties formed since 1971 and some of the smaller old parties unrepresented in Parliament during most of the 1960s.

Table 5.2 Election returns for new and smaller 'old' parties 1973

	1971		1973	
	Seats	% vote	Seats	% vote
Communist Party	–	–	6	3.6
Christian Peoples' Party	x	x	7	4.0
Centre Democrats	x	x	14	7.8
Justice Party	–	–	5	2.9
Progress Party	x	x	28	15.9

Notes: x = Founded after 1971
  – = Contested elections of 1971 but won no seats

parties – the Centre Democrats, the Progress Party and the Christian Peoples' Party.

THE 1973 ELECTION AND AFTER

Superlatives dominate in commentaries on the 1973 election. One commentator asserts that the level of political distrust and partisan instability exhibited during the campaign was unparalleled in the history of western democracies, while the result constituted an apex in political instability.[141] It produced, another claims, the most shattering overnight change in postwar European politics.[142]

General alienation, dissatisfaction with high taxation, or divisions engendered by the EEC debate may explain why 40 per cent of the electorate, discarding traditional loyalties, voted for different parties.[143] The four 'old' or established parties which had dominated Parliament since the 1920s bore the brunt of these defections.

The 1973 election result doubled the number of parties in Parliament from five to ten. One commentator suggests that time will prove this a transient aberration, and he detects a gradual reversion to the pre-1973 pattern.[144] Certainly, the populism of the radical right espoused by Glistrup's Progress Party has lost some support, particularly since his arrest for tax fraud.[145] In elections subsequent to 1973, the party failed to retain its initial number of seats, and by 1981 these had been reduced to 16. After 1977 the Communist Party again vanished from Parliament, but was replaced by the Left Socialists. By the end of the decade, social democracy had made only a partial recovery. On its right, the Centre Democrats continued to flourish intermittently, while the Socialist Peoples' Party had regained all lost ground, even improving slightly on its best performance of 1966. Nevertheless, despite the fluctuating fortunes of various groups, plus running the gauntlet of three general elections between 1973 and 1981 in that latter year, nine parties were returned to Parliament.[146] At the beginning of the 1980s there were no obvious signs of a return to former, less complex parliamentary arrangements. Thus, in the aftermath of 1973, members of the established parties found themselves in a chaotic and unfamiliar Parliament where the standard recipe for majority coalitions was no longer relevant.[147] While it was difficult to form governments during most of this period, it was even more difficult for them to act.[148] In such turbulent waters, proponents of economic democracy could no longer steer for the haven of legislative enactment but merely struggle to stay afloat.

Political disarray was compounded by a deteriorating economic situation. Almost totally dependent on imported energy, the Danish economy experienced in full the adverse effects of the 1973 oil price rises.[149] Indigenous economic maladies kept at bay during the 1960s reappeared with renewed virulence. Consumer prices rose by 9.3 per cent in 1973 and by 15 per cent in the following year. Within the same period, growth in real GDP was more than halved.[150] Unemployment rose from less than 1 per cent of the workforce in 1973 to 6.7 per cent in 1977, and to 7.5 per cent by 1980.[151] During the latter half of the decade, the balance of payments deficit reached record levels.[152]

A loose coalition of centre and right parties under the leadership of the Agrarian Liberals took office early in 1974. Though labelled a 'black compromise' by the left, within the coalition there was only tepid support for a wage freeze, cuts in government expenditure, and taxation proposed by the Liberals as a remedy for economic crisis. Irritation with their partners and the hope of strengthening their hand prompted the Liberals to call another general election at the year's end, but the overall result changed little. Continuing disagreement among the bourgeois parties allowed the Social Democrats to form a minority government.[153] At the opening session of the new Parliament in 1975, the government announced that any proposals it put before Parliament would take account of the prevailing bourgeois majority.[154] It is hardly surprising that a modified version of economic democracy, drawn up a year later, was not put before Parliament.[155] Yet in the absence of such a measure, development of a concerted labour movement policy to tackle the crisis became all the more difficult.

ECONOMIC CRISIS, SOCIAL DEMOCRACY AND THE UNIONS

In many ways, the economic problems of the 1970s, though probably more profound, paralleled those of the early 1960s. At that time a key element in the stabilisation policy adopted by the Social Democrats was wage restraint. In the mid-1970s, confronted by inflation and unemployment, the party attempted to apply a similar remedy. Apart from the severity of the crisis, and the government's precarious parliamentary position, other considerations rendered the success of such an approach extremely problematic.

The experience of the 1960s demonstrated that the pursuit of wage restraint constituted a high-risk strategy for the labour movement leadership. It strained relations not only between members and union leaders, but between individual unions and the LO. Disaffection was also stirred up on the political wing of the movement. Indeed, rank-and-file discontent may have contributed to the rise of the SPP and a subsequent decision by the largest general workers' union no longer to fund exclusively the election campaigns of Social Democrats. Future contributions, the union decided, would be distributed among socialist parties according to their parliamentary strength. This example was followed by the Union of Printers and Typesetters.[156] Given its declining and ageing membership, this was a serious setback for the Social Democratic Party.[157]

None the less, in 1974 the party and LO jointly reaffirmed their commitment to incomes policies. Two considerations make this apparent act of folly comprehensible. First, membership dissatisfaction was not so much with incomes policies *per se* as with their inequitable operation. It was generally believed, with some justification, that the principal and long-term beneficiaries of wage restraint were not workers, but employers and large capital owners. Second, the incomes policy now put forward by the labour movement leadership addressed this problem and proposed a remedy. Prospective incomes policies

would be 'socially just' ones. That is, they would include all forms
of income, not just wages, involve some changes in taxation, and
allocate to workers a share in capital growth. For the LO these were
more than pious aspirations. The union movement, it announced,
would only become party to a formal incomes policy meeting these
requirements.[158] Yet the postponement of economic democracy made
it virtually impossible to satisfy the proviso that workers share in
capital growth. Short of a complete turn-about, the LO could not
now justify income policy participation to its membership.

In negotiating the national wage agreement of 1975, the LO could
not accept a modest settlement for reasons already outlined. The first
act of the minority social democratic government was to legislate a
solution by extending the operation of the existing agreement.[159] This
could only be a temporary expedient, and unless some compromise
were found, relations between the industrial and political wings of the
labour movement would be strained to breaking point. Unfortunately,
the leaders of both wings were largely prisoners of circumstance.
The LO could not countenance incomes policy or wage moderation
without the quid pro quo of economic democracy. To oblige, the
party was very willing but its parliamentary flesh was weak. Yet
wage restraint was a centrepiece of social democratic measures to
check rising inflation and unemployment. The search for a resolution
to this dilemma occupied the labour movement for the remainder of
the decade.

THE WAGE EARNERS' COST OF LIVING FUND

The government's statutory extension of the existing national wage
agreement was due to expire by 1976. In entering negotiations for a
new two-year agreement, the LO was subject to conflicting pressures.
On the one hand, the rank-and-file expected the abjuration of
wage restraint unless accompanied by economic democracy. On
the other, loyalty to its political ally, deepening economic crisis,
and the unpalatable alternatives of non-cooperation, disposed the
Congress leadership to compromise. Consequently, a government
proposal partially to suspend, for the agreement's duration, compensatory payments for rises in the cost of living, was not immediately
rejected. There was little new in this proposal. It merely repeated
a request made by a former social democratic government grappling
with similar economic problems in the late 1960s. At that time
the response of the union movement was unconditionally generous. Now it was cautious, guarded and legalistic, perhaps reflecting

widespread disenchantment with the inequity of wage restraint. To win acceptance, the government proposal would have to guarantee wage earners concrete future returns for any present deferral of gratification.

The compromise hammered out between the government and LO was to operate as follows. For the first three-point rise in the cost of living index, wage earners would as usual be compensated with a corresponding pay increase. However, payments for any subsequent rises in the index within the period covered by the agreement were suspended.[160] Monies forfeited by employees would be paid by the state into the Labour Market Supplementary Pension Fund.

While favouring this arrangement in principle, the unions were unhappy with some of its aspects. On the board set up to administer accumulated monies, employers and employees were equally represented. The employers' presence irritated the unions who argued they should have no voice in the investment of employees' money.[161] No action was taken on this complaint until the wage agreement had run its course. By that time, deferred cost of living payments totalled DKr. 10 billion. An act of Parliament in January 1980 created a special fund for this money, separate from the Labour Market Supplementary Pension Fund.[162]

Though the fund established by the act was officially entitled the Employees' Capital Pension Fund, it was commonly known as the Wage Earners' Cost of Living Fund. The fund's primary purpose was to invest accumulated moneys for the maximum benefit of participants.[163]

Fund administration

On the administrative board created by the act, employers were no longer represented. Of the board's 21 members, six were government appointees while the remainder representing employees were nominated by the unions.[164] Once the fund board elected a chairman, it was only required to meet quarterly. However, four specially selected board members, the presidents of the national bank, the white collar Congress, the LO, and the LO's chief economist would meet monthly. This group can authorise investment of up to nearly DKr. 5 million in any one company. Investment of sums at or above this figure require approval from a full board meeting.[165] Routine fund administration is carried on by five economists and a clerical staff.

Investment criteria

The bulk of fund capital, the act rules, should be used to purchase government bonds or provide loans. Nevertheless, 20 per cent of total fund capital could be used to acquire shares in companies with or without stock market quotations. Such investments were subject to certain restrictions. Not more than 1 per cent of fund capital could be invested in a single company. Furthermore, the share holding of the Cost of Living Fund and the National Pension Fund in any one company singly or combined could not exceed 20 per cent of that company's total share capital.[166] These broad guidelines regarding share purchase were later refined by the fund board. Investment, the board decided, would be confined to Danish companies or multinationals with their headquarters in Denmark. Companies within this group producing for the export market, or where fund investment was likely to increase employment, would receive prior consideration. Many companies quoted on the Danish stock exchange have two classes of shares, one carrying more voting rights. It was board policy to purchase whenever possible this latter class of share. Finally, the board would provide capital to start up new enterprises likely to produce a competitive product and stable employment.[167]

Fund influence

The board of the Cost of Living Fund intended it to be more than a passive shareholder. Representatives would attend shareholders' meetings of companies in which the fund had an equity stake of at least 10 per cent and if necessary block-vote these shares. For instance, it was board policy to oppose all takeover bids unless it judged them to be in the company's long-term economic interest. The fund could also assist in strengthening employee influence. Employees of companies in which the fund invests can request the transfer of voting rights on these shares to their own group. Even where fund shareholding is not significant, it can supply employees with detailed and comprehensible financial information on their firm.[168]

Participant eligibility and benefits

All those employed between 1977 and 1980 are eligible participants in the Wage Earners' Cost of Living Fund. Each year, profits from the fund's investments are transferred to the individual accounts of

2.5 million participants. Money in these accounts is frozen until beneficiaries retire, when they receive a lump sum payment.[169]

The Cost of Living Fund was initially opposed by employers. Opposition gradually subsided and it is now claimed that many welcome fund investment in their firms. This is particularly the case with firms experiencing a temporary shortage of capital but whose future prospects are bright.[170] Spokesmen for employers, however, characterise their attitude as resigned rather than enthusiastic. The fund is tolerable, they suggest, only because it is small.[171] Though the scheme originated within the union movement, there is none the less some dissatisfaction there with its actual operation. Unions desire an increase in the portion of fund capital allocated for the purchase of company shares.[172] Despite its similarity to economic democracy, the LO does not regard the Cost of Living Fund as part of that project.[173] There are at least two possible explanations for this stance. First, because the fund is financed by employees and not employers. Second, the fund is but a temporary expedient. Contributions are limited to a two-year period, and when all participants retire, fund capital will be exhausted.[174] At best, the LO views the fund as a step on the road to economic democracy.[175] Yet could it not also be seen as demonstrating in a small way the practicality of the concept?

DEEPENING ECONOMIC CRISIS

The wage moderation secured by the Cost of Living Fund had little impact. In the autumn of 1978 the Social Democrats took the unusual step of forming a parliamentary liaison with the Agrarian Liberals. The LO reacted by accusing Jorgensen of betraying the working class. However the underlying differences between the coalition parties soon surfaced on the issue of wage restraint.

When national wage negotiations opened early in 1979 there was a wide disparity between the initial positions of the labour market parties. Employers demanded a 3 per cent cut in wages and a three-year freeze while the unions sought an 11 per cent increase. Whereas the Social Democrats allowed that a small increase might be feasible, the Liberals supported the employers. The LO president damned the coalition as a 'lackey of the bourgeoisie' and demanded 'a clearly definable workers' share in the means of production'.[176] Intervention by the government's mediator, the award of a 3–5 per cent wage increase and longer annual holidays narrowly averted a national strike and lockout.

Unfortunately the economic situation, remaining unresponsive to corrective action, continued to deteriorate. By the summer it was clear that a currency devaluation had not only failed to improve the competitiveness of exports but added momentum to the inflationary spiral.[177] The immediate imposition of a wage price freeze without union consent was urged by the Liberals but rejected by the Social Democrats as unworkable. Instead, they proposed to win union agreement with the offer of collective profit sharing or economic democracy. The Liberals' rejoinder, accusing their partners of subservience to the LO leadership which, they charged, was emerging as a quasi super government, signalled the coalition's demise. In the ensuing general election, the Liberals headed a grouping of non-socialist parties pledged to curb union power and end wage indexation. The verdict of the electorate, though as usual not clear-cut (no party gained an overall majority), seemed to endorse the Social Democrats' contention that an incomes policy without union support could not function.[178]

ECONOMIC DEMOCRACY AFTER 1973

Despite the difficulties presented by the changed political landscape after 1973, proponents of economic democracy did not abandon the measure. Even the failure to generate parliamentary discussion on their modified proposal of 1976 left them undaunted. The continuing endeavours of these enthusiasts to maintain economic democracy as a live issue were rewarded in 1977. Late that year a committee was appointed by the minister of labour, charged with the task, 'of examining proposals aimed at initiating implementation of the principles of wage-earners' right to co-ownership and of the concomitant right to co-determination'.[179]

Report on the wage earners' right to co-ownership

The composition of the nine-member committee broke down as follows: union representatives, three; employers, three; association of civil servants, one; government, one; and an independent chairman. A report was produced in November 1978. Its format anticipated that of the Swedish Commission on wage earner funds. Profit sharing in France, Holland, the US and saving schemes in Germany, were described.[180] Submissions from the labour market parties rehearsed familiar arguments. The objections of Danish employers accurately forecast those of their Swedish counterparts. They suggested that economic democracy would undermine a pluralist society by concentrating power in unions.[181] Furthermore, the union movement's likely departure from the investment criterion of profitability could result in a misallocation of capital resources.[182] Finally, employers believed, fund legislation would prove unconstitutional because of its confiscatory element. In principle, it would repeal protection of the right to private property not only in business firms but even in dwelling houses.[183] The Danish report on wage earner funds prefigured the Swedish commission in one other important respect. It was inconclusive, making no recommendation either for or against the establishment of such funds.[184]

This anticlimactic outcome was offset by other developments which kept economic democracy in public view. The general election result of November 1979 allowed the Social Democrats to form a minority government. Determined to overcome chronic economic crisis, Prime Minister Jorgensen introduced the most draconion income stabilisation policy since the war. A compulsory profit sharing scheme was to reciprocate for union co-operation.[185] As a first step in giving effect to the measure, a parliamentary resolution was sponsored by the Social Democrats in December.

COMPULSORY PROFIT SHARING 1979

The resolution contained the draft of a bill for compulsory profit sharing. Yet despite its title and differences in detail, the bill was in essence the 1973 proposal on economic democracy. Certainly, both shared the common objective of collective co-ownership and influence for employees. However, funding of the 1979 scheme was based not on payroll but profit. All companies would pay an annual cash amount equivalent to 10 per cent of post-tax profit into a Joint Investment and Employment Fund.[186] Controlled in the main by elected union representatives, the fund would invest money as liable capital, provide loans to new or old enterprises, or assist in employee buyouts.

Besides the Joint Investment and Employment Fund, there was another possible destination for employer profit sharing contributions. These could be retained within the firm if management and employees were in agreement. In that event, a number of the firm's shares equal in value to the profit sharing cash contribution would be deposited in an enterprise fund. Voting rights on shares in this fund would be exercised by the firm's employees. Dividend payments on these shares would be divided equally between the Joint Investment Fund (adding to its capital) and the employees of the particular firm to be used for their collective benefit.[187] The capital of the

Joint Investment Fund was to be collectively owned by all wage earners in the public and private sectors. Consideration of the form distribution might take was postponed until the scheme would have completed five years of operation.[188] Capital in the enterprise funds would not be distributed. Employee influence was to be exercised through enterprise funds and the equity capital and loans of the Joint Investment and Employment Fund.

THE LABOUR MOVEMENT ON THE DEFENSIVE

When the resolution on compulsory profit sharing was put to a vote, it was overwhelmingly defeated.[189] As might be expected, the parties of the right and centre united in opposition. However, the measure was also voted down by socialist parties to the left of the Social Democrats. Initially, the Parliamentary Party of the SPP were willing to support the Social Democrats. Instructions from the party executive obliged the parliamentary representatives to oppose compulsory profit sharing because of its association with incomes policy.[190] Opposition from the Left Socialists was unequivocal. For them, national wage agreements, incomes policy, and various versions of economic democracy merely institutionalised class collaboration. Capitalists not workers, they argued, would be the real beneficiaries from economic democracy. As the market mechanism would continue to function within capitalist parameters, worker representatives on fund boards would find themselves responsible for decisions creating unemployment. While fomenting new divisions and contradictions in the working-class movement, economic democracy would simultaneously improve the working of capitalism. The Left Socialists believed that support for the reformism epitomised by compulsory profit sharing or economic democracy would be tantamount to urging workers to accept and work within the capitalist system.[191]

The grouping ranged against compulsory profit sharing contained some strange allies with contradictory motivations. Parties of the right opposed economic democracy as destructive of the free market, private property, pluralism and a harbinger of economic totalitarianism. The revolutionary left rejected the measure because they believed it secured for capitalism a new lease of life, curing some of its ills rather than hastening its final and inevitable collapse. Meidner's prophetic observation on the reception of wage earner funds in his country is apposite.[192]

Rejection of compulsory profit sharing in December was followed by the defeat of Jorgensen's budget in January 1980. These events marked a turn for the worse in the fortunes of the labour movement. In the general elections of 1981 and 1984 the Social Democrats lost seats. While there was only a fractional decline in the overall socialist vote, the socialist bloc remained divided within Parliament.[193] More stable coalitions of right and centre were formed under the leadership of a strengthened Conservative Party. Outside Parliament, unions were weakened by the continuing haemorrhage of unemployment.[194] Reluctantly they agreed to experiment with decentralised wage bargaining.[195] Economic democracy was once again in abeyance.

THE EMPLOYERS' CAMPAIGN AGAINST WAGE EARNER FUNDS

Danish employers are convinced there is no majority for the union version of economic democracy, either within Parliament or in the country at large. Consequently their organisation has refused to agitate or stage demonstrations.[196] Until recently, employer opposition was expressed in two ways. First, through publications and submissions to government detailing their objections and predicting unpleasant outcomes from fund operation. These productions have already been considered.

A second approach was to commission surveys among the union movement's rank-and-file and the general public on their attitude to economic democracy. Employers claim that these show only minority support for the concept.[197] Yet the apathetic and uncomprehending seemed to figure prominently within the majority.[198] Unions dispute these findings and are sceptical regarding the impartiality and methodology of polls commissioned by employers. Many of their questions, unions assert, are framed in such a way as to invite negative responses.[199] They point to the findings of a 1981 opinion poll conducted by academic political scientists as contradicting employers' claims. Nevertheless, these findings were not of great comfort to unions. Overall, the respondents for and against the various aspects of economic democracy appeared to be roughly balanced, but a significant percentage did not answer questions or had no opinion.[200] This lends substance to the employers' characterisation of the union proposal for economic democracy as too complex and their contention that subsequent modifications only compounded the difficulty of comprehension.[201] Yet the LO claims to have carried out a massive educational campaign on wage earner funds within the labour movement. The results have been disappointing. While activists have grasped the concept, a majority of the rank-and-file have but hazy notions of economic democracy.[202]

Crusaders for economic democracy were undeterred by the hostile climate prevailing from the early 1980s. Towards the end of 1985 they attempted to revive the issue. Circulation of another proposal precipitated an employer counter-offensive in which a new weapon was deployed. Previously, the official attitude of the employers' organisation (DA) to the voluntary introduction of profit sharing schemes in member firms had been one of neutrality.[203] The revival of economic democracy changed that policy. Now the DA actively encourages its members to introduce such schemes and it provides guidelines for their implementation. A scheme can either be cash- or share-based, but its operation must be confined within the single firm. Profit to be shared should be calculated on the residue or surplus remaining after the firm has fulfilled all its financial commitments and allowed for depreciation, reinvestment, etc. Management should offer profit sharing to the unions as a gift which they can accept or reject in its entirety. Negotiations on the form or details of the scheme must be avoided:[204] a recommendation incidentally that belied an earlier attachment by employers to consultation and democratic management. The DA hopes the proliferation of company profit sharing schemes will constitute a bulwark against union proposals for economic democracy. Indeed, employer spokesmen warn that legislative enactment of such a measure will trigger the immediate termination of all existing profit sharing plans.[205]

The practical and ideological objections of Scandinavian unions to profit sharing plans specific to a single company have already been outlined. Promotion of these plans as antidotes to economic democracy coupled with employers' refusal to negotiate on any of their aspects can only have sharpened labour movement opposition. One anecdote resonant with ironic paradox illustrates how the battle has been joined. In April 1986, management of one company proposed to offer a portion of its shares at favourable prices to employees. One shareholder of significance – the Wage Earners' Cost of Living Fund – attempted to block the proposal. However, an extraordinary general meeting of shareholders overruled the fund and allowed the employee share purchase to proceed.[206] Yet this scheme, Congress spokesmen would claim, is exceptional in apparently offering a modicum of ownership and influence to employees: features absent, Congress contends, in the majority of profit sharing schemes recently introduced by employers. The labour movement leadership remains convinced that genuine ownership and influence for employees can only be achieved through some form of collective profit sharing.[207]

PROPOSAL FOR COMPULSORY PROFIT SHARING, NOVEMBER 1985

In many respects this proposal was similar to its predecessor of 1979. Both shared the common objective of ownership and co-determination for employees. Though the 1985 proposal was more insistent in emphasising the close connection between ownership and control, an absolutely decisive factor in genuine co-determination, it declared, was the wage earner' right to co-ownership in Danish workplaces. This was to be achieved through the introduction of a compulsory and solidaristic profit sharing scheme.[208] All enterprises, irrespective of size or form of ownership, would be covered by the regulation and obliged to share a portion of their profit.[209] For private sector firms, the proposal did not specify the amount or percentage of profit that would make up their contribution. Employers are convinced it will issue as the same figure in the 1979 proposal, namely 10 per cent.[210] Profit sharing contributions from public sector firms will match the average profit share per employee in the private sector.[211]

Enterprise funds

A private sector employer's contribution or the wage earner's profit share may, if the parties mutually agree, remain within the individual enterprise. In that case, the employer's total profit sharing contribution will be deposited as shares in an enterprise fund managed solely by employee representatives. These representatives will be drawn from, and elected by, the company employees. The enterprise fund will perform a dual function. While providing investment for the development and expansion of the firm, it will simultaneously secure for employees an economic basis for enhanced co-determination.[212]

County funds

In private sector firms where one or other of the parties oppose an enterprise fund, the employer's profit sharing contribution will be paid directly into a fund established in each county. These county funds will also receive the total profit sharing contribution of the public sector. The size or value of the portion received by a particular county fund will be determined by population density in the county. Fund management will be carried on by a board composed of county councillors, local businesspeople, and representatives of wage earners' organisations in the area. A majority of seats on these boards must be occupied by wage earners' representatives.

County funds have a variety of aims. First, to stimulate commercial development and employment in the region while, at the same time, strengthening employee influence on enterprise decision making through share purchase. Second, to promote investment, product development, innovation and education within companies. County funds will also support the establishment of new enterprises.[213]

National council

To prevent enterprise or county funds operating at cross purposes, a national council is to co-ordinate their activities. One important task of the council is to initiate and arrange investment projects involving many counties. The council will also provide education, advice, assistance and various services for wage earners in enterprise and county funds. Again, union representatives will be in a majority on the national council. Individuals with economic or business expertise and representatives of government and the central bank will make up the minority.[214]

Profit sharing council

The purpose of this body is to resolve any disputes that might arise between funds operating the scheme. Members of this council will represent unions, government, business and the professions. Finally, like its forerunner of 1979, the proposal postponed consideration of the eventual form of fund distribution to employees.[215]

Today, the 1985 proposal languishes in the doldrums. It awaits from the socialist quarter not the former fitful eddying crosswinds, but a stiff breeze to speed its progress through Parliament, an appropriate moment at which to identify elements of change and continuity in the evolution of Danish wage earner funds since 1973.

The constants of all proposals have been the objectives of increased capital formation, employee influence in enterprise decision making, and a more equitable distribution of wealth. However, the 1985 proposal apparently added another objective to that list. Now compulsory profit sharing is to resolve the intrinsic difficulties of a prices and incomes policy. It will do this first by guaranteeing that increased profits resulting from wage restraint will be reinvested. Second, wage earners' ownership of these investments will prevent their wage moderation buttressing the already skewed distribution of wealth.[216] Can this additional requirement that collective profit sharing ensure the equitable operation of an incomes policy be regarded as a novel development? Earlier, when reviewing the background to the 1973 proposal, a tenuous link was suggested between economic democracy and incomes policy. Thus the proposal of 1979 – and particularly that of 1985 – in clearly establishing this connection, may have merely made explicit an unspoken expectation.

If the objectives of the various proposals advanced between 1973 and 1985 are examples of continuity, the structure of these proposals during this period underwent significant change. The most evident result of successive alterations was the strengthening of employee influence at enterprise level. Admittedly, the original 1973 proposal granted substantial decision making power to local employee groups. Nevertheless, the existence of a central fund representing general labour movement and community interest constituted a potential check on the development of an enterprise consciousness focused exclusively on employee concerns in the individual workplace. Yet subsequent proposals reduced to insignificance any potential for the exercise of central fund power. Indeed, the 1985 proposal was structured to maximise wage earner influence at enterprise level. This dispersion and devolution of total control to enterprise funds, 'and the relegation of central bodies to a purely advisory function' was explained as a response to widespread demands for greater local democracy.[217]

Demands for decentralised decision making are not specific to Denmark, but have been commonplace throughout Scandinavia since the late 1960s.[218] They are likely to have been a factor prompting Swedish proponents of economic democracy to substitute five regional funds for the central fund of Meidner's original proposal. However, devolution of total control to employees at enterprise level was avoided. Exercise of voting rights on total fund shareholding in a particular firm was equally divided between its employees and the regional fund. In contrast, the most recent Danish proposal appears to have virtually abandoned attempts to balance local and wider interests – a claim that seemingly ignores the existence of the profit sharing council, the national council and county funds. Yet apart from moral authority, these bodies seem to have no other means of exercising control.

Voting rights or control of shares held by enterprise or county funds can be exclusively exercised by employee groups within the individual enterprise. Despite the superstructure of county funds, councils, etc., the Danish version of economic democracy comes closer to American employee share ownership schemes than the Swedish model.

What explains the comparatively excessive decentralisation of control in the Danish proposal? A plausible explanation might focus on the much slower pace of Danish industrialisation and the persistence of small firms. One result of this process has been the continuing prominent role played by craft unions within the Danish trade union movement. The traditional desire of these unions to retain autonomy and independence has curbed the central power of Congress.[219] Such concerns may have ensured that structural alterations in subsequent proposals for economic democracy maximised the devolution of influence.

PROSPECTS FOR ECONOMIC DEMOCRACY IN DENMARK

Notwithstanding more than a decade of failure, the Danish labour movement leadership remains committed to the implementation of compulsory profit sharing. Given the broad thrust of its economic policy, this persistence is not surprising. In common with other Scandinavian social democratic parties and trade unions, the Danes reject what they describe as the neo-conservative, neo-liberal strategy of competition in which economic development is to be controlled by free market forces. Operation of these policies, they claim, has resulted in deepened social division and mass unemployment. Instead, the labour movements in all Scandinavian countries have reaffirmed their attachment to a strategy of solidarity.

This strategy aims to achieve full employment, satisfactory growth rates, a more equitable distribution of wealth, and the further development of the welfare state.[220] Of course, proponents realise that a fundamental flaw in this policy is its inflationary tendency. Yet low inflation is an essential prerequisite to harmonise full employment and satisfactory growth rates with economic stability. A negotiated incomes policy which includes all forms of income is the solution proposed by the Scandinavian labour movements.[221] Repetition of previous difficulties with the policy exemplified by the Danish experience will be avoided by fulfilling certain preconditions. Rank-and-file union members must have confidence in government distribution policy and be guaranteed their wage moderation will not become restraint of the weak for the benefit of the well-off.[222]

Compulsory profit sharing, or economic democracy, has been identified as making an important contribution to this outcome.[223] Thus, having become an integral part of Danish labour movement economic policy, the continuance of economic democracy as a live issue is assured.

The crucial question is this: will compulsory profit sharing in Denmark ever transcend its status as a mere issue to become embodied in legislation? In the past, two obstacles have prevented this consummation. First, for Social Democrats to govern, some coalition or loose alliance with other parties has been a continuing necessity. Pressure to maintain such arrangements inevitably encouraged procrastination on controversial issues such as economic democracy. Second, disagreement within the socialist bloc regarding the virtue of the measure has deprived Social Democrats of natural allies. Recent developments point to a loosening of this paralysis. The Socialist Peoples' Party has now come very close to the Social Democrats' position on incomes policy and economic democracy, though some in the SPP believe the 1985 proposal has gone too far with decentralisation. Paradoxically, this modification may explain the positive attitude adopted by the Radical Liberals towards the proposal. Early in 1986 these three parties, the SPP, the Social Democrats and the Radical Liberals, issued a joint statement on co-ownership and co-determination. Any acceptable scheme, they agreed, must be compulsory and involve a genuine transfer of ownership and control to employees' exercised by them collectively.[224] This agreement between the parties brightens the prospects for economic democracy in Denmark.

CONCLUSION

What socio-economic factors peculiar to Sweden and Denmark explain the origin and persistence of demands for economic democracy there? One significant factor was the partnership of unions and government in operating national economic policy. The difficulties and anomalies of wage restraint eventually forced unions to seek greater control over the economic process to ensure that its surplus might be both productively invested and equitably distributed. These developments were not unique to Scandinavia. In many European countries since the war, similar co-operative arrangements have existed between unions and governments and have given rise to similar demands. Examples would be the British Labour Party's document *Capital and Equality* or the European Commission's memorandum

Employee Participation in Asset Formation.[225] The urgency of a concrete response to these proposals, some designed to limit the prerogatives of capital, varied with the extent of union government co-operation. Though probably troublesome to business and government, nevertheless this co-operation was a necessity under conditions of full employment. From the late 1970s the increasing substitution of monetarist for Keynesian policy and the resulting unemployment weakened unions in many western countries. The energies of organised workers were concentrated in fighting what in many instances proved to be less than successful rearguard actions. Documents, reports and initiatives, urging a more equitable distribution of wealth and power, produced by many European unions during the early 1970s, remained as beached curiosities of a high tide that had long since retreated.

The triumphal progress of a revivified economic liberalism was checked in Scandinavia and routed in Sweden. High levels of union membership and the intimate connection between the industrial and political wings of the labour movements in Nordic countries contributed to this outcome. Even more important was the virtual monopoly of government office by Social Democrats since 1945. A unique achievement of the labour movement during that period was to inspire commitment and win support among the electorate for its goals of solidarity and full employment.[226] It was this low level of tolerance for unemployment among the generality of Scandinavians that blighted the prospects of monetarism there, especially as the policy seemed to require substantial numbers of citizens to endure the purgatory of unemployment before the paradise of low inflation, flexible wages, mobile labour and deregulated markets was reached. So, with the continuing application of Nordic versions of Keynesianism, the necessity for union/government co-operation on stabilisation policy remained. Consequently, the problem of the skewed distribution of wealth and power continued to rank highly on the political agenda. Though a solution was first proposed in Denmark, only in Sweden has the initial stage been successfully implemented. The failure of Danish social democracy to match this accomplishment to date can be ascribed to its comparatively weak parliamentary position: a weakness compounded by the fragmentation of Danish parliamentary socialism. Obviously, implementation of the Scandinavian model of economic democracy cannot proceed without a significant power shift favouring workers' political and industrial organisations. That this shift has occurred in Sweden is partly a result of the particular pace and direction of its economic development. Its retardation in

Denmark is partly explained by the formerly dominant position of agriculture in the economy and the nature of its industrial sector.

The above conclusion, explaining the acceptance or postponement of economic democracy in terms of the strength of social forces, may appear less than satisfactory. It might be faulted for its failure to apportion due weight to Danish employers' objections and the effectiveness of their alternative proposals. Indeed, may not the incontrovertible nature of their argument have made the crucial contribution to the postponement of economic democracy? Regarding the employers' alternative proposals, it has been fairly well established they would do little to alter the existing distribution of wealth and power. What of their objections to the union version of economic democracy? Its implementation, employers claimed, would create conditions leading to a dilution of private property rights and less efficient economic decision making by the addition of spurious considerations, such as employment creation, to the criterion of profitability. Yet, it could be argued, these conditions already exist but so far have not given rise to the changes predicted by employers. Since the Second World War, European economic growth has largely resulted from a partnership between private industry and the state. Danish industrial expansion in the 1960s is a case in point. This development has just as important implications for the business enterprise as private property and the goals of economic activity. For instance, can it be claimed with confidence that a private firm in receipt of state grants and subsidies funded by the tax-paying citizen is still totally owned by its shareholders? Such a point may appear irrelevant, as the object of state support for business is not control or ownership but the expansion of the enterprise in the hope of additional employment creation. Nevertheless, state economic involvement could be seen as potentially diluting private property rights in the means of production and implying that, alongside profitability, employment creation should be an additional goal for economic activity. State assistance to private enterprise can be seen as an attempt to integrate the workings of a capitalist, free market economy with the demands of political democracy.[227] So rather than a revolutionary departure, economic democracy merely develops implications inherent in the existing situation. Its establishment might ensure accountability from private enterprise for state support, and, for pious hopes, substitute more rational expectations of employment creation.

The arguments of Danish employers against economic democracy, like those of their Swedish counterparts, are rendered unconvincing by their initially incorrect assumptions. They begin with a mythical view of the economy within which individual private firms operate unaided and alone. An understandable error – for recognition of the reality and extent of state involvement in many modern economies would favour arguments for, rather than against, the establishment of economic democracy. The postponement of this reform in Denmark owes more to the disposition of social forces than the persuasive power of the employers' critique.

Finally, it would be mistaken to assume that the more abject the dependence of private enterprise on the state, the more imperative the pressure for economic democracy. Demand for such reform is only likely to arise within the context of a strong socialistic labour movement. Even then, as the Danish and Swedish experience demonstrates, success will depend not so much on the cogency or justice of the arguments but on the political power wielded by the movement. The example of Ireland, subject of the following chapter, lends substance to these claims. A little over 75 per cent of Irish private sector firms receive some form of state aid or assistance.[228] Employment growth – the primary purpose of these subventions – has not materialised. Nevertheless, native and foreign entrepreneurs remain free of the burden of accountability. That Irish labour has never mounted a campaign around the issues of control and accountability illustrates the politically weak and backward nature of the movement. Though formidable arguments might be advanced for greater democratic control in the Irish economy, they would likely have little practical result given the present balance of social forces.

6   Profit sharing and employee shareholding in Ireland – a review

Financial participation whether through the introduction of profit sharing or employee shareholding schemes, has great potential as a means of developing a company-wide identity and corporate image uniting the variety of different interests (managers, employees, trade unions and shareholders) which contribute to the wealth created by the enterprise.

Worker Participation, Department of Labour, 1980[1]

By having a stake in the business in which they work employees have a greater commitment and incentive in insuring that their firm is efficient and profitable.

Government White Paper on Industrial Policy, July 1984[2]

There is little or no evidence on whether or not the issue of shares contributes to improved industrial relations.

Commission on Taxation, 1985[3]

A continuing theme of this book has been the crucial importance of the participative element in schemes of profit sharing and employee shareholding. In the absence of this participative element or managerial willingness to share a modicum of information and control, then the motivational potential of financial participation is unlikely to be realised. Yet many employers in America, Sweden and Denmark apparently either deny the necessity for employee involvement and shared control, or only partially implement the participative element of such schemes. This chapter, in reviewing recent Irish experience with employee shareholding, will show that the response of Irish employers to these schemes is remarkably similar to that of their American and Scandinavian counterparts. Such a demonstration will support a claim of this book that the generality of employers or managers are reluctant to implement the participative requirements of these schemes. Indeed, the response of Irish employers is particularly significant because of its comparative spontaneity. It is not conditioned by an established tradition or widespread experience of employee shareholding.

Given that schemes of profit sharing and employee shareholding are essentially managerialist conceptions, the apparent general reluctance to share information and control is hardly surprising. Nevertheless, that reluctance will render the schemes ineffectual as vehicles to encourage co-operative striving or for the promotion of economic democracy within the workplace or wider society.

PROFIT SHARING AND EMPLOYEE SHAREHOLDING IN IRELAND, PRE-1982

Prior to the Finance Act of 1982, schemes promoting employee shareholding were apparently a rarity in Ireland. The few that did exist, it is claimed, were mainly confined to employees at senior management level.[4] However, two surveys conducted during the early 1980s give an indication of the extent and nature of the profit sharing and employee shareholding schemes in operation prior to the legislation of 1982.[5]

A survey conducted by Geary and Dempsey (1981–2) selected a random sample of 319 public companies operating in Ireland. Of the 180 companies who replied to the initial questionnaire, 30 operated some form of profit sharing or employee shareholding scheme. Only 22 of the 30 firms replied to a more detailed follow-up questionnaire.[6] All were large by Irish private sector standards, given their approximate average of 1,500 employees per firm. In about half these companies, the majority shareholder was foreign based.[7]

Of the 22 companies, ten had installed a single, cash-based profit sharing scheme with an annual payout. Three operated a share-based scheme in which profit was distributed to employees not in cash but in an equivalent number of their own company shares. Another two companies facilitated employee purchase of their own company shares through a share option scheme. The remaining seven companies offered employees a combination of cash-based profit sharing and share options (five) or cash-based PS and share allocations.[8] All companies had introduced their various schemes with the following objectives or expectations:

Improve industrial relations   (15 mentions)
Stimulate productivity   (14 mentions)
Distributive justice or equity   (13 mentions)
Increase employee motivation   (8 mentions)
Increase profit   (5 mentions)
Retain staff   (1 mention)
Improve competitiveness   (1 mention)[9]

These objectives, and even to some extent their ranking, are not exclusive to Ireland, but common to most profit sharing and employee shareholding schemes. Differences that may exist from country to country are likely to be more of degree than kind. In North America, for instance, considerations of equity would rank much lower in the hierarchy of objectives. Though many American profit sharing and share ownership plans serve primarily as pension substitutes, management equally expects them to affect employee motivation positively.[10]

ORTHODOX PRESCRIPTIONS AND IRISH PRACTICE

As already noted, there is consensus among researchers and some proponents of these schemes that if their potential for employee motivation and co-operative striving are to be realised, then adherence to certain principles is essential. These are:

1 *Broad Coverage* A PS or share scheme must embrace the maximum number of employees.
2 *Consultation* Employees must be consulted by management in formulating the plan and be involved in its administration.
3 *Predetermined formula* The cash bonus or share allocation must be distributed to employees not as a function of managerial discretion but according to a predetermined formula worked out between management and workers.
4 *Additional Benefit* The profit share or share allocation must be an addition to standard wage rates and fringe benefits and not a substitute for either.
5 *Communication* Continuing emphasis on the merits and details of the plan and a willingness on the company's part to disclose financial information.

6 *Direct ownership* With share allocation schemes, employees must be direct rather than beneficial owners – i.e. employees must be able to vote their own shares or at least direct trustee voting.

7 *Minimum percentage of company equity* The percentage of company equity held by employee shareholders must be above a certain minimum. Experts variously estimate this minimum as lying somewhere between 10 per cent and 50 per cent.

The reasoning behind these requirements for potentially successful profit sharing (1–5), or employee share ownership schemes (1–7), has been detailed earlier.[11]

Many of the 22 companies surveyed by Geary and Dempsey failed to meet some of the above requirements. In 15 companies the various schemes covered all employees, while the remainder limited their application to managers and executives.[12] If in a majority of companies employee coverage was generous, most failed badly on the requirement of consultation. In nearly all cases, Geary and Dempsey observe, there was no employee participation in the management of PS in the initiation of the schemes or any consultation regarding them. Profit sharing, they conclude, is the child of management in Ireland.[13] This situation fell far short of the Department of Labour's recommendation that 'financial participation must be based upon agreement and developed through good management and trade union practice as part of a total pattern and philosophy of employee participation'.[14]

With one exception, the schemes in all companies were genuine additional benefits. Distribution of cash or shares to employees in half of these companies was at management's discretion and not according to any predetermined formula.[15] Regarding communication, Geary and Dempsey report there was some action taken by management in most companies to propagate among employees the benefits of their particular schemes, but overall, they suggest, these efforts appeared to be less than energetic.[16] While the small number of share allocation schemes seemed to confer direct ownership on employees, the Geary and Dempsey paper gave no figures for the percentage of equity held by these groups of shareholders. It is likely to have been insubstantial. An earlier study of Irish financial participation by McMahon examined some employee shareholding schemes. He found that all companies operating these schemes had from the outset limited employee shareholding to a maximum of 10 per cent of their own company equity.[17]

Given that all companies in the Geary/Dempsey survey had at best only partially established the necessary preconditions for the potential success of these schemes, they are unlikely to have resulted in any significant alteration in employee attitude or behaviour. Indeed, when asked if their particular scheme had achieved its objectives, four companies answered in the negative, three were doubtful and four believed they were partially successful. Yet ten answered in the affirmative.[18] The researchers did not interpret this response as pointing to the success of these schemes as stimulants to employee productivity and co-operation. In their opinion, company expressions of satisfaction were probably no more than a statement that their scheme was working efficiently.[19] All companies were deeply involved in fringe benefits and their profit sharing or employee share schemes, Geary and Dempsey claimed, were simply extensions of that policy.[20] Apparently, management in these companies had little concern for the results of these schemes beyond their establishment and trouble-free operation.

Organisation theorists claim that the usefulness of fringe benefits is limited to holding employees within the enterprise – an inducement to join and remain. Yet improved industrial relations and productivity were the objectives most frequently mentioned by companies in the Geary/Dempsey survey. A shortfall between managerial expectations of these schemes and their actual outcome is not unique to Ireland. As already noted, this was a common feature of most American profit sharing and employee share schemes. Like their Irish counterparts, American managers introduced these schemes hoping for a positive effect on employee behaviour, but failed to establish many of the necessary preconditions for the potential realisation of this aim. Despite their motivational failure many American managers regard their schemes as successful. The fact that a majority of these schemes function primarily as pension substitutes may partly explain this paradox. However, in some large American companies where PS or employee shareholding operate as genuine additional benefits, the motivational results are no better. Nevertheless, management in these companies also claims to be satisfied with their schemes.[21] In companies like those surveyed by Geary and Dempsey, management satisfaction can plausibly be explained by regarding these plans as fringe benefits. Indeed, given that the majority of Irish and American managers make little or no attempt to establish the conditions (employee involvement, consultation, etc.) for the motivational success of these schemes, they cannot legitimately complain that their effectiveness is limited to encouraging employees to join and remain in the organisation. In these circumstances, managerial hopes that their schemes will transcend the limitations of fringe benefits must remain pious aspirations rather than rational expectations. Finally, it must be borne in mind that managerial evaluation of these schemes, flawed apparently by ideological bias, may be less than reliable.[22]

Of course it could be argued that in the national context it is of little consequence whether these schemes act as stimulants to employee effort and co-operation or merely operate as fringe benefits. Indeed, in the absence of state involvement, the efficiency, cost and conduct of the schemes would seem to be largely the concern of management, employees and unions in particular firms. Even if they fail to motivate staff, the schemes can benefit both parties. For management they may reduce labour turnover and ease recruitment difficulties, while for employees they can represent additional income.

STATE INVOLVEMENT AND
EMPLOYEE FINANCIAL PARTICIPATION

The above argument or defence of these schemes is valid only in the absence of state involvement. However, in Ireland towards the end of the 1970s a group, the Planned Sharing Research Association, was founded to urge the general adoption by industry of Scanlon-type profit sharing as a device to improve industrial relations, productivity and labour–management co-operation.[23] Geary and Dempsey concluded their survey by calling for the establishment of wide-scale employee shareholding in Ireland. While accepting the practical or instrumental arguments favouring the introduction of these schemes, they believed equity should be the most important consideration.[24] Whatever differences there may have been in emphasis, there was consensus among proponents of PS and employee shareholding that government intervention in the form of tax concessions was essential to promote the growth of these schemes.[25]

Once the state becomes associated with the promotion of these schemes, their effectiveness regarding productivity, co-operation, motivation, etc. becomes the concern of the wider society as well as the individual enterprise, simply because tax concessions used in many countries to promote the growth of these schemes involves a loss of revenue to the national exchequer. Undoubtedly, were these schemes to become widespread and realise their proponents' expectations of higher productivity, improved industrial relations and the creation of more equitable economic arrangements, then government and society might be well recompensed. On the other hand, were the schemes to remain confined to a handful of firms and their expected benefits (employee motivation, co-operation, etc.) fail to materialise, then taxpayers would be indirectly funding fringe benefits for a minority of employees. Such an outcome would not only result in a misallocation of government resources but tend to exacerbate any existing inequity.

Proponents of government intervention to encourage profit sharing and employee shareholding were apparently aware of the above pitfalls. To ensure a potentially positive outcome, Geary and Dempsey made a variety of recommendations. Tax policy should favour employee shareholding over cash-based profit sharing as this was more likely to give employees a stake in the business. Relevant legislation should be drawn up in consultation with unions and employers. Firms establishing employee shareholding should only receive favourable tax treatment if their schemes conformed to certain requirements. Schemes should involve the maximum number of employees, who should be consulted on its formulation and involved in its administration. Share distribution should be according to a predetermined formula, and employee shareholders should have the same rights as conventional shareholders.[26] Many of these recommendations repeated some of the traditional prescriptions for the potential success of such schemes.

These recommendations were timely. The Fine Gael election manifesto of 1981 proposed to exempt from income tax any shares issued to workers under a worker shareholding scheme.[27] This proposal was retained in the Fine Gael/Labour joint programme for government.[28] In July 1981, the coalition minister for finance, Mr John Bruton TD, announced that the question of financial participation of workers in their firms was undergoing urgent examination, and he was anxious that government should move forward in this area with the minimum of delay.[29] By January of the following year, relevant provisions had been prepared for inclusion in the forthcoming Finance Act. They closely followed those of the UK Finance Act of 1978. Government haste to effect its commitment on financial participation may explain the absence of prior consultation with the Federated Union of Employers or the Irish Congress of Trade Unions. Nevertheless, Minister Bruton was of the opinion that the legislation 'should help in promoting greater involvement by workers in their employer companies and in a small way contribute to the attainment of more harmonious industrial relations and increased employment'.[30]

THE FINANCE ACTS OF 1982, 1984 AND 1986

The Finance Act of 1982 and subsequent amendments mark the entry of government into the field of employee financial participation. In essence, the relevant portion of the act was designed to encourage the voluntary and hopefully widespread adoption by companies of share-based profit sharing. To that end, government offered tax concessions for companies and their individual employees. However, such concessions would only be granted to companies establishing approved schemes. These were share-based profit sharing or employee shareholding schemes which met certain government requirements.

Through the judicious use of taxation policy, the government was in a position to determine the form and detailed operation of approved schemes. It was an opportunity to ensure that approved schemes would fully implement traditional prescriptions for successful profit sharing/employee shareholding, thus maximising any potential they might have for improving industrial relations, employee co-operation, and productivity. A comparison between the conditions of approval and the prescriptions for successful profit sharing/employee shareholding, will show that it was an opportunity only partially availed of.

Conditions of approval

A company seeking approval for its profit sharing/employee shareholding scheme must first apply in writing to the Revenue Commissioners enclosing relevant details. Approval will be forthcoming if the scheme meets the requirements listed below.

The trust

The company must establish a trust which will acquire shares on behalf of participating employees. Trustees must be resident in the state and will be required to maintain necessary records, e.g. the amount of shares allocated to individual participants. They will also be obliged to pay over dividends or other monies to participants, act on their instructions and inform them of their taxation liabilities. Like any other trust, the profit sharing trust will be subject to general trust law.[31]

Initially, companies intending to install a profit sharing/employee shareholding scheme were expected to draw up their own trust document. This could prove to be an expensive procedure, and according to Mr Con Power of the Confederation of Irish Industry, it was a factor inhibiting the growth in scheme numbers after 1982.[32] To remove this perceived impediment, the CII in 1985 drew up a standard trust deed for profit sharing/employee shareholding schemes.[33] The Confederation document was scrupulous regarding the benefits and entitlements of employee participants. Yet while it did not exclude the possibility of rank-and-file employees or their representatives participating in the administration and control of schemes, there was no encouragement for such a development. This is hardly surprising given the CII view that employee shareholding and profit sharing can be considered in isolation from the wider question of employee participation.[34] A 1980 Department of Labour discussion document took a diametrically opposite view.[35] Nevertheless, government accepted the CII trust document as it stood, and apparently did not insist that it include any positive provision for employee participation. The relevant government department could, for instance, have requested that at least some of the scheme's trustees be appointed or elected by rank-and-file employees. Indeed, an Irish Productivity Centre booklet on employee shareholding advised that trusts be representative of both company and employee interests.[36] The important point here is not the inconsistency or discontinuity in state policy but an opportunity lost. A state requirement that trustees be partly composed of employee representatives would have established one of the necessary preconditions for the potential success of such schemes.

Participant eligibility

Participation in approved schemes must be open to all full-time employees or directors of a company who are chargeable to tax under schedule E in respect of their employment or office. All employees must be eligible to participate on similar terms. A company may decide on a qualifying period for participant eligibility, but this cannot exceed five years. However, the legislation expressly excluded certain persons from participation in approved schemes. These would be individual directors or employees who had already shares appropriated to them within the year of assessment under another approved scheme established by the same company or a controlling company. Also excluded were those who within the previous 12 months had a material interest in a closed company which is either the company issuing the shares or is a consortium with that company. A material interest is defined as a shareholding exceeding 15 per cent.[37]

The above requirement, that approved schemes should in effect embrace the maximum number of employees, fulfilled one of the preconditions for the success of these plans – broad coverage. As already noted, the aim of this precondition is to promote a sense of community or team spirit within the workplace. Indeed, the legislation appeared to reinforce that strategy by requiring that employees eligible to participate in approved schemes should do so on similar terms. However, if the amount of shares appropriated to an employee were to vary with the level of remuneration or length of service, the legislation did not regard this as incompatible with participation on similar terms.[38] Unfortunately, such a generous interpretation may reduce the effectiveness of broad coverage. Admittedly, few within the enterprise could legitimately complain that varying share allocation with length of service was discriminatory, given that all who continued in employment would eventually receive the same favourable treatment. Justifying varying amounts of share allocation according to the principle 'to him who hath more shall be given' may be more problematic. This consideration apart, such a procedure, faithfully reproducing the traditional hierarchies of reward and privilege within a scheme aiming to create a sense of common purpose and co-operative striving, seems paradoxical. While this method of share allocation may not exacerbate the 'them and us' syndrome deplored by proponents of PS and employee shareholding schemes, it is unlikely to reduce its incidence. A stricter interpretation by legislators of 'participation on similar terms' might have placed approved schemes on a more secure foundation from which to build a sense of common purpose and shared identity within the enterprise.

Participant shares

Shares issued to participants in approved employee shareholding schemes must conform to a variety of requirements. First, shares must form part of the ordinary share capital of the company concerned or its controlling parent company. Second, they must be shares of a class quoted on a recognised stock exchange. Third, they must be fully paid up, non-redeemable, and free of any restrictions other than those which attach to all shares of the same class. In short, apart from the contractual obligations imposed on all scheme participants, their shares must carry the same rights and privileges attaching to shares of a similar class held by conventional shareholders. Finally, closed or private unquoted companies were not precluded from establishing approved schemes, provided the Revenue Commissioners were satisfied with their method of share valuation.[39]

The above section of the legislation was meticulous and painstaking, ensuring participant shares would in every respect equal those of conventional shareholders. Success in this endeavour avoided the creation of an inferior class of partially enfranchised employee shareholders possessing paper of dubious value – a feature of some American schemes.[40] The stringent requirements of the legislation regarding employee shares was in marked contrast with its libertarian approach to the establishment of conditions necessary for the potential success of these schemes. This was evident in its generous interpretation of 'participation on similar terms' and in the absence of any requirement that trustees should at least partially represent employee interests. It was most apparent, however, in the neutral position of the legislation as to how the amount of profit or shares to be distributed would be calculated.

Expert opinion and common sense concur in the necessity for a predetermined formula when calculating the amount of profit to be shared. Indeed it is one of the essential preconditions for the success of such schemes and ideally should be a product of labour–management discussion. As already noted, the alternative of leaving the timing and amount of profit to be shared entirely to management discretion renders the motivational potential of the scheme negligible, if not a possible source of discontent.[41] The defects of discretionary profit sharing contributions could possibly be overcome where high levels of trust prevail between workers and management. This is not the case in Irish concerns at any rate, where a majority of workers apparently distrust management.[42] Therefore, leaving aside arguments in its favour, the predetermined formula must be an essential prerequisite in any Irish profit sharing or employee share scheme that seeks to effect positively worker motivation, productivity and co-operation. Nevertheless, companies establishing approved schemes under the legislation are free to choose either the predetermined formula or discretionary contributions. Again it was an opportunity missed.

Conditions of approval – disincentives?

In summary, once a company establishes a trust which will secure and distribute shares that satisfy various criteria to the maximum possible number of participants, then its profit sharing/employee shareholding scheme will qualify for approval and thus the available tax concessions. Of course it could be argued that these are already onerous requirements, and that to impose the further additional refinements suggested in the course of the above review would deter the widespread adoption of these schemes. Certainly, such an outcome would run counter to one of the aims of the legislation. Yet its ultimate objective was that these schemes would improve employee motivation, productivity and co-operation, and would help to create more harmonious industrial relations. However, unless companies establish all the preconditions traditionally judged essential for the success of these schemes, then their effect on the above parameters of employee behaviour is likely to be negligible. Maybe the legislation should be seen as an attempt to resolve this dilemma by steering a middle course between insistence on the implementation of all preconditions resulting in a very small number of potentially successful schemes, or minimal requirements encouraging the widespread adoption of schemes that are simply tax breaks for companies. In this particular case, the *via media* is really a falling between two stools. The effects of many approved schemes will likely be limited to those produced by a combination of employee fringe benefits and company tax concessions.

In reality, how burdensome is the necessity to establish all the preconditions required for the potential motivational success of profit sharing/employee shareholding? This will largely depend on the attitude or perspective of a particular company's management. For those willing to trade a very modest dilution of managerial prerogative and control in return for a possibly more co-operative workforce, the traditional requirements may be less than onerous. Alternatively, those who believe share ownership in itself is sufficient to alter employee behaviour and that the participative aspects of these schemes are unnecessary, then obligations to the contrary may appear as inconvenient impositions. Indeed, where management holds this latter attitude, the prospect for any scheme of financial participation improving employee motivation or co-operation is so decidedly bleak there is little point in its establishment. This, of course, would not apply when a scheme is established with other ends in view, e.g. to provide a fringe benefit or to take advantage of tax concessions. However, legislation designed to promote employee shareholding as an aid to harmonious industrial relations, etc. must demand that approved schemes establish all preconditions traditionally deemed essential for their motivational success.

The operation of approved schemes

Company contributions

First a trust is set up and trustees appointed. The company then passes a sum of money, its profit sharing contribution, to the trust. Trustees use this money to purchase shares in the company on behalf of all eligible employees. A company can shorten this procedure by passing directly to the trust a block of its own newly issued shares as its profit sharing contribution. Individual companies can also decide if the amount or portion of profit to be shared will be purely a function of managerial discretion or calculated according to a predetermined formula. Initially, there was a limit on the amount of tax-deductible profit that could be allocated to the trust.[43]

Share distribution

Once trustees have purchased or received a block of shares from the company, they must be credited to blocked accounts of individual participants. The criteria for allocation, equally dividing the block of shares among eligible employees or varying the amount according to length of service or levels of remuneration, is in the main a company decision. Shares are not immediately released or distributed to employees who must, under the terms of the act, agree to their retention by the trustees for a minumum period of two years. Beyond the obligatory retention period, employees can instruct trustees to release, sell on their behalf, or retain their shares. Employees who instruct trustees to sell or transfer shares to their name will be liable for income tax.[44] The extent of this liability will vary inversely with time elapsed from the end of the retention period. Operation of this sliding scale is illustrated below. Maximum tax advantage is with participants who allow trustees to retain their shares for five years from the date they were first acquired by the trust. Beyond this period, shares held in trust are automatically released or transferred to individual employees free of any liability for tax. These employees now become shareholders in their own company, and enjoy the rights and privileges of conventional shareholders. They may attend general meetings and vote their shares, or dispose of them for cash if they wish. Shares can be sold back to the company or on the open market. Special arrangements might be necessary in closed companies.

Figure 6.1 Sliding scale of percentage of income tax on initial value of shares as per Finance Acts 1982 and 1986

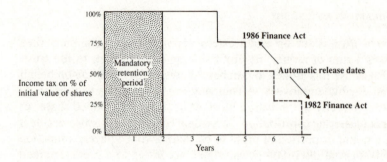

Tax advantages for companies and employees

A company that establishes an approved profit sharing/employee shareholding scheme is allowed to deduct the value of its profit sharing contribution, be it in cash or its equivalent in newly issued shares, from its taxable income. This concession is subject to certain conditions. Under the provisions of the 1982 Finance Act, only contributions up to a maximum of 20 per cent of trading profit less deductions and losses were tax-deductible. Furthermore, the total market value of shares acquired by trustees for an individual employee must not exceed £1,000 per annum.[45] These concessions underwent generous modification in the Finance Act of 1984. Company contributions up to 100 per cent of trading profit less deductions and losses were now tax deductible. The limitation on the market value of shares acquired by trustees for an individual employee was raised from £1,000 to £5,000 per annum.[46] Also tax-deductible were payments to trustees or any administrative expenses incurred by the company operating an approved scheme. These concessions could make a valuable contribution to improving a company's liquidity.

Shares appropriated to employees participating in approved schemes under certain conditions will not be treated as a taxable benefit. These conditions are in Figure 6.1. For optimum tax concessions, employees must allow trustees to retain shares from the time they

Figure 6.2 Tax treatment of cash bonus

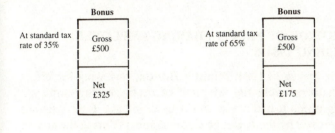

were first acquired on their behalf to the automatic release date. This was a seven-year period under the terms of the 1982 Finance Act, but was later reduced to five years by the 1986 Finance Act. As can be seen from Figure 6.1, employees instructing trustees to sell or transfer shares to their name beyond the mandatory retention period and before the automatic release date will be subject to varying levels of tax. For instance, under the 1986 act, employees issuing either of the above instructions four years after the shares were first acquired will be taxed at the standard rate on 75 per cent of the initial market value of these shares.[47] Beyond the automatic release date, shares received by employees are not regarded as a taxable benefit. Any dividend payments arising from shares held by employees or by trustees on their behalf will be treated as taxable income. If subsequently an employee sells shares, money received from the transaction may become subject to capital gains tax.[48]

The value of these concessions to an individual employee is illustrated by the following example. Assume an employee is granted an annual bonus of £500 which he can choose to take in cash or in an equivalent amount of company shares. This is a feature of schemes operated by Guinness and the Bank of Ireland.[49] Employees opting for the bonus as a cash payment will be treated accordingly. Those opting to have the bonus paid in shares within an approved profit sharing/employee shareholding scheme can, after five years, realise their cash value free of tax. The original cash bonus will now be tax free. This of course assumes that in the interim shares have not fallen in value. On the other hand, sale of shares that have appreciated in value may involve capital gains tax. Finally, tax concessions for companies and employees will only apply to those operating and participating in approved schemes. The Revenue Commissioners can at any time withdraw approval from companies or individual participants contravening conditions of approval.[50]

THE PROMOTION OF PROFIT SHARING/EMPLOYEE SHAREHOLDING 1984–6

In the budget speech of 1984, Minister Bruton, reviewing the effect of legislation to promote the adoption of profit sharing/employee shareholding, noted it had made only a small impact. Four schemes had been approved by the Revenue Commissioners during the course of 1983.[51] The minister ascribed the slow take-up by companies of these schemes to restrictions on tax-deductible profit and the value of shares allocated to individual employees. Consequently, he decided to raise the ceiling on share allocations and that any amount of profit shared would now be tax-deductible.[52] As already noted, these decisions were given effect in the Finance Act of 1984.

The minister, however, was not content to rely solely on legislative inducements. In January 1984, maybe somewhat belatedly, he wrote to the general secretary of the Irish Congress of Trade Unions suggesting they might 'review the whole question of how best to promote a more active and widespread application of worker shareholding and profit sharing'.[53] A similar invitation was extended to the Federated Union of Employers. Furthermore, on at least five occasions during that year, Minister Bruton publicly endorsed profit sharing as a possible solution to a variety of ills.[54] Apparently this enthusiasm was shared by his colleagues in government and the main opposition party. Fianna Fail's shadow spokesman on finance, Mr Michael O'Kennedy TD, in March 1984 announced his support for profit sharing/employee shareholding.[55] Later that year the coalition government's plan for the economy 'Building on Reality 1985–7' stated:

> The government, for their part, have a strong commitment to developing profit sharing and worker shareholding which they consider an effective step to ensure the success and efficiency of Irish industry and the prosperity and security of Irish workers for the future.[56]

The document also commissioned the Irish Productivity Centre to promote dialogue on employee shareholding. To that end the centre published *A Guide to Employee Shareholding Through Profit Sharing*, and organised a number of seminars on the topic in Dublin and provincial cities during 1984–5. Similar seminars were run by the

Planned Sharing Research Association and some finance houses. In November 1984, at the request of the National Economic and Social Council (NESC), the IPC began a preliminary study on profit sharing and employee shareholding.[57] Though completed in the following year, the report was never published.

Promotional activity was continued throughout 1985. The Finance Act of 1986 contained a further improvement in tax concessions for approved profit sharing/employee shareholding schemes. Reviewing progress, Minister Bruton announced that 15 companies had now established approved schemes. This, he claimed, was quite a good result given 'the adversarial concept of industrial relations and the virtual absence of a tradition of employee shareholding in Ireland'. Furthermore, there were clear developments of growing interest in the available incentives from which the minister expected 'big developments'.[58]

The occasion of the minister's speech (June 1986) was a seminar on tax incentives for profit sharing and wider share ownership, organised by the Institute of Taxation in Ireland. It was the inaugural one of a series to be held at various venues throughout the country. There was little novelty in the Institute setting out to travel a road already taken by the IPC, the PSRA and others. Nevertheless its involvement was significant. In nearly all previous seminars on profit sharing/employee shareholding, attention was largely focused on the tax advantages of these schemes. At best, their participative aspects received cursory consideration. Promotion of these schemes by the Institute, given its *raison d'étre*, was likely to confirm this trend. So, over time, the ultimate objective of these schemes (a positive alteration in a range of employee behaviour) could become increasingly obscured. Tax concessions – the mere means to promote the growth of these schemes – might eventually become their very end. In that event, preconditions will be established to qualify the scheme for favourable tax treatment rather than to maximise its motivational potential. However, Minister Bruton's references at the Institute seminars in Dublin and Galway to workers' desire for involvement in decision making, and how shareholding would give trade unionists a concrete means of controlling and contributing to company development, were very much a ritual obeisance.[59] Complaints from ICTU spokesmen at the lack of any provision for employee involvement in the administration of approved schemes had gone unheeded.[60]

The seminars run by the Institute of Taxation mark the end of a period of promotional activity for employee shareholding. With the defeat of the former coalition partners in the general election of

February 1987, public discussion of the topic virtually ceased. The concrete result of the campaign is illustrated in Table 6.1.

Table 6.1 Growth in number of approved shareholding schemes 1982–7

Year	No. of applications for approval	No. of schemes actually approved
1982	1	1
1983	6	4
1984	17	10
1985	10	5
1986	18	10
1987	28	22
1988	27	18
1989	29	19
1990	29	23
1982–90	165	112

Source: Based on figures supplied by the Revenue Commission for approvals up to 1990.

EMPLOYER RESPONSES TO PROFIT SHARING/EMPLOYEE SHAREHOLDING

The FUE survey

Early in 1984 the Federated Union of Employers (FUE) was invited by Minister Bruton to discuss profit sharing/employee shareholding. As the organisation had not previously developed a policy on the topic, it decided to conduct an attitude survey among its corporate members. The result was intended to assist FUE representatives to reflect accurately members' views in discussions with government.[61]

A total of 428 member companies responded to an FUE postal questionnaire. The responses were completed by the chief executive or head of personnel. While nearly 25 per cent or 106 of the companies surveyed operated a profit sharing scheme, the majority of these (75) were confined to managerial personnel. A minority of 31 companies (7.5 per cent) included employees other than managers in their schemes. Nevertheless, a majority of respondents (235 or 54.4 per cent) believed such schemes could contribute to improved company performance and better industrial relations. Approximately 53.7 per cent (230 companies) professed to favour the development of suitable schemes. A smaller majority (227 or 53 per cent) wished the FUE to support the concept.[62]

Apart from lack of profit, companies without profit sharing were asked to list the principal obstacles to the establishment of such schemes. Some of the difficulties cited originated in unfamiliarity with the Finance Acts. A number of respondents with multinational subsidiaries believed they were precluded from establishing approved schemes by their particular company structure (53 mentions). This is not the case.[63] Many respondents appeared to regard an adverse union/workforce response as a major deterrent to the introduction of profit sharing. They anticipated union opposition (22 mentions), worker distrust (13 mentions), and difficulties educating both workers and unions concerning the scheme's operation (29 mentions). Similarly, others implied that fluctuations in profit (35 mentions) would cause employee unrest and attempts might be made to set a precedent from one year to the next (18 mentions).[64] The use of a predetermined profit sharing formula jointly produced by management and workers along with their involvement in the scheme's administration could prevent such misunderstandings. This would probably involve greater disclosure of company financial information – a daunting prospect for some respondents. Indeed, loss of confidentiality (35 mentions), unfavourable reactions of existing shareholders (11 mentions), dilution of ownership (2 mentions), and other dangers (8 mentions) perceived to be associated with these schemes, were all cited as obstacles to their adoption.[65]

These reservations would suggest a reluctance among some employers to establish the preconditions deemed essential for the success of profit sharing/employee shareholding. Furthermore, it might be argued that withholding information and a desire for secrecy sits ill with a scheme ostensibly aiming to foster co-operation and a sense of common purpose and identity. Introduction of profit sharing in firms where these attitudes and practices persist will prove managerial expectations of unfavourable union/employee responses prophetic. In such circumstances, the motivational potential of these schemes is likely to be extremely limited, though their tax advantages may remain attractive.

Reviewing the findings of its survey, the FUE was certain that the majority of family-owned businesses would not be interested in developing profit sharing schemes.[66] Much of the review listed the various obstacles to their establishment. However, a comparatively large amount of attention was devoted to views voiced by a minority of respondents. Profit sharing, they believed, was a useful motivator only at senior management level. It would not act as an incentive to performance of non-executive personnel. This was because such personnel were carrying out fairly routine work which did not demand initiative and judgement. Furthermore, the schemes did not distinguish between persons making an effective contribution to the business and others.[67]

These are questionable assumptions. Take the supposition that employees engaged in routine work devoid of judgement and initiative will have no scope for response to incentives such as profit sharing. Its error is obvious when industrial action such as a work-to-rule is considered. This involves a strict adherence by employees to company instructions and regulations regarding job performance resulting in slowed or disrupted production. It is a weapon often used effectively by low discretion employees, which suggests that few jobs may be totally devoid of opportunity to exercise some judgement and initiative. If in this instance the limited discretion available to employees has been used in a negative way, the introduction of profit sharing might promote more positive applications. Thus profit sharing may retain its motivational potential even when it embraces employees at the lowest reaches of the enterprise hierarchy.

Respondents were also critical of profit sharing schemes which spread their largesse among all employees and so failed to distinguish between those making an effective contribution to the firm and others.[68] This criticism ignores a primary aim of such schemes. They seek to create a collective sense of co-operative striving, not to emphasise or rank individual contributions (a potentially divisive strategy). Indeed, profit sharing schemes can be seen as an attempt to give substance to managerial rhetoric which speaks of the enterprise as a team, ship, etc. in which all – no matter how humble their position – make a valuable contribution.

A policy incorporating the views of the above respondents would confine profit sharing/employee shareholding schemes to senior management. This would run counter both to the precondition of broad coverage and the requirement of the Finance Act that approved schemes be open to all employees. Yet it may have been this requirement that prompted the FUE complaint 'That present legal and administrative considerations are not conducive to the encouragement of profit sharing.'[69] Such a suggestion is, of course, purely speculative, as the employers' organisation did not specify any particular legal or administrative provision uncongenial to the growth of these schemes. Anyway, only a minority of employers surveyed by the FUE appeared to view broad coverage as an obstacle to introducing profit sharing. Nevertheless, within a year another survey was to find a large majority of employers irked by the obligation to include all employees in approved schemes.[70]

Finally, the official attitude adopted by the FUE regarding profit sharing/employee shareholding was hardly enthusiastic. The organisation regarded an entirely voluntary development of these schemes within individual companies as acceptable. However, it was flatly opposed to any element of compulsion in their establishment. Though the schemes were acceptable to the National Executive, it was not prepared to encourage their adoption by member companies: apparently it was sceptical of their merit. The Executive suggested that the development of reward systems, closely relating remuneration to performance at all levels of the enterprise, might be of greater value than profit sharing.[71]

The Sedgwick Dineen survey

In January 1985 Sedgwick Dineen, a firm of consultants who specialise in employee benefits, made submissions to the minister of finance, Mr Alan Dukes TD, and the minister of industry, trade, commerce and tourism, Mr John Bruton TD. Their submissions, the consultants claimed, were based on a comprehensive survey of the views of some major employers, though the number surveyed was not stated. The consultants pointed to the slow take-up of approved profit sharing/employee shareholding schemes, despite the inducement of generous tax concessions. According to their survey, defective legislation explained employer reluctance. Remedial action suggested by the consultants would take the form of 11 amendments to the Finance Acts of 1982 and 84.[72]

The amendment receiving the highest importance weighting (76) from employers proposed to remove or relax the broad coverage requirement that approved schemes be open to all employees. Ranking second in importance (72) was repeal of the obligation that scheme participants be treated on similar terms. Employers instead sought permission to differentiate between participants on the grounds of productivity, attendance or other factors.[73] These suggested amendments amplified themes already heard in the FUE survey. Similarly, worries concerning confidentiality were expressed by employers in both surveys. The consultants' request for the imposition of limits on the amount of information that must be made available to scheme participants received an importance weighting of 36 from employers.[74] Many of the remaining submissions sought simplification of procedures for the valuation and sale of shares in closed or unquoted companies.[75] However, American experience demonstrates that the absence of close government scrutiny and regulation of such transactions can prove detrimental to employee interests.[76] Lastly, one amendment (importance weighting 28) proposed that employees be allowed to forego part of their wage in return for share allocations.[77]

The consultants believed government action on some of their submissions, particularly relaxation of rules requiring equal participation for all employees, would be immediately beneficial. Employers, they were convinced, would then embrace the principle of profit sharing with enthusiasm.[78] Yet many of their submissions, or proposed changes, were in direct opposition to the principles, practice and spirit of profit sharing. On their implementation, employers might be embracing flexible wages or tax effective managerial fringe benefits but not profit sharing. For instance, attempts to limit these schemes to a select group of employees contradict the traditional prescription of broad coverage. Furthermore, such selectivity is inequitable as its tendency would be to exacerbate any existing maldistribution of wealth and power. This, of course, assumes the exclusion of rank-and-file employees – share allocations being confined to managerial personnel. Given employer attitudes in the above surveys, it appears likely that relaxation of the requirement for broad coverage would result in share allocations being largely exclusive to the management group. In that event, lower rank employees and citizens generally would be indirectly funding a managerial fringe benefit – profit sharing in reverse. As the former coalition minister for labour observed:

> If the benefits of these schemes [profit sharing/employee shareholding] and the resulting tax incentives are concentrated with higher income groups and the tax system is not sufficiently progressive, then it may be that the lower income groups will in effect finance the savings and investments of the medium and higher income groups.[79]

Other of the consultants' submissions were mostly either travesties or parodies of profit sharing. The request that employees be allowed to forgo part of their salary in return for share allocations ignored the prescription that profit sharing must be an additional benefit, over and above standard wages and conditions. Practitioners since the nineteenth century had warned against the use of profit sharing as a substitute benefit. One consultant of the Sedgwick Dineen group was aware of this pitfall. Approximately a month after his firm's submission he wrote:

> I would insist that profit sharing should not be considered a substitute for proper wages and terms of employment. To attempt

to introduce a scheme for this purpose would be to court disaster. It would be an expensive charade and potentially counter-productive.[80]

IRISH MARKETING SURVEYS REPORT, MARCH 1985

Early in 1985, Irish Marketing Surveys (IMS) were commissioned by the Irish Productivity Centre to produce a report on attitudes of major commercial concerns to profit sharing and share allocations for employees. The IMS survey was to form part of the IPC study on 'Profit Sharing and Employee Shareholding' being prepared for NESC. Of the top 500 commercial concerns listed in the magazine *Business and Finance* of January 1985, a random selection of 150 received IMS postal questionnaires. Only 65 companies (or 43 per cent) returned completed questionnaires. Telephone follow-up of the 85 non-respondents prompted the IMS team to conclude that non-response could be equated with a complete lack of interest in profit sharing/employee shareholding schemes.[81]

Of the 65 companies who returned questionnaires, two operated a profit sharing/employee shareholding scheme, five operated profit sharing and nine allocated shares to employees.[82] What was the likelihood, respondents were asked, of their introducing a share distribution scheme financed out of profit? A majority answered in the negative, 39 saying they were unlikely even to consider such a step. The remainder were divided between the don't-knows (4), those who might consider (15), and those who would seriously consider (7) establishing a scheme. Only one company definitely intended to proceed.[83] Of the 23 concerns in which the development of profit sharing/employee shareholding was a possibility, 12 intended their schemes to cover all employees, while 11 hoped to restrict participation to executives and other senior staff. There was a similar numerical division between those who insisted that share allocation should be seen as part of total remuneration (12), and those (10) firmly attached to the opposite view.[84]

All 65 respondents were asked to list possible advantages for companies involved in these schemes. A number of concerns either did not answer (9), or believed there was no advantage (10). Some of the remainder saw the advantages of the schemes as follows:

1 Would (or ought to) increase the commitment and loyalty of the workforce to the company (17 mentions)
2 Incentive for better productivity (10 mentions)

3 Improve labour relations (3 mentions)
4 Tax advantages for company and employees (2 mentions)[85]

Respondents' expectations of these schemes appeared at odds with the majority opinion (45) that share allocations would not be of much importance to employees. Even those operating schemes shared this view. Only five employers believed share allocations might be 'fairly important' to employees while the remaining 15 had no opinion. Opportunity for employees to acquire equity, it was generally felt, would be rated very unimportant compared with pay levels, overtime, productivity bonuses and other more conventional benefits.[86] It is difficult to comprehend how such an unimportant benefit for employees was to stimulate their productivity and co-operation. More incredibly, some respondents considering the establishment of schemes hoped to substitute share allocations for a portion of basic salary.

Respondents were also questioned regarding possible disadvantages of the schemes. Some did not answer (8), while others could not think of any disadvantages (14). Familiar themes recurred in the fears expressed by the remainder. The schemes might promote a major breach in the confidentiality of company financial information (11 mentions). Widespread distribution of profits would dilute their worth to individual employees (9 mentions) who might also expect payouts to continue when there was no profit to share (9 mentions). Finally, some respondents feared employee shareholding would lead to conflict with conventional shareholders, influence voting control (3 mentions), and might lead to enforced appointment of worker directors (3 mentions).[87]

One conclusion at any rate can be drawn from these surveys. Among the minority of employers interested in the establishment of profit sharing/employee shareholding, few would be prepared to implement all the traditional prescriptions deemed necessary for their potential motivational success. Though these prescriptions have already been listed in some detail, they can be roughly summarised as employer willingness to share information and control with scheme participants. A majority of respondents who contemplated introducing schemes were apparently anxious to avoid implementation of one or more of these prescriptions. For example, there were the continuing pleas for relaxation of the broad coverage requirement, so that approved profit sharing/employee shareholding could be confined to the managerial strata. Also apparent was a reluctance to disclose financial information and a general apprehension regarding the participative elements of these schemes. Lastly, there was the evident intention to use profit sharing/employee shareholding as a substitute rather than an additional benefit. Schemes introduced in such circumstances are at best unlikely to influence employee behaviour in a positive fashion. At worst, they could act as a source of division and discontent in the workplace and wider society.

THE IRISH CONGRESS OF TRADE UNIONS (ICTU)

At the end of 1984 in response to Minister Bruton's request, the ICTU outlined its position on profit sharing/employee shareholding. Congress claimed its reservations regarding the concept were inspired by practical, not ideological, considerations. Union movement apprehension was aroused by the type of profit sharing/employee shareholding schemes being introduced in Ireland. Congress asserted that these were modelled on American-type profit sharing.[88] In support, the Congress document reproduced a section of this study dealing with profit sharing and the American labour movement. That section clearly demonstrates that a majority of American employers use profit sharing as a cheap pension substitute, and latterly some have attempted to revive its use as a flexible component in wages. Congress opposed a similar usage of the schemes in Ireland.

Reviewing schemes already established, Congress was critical of many aspects of their operation. First, the general absence of employee consultation, involvement or participation either at the introductory stage or in the scheme's subsequent administration. Second, the reluctance of employers to disclose financial information and the small amount of profit distributed among employees which, in most instances, was less than 10 per cent. Certain modifications or additions to the Finance Acts, Congress suggested, would remedy some of these defects. The act should ensure that a significant amount of a firm's share capital be allocated to workers and that they be involved in controlling and administering the scheme. Diversification should be required for part of the workers' shareholding and restrictions placed on its encashment. Yet for Congress, these schemes would remain less than satisfactory even with full implementation of its proposed modifications.[89] None the less, Congress declared that 'the overall approach of the Irish trade union movement to worker shareholding is not a negative one'.[90] However, its expectations of profit sharing/employee shareholding were such as to render unsatisfactory any schemes based at the level of the individual firm.

Congress did not believe that the extra investment capital for growth and job creation could be achieved through individual employee shareholding schemes. Government, according to Congress, assumed that employee shareholding encouraging wage moderation would allow profits to rise, thus stimulating investment and job creation. Yet in the long run only employee shareholders would be guaranteed some recompense for their restraint. Others outside this group seeking compensation might trigger a wage price spiral. Congress insisted that even without this drawback, government strategy could not succeed. It estimated that to create the necessary number of jobs would require an annual capital investment of £350 million. Irish profits and investments had never come near generating such sums in the past, and Congress concluded they were unlikely to do so in the future.[91] Confronted with similar problems of insufficient investment and devising an equitable solution, the Swedish and Danish labour movements put forward a workers' fund system or economic democracy.

Other expectations of Congress from profit sharing/employee shareholding were a redistribution of wealth, increased equity and the introduction of industrial and economic democracy.[92] Obviously none of these objectives can be achieved under existing arrangements. The establishment of profit sharing/employee shareholding schemes in private sector firms is at management's discretion. It is evident from the IMS and FUE surveys that many of these firms would be unwilling to introduce approved schemes. So their potential benefits would be denied to many private sector employees. In addition, all public sector employees would automatically be excluded. Thus, confined to a minority of employees, the schemes might create new disparities in the distribution of wealth. Finally, even within firms operating the schemes, economic or industrial democracy is most unlikely to be realised given employer opposition to disclosure, participation and a significant employee shareholding.

Not surprisingly, Congress proposed to realise its objectives through a Scandinavian-type workers' fund system. A national trust fund was to be established. It would be financed by the 1 per cent youth employment levy, the 1 per cent income levy, and a levy on excess company profits. The trust would be an active risk investor and finance new projects or expansions to existing projects and co-operative ventures. All employees would receive individual fund certificates. Their value would be based on the number of weeks worked by a particular employee in the previous year.[93] In many respects, the ICTU proposal was similar to that developed by the Danish labour movement in 1973.

The Congress document claimed that the above approach to profit sharing was much more realistic than that being advocated by Minister

Bruton.[94] Certainly, a fund system including all workers was much more likely to realise Congress objectives of economic democracy, wealth redistribution, etc. However, in the context of a Parliament dominated by Conservative parties, the expectation of its establishment was totally unreal. The intense opposition similar proposals aroused when put forward by the Swedish and Danish labour movements has already been noted. Politically and industrially, both are more favourably circumstanced than their Irish counterpart. Yet after a 10-year campaign, only the Swedish labour movement has succeeded in implementing a diluted fund proposal. The ICTU espousal was probably a mere strategic manoeuvre designed to checkmate Minister Bruton's profit sharing and flexible wage. After all, Congress had not availed itself of an earlier opportunity to take a step on the road to economic democracy. Though the youth employment levy was in large measure financed by a levy on its own members, the ICTU apparently never requested any say in its investment. The late and sudden conversion of Congress to economic democracy coincided with Minister Bruton's intensification of his profit sharing crusade.

CONCLUSION

Those sections of the Finance Acts 1982, 1984 and 1986 dealing with profit sharing/employee shareholding have two objectives. First, through tax incentives to promote the growth or general adoption by employers of approved schemes. A second objective is a positive alteration in employee behaviour issuing in improved industrial relations, productivity and co-operation. Unfortunately, these objectives are unlikely to be realised.

The above surveys suggest that only a minority of employers would be willing to establish approved schemes in their firms. Consequently, their widespread adoption is very doubtful. In companies where approved schemes are established, their motivational potential or power positively to alter employee behaviour may be negligible. First, because the Finance Acts do not oblige employers to implement all the basic prerequisites traditionally judged essential for the potential motivational success of these schemes. Second, employer attitudes will probably augment the negative effect of these omissions. Within the group of employers who contemplate the introduction of profit sharing/employee shareholding, some fear a loss of confidentiality. Others oppose or hope to limit the participative aspects of these schemes. A reluctance to share information or relinquish a modicum of control renders futile attempts simultaneously to engender co-operative striving. Indeed, the motivational prospects are further darkened with the addition of those employers aiming to establish the schemes as tax-free managerial perks or as flexible components in wages.

Finally, the attitude taken by the FUE and ICTU to profit sharing/employee shareholding may be an important influence retarding the future growth of approved schemes. While the criticism of the schemes made by the social partners are radically different, there are nevertheless some similarities in their approaches and final positions. There are three stages in the process. To begin with, both criticise different aspects of the Finance Acts and suggest what are in effect impossibilist and mutually abhorrent modifications. An example would be the FUE appearing to favour the abolition of broad coverage requirements, while the ICTU argues the legislation should ensure significant transfers of share capital to employee participants. At the next stage, both deny opposition to the profit sharing concept but suggest the present arrangements may not be the most suitable or effective. Lastly, both urge the adoption of their particular approach. The FUE wishes to develop reward systems closely relating remuneration to individual employee performance, while the Congress urges the adoption of a workers' fund system. Again, both are complementary in being mutually unacceptable. In spirit, the social partners are united in opposition to profit sharing/employee shareholding.

In summary, approved schemes are likely to remain confined to a minority of companies where, in many instances, their effect on employee behaviour will be negligible. Their only lasting effect may be the creation of new inequities.

Summary and conclusion

At the micro level, schemes of financial participation such as profit sharing or employee shareholding have in common two principal objectives. These are to stimulate worker motivation and labour–management co-operation. Whether these are achievable objectives is one question addressed by this study. Often, schemes of employee shareholding have an additional macro objective – the resolution of a perceived contradiction between wealth concentrated in the hands of a minority and the democratic ideal. The assumption is that broader ownership of productive assets, in establishing a type of financial or economic democracy, will create conditions in contemporary capitalist economies which will tend to complement rather than contradict political democracy. Can the individualist and voluntary approach of employee shareholding become a vehicle for the realisation of economic democracy at a micro or macro level, or is a compulsory collectivist approach essential? This is the second question addressed by this book.

PROFIT SHARING/EMPLOYEE SHAREHOLDING AND MOTIVATION

Among proponents of financial participation there is virtual unanimity on the necessity to establish certain preconditions for the potential success of such schemes as stimulants to employee effort and co-operation. Surveys of American profit sharing and stock ownership plans demonstrate the absence of one or more of these traditional preconditions. The consequent scepticism as to their effectiveness is challenged by evidence pointing to the superior financial performance of profit sharing against non-profit sharing companies. Again, most comparisons between companies with and without employee stock ownership plans produced similar results. Ambiguities and contradictions apart, a central weakness of these comparisons is the lack of data on changes in employee behaviour, e.g. improved time-keeping, reduced incidence of staff turnover, waste, etc. However, in some of these comparative surveys, managers in companies with profit sharing or employee stock ownership plans were asked to rate their effect on employees. In a majority of cases there was no significant positive alteration in a range of employee behaviour. Thus superior financial performance of these companies cannot easily be ascribed to increased employee effort and co-operation.

A majority of American schemes of financial participation, this book concludes, are motivational failures. Yet this is the result of defective practice rather than defective theory. Indeed, with the establishment of all necessary preconditions, schemes of financial participation seem likely to stimulate employee productivity and engender co-operative striving. This is evident in the case studies of successful profit sharing and employee stock ownership at the Warner Gear and Rath Packing companies respectively.

The most obvious departure from orthodox practice explaining the motivational failure of American schemes of financial participation is their use as cheap pension substitutes. This is the primary function of at least 75 per cent of profit sharing plans and is probably also the case with a similar proportion of employee stock ownership schemes. Yet this is a specifically American aberration rarely found in European schemes. However, some schemes of financial participation operated by the larger American companies function not as pension substitutes but as genuine additions to standard wage rates and fringe benefits. Nevertheless, their concrete result is apparently limited to the attraction and retention of employees within the organisation. There is no evidence of any significant increase in employee effort and co-operation. A common denominator explaining the motivational failure of these schemes, irrespective of their function as additional or substitute benefit, is neglect of the requirement that employees be involved in their initiation, implementation and administration. Neglect of these participative requirements, indicating a reluctance to share a modicum of information and control, is not exclusive to the generality of American employers. A similar reluctance is manifest among many of their counterparts in Ireland and Scandinavia.

THE PARADOX OF MANAGERIAL SCHEMES OF FINANCIAL PARTICIPATION

This tendency among many employers to deprecate or ignore the requirement that employees participate in the establishment and operation of these schemes, highlights a contradiction at the heart of financial participation. Though profit sharing and employee shareholding have long been regarded as managerial tools, their success as stimulants to employee effort and labour–management co-operation apparently involves some dilution of managerial prerogative. Evidence in this book would suggest that many employers or managers are adverse to paying such a price. Instead, they establish schemes of financial participation in which the participative element is either absent or minimal. The financial benefits alone of profit sharing or employee shareholding, it is hoped, will be sufficient to trigger their motivational potential, a hope which, as the American chapters demonstrate, will usually be disappointed.

The reluctance of employers to share a modicum of information and control has a threefold result. First, at the level of the individual enterprise, it largely emasculates the motivational potential of profit sharing and employee shareholding. Second, it neutralises employee shareholding as a vehicle for the realisation of economic democracy. Finally, it raises questions regarding a more ambitious or macro objective for employee shareholding in the wider society. Employers and their spokesmen in America and Scandinavia advance these schemes as resolving a perceived contradiction between political democracy and concentrated wealth and power in the hands of a minority. They are to democratise capitalist economies by spreading share ownership and its material benefits among greater numbers of employees and citizens. However, such diffusion of ownership will do little to democratise economic decision making, a point conceded by its Scandinavian proponents while its American advocates openly opposed such an outcome. Indeed, diffusion of share ownership is much more likely to consolidate or at least leave intact the exercise of economic decision making by a minority of large capital owners.

This is evident in the Scandinavian debates on concentrated capital ownership, which employers and unions agree is excessive. Collective profit sharing or a workers' fund system, the remedy proposed by the Danish and Swedish labour movements, seems likely to increase accountability in economic decision making within the enterprise and wider society. Employers and their spokesmen deployed a variety of less than convincing arguments in opposition to the measure.

At the core of this opposition is employer reluctance to countenance a shift of power and control towards workers and their unions. Yet employers had already agreed on the necessity for some counterweight to concentrated capital ownership. A system maintaining reform or a proposal that apparently tackled the problem of concentration without altering the existing exercise of control would resolve this dilemma. The Swedish and Danish employers' alternative to collective profit sharing or a fund system is the diffusion of individual share ownership among employees and citizens.

OWNERSHIP WITHOUT CONTROL

The approach and objectives of most employers espousing wider share ownership at a macro or micro level appear to be similar. Ownership without the concomitant of control is conferred on employees or citizens. The resulting material benefits will, it is hoped, encourage popular acquiescence and increased legitimacy for the continuing exercise of oligarchic decision making within the enterprise or national economy. This essentially elitist or static conception of economic democracy would be unsatisfactory for those holding a dynamic view of the concept: that is, a belief, common among supporters of wage earner funds or collective profit sharing, that popular participation and control should extend beyond the political process to the workplace and economy generally. Yet weighing the merits of wage earner funds and wider share ownership in terms of ideological preference may be a sterile exercise.

Can a wider dispersion of individual share ownership and its material benefits ensure or at least reinforce popular identification with the prevailing economic arrangements? At the enterprise level, employee share ownership devoid of control failed to stimulate worker effort or labour–management co-operation. The effect of broadening this type of share ownership in the wider society is likely to be equally insignificant. Drucker has shown how beneficial ownership by American workers of a sizeable portion of American industry had no effect on their attitudes or behaviour. Apparently, there is no evidence indicating any different or significant effect on European workers with similar ownership through institutional investments. This would suggest that broadening share ownership may be superfluous, while its results will likely be negligible.

Proponents of share ownership might regard the above reasoning

as flawed because it fails to distinguish between impersonal ownership through pension funds and the individual personal ownership
of shares. Certainly such individualised ownership would seem to
provide a more tangible foundation from which to claim a common
interest between employees or citizens and large capital owners. Yet
in most cases these forms of ownership, individual shareholding
or pension funds, share a common characteristic. Both, in effect,
divorce ownership from the exercise of control. In such circumstances,
attempts to motivate employee shareholders or identify their interests with those of the firm and its management by appealing to a
sense of ownership will, American experience suggests, fail. Indeed,
such appeals might raise expectations which, when frustrated by the
absence of influence and control, could prove counter-productive.
The case study of South Bend Lathe was a dramatic example of such
an outcome. Thus ownership without control, irrespective of its form,
seems unlikely to generate positive responses from employees in the
enterprise or from citizens in the wider society.

Another defect of employee shareholding at a macro level would
be its tendency to exacerbate the maldistribution of wealth. Employer
organisations in Ireland and Scandinavia opposed any legal obligation on their members to adopt these schemes. The inevitable
haphazard and piecemeal establishment of employee shareholding
would exclude many from its benefits. A consequence would be the
creation of new disparities in income between groups of workers.
Again, this could be a source of discontent. Undoubtedly it would
add to the difficulties in operating an incomes policy or national wage
agreement.

Despite the validity of this latter observation, the juxtaposition
of employee shareholding and incomes policies seems somewhat
anachronistic. Employee shareholding after all was conceived at a
time when *laissez-faire* individualism reigned virtually unchallenged
as the dominant orthodoxy and the most effective way of conducting
economic affairs. To this day, employee shareholding retains many
of those assumptions. In the interim, however, developments such
as political democracy, increasing state involvement and support in
industry and the rise in some countries of powerful labour movements
with a collectivist orientation have complicated the picture. These
developments have brought to the fore problems of accountability, maldistribution, the conduct of national economic policy and
the terms of co-operation between capital and labour. Employee
shareholding – an individualist response to these complexities – is
no longer adequate. As already noted, these schemes mostly failed

to alter the distribution of wealth or power, a failing which, in Sweden or Denmark at any rate, condemned them to irrelevance.

COLLECTIVIST AND INDIVIDUALIST APPROACHES TO ECONOMIC DEMOCRACY

For the problems and paradoxes of modern capitalist economies operating within a democratic political framework, a more effective solution would seem to be provided by the Scandinavian labour movement's proposals for collective profit sharing. Yet comparisons between managerial schemes of financial participation and the fund proposals of Danish and Swedish unions might appear unfair. The success or failure of profit sharing or employee shareholding after more than 100 years of practice is relatively easy to assess. On the other hand, the very recent establishment of wage earner funds in Sweden renders any judgement as to their effectiveness largely speculative. Nevertheless, a priori claims for the superiority of the labour movement initiative over its managerialist counterpart may be sustainable. Collective profit sharing or wage earner funds have been specifically developed in response to emerging problems in contemporary capitalist economies. They are designed to secure wage moderation, offset declining investment, increase economic growth, while simultaneously correcting a recurring defect of this strategy – increased maldistribution of wealth. Furthermore, the funds would gradually increase the influence and control of employees and citizens over the economic process. It was, in short, an attempt to purge Keynesian economic policy of its defects while retaining full employement. In sharp contrast, schemes of employee shareholding hope to resolve contemporary problems by re-creating the less complex economic conditions of an earlier time.

Yet even if the superiority of the collectivist approach to economic democracy at a macro level is recognised, critics can point to its weakness at the micro level. For instance, Swedish wage earner funds attempt to balance local trade union interests, general labour movement interests, and the national interest. The resultant complexity of the scheme may make it irrelevant or remote for the individual rank-and-file employee. Certainly, at a micro level, the individualist approach to economic democracy epitomised by the Rath Packing Company case study would appear to have the advantage. However, Swedish proponents of wage earner funds are aware that the scheme could appear remote to rank-and-file employees, but this can be offset, they believe, by increased worker participation in decision making at all levels in the enterprise. Indeed, the Scandinavian labour movement regards economic and industrial democracy as interdependent elements of a strategy to democratise economic decision making within the enterprise and wider society.

Of course, from the viewpoint of orthodox free marketeers, the most pernicious aspect of wage earner funds is their stultifying effect on economic decision making with the introduction of political criteria such as employment creation. Such fears are exaggerated if not disingenuous. Many firms throughout Western Europe benefit from state grants, subsidies or tax concessions. The long-term object of much of this aid is job creation. However, under present arrangements, large capital owners are almost free of accountability. Far from being a revolutionary measure, the establishment of economic democracy will merely serve to regulate an existing situation. By strengthening the economic influence of workers and citizens, it will impose some control and accountability on the state's overmighty subjects, laying the foundation of a more rational and equitable economic order.

IMPLICATIONS FOR THE DEVELOPMENT OF FINANCIAL PARTICIPATION IN IRELAND

The implications of this book for the development of financial participation in Ireland must now be considered. For Irish proponents of financial participation the central question is: how can the objective of these schemes – increased worker motivation and more harmonious industrial relations – be realised? This book demonstrates that such an outcome is only likely where profit sharing/ employee shareholding schemes implement orthodox prescriptions. The Irish chapter shows that minor modifications to existing legislation are necessary to ensure that approved schemes meet traditional requirements.

Amended legislation is likely to have a number of beneficial effects. First, it would maximise the potential of approved profit sharing/employee shareholding schemes to motivate workers and engender co-operative striving. In that event, the tax concessions used to promote the growth of these schemes could be regarded more as an investment than as a loss to the national exchequer. Second, in introducing an element of worker participation, it might encourage more positive union attitudes to these schemes. Admittedly the ICTU's initial response to profit sharing/employee shareholding was to demand a workers' fund system on the Danish model. This cannot be regarded as a practical proposal given the balance of social forces in Ireland. Perhaps it would be more realistic to view this demand as a bargaining counter or opening gambit. The ICTU's criticism of these schemes, unlike that of its Scandinavian counterparts, is based solely on practical and not ideological considerations. One complaint frequently voiced by Congress spokespersons was the absence of any requirement in those sections of the Finance Acts dealing with profit sharing/employee shareholding that employees be involved in a scheme's administration. The suggested legislative amendments would redress this grievance. Furthermore, recent difficulties in Waterford Glass, where unionised workers have requested shares in return for various concessions, may oblige Congress to take a more positive and less detached view of employee shareholding schemes.

However, the suggested legislative amendments have some possible drawbacks. For instance, a requirement that approved profit sharing/employee shareholding schemes should involve workers in their administration could act as a deterrent to some employers contemplating their introduction. In that case, quantity may be sacrificed to quality. Yet as a long-term strategy, this approach may prove more viable. This book suggests that only those profit sharing or employee shareholding schemes that implement traditional prescriptions according to their letter and spirit have a reasonable prospect of realising their objectives. If so, their success may encourage interested but reluctant employers to trade a modest dilution in managerial prerogative for a motivated and co-operative workforce.

At best, these are *ad hoc* suggestions. Yet they reflect the difficulties created by the Irish government approach to financial participation. The sections of the 1982 Finance Act designed to promote employee shareholding (a copy of UK legislation) were introduced without consultation with the social partners or investigation into the appropriateness of such schemes in the Irish context. Nevertheless, as currently operated, employee shareholding constitutes an indirect cost to the state and its taxpayers. Consequently, the schemes should be subject to a cost–benefit analysis. One possible approach would be to establish clearly the expectations of the state from these schemes. After that, a programme of empirical research to discover, at enterprise level, the practical outcome of these schemes, should be initiated. A realistic assessment of their performance would then assist rational decision making regarding their future.

THE PROSPECT FOR ECONOMIC DEMOCRACY

This book suggests that the Scandinavian fund system is the approach most likely to realise economic democracy. Yet it would be naive to assume that the objective merits of the proposal will play a significant part in securing its implementation. Success or failure in this matter will be determined by the balance of social forces. This explains its postponement in Denmark and its partial implementation in Sweden. Such vicissitudes are hardly surprising when the struggles in many European countries to achieve universal suffrage are considered. The proponents of economic democracy may have to travel an even longer and more difficult road to its enactment.

PERSPECTIVES OR FRAMES OF REFERENCE ON FINANCIAL PARTICIPATION

This book attempted to assess the motivational potential of some schemes of financial participation, and to identify among them a likely vehicle for the realisation of economic democracy. Certainly some proponents and practitioners of financial participation had one or other of these objectives in mind. However, throughout this book there were others who could legitimately and convincingly disclaim either an intention to use the schemes as stimulants to employee effort, or a concern with the establishment of economic democracy. Among the aims, objectives and sometimes contradictory expectations of financial participation, there is great scope for confusion. Much of this ambiguity could be reduced by some system of classification. Perspectives on financial participation can be roughly divided into four categories.

1 The traditional perspective

Traditional or altruistic proponents and practitioners of profit sharing/ employee shareholding have existed in Europe, and to a lesser extent in America, since the mid-nineteenth century. Their motivation to share profit is generally inspired by Christian, philanthropic or paternalist sentiments of *noblesse oblige*. Frequently, altruistic practitioners justify their largesse by reference to equity and social justice, or by a claim that employees have a right to share in the profits they help create. For altruistic proponents and practitioners of financial participation, the benefit lies primarily in virtue being its own reward, though there may also be some expectation of more harmonious labour–management relations.

There can be the odd blemish in this otherwise perfect picture. In cases where the decision to share profits is principally animated by paternalism, a union presence in the firm can become a source of tension. Paternalist practitioners might come to regard continuing union loyalty as smacking of ingratitude, while many modern employees may resent any scheme with paternalist overtones, no matter how well intentioned. Yet the John Lewis Partnership, a contemporary example of the traditional or Christian/philanthropic approach to financial participation, remains free of these defects. However, among practitioners of financial participation, traditionalists have generally remained in a minority.

2   The managerial perspective

Schemes of profit sharing or employee shareholding are most frequently used as managerial tools. Invariably, owners or their managerial agents establish schemes to perform a particular function, or to result in some positive outcome for the firm. Yet within this broad managerial goal, motivations and expectations can vary, and the adoption of a particular perspective is to some extent determined by the type, size and market situation of the firm. The managerial perspective can be subdivided into three categories.

(a)   Sophisticated managerialism

This approach to profit sharing/employee shareholding is most commonly found in large, capital-intensive multinational corporations. Cash or shares are distributed to all permanent employees, the amount varying according to the individual's salary or length of service. In some instances, the profit or share scheme is only one element in a package of fringe benefits, additional to standard wage or salary. Management expects this generosity to encourage employee attachment to the firm, and so reduce labour turnover. In the wider society, these benefits help to project an image of the caring, socially responsible corporation and good employer. This is likely to widen the pool of potential recruits, thus facilitating management selection of the most talented. From a strictly economic viewpoint, the apparent intangibility of these benefits to the corporation is offset by tax concessions granted by many governments to companies operating such schemes.

Few, if any, of the corporations which adopt the above perspective use financial participation as an incentive to increased employee effort and productivity. Occasionally, in the course of the chairman's address or in internal company publications, vague references may be made to a connection between employee effort and profit; however, beyond ensuring the efficient and trouble-free functioning of the profit sharing/employee shareholding scheme, little effort is made to give this rhetoric practical effect. This is borne out by the results of the Geary/Dempsey survey and the example of the Harris Trust Savings Bank in Chicago.

There are other less generous versions of the above approach to financial participation. A recent trend in large labour-intensive corporations is to divide the workforce into core and peripheral groups. The peripheral group is composed of unskilled, part-time, contract or seasonal workers, while skilled, technical and professional employees constitute the core. Usually, peripheral workers are relatively easy to replace and require little training. It is the opposite case with core workers. Consequently, as an inducement to join and remain in the organisation, core workers are sometimes offered participation in a company shareholding scheme.[1] A more traditional example of this approach is the executive share option scheme, which restricts participation to the senior management group.

(b) Cost–benefit managerialism

This approach is often adopted in small firms operating in a competitive market. In these circumstances, the introduction of financial participation is expected to result in some concrete economic benefit or competitive advantage for the company. Profit sharing or employee shareholding, it is hoped, will enhance labour–management co-operation and increase the quality and quantity of employee output. For many American managers with a cost–benefit perspective on financial participation, this is not the only, or principal expectation of deferred profit sharing. As Chapter 2 demonstrates, a majority of these schemes primarily function as cheap pension substitutes. Funding a pension through profit sharing is less costly, and avoids many of the obligations and regulations governing defined benefit pension plans. Another example of this approach is a recent attempt to revive the practice where the profit sharing bonus becomes a flexible component in a formerly fixed or standard wage. Here profit sharing is used as a device to control or reduce labour costs. An example of this approach is the United Auto Workers' experience with profit sharing.

The development and growth of ESOPs has created new opportunities for the cost–benefit approach to financial participation. Sophisticated and flexible, these plans have a variety of uses, ranging from being a technique of corporate finance to a high-risk pension benefit. Some applications of an ESOP principally benefit the company owners rather than its employees. Indeed, with some manifestations of the cost–benefit approach to financial participation, the connection with sharing is extremely tenuous.

(c)   Machiavellian managerialism

This approach to financial participation is often adopted by management in non-union firms. Profit sharing/employee shareholding is used as a defence or deterrent against union organising drives. Management suggests to workers that its unforced generosity in sharing profit renders a union superfluous. Sometimes management may threaten to abandon the scheme if workers opt for union membership. As can be seen in Chapter 2, this strategy has met with some success in North America.

In Europe, the Machiavellian approach to financial participation is less overt. Yet, where employee shareholding features as a weapon in the arsenal of the competent human resource manager (HRM), it can darken a union's prospects. Shareholding, apparently providing a personal financial stake, complements HRM attempts to establish an individual relationship between the company and its employees. Effective application of this strategy can weaken the appeal of collectivism and even in the organised enterprise its tendency can be to marginalise the union.

3   The New Right or neo-liberal perspective

Despite its title, this is hardly a novel perspective on financial participation as it has enjoyed an intermittent popularity since the 1880s. Neo-liberal proponents of financial participation see it as a device for resolving a perceived contradiction between capitalism and democracy or between concentrated wealth and power and the democratic ideal. Broadening share ownership among employees and citizens, they believe, will establish a people's capitalism. This approach operates on a micro and macro level.

At the enterprise or micro level, share ownership will provide employees with a financial stake in the company and so dissolve conflicts of interest between capital and labour. Establishing an identity of interest in the workplace will have ramifications in the wider society or at a macro level. Worker owners, it is assumed, will see the world differently from mere wage workers. Thus, worker share ownership will encourage an identification with shareholders generally, an attachment to the prevailing economic arrangements, and diminishing enthusiasm for socialist or collectivist projects. Furthermore, some expect broadened share ownership eventually to issue in popular support for reducing levels of corporate taxation and welfare expenditure. Certainly, this was a hope entertained by Louis O. Kelso.

Other versions of the neo-liberal approach focus more on citizens than on employees. One method of establishing participatory or people's capitalism is to gift a public sector company to the whole population in the form of individual shares. However, privatisation of a state company through a stock exchange flotation is the more favoured device. Initially, a limit may be placed on the number of shares that can be purchased by an individual or institution. This provision appears to have a twofold objective. First, it ensures a wider dispersion of share ownership among citizens and employees. Second, it disarms criticism that privatisation merely involves the metamorphosis of public ownership into oligarchic ownership by a few wealthy individuals. In the long term, the democratic aspect of the above provision is largely illusory as share ownership tends to re-concentrate.

The neo-liberal approach to financial participation, by providing employees and citizens with a financial stake, hopes to secure popular commitment to the prevailing economic arrangements. As to resolving the contradiction between concentrated wealth and power and the democratic ideal, it is no more than a symbolic solution. It is concerned to maintain, not transform, the existing arrangements. Indeed, some proponents see widespread share ownership as constituting a check on what they regard as the dysfunctional effect of political democracy on the business system. This would be a view shared by Kelso and some Danish employers. Finally, among its more utopian proponents, is the belief that people's capitalism can re-create that garden of Eden where *laissez faire* reigns supreme, and into which the serpent of state interventionism had not yet entered.

4 The social democratic or union movement perspective

Compared with other perspectives on financial participation, the social democratic is of fairly recent origin. Indeed, its development owes much to a particular set of circumstances. The operation of Keynesian economic policy, and the maintenance of full employment usually requires wage restraint as an antidote to inflation. Throughout Europe, during the postwar period, many labour movements co-operated with their social democratic governments in this endeavour. Such co-operation was particularly consistent and sustained in Scandinavia. Restraining wages and allowing profits to rise is always a difficult policy for unions. Yet, increased profit for re-investment was essential if full employment was to be maintained. While in Sweden and Denmark the policy was successful, it had unintended consequences. Corporate self-financing, coupled with government taxation policy, resulted in enormous concentration of wealth and power in the hands of a few large capital owners. To the Swedish and Danish labour movements, committed as they are to a more equitable distribution of wealth and power, remedial action was essential.

While profit sharing seemed the obvious answer, it could not conflict with the labour movement ideals of collectivism and class solidarity. Consequently, conventional approaches in which profit in the form of cash or shares is distributed to individual workers in particular firms, was excluded. An examination of the reasoning behind this exclusion throws into sharp relief the social democratic or union movement perspective on financial participation. Cash-based profit sharing was rejected because it withdraws potential investment capital from the enterprise, fuels inflation and cannot contribute to worker influence on economic decision making. Though share ownership can potentially facilitate worker influence on decision making within the individual firm, this was also rejected. First, the benefits of share ownership for individual workers in different firms would be uneven, thus creating new income disparities and undermining union wage policy. Second, even where worker share ownership facilitates worker influence, it may be productive of an enterprise consciousness at odds with the broad socio-economic perspective of the labour movement. Consequently, the approach adopted by the Social Democrats is to base profit sharing on the collective, rather than the individual.

For Social Democrats, collective profit sharing is free of what they regard as the defects of conventional approaches to financial participation. It is non-inflationary and unites rather than divides workers along individual or enterprise lines. Also, it facilitates worker and union influence on economic decision making within the enterprise and at a national level. Furthermore, wage restraint and high profits will no longer exacerbate maldistribution, but instead will speed the transfer of ownership and control from a minority of large capital owners to the labour movement and society generally.

When compared with other approaches, the social democratic perspective on financial participation appears radical if not revolutionary. In large measure this is due to the assumptions underlying conventional approaches to financial participation which are rooted in a less complex, nineteenth-century, social and economic order. Far from constituting a revolutionary new departure, the social democratic perspective on financial participation is merely a response to the growing interdependence of political and economic policy. The democratisation of economic decision making through collective profit sharing is the equitable and logical outcome of this development.

There is an element of artificiality in the above classification of perspectives on financial participation. In reality, boundaries between the perspectives are not rigid and impermeable, but fluid and overlapping. An exception would be the sharp division between the neo-liberal and social democratic perspectives.

SOME CONCLUDING REMARKS

Schemes of profit sharing and employee shareholding have a nineteenth-century origin. Since that time, they have enjoyed a cyclical popularity with managers and owners. Yet with each revival, a majority of practitioners seem fated to repeat the old errors. American use of profit sharing as a pension substitute despite previous failures of this strategy, is a case in point. Another example is the recent attempt to revive profit sharing as a flexible component in wages. Some contemporary proponents of the flexible wage concept appear unaware of its antiquity and previous failures. The obvious explanation is the absence of a historical perspective in much writing on financial participation. Also, the academic, or detached, researchers in the field of financial participation are far outnumbered by enthusiasts. Furthermore, despite the simplicity of the concept, there seems to be some confusion as to what constitutes profit sharing. With some manifestations of profit sharing, it is difficult to see any connection with genuine sharing.

More independent research, with a historical dimension, will help clear confusion that is not simply wilful. However, it is questionable if the individualist approach to financial participation epitomised by profit sharing/employee shareholding, remains relevant in the late twentieth-century. Collective profit sharing is the more relevant response. However, individualist schemes of financial participation are likely to retain an attractiveness for management, as they apparently offer a shortcut to harmonious industrial relations and industrial peace.

Notes

INTRODUCTION

1 Quoted in S. Taylor, *Profit Sharing between Labour and Capital* (London 1884), p. 138.
2 S. Lewis, *Main Street* (London 1973); 1st edn 1921, pp. 54–5. My thanks to John O'Riordan for bringing this quotation to my attention.
3 S. Pollard, *The Genesis of Modern Management* (Harmondsworth 1968), pp. 76, 189.
4 S. Marglin, 'The origins and functions of hierarchy in capitalist production', in T. Nichols (ed.) *Capital and Labour* (London 1980), pp. 237–54.
5 E.P. Thompson, 'Time, work discipline and industrial capitalism', in *Past and Present* (Vol. 38, 1967), pp. 56–97.
6 A. Fox, *Beyond Contract: Work Power and Trust Relations* (London 1974), p. 187.
7 A. Fox, *Man Mismanagement* (London 1974), pp. 52–3.
8 D.F. Schloss, *Methods of Industrial Remuneration*, 3rd edn (London 1898), pp. 241–2.
9 See commentary by D.F. Schloss, ibid., pp. 242–8. See also B.L. Metzger and J.A. Colletti, *Does Profit Sharing Pay?*, Profit Sharing Research Foundation (PSRF) (Evanston, Illinois 1971), p. 5.
10 S. Taylor, *Profit Sharing between . . .*, p. vii.
11 R.A. Church, 'Profit sharing and labour relations in England in the 19th century', *International Review of Social History* (Vol. 14, 1971), p. 6.
12 E. Bristow, 'Profit sharing, socialism and labour unrest', in K.D. Brown (ed.) *Essays in Anti-Labour History* (London 1974), pp. 264–5.
13 Ibid., p. 273; D.F. Schloss, *Methods of Industrial . . .*, Parts 1 and 2, pp. 366–79.
14 E. Bristow, 'Profit sharing, socialism . . .', p. 282.
15 R.A. Church, 'Profit sharing and labour relations . . .', pp. 10,16.
16 M. Derber, *The American Idea of Industrial Democracy 1865–1965* (Illinois 1970).
17 Ibid., pp. 204–20.

18 K.M. Thompson, *Profit Sharing – Democratic Capitalism in American Industry* (New York 1949), p. 8.
19 G.D.H. Cole, *The World of Labour* (London 1913), pp. 328, 333.
20 K.M. Thompson, *Profit Sharing – Democratic Capitalism . . .*, p. 25.
21 S. Taylor, *Profit Sharing between Labour . . .*, p. 25.
22 Council of Profit Sharing Industries (CPSI), *Revised Profit Sharing Manual* (Michigan 1951), p. 4.
23 K.M. Thompson, *Profit Sharing – Democratic Capitalism . . .*, pp. 154–5.
24 A. Flanders, R. Pomeranz and J. Woodward, *Experiment in Industrial Democracy: A Study of the John Lewis Partnership* (London 1968), pp. 181, 242, 246.
25 E. Bristow, 'Profit sharing, socialism . . .', p. 262.
26 See Chapter 2.
27 See Chapter 2.
28 K.M. Thompson, *Profit Sharing – Democratic Capitalism . . .*', p. 180.
29 Ibid., p. 187.
30 G. Copeman, P. Moore and C. Arrowsmith, *Shared Ownership – How to Use Capital Incentives to Sustain Business Growth* (Aldershot 1984), p. 236.
31 See Chapter 4, note 91.
32 See F. Wilken, 'New forms of ownership in industry', in P. Derrick, J.F. Phipps (eds) *Co-ownership, Co-operation and Control* (London 1969), p. 73.
33 C.B. Macpherson, *The Life and Times of Liberal Democracy* (Oxford 1977), p. 111.
34 Quoted in E. Bristow, 'Profit sharing, socialism . . .', p. 263.

AIM AND APPROACH OF BOOK

1 R. Bean, *Comparative Industrial Relations: An Introduction to Cross-National Perspectives* (London 1985); J. Schregle, 'Comparative industrial relations – pitfalls and potential', in *International Labor Review* (Vol. 120, No. 1, Jan.–Feb. 1981).

CHAPTER 1

1 J.A. Schumpeter, *Capitalism, Socialism and Democracy* (London 1943), p. 300.
2 D.F. Schloss, *Methods of Industrial Remuneration* (London 1898), p. 310.
3 J. Dunn, *Western Political Theory in the Face of the Future* (Cambridge 1979), p. 15.
4 R. Williams, *Key Words – A Vocabulary of Culture and Society* (London 1976), p. 83.
5 C. Pateman, *Participation and Democratic Theory* (Oxford 1970), p. 22.
6 J. Dunn, *Western Political Theory . . .*, p. 15; R. Williams, *Key Words . . .*, p. 84.
7 J. Dunn, *Western Political Theory . . .*, pp. 15–16.

8 T.B. Bottomore, *Elites and Society* (Harmondsworth 1982), p. 15.
9 J.H. Meisel, *The Myth of the Ruling Class: Gaetano Mosca and the Elite* (Michigan 1962), pp. 32–3.
10 C. Pateman, *Participation and Democratic Theory*, p. 3.
11 J.P. Schumpeter, *Capitalism, Socialism and Democracy*, p. 254, footnote 3 and p. 265.
12 Ibid., p. 242.
13 Ibid., p. 263.
14 Ibid., pp. 269, 282.
15 Ibid., p. 295.
16 Ibid., p. 299.
17 S. Bowles and H. Gintis, 'The invisible fist: have capitalism and democracy reached a parting of the ways?', *American Economic Review* (May 1978), p. 359. See also G. Hodgson, *The Democratic Economy – A New Look at Planning Markets and Power* (Harmondsworth 1984), pp. 111–25.
18 T. Kempner, K. MacMillan and K.H. Hawkins, *Business and Society – Tradition and Change* (London 1974), pp. 7–8, 110, 243. See also R.L. Heilbroner, *Business Civilization in Decline* (Harmondsworth 1977), p. 20.
19 See K.A. Kennedy, T. Giblin and D. McHugh, *The Economic Development of Ireland in the 20th Century* (London 1988), pp. 172–4, 177, 257–8. See also C. Crouch *The Politics of Industrial Relations* (Glasgow 1979), p. 148.
20 C. Crouch, *The Politics of . . .*, p. 184.
21 Bulletin of the European Communities, *Employee Participation in Asset Formation*, memorandum from the commission, supplement 6/79, p. 28, para. 47. See also Chapters 3,4 and 5.
22 Quoted in P. Bachrach, *The Theory of Democratic Elitism* (London 1969), p. 80.
23 See Department of Trade, *Report of the Committee of Enquiry on Industrial Democracy* (HMSO, London 1977), CMND 6706, pp. 20–5.
24 P. Bachrach, *The Theory of Democratic Elitism*, pp. 4, 24.
25 Ibid., p. 38.
26 J.A. Schumpeter, *Capitalism, Socialism and Democracy*, p. 262.
27 Quoted in J. Banks and K. Jones, *Worker Directors Speak*, Industrial Participation Association (Aldershot 1977), pp. xi–xii.
28 C. Pateman, *Participation and Democratic Theory*, p. 3.
29 W.G. Runciman, *Social Science and Political Theory* (Cambridge 1963), p. 98; S.M. Lipset, *Political Man – The Social Basis of Politics* (New York 1963), p. 228.
30 Quoted in P. Bachrach, *The Theory of Democratic . . .*, p. 52.
31 T.B. Bottomore, *Elites and Society*, p. 117.
32 J. Dunn, *Western Political Theory . . .*, p. 23.
33 T.B. Bottomore, *Elites and Society*, pp. 121–2.
34 R. Dahrendorf, *Class and Class Conflict in an Industrial Society* (London 1967), p. 143.
35 Ibid., pp. 142–3.
36 International Research Group (IDE), *Industrial Democracy in Europe* (Oxford 1981), pp. 11, 328, 333.
37 T. Baumgartner, T.R. Burns and P. De Ville, 'Work, politics and social

structuring under capitalism', in T.R. Burns, L.E. Karlsson and V. Rus (eds) *Work and Power* (London 1979), p. 182.

38 S.M. Lipset, *Political Man . . .*, pp. 100–101.
39 G. Hunnius, 'On the nature of capitalist initiated innovations in the workplace', in T.R. Burns, L.E. Karlsson and K. Rus (eds) *Work and Power*, p. 288.
40 IDE, *Industrial Democracy . . .*, p. 104.
41 G. Hunnius, 'On the nature of . . .', p. 288.
42 C. Pateman, *Participation and Democratic Theory*, pp. 46–9.
43 Ibid., pp. 34–5.
44 Ibid., pp. 49–51, 53. See also S.M. Miller and F. Riessman, 'Working-class authoritarianism – a critique of Lipset', *British Journal of Sociology* (Vol. 12, 1961), pp. 263–72.
45 C.B. Macpherson, *The Life and Times . . .*, p. 1.
46 R.L. Heilbroner, *Business Civilization in Decline*, p. 36.
47 E. Berg, 'Democracy and self-determination', in P. Birnbaum, J. Lively, and G. Parry (eds) *Democracy Consensus and Social Contract* (Vol. 2, London 1978), pp. 169–70.
48 D. Guest and D. Fatchett, *Worker Participation: Individual Control and Performance* (London 1974), pp. 13, 24.
49 D. Wallace Bell, *Industrial Participation* (London 1979), pp. 142–53.
50 P.A. Reilly, *Employee Financial Participation* (BIM Foundation Report No. 41 1978), p. 19; R.C. Geary and M. Dempsey, 'Profit sharing for Ireland?' in *Journal of the Statistical and Social Inquiry Society of Ireland* (Vol. xxiv, Part iv, 1981–2), p. 158.
51 R. Marriott, *Incentive Payment Systems* (London 1971), 4th edn, pp. 44–5.
52 N.C. Hunt, *Methods of Wage Payment in British Industry* (London 1951), p. 142.
53 G.W. Latta, *Profit Sharing, Employee Stock Ownership, Savings and Asset Formation Plans in the Western World* (Pennsylvania 1979), p. 5.
54 R. Marriott, *Incentive Payment Systems* (London 1971), p. 207.
55 S. Shimmin, 'A 1968 survey of recent literature', postscript in R. Marriott, *Incentive Payment Systems*, p. 275.
56 D. McGregor, 'The Scanlon Plan through a psychologist's eyes', in F.G. Lesieur (ed.) *The Scanlon Plan – A Frontier in labour Management Co-operation* (Massachusetts 1958), p. 90.
57 W.F. Whyte, *Money and Motivation – An Analysis of Incentives in Industry* (New York 1955), p. 147.
58 Ibid., p. 227.
59 C.T. Whelan, *Worker Priorities, Trust in Management and Prospects for Workers' Participation* (ESRI Paper no. 111, Dublin, 1982), pp. 5, 64.
60 A. Fox, *Man Mismanagement*, pp. 108–9.
61 Ibid., p. 115.
62 P.A. Reilly, *Employee Financial Participation*, p. 26.
63 Ibid.
64 H. Behrend, 'Financial incentives as the expression of a system of beliefs', *British Journal of Sociology* (Vol. 10, No. 2 1959), p. 138.
65 Ibid., p. 144.
66 D. Katz, 'The motivational basis of organisational behaviour', in V. H.

Vroom and L. Deci (eds) *Management and Motivation* (Harmondsworth 1970), pp. 277–9.

67 J.R. Galbraith, *Organisation Design* (Pennsylvania 1977), p. 299.
68 A. Flanders, R. Pomeranz and J. Woodward, *Experiment in Industrial . . .*, pp. 23, 132–7.
69 Ibid., pp. 42, 102, 118.
70 Ibid., pp. 47, 99, 242.
71 Ibid., p. 130.
72 Ibid., p. 129.
73 Ibid., p. 92.
74 See Chapter 2.
75 A.M. Bowey, R. Thorpe, F.H.M. Mitchell, G. Nicholls, D. Gosnold, L. Savery and P.K. Hellier, *Effects of Incentive Payment Systems United Kingdom 1977–80*, Research Paper No. 36, Department of Employment, September 1982.
76 Ibid., p. 9.
77 Ibid., pp. 9, 12.
78 Ibid., p. 7.
79 Quoted in A.M. Bowey *et al.*, *Effects of Incentive Payment Systems . . .*, p. 7.
80 Ibid., pp. 9, 13.
81 Ibid., pp. 15–16.
82 Ibid., pp. 41–2, 62.
83 Ibid., p. 71.
84 Ibid., p. 63.
85 Ibid., p. 71.
86 Ibid.
87 Ibid.
88 Ibid.
89 Ibid., p. 97.
90 Ibid.
91 Ibid., pp. 97–8.
92 Ibid., p. 97
93 R.W. Davenport, 'Enterprise for everyman' in F.G. Lesieur (ed.) *The Scanlon Plan . . .*, p. 19.
94 F.G. Lesieur, 'The Scanlon Plan – what the plan isn't and what it is', in F.G. Lesieur (ed.) *The Scanlon Plan . . .*, p. 46.
95 Ibid., pp. 45, 66.
96 For the drawbacks of individual incentive schemes, see W.F. Whyte, *Money and Motivation . . .*, p. 261 *passim*.
97 F.G. Lesieur, *The Scanlon Plan . . .*, pp. 47, 49.
98 E.S. Puckett, 'Productivity achievements – a measure of success', in F.G. Lesieur (ed.) *The Scanlon Plan . . .*, pp. 112–13.
99 Ibid., p. 115.
100 C. Hampden-Turner, *Radical Man* (London 1971), p. 237.
101 Quoted in S. Shimmin, postscript in R. Marriott, *Incentive Payment Systems*, p. 262.
102 Ibid.
103 H.A. Turner, G. Clack and G. Roberts, *Labour Relations in the Motor Industry* (London 1967), p. 99.

104 Cited in S. Shimmin, postscript in R. Marriott, *Incentive Payment Systems*, p. 262.
105 M. Schuster, 'Forty years of Scanlon Plan research', in C. Crouch and F.A. Heller (eds) *Organisational Democracy and the Political Process*, International Yearbook of Organisational Democracy, Vol. 1 (Chichester 1983), pp. 69–70.
106 C. Hampden-Turner, *Radical Man*, p. 222.
107 Ibid., p. 225.
108 W.F. Whyte, *Money and Motivation*, p. 176.
109 Ibid., p. 180.
110 M. Rose, *Industrial Behaviour – Theoretical Developments since Taylor* (Harmondsworth 1978), p. 158.
111 D.Q. Mills, Labour Management Relations (New York 1978), pp. 70–1.
112 D. Wallace Bell, *Industrial Participation*, pp. 154–9.
113 N. Mulcahy and J. McConnell, 'Sharing the cake or why should profit be a dirty word?', in *Management* (Vol. xx, No. 9, 1974), pp. 51–6.
114 Manus O'Riordain, 'Applying added value – the slice going to wages does not exhaust the issue', in Management (Vol. xxi, Nos 7, 8), pp. 39–45.
115 See Chapter 4.

CHAPTER 2

1 K.M. Thompson, *Profit Sharing – Democratic Capitalism in American Industry* (New York 1949), p. 79
2 G.W. Latta, *Profit Sharing, Employee Stock Ownership, Savings and Asset Formation Plans in the Western World* (Pennsylvania 1979), p. 3.
3 R.C. Geary and M. Dempsey, 'Profit sharing for Ireland?', in *Journal of the Statistical and Social Inquiry Society of Ireland* (Vol. xxiv, Part iv, 1981–2), p. 163.
4 D. Wallace Bell, *Financial Participation* (London 1973), p. 16.
5 Bulletin of EC, Supp. 6/79, *Employee Participation in Asset Formation*, p. 27.
6 P.A. Reilly, *Employee Financial Participation* (BIM Foundation Report No. 41, 1978), p. 23, Table 3.
7 T.E. Wood, 'Trends in the 1980s: their effects on profit sharing plans and productivity', in B.L. Metzger (ed.) *Increasing Productivity through Profit Sharing*.
8 B.L. Metzger, *Profit Sharing in 38 Large Companies* (PSRF 1975, 2 Vols), Vol. 1, p. 13.
9 T.E. Wood, 'Setting objectives for profit sharing plans', in *Guide to Modern Profit Sharing* (Profit Sharing Council of America (PSCA), Chicago, Illinois 1973), p. 18.
10 Ibid.
11 G.W. Latta, *Profit Sharing . . .*, p. 3.
12 Profit Sharing Council of America (PSCA) *Guide to Modern Profit Sharing*, pp. 15–16.
13 Hewitt Associates in co-operation with the PSCA, *1982 Profit Sharing Survey* (1981 experience) (Chicago 1982), p. 5.

14 PSCA, *Guide to Modern . . .*, p. 14.
15 This figure is based on Hewitt Associates, *1982 Profit Sharing Survey*, pp. 4–5.
16 Ibid.
17 Ibid., p. 4. See also PSCA, *Guide to Modern . . .*, p. ix, Col. 2
18 PSCA, *Guide to Modern . . .*, p. 227.
19 Ibid., p. 230; also Hewitt Associates, *1982 Profit Sharing Survey*, pp. 32–3.
20 PSCA, *Guide to Modern . . .*, p. 149.
21 Ibid., p. 300; Hewitt Associates, *1982 Profit Sharing Survey*, p. 33.
22 Ibid., p. 35. (In a tiny minority of plans, more than 50 per cent of the assets are invested in employer stock or other employer securities.)
23 PSCA, *Profit Sharing Benefits to Business Labour and Capital Markets*. Reprint of a statement on profit sharing presented to the President's Commission on pension policy (Chicago 1980), p. 26.
24 D. Wallace Bell, *Financial Participation*, pp. 56–7.
25 PSCA, *Profit Sharing Benefits . . .*, p. 26.
26 Ibid.
27 Quoted in B.L. Metzger, *Profit Sharing in 38 Large Companies*, Vol. 2, p. 49.
28 B.M. Stewart and W.J. Couper, *Profit Sharing for Wage Earners and Executives* (Industrial Relations Counsellors, New York 1951), p. 57.
29 Quoted in B.L. Metzger and J.A. Colletti, *Does Profit Sharing Pay?*, p. 90.
30 Ibid., pp. 90–1.
31 See Chapter 2.
32 P. Henle and R. Schmitt, 'Pension reform: the long hard road to enactment', *Monthly Labor Review* (Nov. 1974), p. 3.
33 Ibid., p. 4.
34 D.G. Carlson, 'Responding to the pension reform law', *Harvard Business Review* (Nov.–Dec. 1974), p. 133.
35 Ibid., p. 135.
36 PSCA, *Profit Sharing Benefits . . .*, p. 21.
37 This review of ERISA is largely based on articles by Henle/Schmitt and Carlson.
38 Quoted in B.L. Metzger, 'Profit sharing as a system incentive', speech presented at Work in America Institute Conference on 'Sharing the Gains of Productivity', PSRF, p. 1, n.d.
39 B.L. Metzger, 'Profit sharing trends', in B.L. Metzger (ed.) *New Horizons for Capitalism. Post-ERISA Idea Papers* (PSRF 1977), p. 31.
40 'Employee wrath hits profit sharing plans', *Business Week* (18 July 1977), p. 25.
41 Ibid.
42 Ibid.
43 PSCA, *Profit Sharing Benefits . . .*, p. 23.
44 D.G. Carlson, 'Responding to the pension . . .' p. 137; P. Henle and R. Schmitt, 'Pension reforms . . .', p. 8.
45 B.L. Metzger, *Participative Developments in the United States* (PSRF 1978), p. 4, Table 3.
46 P. Henle and R. Schmitt, 'Pension reforms . . .', p. 11.
47 D.G. Carlson, 'Responding to the pension . . .', p. 143.

48 B.L. Metzger, *Profit Sharing in 38 Large* . . ., Vol. 2, p. 44.
49 Ibid., pp. 44–8.
50 B.L. Metzger, *Participative Developments* . . ., p. 9.
51 B.L. Metzger, *Profit Sharing in 38* . . ., Vol. 1, pp. 2, 3.
52 Ibid., Vol. 2, p. 42.
53 PSCA, *Guide to Modern* . . ., p. 14.
54 Hewitt Associates, *1982 Profit Sharing Survey* p. 5.
55 PSCA, *Guide to Modern* . . ., p. 14; Hewitt Associates, *1982 Profit Sharing Survey* . . ., p. 4.
56 B.L. Metzger, *Profit Sharing in 38* . . ., Vol. 1, p. 38, Table 44; see also Chapter 2.
57 B.L. Metzger, *Participative Developments* . . ., p. 9; *Profit Sharing Benefits* . . ., p. 31.
58 See Chapter 2.
59 B.L. Metzger, *Post ERISA Dilemma: Profit Sharing, Pensions or Both?* (PSRF), p. 12, n.d.
60 B.L. Metzger, *Employee Investment Choice in Deferred Profit Sharing* (PSRF 1977), p. 21; *Participative Developments* . . ., p. 4.
61 B.L. Metzger, 'How to motivate with profit sharing', in B.L. Metzger (ed.) *The Future of Profit Sharing. Post-ERISA Idea Papers* (PSRF 1979), p. 16.
62 See Chapter 2.
63 D.V. Nightingale, *Profit Sharing and Employee Ownership: a Review and Appraisal*. Report to the Employment Relations Branch of Labour Canada (Profit Sharing Council of Canada 1980), p. 23. See also D.F. Schloss, *Methods of Industrial Remuneration*, pp. 246–7, 270; CPSI, Revised Profit Sharing Manual (Michigan 1951), p. 7; P.S. Narasimhan, 'Profit sharing: a review', *International Labour Review* (Vol. LXII, No. 6, Dec. 1950), p. 471.
64 PSCA, *Guide to Modern* . . ., p. 59.
65 J.A. Curtis, 'Coverage and eligibility conditions', in PSCA, *Guide to Modern* . . ., p. 57.
66 B.L. Metzger, *Profit Sharing in 38* . . ., Vol. 1, pp. 15–16.
67 Hewitt Associates, *1982 Profit Sharing Survey*, p. 4.
68 Department of Labour, Australia, *Profit Sharing: A Study of the Result of Overseas Experience* (March 1947), p. 25. See also P.S. Narasimhan, 'Profit sharing – a review', pp. 484–5.
69 Department of Labour, Australia, *Profit Sharing: A Study of* . . ., pp. 25–6.
70 K.M. Thompson, *Profit Sharing – Democratic Capitalism* . . ., pp. 91–4.
71 J.A. Curtis, 'Coverage and eligibility . . .', p. 56. See also W.H. Brummond, 'Legal requirements and considerations', in PSCA, *Guide to Modern* . . ., pp. 23–9.
72 PSCA, *Guide to Modern* . . ., p. 184.
73 Ibid.
74 Hewitt Associates, *1982 Profit Sharing Survey*, pp. 16–17.
75 Ibid. (In a small number of plans – 11.4 per cent – there were more than four funds.)
76 Hewitt Associates, *1982 Profit Sharing Survey*, pp. 36–7.
77 *Business Week* (18 July 1977).

78 B.L. Metzger, *Profit Sharing in 38 . . .*, Vol. 2, p. 140.
79 Ibid., p. 142.
80 Hewitt Associates, *1982 Profit Sharing Survey*, p. 35.
81 Department of Labour, Australia, *Profit Sharing – a Study of . . .*, pp. 3, 25.
82 D.V. Nightingale, *Profit Sharing and Employee . . .*, p. 24.
83 B.L. Metzger, 'Achieving motivation through employee stock ownership', speech at the 1st Annual Conference of the ESOP Council of America, Los Angeles, 8 May 1978 (PSRF 1978), p. 8. See also P.S. Narasimhan, 'Profit sharing – a review', p. 471; CPSI, *Revised Profit Sharing Manual*, pp. 25, 34–5; D.F. Schloss, *Methods of Industrial Remuneration*, pp. 245–6.
84 Hewitt Associates, *1982 Profit Sharing Survey*, p. 15.
85 Calculated using figures in Hewitt survey, p. 15.
86 P.A. Knowlton, *Studies in Profit Sharing* (PSRF New York 1952, 1953), p. 26.
87 B.M. Stewart and W.J. Couper, *Profit Sharing for Wage Earners . . .*, p. 36.
88 Department of Labour, Australia, *Profit Sharing: A Study of the Result . . .*, p. 25; CPSI, *Revised Profit Sharing Manual*, pp. 24–5, 34–5; D.V. Nightingale, *Profit Sharing and Employee . . .*, p. 26; D.F. Schloss, *Methods of Industrial . . .*, p. 258; K.M. Thompson, *Profit Sharing – Democratic Capitalism . . .*, p. 79; D. Wallace Bell, *Industrial Participation*, p. 137; P.S. Narasimhan, 'Profit sharing – a review', p. 471.
89 R. Tilove, 'Pensions, health and welfare plans', in L. Ulman (ed.) *Challenges to Collective Bargaining* (Englewood Cliffs, New Jersey 1967), p. 37.
90 K.M. Thompson, *Profit Sharing – Democratic Capitalism . . .*, p. 79.
91 Dept of Labour, Australia, *Profit Sharing: A Study of the Result . . .*, p. 19.
92 T.E. Wood, 'Trends in the 1980s . . .', in B.L. Metzger (ed.) *Guide to Modern . . .*, p. 29.
93 D.V. Nightingale, *Profit Sharing and Employee . . .*, p. 9.
94 Ibid.
95 B.L. Metzger, 'Profit sharing as a system incentive', speech at the Work in America Institute Conference on 'Sharing the Gains of Productivity' (PSRF, n.d.).
96 B.A. Diekman, 'Profit sharing systems', in B.A. Diekman and B.L. Metzger (eds) *Profit Sharing: The Industrial Adrenalin* (Joint Publication of the Institute of Profit Sharing, Canada and PSRF 1975), pp. 15–16.
97 Ibid., p. 16.
98 Ibid., p. 17.
99 Ibid., pp. 17–18. See also K.M. Thompson, *Profit Sharing – Democratic Capitalism . . .*, p. 195; CPSI, *Revised Profit Sharing Manual*, p. 16; D. Wallace Bell, *Industrial Participation*, p. 168; P.S. Narasimhan, 'Profit sharing – a review', p. 485.
100 For a different view of the utility of communication see V.L. Allen, *Militant Trade Unionism* (London 1972), p. 109.
101 B.L. Metzger, *Profit Sharing in 38 . . .*, Vol. 2, p. 49.

102 Ibid., p. 20.
103 Quoted in M. Carnoy and D. Shearer, *Economic Democracy: The Challenge of the 1980s* (New York 1980), p. 258.
104 See Chapters 1 and 6.
105 B.L. Metzger and J.A. Colletti, *Does Profit Sharing Pay?* (PSRF, Illinois 1971).
106 Ibid., p. 72.
107 Ibid., p. 84.
108 Ibid., pp. 78–81.
109 Ibid., p. 81, Table 52.
110 Ibid., p. 84.
111 Ibid.
112 Ibid., p. 81.
113 B.L. Metzger, *Profit Sharing in 38 . . .*, Vol. 2, pp. 17–19.
114 Ibid., Vol. 2, p. 17.
115 Ibid., Vol. 1, p. 14.
116 Ibid., Vol. 1, p. 14.
117 Ibid., Vol. 2, p. 14.
118 K.M. Thompson, *Profit Sharing – Democratic Capitalism . . .*, p. 62.
119 B.L. Metzger, *Profit Sharing in 38 . . .*, Vol. 2, pp. 18–19.
120 Ibid., Charts 6 and 7.
121 B.B. Howard, *A Study of the Financial Significance of PS 1958–1977* (PSCA, Chicago 1979).
122 Ibid., p. 5.
123 Ibid., p. 4.
124 Ibid., p. 5, see also footnote 123.
125 Ibid., pp. 5–6.
126 Ibid., p. 6.
127 B.L. Metzger and J.A. Colletti, *Does Profit Sharing Pay?*, p. 77. See also B.L. Metzger, *Profit Sharing in 38 . . .*, Vol. 2, p. 42.
128 See Chapter 2, Table 2.1
129 See Chapter 2, Figure 2.3.
130 Interview with Mr R.L. Wilson, vice president personnel, Chicago & North Western Transportation Company, 14 March 1984.
131 Interview with Mr L. Perlman, vice president controller, W. Braun Company, Chicago, 14 March 1984.
132 Interview with Mr T.E. Parfitt, vice president of the Harris Trust and Savings Bank, Chicago, 15 March 1984.
133 Harris Bankcorp, *Employee Benefits, Profit Sharing Annual Report*, April 1982.
134 Telephone interview with Mr Dean Boyle, vice president Human resources, Warner Gear (a division of the Borg Warner Corporation), Muncie, Indiana, 19 March 1984.
135 *Muncie Star*, 2 March 1984
136 Interview with Mr Dean Boyle, 19 March 1984.
137 The above paragraphs are based on the monthly newletter issued to employees by Warner Gear. From files in the PSRF, Evanston Illinois.
138 P. Jacobs, 'Comments on Bernstein's paper on the Teamsters' Union', in C. Remus, D. McLaughlin and F. Nesbitt *Labor and American Politics* (Michigan 1978), p. 292.

139 *A Piece of the Action* – subtitle of Metzger's *Profit Sharing in 38 Large Companies*.
140 G.W. Latta, *Profit Sharing* . . ., p. 26.
141 Interview with John L. Zalusky, economist, Dept of Economic Research American Federation of Labor and Congress of Industrial Organization (AFL/CIO), Washington, 26 March 1984.
142 B.L. Metzger, *Participative Developments* . . ., pp. 9–10.
143 'Profit sharing in recession contracts. Permanent or passing fancy?', Employment Relations Report (30 Nov. 1982), p. 5, from files of AFL/CIO, Washington DC.
144 Interview with J.L. Zalusky, 26 March 1984.
145 E.R. Czarnecki 'Effects of profit sharing plans on union organising efforts', *Personnel Journal* (Sept. 1970), p. 765.
146 Interview with J.W. Cooper, vice president of the Harris Trust Bank and treasurer of the PSRF, Chicago, 15 March 1984.
147 Quoted in E.R. Czarnecki, 'Effects of profit sharing plans . . .', p. 764.
148 This was the case in the North Western Railroad Co., Chicago.
149 Interview with J.L. Zalusky, 26 March 1984.
150 E.R. Czarnecki, 'Effects of profit sharing plans . . .', p. 765.
151 Ibid., p. 767.
152 Ibid., p. 770.
153 Ibid., p. 771.
154 Interview with T.E. Parfitt, 15 March 1984.
155 E.R. Czarnecki, 'Effects of profit sharing plans . . .', p. 764.
156 Daily Labor Report (DLR) No. 16 1–25–82 A-12, The Bureau of National Affairs Inc., Washington DC. From the files of the AFL/CIO.
157 Employment Relations Report 'Profit sharing in recession contract . . .', p. 4.
158 DLR No. 5 1–8–82 A-7 A-8.
159 DLR No. 16 1–25–82 A-12 A-13; DLR No.201 10–18–82 A-5.
160 DLR No. 5 1–8–82 A-6 A-7 A-8.
161 DLR No. 5 1–8–82 A-7 A-8.
162 DLR No. 5 1–8–82 A-7.
163 DLR No. 40 3–1–82 A-5.
164 DLR No. 40 3–1–82 A-6.
165 DLR No. 69 4–9–82 A-6.
166 DLR No. 31 2–16–82 E-1 E-4. Joint UAW/Ford summary of National Agreement, DLR No. 58 3–25–82 E-1 E-6. Summary of tentative agreement UAW/General, Motors Corporation.
167 DLR No. 31 2–16–82; DLR No. 58 3–25–82.
168 Employment Relations Report, 'Profit sharing in recession . . .', p. 5.
169 DLR No. 40 3–1–82 A-5.
170 DLR No. 69 4–9–82 A-7.
171 DLR No. 69 4–9–82 A-7.
172 DLR No. 115 6–15–82 A-11.
173 DLR No. 115 6–15–82 A-11 A-13.
174 DLR No. 30 2–14–84 A-9; DLR No. 201 10–18–82 A-4 A-5; DLR No. 204 10–21–82 A-8 A-9; DLR No. 208 10–27–82 A-6 A-7; DLR No. 237 12–9–82 a-12 A-13; DLR No. 244 12–20–82 E-1.

175 P. Drucker, 'Where union flexibility's now a must', *Wall Street Journal* 23 Sept. 1983.
176 *Wall Street Journal* 14 Nov. 1983.
177 *New York Times* 22 Jan. 1984.
178 *Automotive News*, 28 Nov. 1983.
179 DLR No. 30 2–14–84 A-8.
180 R. B. Smith, Chairman, General Motors, Remarks on profit sharing at General Motors. Speech at the National Press Club, Washington DC, 7 Feb. 1984. Distributed by PSRF, p. 2.
181 Ibid., pp. 2–3.
182 Ibid., p. 3.
183 Ibid., p. 5.
184 Ibid., p. 4.
185 Ibid., pp. 4–5.
186 Ibid., p. 7.
187 Ibid., p. 8.
188 DLR No. 30 2–14–84 A-8.
189 DLR No. 26 2–8–84 A-5.
190 DLR No. 30 2–14–84 A-9.
191 DLR No. 30 2–14–84 A-8. The figures mentioned are average payments.
192 *Automotive News*, 27 Feb. 1984.
193 Ibid.
194 Ibid.
195 R.B. Smith, speech at National Press Club, Washington, 7 Feb. 1984 p. 5.
196 Quoted in K.M. Thompson, *Profit Sharing – Democratic Capitalism* . . ., p. 7.
197 Interview with B.L. Metzger, president of PSRF, at Evanston, Illinois, 20 March 1984.
198 D.F. Schloss, *Methods of Industrial Renumeration*, p. 258.
199 K.M. Thompson, *Profit Sharing – Democratic Capitalism* . . ., p. 79; P.S. Narasimham, 'Profit sharing – a review', p. 472.
200 M.L. Weitzman, *The Share Economy* (Harvard 1984).
201 *The Guardian*, 19 March 1986; *The Irish Times*, 15 July 1986; *The Times*, 6 Mar 1986.
202 D. Fouquet, 'An interview with Henk Vredeling', *Multinational Info.* (No.3, Oct. 1983), IRM Geneva.
203 Quoted in K.M. Thompson, *Profit Sharing – Democratic Capitalism* . . ., p. 49.
204 See Chapter 1.
205 B.L. Metzger, 'Elements of a sharing-participative system', in B.L. Metzger (ed.) *New Horizons for Capitalism* . . ., p. 28.
206 See Chapter 1.
207 B.L. Metzger; PSRF.
208 R. Tilove, 'Pensions, health and welfare plans', in L. Ulman (ed.) *Challenges to Collective Bargaining*, p. 37.

CHAPTER 3

  1 Quoted in J.R. Gates, 'The history, strengths and weaknesses of employee stock ownership plans in the United States – what can we

learn from the US experience?', speech delivered at a conference on 'Retirement Programs of the Future', sponsored by the Canadian Pension Conference, Personnel Association of Toronto, 20 November 1979, pp. 12–13.

2 D. Kruse, *Employee Ownership and Employee Attitudes: Two Case Studies* (Norwood, 1984), pp. 61–2.

3 See Chapter 1.

4 See Introduction, Chapters 1 and 2.

5 R.J. Patard, 'Employee stock ownership in the 1920s', in *The Employee Ownership Reader*, National Center for Employee Ownership (NCEO) (Arlington, Virginia 1983), p. 53.

6 D. Yoder, *Labor Economics and Labor Problems* (New York 1939, 2nd edn), p. 596.

7 Ibid., p. 597.

8 Ibid.

9 Ibid., p. 471.

10 R.J. Patard, 'Employee stock ownership . . .', in *The Employee Ownership Reader*, p. 53.

11 D. Yoder, *Personnel Management and Industrial Relations* (London 1958, 4th edn), p. 500.

12 R.J. Patard, 'Employee stock ownership . . .', p. 53.

13 K.M. Thompson, *Profit Sharing – Democratic Capitalism in American Industry* (New York 1949), p. 168.

14 R.J. Patard, 'Employee stock ownership . . .', p. 53.

15 L.O. Kelso, 'Karl Marx: the almost capitalist', in *American Bar Association Journal* (Vol.43, March 1957), p. 238.

16 Ibid.

17 L.O. Kelso and M.J. Adler, *The Capitalist Manifesto* (New York 1958), p. 41.

18 Ibid., pp. 183–9, 258–65.

19 L.L. Granados, 'Employee stock ownership plans: an analysis of current reform proposals', in *University of Michigan Journal of Law Reform* (Vol.14, No.1, Fall 1980), pp. 17–18.

20 L.O. Kelso and P. Hetter, *Two Factor Theory: The Economics of Reality* (New York 1967), p. 6.

21 L.O. Kelso and P. Hetter, *How to Turn Eighty Million Workers into Capitalists on Borrowed Money* (New York 1967), p. 11.

22 L.O. Kelso and P. Hetter, *Two Factor Theory . . .*, p. 41

23 L.O. Kelso and P. Hetter, *How to Turn Eighty . . .*, p. xxi.

24 L.O. Kelso and P. Hetter, *Two Factor Theory . . .*, p. 26.

25 Ibid., pp. 8–9.

26 C.G. Burck, 'There's more to ESOP than meets the eye', *Fortune* (March 1976), p. 132.

27 J.R. Gates, 'The history, strengths . . .', pp. 3–4

28 Hewitt Associates, *ESOPs: An Analytical Report*. Prepared for the Profit Sharing Council of America by the staff of Hewitt Associates (Illinois 1975), p. 8.

29 T.R. Marsh and D.E. McAllister, 'ESOP tables: a survey of companies with employee stock ownership plans', *Journal of Corporation Law* (Spring 1981), p. 560.

30 See Chapter 2.
31 L.L. Granados, 'Employee stock ownership plans . . .', p. 19.
32 Hewitt Associates, *ESOPs: An Analytical . . .*, p. 10.
33 T.R. Marsh and D.E. McAllister, 'ESOP tables . . .', p. 561.
34 L.L. Granados, 'Employee stock ownership . . .', p. 19. See also T.R. Marsh and D.E. McAllister, 'ESOP tables . . .', p. 561.
35 Hewitt Associates, *ESOPs: An Analytical . . .*, p. 11.
36 National Center for Employee Ownership (NCEO), *Employee Ownership Resource Guide* (Arlington, Virginia 1984), p. 13. See also L.L. Granados, 'Employee stock ownership plans . . .', pp. 19–20.
37 Comptroller General of the United States, General Accounting Office (GAO), report to the Committee on Finance, United States Senate, *Employee Stock Ownership Plans: Who Benefits Most in Closely Held Companies?* (HRD 80. 88 Washington DC, 20 June 1980), p. 3.
38 S. Coll, 'ESOP's fables: with employee stock ownership plans everybody gets a little bit rich', *California Magazine* (Sept. 1983).
39 J. Carrol, 'Crazy Lewis and his creeping two-factorism', in *The Village Voice* (28 April 1975).
40 Quoted in J.R. Gates, 'The history, strengths . . .', p. 9.
41 Statement by P.A. Samuelson, *US Senate Congressional Record* (8 June 1972), p. 20207.
42 T.P. Roth, 'Employee Stock Ownership Trusts, myopia, and intertemporal profit maximisation', *Quarterly Review of Economics and Business* (Vol. 18, Summer 1978), p. 84.
43 P. Drucker, *The Unseen Revolution – How Pension Fund Socialism Came to America* (London 1976), pp. 36–7, 40.
44 C.G. Burck, 'There's more to ESOP . . .', p. 172.
45 A. Sloan, 'An idea whose time has come', *Forbes Magazine* (20 July 1981), p. 78.
46 Quoted in J.R. Gates, 'The history, strengths . . .', p. 18.
47 A. Schonfield, *Modern Capitalism* (London 1970), p. 312.
48 L.L. Granados, 'Employee Stock Ownership . . .', p. 18.
49 Quoted in J.R. Gates, 'The history, strengths . . .', p. 18.
50 J.R. Blasi, P. Mehrling and W.F. Whyte, 'The politics of worker ownership in the United States', in C. Crouch and F.A. Heller (eds) *Organisational Democracy . . .*, pp. 638–9.
51 Ibid., p. 650.
52 J. Rothschild-Whitt, 'Worker ownership in relation to control: a typology of work reform', in C.Crouch and F.A. Heller (eds) *Organisation Democracy . . .*, p. 394.
53 A. Beltran-Del-Rio, R.D. Hamrin and S.M. Speiser, 'Increasing capitalism's capitalists – a challenge for economists', *Journal of Post-Keynesian Economics* (Spring 1979, Vol. 1, No. 3), pp. 41–54.
54 Interview with L.L. Granados, managing director ESOP Association of America, Washington DC, 26 March 1984.
55 Interview with Corey Rosen, executive director National Center for Employee Ownership, Arlington, Virginia, 26 March 1984.
56 Hewitt Associates, *Employee Stock Ownership Plans*, prepared by the research staff of Hewitt Associates (Illinois 1982), p. 4.
57 See US Government Internal Revenue Code: IRC 410 (a) (1) (A); IRC

410 (b) (1) (A); IRC 410 (b) (1) (B); IRC 410 (b) (3) (A); IRC 410 (b) (3) (B).

58 See US Government Treasury Regulations: Treasury Reg. 1 401 1 (b) (i) (ii) (iii).

59 Staff of the Committee on Finance, US Senate, Chairman R.B. Long, *Employee Stock Ownership Plans – An Employer's Handbook*, US Government Printing Office, Washington DC (April 1980), p. 9.

60 See Chapter 2.

61 IRC 409 A (c).

62 US Senate Finance Committee, ESOPs – *An Employer's Handbook*, p. 12.

63 Ibid., pp. 12–13.

64 IRC 409 A (h) (1) (A); IRC 4975 (e) (7); Treasury Reg. 54. 4975–7 (b) (ii) 1977; Treasury Reg. 1.46–8 (g) (5) 1979.

65 C.G. Burck, 'There's more to ESOP . . .', pp. 130–1.

66 US Treasury Reg. 1.401.1 (a) (ii) (1956); Treasury Reg. 1.401.2 (a) (1956); IRC 401 (a) (2).

67 ERISA 408 (e) (1) 29 USC 1108 (e) (1) (1976).

68 ERISA 406 (a) (1) (A) 29 USC 1106 (a) (1) (1976).

69 IRC 4975 (e) (7); IRC 409A (h) (1) (B); Treasury Reg. 54.4975–7 (b) (11) (1977).

70 R.N. Stern and P. Comstock, *Employee Stock Ownership Plans (ESOPs) – Benefits for Whom?*, Key Issues No. 23, New York State School of Industrial and Labor Relations (New York 1978), p. 39.

71 B. Bluestone, B. Harrison and L. Baker, *Corporate Flight – The Causes and Consequences of Economic Dislocation* (Washington DC 1981), pp. 57–8.

72 C. Rosen and W.F. Whyte, 'Employee ownership saving businesses, saving jobs', *Commentary* (Spring 1982), reprinted in *The Employee Ownership Reader*, p. 24.

73 W.R. Reum and S.M. Reum, 'Employee stock ownership plans – pluses and minuses', *Harvard Business Review* (July – Aug. 1976), p. 140.

74 Ibid., p. 140.

75 See Chapter 2.

76 Senate Finance Committee, *ESOPs – An Employer's . . .*, p. 27.

77 P.T. Taplin, 'Goal is shared ownership not retirement benefits', *Employee Benefit Plan Review* (Nov. 1980), p. 43.

78 A.L. Adams, 'A leveraged ESOP's no fable', *Investment Dealers' Digest* (25 Oct. 1983), p. 13.

79 J.R. Gates, 'The history, strengths . . .', pp. 18–19.

80 Interview with Ms Eileen Pollak, Staff Associates Pension Planning, Pan American World Airways, New York, 5 April 1984.

81 See Chapter 2.

82 Hewitt Associates, *ESOPs: An Analytical Report*, p. 12.

83 T.R. Marsh and D.E. McAllister, 'ESOP tables . . .', p. 589, Table 1.

84 M.J. Bonaccorso, S.M. Cranmer, D.G. Greenhut, D.T. Hoffman and N. Isbrandtsen, *Survey of Employee Stock Ownership Plans: Analysis and Evaluation of Current Experience*. A report submitted in partial fulfilment of the requirements for a Masters of Business Administration

degree, University of California, Los Angeles Graduate School of Management (Dec. 1977), p. 7.

85 The ESOP Association, *ESOP Survey 1983* (Washington DC 1984), p. 11.
86 T.R. Marsh and D.E. McAllister, 'ESOP tables . . .', p. 589, Table 1.
87 M.J. Bonaccorso *et al.*, *Survey of Employee* . . ., p. 8.
88 See Chapter 2.
89 See Chapter 2.
90 T.R. Marsh and D.E. McAllister, 'ESOP tables . . .', p. 591, Table 4.
91 Ibid., p. 592, Table 5.
92 ESOP Association Survey 1983, p. 8, unionised 31 per cent; Bonaccorso *et al.*, 'Survey of Employee . . ., p. A–4, unionised 27.3 per cent; T.R. Marsh and D.E. McAllister, 'ESOP tables . . .', p. 600, unionised 34 per cent.
93 ESOP Association Survey 1983, p. 49, Question 11; see also T.R. Marsh and D.E. McAllister, 'ESOP tables . . .', p. 601, Table 22.
94 T.R. Marsh and D.E. McAllister, 'ESOP tables . . .', p. 601.
95 See Chapter 2.
96 T.R. Marsh and D.E. McAllister, 'ESOP tables . . .', p. 592, Table 6.
97 T.R. Marsh and D.E. McAllister, 'ESOP tables . . .', p. 594, Table 8; ESOP Survey 1983, p. 35.
98 Ibid.
99 See Chapter 2.
100 ESOP Association Survey 1983, p. 17.
101 K. Bradley and A. Gelb, *Worker Capitalism – The New Industrial Relations* (London 1983), p. 69.
102 ESOP Association Survey 1983, p. 13.
103 Ibid., p. 12.
104 M.J. Bonaccorso *et al.*, *Survey of Employee* . . ., Question 15 (B), p. 12.
105 See Chapter 2.
106 T.R. Marsh and D.E. McAllister, 'ESOP tables . . .', p. 611, Table 33.
107 ESOP Association Survey 1983, p. 31.
108 M.J. Bonaccorso *et al.*, *Survey of Employee* . . . , p. 20
109 ESOP Association Survey, 1983, p. 31
110 General Accounting Office (GAO) Report, *Employee Stock Ownership Plans* . . ., p. 1.
111 L.L. Granados, 'Employee stock ownership . . .', pp. 26–7.
112 Ibid.
113 GAO Report, *Employee Stock Ownership Plans* . . ., p. 6.
114 Ibid., pp. 8–9.
115 Ibid., p. 10.
116 M.J. Bonaccorso *et al.*, *Survey of Employee* . . ., p. A-19.
117 GAO Report, *Employee Stock Ownership Plans* . . ., p. 13.
118 Ibid., p. 8.
119 Ibid., pp. 17–18.
120 Ibid., p. 22.
121 Ibid., pp. 23–4.
122 T.R. Marsh and D.E. McAllister, 'ESOP tables . . .', p. 596, Table 12.
123 M.J. Bonaccorso *et al.*, *Survey of Employee* . . ., p. A-16, Question 20.

124 ESOP Association Survey, p. 43.

125 Ibid., p. 45.

126 GAO Report, *Employee Stock Ownership* . . ., p. 24.

127 Ibid., p. 25.

128 Ibid., p. 26.

129 See ESOP Association Survey 1983; T.R. Marsh and D.E. McAllister 'ESOP tables . . .'; M.J. Bonaccorso *et al.*, *Survey of Employee.* . . .

130 GAO Report, *Employee Stock Ownership Plans* . . ., pp. 24, 26–7.

131 Ibid., p. 26.

132 Ibid., p. 22.

133 The Department of Labour, the GAO pointed out, has not promulgated any special regulations or guidelines for the valuation of closed company stock. Consequently, the primary guidance available is Revenue Ruling 59–60. See GAO Report, *Employee Stock Ownership Plans* . . ., pp. 9, 10–21.

134 GAO Report, *Employee Stock Ownership Plans* . . ., pp. 10, 19.

135 Ibid., p. 27.

136 Ibid.

137 M. Conte and A.S. Tannenbaum, 'Employee owned companies: is the difference measurable?', *Monthly Labor Review* (July 1987), p. 27.

138 Ibid., p. 25.

139 Ibid., pp. 25–6.

140 C. Rosen, 'Making employee ownership work', *National Productivity Review* (Winter 1982–3). Reprinted in *The Employee Ownership Reader* Virginia 1983), pp. 11, 15.

141 T.R. Marsh and D.E. McAllister, 'ESOP tables . . .', p. 598, Table 16.

142 Ibid.

143 M. Conte and A.S. Tannenbaum, 'Employee owned companies . . .', p. 24, Table 1.

144 T.R. Marsh and D.E. McAllister, 'ESOP tables . . .', p. 598, Table 15; ESOP Association Survey 1983, p. 27.

145 K. Bradley and A. Gelb, *Worker Capitalism – The New* . . ., p. 4.

146 Ibid., p. 33.

147 L.O. Kelso, Testimony before the House Committee on Small Business 1979. Quoted in D.P. Ellerman's *Notes on the Co-op/ESOP Debate*, Industrial Co-operative Association, Somerville, Mass. (June 1983), p. 8.

148 L.O. Kelso, quoted in D.P. Ellerman *Notes on the Co-op/ESOP Debate*, p. 8.

149 Quoted in T.C. Jochim, *Employee Stock Ownership and Related Plans* (London 1982), p. 137.

150 C. Gunn, 'The fruits of Rath – a new model of self-management', in *Working Papers* (March–April 1981). Reprinted in C. Rosen (ed.) *Employee Ownership: Issues, Resources and Legislation. A Handbook for Employees and Public Officials* (Arlington, Virginia 1982), p. 52. See also D. Kruse, *Employee Ownership* . . ., p. iv.

151 D.P. Ellerman, *Notes on the Co-op/ESOP Debate*, pp. 8–10.

152 C. Rosen, 'ESOPs – making employees owners', *Business* (April–June 1983). Reprinted in *The Employee Ownership Reader*, p. 7.

153 D. Kruse, *Employee Ownership* . . ., p. 51.

154 C. Rosen, 'Making employee ownership work', reprinted in *The Employee Ownership Reader*, p. 17.

155 T.R. Marsh and D.E. McAllister, 'ESOP tables . . .', p. 618.

156 ESOP Association Survey 1983, p. 36.

157 R.J. Long, 'Job attitudes and organisational performance under employee ownership', *Academy of Management Journal* (Vol. 23, No. 4, 1980), p. 735.

158 R.J. Long 'The relative effects of share ownership versus control on job attitudes in an employee-owned company', *Human Relations* (Vol. 31, No. 9, 1978), p. 761.

159 D. Kruse, *Employee Ownership* . . ., pp. 146–7, 150.

160 J. O'Toole, 'The uneven record of employee ownership', *Harvard Business Review* (Nov.–Dec. 1979), p. 194.

161 Ibid., p. 195.

162 L.L. Granados, 'Employee stock ownership plans . . .', p. 33.

163 GAO Report, p. 25.

164 ESOP Association Survey 1983, p. 34.

165 Ibid., p. 35.

166 Ibid., p. 50, Question 24.

167 W.R. Reum and S.M. Reum, 'Employee stock ownership plans . . .', pp. 140–1.

168 M. Conte and S. Tannenbaum, 'Employee owned companies . . .', p. 25.

169 Ibid., p. 24, Table 1.

170 See Chapter 3.

171 M.J. Bonaccorso *et al.*, *Survey of Employee* . . ., p. 19.

172 Ibid., p. 18.

173 Ibid., p.A-8.

174 Ibid., p. 18.

175 Ibid., p. 22.

176 Ibid., p. 21.

177 ESOP Association Survey 1983, p. 36.

178 Ibid., p. 37.

179 T.R. Marsh and D.E. McAllister, 'ESOP tables . . .', p. 614.

180 Ibid., p. 615.

181 Ibid., p. 613, Table 35.

182 See Chapter 1.

183 T.R. Marsh and D.E. McAllister, 'ESOP tables . . .', p. 619.

184 Ibid.

185 Ibid.

186 D.T. Livingston and J.B Henry, 'The effect of employee stock ownership plans on corporate profits', *Journal of Risk and Insurance* (Vol. 47 1980), pp. 492–3, 502.

187 Ibid, p. 502.

188 See T.R. Marsh and D.E. McAllister, 'ESOP tables . . .'.

189 National Center for Employee Ownership (NCEO) 'How consultants view employee ownership', *Employee Ownership* (Vol. IV, No. 1, March 1984).

190 J.R. Boulis's, testimony to the US Senate Finance Committee 1978, quoted in T.C. Jochim, *Employee Stock Ownership* . . ., p. 131.

191 D.G. Olson, 'Union experiences with worker ownership: legal and practical issues raised by ESOPs, TRASOPs, stock purchases and co-operatives', in *Wisconsin Law Review* (No.5, 1982), p. 749, Note 98.
192 Ibid.
193 Ibid., pp. 751–2. By 1980, of the 16,884 shares of common stock in the ESOP, only 3,775.69 were vested and eligible for participant voting.
194 W.F. Whyte and J.R. Blasi, 'Worker ownership, participation and control: towards a theoretical model', *Policy Sciences* (14–1982), p. 146.
195 D.G. Olson, 'Union experiences with worker . . .', pp. 748–50.
196 'More worker-owners' *Time Magazine* (4 Oct. 1976).
197 J.R. Boulis's testimony to US Senate Finance Committee, quoted in T.C. Jochim, *Employee Stock Ownership* . . ., pp. 131–2.
198 D.G. Olson, 'Union experiences with worker . . .', p. 753.
199 Ibid., pp. 750, 752 (footnote 119), 753.
200 'When workers strike the company they own', *Business Week* (22 Sept. 1980)
201 I. Ross, 'What happens when the employees buy the company?', *Fortune* (22 June 1980), pp. 109–10.
202 W.F. Whyte and J.R. Blasi, 'Worker ownership, participation . . .', p. 146.
203 *Business Week* (22 Sept. 1980).
204 Ibid.
205 Ibid.
206 W.F. Whyte and J.R. Blasi, 'Worker ownership, participation . . .', p. 146. See also *Business Week* (22 Sept. 1980).
207 *Washington Post* (30 Sept. 1980), quoted in W.F. Whyte and J.R. Blasi, 'Worker ownership, participation . . .', p. 146.
208 W.F. Whyte and J.R. Blasi, 'Worker ownership, participation . . .', p. 147.
209 Ibid.
210 W.F. Whyte, 'Restructuring work at Rath Packing', in *The Employee Ownership Reader* (NCEO, Virginia 1983), p. 58.
211 J. O'Toole, 'The uneven record of . . .', p. 193.
212 *Business Week* (22 Sept. 1980).
213 D.G. Olson, 'Union experiences with worker . . .', p. 751, footnote 113.
214 C. Gunn, 'The fruits of Rath . . .', p. 49.
215 D.G. Olson, 'Union experiences with worker . . .', p. 754, footnote 127.
216 Ibid., pp. 754–5.
217 C. Rosen and W.F. Whyte, 'Employee ownership saving . . .', p. 22, Col. 2.
218 C. Gunn, 'The fruits of Rath . . .', p. 49, Col. 3.
219 D.G. Olson, 'Union experiences with worker . . .', p. 754.
220 W. Woodworth, 'Creating a culture of participation', in *The Employee Ownership Reader*, p. 54, Col. 2.
221 D.G. Olson, 'Union experiences with worker . . .', pp. 755–8; C. Gunn, 'The fruits of Rath . . .', p. 49, Col. 3; p. 50.
222 W.F. Whyte, 'Restructuring work at Rath . . .', p. 58, Cols 2–3.

223 W.F. Whyte and J.R. Blasi, 'Worker ownership, participation . . .', p. 149.
224 Ibid., p. 150.
225 C. Gunn, 'The fruits of Rath . . .', p. 50, Cols 2–3.
226 'An acid test for worker-owners', *Business Week* (2 Aug. 1982).
227 C. Rosen and W.F. Whyte, 'Employee ownership saving . . .', p. 22, Col. 2.
228 D.G. Olson, 'Union experiences with worker . . .', p. 760.
229 Ibid., p. 759.
230 Ibid.
231 Ibid.
232 Quoted in T.C. Jochim, *Employee Stock Ownership . . .*, p. 154.
233 Ibid., p. 153.
234 E. Sachar, 'Taking stock of ESOP experience', *Newsday Graphic*. (Clippings of newspapers in booklet form for the year 1983, published by the ESOP Association.) (Washington 1984), p. 69.
235 UAW Social Security Department, *Employee Stock Ownership Plans ESOPS* (March 1977), quoted in T.C. Jochim, *Employee Stock Ownership . . .*, pp. 148–9.
236 Ibid., pp. 149–52.
237 'Labor's quid pro quo in the Chrysler rescue', *Business Week* (1 Oct. 1979).
238 T.C. Jochim, *Employee Stock Ownership . . .*, p. 147.
239 T.R. Marsh and D.E. McAllister, 'ESOP tables . . .', p. 618.
240 R.N. Stern and R.A. O'Brien, *National Unions and Employee Ownership*, Department of Organizational Behavior, New York State School of Industrial and Labor Relations (May 1977), pp. 6–8.
241 Ibid., p. 8.
242 D. Kruse, *Employee Ownership . . .* p. 118.
243 Ibid.
244 Ibid., p. 148.
245 ESOP Association Survey 1983, p. 34.
246 D. Kruse, *Employee Ownership . . .*, p. 148.
247 D.G. Olson, 'Union experiences with worker . . .', pp. 814, 822–3.
248 J. Rothschild-Whitt, 'Worker ownership in relation . . .', p. 397.
249 R.B. Rose, 'Employee stock ownership and the Community Bank', *American Banker* (Oct. 1983), from ESOP Association's book of clippings for 1983 (Washington DC 1984), pp. 46–7.
250 Senate Finance Committee, *ESOPs: An Employer's Handbook*, p. 9.
251 B. Wotton, *The Social Foundations of Wage Policy* (London 1962, 2nd edn), pp. 146, 165.
252 A.M. Okun, *Equality and Efficiency – The Big Trade-off*, The Brookings Institute (Washington DC 1975), p. 42.
253 D.P. Ellerman, *Notes on the Co-op/ESOP Debate*, pp. 10–18.
254 A.M. Okun, *Equality and Efficiency . . .*, p. 48.
255 J.A. Banks, *Trade Unionism* (London 1974), pp. 73, 76.
256 See Chapter 2.
257 GAO Report, *Employee Stock Ownership Plans . . .*, p. 42.
258 Quoted in J. Perham, 'Upsurge in ESOPS', *Duns Business Month* (Feb. 1983).

259 GAO Report, *Employee Stock Ownership Plans* . . ., p. 3.
260 'New tax law causes surge in interest in employee ownership', in *Employee Ownership* (Vol. v, No. 1, Feb. 1985), p. 5.

CHAPTER 4

1 Quoted in T.A. Tilton, 'A Swedish road to socialism: Ernst Wigforss and the ideological foundations of Swedish social democracy', *American Political Science Review* (Vol. 73, 1979), p. 512.
2 Quoted in R. Ball, 'How Electrolux cleans up in socialist Sweden', *Fortune* (March 1976), pp. 154, 155, 156.
3 E. Schwartz, *Trouble in Eden – A Comparison of the British and Swedish Economies* (New York 1980), pp. 66, 77.
4 K. Kvist and G. Agren, 'Social Democracy in the Seventies', in J. Fry (ed.) *Limits of the Welfare State*, (Aldershot 1979), p. 25.
5 A. Lindbeck, *Swedish Economic Policy* (London 1975), p. 247.
6 Quoted in J. Fry, 'Introduction to limits of welfare state', in *Limits of the Welfare State*, p. 1.
7 Industrial Democracy in Europe (IDE), 'The Swedish industrial relations system', in *European Industrial Relations*, (Oxford 1981), p. 37.
8 See A. Lindbeck, *Swedish Economic Policy*, pp. 214–15.
9 Quoted in 'Ownership and influence in the economy', a summary and translation of the Commission on Industrial and Economic Concentration 1968, in R. Scase (ed.) *Readings in the Swedish Class Structure* (Oxford 1976), p. 43.
10 See Chapter 3.
11 R. Aberg, 'Market-independent income distribution: efficiency and legitimacy', in J.H. Goldthorpe, *Order and Conflict in Contemporary Capitalism* (Oxford 1984), p. 210.
12 Ibid., p. 229. See also G. Esping-Andersen and W. Korpi, 'Social policy as class politics in postwar capitalism: Scandinavia, Austria and Germany', in J.H. Goldthorpe (ed.) *Order and Conflict* . . ., p. 202.
13 J.H. Goldthorpe, 'The end of convergence: corporatist and dualist tendencies in modern western societies', in J.H. Goldthorpe (ed.) *Order and Conflict* . . ., pp. 320–1.
14 B. Gustafsson, 'Co-determination and wage earner funds', in J. Fry (ed.) *Towards a Democratic Rationality: Making the Case for Swedish Labour* (Aldershot 1986), p. 88.
15 A. Lindbeck, *Swedish Economic Policy*, p. 1.
16 N. Elvander, 'In search of new relationships: parties, unions and salaried employees' associations in Sweden', *Industrial and Labour Relations Review* (Vol. 28, No.1, 1974), p. 62.
17 W. Korpi, *The Democratic Class Struggle* (London 1983), p. 46.
18 Ibid., pp. 48–9. See also W. Korpi, 'Sweden: conflict, power and politics in industrial relations', in P. Doeringer, P. Gourevitch, P. Lange and A. Martin (eds) *Industrial Relations in International Perspective* (London 1981), pp. 195–6.
19 T.A. Tilton, 'A Swedish road to socialism . . .', pp. 509–17.
20 A.L. Thimm, *The False Promise of Co-determination* (Lexington 1980), p. 190.

21 M.D. Hancock, *Sweden: the Politics of Post-Industrial Change* (Illinois 1972) pp. 208–9.
22 A. Martin, 'The dynamics of change in a Keynesian political economy: the Swedish case and its implications', in C. Crouch (ed.) *State and Economy in Contemporary Capitalism* (London 1979), p. 104.
23 D. Robinson, *Solidaristic Wage Policy in Sweden* (OECD Paris 1974), pp. 18–19.
24 A. Martin, 'The dynamics of change . . .', pp. 104–5.
25 J. Fulcher, 'Class conflict: joint regulation and its decline', in R. Scase (ed.) *Readings in the Swedish Class Structure*, p. 54. See also A. Martin, 'Trade unions in Sweden: strategic responses to change and crisis', in P. Gourevitch, A. Martin, G. Ross, C. Allen, S. Bornstein and A. Markovits (eds) *Unions and Economic Crisis: Britain, West Germany and Sweden* (London 1984), pp. 320–3.
26 L. Ulman and R.J. Flanagan, *Wage Restraint: A Study of Incomes Policies in Western Europe* (University of California Press 1971), p. 93.
27 D. Robinson, *Solidaristic Wage Policy . . .*, p. 38.
28 M.D. Hancock, *Sweden: the Politics of . . .*, pp. 215, 216, 222.
29 C. Van Otter, 'Sweden: Labour reformism reshapes the system', in S. Barkin (ed.) *Worker Militancy and Its Consequences 1965–75: New Directions in Industrial Relations* (New York 1975), p. 212.
30 Swedish Trade Union Confederation (LO), *Employee Investment Funds in Sweden in 1984* (Stockholm 1984), p. 6, Diagram 3.
31 D. Robinson, *Solidaristic Wage Policy . . .*, p. 35.
32 J. Israel, 'Swedish socialism and big business', *Acta Sociologica* (Scandinavian Sociological Association) (Vol. 21, No. 4, 1978), p. 345.
33 A. Lindbeck, *Swedish Economic Policy*, p. 223, Chart 11:8.
34 A. Martin, 'Trade unions in Sweden . . .', in P. Gourevitch *et al.* (eds) *Unions and Economic Crisis . . .*, pp. 268–9.
35 J. Fulcher, 'Joint regulation and its decline', in R. Scase (ed.) *Readings in the Swedish Class . . .*, pp. 75–6.
36 L. Berntson 'Postwar Swedish Capitalism', in J. Fry (ed.) *Limits of the Welfare . . .*, p. 75.
37 J. Fulcher, 'Joint regulation and . . .', p. 75.
38 C. Van Otter, 'Sweden: labour reformism . . .', in S. Barkin (ed.) *Worker Militancy . . .*, p. 201.
39 P. Scase, *Social Democracy in Capitalist Society* (London 1977), p. 69.
40 C. Van Otter, 'Joint regulation . . .', p. 201.
41 W. Korpi, *The Democratic Class Struggle*. p. 23.
42 H.-G. Myrdal, 'The Swedish model – will it survive?', *British Journal of Industrial Relations* (Vol. xviii, No. 1, March 1980), p. 58.
43 Commission on Industrial and Economic Concentration, 'Ownership and influence in the economy', summarised in R. Scase (ed.) *Readings in the Swedish . . .*, p. 30.
44 A. Lindbeck, *Swedish Economic Policy*, p. 223, Chart 11:8.
45 Commission on Industrial and Economic Concentration, 'Ownership and influence in the economy', summarised in R. Scase (ed.) *Readings in The Swedish . . .*, p. 47.
46 Ibid., p. 33.
47 Ibid., p. 38.

48 Ibid., p. 34.
49 J. Israel, 'Swedish socialism and big business', in *Acta Sociologica*, p. 346.
50 Commission on Industrial and Economic Concentration, 'Ownership and influence in the economy', p. 37.
51 Ibid.
52 Ibid., p. 46.
53 Ibid., p. 47.
54 IDE, 'The Swedish industrial . . .', p. 54; see also W. Korpi, *The Working Class in Welfare Capitalism: Work Unions and Politics in Sweden*, p. 324.
55 A. Martin, 'Sweden: Industrial democracy . . .', p. 72
56 C. Van Otter, 'Sweden: labour reformism . . .', p. 212.
57 W. Korpi, *The Working Class* . . ., p. 325.
58 J. Fulcher, 'Class conflict in Sweden', *Sociology* (Vol. 7, 1973), 59.
59 Ibid., p. 58.
60 C. Van Otter, 'Sweden: labour reformism . . .', pp. 213–14.
61 W. Korpi, 'Unofficial strikes in Sweden', *British Journal of Industrial Relations* (Vol. 19, March 1981), p. 69, Table 3, pp. 82–3.
62 R. Eidem and B. Ohman, *Economic Democracy through Wage Earner Funds*, Swedish Centre for Working Life (Stockholm 1979), pp. 39–41.
63 H.-G. Myrdal, 'The Swedish model . . .', p. 58.
64 A. Martin, 'Sweden: industrial democracy . . .', p. 68.
65 IDE, 'The Swedish industrial . . .', p. 50.
66 A. Larsson *et al.*, *Labour Market Reforms in Sweden: Facts and Employee Views*, The Swedish Institute (Uppsala 1979), pp. 21–5.
67 Ibid., pp. 35–6; see also IDE, 'The Swedish industrial relations . . .', p. 53.
68 L. Forseback, *Industrial Relations and Employment in Sweden*, The Swedish Institute (Uppsala 1980), pp. 101–2. See also A. Larsson *et al.*, *Labour Market Reforms*, p. 59.
69 IDE, 'The Swedish industrial relations . . .', pp. 49–53; A. Larsson *et al.*, *Labour Market Reforms*, p. 27; L. Forseback, *Industrial Relations*, pp. 41–3.
70 E. Asard, 'Employee participation in Sweden 1971–79: the issue of economic decomcracy', in *Economic and Industrial Democracy* (Vol. 1, 1980), pp. 381–2.
71 IDE, 'The Swedish industrial relations . . .', p. 57.
72 R. Eidem and B. Ohman, *Economic Democracy through* . . ., p. 40.
73 See J. Fry, 'The co-determination act in practice: the case of the mining industry', in J. Fry (ed.) *Towards a Democratic Rationality* . . ., pp. 122–66. See also A. Hass, 'The aftermath of Sweden's co-determination law: workers' experiences in Gothenburg 1977–80', *Economic and Industrial Democracy* (Vol. 4, No. 1, Feb. 1983), pp. 19–46.
74 Swedish Trade Union Confederation (LO), *Wage Policy – A Report to the 1971 Congress of the Swedish Trade Union Confederation* (Stockholm 1972), p. 74.
75 Ibid., p. 80.
76 R. Eidem and B. Ohman, *Economic Democracy through* . . ., pp. 39–40.

77 W. Korpi, *The Working Class* . . ., p. 327; B. Gustafsson, 'Co-determination and wage earner . . .', p. 90.
78 A. Martin, 'Trade unions in Sweden . . .', p. 271.
79 R. Meidner, *Employee Investment Funds. An Approach to Collective Capital Formation* (London 1978), p. 15.
80 Ibid., pp. 16–17.
81 Ibid., pp. 26–7.
82 Ibid., pp. 27–8.
83 Ibid., p. 28.
84 Ibid., p. 17.
85 Ibid., pp. 96–7.
86 Ibid., p. 119.
87 Ibid., pp. 45–6.
88 SAF, *Company Profits, Sources of Investment Capital and Wage Earner Funds. A Brief Background and Summary of the Waldenstrom Report* (SAF Doc. No. 1444 1976–07–09), p. 6.
89 R. Meidner, *Employee Investment Funds* . . ., pp. 39–40.
90 'Zanussi's new Swedish godfathers', in *International Management Europe* (Sept. 1985), pp. 24–8.
91 R. Meidner, *Employee Investment Funds* . . ., p. 40. See also V. Perlo, 'People's capitalism and stock ownership', *The American Economic Review* (Vol. 48, No. 3, June 1958), pp. 333–47, 337–8, 345.
92 R. Meidner, *Employee Investment Funds* . . ., pp. 47, 56.
93 Ibid., pp. 70–1.
94 Ibid., p. 74.
95 Ibid., p. 91.
96 Ibid., pp. 69, 74.
97 Ibid., p. 47.
98 Ibid., p. 103.
99 Ibid., p. 83.
100 Ibid., pp. 86–9.
101 Ibid., p. 99.
102 Ibid., p. 101.
103 Ibid., pp. 98, 125.
104 Ibid., p. 94.
105 Ibid., pp. 98–9.
106 Ibid., p. 106.
107 Ibid., p. 77.
108 Ibid., p. 107.
109 Ibid., p. 124.
110 Ibid., p. 126.
111 B. Ohman, 'The debate on wage earner funds in Scandinavia', in C. Crouch and F.A. Heller *Organisation Democracy* . . ., p. 41.
112 A. Martin, 'Trade unions in Sweden . . .', pp. 285–6.
113 E. Asard, 'Employees participation in Sweden . . .', pp. 382–3.
114 A. Martin, 'Trade unions in Sweden . . .', p. 284.
115 E. Asard, 'Employee participation in Sweden . . .', p. 379.
116 Ibid., p. 382.
117 Quoted in R. Ball, 'How Electrolux cleans up . . .', p. 156.
118 E. Asard, 'Employee participation in Sweden . . .', p. 388.

119 H.-G. Myrdal, 'The Swedish model . . .', p. 65.

120 A.L. Thimm, *The False Promise of . . .*, p. 194.

121 W. Korpi, *The Democratic Class Struggle*, pp. 142–4.

122 These two paragraphs are based on an interview with Mr Clas Nikvist, Economic Research Section, TCO, Stockholm 28 Nov. 1984.

123 Stahl, quoted in P.-M. Meyerson, *Company Profits – Sources of Investment Finance and Wage Earners' Investment Funds in Sweden: Proposals, Debate, Analysis*, Federation of Swedish Industries (SI) (Stockholm 1976), p. 15.

124 Ibid., pp. 15–16.

125 Ibid., p. 16.

126 Ibid.

127 Ibid.

128 H.-G. Myrdal, 'Collective wage earner funds in Sweden – a road to socialism and the end of freedom of association', *International Labour Review* (Vol. 120, No. 3, May–June 1981), p. 333.

129 R. Meidner, *Employee Investment Funds . . .*, pp. 118–19.

130 Ibid.

131 U. Himmelstrand, G. Ahrne, Leif Lundberg and Lars Lundberg, *Beyond Welfare Capitalism – Issues, Actors and Forces in Societal Change* (London 1981), p. 276.

132 A. Lindbeck, quoted in P.-M. Meyerson, *Company Profits . . .*, pp. 12–13. See also B. Abrahamsson and A. Brostrom, *The Rights of Labour* (London 1980), pp. 212–13.

133 R. Meidner, 'Our concept of the third way – some remarks on the socio-political tenets of the Swedish labour movement', *Economic and Industrial Democracy* (Vol. 1, No. 3, Aug. 1980), p. 364.

134 P.-M. Meyerson, *Company Profits . . .*, p. 12. See also H.-C. Myrdal, 'Collective Wage Earner Funds . . .', pp. 330–2.

135 P. Meidner, 'Our concept of the third . . .', p. 364.

136 B. Abrahamsson and A. Brostrom, *The Rights of Labour*, pp. 213–14.

137 U. Himmelstrand *et al.*, *Beyond Welfare Capitalism . . .*, p. 283.

138 R. Meidner, 'Our concept of the third . . .', p. 365.

139 Ibid., pp. 365–6.

140 SAF, translation of Lindbeck article in *Dagens Nyheter* (15 Aug. 1976). Reproduced in SAF Doc. No. 1446 (2) 27 Sept. 1976, pp. 1–2.

141 SAF, Doc. No. 1446 (2) 27 Sept. 1976, pp. 2–3.

142 P.-M. Meyerson, *Company Profits . . .*, p. 14.

143 Ibid.

144 K. Kumar, *Prophecy and Progress – The Sociology of Industrial and Post-Industrial Society* (Harmondsworth 1978), pp. 126–31.

145 R. Meidner, *Employee Investment Funds . . .*, pp. 86–9.

146 U. Himmelstrand *et al.*, *Beyond Welfare Capitalism*, pp. 63, 119.

147 P.M. Meyerson, *Company Profits . . .*, p. 13.

148 Ibid., pp. 13–15

149 B. Abrahamsson and A. Brostrom, *The Rights of Labour*, pp. 216–17.

150 U. Himmelstrand *et al.*, *Beyond Welfare Capitalism*, p. 277.

151 Ibid., pp. 277–8.

152 Ibid., pp. 278–9.

153 B. Abrahamsson and A. Brostrom, *The Rights of Labour*, pp. 217–18.

154 SAF, *The Collective Wage Earner Funds. Brief Survey in July 1984*, Doc. No. 1449/BWn 1984-08-23, p. 4.
155 SAF, Doc. No. 1444, p. 6.
156 Ibid.
157 P.-M. Meyerson, *Company Profits . . .*, p. 23.
158 R. Eidem and B. Ohman, *Economic Democracy through . . .*, p. 47.
159 Ibid., p. 48; see also P.-M. Meyerson, *Company Profits . . .*, p. 24.
160 P.-M. Meyerson, *Company Profits . . .*, pp. 24–5.
161 SAF, Doc. No.1444, p. 7.
162 Ibid.
163 Ibid.
164 Ibid., p. 8.
165 Ibid.
166 Ibid., p. 10.
167 Ibid., p. 9.
168 Ibid., p. 8.
169 Ibid., p. 10.
170 Ibid., pp. 6–10.
171 R. Eidem and B. Ohman, *Economic Democracy through . . .*, p. 49.
172 SAF, *SAF and the Free Market Economy: Income Earners and Capital Formation*, Doc. No. 1448, 1977-10-20.
173 Ibid.
174 A. Martin, 'Trade unions in Sweden . . .', p. 303.
175 Ibid., p. 304.
176 Ibid., pp. 307–8.
177 Ibid., pp. 295–6.
178 W. Korpi, *The Democratic Class . . .*, pp. 200–7.
179 A. Martin, 'Trade unions in Sweden . . .', pp. 296–7.
180 Ibid., p. 303.
181 L. Forseback, *Industrial Relations*, p. 133.
182 Ibid., pp. 133–4.
183 E. Asard, 'Employee participation in Sweden . . .', p. 383.
184 C.G. Gill, 'Swedish wage earner funds: the road to economic democracy?' *Journal of General Management* (Vol. 9, No. 3, Spring 1984), p. 51.
185 R. Meidner, 'Collective asset formation through wage earner funds', *International Labour Review*, (Vol. 120, No. 3, May–June 1981), p. 312.
186 C.G. Gill, 'Swedish wage earner . . .', pp. 51–2.
187 H.-G. Myrdal, 'The Swedish model . . .', p. 66.
188 C.G. Gill, 'Swedish wage earner . . .', p. 52.
189 R. Meidner, 'Collective asset formation . . .', p. 312.
190 Ibid., pp. 312–13.
191 H.-G. Myrdal, 'The Swedish model . . .', p. 67.
192 W. Korpi, *The Democratic Class . . .*, p. 144.
193 A. Martin, 'Trade unions in Sweden . . .', p. 310.
194 L. Forseback, *Industrial Relations*, p. 125.
195 A. Martin, 'Trade unions in Sweden . . .', p. 311.
196 R. Meidner, 'Collective asset formation . . .', p. 313.
197 B. Ohman, 'The debate on wage earner funds . . .', p. 46.

198 Interview with Clas Nykvist.
199 Ibid.
200 Interview with B.E. Carlsson, Economic Section SAF, Swedish Employers' Federation, Stockholm (30 Nov. 1984).
201 Interview with Mrs Anne Wibble, economist with Liberal Party and member of three-party working group on fund abolition, Stockholm (30 Nov. 1984).
202 Federation of Swedish Industries (SI), *Collective Wage Earner Funds*, Stockholm (March 1982), pp. 3–5.
203 B. Ohman, 'The debate on . . .', p. 50.
204 SI, *Collective Wage Earner Funds* (March 1982), p. 5.
205 B. Ohman, 'The debate on wage earner . . .', p. 50.
206 Quoted in 'Another Swedish pink movie?', *Economist* (28 Aug. 1982), p. 41.
207 SAF, *Collective WEFs Will Harm Sweden*, Doc. No. 1442 (Stockholm 1981), pp. 14–15.
208 A. Martin, 'Trade unions in Sweden . . .', p. 328.
209 Ibid. See also B. Gustafsson, 'Co-determination and wage earner . . .', in J. Fry (ed.) *Towards a Democratic . . .*, p. 100.
210 SAF, *Collective WEFs Will Harm Sweden*, pp. 14–17.
211 Ibid., p. 19.
212 Ibid., p. 21.
213 Ibid.
214 A. Martin, 'Trade unions in Sweden . . .', p. 328.
215 *Economist* (28 Aug. 1982); *Irish Times* (4 Oct. 1983).
216 SI, reproduced in *The Debate on Collective Wage Earner Funds in Sweden* (Stockholm, Sept. 1983), p. 2.
217 B. Ohman, 'The debate on wage earner . . .', p. 50.
218 Ibid.
219 *Economist* (28 Aug. 1982), p. 42.
220 *Irish Times* (10 Sept. 1985).
221 Ministry of Finance, Sweden, *Employee Investment Funds* (Stockholm 1984), pp. 13–14.
222 SI, *The Debate on Collective Wage Earner . . .*, pp. 1–2.
223 Ibid. See also SAF Doc. No. 1445.
224 Ministry of Finance, *Employee Investment Funds*, p. 15.
225 SI, *The Debate on Collective Wage . . .*, pp. 7–8.
226 SAF, *The Collective Wage Earner . . .*, Doc. No. 1449, p. 1.
227 Ministry of Finance, *Employee Investment Funds*, pp. 14–15.
228 Ibid., p. 15.
229 Ibid., pp. 15–16.
230 Ibid., pp. 17–18.
231 Interviews with C. Nykvist, A. Wibble and K. Kvist.
232 SAF, *The Collective Wage Earner . . .*, Doc. No. 1449, p. 1.
233 Interview with K. Kvist, secretary of the Parliamentary Group, Left Party Communists, Stockholm, 29 Nov. 1984.
234 Ministry of Finance, *Employee Investment Funds*, pp. 5, 19.
235 LO, *Employee Investment Funds . . .*, p. 10.
236 Ministry of Finance, *Employee Investment Funds*, Appendix 1, pp. 24–5; Appendix 2, pp. 26–9.

237 Ibid., p. 20. See also LO, *Employee Investment Funds* . . ., p. 13.
238 Ministry of Finance, *Employee Investment Funds*, p. 22.
239 Ibid., pp. 20–2.
240 Ibid., p. 21.
241 Ibid.
242 LO, *Employee Investment Funds* . . ., p. 14.
243 A. Martin, 'Trade unions in Sweden . . .', p. 326.
244 Ministry of Finance, *Employee Investment Funds*, p. 19; LO, *Employee Investment* . . ., p. 14.
245 Ibid.
246 LO, *Employee Investment Funds* . . ., p. 14.
247 Ibid., p. 15.
248 Interview with L.O. Pettersson, economist with LO, Stockholm, 27 Nov. 1984.
249 Ministry of Finance, *Employee Investment Funds*, p. 22; see also Pettersson interview.
250 SAF, *The Collective Wage Earner* . . ., Doc. No. 1449, p. 3.
251 Ibid., p. 4.
252 Interviews with C. Nykvist and L.O. Pettersson.
253 Interview with K. Kvist.
254 Interview with C. Nykvist.
255 Ministry of Finance, *Employee Investment Funds*, p. 20.
256 Ibid., p. 18.
257 J.M. Keynes, *The General Theory of Employment Interest and Money* (London 1967), p. 378.
258 J. Strachey, *Contemporary Capitalism* (London 1956), p. 207.
259 A. Martin, 'The dynamics of change . . .', p. 117.

CHAPTER 5

1 L. Ulman and R. Flanagan, *Wage Restraint: A Study of Incomes Policies in Western Europe* (California 1971), p. 229.
2 Ministry of Foreign Affairs, Denmark, *Recommendations for Economic Democracy*, Factsheet Denmark Code 010772, p. 2, Col. 2.
3 First interview with Jorgen Freddy Hansen, economist and expert on economic democracy with the Danish Congress of Trade Unions LO, Copenhagen, 4 Dec. 1984.
4 First interview with J.F. Hansen.
5 J. Fitzmaurice, *Politics in Denmark* (London 1981), p. 21.
6 Ibid., p. 1.
7 W.M. Lafferty, *Economic Development and the Response of Labour in Scandinavia – a Multi-Level Analysis* (Universitetsforlaget Oslo 1971), pp. 71–4. Also see W. Galenson, *The Danish System of Labor Relations* (Harvard 1952), p. 9.
8 L. Jorberg and O. Krantz, 'Scandinavia 1914–1970', in C.M. Cipolla (ed.), *The Fontana Economic History of Europe: Contemporary Economies* (Glasgow 1976), Vol. 6, Part 2, pp. 418–19.
9 Industrial Democracy in Europe (IDE), 'The Danish industrial relations system', in *European Industrial Relations*, International Research Group (Oxford 1981), p. 63.

10 F. Valentin, 'Self-management – strategy for autonomy or integration', in T.R. Burns, L.E. Karlsson and V. Rus (eds) *Work and Power . . .*, pp. 323, 330.
11 IDE, 'The Danish industrial relations . . .', pp. 63–6.
12 L. Ulman and R. Flanagan, *Wage Restraint . . .*, p. 129.
13 Ibid., pp. 129–30.
14 Ibid., p. 141.
15 J. Logue, *Trade Unions in the Corporate State. The Effects of Corporatism on Party Competition, Contract Referenda and Internationalism in Danish Trade Unions* (Publication No. 5, University of Gothenburg, Dept of History 1976), p. 45.
16 Ibid., p. 10
17 First interview with J.F. Hansen.
18 N. Elvander, 'Collective bargaining and incomes policy in Nordic countries – a comparative analysis', *British Journal of Industrial Relations* (Vol. 12, No. 3, 1974), p. 420.
19 Ibid., p. 420.
20 L. Ulman and R. Flanagan, *Wage Restraint . . .*, p. 227.
21 J. Logue, *Trade Unions in the Corporate . . .*, pp. 33–6.
22 Under the terms of the September agreement (1889), the labour market parties are bound by a 'peace obligation' to refrain from any industrial action for the duration of a collective agreement.
23 L. Ulman and R. Flanagan, *Wage Restraint . . .*, pp. 229–30. See also N. Elvander, 'Collective bargaining . . .', p. 420.
24 L. Ulman and R. Flanagan, *Wage Restraint . . .*, p. 140.
25 First interview with J.F. Hansen.
26 N. Elder, A. Thomas and D. Arter, *The Consensual Democracies? The Government and Politics of the Scandinavian States* (Oxford 1982), p. 109.
27 M. Lykketoft, 'Towards economic democracy: wage earner funds', *Scandinavian Review* (Part 2, 1977), p. 41.
28 Second interview with J.F. Hansen, LO, Copenhagen, 5 August 1986.
29 L. Ulman and R. Flanagan, *Wage Restraint . . .*, pp. 136, 145–6.
30 Ibid., pp. 141–2.
31 Ibid., p. 145.
32 J. Logue, *Trade Unions in the Corporate . . .*, pp. 40–3.
33 First interview with J.F. Hansen.
34 G. Karlsson, *Trade Unions and Collective Capital Formation – A Review of Initiatives in Western European Countries*, European Trade Union Institute (ETUI) (Brussels 1983), p. 26.
35 R.C. Geary and M. Dempsey, 'Profit sharing for Ireland?', *Journal of the Statistical . . .*, Vol. xxiv, Part iv, p. 167.
36 C. Gill, 'Industrial relations in Denmark – problems and perspectives', *Industrial Relations Journal* (No. 15, 1984), p. 52.
37 The Danish Employers' Confederation (DA) and the Federation of Danish Industries (I), 'Co-worker – co-owner', a discussion paper on economic democracy (Copenhagen, March 1972), p. 44.
38 First interview with J.F. Hansen.
39 C. Gill, 'Industrial relations . . .', pp. 54–5.
40 DA/LO, *Agreement on Cooperation and Cooperation Committees*

between the Danish Employers' Confederation and the Danish Federation of Trade Unions, 2 Oct. 1970. Text of agreement and notes (Copenhagen 1978, 2nd edn), p. 4.

41 Ibid., pp. 28–9, 32–3.

42 Ibid., pp. 4–6.

43 Ibid., pp. 35–7.

44 C. Gill, 'Industrial relations . . .', p. 54.

45 DA/LO, *Agreement on Co-operation* . . ., p. 5.

46 Ibid., p. 41.

47 A. Westenholz, 'Workers' participation in Denmark', *Industrial Relations* (Vol. 18, No. 3, Fall 1979), p. 377.

48 A. Slok, *Participation and Co-Operation on the Danish Labour Market* (DA Copenhagen, June 1979, 2nd edn), p. 9.

49 First interview with J.F. Hansen.

50 A. Slok, *Participation and Co-operation* . . ., pp. 12–13.

51 First interview with J.F. Hansen.

52 W. Galenson, 'Current problems of Scandinavian trade unionism', in K.H. Cerny (ed.) *Scandinavia at the Polls*, American Enterprise Institute for Public Policy Research (Washington DC 1977), p. 289.

53 A. Westenholz, 'Wrokers' participation . . .', p. 378.

54 Ibid.

55 C. Gill, 'Industrial relations . . .', p. 53.

56 Ministry of Labour, *Economic Democracy – Introduction and Bill* (Copenhagen, March 1973), p. 1.

57 F. Valentin, 'Self-management – strategy for . . .', in T.R. Burns, L.E. Karlsson and R. Veljko, *Worker and Power* . . ., p. 330. See also G.W. Latta, *Profit Sharing* . . ., p. 93.

58 DA/I, 'Co-worker – co-owner', p. 45.

59 Ministry of Labour, *Economic Democracy* . . ., pp. 1,3.

60 Ibid., pp. 18–21.

61 Ibid., p. 29.

62 Ibid., p. 30.

63 Ibid.,

64 Ibid., pp. 11, 13, 30, 34, 41.

65 Ibid., p. 30.

66 Ibid., p. 4.

67 Ibid., pp. 30–1.

68 Ibid., p. 31.

69 Ibid., pp. 5, 17.

70 Ibid., pp. 31, 39.

71 Ibid., pp. 6, 16–18, 34.

72 Ibid., pp. 6, 31–2.

73 Ibid., p. 18.

74 Ibid., pp. 2–3, 9–11, 26, 28–9.

75 M. Lykketoft, 'Towards economic democracy . . .', p. 45.

76 Ministry of Labour, *Economic Democracy* . . ., p. 23.

77 Ibid., p. 42.

78 Ibid., p. 26.

79 Ibid., pp. 26–7.

80 Ibid., p. 25.

81 DA/I, 'Co-worker – co-owner . . .', pp. 8, 12.
82 Ibid., p. 11.
83 Ibid., pp. 11–12.
84 Ibid.
85 Ibid., pp. 16–18
86 Ibid., p. 28.
87 Ibid., p. 34.
88 Ibid., p. 39.
89 Ibid., p. 48.
90 Ibid., p. 18.
91 Ibid., pp. 18–20, 24.
92 Ibid., pp. 26–7, 48–9.
93 Ibid., pp. 50–1.
94 Ibid., p. 26.
95 Ibid., pp. 26, 47.
96 Ibid., pp. 19–20.
97 Ibid., p. 54.
98 Ibid., pp. 22–3.
99 P.F. Drucker, *The Unseen Revolution – How Pension Fund Socialism Came to America* (London 1976), pp. 1, 107.
100 Ibid., p. 97.
101 Ibid., pp. 164–5.
102 J. Scott, *Corporations, Classes and Capitalism* (London 1979), p. 143. See also T. Nichols, *Ownership, Control and Ideology* (London 1969), pp. 104–5, 109, 225, 241.
103 G.E. Jackson, *How To Stay Union Free* (Memphis 1978), pp. 41–7. See also G. Salaman, *Work Organisations Resistance and Control* (London 1979), p. 208.
104 DA/I, 'Co-worker – co-owner . . .', pp. 18–19, 54.
105 DA, *The Consequences of Economic Democracy* (Copenhagen, Sept. 1973), p. 4.
106 Ibid., pp. 9, 16, 25.
107 Ibid., p. 17.
108 Ibid., p. 16.
109 Ibid., p. 26.
110 S. Ward, *Pensions* (London 1981), pp. 202–5. See also R. Barber 'Pension funds in the US – issues of investment and control', *Economic and Industrial Democracy* (Vol. 3, No. 1, Feb. 1982), p. 31.
111 DA, *The Consequences* . . ., p. 27.
112 Ibid., p. 12.
113 Ibid., pp. 12, 29.
114 Ibid., p. 28.
115 Ibid., p. 29.
116 *Problems of Long-Term Economic Planning in Denmark 1970–1985*, summary and conclusion of a report presented by a working party set up by government in November 1968 (Copenhagen, March 1971), p. 30.
117 DA, *The Consequences* . . ., p. 29.
118 N. Elder, A. Thomas and D. Arter, *The Consensual* . . ., p. 83.
119 A.H. Thomas, 'social democracy in Denmark', in W.E. Patterson and A.H. Thomas (eds) *Social Democratic Parties in Western Europe*

(London 1977), p. 240. See also, O. Borre, 'Recent trends in Danish voting behaviour', in K.H. Cerny *Scandinavia at the Polls* (Washington DC 1977), p. 6.

120 J. Fitzmaurice, *Politics in Denmark*, pp. 109–10.

121 N. Elder, A. Thomas and D. Arter, *The Consensual* . . ., p. 85, Table 3.9.

122 A.H. Thomas, 'Social democracy in Denmark', p. 243. See also O. Borre 'Recent trends . . .', p. 6.

123 J. Fitzmaurice, *Politics in Denmark*, p. 105. See also A.H. Thomas, 'Social democracy . . .' pp. 252–3.

124 J. Fitzmaurice, *Politics in Denmark*, p. 104.

125 A.H. Thomas, 'Social democracy . . .', p. 259.

126 J. Fitzmaurice, *Politics in Denmark*, p. 115.

127 Ministry of Foreign Affairs, *The Political Parties in Denmark*, Factsheet Denmark (2nd revised edn 1983), p. 3, Col. 1. See also A.H. Thomas, 'Social democracy . . .', pp. 252–3; J. Fitzmaurice, *Politics in Denmark*, p. 166.

128 N. Elder, A. Thomas and D. Arter, *The Consensual* . . ., pp. 91–2.

129 P. Kosonen, 'Public expenditure in the Nordic nation states – the source of prosperity or crisis?', in R. Alapuro, M. Alestalo, E. Haavio-Mannila and R. Vayrynen (eds) *Small States in Comparative Perspective* (Norwegian University Press 1985), p. 110.

130 N. Elder, A. Thomas and D. Arter, *The Consensual* . . ., p. 163; see also J. Fitzmaurice, *Politics in Denmark*, p. 131.

131 J. Fitzmaurice, *Politics in Denmark*, p. 131.

132 DA, *The Consequences* . . ., pp. 27–8.

133 J. Fitzmaurice, *Politics in Denmark*, pp. 116–17.

134 O. Borre, 'Recent trends . . .', p. 8.

135 N. Elder, A. Thomas and D. Arter, *The Consensual* . . ., p. 86.

136 N. Andren, *Government and Politics in the Nordic Countries* (Stockholm 1964), p. 58. See also Ministry of Foreign Affairs, *Political Parties in Denmark*, Factsheet Denmark (n.d.), p. 2, Col. 2.

137 J. Fitzmaurice, *Politics in Denmark*, pp. xii, 122.

138 O. Borre, 'Recent trends . . .', p. 8.

139 A.H. Thomas, 'Social democracy . . .', p. 253.

140 O. Borre, 'Recent trends . . .', p. 8.

141 Ibid., pp. 9, 12.

142 Ministry of Foreign Affairs, *The Political Parties* . . ., p. 2, Col. 3.

143 O. Borre, 'Recent trends . . .', p. 9.

144 J. Fitzmaurice, *Politics in Denmark*, p. xii.

145 N. Elder, A. Thomas and D. Arter, *The Consensual* . . ., p. 215.

146 Ibid., p. 85, Table 3.9.

147 O. Borre, 'Recent trends . . .', p. 9.

148 J. Fitzmaurice, *Politics in Denmark*, p. xii.

149 Ibid., p. 34.

150 W. Galenson, 'Current problems of Scandinavian trade unionism', in K.H. Cerny, *Scandinavia at the Polls*, p. 269.

151 J. Fitzmaurice, *Politics in Denmark*, p. 32.

152 A.L. Thimm, *The False Promise* . . ., p. 206, Fig. 6.2.

153 O. Borre, 'Recent trends . . .', pp. 9–12.

154 Ibid., p. 12.
155 G. Karlsson, *Trade Unions and Collective* . . ., p. 24.
156 J. Logue, *Trade Unions in the Corporate* . . ., p. 24.
157 A.H. Thomas, 'Social democracy in Denmark', p. 239, Fig. 1, p. 241.
158 W. Galenson, 'Current problems of Scandinavian . . .', pp. 283–4.
159 B. Bye and M. Doyle, *Workers in Europe*. Study booklet in European Trade unionism No. 10, Scandinavian Workers' Educational Association (London, n.d.), p. 14.
160 Interview with Peter Vognbjerg – economist with Wage Earners' Cost of Living Fund (Lonmodtagernes Dyrtidsfond), Copenhagen, 7 Dec. 1984.
161 Interview with P. Vognbjerg.
162 G. Karlsson, *Trade Unions and Collective* . . ., p. 30.
163 Ministry of Labour, *Act To Set Up the Employees' Capital Pension Fund* (Wage Earners' Cost of Living Fund), Act No. 7 (Copenhagen, 9 Jan. 1980), p. 4, Part 4.
164 Ibid.
165 Interview with P. Vognbjerg.
166 Ministry of Labour, *Act to Set up the Employees'* . . ., p. 4, Part 4.
167 Interview with P. Vognbjerg.
168 Interview with P. Vognbjerg.
169 G. Karlsson, *Trade Unions and Collective* . . ., p. 30.
170 Interview with P. Vognbjerg.
171 Interview with Torben A. Sorensen, spokesman for the Danish Employers' Confederation, Copenhagen, 4 Dec. 1984.
172 G. Karlsson, *Trade Unions and Collective* . . ., p. 31.
173 Ibid., p. 32.
174 Ibid., p. 31.
175 Interview with P. Vognbjerg.
176 A.L. Thimm, *The False Promise* . . ., p. 203.
177 Ibid.
178 'Ungovernable Denmark turns a shade less so', *Economist* (Oct./Nov. 1979), p. 51.
179 DA, *Wage Earners' Right To Co-Ownership*. Extracts from the Committee report, translated at the request of the Danish Employers' Federation (Copenhagen 1979), p. 1.
180 Ibid., pp. 3–4.
181 Ibid., p. 31.
182 Ibid., p. 30.
183 Ibid., pp. 37–8.
184 Interview with T.A. Sorensen.
185 A.L. Thimm, *The False Promise* . . ., p. 205.
186 Ministry of Labour, *Proposed Parliamentary Resolution Regarding the Right of Co-Ownership and Co-Determination* (Introduction of PS), presented by the minister of labour, 4–12–1979, p. 1.
187 Ibid., p. 2.
188 Ibid., pp. 1–2.
189 LO, *Economic Democracy – Co-Ownership and Co-Determination of Employees as Seen from the Point of View of the Danish Trade Union Movement* 1–4–1980 – JFM/GM, p. 8. See also A.L. Thimm, *The False Promise* . . ., pp. 205–6.

190 First interview with J.F. Hansen.
191 Interview with Bjorn Pedersen, industrial secretary, Left Socialist Party, (Venstresocialisterne), Copenhagen, 7–12–1984.
192 R. Meidner, *Employee Investment Funds* . . ., p. 124.
193 N. Elder, A. Thomas and D. Arter, *The Consensual Democracies* . . ., pp. 215–16.
194 IDE, 'The Danish industrial . . .', p. 80.
195 LO, *Danish Labour News* (April 1983), No.85, pp. 1–5. See also Hansen interview.
196 Sorensen interview.
197 Ibid.
198 See C. Gill, 'Industrial relations . . .', p. 57, Note 22.
199 First interview with J.F. Hansen.
200 J.A. Buksty, O.P. Kristensen and P. Svensson, 'The people's attitude or opinion towards profit sharing', Institute for Political Science, University of Aarhus. Figures from this study in Danish were provided by J.F. Hansen at the first interview.
201 Sorensen interview.
202 Second interview with J.F. Hansen, Copenhagen, 5–8–1986.
203 Interview with O. Olsen, spokesman for Danish Employers' DA, Copenhagen, 5–8–1986.
204 Olsen interview.
205 Olsen interview.
206 Olsen interview.
207 Second interview with J.F. Hansen.
208 LO, *Proposal for a Parliamentary Resolution on the Right of Co-Ownership and Co-Determination* (the introduction of profit sharing), 1 Nov., 1985, p. i, para. 1. Translated from Danish by Alan Matthews, FTCD.
209 Ibid.
210 Olsen interview.
211 LO, *Proposal for* . . ., p. i, para. 1.
212 Ibid., p. i, para.2.
213 Ibid., p. ii, para.3.
214 Ibid., p. 2, para.4.
215 Ibid., p. ii, para.5.
216 Ibid., p. 1.
217 Ibid., p. 3 and Addendum No. 2.
218 N. Elder, A. Thomas and D. Arter, *The Consensual Democracies* . . ., p. 93.
219 G.K. Ingham, *Strikes and Industrial Conflict: Britain and Scandinavia* (London 1974), p. 64. See also W. Galenson, 'Current problems . . .', p. 32.
220 SAMAK (The Joint Committee of the Nordic labour movement), *Solidarity for Growth and Employment*. Report from a working group on economic policy (Copenhagen, Nov. 1985), p. 7.
221 Ibid., pp. 50–4.
222 Ibid., pp. 59–61.
223 Ibid., pp. 63–4.
224 Interview with Svend Auken, former minister of labour and vice president of the Social Democratic Party, SAP (Copenhagen 5–8–1986).

225 C. Karlsson, *Trade Unions and Collective* . . . See also British Labour Party, *Capital and Equity*, report of Labour Party study group (London 1973). See also Bulletin of EC, Supplement 6/79.
226 SAMAK, *Solidarity for Growth* . . ., p. 14.
227 S. Bowels and H. Gintis, 'The invisible fist . . .', p. 361.
228 J. Fitzpatrick, *What Do Companies Think about Industrial Policy*, Industrial Studies Association, Fitzpatrick and Associates Economic Consultants (Dublin 1987).

CHAPTER 6

1 Department of Labour, *Worker Participation – A Discussion Paper* (Dublin 1980), p. 12.
2 White Paper, *Industrial Policy* (Dublin 1984), p. 45.
3 *Commission on Taxation* (Dublin 1985), p. 107.
4 Irish Productivity Centre (IPC), *A Guide to Employee Shareholding through Profit Sharing* (Dublin 1985), p. 4.
5 G.V. McMahon, *Financial Participation in Ireland*, MBS thesis (UCD 1981). See also R.C. Geary and M. Dempsey, 'Profit sharing for Ireland?' *Journal of the Statistical* . . ., Vol. xxiv, Part iv, p. 167.
6 R.C. Geary and M. Dempsey, 'Profit sharing . . .', p. 155.
7 Ibid., p. 156, Table 3.1, p. 158.
8 Ibid., p. 156, Table 3.1.
9 Ibid., pp. 156–7, Table 3.1.
10 See Chapters 2 and 3.
11 See Chapters 2 and 3.
12 R.C. Geary and M. Dempsey, 'Profit sharing . . .', p. 156, Table 3.1.
13 Ibid., p. 158.
14 Department of Labour, *Worker Participation* . . ., p. 12.
15 R.C. Geary and M. Dempsey, 'Profit sharing . . .', p. 156, Table 3.1.
16 Ibid., p. 158.
17 G.V. McMahon, *Financial Participation* . . ., pp. 274–5.
18 R.C. Geary and M. Dempsey, 'Profit sharing . . .', p. 156, Table 3.1.
19 Ibid., p. 159.
20 Ibid., p. 158.
21 See Chapter 2.
22 See Chapter 1.
23 J.I. Fitzpatrick, *Planned Sharing – Pratical Profit Sharing*, Planned Sharing Research Association (PSRA) (Dublin 1983), pp. 38–43.
24 R.C. Geary and M. Dempsey, 'Profit sharing . . .', p. 163.
25 Ibid. See also J.I Fitzpatrick, *Planned Sharing* . . . pp. 89, 95–6.
26 R.C. Geary and M. Dempsey, 'Profit sharing . . .', p. 163.
27 Fine Gael, *A Better Future*, election manifesto (Dublin 1981), p. 11.
28 Fine Gael/Labour, *Joint Fine Gael/Labour Programme for Government 1981/1986* (Dublin 1981), p. 19.
29 Dail Eireann, *Parliamentary Debates*, Vol. 329, p. 589, 21 July 1981.
30 Dail Eireann, *Parliamentary Debates*, Vol. 331, p. 346, 27 Jan. 1982.
31 Acts of the Oireachtas, *Finance Act 1982*, No. 14, 3rd schedule, Part 1, pp. 96–8.

32 Telephone conversation with Mr Con Power, director of economic policy, Confederation of Irish Industry (CII), 8 Oct. 1987.
33 CII, *Standard Trust Deed for Profit Sharing Schemes*, CII Information Sheet No. 1, April 1985.
34 Mr C. Power, letter to Mr Paul Turpin, secretary NESC, 12 March 1984, p. 2.
35 Department of Labour, *Worker Participation* . . ., p. 12
36 IPC, *A Guide to Employee* . . ., p. 21.
37 *Finance Act 1982*, No. 14, 3rd Schedule, Part 3, pp. 99–100.
38 Ibid., Part 1, p. 97.
39 Ibid., Part 2, pp. 98–9.
40 See Chapter 3.
41 See Chapter 2.
42 C.T. Whelan, *Worker Priorities, Trust in Management and Prospects for Worker's Participation*, Economic and Social Research Institute Paper No. 111 (Dublin 1982), p. 64.
43 *Finance Act 1982*, No. 14, pp. 65–6, 3rd Schedule, Part 1, pp. 96–7.
44 Ibid., pp. 59–62.
45 Ibid., pp. 64–5.
46 *Finance Act 1984*, No. 9, pp. 38–9.
47 *Finance Act 1982*, No. 14, p. 60; *Finance Act 1986*, No. 13, pp. 19–20.
48 *Finance Act 1982*, No. 14, pp. 57–63.
49 Arthur Guinness & Sons plc, *Irish Profit Sharing Scheme – An Explanatory Guide* (n.d.); Bank of Ireland, *Employee Capital Stock Issue Scheme: A Guide for Employees* (Dublin 1984), pp. 6–7.
50 *Finance Act 1982*, No. 14, 3rd Schedule, Part 1, pp. 96–8.
51 See Chapter 6, Table 6.1.
52 Dail Eireann *Parliamentary Debates*, Vol. 347, pp. 829–30, 25 Jan. 1984.
53 Irish Congress of Trade Unions (ICTU), *Worker Shareholding and Collective Capital Formation: A Confidential Report* (Dublin 1984).
54 IPC, *Profit Sharing and Employee Shareholding in Ireland*. A preliminary report for NESC, second draft (Dublin 1985), p. 97, Note 3.
55 Ibid., p. 73.
56 Ibid.
57 Ibid., pp. 1–2; see also IPC, *A Guide to Employee* . . ., p. 2.
58 Address by Mr J. Bruton, TD, minister of finance, to the seminar on 'Tax Incentives for Wider Share Ownership', Institute of Taxation in Ireland, Burlington Hotel, (Dublin 9–6–1986).
59 Address by Mr J. Bruton, TD, minister of finance, to Institute of Taxation seminars at Dublin (9–6–1986) and Galway (10–9–1986).
60 Complaint made by Mr Stephen McCarthy, ICTU, at number of IPC seminars on employee shareholding.
61 D.J. McAuley, director general FUE, letter to all members (2 Feb. 1984), attached to Profit Sharing Survey.
62 Federated Union of Employers (FUE), *Profit Sharing Schemes Survey* (Dublin 1984).
63 See *Finance Act 1982*; See also IPC, *A Guide to* . . ., p. 8.
64 Federated Union of Employers (FUE), *Profit Sharing* . . .,
65 Ibid.

66 Ibid.
67 Ibid.
68 Ibid.
69 Ibid.
70 Sedgwick Dineen, *Survey 1984–1985 and Suggested Amendments to Existing Legislation* (Dublin 1985).
71 FUE, *Profit Sharing* . . .
72 Sedgwick Dineen, *Survey 1984–1985* . . .
73 Ibid.
74 Ibid.
75 Ibid.
76 See Chapter 3.
77 Sedgwick Dineen, *Survey 1984–1985* . . .
78 Ibid.
79 Quoted in A. O'Toole, 'Is profit sharing such a big deal?', *Business and Finance* (11 April 1985), p. 29.
80 S. Lalor, 'Profit sharing – the cure for industrial relations', *Industry and Commerce* (Feb. 1985), p. 11.
81 Irish Marketing Surveys (IMS), *Attitudes of Major Commercial Concerns to Profit Sharing and Share Allocations for Employees*, report prepared for IPC by IMS (March 1985), pp. i-iii.
82 Ibid., p. 1
83 Ibid., p. 3.
84 Ibid., p. 4.
85 Ibid., pp. 1–2.
86 Ibid., p. 7.
87 Ibid., p. 2.
88 Irish Congress of Trade Unions (ICTU), *Worker Shareholding* . . .
89 Ibid.
90 Ibid.
91 Ibid.
92 Ibid.
93 Ibid.
94 Ibid.
95 Ibid.

SUMMARY AND CONCLUSION

1 F. Wilkinson (ed.), *The Dynamics of Labour Market Segmentation* (London 1981). See also M.J. Piore, 'The dual labour market: theory and implications', in D.M. Gordon (ed.) *Problems in Political Economy: An Urban Perspective* (Lexington 1971).

References

OFFICIAL PUBLICATIONS AND REPORTS

Acts of the Oireachtas, *Finance Acts 1982, 1984, 1986*.

Bulletin of the European Communities, *Employee Participation in Asset Formation*. Memorandum from the commission, Supplement 6/79, Commission of the European Communities (August 1979).

Comptroller General of the US, General Accounting Office (GAO), *Employee Stock Ownership Plans: Who Benefits Most in Closely Held Companies?*, report of the Committee on Finance, United States Senate, (HRD 80 88, 20 June 1980, Washington DC).

Dail Eireann, *Parliamentary Debates*, Vol. 329, July 1981, Vol. 331, January 1982, Vol.347, January 1984.

Department of Employment (UK), *Effects of Incentive Payment Systems United Kingdom 1977–80*, Research Paper No.36, September 1982 A. M. Bowey, R. Thorpe, F. Mitchell, G. Nicholls, D. Gosnold, L. Savery and P. Hellier.

Department of Trade (UK), *Report of the Committee of Inquiry on Industrial Democracy*, Chairman Lord Bullock (HMSO London 1977), Cmnd. 6706.

Department of Labour (S. Ireland), *Worker Participation: A Discussion Paper*. Government Publications (Dublin, 1980).

Department of Labour and National Service, Commonwealth of Australia Industrial Welfare Division, *Profit Sharing: A Study of the Results of Overseas Experience* (March 1947).

Government Commission (S. Ireland), *Commission on Taxation* (Dublin 1985).

Ministry of Finance (Sweden), *Employee Investment Funds* (Stockholm 1984).

Ministry of Foreign Affairs (Denmark), *Recommendations for Economic Democracy*, Fact Sheet Denmark Code 010772 (Copenhagen n. d.).

Ministry of Foreign Affairs (Denmark), *The Political Parties in Denmark*, Fact Sheet Denmark (2nd rev. edn, Copenhagen 1983).

Ministry of Labour (Denmark), *Act to Set up the Employees' Capital Pension Fund*, Act No.7, (Copenhagen 1980).

Ministry of Labour (Denmark), *Economic Democracy – Introduction and Bill*, (Copenhagen 1973).

Staff of the Committee on Finance, US Senate, Chairman R.B. Long, *Employee Stock Ownership Plans: An Employer's Handbook*, US Government Printing Office (Washington DC 1980).

White Paper, *Industrial Policy*, (Dublin 1984).

PUBLICATIONS OF ASSOCIATIONS AND ORGANISATIONS

American Federation of Labor/Congress of Industrial Organizations (AFL/CIO), Various Daily Labor Reports for 1982 from the file of the AFL/CIO Washington DC.

Confederation of Irish Industry (CII), *Standard Trust Deed for Profit Sharing Schemes*, Information Sheet No.1, April 1985.

Council of Profit Sharing Industries (CPSI), *Revised Profit Sharing Manual Containing a Digest and Analysis of Ninety-One Representative Profit Sharing Plans*, (Michigan 1951).

Danish Employers' Confederation (DA), *The Consequences of Economic Democracy*, (Copenhagen 1973).

Danish Employers' Confederation (DA) and The Federation of Danish Industries (I) 'Co-worker – co-owner', a discussion paper on economic democracy (Copenhagen 1972).

Danish Employers' Confederation (DA) and Danish Federation of Trade Unions (LO), *Agreement on Cooperation and Cooperation Committees*, Text of agreement and notes (2 October 1970) 2nd edn (Copenhagen 1978).

Federated Union of Employers (FUE), *Profit Sharing Schemes Survey* (Dublin 1984).

Fine Gael, *A Better Future*, election manifesto (Dublin 1981).

Fine Gael/Labour, *Programme for Government 1981–1986* (Dublin 1981).

Government Committee, *Wage Earners' Right to Co-Ownership*, extracts from the committee report, translated at the request of the Danish Employers' Federation (DA), (Copenhagen 1979).

Hewitt Associates, *ESOPs: An Analytical Report*, prepared for the Profit Sharing Council of America by the staff of Hewitt Associates (Illinois 1975).

Hewitt Associates, *Employee Stock Ownership Plans*, prepared by the research staff of Hewitt Associates (Illinois 1982).

Hewitt Associates in co-operation with PSCA, *1982 Profit Sharing Survey*, (1981 Experience), (Chicago 1982).

Irish Congress of Trade Unions (ICTU) *Worker Shareholding and Collective Capital Formation* (Dublin 1984).

Irish Marketing Surveys (IMS), *Attitudes of Major Commercial Concerns to Profit-Sharing and Share Allocation for Employees*. Report prepared for IPC by IMS (Dublin 1985).

Irish Productivity Centre (IPC), *A Guide to Employee Shareholding through Profit Sharing*, (Dublin 1985).

IPC, *Profit Sharing and Employee Shareholding in Ireland: A Preliminary Report*, prepared for the National Economic and Social Council (NESC), Second draft (Dublin 1985).

Labour Party, *Capital and Equality*, report of a Labour Party study group (London 1973).

LO (Denmark) (Danish Federation of Trade Unions) *Economic Democracy – Co-Ownership and Co-Determination of Employees as Seen from the Point of View of the Danish Trade Union Movement* (Copenhagen 1980 – JFM/GM).

LO (Denmark) *Danish Labour News* No. 85 (April 1983).

LO (Denmark), *Proposal for a Parliamentary Resolution on the Right of Co-Ownership and Co-Determination* (The Introduction of Profit Sharing) (Copenhagen 1985), Translated from Danish by Alan Matthews, FTCD.

LO, (Swedish Trade Union Confederation) *Employee Investment Funds in Sweden in 1984*, L.-O. Pettersson, S-105 53 (Stockholm 1984).

LO (Sweden) *Wage Policy – A Report to the 1971 Congress of the Swedish Trade Union Confederation* (Stockholm 1972).

National Center for Employee Ownership (NCEO), *Employee Ownership Resource Guide* (Arlington Virginia, 1984).

NCEO, *The Employee Ownership Reader* (Virginia 1983).

NCEO, *How Consultants View Employee Ownership* Vol.IV, No.1 (March 1984).

NCEO, *New Tax Law Causes Surge in Interest in Employee Ownership* Vol.V, No.1 (Feb. 1985).

Profit Sharing Council of America (PSCA), *Guide to Modern Profit Sharing* Illinois 1973).

PSCA, *Profit Sharing Benefits to Business, Labour and Capital Markets*. Reprint of statement on profit sharing presented to president's Commission on Pension Policy (Chicago 1980).

SAF (Swedish Employers' Federation) *Collective Wage Earner Funds Will Harm Sweden* Doc. No. 1442 (Stockholm 1981).

SAF, *Company Profits, Sources of Investment Capital and Wage-Earner Funds*, a brief background and summary of the Waldenstrom Report, Doc. No. 1444 (MB 1976–07–09).

SAF, *SAF and the Free Market Economy: Income Earners and Capital Formation*, Doc. No. 1448 (1977–10–20).

SAF, *The Collective Wage-Earner Funds*, brief survey in July 1984, Doc. No. 1449 (BWN 1984–08–23).

SAF, Translation of article in *Dagens Nyheter* on 15 August 1976 by Professor Assar Lindbeck, Doc. No. 1446 (2) (MO 1976–09–27).

SAMAK (Joint Committee of the Nordic labour movement) *Solidarity for Growth and Employment Report from a Working Group on Economic Policy* (Copenhagen 1985).

SI (Federation of Swedish Industries) *Collective Wage Earner Funds* (Stockholm 1982).

SI, *The Debate on Collective Wage Earner Funds in Sweden* (Stockholm 1983).

The ESOP Association, *ESOP Survey 1983* (Washington DC 1983).

BOOKS AND ARTICLES

Aberg, R., 'Market-independent income distribution: efficiency and legitimacy', in J. H. Goldthorpe *Order and Conflict in Contemporary Capitalism* (Oxford 1984).

Abrahamsson, B. and Brostrom, A. *The Rights of Labour* (London 1980).

Alapuro, R. and Haavio-Mannila E. *Small States in Comparative Perspective. Essays for Erik Allardt* (Oslo 1985).

Allen, V.L. *Militant Trade Unionism* (London 1972, 3rd Imp.).

Andren, N. *Government and Politics in the Nordic Countries* (Stockholm 1964).

Bachrach, P. *The Theory of Democratic Elitism -A Critique* (London 1969).

Banks, J.A. *Trade Unionism* (London 1974).

Banks J. and Jones, K. *Worker Directors Speak*, Industrial Participation Association (Aldershot 1977).

Barkin, S. (ed.) *Worker Militancy and its Consequences 1965–75 New Directions in Western Industrial Relations* (New York 1975).

Baumgartner, T., Burns, T.R. and De Ville, P. 'Work, politics and social structuring under capitalism; in T.R. Burns, L.E. Karlsson and V. Rus (eds). *Work and Power*, (London 1985).

Bean, R. *Comparative Industrial Relations: An Introduction to Cross-National Perspectives* (London 1985).

Bell, W.D. *Financial Participation* Industrial Participation Association (London 1973).

Bell, W.D. *Industrial Participation* (London 1979).

Berg, E. 'Democracy and self-determination', in P. Birnbaum, J. Lively and G. Parry (eds) *Democracy, Consensus and Social Contract* (London 1978).

Berntson, L. 'Post-war Swedish capitalism', in J. Fry (ed.) *Limits of the Welfare State* (Aldershot England 1979).

Birnbaum, P., Lively, J. and Parry, G. (eds) *Democracy, Consensus and Social Contract* Sage Modern Politics Series, Vol.2 (London 1978).

Blasi, J.R., Mehrling, P. and Whyte, W.F. 'The politics of worker ownership in the United States', in C. Crouch and F.A. Heller (eds) *Organisational Democracy and Political Processes*, Vol.1 (Chichester 1983).

Bluestone, B., Harrison, B. Baker, L. *Corporate Flight; The Causes and Consequences of Economic Dislocation* (Washington DC 1981).

Bonaccorso M.J., Cranmer, S.M., Greenhut, D.G., Hoffman, D.T. and Isbrandtsen, N. *Survey of Employee Stock Ownership Plans: Analysis and Evaluation of Current Experience*. A report offered in partial fulfilment of the requirements for a Master of Business Administration degree, Graduate School of Management, University of California, Los Angeles (December 1977).

Borre, O. 'Recent trends in Danish voting behaviour', in K.H. Cerny (ed.) *Scandinavia at the Polls* (Washington DC 1977).

Bottomore, T.B. *Elites and Society* (Harmondsworth 1982).

Bradley, K. and Gelb, A. *Worker Capitalism; The New Industrial Relations* (London 1983).

Bristow, E. 'Profit sharing, socialism and labour unrest', in K.D. Brown (ed.) *Essays in Anti-Labour History* (London 1974).

Brummund, W.H. 'Legal requirements and considerations'. *Guide to Modern Profit Sharing* (PSCA, Chicago 1973).

Burns T.R., Karlsson, L.E. and Rus V. (eds) *Work and Power; The Liberation of Work and the Control of Political Power* (London 1979).

Bye B. and Doyle, M. *Workers in Europe* Study Booklet in European Trade Unionism No.10, Scandinavian Workers' Educational Assoc. (London n.d.)

Carnoy, M. and Shearer, D. *Economic Democracy; The Challenge of the 1980s* (New York 1980).

Cerny, K.H. (ed.) *Scandinavia at the Polls; Recent Political Trends in Denmark, Norway and Sweden*, American Enterprise Institute for Public Policy Research (Washington DC 1977).

Cipolla, C.M. (ed.) *The Fontana Economic History of Europe: Contemporary Economies*, Vol.6, Part 2 (Glasgow 1976).

Cole, G.D.H. *The World of Labour; A Discussion of the Present and Future of Trade Unionism* (London 1913).

Copeman, G., Moore, P. and Arrowsmith, C. *Shared Ownership; How to Use Capital Incentives to Sustain Business Growth* (Aldershot 1984).

Crouch, C. *The Politics of Industrial Relations* (Glasgow 1979).

Crouch, C. (ed.) *State and Economy in Contemporary Capitalism* (London 1979).

Crouch, C. and Heller, F.A. (eds) *Organisational Democracy and the Political Processes* International Yearbook of Organisational Democracy, Vol.1 (Chichester 1983).

Curtis, J. A. 'Coverage and eligibility conditions', in *Guide to Modern Profit Sharing* (PSCA Chicago 1973).

Dahrendorf, R. *Class and Class Conflict in an Industrial Society* (London 1959).

Davenport, R.W. 'Enterprise for Everyman', in F. G. Lesieur (ed.) *The Scanlon Plan* (Massachusetts 1958).

Derber, M. *The American Idea of Industrial Democracy 1865–1965* (Illinois 1970).

Derrick P. and Phipps, J.F. (eds) *Co-ownership, Co-operation and Control*, Management Studies Series (London 1969).

Diekman, B.A. 'Profit sharing systems', in *Profit Sharing the Industrial Adrenalin* B.A. Diekman and B.L. Metzger (eds) (Canada/Illinois 1975).

Diekman, B.A. and Metzger, B.L. *Profit Sharing the Industrial Adrenalin* Joint Publication of Institute of Profit Sharing, Ontario, Canada and PSRF (Evanston, Illinois 1975).

Doeringer, P.B., Gourevitch, P. Lange, P. and Martin, A. *Industrial Relations in International Perspective* (London 1981).

Drucker, P.F. *The Unseen Revolution – How Pension Fund Socialism Came to America* (London 1976).

Dunn, J. *Western Political Theory in the Face of the Future* (Cambridge University Press 1979, reprint 1983).

Eidem, R. and Ohman, B. *Economic Democracy through Wage Earner Funds* Swedish Centre for Working Life (Stockholm 1979).

Elder, N., Thomas, A.H. and Arter, D. *The Consensual Democracies? The Government and Politics of the Scandinavian States* (Oxford 1982).

Ellerman, D.P. *Notes on the Co-Op./ESOP Debate* Industrial Cooperative Association, Somerville MA (June 1983).

Esping-Andersen, G. and Korpi, W. 'Social policy as class politics in post-war capitalism: Scandinavia, Austria and Germany', in J.H. Goldthorpe (ed.) *Order and Conflict in Contemporary Capitalism* (Oxford 1984).

Fitzmaurice, J. *Politics in Denmark* (London 1981).

Fitzpatrick, J. *What Do Companies Think about Industrial Policy*. Industrial Studies Association, Fitzpatrick and Associates Economic Consultants (Dublin 1987).

Fitzpatrick, J.I. *Planned Sharing Practical Profit Sharing* Planned Sharing Research Association (Dublin 1983).

Flanders, A., Pomeranz, R. and Woodward, J. *Experiment in Industrial Democracy. A Study of the John Lewis Partnership* (London 1968).

Forseback, L. *Industrial Relations and Employment in Sweden* (Uppsala 1980).

Fox, A. *Beyond Contract: Work Power and Trust Relations* (London 1974).

Fox, A. *Man Mismanagement* (London 1974).

Fry, J. (ed.) *Limits of the Welfare State. Critical Views of Post-War Sweden* (Aldershot England 1979).

Fry, J. (ed.) *Towards a Democratic Rationality: Making the Case for Swedish Labour* (Aldershot 1986).

Fry, J. 'The co-determination act in practice: the case of the mining industry', in J. Fry (ed.) *Towards a Democratic Rationality* (Aldershot 1986).

Fulcher, J. 'Class conflict: joint regulation and its decline', in R. Scase (ed.) *Readings in the Swedish Class Structure* (Oxford 1976).

Galbraith, J.R. *Organisation Design* (Pennsylvania 1977).

Galenson, W. *The Danish System of Labour Relations: A Study in Industrial Peace* (Harvard 1952).

Galenson, W. 'Current problems of Scandinavian trade unionism', in K.H. Cerny (ed.) *Scandinavia at the Polls* (Washington DC 1977).

Garson, D. (ed.) *Worker Self Management in Industry: The West European Experience* (New York 1977).

Goldthorpe, J.H. (ed.) *Order and Conflict in Contemporary Capitalism* (Oxford 1984).

Goldthorpe, J.H. 'The end of convergence: corporatist and dualist tendencies in modern western societies,' in J.H. Goldthorpe (ed.) *Order and Conflict in Contemporary Capitalism* (Oxford 1984).

Gordon, D.M. (ed.) *Problems in Political Economy: An Urban Perspective* (Lexington 1971).

Gourevitch, P., Martin, A., Ross, G., Allen, C., Bornstein, S. and Markovits, A. (eds) *Unions and Economic Crisis: Britain, West Germany and Sweden* (London 1984).

Guest, D. and Fatchett, D. *Worker Participation: Individual Control and Performance*, Institute of Personnel Management (London 1974).

Gunn, C. 'The Fruits of Rath: a new model of worker self-management. Working papers for a new society', reprinted in R. Corey (ed.) *Employee Ownership: A Handbook for Employees and Public Officials* (NCEO, June 1982).

Gustafsson, B. 'Co-determination and wage earners' funds', in J. Fry (ed.) *Towards a Democratic Rationality* (Aldershot 1986).

Hancock, D.M. *Sweden: The Politics of Post-Industrial Change* (Illinois 1972).

Heilbroner, R. L. *Business Civilization in Decline* (Harmondsworth Books 1977).

Himmelstrand, U., Ahrne, G., Lundberg, Leif and Lundberg, Lars, *Beyond*

Welfare Capitalism: Issues, Actors and Forces in Societal Change (London 1981).

Hodgson, G. *The Democratic Economy: A New Look at Planning Markets and Power* (Harmondsworth Books 1984).

Howard, B.B. *A Study of the Financial Significance of Profit Sharing 1958–1977*, Graduate School of Management, Northwestern University, Evanston Illinois (PSCA Chicago 1979).

Hunnius, G., 'On the nature of capitalist initiated innovations in the workplace'., in T.R. Burns, L.E. Karlsson and V. Rus (eds) *Work and Power* (London 1979).

Hunnius, G., Garson, and Case, J., (eds) *Workers' Control: A Reader in Labour and Social Change* (New York 1973).

Hunt, N.C. *Methods of Wage Payment in British Industry* (London 1951).

Industrial Democracy in Europe (IDE) International Research Group *European Industrial Relations* (Oxford 1981).

Industrial Democracy in Europe (IDE), International Research Group *Industrial Democracy in Europe* (Oxford 1981).

IDE 'The Danish industrial relations system', in *European Industrial Relations* (Oxford 1981).

Ingham, G.K. *Strikes and Industrial Conflict: Britain and Scandinavia* (London 1974).

Jackson, G.E. *How to Stay Union Free* (Memphis 1978).

Jacobs, P. 'Comments on Bernstein's paper on the Teamsters' Union', in C.M. Rehmus, D.B. McLoughlin and F.H. Nesbitt (eds) *Labour and American Politics* (Michigan 1978).

Jepsson, O. and Agren, G. 'Work milieu Part I', in J. Fry (ed.) *Limits of the Welfare State* (Aldershot 1979).

Jochim, T.C. *Employee Stock Ownership and Related Plans: Analysis and Practice* (London 1982).

Jorberg, L. and Krantz, O. 'Scandinavia 1914–1970', in C. M. Cipolla (ed.) *Fontana Economic History of Europe* Vol. 2 (Glasgow 1976).

Karlsson, G. *Trade Unions and Collective Capital Formation: A Review of Initiatives in Western European Countries*, European Trade Union Institute (Brussels 1983).

Katz, D. 'The motivational basis of organisational behaviour', in V.H. Vroom and E.L. Deci (eds) *Management and Motivation* (Harmondsworth 1970).

Kelso; L.O. and Adler, M.J. *The Capitalist Manifesto* (New York 1958).

Kelso, L.O. and Hetter, P. *How to Turn Eighty Million Workers into Capitalists on Borrowed Money* (New York 1967).

Kelso, L.O. and Hetter, P. *Two Factor Theory: The Economics of Reality* (New York 1967).

Kempner, T., MacMillan, K. and Hawkins, K.H. *Business and Society, Tradition and Change* (London 1974).

Kennedy, K. A., Giblin, T. and MacHugh, D. *The Economic Development of Ireland in the Twentieth Century* (London 1988).

Keynes, J.M. *The General Theory of Employment Interest and Money* (London 1967).

Knowlton, P.A. *Studies in Profit Sharing* (PSRF, New York 1952–3).

Korpi, W. *The Working Class in Welfare Capitalism: Work Unions and Politics in Sweden* (London 1978).

Korpi, W. *The Democratic Class Struggle* (London 1983).

Korpi, W. 'Sweden: conflict, power and politics in industrial relations', in P.Doeringer, P.Gourevitch, P.Lange and A. Martin (eds) *Industrial Relations in International Perspective* (London 1981).

Kosonen, P. 'Public expenditure in the Nordic nation states – the source of prosperity or crisis?', in R.Alapuro, M. Alestalo, E. Haavio-Mannila and R.Vayrynen (eds) *Small States in Comparative Perspective* (Oslo 1985):

Kruse, D. *Employee Ownership and Employee Attitudes: Two Case Studies* (Norwood PA 1984).

Kumar, K. *Prophecy and Progress: The Sociology of Industrial and Post Industrial Society* (Harmondsworth 1978).

Kvist, K. and Agren, G. 'Social democracy in the seventies', in J. Fry (ed.) *Limits of the Welfare State* (Aldershot 1979).

Lafferty, W.M. *Economic Development and the Response of Labour in Scandinavia: A Multi-Level Analysis* (Oslo 1971).

Larsson, A. *Labour Market Reforms in Sweden: Facts and Employee Views* (Uppsala 1979).

Larsson, K.A. 'The international dependence of the Swedish economy', in J. Fry (ed.) *Limits of the Welfare State* (Aldershot 1979).

Latta, G.W. *Profit Sharing, Employee Stock Ownership, Savings and Asset Formation Plans in the Western World* University of Pennsylvania, The Wharton School Industrial Research Unit (1979).

Lesieur, F.G.'The Scanlon Plan – what the Plan Isn't and What It Is', in F. G. Lesieur (ed.) *The Scanlon Plan* (Massachusetts 1958)

Lesieur, F.G.(ed.) *The Scanlon Plan: A Frontier in Labour Management Cooperation* (Massachusetts 1958).

Lewis, S. *Main Street* (1st ed. 1921; rep. London 1973).

Lindbeck, A. *Swedish Economic Policy* (London 1975).

Lipset, S.M. *Political Man: The Social Bases of Politics* (New York 1963).

List, W. 'In Sweden the byword is co-operation', in G. Hunnius, G. Garson and J. Case (eds.) *Workers' Control* (New York 1973).

Logue, J. *Trade Unions in the Corporate State: The Effects of Corporatism on Party Competition, Contract Referenda and Internationalism in Danish Trade Unions*, Publication No.5 (Gothenburg 1976).

Macpherson, C.B. *The Life and Times of Liberal Democracy* (Oxford 1977).

McGregor, D. 'The Scanlon Plan through a psychologist's eyes', in F.G. Leiseur (ed.) *The Scanlon Plan* (Massachusetts 1958).

Marglin, S. 'The origins and function of Hierarchy in capitalist production', in T. Nichols (ed.) *Capital and Labour* (Glasgow 1980).

Marriott, R. *Incentive Payment Systems: A Review of Research and Opinion* (London 1971, 4th).

Martin, A. 'Sweden: industrial democracy and social democratic strategy', in D. Garson (ed.) *Worker Self-Management in Industry: The West European Experience* (New York 1977).

Martin, A. 'The dynamics of change in Keynesian political economy: the Swedish case and its implications', in C. Crouch (ed.) *State and Economy in Contemporary Capitalism* (London 1979).

Martin, A. 'Trade unions in Sweden: strategic responses to change and crisis', in P. Gourevitch, A. Martin, G. Ross, C. Allen, S. Bornstein and A. Markovits (eds) *Unions and Economic Crisis: Britain, West Germany and Sweden* (London 1984).

Meidner, R. *Employee Investment Funds: An Approach to Collective Capital Formation* (London 1978).

Meisel, J. H. *The Myth of the Ruling Class: Gaetano Mosca and the Elite* (Michigan 1962).

Metzger, B.L. *Profit Sharing in 38 Large Companies – A Piece of the Action for 1,000,000 Participants* (PSRF, Illinois 1975, 2 Vols).

Metzger B. L. 'Elements of a sharing-participative system', in B. L. Metzger (ed.) *New Horizons for Capitalism* (PSRF, Evanston Illinois 1977).

Metzger, B. L. *Employee Investment Choice in Deferred Profit Sharing* (PSRF, Evanston Illinois 1977, 2nd. eds).

Metzger, B. L. *New Horizons for Capitalism – Post ERISA Idea Papers* (PSRF, Illinois 1977).

Metzger, B.L. *Post-ERISA Dilemma: Profit Sharing, Pension or Both?* (PSRF, Illinois, n. d.).

Metzger, B.L. 'Profit sharing trends', in B.L. Metzger (Ed.) *New Horizons for Capitalism* (PSRF, Illinois 1977).

Metzger, B.L. *Participative Developments in the United States* (PSRF, Illinois 1978).

Metzger, B.L. *The Future of Profit Sharing – Post ERISA Idea Papers* (PSRF, Illinois 1979).

Metzger, B.L. 'How to motivate with profit sharing', in B.L. Metzger (ed.) *The Future of Profit Sharing* (PSRF, Illinois 1979)

Metzger, B.L. and Colletti, J.A. *Does Profit Sharing Pay?* (PSRF, Illinois 1971).

Meyerson, P.-M. *Company Profits, Sources of Investment Finance – Wage Earners' Investment Funds in Sweden. Proposals, Debate Analysis*, SI (Federation of Swedish Industries) (Stockholm 1976).

Mills, D.Q. *Labour Management Relations*, McGraw Hill Studies in Management (New York 1978).

Nichols, T. *Ownership, Control and Ideology* (London 1969).

Nichols, T. (ed.) *Capital and Labour: A Marxist Primer* (Glasgow 1980).

Nightingale, D.V. *Profit Sharing and Employee Ownership: A Review and Appraisal*, a report to the Employment Relations Branch of Labour Canada (Profit Sharing Council of Canada, Ontario 1980).

Ohman, B. 'The debate on wage earner funds in Scandinavia', in C. Crouch and F.A. Heller (eds) *Organisational Democracy and the Political Processes*, Vol. 1 (London 1983).

Okun, A.M. *Equality and Efficiency: The Big Trade-Off*, Brookings Institution (Washington DC 1975).

Otter C. Van 'Sweden: labour reformism reshapes the system', in S. Barkin (ed.) *Worker Militancy and its Consequences* (New York 1975).

'Ownership and influence in the economy', a summary and translation of The Commission on Industrial and Economic Concentration, reproduced in R. Scase (ed.) *Readings in the Swedish Class Structure* (Oxford 1976).

Patard, R. J. 'Employee stock ownership in the 1920s', in *The Employee Ownership Reader* (NCEO, Arlington Virginia 1983).

Pateman, C. *Participation and Democratic Theory* (Cambridge, England 1970).

Paterson, W.E. and Thomas, A.H. *Social Democratic Parties in Western Europe* (London 1977).

Piore, M.J. 'The dual labour market: theory and implications', in D.M. Gordon (ed.) *Problems in Political Economy: An Urban Perspective* (Lexington 1971).

Pollard, S. *The Genesis of Modern Management – A Study of the Industrial Revolution in Great Britain* (Harmondsworth 1968).

Puckett, E.S. 'Productivity achievements – a measure of success', in F.G. Lesieur (ed.) *The Scanlon Plan* (Massachusetts 1958).

Rehmus, C.M., McLaughlin, D.B. and Nesbitt, F.H. (eds) *Labour and American Politics* (Michigan 1978, rev. edn).

Reilly, P.A. *Employee Financial Participation*, British Institute of Management, Foundation Management Survey, Report No. 41 (1978).

Robinson, D. *Solidaristic Wage Policy in Sweden* (OECD, Paris 1974).

Rose, M. *Industrial Behaviour: Theoretical Developments since Taylor* (Harmondsworth 1978).

Rosen, C. (ed.) *Employee Ownership: Issues, Resources and Legislation: A Handbook for Employee and Public Officials*, National Center for Employee Ownership (Arlington Virginia 1982).

Rosen C. 'Making employee ownership work', *National Productivity Review* (Winter 1982/3); reprinted in *The Employee Ownership Reader* (NCEO, Arlington Virginia 1983).

Rosen C. 'Making Employees Owners', *Business* (April–June 1983); reprinted in *The Employee Ownership Reader* (NCEO, Arlington Virginia 1983).

Rothschild-Whitt, J. 'Worker ownership in relation to control: a typology of work reform', in C. Crouch and F.A. Heller (eds) *Organisational Democracy and the Political Processes*, Vol. 1 (London 1983).

Runciman, W.G. *Social Science and Political Theory* (Cambridge, England 1963).

Salaman, G. *Work Organisations Resistance and Control* (London 1979).

Scase, R. (ed.) *Readings in the Swedish Class Structure* (Oxford 1976).

Scase, R. *Social Democracy in Capitalist Society* (London 1977).

Schloss, D.F. *Methods of Industrial Remuneration* (London 1898, 3rd edn).

Schumpeter, J.A. *Capitalism, Socialism and Democracy* (London 1943).

Schuster, M. 'Forty years of Scanlon Plan research: a review of the descriptive and empirical literature', in C. Crouch and F.A. Heller (eds) *Organisational Democracy and the Political Processes*, Vol. 1 (London 1983).

Schwartz, E. *Trouble in Eden: A Comparison of the British and Swedish Economies* (New York 1980).

Scott, J. *Corporations, Classes and Capitalism* (London 1979).

Shimmin, S. 'A 1968 survey of recent literature', postscript in R. Marriott (ed.) *Incentive Payment Systems* (London 1971).

Shonfield, A. *Modern Capitalism: The Changing Balance of Public and Private Power* (Oxford 1970, 1st edn 1965).

Slok, A. *Participation and Cooperation on the Danish Labour Market*, Danish Employers' Confederation (2nd edn, Copenhagen 1979).

Stern, R.N. and Comstock, P. *Employee Stock Ownership Plans (ESOPs):*

Benefits for Whom?, Key Issues No. 23, New York State School of Industrial and Labor Relations (New York 1978).

Stern, R.N. and O'Brien R.A. *National Unions and Employee Ownership*, Dept. of Organizational Behavior, New York State School of Industrial and Labor Relations (New York 1977).

Stewart, B.M. and Couper, W.J. *Profit Sharing for Wage Earners and Executives*, Industrial Relations Monograph No. 15, Industrial Relations Counsellors (New York 1951).

Strachey, J. *Contemporary Capitalism* (London 1956).

Taylor, S. *Profit Sharing Between Capital and Labour – Six Essays* (London 1884).

Thimm, A.L. *The False Promise of Co-Determination – The Changing Nature of European Workers, Participation* (Lexington 1980)

Thomas, A.H. 'Social Democracy in Denmark' in W.E. Patterson and A.H. Thomas (eds) *Social Democratic Parties in Western Europe* (London 1977).

Thompson, K.M. *Profit Sharing – Democratic Capitalism in American Industry* (New York 1949).

Tilove, R. 'Pensions, health and welfare plans', in L. Ulman (ed.) *Challenges to Collective Bargaining* (Englewood Cliffs, N.J. 1967).

Turner, H.A., Clack, G. Roberts, G. *Labour Relations in the Motor Industry* (London 1967).

Turner, C.H. *Radical Man* (London 1971).

Ulman, L. (ed.) *Challenges to Collective Bargaining* (Englewood Cliffs, N.J. 1969).

Ulman, L. and Flanagan, R.J. *Wage Restraint: A Study of Incomes Policies in Western Europe* (California 1971).

Valentin, F. 'Self-Management – strategy for autonomy or integration', in T.R. Burns, L.E. Karlsson and V. Rus (eds) *Work and Power* (London 1979).

Vroom, V.H. and Deci, E.L. *Management and Motivation* (Harmondsworth 1970).

Ward, S. *Pensions* (London 1981).

Weitzman, M.L. *The Share Economy – Conquering Stagflation* (Harvard 1984).

Whelan, C.T. *Worker Priorities, Trust in Management and Prospects for Workers' Participation*, Economic and Social Research Institute, Paper No. 111 (Dublin 1982).

Whyte, W.F. *Money and Motivation – An Analysis of Incentives in Industry* (New York 1955).

Whyte, W.F. 'Restructuring work at Rath Packing', in *The Employee Ownership Reader* (NCEO, Arlington Virginia 1983).

Wilken, F. 'New forms of ownership in industry', P. Derrick and J.F. Phipps *Co-Ownership, Co-operation and Control* (London 1969).

Wilkinson, F. (ed.) *The Dynamics of Labour Market Segmentation* (London 1981).

Williams, R. *Key Words. A Vocabulary of Culture and Society* (Glasgow 1976).

Wood, T.E. 'Setting objectives for profit sharing plans', in *Guide to Modern Profit Sharing* (PSCA, Chicago 1973).

Wood, T.E. 'Trends in the 1980s: their effects on profit sharing plans and productivity' in B. L. Metzger (ed.) *Increasing Productivity through Profit Sharing* (PSRF, Evanston Illinois 1980).

Woodworth W. 'Creating a culture of participation', in *The Employee Ownership Reader* (NCEO, Arlington Virginia 1983).

Wootton B. *The Social Foundations of Wage Policy* (London 1962, 2nd edn).

Yoder, D. *Labour Economics and Labour Problems* (New York 1939, 2nd edn).

Yoder, D. *Personnel Management and Industrial Relations* (London 1958, 4th edn).

ARTICLES IN JOURNALS AND PERIODICALS

Adams, A.L. 'A leveraged ESOP's no fable', *Investment Dealers' Digest* (25 Oct. 1983).

Asard, E. 'Employee participation in Sweden 1971–1979. The issue of economic democracy', *Economic and Industrial Democracy* (Vol. 1 1980, pp. 371–93).

Ball, R. 'How Electrolux cleans up in socialist Sweden', *Fortune* (March 1976, pp. 150–6)

Barber, R. 'Pension funds in the United States: issues of investment and control', *Economic and Industrial Democracy* (Vol. 3, No. 1, Feb. 1982, pp. 31–73).

Behrend, H. 'Financial incentives as the expression of a system of beliefs', *British Journal of Sociology* (Vol. 10, No. 2, 1959).

Beltran-Del-Rio, A., Harmin, R.D. and Spicer, S.M. 'Increasing capitalism's capitalists – a challenge for economists', *Journal of Post Keynesian Economics* (Vol. 1, No. 3, Spring 1979, pp. 41–54).

Bowles, S. and Gintis, H. 'The invisible fist: have capitalism and democracy reached a parting of the ways?', *American Economic Review* (May 1978, pp. 358–63).

Burck, C. G. 'There's more to ESOP than meets the eye', *Fortune* (March 1976, pp. 129–33, 170–2).

Carlson, D.G. 'Responding to the pension reform law', *Harvard Business Review* (Nov.–Dec. 1974, pp. 133–44).

Carroll, J. 'Crazy Louis and his creeping two-factorism', *The Village Voice* (New York, 28 April 1975).

Church, R.A. 'Profit sharing and labour relations in England in the nineteenth century', *International Review of Social History* (Vol. 14, No. 1, 1971, pp. 2–16).

Coll, S. 'ESOP's fables – with employee stock ownership plans everybody gets a little bit rich', *Calfornia Magazine* (Sept. 1983).

Conte, M. and Tannenbaum, A.S. 'Employee-owned companies: is the difference measurable?', *Monthly Labor Review* (July 1978, pp. 23–8).

Czarnecki, E.R. 'Effect of profit sharing plans on union organizing efforts', *Personnel Journal* (Sept. 1970, pp. 763–73).

Drucker, P.F. 'Where union flexibility's now a must', *Wall Street Journal* (23 Sept. 1983).

Elvander, N. 'Collective bargaining and incomes policy in the Nordic countries: a comparative analysis', *British Journal of Industrial Relations* (Vol. 12, No. 3, 1974, pp. 417–37).

Elvander, N. 'In search of new relationships: parties, unions and salaried employees' associations in Sweden', *Industrial and Labour Relations Review* (Vol. 28, No. 1, 1974, pp. 60–74).

Fouquet, D. 'An interview with Henk Vredeling', *Multinational Info* (No. 3, Oct. 1983, IRM Geneva).

Fulcher, J. 'Class conflict in Sweden', *Sociology* (Vol. 7, 1973, pp. 49–70).

Geary, R.C. and Dempsey, M. 'Profit sharing for Ireland?', *Journal of the Statistical and Social Inquiry Society of Ireland* (Vol. xxiv, Part iv, 1981/82; pp. 139–74).

Gill, C.G. 'Swedish wage earner funds: the road to economic democracy?', *Journal of General Management* (Vol. 9, No. 3, Spring 1984, pp. 37–59).

Gill, C.G. 'Industrial relations in Denmark: problems and perspectives', *Industrial Relations Journal* (No. 15, 1984, pp. 46–57).

Granados, L.L. 'Employee stock ownership plans: an analysis of current reform proposals', *University of Michigan Journal of Law Reform* (Vol. 14, No. 1, Fall 1980, pp. 15–50).

Hass, A. 'The aftermath of Sweden's co-determination law: workers' experiences in Gothenburg 1977–80', *Economic and Industrial Democracy* (Vol. 4, No. 1, Feb. 1983, pp. 16–46).

Henle, P. and Schmitt, R. 'Pension reform: the long hard road to enactment', *Monthly Labor Review* (Nov. 1974, pp. 3–12).

Israel, J. 'Swedish socialism and big business', *Acta Sociologica* (Vol. 21, No. 4, 1978, pp. 341–53).

Kelso, L.O. 'Karl Marx: the almost capitalist', *American Bar Association Journal* (Vol. 43, March 1957, pp. 235–8, 275–6).

Korpi, W. 'Unofficial strikes in Sweden', *British Journal of Industrial Relations* (Vol. 19, March 1981, pp. 66–86).

Lalor, S. 'Profit sharing the cure for industrial relations?', *Industry and Commerce* (Feb. 1985, pp. 7–12).

Livingston, D.T. and Henry, J.B. 'The effect of employee stock ownership plans on corporate profits', *The Journal of Risk and Insurance* (Vol. 47, 1980, pp. 491–505).

Long, R.J. 'The relative effects of share ownership vs control on job attitudes in an employee-owned company', *Human Relations* (Vol. 31, No. 9, 1978, pp. 753–63).

Long, R.J. 'Job attitudes and organisational performance under employee ownership', *Academy of Management Journal* (Vol. 23, No. 4 1980, pp. 726–37).

Lykketoft, M. 'Towards economic democracy: wage earner funds', *Scandinavian Review* (Part 2, 1977, pp. 40–5).

Marsh T.R. and McAllister, D.E. 'ESOP tables: a survey of companies with employee stock ownership plans', *Journal of Corporation Law* (Spring 1981, pp. 551–623).

Meidner, R. 'Our concept of the third way: some remarks on the socio-political tenets of the swedish labour movement', *Economic and Industrial Democracy* (Vol. 1, No. 3, August 1980, pp. 343–69).

Meidner, R. 'Collective asset formation through wage earner funds', *International Labour Review* (Vol. 120, No. 3, May–June 1981, pp. 303–17).

Miller, S.M. and Riessman, F. 'Working class authoritarianism: a critique of Lipset.' *British Journal of Sociology* (Vol. 12, 1961, pp. 263–72).

Mulcahy, N.and McConnell, J. 'Sharing the cake or why should profit be a dirty word?', *Management* (Vol. xx, No. 9, 1974, pp. 51–6).

Myrdal, H.-G. 'The Swedish model – will it survive?' *British Journal of Industrial Relations* (Vol. xviii, 1 March 1980, pp. 57–69).

Myrdal, H.-G. 'Collective wage earner funds in Sweden: a road to socialism and the end of freedom of association', *International Labour Review* (Vol. 120, No. 3, May–June 1981, pp. 319–34).

Narasimhan, P.S. 'Profit sharing: a review', *International Labour Review* (Vol. lxii, No. 6, Dec. 1950, pp. 469–99).

Olson D.G. 'Union experiences with worker ownership: legal and practical issues raised by ESOPs, TRASOPs, stock purchases and co-operatives.', *Wisconsin Law Review* (No. 5 1982, pp. 729–823).

O'Riordan, M. 'Applying added value: the slice going to wages does not exhaust the issue' *Management* (Vol. xxi, Nos. 7 and 8 1974, pp. 39–45).

O'Toole, A. 'Is profit sharing such a big deal?' *Business and Finance* (11 April 1985, pp. 28–9).

O'Toole, J. 'The uneven record of employee ownership', *Harvard Business Review* (Nov.–Dec. 1979, pp. 185–97).

Perham, J. 'Upsurge in ESOPs', *Duns Business Month* (Feb. 1983) in ESOP Assoc. Book of Clippings for 1983 (ESOP Association, Washington DC 1984).

Perlo, V. '"People's capitalism" and stock ownership', *American Economic Review* (Vol. 48, No. 3, June 1958, pp. 333–47).

Reum, W.R. and Reum, S.M. 'Employee stock ownership plans: pluses and minuses'. *Harvard Business Review* (July–Aug. 1976, pp. 133–43).

Rose, R.B. 'Employee stock ownership and the Community Bank', *American Banker* (Oct. 1983), in ESOP Assoc. Book of Clippings for 1983 (ESOP Association, Washington DC 1984).

Ross, I. 'What happens when the employees buy the company', *Fortune* (2 June 1980, pp. 108–11).

Roth, T.P. 'Employee stock ownership trusts, myopia and intertemporal profit maximization'. *Quarterly Review of Economics and Business* (Vol. 18, Summer 1978, pp. 73–85).

Sachar, E. 'Taking stock of ESOP experience', *Newsday Graphic*, in ESOP Assoc. Book of Clippings for 1983 (ESOP Association, Washington DC 1984).

Schregle, J. 'Comparative industrial relations: pitfalls and potential', *International Labor Review* (Vol. 120, No. 1, Jan. Feb. 1981).

Sloan, A. 'An idea whose time has come', *Forbes Magazine* (20 July 1981).

Taplin, P.T. 'Goal is shared ownership not retirement benefits', *Employee Benefit Plan Review* (Nov. 1980, pp. 43, 91).

Thompson, E.P. 'Time, work, discipline and industrial capitalism', *Past and Present* (Vol. 38, 1967, pp. 56–97).

Tilton, T.A. 'A Swedish road to socialism: Ernst Wigforss and the ideological foundations of Swedish social democracy, *American Political Science Review* (Vol. 73 1979, pp. 505–520)

Westenholz, A. 'Workers' participation in Denmark', *Industrial Relations* (Vol. 18, No. 3, Fall 1979, pp. 376–80).

Whyte, W. F. and Blasi, J. R. 'Worker ownership, participation and control: towards a theoretical model', *Policy Sciences* (14, 1982, pp. 137–63).

MISCELLANEOUS

Bank of Ireland (Personnel Dept.) *Employee Capital Stock Issue Scheme: A Guide for Employees* (Dublin 1984).

Arthur Guinness Sons, PLC *Irish Profit Sharing Share Scheme: An Explanatory Guide* (n.d., n.p)

Gates, Jeffrey R. (Hewitt Assiociates) *The History, Strengths and Weaknesses of Employee Stock Ownership Plans (ESOPs) in the United States – What Can We Learn from the US Experience*? Speech at Conference on 'Retirement Programs of the Future' sponsored by Canadian Pension Conference, Personnel Association of Toronto (27 Nov. 1979).

Harris Bankcorp *Employee Benefits: Profit Sharing Annual Report* (April 1982 Chicago).

Metzger, B.L. 'Achieving motivation through employee stock ownership'. Speech at 1st Annual Conference of ESOP Council of America, 8 May 1978, Los Angeles, California (PSRF 1978).

Metzger, B.L. *'Profit sharing as a system incentive'*. Speech presented at Work in America Institute Conference, 'Sharing the Gains of Productivity' (PSRF, n. d.).

Sedgwick Dineen Consultants Ltd *Approved Profit Sharing Schemes Survey 1984/85 and Suggested Amendments to Existing Regulations*, P.H. Prost (M.D.), Sedgwick Dineen Consultants (11 Jan., Dublin 1985).

Smith, R.B., Chairman, General Motors 'Remarks on profit sharing at General Motors', Speech at National Press Club, Washington DC, 7 Feb. 1984; Distributed by PSRF (Evanston, Illinois).

Index